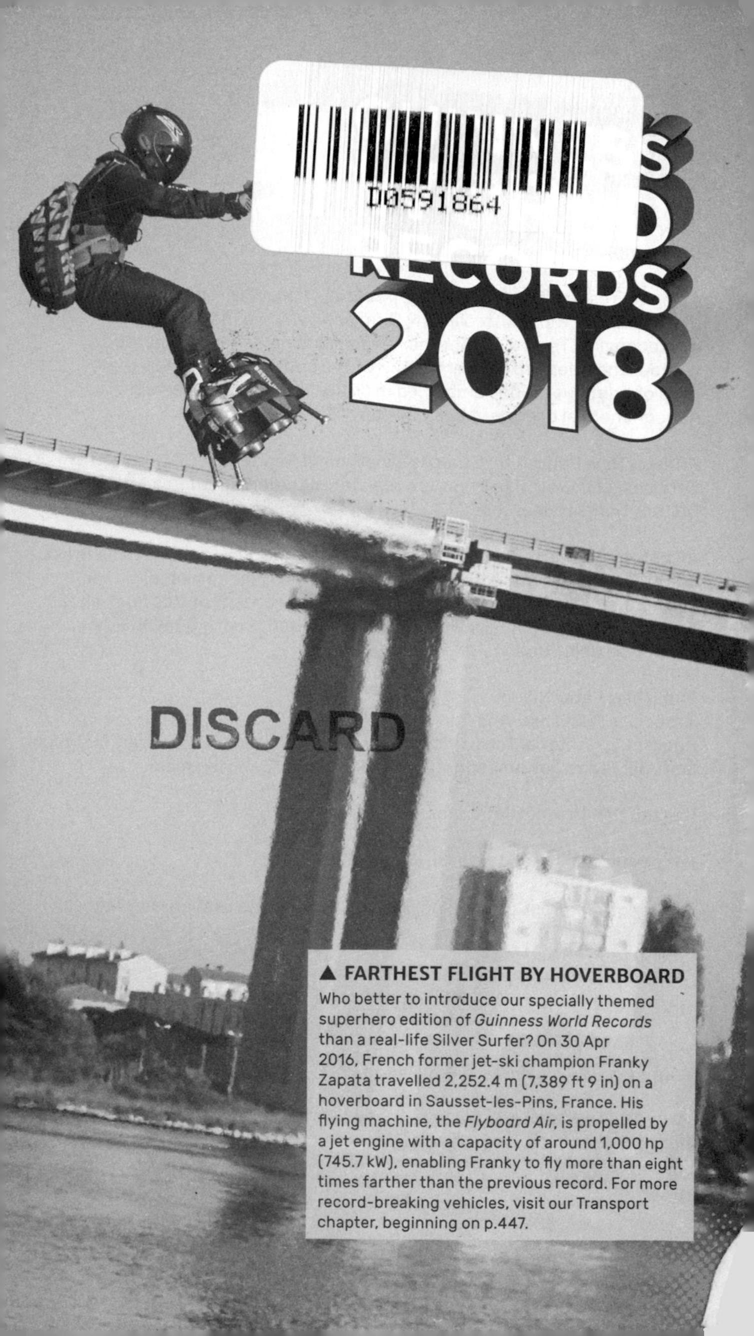

RECORDS

2018

DISCARD

▲ FARTHEST FLIGHT BY HOVERBOARD

Who better to introduce our specially themed superhero edition of *Guinness World Records* than a real-life Silver Surfer? On 30 Apr 2016, French former jet-ski champion Franky Zapata travelled 2,252.4 m (7,389 ft 9 in) on a hoverboard in Sausset-les-Pins, France. His flying machine, the *Flyboard Air*, is propelled by a jet engine with a capacity of around 1,000 hp (745.7 kW), enabling Franky to fly more than eight times farther than the previous record. For more record-breaking vehicles, visit our Transport chapter, beginning on p.447.

Portable Press
An imprint of Printers Row Publishing Group
10350 Barnes Canyon Road, Suite 100, San Diego, CA 92121
www.portablepress.com • e-mail: mail@portablepress.com

Printers Row Publishing Group is a division of Readerlink Distribution
Services, LLC. Portable Press is a registered trademark of Readerlink
Distribution Services, LLC.

All notations of errors or omissions should be addressed to Portable Press,
Editorial Department, at the above address. All other correspondence
(author inquiries, permissions) concerning the content of this book should
be addressed to Guinness World Records Limited, South Quay Building,
189 Marsh Wall, London, E14 9SH

Publisher: Peter Norton
Associate Publisher: Ana Parker
Publishing/Editorial Team: Vicki Jaeger, Tanya Fijalkowski, Lauren Taniguchi
Editorial Team: JoAnn Padgett, Melinda Allman, Dan Mansfield

Design: Dan Prescott at Couper Street Type Co.

For permissions credits please see p. 577

Library of Congress Cataloging-in-Publication Data available on request.

ISBN: 978-1-68412-146-5

Printed in USA by Worzalla Publishing Co

22 21 20 19 18 2 3 4 5 6

GUINNESS WORLD RECORDS 2018

Contents

45,000 claims researched · 3,000 new and updated records published 1,000 photographs sourced · 60 exclusive photoshoots attended

This year's edition is divided into 11 sections, including a special feature chapter on superheroes, plus our free-to-download superlative posters. These chapters cover a wide range of topics, from buccaneering adventures on oceans and mountaintops to blockbuster movies and TV streaming hits. There's also a fascinating look at some of the finest specimens of the animal world – including majestic whales and adorable panda bears – plus cutting-edge science and technology, and record-breaking highlights from the past year of sports.

The book is organized into 11 unique chapters, and each chapter kicks off with a dramatic double-page photograph illustrating one of the records from that section.

Every edition of *GWR* features more than 1,000 photos – many exclusive to us and seen for the first time. Our dedicated picture team has travelled the world to capture the most visually striking record holders.

MOST PEOPLE DRESSED AS...

Dragon Ball characters
On 1 Nov 2015, Editorial Planeta (ESP) arranged for 307 people to dress as characters from the manga series *Dragon Ball* at the Saló de Manga comic festival in Barcelona, Spain.

Spider-Man
Recruitment company Charterhouse (AUS) assembled 438 individuals dressed as the fan favourite web-slinger in Sydney, New South Wales, Australia, on 28 Jul 2015.

Ben 10
On 25 Mar 2016, a group of 475 participants became certain heroes Ben 10 for a day at Red Sea Mall in Jeddah, Saudi Arabia. The event was organized by Rainbow Paint and Mills (SAU).

Batman
A total of 542 individuals donned the famous caped crusader's attire in Calgary, Alberta, Canada, on 18 Sep 2014. The mass costuming was staged by Nexen Energy (CAN).

LARGEST GATHERING OF PEOPLE DRESSED AS COMIC-BOOK CHARACTERS
On 29 Sep 2015, a cape participants dressed as familiar comic-book characters at the Salt Lake Comic Con in Salt Lake City, Utah, USA.

SUPERHEROES

COSPLAY

Fastest half marathon in a superhero costume
On Sunday, 2 Oct 2016, Morgan Valentine (GBR) ran the Cardiff Half Marathon in Wales, UK, in 1 hr 4 min 33 sec dressed as Batman (aka Clemens Jones) finished taking him to the 10 min 45 sec.

Longest-running dedicated cosplay event
The World Cosplay Summit has run annually in Nagoya, Japan, for 15 years as of the 2016 event, held from 30 Jul to 7 Aug.
Delegates videogames, anime, manga and cosplay.
The finale of the event is the World Cosplay Championship. The record for **most World Cosplay Championship victories** is three, shared by four teams: Brazil won in 2006, 2008 and 2011, while the winner in 2006, 2008 and 2011. Paranormales Japan have won twice, in 2014 and 2015, and Italy won the title in 2016.
The **most countries at a dedicated cosplay tournament** is 30, at the 2016 World Cosplay Championship, staged on 6–7 Aug in Nagoya. The participants included China, Australia, India, Kuwait, Denmark and Mexico.

LARGEST COSPLAY COSTUME
BUMBLE VERSION
Designed and built by Thomas DePetrillo (USA), the Extreme Hulkbuster is 9 ft 6 in (2.89 m) tall, has a shoulder width of a ft 4 in (1.95 m) and weighs 100 lb (45.08 kg). It takes Thomas 20 min to don the suit, which both helmet fitted to make 1 in (17.7 cm) taller than the tallest man ever, Robert Wadlow.

Starting on p.177 is our 39-page section devoted to superheroes, from the original comic-book characters via TV shows and movies to videogamers and cosplayers. And just for fun, we ask which fictional heroes would be record-breakers in the real world!

Still hungry for more? Our bite-sized fact bubbles offer a unique mix of quirky trivia and extraordinary stats that will satisfy even the most voracious of record addicts.

Look out for "Round-Ups" at the end of each chapter – you'll find records here that don't fit on to any of the regular themed pages, plus some last-minute additions to the GWR archive.

Whenever you see the 100% icon, you know you're looking at a record holder in its actual size – whether that's a humongous beetle or an extra-long ear hair!

Put your general knowledge to the test with our quiz questions. See how many you can get, then turn quiz master for your friends and family.

Our fact-packed tables will provide you with even more information. From musical chart-toppers to fitness fanatics and incredible strongmen and women, you will have all the raw data you need at your fingertips.

Our infographic columns provide a fun and snappy way of delivering you instantaneous information.

Keep an eye out for even more pull-out facts in the oval boxes, getting you closer to the extraordinary record-breakers who populate the book and the truth behind their Officially Amazing feats!

▶ SUPERLATIVE POSTERS

Designed specially for *GWR 2018*, our exciting new superlative spreads bring records to life in all their infographic glory. These two-page poster features appear throughout the book between each chapter, and each one is based on a single superlative – such as **Tallest**, **Longest**, **Highest** and **Heaviest**.

The records that you'll find on these pages are presented in increasing (or decreasing) order, allowing you to compare holders side by side. What's faster: Usain Bolt or a cheetah? Does the **tallest Christmas tree** outstretch the **tallest snowman**? And what would cost you more: the **most expensive guitar** or the **most expensive sandwich**?

To download your free posters, visit **guinnessworldrecords.com/2018**.

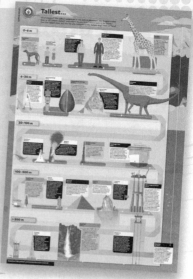

Editor's Letter

Between them, North Americans were responsible for making more than a quarter of all applications to Guinness World Records in the past 12 months.

Welcome to this superpowered, superlative edition of the record-breaking record book. We believe that anyone can unleash their inner superhero, and this edition is proof of that. It's packed with thousands of incredible tales of everyday heroes overcoming the odds to become the best in the world.

▲ MOST MEDICATION DONATED IN 24 HOURS (MULTIPLE VENUES)
On 30 Jan 2017, Uniting to Combat NTDs (UK) oversaw the donation of 207,169,292 doses of medication at various venues in India, South Africa, Portugal, Mexico, France and Belgium. On 18 Apr 2017, a GWR certificate acknowledging this incredible achievement was presented to Thoko Elphick-Pooley, Director of the Uniting to Combat NTDs Support Centre in Geneva, Switzerland. She is shown above next to Bill Gates, in a line-up of individuals who play pivotal roles in the fight against NTDs (neglected tropical diseases).

As ever, you'll find thousands of new and updated world records – plus some favourite classics from the archives – but this year we've put an exciting new spin on things. We've taken our inspiration for this edition from the fantastical world of the superhero, both fictional and real life.

I've always thought of our record holders as living, breathing superheroes. With their heightened powers – be it strength, stamina, intelligence, persistence, determination or a combination of all five – they're certainly the closest thing you'll find to Superman, Wonder Woman and Iron Man in the real world. If we had to assemble a team of superheroes, we've certainly got plenty of people to choose from! In fact, you'll find my suggestion for this very thing on pp.xx–xxii: the Superlative Squad – a team of real-life record holders that epitomizes the range and diversity of record-breaking.

▼ LARGEST HUMAN LETTER

Over the years, NBC's *Today* show has witnessed a wealth of record-breaking (see table below). On 29 Mar 2017, The University of Tennessee (USA) assembled 4,223 students in the shape of the letter "T" in Neyland Stadium, Knoxville, Tennessee. It took place during Rokerthon 3, a series of record attempts hosted by *Today*'s weatherman Al Roker. Two days later, Rokerthon 3 claimed another GWR record with the **longest conga on ice** (below centre), by 593 students from the State University of New York at Oswego in New York, USA.

The **most balloons burst with the mouth in 30 seconds** is 19, by Ashrita Furman (USA; bottom left) on the set of *Today* in New York City, USA, on 7 Sep 2016. And Raymond Butler (USA; below right) performed the **longest backflip into a pair of trousers** (259 cm; 8 ft 6 in) two days beforehand, also on *Today*'s set. Butler achieved the record on his second attempt.

AS SEEN ON THE *TODAY* SHOW...			
Title	Record	Holder (all USA)	Date
Most skips with a leg behind the head in one minute	35	Bria Roberts	8 Sep 2016
Largest street dance	253 dancers	PMT Dance Studio	9 Sep 2016
Largest human image of a cloud	490 people	The University of Oklahoma	27 Mar 2017
Largest human image of a lightning bolt	280 people	The University of Oklahoma	27 Mar 2017
Largest game of freeze tag	634 people	Northern Michigan University	28 Mar 2017
Most people crab walking	494 people	Loyola University Maryland	30 Mar 2017

As this line-up shows, you don't have to wear your underpants on the outside of your trousers to be a record-breaker. (On saying that, it worked for Morgan Reardon and Natalie Edwards, holders of the record for **most underpants pulled on in one minute (team of two)**, with 18 pairs!) We believe that everyone has the potential to be the very best at something, and that's what Guinness World Records is here for: to give you the chance to be a hero in any field of endeavour. I hope the heroes you meet in this year's book will inspire you to become the best you can be, whatever it is you want to achieve.

Neff pushed his 11-month-old daughter Holland in a pram during the marathon. The duo attracted attention from all over the world as they live-streamed their record attempt via Periscope.

▲ SCOTIABANK TORONTO WATERFRONT MARATHON

Inaugurated in 2000, this annual event is held in Toronto, Canada. On 16 Oct 2016, it was the stage for Calum Neff (CAN) to run the **fastest marathon while pushing a pram**: 2 hr 31 min 22 sec. The previous year, Neff ran the **fastest half marathon pushing a pram**: 1 hr 11 min 27 sec at the Katy Half Marathon in Katy, Texas, USA, on 6 Feb 2016.

The **fastest half marathon in motocross gear (female)** took 2 hr 14 min 34 sec and was achieved by Bridget Burns (CAN, right) during the Toronto marathon on 16 Oct 2016. On the same day, Daniel Janetos and Jasper Moester (both CAN) set new records for the **fastest marathon dressed as a chef** and **fastest half marathon dressed as a chef**, although both have now been broken. For more speedy runs in fancy dress set at the same event, see below.

FASTEST HALF MARATHONS			
DRESSED...	Time	Holder	Date
In a suit (female)	1 hr 42 min 42 sec	Jennifer Wilson (CAN)	16 Oct 2016
As a swimmer (male)	1 hr 47 min 51 sec	Robert Winckler (CAN)	16 Oct 2016

◄ MOST PEOPLE USING VIRTUAL REALITY DISPLAYS SIMULTANEOUSLY

On 3 Mar 2017, Israeli technology company Mobileye brought together 1,867 people to don virtual reality displays during the 2017 YPO EDGE event in Vancouver, British Columbia, Canada. The participants viewed a video that placed them inside a virtual car, highlighting Mobileye's cutting-edge technology in advanced collision-avoidance systems. The attempt took place during the keynote presentation by Ziv Aviram, CEO of Mobileye.

In the past 12 months, we've had more than 45,000 applications for world records, from all around the planet. The majority of claimants, however, won't find their names in the book – our rigorous adjudication procedures mean that only a very small percentage of applicants, about 5%, actually make it all the way through to record-breaking success. If you've made a claim that's been unsuccessful, don't be too disheartened – just give it another go and try your very best to prove how amazing you are. If you *have* received that official Guinness World Records certificate, congratulations - you're part of a very small elite of record-breakers. You're Officially Amazing!

MEET THE EXPERTS

Not all records are sourced from the general public, however. We're supported by an invaluable team of experts and advisors who are constantly on the look-out for the latest record-breaking happenings. This international panel allows us to cover the vast spectrum of topics that you'll find in the book. We call this "extracting the -ests from the -ists" – that is, sourcing the fastest, tallest, oldest and longest from the archaeologists, gerontologists, meteorologists and zoologists. I'd like to say a personal thank you to all of our experts – we couldn't do it without you.

For this edition, we welcome on board some new consultants for topics we've never covered before, or at least never in such detail. Ian Sumner, for example, is the librarian of the Flag Institute and has provided the new flag records on p.336. Warren Dockter, from the Department of International Politics at Aberystwyth University, supplied us with records about superpowers – political ones, that is! – on p.316, and comic-book experts Rob Cave and TQ Jefferson supplied superlatives regarding the other kind of superpowers – those possessed by fictional superheroes, which you'll find throughout the feature chapter starting on p.177.

◄ MOST AMERICAN FOOTBALL FIELD GOALS MADE IN ONE MINUTE

On 3 Feb 2017, Adam Vinatieri (USA) kicked 28 field goals in 60 sec for NFL Extra Points Credit Card (issued by Barclaycard) at the NFL Experience in Houston, Texas, USA. Upon completion of the attempt, Barclaycard made a donation to the Pat Tillman Foundation for military veterans.

Vinatieri is placekicker for the Indianapolis Colts. His GWR records include **most consecutive field goals by an NFL kicker** (44) and **most field goals by an individual in a Super Bowl career** (48).

◀ **TALLEST STACK OF TORTILLAS**

On 10 Mar 2017, Ben Leventhal – with the support of multi-platform media company Mashable (both USA) – created a 58.03-cm (22.85-in) pile of Freeb!rds World tortillas. The record attempt took place at Mashable House at the SXSW festival in Austin, Texas, USA, and was performed live during Mashable's Twitter show. Leventhal is a co-founder of Resy, a mobile app for making restaurant reservations, and the food blog network Eater.

Also joining the team this year is Star Wars historian James Burns – you'll find his records not too far, far away on p.384 – and James Proud, who has unearthed some incredible records associated with transhumanism and cyborgs (p.142).

Thanks are also due to the Fédération Aéronautique Internationale (FAI) for providing us with air sports records (p.298), and to box-office analyst Bruce Nash at The Numbers for all the statistical records from the movie industry.

Other new topics this year include wildfires (p.29), Rubik's Cubes (p.254), emojis (p.331) and fireworks (p.432) – proof, if it were needed, that Guinness World Records covers a wider range of topics than most annuals! And if you're reading this on the toilet, pop over to p.346 to find an exploration of all things lavatorial – a surprising and important topic, given the fact that more people on the planet have access to mobile phones than clean water...

In addition to the many new topics – and a fresh new look from our designers at 55 Design – we've introduced a range of features unique to this edition. The first is a series of poster pages, each based on a single superlative, such as Tallest, Longest, Heaviest and Oldest. These infographic-style pages – found between each of the chapters – can be downloaded and printed off at home.

◀ **CARLI LLOYD**

Above, US soccer legend Carli Lloyd (b. 16 Jul 1982) shows off the certificates for her three GWR titles. From left to right:
· **fastest goal scored in the FIFA Women's World Cup final**: 3 min, for the USA vs Japan in the 2015 Women's World Cup final at BC Place, Vancouver, Canada, on 5 Jul 2015.
· **most goals scored in the FIFA Women's World Cup final by an individual**: 3, at the same event.
· **oldest goalscorer in the FIFA Women's World Cup final**: aged 32 years 354 days, at the same event.

▲ LARGEST BANNER FLOWN BY A VEHICLE

On 19 Nov 2016, Ford Motor Company (USA) flew a 383.18-m² (4,124.51-sq-ft) US flag at the Ford Championship Weekend at Homestead-Miami Speedway in Florida, USA. The banner was around three-quarters the size of a basketball court, or one-and-a-half times the size of a tennis court. The giant Stars and Stripes was trailed behind a Ford F450 Crew Cab.

A dozen volunteers held the flag while the driver drove away, letting it unfurl without touching the ground. The record was achieved on a closed course before the raceway opened to the public.

▲ LONGEST PINEWOOD DERBY TRACK

The Boy Scouts of America Mid-America Council (USA) put together a 554.53-m (1,819-ft 3.84-in) pinewood derby track at Eugene T Mahoney State Park in Ashland, Nebraska, USA, on 15 Oct 2016. The winning car was provided by Glenn Jewkes of Jewkes Engineering. It weighed 137 g (4.83 oz) and completed the run in 1 min 16.7 sec.

At the end of each chapter, you'll see Round-Up pages. These features allow us to include records that would otherwise not fit into the regular themed pages, and give us the chance to include some late additions to the records archive. The Round-Up at the end of the book (p.604) also includes the very latest records approved after the official closing date for submissions.

This year's Sports chapter – which starts on p.485 – features exclusively world records set in the past year. And the Animals chapter (pp.55–113), curated by consultant Dr Karl Shuker, focuses on a handful of superlative creatures rather than covering the entire animal kingdom; the idea is to explore each animal in greater depth.

Finally, we say happy birthday to Robert Pershing Wadlow, the tallest man who ever lived. February 2018 marks the 100th anniversary of his birth, and our feature on p.112 celebrates his remarkable – and tragically short – life. Wadlow is probably the

FASTEST MARATHON

Dressed…	Time	Holder
In pyjamas (male)	3 hr 44 min 55 sec	Fred Perez (USA)
As a three-dimensional bird	5 hr 31 min 5 sec	Jean-Baptiste Bourdu (FRA)
As a boxer	3 hr 4 min 57 sec	Christian Aarstad Odgaard (NOR)

▲ SKECHERS PERFORMANCE LOS ANGELES MARATHON

The LA Marathon was set up in 1986, prompted by the success of the 1984 Summer Olympic Games, which were held in the city. On 19 Mar 2017, Kevin Odle (USA) ran the **fastest marathon dressed as a tennis player (male)** in 3 hr 44 min 52 sec. Jerry Knox (USA) took just over five minutes longer to complete the **fastest marathon wearing lederhosen**: 3 hr 50 min.

On the day, Craig Handy and Lawrence Pitkin (both USA) set new records for the fastest marathons **as a swimmer** and **as a fast-food item** respectively, although both these records have since been broken. All four are shown above, while below we list three more records set at the marathon.

most famous record-breaker of them all – a true superhuman who continues to amaze everyone who discovers his extraordinary story.

If you think you've got what it takes to become a record holder, let us know about it by visiting guinnessworldrecords.com and making an application. On p.xxvii you can read about Guinness World Records Day – our annual international celebration of the superlative. Why not choose that day to try your hand at a world record? Perhaps you could be one of the 5% to have your achievement recognized by our Records Managers. And if you want to attempt your record with your underpants on the outside, that's fine by us too…

Craig Glenday
Editor-in-Chief

▲ LARGEST LEGO® MOSAIC OF A LEGO MINIFIGURE

On 17 Sep 2016, Brick Fest Live! (USA) presented a 37.62-m² (404.93-sq-ft) mosaic of a Darth Vader LEGO Minifigure in Richmond, Virginia, USA. It included 59,176 bricks and was completed during the course of a day's record attempts for GWR Live! Various families entered the record area to put individual parts of the mosaic together. These were then placed together to form the final artwork.

▲ MOST SUBSCRIBERS FOR A STUNT/TRICK-SHOT CHANNEL ON YOUTUBE

Videos of people doing amazing stunts and trick shots – aka "sports entertainment" – rack up millions of views on YouTube. No other channel in this genre is more popular than "Dude Perfect" (USA), with 18,125,930 subscribers as of 5 May 2017. Dude Perfect consists of Cody Jones, Tyler Toney, Garrett Hilbert, and Coby and Cory Cotton (all USA). Here's a selection of their GWR records, all achieved at Texas Christian University in Fort Worth, Texas, USA.

DUDE PERFECT AND AMERICAN FOOTBALL

Record title	Feat	Holder (all USA)	Date
Most consecutive punt return catches caught and held	5	Cody Jones	23 Jan 2017
Most one-handed American football catches in one minute	42	Stephen Baca and Tyler Toney	23 Jan 2017
Farthest behind-the-back catch of an American football	41.3 yd	Garrett Hilbert	23 Jan 2017
Farthest blindfold catch of an American football (in motion)	22.3 yd	Cory Cotton	23 Jan 2017
Farthest American football throw into a target	50 yd	Tyler Toney	23 Jan 2017
Most American football snaps in one minute (pair)	61	Coby and Cory Cotton	23 Jan 2017
Farthest American football field goal kick into a target	30 yd	Garrett Hilbert (above)	24 Jan 2017
Greatest height from which an American football is caught	171.6 m (563 ft)	Tyler Toney	24 Jan 2017

▶ LONGEST 50-50 AND MOST FAKIE KICKFLIPS

Jagger Eaton (USA) performed a 204-ft (62.1-m) 50-50 rail grind on a skateboard on 17 Oct 2016. The record took place on the set of Nickelodeon's *Jagger Eaton's Mega Life* in Los Angeles, California, USA. The rail used had a number of kinks and curves – Jagger had the choice to use a straight rail, but wanted to make the record look as extreme as possible.

The **most fakie kickflips on a skateboard in one minute** is 24, by Chris Cole (USA) at the same location and on the same date. He broke the record at the first attempt.

INTRODUCTION
SUPERHEROES

The theme of this year's edition is the superhero, from the fictional crimefighters of the comic-book world to the real-life superhumans who do extraordinary things in the name of world records. Our special feature chapter on fictional heroes starts on p.177, but introducing the topic here are a selection of record holders from the real world who are inspired by superheroes. Plus, meet the new big-screen Spider-Man, Tom Holland...

MICHAEL KALLENBERG

It's not uncommon to see athletes racing in superhero outfits, especially when running for charity. Michael Kallenberg (UK, left), for example, ran the **fastest half marathon in superhero costume (male)** to raise money for an injured RAF serviceman, finishing the Cardiff Half Marathon in Wales, UK, in just 1 hr 9 min 33 sec on 2 Oct 2016. You'll find more costumed heroes running for charity on p.202 and pp.546–50.

Have you got what it takes to be a superhero?

The idea of a crimefighting hero hiding behind a mask and secret identity emerged in the 1930s, inspired by folkloric and fictional characters such as Robin Hood, The Scarlet Pimpernel and Tarzan. The resulting Golden and Silver Ages of comic books saw the creation of thousands of heroes (and anti-heroes) who continue to entertain and inspire us, and today our movie theatres are overrun with caped crusaders and men (and women) of steel.

But you don't need to fly faster than a speeding bullet or be

UNITE

XI SHUN
Former **tallest man** Xi Shun (CHN, 2.361 m; 7 ft 8.95 in) is proof that superheroes come in all shapes and sizes. In 2006, the Chinese giant was drafted in to save the lives of two dolphins choking on plastic. Only the world's tallest man had arms long enough to reach down into the dolphins' stomachs to extract the plastic, sparing the need for dangerous surgery.

bitten by a radioactive spider to become a superhero. We believe that everyone has a superpower that could one day be recognized by Guinness World Records. We like to think of ourselves as a real-world recruiter of superhumans – a S.H.I.E.L.D. or League of Extraordinary Gentlemen! – and we hope that this year's book will inspire you to find your inner superhero and join our world-beating team.

NATHAN SAWAYA
A life-long comics fan, artist Nathan Sawaya (USA) was inspired to create the **largest display of life-sized LEGO® brick superheroes**, crafting 11 DC characters – including Batman, Superman and The Flash – in London, UK, on 28 Feb 2017.

Nathan's sculptures formed part of his touring exhibit "The Art of the Brick: DC Super Heroes", which was built from nearly 2 million bricks!

STAN LEE

Stan "The Man" Lee (USA) is the record-breaking father of modern comic books. He's been creating incredible characters since 1941 and has gone on to inspire countless other comic artists to produce superheroes of their own. Find out about his heroic contribution to pop culture between p.180 and p.215.

TOM HOLLAND

British actor Tom Holland was aged just 20 years 123 days when filming wrapped on *Spider-Man: Homecoming* (USA, 2017), making him the **youngest actor to play a title role in the Marvel Cinematic Universe (MCU)**. Here, he talks exclusively to Guinness World Records about the daunting task of playing one of the world's most popular superheroes, and which real-life superhero he's most inspired by...

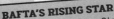

BAFTA'S RISING STAR

Tom won the EE Rising Star award at the 2017 British Academy of Film and Television Arts (BAFTA) ceremony. His big break in acting came in 2008, when he took the lead role in the stage musical version of *Billy Elliot* in London. He appeared on the big screen in *The Impossible* (ESP/USA, 2012), and made his first (brief) appearance as Spider-Man in *Captain America: Civil War* (USA, 2016).

Interview: TOM HOLLAND

How does it feel to be playing such an iconic superhero?
It's a huge, huge honour. The fact that I'm getting to portray Spider-Man is unreal to me! It still hasn't quite sunk in yet. This is a character that I've loved so much as a kid so it's like my dreams are coming true.

Why are superheroes still so popular?
These movies appeal to such large audiences – they're funny, they're dramatic, they're exciting, they're action-packed. And Spider-Man is so loved because he's such a relatable character. There's not a kid who's gone to high school and not experienced the awkwardness of talking to a girl for the first time, or struggled with homework or been late for class. It's refreshing for the younger generation to see a superhero going through similar things to what they're going through. Also, the older generation can reminisce about their time at high school.

And they're inspirational too...
If you look at Peter Parker, he's a kid that's been given these incredible powers, and instead of committing crimes he does good with it and uses his powers to make his city a better place. This is an amazing message for kids to hear. If I'm honest, I don't know if I'd necessarily do the best things if I was given superpowers... I might rob a bank or two! But seriously, Peter Parker represents the best in us and is a good role model for young kids.

If you could have just one superpower, what would it be?
I'd ask for the power of teleportation! In my job, I'm on an aeroplane so often that being able to teleport would be such a handy little tool.

You've had a busy career and you're only 20 years old. What's the secret of your success?
I think the best thing to do is keep your head down and just keep grinding. As much as it's difficult, the harder you work, the more you get out of any situation, whether you're in school, at work or on a movie set. I'm a huge advocate of working hard and being the hardest worker in the room.

Which real-life superheroes do you look up to?
We all need heroes in our lives, and at the moment my biggest inspiration is The Rock [Dwayne Johnson]. I was lucky enough to meet him the other day and he's a very nice, kind, loving man. I've heard from other people that he just doesn't take any time off – he's working every single day. If I'm ever tired, I remind myself that Dwayne is probably in the gym, pushing it. And I think, "I have to work harder if I want to get to where I want to be." If I'm ever challenged, I say to myself, "What would The Rock do?!"

The Rock is also a GWR title holder!
No way?! This means I'm one step closer to being The Rock. I could be the next Rock. Or Little Rock!

How does it feel to be a GWR record holder?
I'm a big fan of the book. I'm not going to lie – there it was in my stocking every Christmas. I love the *GWR* books and it's crazy to now be in there! I'm so happy – it's such an amazing thing to have a record, and I'm looking forward to getting the certificate up on my wall. Probably next to my BAFTA!

SUPERLATIVE

If Guinness World Records had to bring together a team of superheroes from our long list of record-breakers, we'd be spoiled for choice. Here's just one possible line-up of Officially Amazing individuals – every one a real-life superhuman.

THE SAMURAI

For a cutting-edge hero to rival Wolverine, we'll take Isao Machii (JPN). In 2011, the sword-wielding record-breaker delivered the **most sword cuts to straw mats in three minutes** (252) in Milan, Italy. Four years later, he applied the **most martial arts sword cuts to one mat** (8) in Tokyo, Japan.

KILO-GIRL

Look away now, She-Hulk… Ukraine's Nina Geria has got strength to spare! On 28 Mar 2012, she took just 12.33 sec to carry out the **fastest 20 m duck walk carrying 120 kg**, on the set of *Lo Show dei Record* in Rome, Italy. What does 120 kg feel like? More than 17 times heavier than a bowling ball!

ELASTIC MAN

Who better to mimic Mr Fantastic's extreme plasticity than Garry Turner (UK), the man with the **stretchiest skin**? Garry can pull the skin of his stomach out to 15.8 cm (6.22 in) owing to Ehlers-Danlos syndrome – a disorder of the connective tissues affecting the skin, ligaments and internal organs. It results in a loosening of the skin and "hypermobility" of the joints.

SQUAD

"Superlative" /soo-PER-la-tiv/; **1** adj. A high (or the very highest) degree of an attribute; the best. **2** n. someone or something of unmatched excellence.

SUPER HOOPER

Whirling up a storm is extreme hula hooper Marawa Ibrahim (AUS). Her records include **longest duration on high-heeled roller skates while spinning three hoops** (2 min 29 sec) and **farthest distance on high-heeled roller skates spinning eight hula hoops** (43.2 m; 141 ft 8 in).

THE FLAME

When it comes to hot-heads, the Human Torch has got stiff competition in the shape of Josef Tödtling (AUT). On 23 Nov 2013, Josef endured the **longest duration full-body burn without oxygen** – lasting 5 min 41 sec – at Salzburg Fire Department in Salzburg, Austria.

APPLE CRUSH

Looking for the super-strength of Captain Marvel? Step forward Linsey Lindberg (USA)! Among her many power records are **most apples crushed with the bicep in one minute (female)** - 10 - and **most telephone directories torn in one minute (female)** - 5.

CAPTAIN FREEZE

When you're in danger, you need someone with a cool head – and no one's head gets cooler than Jin Songhao's (CHN). This living Iceman endured the **longest time spent in direct, full-body contact with ice** (1 hr 53 min 10 sec) in Xiamen, Fujian, China, on 4 Sep 2014.

THE HUMAN SPIDER

He's earned the nickname "Spider-Man" for his habit of going up skyscrapers – the hard way. Alain Robert (FRA) holds the GWR record for the **most buildings climbed externally by a person** (121). He started climbing towers, monuments and skyscrapers in 1994 and completed his latest climb on the 306-m-tall (1,003-ft) Cayan Tower in Dubai, UAE, on 12 Apr 2015.

NEVER MISS

We'd surely want the Hawkeye-like skills of Nancy Siefker (USA). This awesome archer achieved the **farthest arrow shot into a target using the feet** (20 ft; 6.09 m) on the set of *Guinness World Records Unleashed* in Los Angeles, California, USA, on 20 Jun 2013.

WONDER WHEELS

Professor X may be telepathic, but when it comes to two-wheeled talents, Aaron Fotheringham (USA) is simply X-traordinary! He landed the **first wheelchair backflip** in 2008, the **highest ramp jump in a wheelchair** (60 cm; 1 ft 11.6 in) in 2010 and the **longest duration balancing a side wheelie in a manual wheelchair** (18.22 sec) in 2012.

Reebok Record-Breakers

Twenty-four hours. Four cities. Three countries. One team of awesomely talented athletes. And a whole host of records.

When Reebok goes big, they go above and beyond – especially when it comes to breaking world records. For their launch of the new Reebok CrossFit Nano 7 shoe, Reebok assembled a task force of talented athletes who achieved 44 Guinness World Records titles in 24 hr in cities across the globe.

An ensemble of some of the world's strongest and fastest athletes gathered in four cities in Australia, the UK and the USA on 1 Feb 2017 for an intense day under the watchful eye of GWR adjudicators.

Sydney, London, New York City and Los Angeles were the cities chosen to host masses of athletes sporting the Nano 7. The athletes – who came from varied fitness disciplines – achieved a total of 44 Guinness World Records titles, pushing their bodies to the limit in the name of excellence. Listed on the following pages is every successful attempt.

▼ MOST ONE-ARM, ONE-LEG PUSH-UPS IN ONE MINUTE (MALE)

CrossFit coach Logan Aldridge (USA) achieved 26 one-arm, one-leg push-ups in 60 sec in Brooklyn, New York City, USA. It was one of two records set by adaptive athlete Logan, whose left arm was amputated after a 2004 wakeboarding accident.

UK – LONDON (2)		
Record	**No.**	**Holder**
Most barbell back somersaults in one minute (male)	4	Eirik Lundstein (NOR)
Most kettlebell back somersaults in one minute (male)	16	Eirik Lundstein (NOR)

▶ MOST WEIGHT LIFTED BY BARBELL THRUSTS IN ONE MINUTE

Canadian strongman Paul Tremblay lifted 2,128.81 kg (4,693 lb 3.5 oz) in 60 sec in New York City, USA. It was one of three world records he set in one Herculean day, including the most weight lifted by barbell thrusts in three minutes – 3,398.68 kg (7,492 lb 12 oz).

◀ MOST KETTLEBELL BACK SOMERSAULTS IN ONE MINUTE (MALE)

Carrying a 6-kg (13-lb 3.6-oz) kettlebell in each hand, Eirik Lundstein (NOR) completed 16 back somersaults in 60 sec in London, UK. Eirik wasn't finished there: carrying a barbell and weights totalling 20.1 kg (44 lb 5 oz), he made the **most barbell back somersaults in one minute (male)** – four.

USA – NEW YORK CITY (15)

Record	Measurement	Holder (USA unless stated)
Most knuckle push-ups in one minute (male)	91	Ron Cooper
Most wall ball squats in one minute with 20-lb medicine ball (male)	35	Paul Tremblay (CAN)
Most handstand push-ups in one minute (female)	12	Rachel Martinez
Most switch grip pull-ups in one minute (male)	26	Ron Cooper
Most weight lifted by barbell thrusts in one minute (male)	2,128.81 kg (4,693 lb 3.5 oz)	Paul Tremblay (CAN)
Most weight lifted by barbell thrusts in three minutes (male)	3,398.68 kg (7,492 lb 12 oz)	Paul Tremblay (CAN)
Most one-arm, one-leg push-ups in one minute (male)	26	Logan Aldridge
Most weight lifted by clean and jerk in one minute (male)	1,155.64 kg (2,547 lb 12 oz)	Scott Panchik
Most weight lifted by clean and jerk in one minute (female)	809.66 kg (1,785 lb)	Annie Thorisdottir (ISL)
Most weight lifted by overhead squats in three minutes (male)	4,902.75 kg (10,808 lb 11 oz)	Frederik Aegidius (DNK)
Most weight lifted by barbell snatch in one minute (male)	1,338.11 kg (2,950 lb 0.4 oz)	Scott Panchik
Most weight lifted by barbell snatch in one minute (female)	1,038.74 kg (2,290 lb 0.4 oz)	Annie Thorisdottir (ISL)
Most weight lifted by barbell snatch in three minutes (male)	2,145.3 kg (4,729 lb 9.2 oz)	Dan Bailey
Most weight lifted by overhead squats in one minute (female)	1,877.87 kg (4,140 lb)	Emily Bridgers
Most weight lifted by single-arm barbell cleans in one minute (male)	918.53 kg (2,025 lb)	Logan Aldridge

▶ LOS ANGELES

Reebok ended its record-breaking day in California, USA, where athletes including Rebecca Voigt, Tommy Hackenbruck and Stacie Tovar (from left, all USA) came together to set 18 new records. DJ Dillon Francis and hula hooper "Marawa the Amazing" added some celebrity glamour with their own record attempts.

In order to set her record above, Stacie Tovar lifted the equivalent of five grizzly bears in three minutes!

AUSTRALIA – SYDNEY (9)

Record	No.	Holder (all AUS)
Most pistol squats in one minute (male)	49	Ben Garard
Most pistol squats in one minute (female)	42	Kara Webb
Most chin-ups in one minute with 100-lb pack	12	Marcus Bondi
Most lunges in one minute (male)	70	Ricky Garard
Most lunges in one minute (female)	64	Sammy Wood
Most toe-to-bar touches in one minute (male)	46	Ricky Garard
Most toe-to-bar touches in one minute (female)	41	Maddie Sturt
Most consecutive tandem push-ups (male/male)	28	Ben Garard & Ricky Garard
Most consecutive tandem push-ups (female/female)	21	Kara Webb & Sammy Wood

USA – LOS ANGELES (18)

Record	Measurement	Holder (USA unless stated)
Fastest time to climb a peg board (male)	15.22 sec	Tommy Hackenbruck
Fastest time to climb a peg board (female)	15.97 sec	Camille Leblanc-Bazinet (CAN)
Most wall ball squats in one minute (female)	36	Rebecca Voigt
Most wall ball squats in three minutes (male)	89	Conor Murphy
Most wall ball squats in three minutes (female)	92	Rebecca Voigt
Most burpee pull-ups in one minute (male)	17	Andy Doolty
Most burpee pull-ups in one minute (female)	19	Michelle Kinney
Most weight lifted by overhead squat in three minutes (female)	2,740.6 kg (6,042 lb)	Stacie Tovar
Most weight lifted by overhead squat in one minute (male)	1,833.42 kg (4,042 lb)	Conor Murphy
Most toe-to-bar touches in one minute (female)	41	Camille Leblanc-Bazinet (CAN)
Most consecutive tandem push-ups (mixed)	25	Camille Leblanc-Bazinet (CAN) & David Lipson
Most weight lifted by Atlas stone lifts in one minute (male)	1,122.64 kg (2,475 lb)	Logan Gelbrich
Most weight lifted by Atlas stone lifts in one minute (female)	539.77 kg (1,190 lb)	Michelle Kinney
Most weight lifted by Atlas stone lifts in three minutes (male)	2,694.34 kg (5,940 lb)	Tommy Hackenbruck
Most weight lifted by Atlas stone lifts in three minutes (female)	1,397.06 kg (3,080 lb)	Michelle Kinney
Most consecutive muscle-ups (female)	45	Camille Leblanc-Bazinet (CAN)
Fastest 100 m hula hooping (female)	17.87 sec	Marawa Ibrahim (AUS)
Fastest mile hula hooping (female)	8 min 0.4 sec	Marawa Ibrahim (AUS)

▲ Q&A WITH ANNIE THORISDOTTIR

Why did you choose to get involved with fitness?
I've always been involved in sports. I started out in gymnastics, reaching national level in Iceland. I also practised ballet and, later, pole vaulting, with the goal of representing Iceland at the 2012 Olympics. Then I happened to sign up for a CrossFit competition in Iceland, which I won, and this qualified me for the CrossFit Games in LA. I haven't looked back since.

Can you describe growing up in Iceland, and how that has influenced your journey?
Iceland is a very harsh place to grow up if you judge it by the weather. But I am very proud of where I am from, and I try to make that shine through who I am. Growing up in a town with only 200 people is something that gives you a sense of freedom and independence. I was taught that I could do anything I set my mind to.

Of all your fitness achievements, which one was your proudest moment, and why?
My biggest moment in my athletic career was winning the CrossFit Games for the first time in 2011. I set a goal when I participated in my first competition in 2009 that I would one day stand on top of the podium.

Many would say you have superhuman strength. In your opinion, what would be your superpower?
A burning desire to pursue my goal, no matter what stands in my way.

Can you explain a moment in fitness you defied the odds?
In Mar 2013, I was slowly getting back into training after suffering a severe back injury in 2012 when I had another setback that kept me out of the 2013 CrossFit Games. Mentally this was devastating, but I was not ready to let go of my dream of getting back to the podium. In my return season of 2014, I secured a second-place finish at the CrossFit Games – proving to myself that I could do anything I set my mind to.

What training and regiments are necessary to maintain your incredible strength and agility?
I spend 5-6 hours at the gym every day, but my whole life evolves around being at my best physically. Proper nutrition and sleep are just as important as what you do in the gym, so this is more than a full-time job.

How do you think your fitness journey has inspired or impacted on others?
I love hearing young girls talking about being strong when they grow up. I am hoping that one of these days fit and healthy will be the new beautiful for women.

Who is your hero, and why?
I think I will have to be corny and say my parents! They've always taught me by example that I can do anything I want, if I'm willing to put in the work.

What advice would you give to someone who wants to be extraordinary in their own activity?
You have to make up your mind if this is something you really want, something you are passionate about and willing to work hard for. Have people around you who will lift you up when you need it.

How did it feel to attempt a Guinness World Records title?
Walking up to the bar, knowing that if I did my best I would be part of the legendary books that I read often as a child, gave me chills down my back. Being an official part of something as renowned as Guinness World Records makes me feel like a superhero!

◀ MOST CONSECUTIVE TANDEM PUSH-UPS (MIXED)

Actor, star of *New Girl* and CrossFit devotee Max Greenfield (USA, right) tried his hand at the world record for mixed consecutive tandem push-ups, along with Stacie Tovar. But they were unable to match the efforts of super-fit husband-and-wife team Camille Leblanc-Bazinet (CAN) and David Lipson (USA), who achieved 25 in Venice, California, USA.

GWR Day

Guinness World Records Day is our global celebration of record-breaking. Just look what happened on 17 Nov 2016...

Largest display of origami elephants

When the Wildlife Conservation Society (WCS) at the Bronx Zoo in New York City, USA, sent out requests for origami elephants to show in a record-breaking display, they received 78,564 samples from countries including Egypt, Iran and Kazakhstan. Each elephant then had to be individually mounted. The exhibition was put together as part of WCS's "96 Elephants" campaign, which highlights the fact that 96 elephants are killed each day for their ivory.

Largest human image of a cloud

To publicize their cloud-computing services, enterprise software firm Deltek (USA) invited participants at their Insight 2016 user conference at the Gaylord National Resort & Convention Center in National Harbor, Maryland, USA, to take part in a record attempt. In total, 468 people joined in, donning white and royal-blue ponchos and arranging themselves inside a cloud-shaped outline. At 11.38 x 19.40 m (37 ft 4 in x 63 ft 8 in), Deltek's cloud measured twice the length of a London bus.

Largest human jigsaw puzzle piece

To celebrate the unveiling of a new puzzle artwork decorating their 132-m (433-ft) industrial chimney, Covestro Deutschland AG (DEU) made a giant jigsaw piece of their own. Donning pink hoodies, 548 employees formed the distinctive shape in Brunsbüttel, Germany.

▼ MOST RINGS PLACED ON A TARGET BY A PARROT IN ONE MINUTE

In 2015, a video of Otto the skateboarding bulldog became an internet sensation, earning more than 2.5 million views on YouTube. For GWR Day 2016, a macaw named Skipper Blue stepped into the spotlight. The talented parrot, prompted by her trainer "Wildlife" Wendy Horton (USA), managed to place 19 rings around a target in 60 sec in Los Angeles, California, USA.

Why not attempt a record to celebrate GWR Day? Head to **guinnessworldrecords.com** to find out how you can apply.

▲ MOST PEOPLE PERFORMING SQUATS
Fitness guru Kayla Itsines (AUS) marked GWR Day by leading a supersized exercise class in Melbourne, Australia. A total of 2,201 people performed squats, smashing the previous best of 665. It was one of five mass-participation records set at Kayla's "boot camp", along with **most people performing lunges** (2,201), **star jumps** (2,192), **sit-ups** (2,005) and **running on the spot** (2,195).

Longest duration to juggle four basketballs
Marko Vermeer (NLD) kept four basketballs in the air for 5 min 26 sec in Utrecht, Netherlands. In order for the record to stand, Vermeer could only use juggling patterns that switched the balls continuously between left and right hands.

Most hula hoops spun while suspended from the wrists
In a live Facebook record attempt, Marawa Ibrahim (AUS) spun 50 hula hoops at Hollywood Aerial Arts in Los Angeles, California, USA. For the record to count, she had to maintain three full revolutions in mid-air. Marawa smashed the previous record of 41, set by Kareena Oates (AUS) on the set of *Guinness World Records* in Sydney, New South Wales, Australia, on 4 Jun 2005.

Most ABBA songs identified by lyrics
Live on his show on Radio Suffolk in Ipswich, UK, DJ Luke Deal (UK) recognized 15 songs by the Swedish pop quartet in one minute. Nine other DJs at UK local radio stations took a chance on beating Deal's record, but when all was said and done the winner took it all.

▲ MOST FLOWERS PICKED WITH THE MOUTH IN A CONTORTION BACKBEND IN ONE MINUTE
Liu Teng (CHN) picked 15 flowers from a vase positioned beneath her feet, using her teeth, before placing them by hand in a vase – and all in just 60 sec. The record was set at an event in Yongcheng in Henan, China. Teng has enjoyed a friendly rivalry with fellow contortionist "Zlata", aka Julia Günthel (DEU), who held the previous highest mark of 11 roses, achieved in Jiangyin, Jiangsu, China, on 5 Jan 2015.

▲ MOST DOUBLE-DUTCH-STYLE SKIPS IN 30 SECONDS

In "Double Dutch" skipping, two long ropes are turned in opposite directions for one or more players to jump over. Ayumi Sakamaki (JPN) and the other members of the Double Dutch team "Diana" performed an unprecedented 129 skips in half a minute in Toride, Ibaraki, Japan. In order to count the skips and make sure that each one met the official guidelines, the Guinness World Records adjudicators had to review the attempt in slow motion.

Farthest basketball shot under one leg

Thunder Law (USA) of the Harlem Globetrotters (see box p.xxx) sank a basket from a distance of 15.98 m (52 ft 5 in) at the AT&T Center in San Antonio, Texas, USA. Not content with one record, Law also managed the **farthest basketball shot made while sitting** – 17.91 m (58 ft 9 in).

Continuing his record tussle with YouTube sports entertainers Dude Perfect, Globetrotter Big Easy Lofton (USA) reclaimed his record for the **longest blindfolded basketball hook shot**, notching up an incredible distance of 17.74 m (58 ft 2 in). He also took back the **longest basketball hook shot** from the no-doubt disappointed Dudes, sinking from 22.1 m (72 ft 6 in).

Fellow Globetrotter Zeus McClurkin (USA) joined the on-court fun with the **most basketball slam dunks in one minute (individual)** – 16.

▲ MOST TRAFFIC CONES BALANCED ON THE CHIN

Despite a sleepless night owing to excitement, Keisuke Yokota (JPN) balanced 26 traffic cones on his chin in his garden in Shibuya, Tokyo, Japan. In order to hone his cone skill, Yokota practises for 2–3 hr every day. He says that the secret to his success is having a strong core, as the 26 cones weigh more than a bicycle. Yokota beat his previous record of 22 cones, set at Alios Park Fes in Iwaki, Japan, on 9 Oct 2016. The event was held in aid of the disaster-stricken region of Fukushima.

▲ MOST MAGIC TRICKS PERFORMED ON A SINGLE SKYDIVE

Martin Rees (UK) performed 11 mid-air magic tricks at GoSkydive at Old Sarum Airfield in Salisbury, Wiltshire, UK. A velocity of 120 mph (193 km/h) wasn't enough to put off the daredevil magician, who carried out tricks during both freefall and under parachute. The event was organized as part of GWR Day and also in aid of a children's charity.

▲ MOST BASKETBALL THREE-POINTERS IN ONE MINUTE (SINGLE BALL)

The AT&T Center in San Antonio, Texas, USA, hosted the Harlem Globetrotters (from left, Thunder Law, Cheese Chisholm, Big Easy Lofton, Ant Atkinson and Zeus McClurkin, all USA) for a day of record-breaking basketball fun. Ant and Cheese each hit 10 three-pointers in 60 sec using just one ball, which had to be retrieved after every shot.

GWR Day was first held in 2005 to commemorate *Guinness World Records* selling its 100 millionth copy. Now, every November, new records are set in a global celebration of excellence.

▲ LARGEST LIGHT-BULB DISPLAY IN AN INDOOR VENUE

Constructed by Universal Studios Singapore in Resorts World Sentosa, Singapore, this stunning wintery display is made up of 824,961 individual light bulbs. It forms the showpiece of the attraction's Universal Journey – a spectacular experience created for the Christmas season that gives visitors the opportunity to visit eight themed zones and encounter lookalikes of Charlie Chaplin and Marilyn Monroe. The display took two months to construct.

▶ HIGHEST BUNGEE DUNK

With the help of Experience Days, death-defying dunker Simon Berry (both UK) dipped a biscuit into a mug of tea from a height of 73.41 m (240 ft 10 in) at Bray Lake Watersports in Berkshire, UK. Berry had to be incredibly precise with his jump, as the guidelines for the record stated that the mug used could measure no more than 15 cm (6 in) in both height and diameter.

Earth

Today is the longest day in Earth's history...
The planet's rotation is slowing down by
around 1.4 milliseconds every hundred years.
In 140 million years, a day will be 25 hr long.

▲ LONGEST RECORD OF VOLCANIC ERUPTIONS

The first documented eruption of Mount Etna, on the Italian island of Sicily, dates back to c. 1500 BCE, when it was written that the Sicani people were made homeless following a cataclysmic explosion. Etna – a stratovolcano with a summit height of 3,329 m (10,921 ft) – has erupted approximately 200 times since, most recently in Mar 2017.

On 3 Dec 2015 local photographer Fernando Famiani captured the drama of an eruption from the safety of the nearby province of Messina. "The eruption lasted around 30 minutes," reported Famiani, "but days followed of copious lava spills." The explosion fired lava 1 km (3,300 ft) into the sky, and a few days later the resulting ash plume had reached a height of around 7 km (23,000 ft).

Stratovolcanoes are cone-shaped volcanoes, typically with steep sides. They are built up from alternate strata (layers) of lava, pumice and ash. Etna has been growing for c. 500,000 years.

CONTENTS

Swamps, Bogs & Mangroves

Found everywhere on Earth, from equatorial latitudes to frozen climes, wetlands account for around 6% of the world's terrestrial surface.

▲ OLDEST BOG BODY
Koelbjerg Man was discovered in 1941 in a peat bog near Odense in Denmark. Only the skull and a few bones were found. Radiocarbon dating suggests that he lived around 8000 BCE, as part of the Maglemosian culture in northern Europe. At the time of his death, he was about 25 years old. His remains exhibit no signs of violence, and it is possible that he simply drowned.

Oldest bog butter
Butyrellite is a man-made butter-like, waxy substance that can be found buried in wooden containers within peat bogs. It is thought to be an ancient example of food preservation, one that makes use of the cool, acidic, low-oxygen environment in peat bogs. Found mainly in Ireland and the UK, these reserves are either dairy-based or composed of animal fats, with the appearance and texture of paraffin wax. The oldest known example was found at Ballard Bog in Tullamore, County Offaly, Ireland, in 2013. Some 5,000 years old, it still had a dairy smell when unearthed. The butter was found in a wooden vessel 1 ft (30.4 cm) wide, almost 2 ft (60.9 cm) high and weighing more than 100 lb (45.3 kg).

LARGEST...

Peatland
The West Siberian Plain lies between the Ural Mountains to the west and the Yenisei River to the east. It covers an area of approximately 2.6–2.7 million km² (1–1.04 million sq mi) – around four times larger than the US state of Texas – of which peatlands occupy 603,445 km² (233,000 sq mi). The peat here can be 10 m (32 ft 9 in) deep and formed in cool, wet conditions where dead plants do not fully decompose.

Mangroves are shrubs or trees that live in coastal swamps. Their dense roots help them remain upright on unstable ground. Mangrove swamps are found throughout the tropics and sub-tropics.

Q: What name was given to the moist, rich land including Mesopotamia that is seen as one of the birthplaces of civilization?

A: The Fertile Crescent

Bog

The Great Vasyugan Mire is in the central West Siberian Plain. Covering around 55,000 km² (21,235 sq mi) – larger than Switzerland – it accounts for around 2% of all peat bogs.

Frozen peat bog

The western Siberian sub-Arctic region is a frozen peat bog covering some 1 million km² (386,100 sq mi). Scientists discovered in 2005 that this region is beginning to thaw for the first time since its formation some 11,000 years ago.

Peatland reclamation project

The Mega Rice Project was a disastrous scheme introduced by the Indonesian government in 1996. The aim of the project was to transform vast amounts of land from peatland to paddies for large-scale rice farming to feed Indonesia's growing population. Nearly 1 million ha (2,471,050 acres) of peatland – around the same size as the island of Hawaii – was drained for paddies. Unfortunately, the acidic, nutrient-poor soil was unsuitable for rice growth. The project was abandoned in 1998, having produced an insignificant amount of rice.

Reed bed

The Danube River Delta, which is located in Romania and Ukraine, formed some 6,500 years ago by the action of sediments washing into the Black Sea. It consists of natural canals, lakes and ponds, and is growing by around 24 m (78 ft 8 in) per year into the Black Sea. The Danube Delta is also home to a reed bed that covers an area of 1,563 km² (603 sq mi), and the delta as a whole hosts more than 300 species of birds and 45 species of freshwater fish.

The many types of wetland include:

Bogs
Higher than the surrounding land, a bog receives most of its water from rain.

Marshes
Usually permanently waterlogged. They flood at high tide, or during wet seasons.

Swamps
Found in flat, low-lying areas; shallow and can support tree growth. Often found along rivers.

◄ OLDEST WORKABLE WOOD

The coniferous tree *Agathis australis*, best known by its Maori name kauri, is one of New Zealand's largest trees. Prehistoric kauri can be found buried in peat, which has preserved both the wood and sometimes the bark and seed cones. These "swamp kauri" are usually c. 3,000 years old, but some excavated trees have been radiocarbon-dated to around 50,000 years old. The wood itself is often in excellent condition and, once dried, can be used to make furniture. The grain in ancient kauri pieces is termed "whitebait", as it is thought to be similar to the shimmering effect created when sunlight strikes a moving shoal of these fish. Shown here is a "whitebait" serving platter.

BOG FINDS

The chemistry of bogs in northern Europe – particularly their high acidity and low oxygen content – means that objects buried in the soil are preserved. This gives historians access to intact ancient artefacts made of wood, leather and metal... and even human flesh.

Bog butter

Barrels of butter ("butyrellite") – often dating back thousands of years – have been found in bogs in the UK and Ireland

Human bodies

Dead bodies are typically mummified by bog soil, which preserves the skin and soft tissues

Weapons

Medieval swords, shields and garottes have been found preserved in bogs – often next to a human victim

Book

In 2006, a leather-bound, still-readable Book of Psalms was discovered in a bog in Ireland; it is thought to date back to 800–1000 CE

Canoe

The Pesse canoe was found by road workers in Hoogeveen, Netherlands, in 1955; some 2.98 m (9 ft 9 in) long, it has been radiocarbon-dated to 8040–7510 BCE

Settlement

An entire Bronze Age village was unearthed from a bog in Cambridgeshire, UK, in 2016; among the remnants were cooking pots with meals still inside

Unbroken intertidal mudflats

The Wadden Sea stretches along some 500 km (310 mi) of the northern European coastline from the Netherlands to Denmark. Its shallowness gives it a rich diversity of habitats including tidal channels, sea-grass meadows, sandbars, mussel beds and salt marshes. It covers the area between the shore and the Frisian Islands archipelago, and is some 10,000 km² (3,860 sq mi) in size. The Wadden Sea is a key area for migratory birds: 10–12 million pass through each year, with up to 6.1 million present at any one time.

Indoor swamp

Occupying 0.1 ha (0.25 acres) and containing almost 160,000 US gal (605,665 litres) of water, the most extensive indoor swamp lies in the 53-ha (130.9-acre) grounds of the Henry Doorly Zoo in Omaha, Nebraska, USA. It is home to 38 species of swamp-dwelling animal, including nine specimens of the American alligator (*Alligator mississippiensis*). One of these is a rare white or leucistic alligator, of which there are thought to be fewer than 15 in the world.

▲ LARGEST PROTECTED WETLAND

On 2 Feb 2013, the government of Bolivia declared that more than 69,000 km² (26,640 sq mi) of the Llanos de Moxos would be protected as part of the Ramsar Convention. The Llanos de Moxos is a tropical wetland consisting of savannahs that alternate between seasons of drought and flood, and is located near the borders of Bolivia, Peru and Brazil. Each year, World Wetlands Day is marked on 2 Feb.

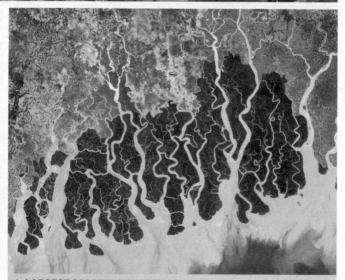

▼ LARGEST PROTECTED SWAMP

The Sudd is a swamp in the lowlands of South Sudan. In the dry season, it is some 30,000 km² (11,580 sq mi) in size, but during the wet season it can more than quadruple to approximately 130,000 km² (50,190 sq mi). Around half of its water is lost each year to evaporation. Since 2006, some 57,000 km² (22,000 sq mi) has been protected by the Convention on Wetlands of International Importance, aka the Ramsar Convention, a global treaty intended to help preserve such habitats. It is named after the city of Ramsar in Iran, where the convention was first signed in 1971.

▲ LARGEST COASTAL MANGROVE FOREST

The Sundarbans (satellite picture, above) stretches for almost 6,000 sq mi (15,540 km²) across India and Bangladesh, and acts as a natural barrier against the tsunamis and cyclones that often blow in from the Bay of Bengal. With saltwater-tolerant roots, this forest's mangrove trees may exceed 70 ft (21 m) in height. They sit on islands of layered sand and grey clay, which have been deposited by rivers that flow for more than 1,000 mi (1,600 km) from the Himalayas to the Bay of Bengal.

▼ LARGEST SWAMP

Located principally in south-western Brazil, but with small areas within neighbouring Bolivia and Paraguay too, the Pantanal (Spanish for "marshland") covers 150,000 km² (57,915 sq mi) – greater than the total surface area of England. During the rainy season (December–May), 80% of the Pantanal is flooded and it contains the greatest diversity of water plants in the world.

▼ GREATEST MANGROVE COVER (COUNTRY)

According to a report by US scientists Stuart Hamilton and Daniel Casey, Indonesia has the greatest mangrove growth. The duo calculated that as of 2014, Indonesia had 42,278 km² (16,323 sq mi) of mangrove biome, 25.79% of the global total. Hamilton and Casey analysed data from three databases: Global Forest Change, Terrestrial Ecosystems of the World, and Mangrove Forests of the World. Seen below and right are mangroves in a remote part of Raja Ampat, Indonesia.

Hard Rock

Granite makes up most of Earth's crust and is found on every continent. But to date, no trace of it has been found anywhere else in the Solar System.

Deepest-forming rocks

On 19 May 2000, geologists from the University of Queensland in Australia announced their discovery of rocks on Malaita in the Solomon Islands. These samples contained minerals that only form under very high pressures, including microdiamond and majorite – a form of the mineral garnet that is rich in silica. Examining the structure of the majorite crystals, the team concluded that they had experienced pressures of up to 23 gigapascals, around a quarter of a million times greater than atmospheric pressure at the surface, indicating that the rocks originated 400–670 km (248–416 mi) underground.

Greatest eruption (by pumice ejected)

The amount of ejecta in the Taupo eruption, which took place in New Zealand in around 186 CE, has been put at 30,000 million tonnes of pumice. It flattened an area of 16,000 km² (6,200 sq mi).

In 1996, the *Mars Global Surveyor* spacecraft took off, carrying a grain of the Zagami meteorite. In time, the craft will smash into Mars, thereby returning the fragment to its place of origin.

▼ LARGEST MARTIAN METEORITE

The Zagami meteorite, which weighed approximately 40 lb (18 kg), making it around 6.5 times heavier than a house brick, landed on Earth on 3 Oct 1962. It fell into a field near the village of Zagami in Nigeria, about 10 ft (3 m) away from a farmer who was attempting to clear cows out of his corn field and who was buffeted by the blast. He subsequently discovered the extraterrestrial rock in a 2-ft-deep (0.6-m) crater. An estimated 32 meteorites from Mars have landed on Earth to date.

It took 14 years for 400 men to carve the likenesses of four US presidents into the granite at Mount Rushmore in South Dakota

Mount Rushmore eyes (width):

11 ft (3.35 m)

Mount Rushmore noses (length):

20 ft (6 m)

If it was a whole figure, the likeness of George Washington on Rushmore would stand:

465 ft (141.7 m)

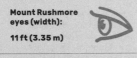

The Earth's crust is made of 64.7% igneous, 7.9% sedimentary and 27.4% metamorphic rocks

Hardest substance on the Mohs scale

In 2005, researchers at the Bayerisches Geoinstitut in Bayreuth, Germany, produced an aggregated diamond nanorod (ADNR) that is 11% less compressible than diamond

Most common rock type at the surface of the continental crust

Approximately 75% of Earth's continental crust has sedimentary rocks at its surface. Usually present as a thin veneer over igneous and metamorphic rocks, these sedimentary rocks include sandstone, mudstone, chalk and breccias. They formed when small particles became buried over time and were subjected to great pressures. Erosional and tectonic forces can expose them on the surface again.

The **most common sedimentary rocks** are mudrocks, which include mudstone, shale and siltstone and are made up of particles smaller than 0.0625 mm. They account for around 65% of all sedimentary rocks on Earth, and possibly up to 80%. Mudrocks consist mainly of clay minerals and most of them formed at the bottoms of oceans and lakes. Dead organic material, mixed with the original sediments, is responsible for the occurrence of fossil fuels in rocks such as shale.

Youngest Moon rocks

A type of volcanic basalt, Moon rocks begin to form in the dark lunar *maria* (seas). The most recent examples date back some 3.2 billion years – making them not dissimilar in age to the oldest dateable rocks on Earth. Lunar samples measuring 382 kg (842 lb) from the Apollo missions have been returned to Earth.

▲ THICKEST CRUST

The Earth's crust is the cold, solid, outermost layer of its lithosphere, which sits above the hot convecting asthenosphere (semi-molten rock at the upper levels of the mantle). It is divided into plates and consists of two types: the dense ocean crust and the lighter continental crust. The Earth's crust is at its thickest in the Himalaya mountains in China, where it reaches 75 km (46 mi).

Q: What is the difference between lava and magma?

A: Magma is molten rock below the Earth's surface.
When it erupts above ground, it is called lava.

▲ **LARGEST GLACIAL ERRATIC BOULDER**
Glacial erratics are rocks that have been carried by glaciers before being deposited on the ground as the ice melted. The Okotoks Erratic is one such boulder, located near the town of Okotoks in the Canadian Prairies in Alberta, Canada. Composed of the metamorphic rock quartzite, it measures approximately 41 x 18 m (134 x 59 ft) and is some 9 m (29 ft) high, with a mass of around 16,500 tonnes (18,188 tons).

LARGEST...

Meteorite
A block 9 ft (2.7 m) long by 8 ft (2.4 m) wide, estimated to weigh 130,000 lb (59 tonnes), is the largest known meteorite. It was found in 1920 at Hoba West, near Grootfontein in Namibia.

The **largest lunar meteorite** is Kalahari 009, with a mass of 13.5 kg (29 lb 12 oz). It was found in Kalahari in Botswana in Sep 1999. Around 50 meteorites on Earth originated from the Moon.

Stone run
During the last ice age, intense freezing followed by thawing gave rise to accumulations of boulders known as "stone runs". Princes Street, located north-east of Stanley in the Falkland Islands, is a stone run measuring 4 km (2.4 mi) long and 400 m (1,312 ft) wide. It consists of thousands of boulders of hard quartzite rock, mostly 0.3–2 m (11 in–6 ft 6 in) across.

▲ **MOST RECENT FLOOD BASALT ERUPTION**
When a huge volcanic eruption covers large areas of land or sea floor in basalt lava, the result is known as a "flood basalt". In 1783, Laki – a system of volcanic fissures in Iceland – began exploding, in one of only two episodes of flood basalt eruption in historic times. For eight months, it emitted some 15 km³ (3.5 cu mi) of lava, along with 122 million tonnes (134 million tons) of sulphur dioxide. The effects of this gas at least partially caused the devastatingly cold winters of 1783–84 and 1784–85 and the cool summer of 1784.

Anorthosite body

An igneous rock, anorthosite consists mostly of the mineral plagioclase feldspar. On Earth, there are two types of anorthosite – Archaean and Proterozoic – which formed 3.8–2.4 billion years ago and 2.5–0.5 billion years ago, respectively. They are thought to have formed in underground magma chambers where partially melted mantle material separated into denser "mafic" minerals and lighter "felsic" ones. A body of anorthosite, estimated at 20,000 km² (7,722 sq mi), underlies an area north of Lake St John in Quebec, Canada.

▲ LARGEST SANDSTONE MONOLITH ROCK FORMATION

Uluru rises 348 m (1,141 ft) above the surrounding desert plain in Northern Territory, Australia. Also known as Ayers Rock, this exposed sandstone monolith is 2.5 km (1.5 mi) long and 1.6 km (1 mi) wide. In fact, a further 2.5 km of this Australian landmark lies underground. The characteristic red hue of Uluru is caused by the rusting of the iron content in the rock at its surface.

▲ MOST COMMON VOLCANIC ROCK

Basalt accounts for more than 90% of all volcanic rock at the Earth's surface. It is the largest component of the oceanic crust and also constitutes the main rock type seen in many of the Earth's mid-ocean land forms, including the Hawaiian islands and Iceland. Basalt is fine-grained in texture and dark in colour. Approximately 50% of this rock is composed of silica; it also contains significant amounts of iron and magnesium. Pictured above is the Giant's Causeway – on the coast of County Antrim in Northern Ireland – which is formed from basalt.

Craton

This term describes large parts of continental crust that are stable and have remained relatively unmodified by plate tectonics since the end of the Precambrian period, 542 million years ago. They are normally located in the interior of continents and contain some of the oldest rocks on Earth. The North American craton is the largest, covering around 70% of the continent. It was formed some 2 billion years ago by the collision of several smaller microcontinents.

Native American tribes call this monolith by a number of different names. To the Kiowa, it is "Tree Rock" or "Aloft on a Rock", while the Lakota know it as "Grizzly Bear's Lodge".

▶ TALLEST VOLCANIC COLUMNS

Devils Tower in Wyoming, USA, began as an underground intrusion of igneous rock more than 50 million years ago. The surrounding softer sedimentary rock has eroded, leaving this towering monolith. Its volcanic columns, some 585 ft (178 m) tall, formed as the magma intrusion cooled and shrank. The Giant's Causeway (see above) is another example of this type of volcanic column.

Heavy Metal

As of 1700, only seven of the 84 metal elements on the periodic table were identified. These "Metals of Antiquity" were gold, copper, silver, lead, tin, iron and mercury.

ELEMENTARY SCHOOL

lead
82
Pb
207.2

Every element on the periodic table has its own atomic number, atomic weight and chemical symbol. Lead, for example, has an atomic number of 82, which means there are 82 protons in every atom. Its atomic weight (or relative atomic mass) is 207.2, which is the ratio of the average mass of an atom of lead compared to 1/12th of the mass of an atom of a carbon-12 isotope. Lead's chemical symbol is Pb. It derives from the Latin word *plumbum*, which means "liquid silver".

▼ MOST ABUNDANT METAL IN THE UNIVERSE

Iron (Fe) accounts for approximately 0.11% of all matter in the universe. The sixth most common element overall, it makes up around 0.1% of the Sun and 0.006% of a human being. It also accounts for around 22% of meteorite material found on Earth – such as the famous Willamette Meteorite (below), a giant chunk of iron-nickel space debris weighing 14.15 tonnes (31,195 lb) that was discovered in the US state of Oregon.

Longest half-life by alpha decay

Half-life is the measure of how long it takes an unstable element to decay. A half-life of one day means that it would take that time for half the atomic nuclei in a sample to decay into a more stable element. In 2003, French scientists discovered that bismuth-209, previously believed to be radioactively stable, in fact gradually decays with a half-life of around 20 billion billion years – more than a billion times the age of the universe.

iron
26
Fe
55.845

Ellis Hughes, a settler living in Oregon, moved the Willamette meteorite to his own land in 1903, with the help of his son. It took them 90 days to shift the vast stone just 1,200 m (3,940 ft)!

Q: Which element makes up most of the human body?

A: Oxygen. It accounts for around 65% of all the elements in us.

First artificially produced element
Technetium (Tc) was discovered in 1937 by Carlo Perrier and Emilio Segrè (both ITA) at the University of Palermo in Sicily, Italy. They isolated the element from a sample of molybdenum (Mo), which had been exposed to high levels of radiation in a particle accelerator known as a cyclotron. Its most stable isotope, technetium-98, has a half-life of around 4.2 million years, meaning that any significant mineral deposits in the Earth's crust have long since radioactively decayed into ruthenium-98.

Largest cluster of francium atoms made in a laboratory
In Dec 2002, scientists at the State University of New York, USA, managed to create francium (Fr) atoms using a heavy ion nuclear fusion reactor, collecting more than 300,000 together in a magneto-optical trap. Francium's most stable isotope has a half-life of just 22 min, making it the **most unstable naturally occurring element**. It has no practical uses.

Largest civil stockpile of plutonium
As of 2016, the UK held around 126 tonnes (277,782 lb) of plutonium (Pu), 23 tonnes (50,706 lb) of which is owned by other nations. A by-product of uranium used in nuclear reactors, the plutonium is stored at the Sellafield nuclear site in Cumbria. It exists in powdered form and is kept in steel and aluminium containers.

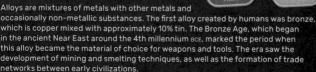

tin
50
Sn
118.71

copper
29
Cu
63.546

▲ FIRST ALLOY
Alloys are mixtures of metals with other metals and occasionally non-metallic substances. The first alloy created by humans was bronze, which is copper mixed with approximately 10% tin. The Bronze Age, which began in the ancient Near East around the 4th millennium BCE, marked the period when this alloy became the material of choice for weapons and tools. The era saw the development of mining and smelting techniques, as well as the formation of trade networks between early civilizations.

On Venus, it "snows" lead and bismuth sulphides, so the mountains are capped with metal

Toxic arsenic trioxide was mixed with chalk and vinegar in Victorian times to make face cream!

The element cobalt (Co) was named after "kobalt", the German word for goblin

More than half of the world's output of lead is used to make car batteries

Cigarettes often contain the heavy metals cadmium, lead, arsenic and nickel

An average 70-kg (154-lb) human body comprises about 0.01% heavy metals (7 g, the weight of two dried peas)

Tooth cavities are filled with "dental amalgam" – a liquid alloy of mercury and other metals. The technique dates to 658 CE.

HEAVIEST...

Naturally occurring element
In 1971, US scientist Darleane Hoffman published her discovery of small amounts of plutonium-244 in Precambrian phosphate deposits found in California, USA. Plutonium has an atomic number of 94.

Alkali metal to occur in significant quantities
Occupying group 1, or the left-most column of the periodic table, alkali metals are soft and highly reactive, with low density. Although caesium's atomic number of 55 is lower than that of francium (87), francium is only visible in microscopic amounts in the Earth's crust and is invisible to the naked eye.

Lanthanide metal
The lanthanide metals consist of the 15 elements with atomic numbers 57 to 71 and are sometimes known as the "rare earth elements", along with yttrium and scandium. Lutetium's atomic number of 71 makes it the heaviest of the group.

▲ **HEAVIEST ALKALINE EARTH METAL**
The alkaline earth metals occupy group two of the periodic table. They all occur naturally and have a shiny, silvery-white appearance. The heaviest is radium (Ra), with an atomic number of 88. Discovered by Marie and Pierre Curie (both FRA) in 1898, it is the only radioactive member of the alkaline earth metals. Radium is used in industrial imaging and radioluminescent devices.

▲ SOFTEST METALLIC ELEMENT

With a Mohs value of just 0.2, caesium (Cs) is soft enough to be cut with a butter knife. It melts at just 28°C (82°F) and explodes violently when dropped in water. Caesium was discovered in 1860 by the German scientists Robert Bunsen and Gustav Kirchhoff, who isolated it from a sample of mineral water using the recently developed technique of flame spectroscopy. Silvery-gold in colour, caesium's most notable use is in super-accurate atomic clocks.

Caesium is so reactive that it ignites on contact with air. It is stored in glass tubes inside inert gas, or in a vacuum, to keep it safe.

▲ LIGHTEST METAL THAT IS LIQUID NEAR ROOM TEMPERATURE

Discovered in 1875, the unusual metal gallium (Ga) possesses an atomic number of 31 and melts at just 29.76°C (85.56°F). Unlike liquid mercury, which is highly toxic, gallium is safe to handle and will melt in your hand. These properties have made it a key ingredient of a popular practical joke among some chemists, who serve tea with a gallium spoon that rapidly disappears upon stirring.

Transition metal

All elements in groups 3–12 of the periodic table (with the exception of lutetium and lawrencium) are known as transition metals. Less reactive than alkali metals, transition metals are good conductors of heat and electricity and include gold, copper and iron. With an atomic number of 112, copernicium (Cn) is the heaviest of these metals. First created in 1996, it is a man-made element that does not occur in nature.

Element to produce a net release of energy via nuclear fusion

Elements are created in the cores of stars by a process called stellar nucleosynthesis, in which the protons and neutrons of lighter elements are bonded together to form heavier ones. Iron (atomic number 26) is the heaviest element that can be created without requiring additional energy. Stars producing elements heavier than iron suffer a dramatic drop in energy output, leading to collapse and eventual supernova.

◄ HIGHEST BOILING POINT OF ANY METAL

As established by the International Tungsten Industrial Association (ITIA), Tungsten (W) has a boiling point of 5,700°C (10,292°F), with a 200°C (392°F) margin of error each side. This is equivalent to the surface temperature of the Sun. Tungsten also has the **highest melting point of any metal**, at 3,422°C (6,191°F), with a 15°C (59°F) margin of error. Its extraordinary heat resistance makes tungsten a useful metal for industrial applications such as drill-bits and furnaces.

osmium
76
Os
190.23

▲ DENSEST METAL

Discovered in 1803 by Smithson Tennant and William Hyde Wollaston (both UK), osmium (Os) has a density of 22.59 g/cm³, about twice that of lead. The toxic nature of osmium's oxides mean that it is rarely used in its natural form. However, its hardwearing qualities make it ideal for use in alloys for electrical contacts and fountain-pen nibs. The **least dense metal** at room temperature is lithium, at 0.5334 g/cm³.

▶ HARDEST METALLIC ELEMENT

Chromium (Cr) boasts a value of 8.5 on the Mohs scale, which measures the hardness of minerals by their scratch resistance to other materials. Lustrous and steely grey, chromium has both a high melting point and corrosion resistance. When added to iron in sufficient quantities, it forms the corrosion-proof alloy known as stainless steel. Chromium takes its name from the Greek word for "colour" – trace amounts of the element are what make rubies red. They are also responsible for the brilliant red hue of the samples of crocoite mineral (shown left), which were retrieved from a Tasmanian lead mine.

chromium
24
Cr
51.996

Tectonics

Most of Earth's geological activity occurs at the points where tectonic plates come together or divide.

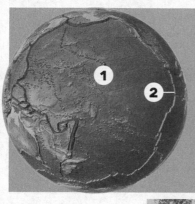

◄ LARGEST AND SMALLEST TECTONIC PLATES

The Earth's rocky outer shell is broken into large pieces called "plates", which constantly move. The Pacific plate (1) is more than 103,000,000 km² (39,768,522 sq mi) in area. It is moving north-west in relation to North America around 7 cm (2.75 in) per year, as measured around the Hawaiian islands.

The North Galápagos microplate (2) is in the Pacific Ocean, off the west coast of South America. Only around 1,559 km² (602 sq mi) in size, it sits at the junction of the Nazca, Cocos and Pacific plates.

Widest continental shelf

Continental shelves are an extension of coastal plains and are characterized by broadly sloping submerged plains. Around 7.4% of the world's ocean surface sits above continental shelves. The widest one extends 1,210 km (750 mi) off the coast of Siberia, Russia, into the Arctic Ocean.

Largest continental collision zone

Some 40–50 million years ago, the Indian subcontinent collided with the Eurasian continent. The impact, which is still ongoing along a zone roughly 2,400 km (1,490 mi) in length, created the Himalayan mountains.

Nanga Parbat, a mountain in Pakistan, began forming when this continental collision occurred. It is the **fastest-rising mountain**, growing taller at a rate of 7 mm (0.27 in) per year.

▲ HIGHEST EARTHQUAKE DEATH TOLL IN MODERN TIMES

At 21:53 Coordinated Universal Time (UTC) on 12 Jan 2010, a magnitude-7 quake struck with an epicentre around 25 km (15.5 mi) west of the Haitian capital Port-au-Prince. Haiti's government later put the death toll at 316,000, although lower estimates put the figure at 100,000. Some 1.3 million people were displaced by the earthquake and 97,294 houses destroyed.

◀ MOST RECENT SUPERCONTINENT

In the distant past, tectonic plate movement combined Earth's continental crust into one landmass – a supercontinent. There have been perhaps seven in all; each one broke up due to the same tectonic processes that created them. This last happened some 300 million years ago, when the crust gathered in the southern hemisphere to create the supercontinent that we call Pangea.

▼ LARGEST OPHIOLITE

Ophiolites are formed by tectonic activity that lifts sections of Earth's oceanic crust above sea level and sometimes places them into the continental crust. The Semail ophiolite in Oman's Hajar Mountains measures around 550 x 150 km (341 x 93 mi) and covers an area of approximately 100,000 km^2 (38,610 sq mi). It formed around 96–94 million years ago, in the Late Cretaceous period, and is rich in copper and chromite. The inset picture provides a close-up of "pillow lavas" at this location – rounded shapes of lava that originally formed underwater.

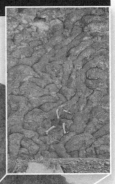

Q: We live at the top of Earth's crust. How far below the surface does it extend for?

A: Around 70 km (44 mi)

Fastest-moving strike-slip fault

New Zealand's Alpine Fault runs along most of South Island and marks the point where the Pacific and Australian plates meet. These plates are moving relative to each other in a strike-slip fault (the transform fault is one such – see p.22). On 8 Mar 2016, scientists from Victoria University of Wellington and GNS Science (both NZ) revealed that the plates are moving 4.7 cm (1.8 in) per year in relation to each other, and have covered 700 km (434 mi) in the past 25 million years.

▲ LONGEST RIFT SYSTEM

Rift valleys form when Earth's plates pull apart. The East African Rift System is around 4,000 mi (6,400 km) long – almost as long as the Amazon River – with an average width of some 30–40 mi (50–65 km). It runs from Jordan to Mozambique. The escarpments at the valley's edge have an average height of 600–900 m (1,968–2,952 ft). It has been forming for some 30 million years, as the Arabian Peninsula has separated from Africa.

Fastest seafloor spreading centre

The East Pacific Rise is a tectonic plate boundary that runs from Antarctica to the west coast of the USA. A portion of the East Pacific Rise called the Pacific-Nazca boundary is pushing the Pacific and Nazca continental plates apart at a rate of around 15 cm (5.9 in) per year.

The **slowest seafloor spreading centre** is the Gakkel Mid-Ocean Ridge, the northern extension of the Mid-Atlantic Ridge. Separating the North American and Eurasian plates, it runs for 1,800 km (1,118 mi) from the north of Greenland to Siberia. The rate of spread ranges from 13.3 mm (0.52 in) per year near Greenland to 6.3 mm (0.24 in) per year at the other end, close to Siberia.

Newest ocean

In 2005, a rift 56 km (34.7 mi) long opened in the Afar Depression in Ethiopia (aka the Danakil Depression, the lowest point in Africa). In Nov 2009, geologists heralded it as a new ocean.

The Pacific is the **oldest ocean**. Some rocks on its floor are approximately 200 million years old.

Oldest evidence for plate tectonics

On 8 Jul 2002, a team of Chinese and US geologists announced their discovery of rocks indicating that plate tectonics were active on Earth some 2.5 billion years ago. This is around 500 million years earlier than previously thought.

Three types of plate boundaries:

Transform
Tectonic plates slide sideways past each other

Divergent
The plates slide apart

Convergent
The plates slide towards each other

▲ LONGEST SUBDUCTION

"Subduction" describes the movement of one tectonic plate beneath another (see convergent plate boundary illustration, above right). The Andean Subduction Zone runs for some 7,000 km (4,350 mi) along the western coast of South America. Here, the denser ocean crust of the Nazca plate plunges below the lighter continental crust of South America and is recycled in the Earth's upper mantle.

▲ LONGEST EARTHQUAKE

The Sumatra-Andaman Islands earthquake in the Indian Ocean, on 26 Dec 2004, was the longest-lasting ever recorded. Its duration was measured at 500–600 sec – around 10 minutes! The magnitude-9.1–9.3 earthquake triggered a massive tsunami (damage pictured) that devastated low-lying regions around the Indian Ocean and caused damage as far away as Somalia.

The Mid-Atlantic Ridge moves at 10–40 mm (0.39–1.5 in) a year – or about the same rate that your fingernails grow

The Nazca plate travels at 160 mm (6.29 in) a year, or about the same rate that your hair grows

Tectonic plates are around 100 km (62 mi) thick – about the same as the thickness of the Earth's atmosphere

Atmosphere

Tectonic plate

Magma

FIRST...

Continent
Geological evidence suggests that there was a single continental landmass on Earth from 3.6 billion to 2.8 billion years ago. Named Vaalbara, it was smaller than any of today's continents.

Suggestion of continental drift
Looking at any map of Earth, it is clear that the coastlines of west Africa and east South America complement each other. The first person to have noticed this is believed to have been the Flemish mapmaker Abraham Ortelius (1527–98). He argued that the two continents were once joined together before being pulled apart "by earthquakes and flood". Continental drift only became accepted by mainstream academia in the second half of the 20th century.

Earthquake registered from orbit
The European Space Agency's (ESA) Gravity Field and Steady-State Ocean Circulation Explorer (GOCE) satellite was launched on 17 Mar 2009. It mapped the Earth's gravity field until 11 Nov 2013, when it re-entered the atmosphere and was destroyed. On 11 Mar 2011, as it passed through Earth's ultra-thin thermosphere, GOCE picked up weak sound waves caused by a devastating earthquake that struck Japan.

▲ LONGEST SUBMARINE MOUNTAIN RANGE
The Mid-Ocean Ridge is an underwater mountain range that extends 40,000 mi (65,000 km) from the Arctic Ocean to the Atlantic Ocean, around Africa, Asia and Australia, and under the Pacific Ocean to the west coast of North America. At its apex, it stands 13,800 ft (4,200 m) above the base ocean depth – around half as tall as Everest, the **highest mountain**.

Pollution & Environment

In 2016, scientists announced that the hole in the ozone layer above Antarctica was healing. If the current trend persists, it will have closed by 2050.

Warmest month on record

On 12 Sep 2016, NASA revealed that the warmest months on record were Jul and Aug 2016. The analysis by scientists at NASA's Goddard Institute for Space Studies in New York City, USA, showed that Aug 2016 was 0.98°C (1.76°F) hotter than the mean August temperature from 1951 to 1980. It was also 0.16°C (0.28°F) hotter than the previous warmest August, in 2014.

Smallest recorded size of the Arctic ice cap

The extent of the ice floating on the surface of the Arctic Ocean changes with the seasons, shrinking to a minimum at the end of summer. Its smallest size was registered on 17 Sep 2012, with an area of 3.41 million km² (1.31 million sq mi).

After its 2016 expansion, the Papahānaumokuākea Marine National Monument has quadrupled in size, making it almost equal in area to the Gulf of Mexico.

Largest dead zone

Waters in some coastal areas have very low concentrations of oxygen (hypoxia), making life impossible for many species; such areas are called "dead zones". The largest is in the Baltic Sea, with an average area of 49,000 km² (18,919 sq mi) over the last 40 years. In 1971, the area peaked at 70,000 km² (27,027 sq mi), more than twice the area of Belgium.

▼ LARGEST TROPICAL MARINE RESERVE

On 26 Aug 2016, US president Barack Obama (left) announced the expansion of the Papahānaumokuākea Marine National Monument around the Hawaiian archipelago. It is now 582,578 sq mi (1.5 million km²) in size.

Until 28 Oct 2016, it was also the **largest marine reserve overall**. But on that date, 24 countries and the European Union agreed to declare 1.55 million km² (600,000 sq mi) of the Ross Sea in Antarctica a protected marine area. As a "no-take" zone, nothing can be removed, including marine life and minerals, for 35 years.

▼

Largest extent of the Antarctic sea ice

The Antarctic continent is surrounded by frozen sea; the extent of this ice sheet peaks at the end of the southern winter. On 20 Sep 2014, the Antarctic sea ice peaked at 20.201 million km² (7.8 million sq mi). The additional area of sea ice created by this erratic growth is dwarfed by the area of ice lost in the shrinking Arctic.

Highest level of carbon dioxide in the atmosphere

In 2015, the average concentration of carbon dioxide in the atmosphere reached a level of 400 ppm for the first time. Such high concentrations had been reached before, for short periods, but never as an annual average.

Highest level of acidity in ocean waters

On 4 Jun 2004, in the Beaufort Sea north of Alaska, USA, the water pH level was 6.9718 at a depth of 2 m (6 ft 6 in). This concentration of acids is about 10 times higher than average.

Measuring the pressure of a gas in water is a way of quantifying how much of that gas is dissolved. The higher the quantity dissolved, the higher the pressure. The water samples taken on 4 Jun 2004 had a carbon dioxide pressure reading of 3,796.8 micro atmosphere (384.71 Pa). Some 10 times greater than average, this is the **highest level of carbon dioxide in ocean waters**.

Longest global coral bleaching event

Higher atmospheric concentrations of carbon dioxide result in more of this acidic gas being absorbed in oceanic waters. Ocean acidification

▲ HIGHEST ANTARCTIC CO2 LEVELS

According to the National Oceanic and Atmospheric Administration (NOAA), the South Pole Observatory's carbon dioxide station measured 400 ppm (parts per million) for the first time on 12 May 2016. Carbon dioxide (CO_2) levels have taken time to reach the South Pole as most of the world's population (and its pollution) are in the northern hemisphere.

may be one cause of coral bleaching. Earth's coral reefs are currently undergoing a global bleaching event first seen in mid-2014 in the western Pacific Ocean. As of Jan 2017, this event had lasted more than two-and-a-half years.

On 29 Nov 2016, scientists revealed that two-thirds of a 700-km (435-mi) stretch of the Great Barrier Reef – located off Queensland, north-eastern Australia – had been killed off, the **greatest coral die-off on the Great Barrier Reef**. A rise in ocean temperature was the cause of the damage. Teams of divers led by Professor Andrew Baird, of the Australian Research Council (ARC) Centre of Excellence for Coral Reef Studies, inspected the reef in Oct and Nov 2016.

100+

petrol stations in the Nigerian city of Onitsha (population: 1 million), the worst city for air pollution

India is home to 16 of the world's 30 most polluted cities; of these, the most contaminated is Delhi

Air pollution promotes a higher risk of stroke, heart disease, lung cancer and respiratory problems

3 million

deaths each year are attributable to air pollution

80%

of the planet's urban population is exposed to levels of air pollution greater than the limit established by the World Health Organization (WHO)

▲ HIGHEST SCORE ON THE ENVIRONMENTAL PERFORMANCE INDEX

Finland is the country with the best environmental performance, according to research findings presented to the World Economic Forum on 23 Jan 2016 by scientists from the USA's Yale and Columbia universities. In all, 180 countries were studied, using more than 20 key indicators under nine categories: health impacts, air quality, water and sanitation, water resources, agriculture, forests, fisheries, biodiversity and habitat, and climate and energy.

▲ WORST CITY FOR AIR POLLUTION

PM_{10}s are "particulate matter" such as soot (carbon), metal or dust with a diameter of 10 microns or less. According to the WHO's Ambient Air Pollution report for 2016, the port of Onitsha in south-eastern Nigeria recorded levels of 594 micrograms per m³ of PM_{10}s. This is around 30 times the WHO's recommended level of 20 micrograms per m³, making it the city with the most contaminated air.

First global survey of ocean plastic pollution

On 10 Dec 2014, an international team of scientists, led by the Five Gyres Institute (USA), published the results of a massive survey of plastic pollution in the world's oceans. The team's estimate – based on surveys of beach debris around the world, sample-taking voyages and computer models – was that there were 5.25 trillion pieces of plastic in the oceans.

More recently, the United Nations Environment Programme has studied the composition of this plastic plague. In Aug 2016 the UNEP found that the **most common ocean pollutant** – forming around 50% of all plastic matter in the oceans – is discarded carrier bags.

▲ LARGEST PRODUCER OF CARBON DIOXIDE (COUNTRY)

The Emissions Database for Global Atmospheric Research (EDGAR) is a joint project between the Netherlands Environmental Assessment Agency and the European Commission Joint Research Centre. According to the database, in 2015 China was responsible for 10.64 billion tonnes (11.72 billion tons) of carbon-dioxide emissions. To put that in context, the global carbon-dioxide emissions for 2015 totalled 36.24 billion tonnes (39.94 billion tons).

▲ WORST RIVER POLLUTION INCIDENT

On 1 Nov 1986, firemen fighting a blaze at the Sandoz chemical works in Basel, Switzerland, flushed around 30 tonnes (66,138 lb) of agricultural chemicals into the river Rhine, along with the water they were using to combat the fire. The river water turned red from the influx of chemicals, which included pesticides and mercury. Within 10 days, the pollution had reached the North Sea. Half a million fish died from the toxic chemicals.

▲ LOWEST GLOBAL TREE POPULATION

On 2 Sep 2015, a report by an international team of scientists led by Yale University, USA, revealed that there were around 3.04 trillion trees on Earth, or around 422 trees for each person. The survey also suggests that, since the beginning of human civilization, Earth has lost nearly 46% of its trees and is now less forested than at any time in recorded history. Human activity destroys some 15 billion trees each year.

▲ LARGEST DARK-SKY PRESERVE

On 28 Jun 2013, Wood Buffalo National Park in Canada was declared a dark-sky preserve by the Royal Astronomical Society of Canada. At 44,807 km² (17,300 sq mi), it is Canada's largest national park. Dark-sky preserves implement policies to protect the night sky from light pollution so as to prevent disruption to the diurnal cycles of plants and animals, as well as allowing people to see the night sky without the dimming caused by light pollution.

▼ BIGGEST GLOBAL TOXIC THREAT

In 2015, the not-for-profit organization Pure Earth, formerly known as the Blacksmith Institute, published a report naming the top six worst global pollution problems. Lead pollution was seen as the biggest threat, with as many as 26 million people at risk worldwide. The other five were mercury, radionuclides, chromium, pesticides and cadmium.

Lead-acid storage batteries, used in car engines, contain highly toxic lead and sulphuric acid. This car battery dump is in the town of Athi River in Kenya.

Wildfires

"Fire chaser" beetles (genus *Melanophila*) use their infra-red sensors to seek out forest fires. Burnt trees have no chemical defences to attack their eggs.

The area devastated by the 1871 wildfire in Wisconsin and Michigan (see below) was slightly larger than Belgium – or twice the size of Kuwait.

Earliest known wildfire

In Apr 2004, scientists from Cardiff University's School of Earth, Ocean and Planetary Science (UK) found evidence that a low-intensity wildfire began smouldering c. 419 million years ago, in the Silurian period. The fire was likely started by a lightning strike. The discovery was made while the team was studying charred fossils of small plants found in rocks near Ludlow, UK.

Longest-burning fire

The fire in a burning coal seam beneath Mount Wingen in New South Wales, Australia, is believed to have started 5,000 years ago. It ignited when lightning struck the seam at the point where it reached the Earth's surface. Today, the fire is burning around 100 ft (30 m) underground, as it has slowly eaten away at the seam.

◄ HIGHEST DEATH TOLL FROM A WILDFIRE

On 8 Oct 1871, forest fires ravaged north-east Wisconsin and upper Michigan, USA, killing around 1,200 to 2,500 people. More than 1,500 sq mi (3,885 km²) of forest and farmland were also destroyed (see illustration, left).

Under certain circumstances, tornado-like phenomena known as "fire whirls" can occur within fires. They are caused by heat rising and forming eddies. The **highest death toll from a fire whirl** happened as a result of the Great Kanto Earthquake on 1 Sep 1923, which struck the Kanto region of Honshu in Japan (see photograph, left). Tragically, 38,000 people were incinerated by a fire whirl while packed into a former army clothing depot in Tokyo.

Wildfires can start from the spontaneous combusting of dead leaves, twigs and branches

More than 80% of wildfires are begun by humans - either deliberately or by accident

Lightning strikes can ignite a wildfire under certain conditions

Wildfires can travel at speeds of **14 mph (23 km/h)**

10.1 million

acres (40,873,249,866 m²) of the USA were destroyed by wildfires in 2015 - equivalent to more than...

20,000

American football fields every day!

WILDFIRES

The picture right shows a wildfire in Brazil's Cerrado ecoregion. Such conflagrations are usually man-made, but wildfires can also start naturally. Dry forest debris can catch fire, and lightning strikes may ignite fires. There are positive aspects to less destructive forest fires, however. Old growth and weeds are burned off, stimulating regeneration. Minerals and nutrients are released from burning plants and returned to the soil. Forest canopies are opened up too, allowing more sunlight to reach plants on the ground.

First use of a fire shelter

The last resort used by firefighters faced with wildfires that have surrounded them is to build a fire shelter. Designed to reflect heat, keep out convective heat and contain breathable air, they resemble a shallow one-person tent and are deployed on the ground or in a dug-out hollow. The earliest known use of a fire shelter was noted by explorer William Clark in a journal entry dated 29 Oct 1804. Reporting the outbreak of a prairie wildfire near Fort Mandan in North Dakota, USA, Clark related an incident in which an American mother threw a "Green buffalow Skin" [sic] over her son to protect him from the flames.

Most energy released by a burning tree

The heat content of any fire depends upon wood density, resin, ash and moisture, but the tree that produces the most heat when burned is the osage-orange or horse-apple (*Maclura pomifera*), a large deciduous shrub-like plant belonging to the mulberry family, and distributed widely across North America. When burned, this species produces some 34.8 billion joules per 20% air-dried moisture content cord. A cord is defined as a stack of wood 4 ft wide by 4 ft high by 8 ft long (1.21 m x 1.21 m x 2.43 m), with an average 80 cu ft (2.2 m³) of burnable wood, the remainder being pockets of air.

Longest firebreak

A firebreak is a break in vegetation that acts to block the progress of wildfires. Man-made firebreaks are often created in the form of roads strategically constructed in places at high risk of wildfires. In 1931, construction began on the Ponderosa Way on the western slope of the Sierra Nevada Mountains in California, USA. Eventually reaching a length of some

A: Buildings in its path were blown up, to stop the flames spreading

This Boeing 747-400 drops its load from a height of just 120–240 m (393–787 ft), travelling at around 260 km/h (160 mph).

▲ LARGEST FIREFIGHTING AIRCRAFT

Global SuperTanker Services uses a converted Boeing 747-400 jumbo jet as an aerial firefighter. The aircraft can transport 74,200 litres (19,601 US gal) of water or fire retardant.

Introduced in 1994, the Mi-26TP is the **largest firefighting helicopter** at 33.73 m (110 ft 7 in) long, with a maximum take-off weight of 56 tonnes (123,459 lb). It can be equipped with the VSU-15 water drop system – essentially a sack of tough parachute material that can be lowered into a reservoir and filled with 15 tonnes (16.5 tons) of water in around 30 sec.

800 mi (1,287 km) – around the same as the Rhine river – the Ponderosa Way was built by around 16,000 members of the Civilian Conservation Corps. In 1934 alone, the firebreak was responsible for containing nine of the 11 large wildfires that hit the region that year.

Most smokejumpers per country

Smokejumpers are elite firefighters who are deployed to remote wildfires as soon as they are identified. They are dropped by parachute near a wildfire, along with their equipment, including food and water to make them self-sufficient for a day or two. Once deployed, smokejumpers use chainsaws and other equipment to cut down trees, scrape away topsoil and create firebreaks. Russia, which introduced smokejumpers in around 1936, currently employs approximately 4,000 of them.

▲ WORST YEAR FOR DESTRUCTION OF THE NATURAL ENVIRONMENT BY FIRE

According to the World Wide Fund for Nature, forest fires that had been deliberately lit made 1997 the worst year in history for the devastation of the natural environment. The largest and most numerous were in Brazil, where they raged along a 1,000-mi (1,600-km) front. Although the droughts in the Amazon Basin and South-east Asia (caused by the El Niño effect) were partially to blame for the forest fires, the deliberate lighting of fires to clear forest was the main cause of the disaster.

In this picture, a firefighter shovels sand on to encroaching forest-fire flames, having turned a sapling into a makeshift handle for his spade.

▼ LARGEST WILDFIRE (CURRENT)

According to Greenpeace, as of Jun 2016 wildfires covered some 35,000 km² (13,513 sq mi) of Siberia. Recent very dry weather has exacerbated Siberia's seasonal wildfires. Climate change in Russia is almost certainly to blame; from 1976 to 2012, the average temperature rose by more than twice the global average. Siberia is one of Earth's most forested regions, containing great biodiversity and species such as bears, wolves and golden eagles.

Most coal fires underground (country)

China, the world's **largest producer of coal**, has hundreds of subterranean fires across its coal belt. Some have been burning for centuries. Around 20 million tonnes (19.6 million tons) of coal per year are destroyed and 10 times that amount rendered inaccessible owing to the fires.

▲ **HIGHEST CLOUDS FORMED BY WILDFIRES**

The intense heat from wildfires can make weather. The powerful updrafts of air can carry water vapour and ash high into the atmosphere, creating a type of cumulus cloud known as pyrocumulus. These clouds can reach around 10,000 m (32,800 ft) in height. Even more powerful are pyrocumulonimbus clouds (above), which can reach altitudes of around 16,000 m (52,490 ft).

Fungi

Approximately 50% of mushrooms are inedible; 25% are tasteless; 20% cause sickness; 4% are tasty; and 1% can kill you.

Cap

Scales

Margin (edge)

Gills

Ring (annulus)

Stem (stipe/stalk)

Volva (base or bulb)

Earliest lichen
The lichen *Winfrenatia* evolved approximately 400 million years ago, in the early Devonian period. Some of its fossilized remains were found in the Rhynie Chert – a sedimentary deposit containing exceptionally well-preserved plant, fungus, lichen and animal material. The site is named after the nearby village of Rhynie in Aberdeenshire, UK.

Tallest fungus
Prototaxites was a prehistoric fungus dating from the late Silurian to the late Devonian periods (420 to 370 million years ago). This terrestrial North American life-form produced relatively massive tree-trunk-like structures that grew to 1 m (3 ft 3 in) wide and 8 m (26 ft 2 in) in height – taller than a giraffe. These trunks were composed of numerous interwoven tubes, each of which was no more than 50 μm (micrometres) across. Its dimensions also mean that *Prototaxites* was by far the tallest organism of any kind known to have existed during that particular time period.

Heaviest single fungus
On 2 Apr 1992, a single living clonal growth of the soil fungus *Armillaria bulbosa* was reported to be covering some 15 ha (37 acres) of forest in Michigan, USA. It was calculated to weigh more than 100 tonnes (220,462 lb) – or around 30 hippos. The fungus is thought to have begun at least 1,500 years ago, from one fertilized spore.

Most sexes within one species
In some fungi, two different genes yield two different sexes – male and female – as with animals and plants. But in other fungi, each of these two genes can have several different versions (or "alleles"), resulting in a far larger number of sexes. Slightly more than 28,000 different sexes have been documented from the split gill fungus (*Schizophyllum commune*), an extremely common mushroom species with a global distribution. One of its two sex genes has more than 300 alleles, and the other has in excess of 90 alleles, yielding more than 28,000 different allele combinations – and therefore sexes – from just these two genes.

▲ WHAT IS A MUSHROOM?
Mushrooms fulfil the same purpose for a fungus as fruits and flowers do for plants: they help the organism to germinate. Each mushroom produces microscopic spores, which are rather like seeds or pollen. Some species may produce trillions of these tiny reproductive units.

▲ LARGEST PHYLUM OF FUNGI

The most extensive of the seven phyla (highest taxonomic groups) of fungi is Ascomycota, or "sac fungi". It contains more than 64,000 species known to science, although many as-yet-undiscovered species are thought to exist. Shown here, clockwise from top left, are four colourful Ascomycota species: scarlet elfcup (*Sarcoscypha austriaca*), green elfcup (*Chlorociboria aeruginascens*), cup fungi (*Cookeina* sp.) and devil's matchstick (*Cladonia floerkeana*).

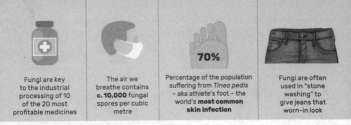

Fungi are key to the industrial processing of 10 of the 20 most profitable medicines

The air we breathe contains c. **10,000** fungal spores per cubic metre

70%
Percentage of the population suffering from *Tinea pedis* – aka athlete's foot – the world's **most common skin infection**

Fungi are often used in "stone washing" to give jeans that worn-in look

Most aquatic species of mushroom

Psathyrella aquatica is native to the Rogue River in Oregon, USA. It is the only basidiomycete species whose fruiting body exists underwater. It is anchored up to 0.5 m (1 ft 7 in) deep in sediment, in order to withstand the river's strong, fast-moving currents. All of the other higher-fungi mushrooms presently known to science are terrestrial.

LARGEST...

Truffle

On 6 Dec 2014, a 1,786-g (3-lb 14.9-oz) *Tuber magnatum pico* was sold by Sabatino Tartufi (ITA/USA) to a bidder in Chinese Taipei for $61,250 (£39,154) at Sotheby's in New York City, USA. In the week after its discovery in Italy, evaporation reduced it from a reported 1,890 g (4 lb 2.6 oz).

Fungal growth

A fungus in the Malheur National Forest in the Blue Mountains of eastern Oregon, USA, covers 890 ha (2,199 acres) – equivalent to around 1,220 soccer fields. Named *Armillaria ostoyae* (and commonly known as the honey mushroom), it is thought to be at least 2,400 years old.

This growth is also the **largest bioluminescent organism**. The honey mushroom is known for its glowing surface, caused by bioluminescent bacteria, although most of its tissue is 1 m (3 ft) underground, in the form of root-like mycelia.

Tree fungus

In 1995, a bracket fungus (*Rigidoporus ulmarius*) growing from dead elm wood in the grounds of the Mycological Herbarium at the Royal Botanic Gardens in Kew, Surrey, UK, was found to measure 1.6 x 1.4 m (5 ft 4 in x 4 ft 7 in). The record-breaking growth had a circumference of 4.8 m (15 ft 9 in).

◀ MOST EXPENSIVE FUNGUS

The edible white truffle (*T. magnatum pico*) is the world's priciest fungus, commanding up to $3,000 (£2,431) per kg. It is found only in the Italian regions of Piedmont, Emilia-Romagna, Tuscany and Marche, and the Istrian peninsula of Croatia. Because this truffle grows around 30 cm (1 ft) underground, it can only be located with the help of pigs or trained dogs.

Mushrooms can be used to make paper

Fungi play a major role in the production of beer, spirits, wine, bread and cheese

Estimates suggest that there are 5.1 million different fungal species in existence

▶ FASTEST-ACCELERATING ORGANISM

The hat-throwing fungus (*Pilobolus crystallinus*) is native to Eurasia, North America and Australia. Its asexual fruiting structure (the sporangiophore) is a stalk that resembles a tiny translucent snake, bearing at one end a sporangium, or sac of spores. When it is mature, a huge increase in internal pressure causes the sporangiophore to "throw" its hat-shaped sporangium with an acceleration of 0–20 km/h (0–12.4 mph) in only 2 µs (microseconds), subjecting it to a force of more than 20,000 g. This is a greater rate of acceleration than that of a speeding bullet, the equivalent of a human being launched at 100 times the speed of sound.

Basidiospore

Basidiomycetes, known as the "higher fungi", include mushrooms, toadstools, puffballs, bracket fungi and rust fungi. Most reproduce sexually, producing minuscule specialized spores known as basidiospores. The largest of these spores are those produced by *Aleurodiscus gigasporus*, a species of crust (corticioid) fungus from China. They measure 34 x 28 µm (micrometres), with an estimated mass of 17 ng (nanograms) and a volume of 14 pL (picolitres). To put that in context, they are about a tenth of the size of a full stop on this page.

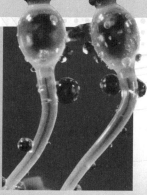

◀ MOST POISONOUS FUNGUS

The death cap (*Amanita phalloides*) can be found worldwide and is responsible for 90% of fatal poisonings caused by fungi. Its toxin content is 7–9 mg (0.1–0.13 grains) per gram of the mushroom's dry weight. The amount of amatoxins (i.e., a set of related toxins) considered lethal for humans, depending on bodyweight, is only 5–7 mg (0.07–0.1 grains), the equivalent of less than 50 g (1.76 oz) of a fresh fungus.

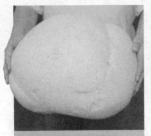

▲ LARGEST PUFFBALL

The giant puffball (*Calvatia gigantea*) fungus is native to temperate areas worldwide. Its spheroid fruiting body (the fleshy part where the spores develop) can reach 1.5 m (4 ft 11 in) in diameter and weigh 20 kg (44 lb). The species develops during late summer and autumn, and occurs in fields, meadows and deciduous forests.

▲ HEAVIEST EDIBLE FUNGUS

On 15 Oct 1990, Giovanni Paba of Broadstone, Dorset, UK, found a huge "chicken of the woods" mushroom (*Laetiporus sulphureus*) in the New Forest, Hampshire, UK. The outsized fungus weighed 100 lb (45.35 kg). Its common name derives from the fact that the fungus is said to have a chicken-like taste.

▲ LONGEST EDIBLE MUSHROOM

A *Pleurotus eryngii* grown by HOKUTO Corporation (JPN) measured 59 cm (1 ft 11.22 in) long at the company's Mushroom Research Laboratory in Nagano, Japan, on 25 Jul 2014. The fungus, which weighed 3.58 kg (7 lb 14.2 oz), took 66 days to grow and the team had to make sure it did not fall and break under its own weight.

The Deep

Below 200 m (656 ft), you are in "deep sea": beyond this, the temperatures near 0°C (32°F), the light fades and the pressure is hundreds of times greater than at sea level.

Largest shipwreck

The 153,479-gross-tonnage VLCC (Very Large Crude Carrier) *Energy Determination* blew up on 13 Dec 1979 and later broke in two in the Strait of Hormuz, Persian Gulf. It was not carrying cargo, but its hull value was $58 m (£26 m at 1979 rates).

Largest deep-sea research submersible

The *Ben Franklin* (PX-15) measured 48 ft 9 in (14.85 m) in length, with a displacement mass of around 295,000 lb (133.8 tonnes). She was developed by NASA and Northrop Grumman (both USA) and built in Switzerland. On 14 Jul 1969 she was launched, with a crew of six, on a 30-day mission to drift in the Gulf Stream at a maximum depth of some 600 m (1,970 ft). She was sold privately in 1971 and now is on display at the Vancouver Maritime Museum in Canada.

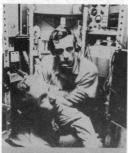

▲ DEEPEST MANNED DESCENT

On 23 Jan 1960, Dr Jacques Piccard (CHE, top) and Lt Donald Walsh (USA, bottom) piloted the Swiss-built US Navy bathyscaphe *Trieste* to a depth of 10,911 m (35,797 ft) in the Challenger Deep section of the Mariana Trench.

Boaty McBoatface will be the name of one of the remotely operated submersibles on the RRS *Sir David Attenborough*, which is under construction in Birkenhead, UK, and will sail in 2019.

▼ MOST PUBLIC VOTES TO NAME A RESEARCH VESSEL

In Mar 2016, the UK's National Environment Research Council (NERC) announced that their new research ship, which would replace the RRS *James Clark Ross* and the RRS *Ernest Shackleton*, would be named by the public via an online vote. The polls closed on 16 Apr 2016; the winner, with 124,109 votes, was "Boaty McBoatface". Despite this, NERC decided to name the vessel RRS *Sir David Attenborough*, after the British natural history broadcaster, whose name came fourth in the poll.

FIRST...

Scientific instrument used in deep-sea exploration
In 1840, while leading an expedition to the Antarctic, British explorer Sir James Clark Ross used a sounding weight to reach a depth of 3,700 m (12,139 ft). This instrument comprised a lead weight attached to rope, which was lowered until it touched the sea floor.

Phone call from the ocean floor to space
On 29 Aug 1965, during NASA's Gemini V mission, the orbiting crew of Gordon Cooper and Charles Conrad received a radiotelephone call from fellow astronaut Scott Carpenter (all USA). Carpenter was on board the experimental marine habitat *Sealab II*, at a depth of 62 m (203 ft) off the coast of California, USA. He spent 30 days living on *Sealab II*, during which he performed research on physiology.

▲ DEEPEST-DIVING SUBMERSIBLE IN SERVICE
Of the submersibles currently in service, the Chinese research submarine *Jiaolong* is capable of diving the deepest. On 24 Jun 2012, piloted by Ye Cong, Liu Kaizhou and Yang Bo (all CHN), it descended to a depth of 7,020 m (23,031 ft) in the Mariana Trench in the western Pacific Ocean. During an 11-hr submersion, the "oceanauts" spent 3 hr exploring the ocean floor, taking sediment and water samples and positioning markers.

Recorded whale fall
In 1956, a research paper was published detailing the fate of whale carcasses that fall to the seabed. It was not until 1977, however, when the bathyscaphe *Trieste II* was exploring the Santa Catalina Basin off the USA's west coast, that the first natural whale fall was discovered. The ocean floor is poor in nutrients, and many species rely on the constant fall of organic particles from above known as "marine snow". One 40-tonne (88,000-lb) whale carcass provides a source of carbon equivalent to 100–200 years' worth of marine snow falling on 1 ha (2.47 acres) of ocean floor.

▶ DEEPEST HYDROTHERMAL VENTS
On 21 Feb 2013, a team of British scientists on board the research ship RRS *James Cook* announced that they had found hydrothermal vents at a depth of 4,968 m (16,299 ft). The vents were discovered in the Cayman Trough in the Caribbean Sea by means of a remotely operated underwater vehicle (ROV). The ROV measured the temperature of the mineral-rich water emanating from the vents at 401°C (753.8°F).

A: The deepest parts of the ocean. It is named after Hades, the god of the underworld in Greek myth.

DEEPEST...

Salvage with divers

On 2 May 1942, British warship HMS *Edinburgh* sank in 245 m (803 ft) of water in the Barents Sea off northern Norway, inside the Arctic Circle. Over the course of 31 days (from 7 Sep to 7 Oct 1981), 12 divers working for a consortium of companies recovered 431 gold ingots. Five years later, a further 29 ingots were reclaimed.

Dive by a combat submarine

A Russian K-278 submarine descended to 1,027 m (3,346 ft) in the Norwegian Sea on 4 Aug 1984. The first (and only) K-278 was commissioned on 28 Dec 1983. A prototype nuclear-powered attack sub, it featured a double hull (including a titanium inner hull) that allowed for deeper operations than any other combat sub.

▶ DEEPEST DIVE USING AN ATMOSPHERIC DIVING SUIT

On 1 Aug 2006, Chief Navy Diver Daniel Jackson of the US Navy dived 2,000 ft (610 m) off the coast of La Jolla in California, USA. He was testing the Navy's latest atmospheric diving suit (ADS), the Hardsuit 2000, which was designed to be used in submarine rescue scenarios. Its robust design enables the user to walk on the seabed, although dual-plane propellers provide most of its propulsion.

▶ YOUNGEST PERSON TO DIVE TO THE *TITANIC*

On 4 Aug 2005, aged 13 years 319 days, Sebastian Harris (USA, b. 19 Sep 1991) dived down to the wreck of the *Titanic* with his father Michael on board the Russian submersible *Mir–2*. The pair spent 8 hr exploring the wreck. Shown right is a styrofoam cup that the duo took on their dive. It was compressed almost to the size of a shot glass by the intense pressures on the seabed.

Shipwreck

On 28 Nov 1996, using side-scanning sonar, Blue Water Recoveries Ltd (UK) found the wreck of the SS *Rio Grande*, a World War II German blockade runner, at the bottom of the South Atlantic Ocean. It lies 5,762 m (18,904 ft) deep.

Point in the ocean

The Challenger Deep is located within the Mariana Trench in the Pacific Ocean, about 300 km (186 mi) south-west of Guam. According to measurements taken in Oct 2010 by the USNS *Sumner*, the bottom of the Challenger Deep lies 10,994 m (36,070 ft) below sea level.

▲ DEEPEST MANNED DESCENT (SOLO)

On 25 Mar 2012, film-maker James Cameron (CAN) made a solo two-hour descent of the Challenger Deep, reaching a depth of 10,898 m (35,755 ft) on board the *DEEPSEA CHALLENGER*, a specially designed one-man "vertical torpedo" submersible. The director of ocean-based dramas *Titanic* (USA, 1997) and *The Abyss* (USA, 1989) spent several hours in the trench, during which he encountered a fine silt and a few small, unidentified life forms.

▲ DEEPEST SALVAGE OF CARGO FROM A SHIPWRECK

The British passenger steamship SS *City of Cairo* was torpedoed on 6 Nov 1942 and sank with the loss of 104 lives. In Apr 2015, it was revealed that the wreck had been found at a depth of 5,150 m (16,896 ft) by salvage company Deep Ocean Search in 2011. The ship had been carrying 100 tonnes (220,460 lb) of silver coins. The salvage team was able to recover almost £34 m ($52.2 m) worth of coinage from the wreck.

Fish

Specimens of the cusk eel *Abyssobrotula galatheae* have been collected from the Puerto Rico Trench at a depth of 8,370 m (27,460 ft).

▲ DEEPEST OBSERVED VOLCANIC ERUPTION

On 6–7 May 2009, US scientists filmed a volcanic eruption that took place more than 1,208 m (3,963 ft) deep in the Pacific Ocean near Samoa. The footage, which was captured by a robotic submersible named *Jason 2*, shows molten lava erupting from the West Mata volcano. One of the most active submarine volcanoes in the world, it is located around 200 km (125 mi) south-west of the Samoan Islands.

Sea level	0 m
Deepest salvage with divers	245 m
Deepest dive in a diving suit	610 m
Deepest combat submarine	1,027 m
Deepest observed volcanic eruption	1,208 m
Wreck of *Titanic*	3,800 m
Deepest hydrothermal vents	4,968 m
Deepest salvage of cargo	5,150 m
Deepest shipwreck	5,762 m
Deepest-diving submersible in service	7,020 m
Deepest fish	8,370 m
Deepest point reached by DEEPSEA CHALLENGER	
Deepest point reached by *Trieste*	10,898 m
	10,911 m
Deepest point in the Mariana Trench	10,994 m

Earth Round-Up

The temperature at Earth's core is around 6,000°C (10,830°F); the average surface temperature is nearer to 14°C (57.2°F).

Longest duration for a lightning flash

In Sep 2016, the World Meteorological Organization announced that on 30 Aug 2012, a 7.74-sec cloud-to-cloud bolt had been tracked travelling horizontally for approximately 200 km (124 mi) over south-east France. The average duration for a lightning bolt is just 0.2 sec.

The **hottest place on Earth** is the air around a lightning strike, which momentarily reaches 30,000°C (54,032°F), or some five times hotter than the surface of the Sun.

Youngest volcano

Parícutin in Mexico is a volcanic cone that erupted from a corn field on 20 Feb 1943, and was volcanically active until 1952. Most of the activity occurred in the first year, during which the volcanic cone grew to a height of 335 m (1,100 ft). Parícutin offered geologists a rare opportunity to witness the birth, evolution and death of a volcano.

▼ HIGHEST TREE

Polylepis tomentella grows at altitudes of 4,000–5,200 m (13,123–17,060 ft) above sea level. It is found all across the semi-arid ecosystem of the Altiplano, which runs through the Central Andes.

The **tallest trees** are redwoods (genera *Sequoia* and *Sequoiadendron*) and eucalyptuses (genus *Eucalyptus*), both of which can top 113 m (370 ft).

The speed of the molten iron in Earth's outer core is around one-fiftieth the average speed of a sloth in motion – but some 35,000 times faster than the rate at which grass grows.

Oldest water (non-meteoritical)

On 13 Dec 2016, a team of scientists led by Barbara Sherwood Lollar (CAN) presented results at a meeting of the American Geophysical Union that showed the discovery of 2-billion-year-old water 3 km (1.8 mi) below the Earth's surface at Kidd Creek Mine in Timmins, Ontario, Canada. Ancient water that becomes trapped at this depth in the crust can preserve evidence of the conditions at the time at which it became trapped. Dissolved elements including helium, neon, krypton, xenon and argon allowed analysis of the age of the water, which is around eight times saltier than seawater.

▲ FASTEST MOTION IN EARTH'S CORE

On 19 Dec 2016, scientists announced their discovery of a "jet stream" of molten iron in Earth's outer core, moving at around 50 km (31 mi) per year. The team – from DTU Space Institute (DEN) and the University of Leeds (UK) – used data from ESA's three *Swarm* satellites, designed to study Earth's magnetic field, and found the mass of molten iron at a depth of around 3,000 km (1,860 mi). It is some 420 km (260 mi) wide and wraps around half the planet.

Most powerful tsunami from an asteroid impact

Sixty-five million years ago, an asteroid measuring at least 10 km (6.2 mi) across struck the Yucatán Peninsula in what is now Mexico. The impact released approximately 2 million times more energy than the most powerful man-made nuclear explosion and resulted in a crater around 180 km (111 mi) across. The resulting tsunami from this event has been estimated to have been around 1 km (0.62 mi) high in places, and would have been much taller had the asteroid landed in the deep ocean rather than in the shallow waters of the peninsula.

Tallest single wave

The highest officially recorded sea wave - dependent on weather or climate - was calculated to have reached 112 ft (34 m) from trough to crest. It was measured from the USS *Ramapo*, proceeding from Manila in the Philippines to San Diego, California, USA, on the night of 6–7 Feb 1933, during a hurricane that reached 126 km/h (78 mph).

Remotest spot from land

At 48°52.6'S, 123°23.6'W, there is a point in the South Pacific Ocean 2,699 km (1,450 nautical mi) from land. It is known as Point Nemo, or the Pacific Pole of Inaccessibility. If you were at this spot, and the *International Space Station* were orbiting directly above, at an altitude of around 400 km (248 mi), you would be nearer to its crew than to anyone on Earth.

LARGEST...

Continent

Of all the continents (Europe, Africa, Asia, North America, South America, Australasia/Oceania and Antarctica), Asia is the largest at 45,036,492 km² (17,388,686 sq mi). Africa ranks second with a land area of 30,343,578 km² (11,715,721 sq mi).

▼ **GREATEST HEAT OUTPUT FOR A VOLCANO**

From 2000 to 2014, Hawaii's Kīlauea volcano emitted 9.8×10^{16} joules of thermal energy, according to a study from 28 Jan 2015 by US and UK geologists. Their analysis used satellite data from Earth's 95 most active volcanoes.

The inset below was created by using radar data from Jan 2010 and May 2011. It shows subtle changes in the landscape as the volcano inflated or deflated during and between eruptions. Each change of colour represents an uplift of 1.5 cm (0.6 in). The more concentrated the rings, the steeper the uplift.

The study showed similarities between the chemistry of this smog and current urban air pollution in China.

▲ MOST LETHAL SMOG

The term "smog" derives from the words "smoke" and "fog". On 5–9 Dec 1952, London experienced thick smog, caused by cold weather coupled with an anticyclone that facilitated a build-up of pollutants. There were around 12,000 fatalities.

In Nov 2016, an international team of scientists published their analysis of the disaster, noting that sulphur dioxide and nitrogen dioxide from residential and power-plant coal burning had formed sulphuric acid when mixed with fog. This led to lung inflammation and, in many cases, death by suffocation. A performance of the opera *La Traviata* at the city's Sadler's Wells Theatre had to be abandoned when smog infiltrated the auditorium, making the audience cough and rendering the stage invisible to those at the back. On the Isle of Dogs in London's East End, the smog became so thick that people could not see their own feet.

▶ LARGEST MUD VOLCANO ERUPTION

Since May 2006, a mud volcano has been erupting in East Java, Indonesia. Expelling a mixture of clay and water, the eruption and its mudflow has buried more than 6.5 km² (2.5 sq mi) of the city of Sidoarjo in up to 40 m (131 ft) of mud, displacing nearly 40,000 people. At its peak, the volcano was discharging around 180,000 m³ (6,356,640 cu ft) of mud per day. That's the equivalent of the volume of the Great Pyramid of Giza in Egypt every two weeks. The eruption is expected to last for 25–30 years.

Island

Apart from Australia, which is usually regarded as a continental land mass, Earth's largest island is Greenland, with an area of about 2,175,600 km² (840,000 sq mi).

The **largest sand island** in the world is Fraser Island, located off the south coast of Queensland, Australia. It covers some 1,630 km² (629 sq mi) and is home to a sand dune 120 km (75 mi) long (and more than 100 freshwater lakes). In 1992, the island was recognized by the United Nations Educational, Scientific and Cultural Organization (UNESCO) as a World Heritage Site.

The world's **highest measured sand dunes** are those in the Saharan sand sea of Isaouane-n-Tifernine in east central Algeria. They are 5 km (3 mi) long and reach a height of 465 m (1,525 ft).

Glacier

The Lambert Glacier in Antarctica covers an area of 1 million km² (386,100 sq mi) and delivers an estimated 33 billion tonnes (36.3 billion tons) of ice from the East Antarctic Ice Sheet to the Southern Ocean every year.

Extending for more than 400 km (250 mi), the Lambert Glacier is also the world's **longest glacier**.

Lava lake

The shield volcano Mount Nyiragongo in the Democratic Republic of the Congo contains an active lava lake in its crater around 250 m (820 ft) across. The volcano has erupted some 34 times since 1882.

▲ FIRST GEOLOGICAL EPOCH OF THE MODERN AGE
On 29 Aug 2016, members of the Anthropocene Working Group of the International Union of Geological Sciences presented their evidence of a new geological epoch. The Anthropocene is defined as the point at which human activities began to impact on Earth's ecosystems. The group recommended that the Anthropocene should formally begin around 1950, when nuclear weapons tests spread radioactive elements across the planet.

Lake database

On 15 Dec 2016, a team of geographers from McGill University in Montreal, Canada, published the most complete global database of lakes. Known as HydroLAKES, the database contains measurements, including volume of water and shoreline length, for 1.42 million lakes larger than 10 ha (24.7 acres). The McGill University team put the overall volume of water in these lakes at around 181,900 km³ (43,640 cu mi). The total length of shorelines for the 1.42 million lakes is an estimated 7,200,000 km (4,473,870 mi).

Subglacial mountain range

Located in eastern Antarctica, the Gamburtsev Mountains extend some 1,200 km (745 mi) across the continent and are around 2,700 m (8,860 ft) tall. No one has ever seen the mountains first-hand as they are permanently buried beneath more than 600 m (1,970 ft) of ice. Discovered in 1958 by a Soviet team using seismic surveys, the range is believed to be c. 500 million years old.

The mass of the technosphere estimated in the study (below) is equivalent to more than 50 kg per m² (10 lb per sq ft) of Earth's surface. That's about the same as four gold bars, or 80 basketballs.

▼ FIRST ESTIMATE OF THE MASS OF THE TECHNOSPHERE

An offshoot of Earth's biosphere, the technosphere comprises every human structure and object that may one day become "technofossils". Everything from roads and cities (New York City, below) to landfill sites (inset) and vehicles – and all the waste generated by them – counts towards the technosphere. On 28 Nov 2016, an international team led by geologists from the University of Leicester, UK, presented their estimate of the mass of Earth's technosphere in the journal Anthropocene Review. They put the technosphere's mass at 30 trillion tonnes (33 trillion tons) – or around 90 million Empire State Buildings.

SUPERLATIVES

Tallest...

What's bigger? The tallest snowman or the tallest dinosaur?
The largest cruise liner or the tallest statue? And where do
you fit in? You're sure to be shorter than the tallest man, but
how do you compare to the tallest dog? Find out here!

0–6 m

Dog (ever)
1.11 m

When measured on
4 Oct 2011, Zeus
(2008–14), a Great
Dane owned by the
Doorlag family of
Otsego in Michigan,
USA, measured
1.11 m (3 ft 8 in)
to the shoulder.

Average
height
of a human
1.66 m
(5 ft 5 in)

Woman (ever)
2.46 m

Zeng Jinlian
(1964–82) of
Yujiang village in
the Bright Moon
Commune, Hunan
Province, China,
measured 2.46 m
(8 ft 1 in) at
the time of
her death
on 13 Feb
1982.

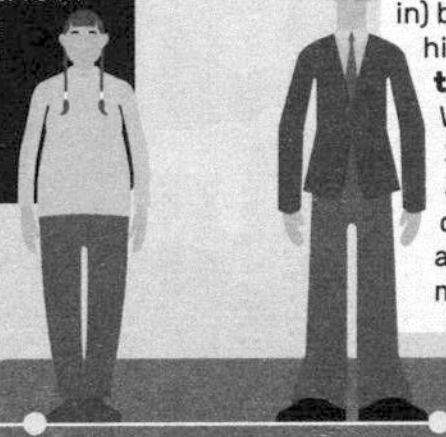

Man (ever)
2.72 m

The tallest man in medical
history is Robert Pershing
Wadlow (USA), who, when
last measured on 27 Jun
1940, was 2.72 m (8 ft 11.1 in)
tall. He was already 1.63 m
(5 ft 4 in) at the age of five,
and passed 2.45 m (8 ft 0.5
in) by the age of 17, making
him – not surprisingly – the
tallest teenager (ever).
When he died, aged just
22, he was buried in a
3.28-m-long (10-ft 9-in)
coffin. To find out more
about this remarkable
man, turn to p.122.

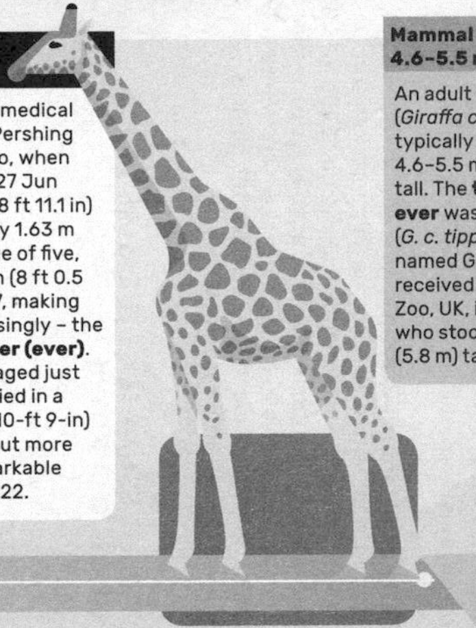

Mammal
4.6–5.5 m

An adult male giraffe
(Giraffa camelopardalis)
typically measures
4.6–5.5 m (15–18 ft)
tall. The **tallest giraffe
ever** was a Masai bull
(G. c. tippelskirch)
named George who was
received at Chester
Zoo, UK, in 1959, and
who stood c. 19 ft
(5.8 m) tall.

6-30 m

Bicycle
6.15 m

Helping Richie Trimble (USA) see over the top of the **tallest giraffe** is the 6.15-m (20-ft 2.5-in) *Stoopidtaller*. To prove that it could be ridden, Richie cycled for a minimum distance of 100 m (328 ft) in Los Angeles, California, USA, on 26 Dec 2013.

Moai (standing)
9.8 m

The tallest of the statues – or *moai* – that remain standing on Easter Island (Rapa Nui) measures 9.8 m (32 ft 1 in). The 74.39-tonne (82-US ton) figure is located at Ahu Te Pito Kura and has been named "Paro".

Chocolate Easter egg
10.39 m

A chocolate Easter egg measuring 10.39 m (34 ft 1 in) tall was made by Tosca (ITA) and measured at Le Acciaierie Shopping Village in Cortenuova, Italy, on 16 Apr 2011. It had a circumference of 19.6 m (64 ft 3.6 in) at its widest point and weighed an elephantine 7.2 tonnes (15,873 lb).

Sandcastle
13.97 m

It took two weeks for Ted Siebert and his team from the Sand Sculpture Company (USA) to build the world's **tallest sandcastle**. Erected on Virginia Key Beach in Miami, Florida, USA, in Oct 2015, it measured 13.97 m (45 ft 10.25 in) tall.

Dinosaur
18 m

Dinosaur remains discovered in 1994 in Oklahoma, USA, belong to what is believed to be the largest creature to have ever walked the Earth. *Sauroposeidon* stood at 18 m (60 ft) tall – the size of a four-storey house – and weighed 60 tonnes (132,277 lb).

30–100 m

Snowman
37.21 m

In Feb 2008, residents of Bethel in Maine, USA, built a snowman (named Olympia, so technically a snowwoman) measuring 37.21 m (122 ft 1 in) tall. The lengthy lady had spruce trees for arms and skis for eyelashes.

Bonfire
47.39 m

A bonfire standing 47.39 m (155 ft 5 in) high was erected by Slinningsbålet (NOR) and lit on 25 Jun 2016 in Ålesund, Norway. The bonfire was built by hand over the course of about three months.

Christmas tree
67.36 m

In Dec 1950, Northgate Mall in Seattle, Washington, USA, unveiled their new Christmas tree: a fully decorated Douglas fir (*Pseudotsuga menziesii*) that reportedly reached a height of 67.36 m (221 ft).

Passenger liner
81 m

Launched in 2009 and 2010 respectively, Royal Caribbean's *Oasis*-class cruise ships MS *Oasis of the Seas* and MS *Allure of the Seas* have a keel-to-funnel height of 81 m (265 ft 8 in) when the 7-m (22-ft-11-in) telescopic part of the funnel is fully extended.

100–500 m

Tree (living) 115.54 m

"Hyperion" is a coast redwood (*Sequoia sempervirens*) that reached 115.54 m (379 ft) tall when measured in Sep 2006. It was discovered by Chris Atkins and Michael Taylor (both USA) in the Redwood National Park, California, USA, on 25 Aug 2006. It is nearly twice the height of the **tallest Christmas tree**.

Statue 127.64 m

The Zhongyuan Buddha in Lushan County, Henan Province, China, towers 127.64 m (418 ft 9 in) over the landscape. It was consecrated on 1 Sep 2009 and was measured on 2 Dec that year. It is more than 7,600 times taller than the average person.

Pyramid 146.7 m

The Pyramid of Khufu at Giza, Egypt, is the world's tallest. Also known as the Great Pyramid, it was 146.7 m (481 ft 3 in) high when completed around 4,500 years ago, but erosion and vandalism have reduced its height to 137.5 ft (451 ft 1 in) today.

Iceberg 167 m

An iceberg estimated to rise 167 m (550 ft) tall – or 55 storeys – above the water line was reported off western Greenland by the icebreaker USCGC *Eastwind* in 1957.

Flagpole 171 m

The flagpole in King Abdullah Square in Jeddah, Saudi Arabia, is 171 m (561 ft) tall. It flies a flag that measures 49.35 m (161 ft 10 in) in length – the size of an Olympic swimming pool!

Offshore gas platform 472 m

The Troll A gas installation, located off the coast of Norway in the North Sea, measures 472 m (1,548 ft) tall and weighs c. 683,600 tonnes (672,800 tons). It stands 303 m (994 ft) below the water's surface. Troll A is made from enough steel to build 15 Eiffel Towers, and enough concrete to build the foundations of 215,000 homes. It is also the **tallest man-made object ever moved**, having been towed out to its current location.

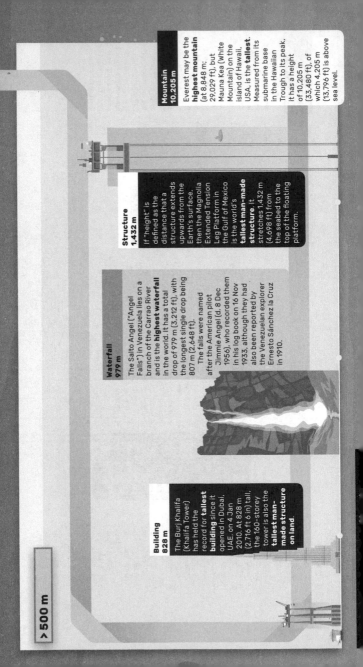

> 500 m

Mountain 10,205 m

Everest may be the **highest mountain** (at 8,848 m; 29,029 ft), but Mauna Kea (White Mountain) on the island of Hawaii, USA, is the **tallest**. Measured from its submarine base in the Hawaiian Trough to its peak, it has a height of 10,205 m (33,480 ft), of which 4,205 m (13,796 ft) is above sea level.

Structure 1,432 m

If "height" is defined as the distance that a structure extends upwards from the Earth's surface, then the Magnolia Extended Tension Leg Platform in the Gulf of Mexico is the world's **tallest man-made structure**. It stretches 1,432 m (4,698 ft) from the seabed to the top of the floating platform.

Waterfall 979 m

The Salto Angel ("Angel Falls") in Venezuela lies on a branch of the Carrao River and is the **highest waterfall** in the world. It has a total drop of 979 m (3,212 ft), with the longest single drop being 807 m (2,648 ft).

The falls were named after the American pilot Jimmie Angel (d. 8 Dec 1956), who recorded them in his log book on 16 Nov 1933, although they had also been reported by the Venezuelan explorer Ernesto Sánchez la Cruz in 1910.

Building 828 m

The Burj Khalifa (Khalifa Tower) has held the record for **tallest building** since it opened in Dubai, UAE, on 4 Jan 2010. At 828 m (2,716 ft 6 in) tall, the 160-storey tower is also the **tallest man-made structure on land.**

Animals

Researchers estimate that there may be as many as 1 trillion species of micro and macro lifeforms on Earth. A single spoonful of soil may contain 10,000 different species of bacteria.

▲ MOST SOPHISTICATED EYES OF ANY ANIMAL

As it patrols the warm waters of the Indian and Pacific oceans, the colourfully costumed peacock mantis shrimp (*Odontodactylus scyllarus*) can see trouble coming a mile off. Its protruding eyes move independently of one another, and contain millions of light-sensitive cells with 16 colour-receptive cones (compared with just three in humans).

The mantis shrimp also has a powerful secret weapon: the **strongest self-powered strike by an animal**. The stomatopod can strike out with its club-shaped front leg at a speed of 23 m/sec (75 ft/sec), delivering a blow with a force of 1,500 N. This shatters the shells of its prey and can also be used to ward off unwary predators.

Contents

The big-punching peacock mantis shrimp lashes out with a force a hundred times its body weight of 0.6 kg (1 lb 5 oz). Each strike is delivered 50 times faster than a blink of a human eye!

CONTENTS

Beetles

Coleopterists (beetle experts) estimate that 85% of all beetle species are still undiscovered and unnamed by science.

Largest taxonomic group

The term "taxonomy" refers to the scientific classification of organisms. Beetles constitute the taxonomic insect order Coleoptera, the largest taxonomic group. They account for one in every five living species of organism, including all animals, plants and fungi. Approximately 40% of all living insect species known to science are beetles.

Beetles are of almost global distribution, absent only from Antarctica, northern polar regions and marine habitats. Around 400,000 species have been scientifically described so far, with many additional ones revealed every year. It has been estimated that even this number only represents 15% of all beetle species inhabiting our planet.

A beetle hatches from its egg in larval form (see opposite) and then undergoes a series of development phases known as "instars". Finally, it "pupates", emerging as an adult insect.

▼ HEAVIEST ADULT BEETLE (AND INSECT)

In their fully grown adult forms, the goliath beetles (Scarabaeidae) of Equatorial Africa are the heavyweights of the beetle world. The male measures up to 11 cm (4.33 in) from the tips of the frontal horns to the end of the abdomen, and weighs a hefty 70–100 g (2.5–3.5 oz) – one-and-a-half times heavier than a tennis ball.

Elytron: hardened wing case protecting the underlying wings

Scutellum: small triangular shield plate on the thorax

Abdomen

Thorax

Antenna

Compound eye

Head

Horns

Femur

Mouth

Tibia

Tarsus: the last multi-segmented part of the leg, ending in a claw

Q: Which type of beetle was used as a sacred symbol
in ancient Egypt?

A: The scarab beetle

▲ LONGEST WEEVIL

There are more than 60,000 species of weevil currently known to science, making them among the most numerous of all beetle types. Many weevils are very small, but the giraffe weevil (*Lasiorhynchus barbicornis*, above) attains a total length of up to 9 cm (3.54 in) in adult males.

In relation to its body size, South Africa's long-snouted cycad weevil (*Antliarhinus zamiae*) has the **longest snout of any beetle**. At 2 cm (0.79 in), its snout accounts for two-thirds of the weevil's total length.

First beetle-like species

The earliest insects that resemble modern-day beetles date from deposits of the early Permian age (c. 280 million years ago) found in Moravia in the Czech Republic and also in Russia's Ural Mountains. They are housed in the taxonomic family Tshekardocoleidae, within the prehistoric taxonomic order Protocoleoptera, whose name translates as "first beetles".

Heaviest beetle larva

The larva of the actaeon beetle (*Megasoma actaeon*), which is native to the northern regions of South America, averages 200 g (7 oz) when fully grown. The heaviest specimen on record was a male (right), bred in Japan in 2009, that in its larval state weighed 228 g (8 oz) – almost as much as an adult female common rat! This same specimen also holds the record for the **heaviest beetle** of any type and the **heaviest insect** of any type.

Smallest insects

There are two contenders for the title of world's smallest insect, both of which also qualify as the **smallest beetles**. The "feather-winged" beetles of the family Ptiliidae (or Trichopterygidae) measure 0.25–0.30 mm (0.01–0.012 in), as do certain species of featherwing beetle belonging to the taxonomic tribe Nanosellini, such as *Scydosella musawasensis*.

Claw

Largest tiger beetle

The aptly named monster tiger beetle (*Manticora latipennis*) – native to South Africa, Botswana and Mozambique – often attains a total length of 6.5 cm (2.55 in). The male is rendered additionally formidable by virtue of its huge antler-like mandibles, which resemble those of the familiar stag beetle. Yet whereas the stag beetle's mandibles are principally ritualistic, they are fully functional in the monster tiger: it uses them to hold and manipulate its prey while chopping it to pieces before devouring the chunks.

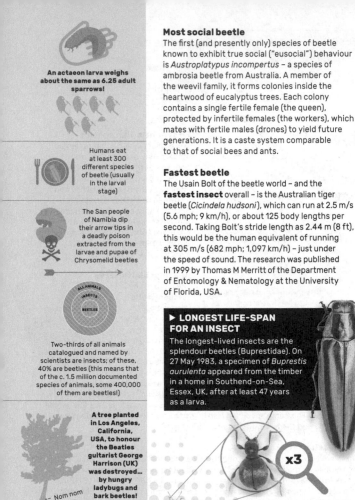

An actaeon larva weighs about the same as 6.25 adult sparrows!

Humans eat at least 300 different species of beetle (usually in the larval stage)

The San people of Namibia dip their arrow tips in a deadly poison extracted from the larvae and pupae of Chrysomelid beetles

Two-thirds of all animals catalogued and named by scientists are insects; of these, 40% are beetles (this means that of the c. 1.5 million documented species of animals, some 400,000 of them are beetles!)

A tree planted in Los Angeles, California, USA, to honour the Beatles guitarist George Harrison (UK) was destroyed... by hungry ladybugs and bark beetles!

Nom nom nom

True (modern-day) beetles first appeared c. 280 million years ago, which means they survived whatever killed the dinosaurs

Most social beetle

The first (and presently only) species of beetle known to exhibit true social ("eusocial") behaviour is *Austroplatypus incompertus* – a species of ambrosia beetle from Australia. A member of the weevil family, it forms colonies inside the heartwood of eucalyptus trees. Each colony contains a single fertile female (the queen), protected by infertile females (the workers), which mates with fertile males (drones) to yield future generations. It is a caste system comparable to that of social bees and ants.

Fastest beetle

The Usain Bolt of the beetle world – and the **fastest insect** overall – is the Australian tiger beetle (*Cicindela hudsoni*), which can run at 2.5 m/s (5.6 mph; 9 km/h), or about 125 body lengths per second. Taking Bolt's stride length as 2.44 m (8 ft), this would be the human equivalent of running at 305 m/s (682 mph; 1,097 km/h) – just under the speed of sound. The research was published in 1999 by Thomas M Merritt of the Department of Entomology & Nematology at the University of Florida, USA.

▶ LONGEST LIFE-SPAN FOR AN INSECT

The longest-lived insects are the splendour beetles (Buprestidae). On 27 May 1983, a specimen of *Buprestis aurulenta* appeared from the timber in a home in Southend-on-Sea, Essex, UK, after at least 47 years as a larva.

x3

▲ HARDIEST BEETLE

The most indestructible beetle is a small species known as *Niptus hololeucus*. Entomologist Dr Malcolm Burr revealed that 1,547 specimens were discovered alive and well inside a bottle of the protein casein that had been stoppered for 12 years. He also reported that another collection of specimens had survived 15 years inside a tin of leaves from the poison plant *Datura stramonium*.

▶ LONGEST BEETLE SPECIMEN

The giant sawyer beetle (*Macrodontia cervicornis*) typically measures 99–170 mm (3.89–6.69 in) in length, although a specimen collected in Peru in 2007 had a total length of 177 mm (6.96 in). A third of this beetle's length in male specimens is accounted for by its huge serrated jaws.

◀ FIRST NON-HUMAN ANIMAL TO NAVIGATE VIA THE MILKY WAY

The African dung beetle *Scarabaeus satyrus* orients itself by using the glow from the Milky Way. In 2013, scientists discovered that these scarabs use the light from the Milky Way on cloudless, moonless nights to ensure that they keep rolling their balls of dung in a straight line. Other animals use stars for orientation, but this dung beetle species is the first animal proven to use the entire galaxy for this purpose.

◀ LONGEST BEETLE SPECIES (BODY)

In terms of its body size alone – i.e., minus horns – the titan beetle (*Titanus giganteus*) of South America is the longest species of beetle, with an average head-to-abdomen length of 150 mm (6 in).

▲ BRIGHTEST BIOLUMINESCENCE

The fire beetle (*Pyrophorus noctilucus*) of the tropical regions of the Americas has a brightness of 45 millilamberts – as bright as a modern single LED torch. There are two dots on the beetle's head and one on its abdomen (only visible when it is flying). It uses its light to signal to other fire beetles.

▲ STRONGEST INSECT

Larger members of the Scarabaeidae beetle family – such as this five-horned rhinoceros beetle (*Eupatorus gracilicornis*) – can support up to 850 times their own body weight. The average human can support around 17 times their own weight, so this is the equivalent of a man holding aloft 10 fully grown African elephants.

◀ LONGEST BEETLE SPECIES (OVERALL)

Hercules beetles (*Dynastes hercules*, aka rhinoceros beetles) typically measure between 44 mm and 172 mm (1.7–6.7 in), much of which is accounted for by a long pair of horns. The longest sub-species is *D. h. hercules* (pictured).

Deer

Having their eyes positioned on the sides of the head gives deer a field of vision of around 310°. They can see behind them.

First antler-shedding deer species
The earliest antler-shedding deer currently known to science is *Dicrocerus elegans*. The species lived in Europe during the Miocene period (20 million–5 million years ago), with fossil records from France, Germany, Portugal, Slovakia and Serbia, as well as China. Its antlers were simple, and hence are dubbed "proantlers". They were forked (*Dicrocerus* translates as "forked antlers"), but lacked tines (prongs, or points) and had a thickened base. Antlers were borne only by males, and were shed annually. The main stem of each antler became shorter with each shedding, as occurs in modern-day muntjacs.

Largest prehistoric fallow deer species
Based upon fossil evidence and depictions in cave paintings, the giant deer (*Megaloceros giganteus*) is believed to have reached a height of 2 m (6 ft 7 in) at the shoulder. It is also known as the Irish elk, owing to the many fossil specimens found in Ireland, but was not closely related to the elks. Genetic studies have confirmed that its closest relative was the modern-day fallow deer.

▼ LARGEST DEER
No deer species is larger than moose. They eat around 73 lb (33.1 kg) a day in the summer – mainly vegetation such as woody plants and shrubs. In winter, they eat plant buds and their daily feed drops to 34 lb (15.4 kg). In Sep 1897, an Alaskan moose bull (*Alces alces gigas*) standing 7 ft 8 in (2.34 m) at the shoulders and weighing 1,800 lb (816 kg) was shot in the Yukon Territory of Canada.

The farthest distance travelled by a migrating land animal is that of Grant's caribou (*Rangifer tarandus*) of Alaska and the Yukon Territory in North America, which travel up to 4,800 km (2,982 mi) per year. In the summer, they eat grasses and shrubs on northern tundra. When winter arrives, however, they trek south to the Yukon to forage for lichens and similar vegetation.

Largest muntjac species

The giant muntjac (*Muntiacus vuquangensis*) is native to Vietnam and Cambodia. Weighing 30–50 kg (66–110 lb), it is twice as heavy as other muntjacs and a third longer, too, with antlers up to four times as large. It is all the more remarkable, then, that this sizeable species remained undescribed by science until as recently as 1994.

Newest species of mouse-deer

Despite their vernacular name, mouse-deer or chevrotains constitute a separate taxonomic family (Tragulidae) from true deer (Cervidae), and with the exception of a single African species are found only in Asia. The latest species of mouse-deer to be formally recognized by science is the yellow-striped chevrotain (*Moschiola kathygre*), officially described and named in 2005. It is native to the island of Sri Lanka.

The **smallest ungulate** is the lesser Malay mouse-deer (*Tragulus javanicus*), with a shoulder height of 20–25 cm (7.8–9.8 in), a body length of 42–55 cm (16.5–21.6 in) and a body weight of 1.5–2.5 kg (3 lb 4 oz–5 lb 8 oz). Mature males are identified by their tusk-like upper canines that protrude from the jaw; females of the species are noted for their ability to conceive within two hours of giving birth.

▲ LARGEST DEER GENUS

Muntiacus, which houses the muntjacs or barking deer, is generally thought to contain 12 species, although a few researchers recognize 16. The extra four are subspecies of the Javan muntjac (*M. muntjak*) elevated by these researchers to full species status. Muntjacs are native to Asia, but some species have been introduced elsewhere, including the UK.

A: Around 100. They are native to every continent, except Antarctica and Australia.

Smallest distribution range for a deer species

The critically endangered Bawean deer (*Hyelaphus kuhlii*), aka Kuhl's hog deer, is entirely confined to the tiny Indonesian island of Bawean, located between Borneo and Java, which has a total area of around 200 km² (77.2 sq mi) and measures only 15 km (9.3 mi) across at its widest point. Only 250 or so individuals still exist there in the wild, in two small, topographically separate populations. Captive breeding programmes have been instigated elsewhere to secure its survival, but it remains the **rarest deer species**.

Most common musk deer species

All seven species of musk deer are rare and threatened with extinction, but the most common species is currently the Siberian musk deer (*Moschus moschiferus*), which is classed as "Vulnerable" by the International Union for Conservation of Nature (IUCN). All the other six species are classed as "Endangered". The world population of Siberian musk deer is decreasing as a result of hunting for the precious musk-secreting gland possessed by the adult males. It is estimated at around 230,000 individuals, of which approximately 150,000 constitute the population inhabiting the Russian Federation's Far Eastern region.

▲ **MOST BLOODTHIRSTY UNGULATES**
(The term "ungulate" denotes hoofed animals, such as deer.) On the Inner Hebridean island of Rùm, UK, the vegetation lacks minerals such as calcium and phosphorus. To meet their dietary requirements, the island's red deer (*Cervus elaphus*) kill the fledglings of ground-nesting seabirds, particularly Manx shearwaters (*Puffinus puffinus*, inset). They bite the birds' heads off and chew on the bones to get the minerals they need.

Some caribou herds contain as many as 100,000 members

100,000

Four stomachs
Like cows, deer have one main stomach split into four compartments. This is true of all "ruminants" – animals who chew cud (i.e., regurgitate and chew food that has been swallowed) as part of the digestion process.

Chinese water deer (*Hydropotes inermis inermis*) **have long, fang-like tusks, but no antlers**

Smallest antlers
The antlers of the tufted deer (*Elaphodus cephalophus*) of Asia are only 5 cm (1.9 in) or so long. They are often hidden from sight beneath the tuft of black hair on its brow, from which this species derives its name.

Oldest deer
Owned by the Fraser family (UK), a hand-reared Scottish red deer (*Cervus elaphus*) named Bambi was born on 8 Jun 1963 and died on 20 Jan 1995, aged 31 years 226 days. Deer in the wild that survive the hazards facing them as fawns usually go on to live for 10–20 years.

▲ SMALLEST REINDEER SUBSPECIES
Native to Norway's Svalbard islands, an average male Svalbard reindeer (*Rangifer tarandus platyrhynchus*) is 160 cm (63 in) long and weighs 65–90 kg (143–198 lb). Females can reach 150 cm (59 in) and 53–70 kg (116–154 lb). Their weight rises from spring to autumn.

◄ LARGEST DEER EVER
The broad-fronted moose (*Cervalces latifrons*) lived during the Pleistocene period. Based upon fossil evidence, it grew to 2.1 m (6 ft 10 in), only slightly taller than the giant deer *Megaloceros giganteus* (left), but weighed about twice as much, at 1,200 kg (2,645 lb).

Antler tissue

This is the **fastest-growing mammal tissue**. It can grow at a rate of an inch (2.5 cm) per day, far faster than human fingernails.

Some species, such as the white-tailed deer (*Odocoileus virginianus*), can jump distances of 30 ft (9.1 m). They are also capable of leaping nearly 8 ft (2.4 m) into the air.

30 ft

◀ SMALLEST DEER SPECIES

The northern pudú (*Pudu mephistophiles*) grows to a height of just 35 cm (13.7 in) at the shoulder, and can reach a weight of 6 kg (13 lb 3 oz). It is native to the Andes mountains of Colombia, Ecuador and Peru. Male pudú have short, spiked antlers that are shed annually, although – unlike other deer species – these are not forked. Female pudú do not have antlers.

The scientific term "palmated" describes a shape like an open hand, or palm, with the fingers extended.

▶ LARGEST ANTLERS

The antler spread, or "rack", of a moose (*Alces alces*) killed near the Stewart River in Yukon, Canada, in Oct 1897 measured 6 ft 6.5 in (1.99 m).

The prehistoric giant deer (*Megaloceros giganteus*) had the **longest antlers of any known animal**. One specimen discovered in an Irish bog had greatly palmated antlers measuring 4.3 m (14 ft) across.

Eagles

Relative to their size, eagles have eyes that are 20 times as big as a human's. A truly "eagle-eyed" human would have eyes twice the size of bowling balls!

Largest genus of eagles
The largest taxonomic genus of eagles is *Aquila*, housing the so-called "true" eagles, and currently containing 15 species. These include the golden eagle (*A. chrysaetos*) of Eurasia and North America, the huge Australian wedge-tailed eagle (*A. audax*), Africa's predominantly black-plumaged Verreaux's eagle (*A. verreauxii*) and the magnificent Spanish imperial eagle (*A. adalberti*).

First *Aquila* ("true") eagle
The first "true" eagles of the genus *Aquila* that are currently known to science all date back to the mid-to-late Miocene epoch, approximately 12 million years ago. There are three species: *A. bullockensis*, *A. delphinensis* and *A. pennatoides*. The first of these lived in Australia; the latter two are known from fossils found in deposits in Grive-Saint-Alban, France.

The harpy eagle is a patient and deadly hunter that can perch silently for up to 23 hr in trees while stalking its prey. Below is one of this eagle's talons, shown at actual size.

100%

▼ LONGEST EAGLE TALONS
The back talons of the South American harpy eagle (*Harpia harpyja*) grow to 13 cm (5.12 in) long, making them even longer than the claws of many grizzly bears. Its legs can reach the thickness of a small child's wrist. The harpy eagle hunts the rainforest canopy for its prey, using its talons to exert a pressure of more than 50 kg (110 lb) on its victims, enough to crush their bones.

RAREST EAGLES IN THE WILD		
NAME	**STATUS**	**NUMBERS**
1 Madagascan fish eagle *Haliaeetus vociferoides*	CE	c. 240
2 Flores hawk-eagle *Nisaetus floris*	CE	<255
3 Philippine eagle *Pithecophaga jefferyi*	CE	c. 600
4 Spanish imperial eagle *Aquila adalberti*	V	c. 648
5 Philippine hawk-eagle *Nisaetus philippensis*	V	600-900
6 Pallas's fish eagle *Haliaeetus leucoryphus*	V	2,500-10,000
7 Sanford's sea eagle *Haliaeetus sanfordi*	V	c. 5,000
8 Greater spotted eagle *Clanga clanga*	V	<8,000
=9 Indian spotted eagle *Clanga hastata*	V	3,500-15,000
=9 Beaudouin's snake eagle *Circaetus beaudouini*	V	3,500-15,000
=9 New Guinea eagle *Harpyopsis novaeguineae*	V	3,500-15,000
=9 Mountain serpent eagle *Spilornis kinabaluensis*	V	3,500-15,000
=9 Wallace's hawk-eagle *Nisaetus nanus*	V	3,500-15,000
=9 Eastern imperial eagle *Aquila heliaca*	V	3,500-15,000

CE: Critically endangered; V: Vulnerable (IUCN)

Largest eagle species ever

First discovered in 1871 by the German geologist Julius Haast in the remains of a swamp, Haast's eagle (*Harpagornis moorei*) was a giant bird of prey native to New Zealand's South Island. Adult female Haast's eagles are estimated to have weighed 10–15 kg (22–33 lb), while their adult male counterparts tipped the scales at 9–12 kg (20–26 lb). In terms of body size, even the largest eagle species living today are around 40% smaller than Haast's eagle.

The raptor's size made it a fearsome predator capable of killing moas – flightless birds that were even taller and heavier than ostriches. However, the arrival of the first Maori settlers on South Island led to over-hunting of the moas, condemning both them and the Haast's eagle to extinction in around 1400.

The official symbol of the Holy Roman Empire was a two-headed eagle

Female eagles are much larger than male eagles

Pound for pound, an eagle's wing is stronger than that of an aeroplane

71 Total number of living species of eagle currently recognized by science

CONVOCATION

Collective noun for a group of eagles

Bald eagles are not bald – the term is used to describe the eagle's white head

▲ GREATEST WING-SPAN FOR AN EAGLE

Formerly known as the monkey-eating eagle, the Philippine eagle (*Pithecophaga jefferyi*) has produced confirmed wing-spans of up to 2.2 m (7 ft 2 in) – greater than the median wing-span of any other species. Given its body size and weight, this species is actually relatively short-winged. In the dense forests of the Philippines, longer wings would only impede the swift bursts of speed the eagle requires to catch the monkeys, birds and reptiles upon which it feeds.

Rarest eagle

Only around 120 pairs of the Madagascan fish eagle (*Haliaeetus vociferoides*, see p.69) are believed to exist in the forests of north-western Madagascar. The Indian Ocean island was once home to a larger raptor, the Malagasy crowned eagle (*Stephanoaetus mahery*), but it became extinct around 1500. An *Aquila* species of eagle in the region also died out. Although neither raptor has survived, their impact can be detected in Madagascar's lemurs, which still display characteristics of raptor-avoidance behaviour.

Rarest hawk-eagle

Fewer than 255 Flores hawk-eagles (*Nisaetus floris*) are thought to remain in existence. The species is entirely confined to the small Indonesian islands of Flores, Lombok, Sumbawa and Alor in the Lesser Sundas group, as well as the two islets of Satonda and Rinca.

▲ LONGEST EAGLE BEAK
A fossil of the now-extinct Haast's eagle (*Harpagornis moorei*) boasts a lower mandible measuring 11.4 cm (4.4 in). This is almost twice the length of the longest beaks of surviving eagle species such as the Philippine eagle (*Pithecophaga jefferyi*) and Steller's sea eagle (*Haliaeetus pelagicus*), which have been recorded at more than 7 cm (2.7 in).

Largest recorded eagle prey
A young male Venezuelan red howler monkey (*Alouatta seniculus*) weighing 7 kg (15 lb 7 oz) was killed and carried off by a South American harpy eagle (see p.68 and p.72) in Peru's Manú National Park in 1990.

▲ SMALLEST EAGLE
The South Nicobar serpent eagle (*Spilornis klossi*) weighs 450 g (15.8 oz) and measures just 40 cm (15.7 in) long, making it only slightly larger than a female sparrowhawk. It is found in forests on the island of Great Nicobar, north of the Indonesian island of Sumatra. The serpent eagle was not formally described until 1902, whereupon it was named after the English zoologist Cecil B Kloss.

▶ LARGEST EAGLE
Named after the German botanist Georg Steller, the Steller's sea eagle (*Haliaeetus pelagicus*) weighs 5–9 kg (11–20 lb). Its average body mass of 6.7 kg (15 lb) is greater than that of any other eagle. Found mainly in Russian coastal regions and parts of Korea and Japan, Steller's sea eagle survives on fish such as salmon, trout and Pacific cod – although it has also been known to dine upon crabs, ducks, squid and even seals! The heavyweight bird also boasts an impressive wing-span, with individual specimens matching that of the Philippine eagle (see opposite). However, a median wing-span of 212.5 cm (7 ft) is only the third-highest among eagles.

▲ LARGEST BIRD'S NEST

Examined on 1 Jan 1963, a nest built by a pair of bald eagles (*Haliaeetus leucocephalus*) near St Petersburg in Florida, USA, was found to measure 9 ft 6 in (2.9 m) wide and 20 ft (6 m) deep. It was estimated that the vast nest weighed more than 4,400 lb (1,995 kg).

However, this is dwarfed by the incubation mounds of the Australian malleefowl (*Leipoa ocellata*). These insulated egg chambers, the **largest incubation mounds**, can involve material weighing as much as 300 tonnes (661,387 lb) – as heavy as the average 747 jumbo jet!

▶ STRONGEST BIRD OF PREY

The female harpy eagle (*Harpia harpyja*) is capable of killing and carrying away animals of a similar body weight, which can reach 9 kg (20 lb, see p.71). As it swoops down upon its prey at speeds of 32 km/h (20 mph), the harpy eagle generates energy approximate to 2,258 joules (1,665 ft-lb) – equivalent to almost three times the muzzle energy of a bullet shot from a .357 Magnum handgun. It is an apex predator that sits at the top of the food chain, and counts sloths and howler monkeys among its prey.

Pandas

A panda's sense of smell is so well developed that it can find bamboo at night by its scent alone.

Oldest known fossil of a giant panda

In 2007, a fossilized skull of the pygmy giant panda (*Ailuropoda microta*) was discovered in the Jinyin limestone cave in Guangxi, southern China. The panda lived in tropical bamboo forests in southern China approximately 2–4 million years ago, during the late Pliocene epoch.

The pygmy giant panda was also the **smallest giant panda**. At 1 m (3 ft 3 in) long, it was smaller than today's giant panda (*A. melanoleuca*) and in appearance resembled a fat domestic dog. From the distinctive wear pattern present on its teeth, scientists have suggested that it fed on bamboo shoots, like its larger, modern-day relative.

Most primitive living bear

In terms of its evolutionary development and delineation, the giant panda diverged from other bears 18–25 million years ago. It is housed within its own subfamily, Ailuropodinae (meaning "black-and-white cat foot").

At just 4.2 km² (1.6 sq mi) – slightly larger than New York's Central Park – the home range of female giant pandas in the Qinling Mountains in Shaanxi Province, China, is the **smallest home range recorded for a bear species**.

▼ OLDEST PANDA IN CAPTIVITY (EVER)

Jia Jia ("good"), a female giant panda, was born in 1978. She arrived at Ocean Park Hong Kong in Mar 1999 and remained there until passing away on 16 Oct 2016 at the age of 38. The average life-span of giant pandas is 18–20 years in the wild, and 30 years in captivity.

Wild pandas were once found all over southern and eastern China and well into Myanmar and Vietnam, but habitat loss and poaching have seen them become one of the world's most endangered animals.

The panda's black-and-white colouration has been compared to the Yin and Yang symbol (above), which the Chinese believe represents the balance of opposing forces in the universe

The lesser (or red) panda's scientific name, *Ailurus fulgens*, translates as **"fiery cat-bear"**

Giant pandas are very short-sighted

EMBARRASSMENT
The collective term for a group of pandas

In 2011, entrepreneur An Yanshi (CHN) began growing green tea fertilized with panda poo; the tea sells for 440,000 yuan (£51,954; $65,065) per kg

Most pandas born in one year

The record year for panda births was 2006, during which 30 cubs were successfully born into captivity. The majority of the cubs were born at Wolong Panda Research Center in south-west China, but the 30th was born at Adventure World in Wakayama, Japan, on 23 Dec 2006.

Most expensive species in captivity

The global population of giant pandas is indigenous to – and owned by – China alone. Four zoos in the US cities of San Diego, Atlanta, Washington and Memphis each pay an annual leasing fee of $1 m (£807,291) to the Chinese government for a pair of these rare creatures. If cubs are born, and twins sometimes result, a one-off payment of $600,000 (£484,374) per offspring must also be made. The money goes towards China's panda conservation projects. A panda's upkeep (including bamboo production and security) makes it five times more costly to maintain than the second most expensive species: the elephant.

▲ NEWEST GIANT PANDA SPECIES

The Qinling giant panda (*Ailuropoda melanoleuca qinlingensis*) was formally recognized as a separate subspecies in 2005. Unlike the more familiar black-and-white fur of the giant panda (*A. melanoleuca*), the Qinling giant panda's fur is dark brown and light brown. Its head is also rounder and smaller than that of the typical giant panda. Only 200–300 specimens are believed to exist in the wild.

▶ FIRST PANDA MADE KNOWN TO SCIENCE

Ailurus fulgens, from south-western China and the eastern Himalayas, was formally described and named in 1825 by French naturalist Frédéric Cuvier. Four years earlier, Major General Thomas Hardwicke had presented a paper to London's Linnean Society describing and naming this species. However, Hardwicke's paper was not published until 1827.

Most restricted diet for a bear

More than 99% of the giant panda's diet consists of bamboo. The remaining <1% consists of other plant material, small birds or rodents and occasionally carrion. In captivity, it also eats eggs, fruit, honey and fish. Pandas actually derive little nutritional sustenance from bamboo, a very poor source of protein and energy, and must eat large quantities – up to 14 kg (30 lb 13 oz) of bamboo shoots per day – to remain healthy.

FIRST...

Written record of the lesser panda

References to the lesser or red panda (*A. fulgens*) exist in a 13th-century Chinese scroll. This document features a hunting scene depicting the species and its human pursuers. However, the lesser panda did not become known to western science until 1821, by way of a paper written by Major General Thomas Hardwicke (see above).

◀ FIRST GIANT PANDA BORN IN CAPTIVITY

On 9 Sep 1963, a male giant panda named Ming-Ming (meaning "bright") became the first of his species to be born in captivity. His birth took place at Beijing Zoo in China. Ming-Ming's father was named Pi-Pi and his mother was Li-Li.

Almost exactly one year later, on 4 Sep 1964, Li-Li gave birth to a second cub. The newborn panda was female and was named Lin-Lin (meaning "pretty jade").

These giant panda sanctuaries cover an area roughly three times the size of the US state of Rhode Island.

▲ LARGEST GIANT PANDA HABITAT

Located in the Qionglai and Jiajin Mountains of Sichuan Province, China, the Sichuan Giant Panda Sanctuaries represent the largest contiguous habitat of the giant panda. More than 30% of the world panda population lives in this 9,245-km² (3,569-sq-mi) network of nature reserves and scenic parks. In 2006, the area was officially designated a UNESCO World Heritage Site.

Living giant panda seen by a westerner

German zoologist Hugo Weigold purchased a giant panda cub in 1916 while in the Chinese province of Wassu, east of the Min River. At that time, Weigold was participating in the Stoetzner Expedition to western China and eastern Tibet, and had been searching for giant pandas without success. Despite his attempts to hand-rear the cub, however, it died shortly afterwards, owing to a lack of suitable food.

▲ MOST RECENT BIRTH OF GIANT PANDA TRIPLETS

Only four cases of triplet births have ever been recorded for giant pandas living in captivity. The most recent such birth occurred on 29 Jul 2014 at Chimelong Paradise amusement park in Guangzhou, Guangdong Province, south-eastern China. All three of the panda cubs were born within four hours of one another, and as of 6 Oct 2016 they were all still alive, after being hand-reared at the park. Their mother, Ju Xiao, had been artificially impregnated in Mar 2014.

Giant panda maintained outside China

Su-Lin (meaning "a little bit of something precious"), a giant panda cub, was around nine weeks old when found abandoned in a tree hollow near the Min River of Sichuan Province, China, in 1936. It was discovered by American explorer Ruth Harkness, who took Su-Lin back with her to the USA in December of that year. Thought by Harkness to be a female, the cub was actually a male. Su-Lin was bottle-fed by Harkness and then, in Apr 1937, sold to Chicago's Brookfield Zoo. He lived there until spring 1938, when he died from choking on a twig, according to the official post-mortem.

▶ HUNGRIEST BEAR SPECIES

In order to survive, the giant panda eats as much as 38% of its own weight in bamboo shoots every day, or 15% of its weight in bamboo leaves and stems. This is because it can only digest up to 21% of all the bamboo that it consumes, which means that it has to eat throughout the winter rather than hibernate like other bears. It spends up to 15 hr per day eating, consuming more food in relation to its body weight than any other species of bear.

Parrots

Parrots can mimic the calls of their predators' own predators! As pets, they copy sounds in the home, from speech to ringing phones and doorbells.

Largest superfamily of parrots

Psittaciformes, the taxonomic order of parrots, contains almost 400 modern-day species and is divided into three superfamilies: Psittacoidea ("true parrots"), Cacatuoidea (cockatoos) and Strigopoidea (New Zealand parrots). The largest is Psittacoidea, with about 350 species, found mostly in the Southern Hemisphere, in tropical and subtropical regions.

The **smallest superfamily of parrots** by far is Strigopoidea, with only three surviving species. All are indigenous to New Zealand, and genetically distinct to other living parrots. The trio consists of the kakapo (see p.80), the kea (*Nestor notabilis*) and the kaka (*N. meridionalis*).

First talking pet budgerigar

In 1788, English convict Thomas Watling was transported to New South Wales in Australia as punishment for counterfeiting banknotes in London. He kept a pet budgerigar (*Melopsittacus undulatus*), which he taught to say "How do you do, Dr White?" – a homage to the convict colony's physician Dr John White, a keen naturalist.

Most extreme sexual dimorphism exhibited by a parrot

Sexual dimorphism is a distinct difference in size or appearance between the two sexes of a given species. The male eclectus parrot (*Eclectus roratus*) has a plumage that is mostly bright green, while the female's is bright red with a bold blue-purple nape band. As recently as the 1920s, this dramatic difference in colour had led to the assumption that the male and female eclectus parrot were entirely separate species.

Largest conure

Native to forests and woodlands in Peru, Bolivia and Argentina, the mitred conure (*Psittacara mitratus*) measures up to 38 cm (14.96 in) long, due in part to its relatively long tail. The green-plumaged parakeet was traditionally housed in the "true" conure genus *Aratinga*, but after a major study in 2013 was moved to *Psittacara*.

▲ **OLDEST EVER PARROT**

A Major Mitchell's cockatoo (*Cacatua leadbeateri*) named Cookie first appeared at Brookfield Zoo in Chicago, Illinois, USA, in May 1934. Estimated to be a year old, he was given a hatch date of 30 Jun 1933. He became so popular that his birthdays were celebrated with an outdoor event, during which Cookie would receive a muffin-sized cake. He died on 27 Aug 2016, aged at least 82 years 88 days.

Q: Prior to "parrot", what was the common term used for these birds?

A: "Popinjay". The term was also used for a trivial, foppish person

Largest lovebird
The Abyssinian or black-winged lovebird (*Agapornis taranta*) can grow to 16.5 cm (6.5 in) long. Mainly green but with a striking red forehead in males, it is native to the east African countries of Ethiopia and Eritrea.

Smallest macaw
Found in South America, the red-shouldered macaw (*Diopsittaca nobilis*) is the only member of its species. A popular pet on account of its small size and docile temperament, it is often dubbed the "mini-macaw" by the pet trade. It measures no more than 30 cm (11.8 in) long and weighs just 165 g (5.8 oz).

Smallest species of amazon parrot
Almost 30 species of amazon parrot are currently recognized. At just 25 cm (9.8 in) long, the black-billed amazon (*Amazona agilis*) is the smallest. Native to mountainous rainforests in the heart of Jamaica, the numbers of this once-common species have dwindled owing to deforestation, specimen collection for the pet trade and poaching. It is now categorized as "Vulnerable" by the IUCN.

Oldest caged budgerigar
Born in Apr 1948, Charlie died aged 29 years 60 days on 20 Jun 1977. He had been cared for by J Dinsey of London, UK.

RAREST...

Cockatoo
Categorized as "Critically Endangered" by the IUCN, the red-vented cockatoo (*Cacatua haematuropygia*) is estimated to number only 560–1,150 individual birds. The species has suffered an extremely rapid decline owing to destruction of its lowland forest habitat and capture by the cage-bird trade. Only remnant populations remain, scattered across certain islands of the Philippines.

Many parrots are omnivores and will eat anything – including meat! The kea parrot of New Zealand has been filmed attacking healthy sheep and using its beak to rip fat from their backs.

100%

▼ SMALLEST PARROT
Native to both Papua and Papua New Guinea, the buff-faced pygmy parrot (*Micropsitta pusio*) measures as little as 8 cm (3.1 in) when fully grown and weighs just 11.5 g (0.4 oz). There are six species of pygmy parrot in total – unusually, all efforts to breed them in captivity have failed. This has been attributed in part to problems maintaining the pygmy parrots' diet of fungi and lichen.

Hanging parrots (*Loriculus*) dangle from branches by their feet when sleeping

393

The most widely accepted number of modern-day parrot species

A gathering of New Zealand kea parrots is called a "circus"

3,000

Average number of feathers possessed by a budgerigar

Parrots have **"Zygodactyl feet"**

This means they have four toes on each foot: two facing forward and two facing backward

The budgerigar is the most popular pet bird in the world

Lorikeet

Entirely confined to the island of New Caledonia off Australia, the last confirmed record of the New Caledonian lorikeet (*Charmosyna diadema*) was in 1913. However, a number of reliable eyewitness sightings have led the IUCN to conclude the species may still exist within the island's wild and inaccessible areas of highland rainforest. Therefore the lorikeet is classified as "Critically Endangered" rather than "Extinct".

True macaw in the wild

Also known as the Caninde or Wagler's macaw, the blue-throated macaw (*Ara glaucogularis*) is confined to Los Llanos de Moxos, a small locality in northern Bolivia. Surveys of the species in the wild by the Armonia Association and the Loro Parque Fundación estimate the number of individuals to be 350–400. It is categorized as "Critically Endangered" by the IUCN, and confined to a special reserve currently occupying 4,600 ha (11,366 acres).

▼ HEAVIEST PARROT

Found only on three tiny islets off New Zealand, the kakapo (*Strigops habroptilus*) is as unusual as it is rare. In addition to being the only flightless species of parrot, it also has a unique ability to retain body fat for the purposes of energy storage. It is therefore perhaps no surprise that the kakapo is the heavyweight of the parrot world, with mature specimens having tipped the scales at 4 kg (8 lb 13 oz).

▲ GREATEST CONCENTRATION OF PARROTS

Set on the outskirts of Puerto de la Cruz on the Spanish island of Tenerife, Loro Parque ("Parrot Park") is home to around 4,000 birds, with around 350 species and subspecies. Loro Parque has been able to breed chicks from rare species such as Spix's macaw (*Cyanopsitta spixii*), which is listed as "Critically Endangered" by the IUCN. The park's residents include scarlet macaws (*Ara macao*; below right), rainbow lorikeets (*Trichoglossus moluccanus*; above) and golden parakeets (*Guaruba guarouba*; below left).

◄ LOUDEST PARROT

Research conducted at San Diego Zoo in California, USA, recorded shrieks from the Moluccan or salmon-crested cockatoo (*Cacatua moluccensis*) reaching an ear-splitting volume of 135 decibels. The cacophonous cockatoo is native to the Moluccas, an archipelago in Indonesia. It has a predominantly white plumage with a pink crest, which it erects whenever it is agitated or excited. An affectionate creature, the cockatoo's scream ensures it gets the attention it craves!

▲ LARGEST VOCABULARY FOR A LIVING BIRD

Owned by Gabriela Danisch of Bad Oeynhausen in Germany, Oskar the budgerigar could recite 148 words when tested on 8 Sep 2010. His repertoire included words in German, English and Polish.

The **largest ever vocabulary for a bird** is 1,728 words, achieved by a budgerigar named Puck. Owned by Camille Jordan of Petaluma in California, USA, Puck died in 1994.

▶ LONGEST PARROT

Native to central and eastern regions of South America, the hyacinth or hyacinthine macaw (*Anodorhynchus hyacinthinus*) measures up to 100 cm (39 in). Its weight can reach as much as 1.7 kg (3 lb 12 oz) – the only heavier parrot is the kakapo or owl parrot (see p.80). Habitat destruction and trapping for the pet trade have led to a decline in the numbers of the hyacinth macaw. With just 4,300 estimated mature individuals, it has been listed as "Vulnerable" by the IUCN.

Many parrots are omnivores and will eat anything – including meat! The kea parrot of New Zealand has been filmed attacking healthy sheep and using its beak to rip fat from their backs.

▲ SMALLEST COCKATOO

Found only in Australia, the cockatiel (*Nymphicus hollandicus*) measures 30–33 cm (11.8–13 in) long. In contrast to other cockatoo species, its long tail feathers account for roughly half its length. Historically, there has been debate as to whether the cockatiel is in fact a parakeet, but recent biochemical and molecular tests have proved that it is indeed a true cockatoo.

Pigs

If babirusas (see p.85) don't grind their inwardly curving canine tusks, they can grow long enough to penetrate their own skulls!

Largest genus of pigs

The *Sus* genus contains 10 modern-day species of typical pigs and wild boars. These include not only the Eurasian wild boar (*S. scrofa*), the direct ancestor of the domestic pig, but also rare Asian island species including the Palawan bearded pig (*S. ahoenobarbus*) and the Mindoro warty pig (*S. oliveri*).

Largest wild pig ever

The unicorn pig (*Kubanochoerus gigas*) lived 7–20 million years ago during the Miocene epoch in modern-day Russia and China. It stood up to 1.2 m (3 ft 11 in) at the shoulder and weighed as much as 500 kg (1,102 lb).

▼ LARGEST WILD PIG

Undescribed by science until 1904, the giant forest hog (*Hylochoerus meinertzhageni*) of central Africa certainly lives up to its name. The huge hog has a head–body length of 1.3–2.1 m (51–83 in), a shoulder height of 85–105 cm (33.5–41.33 in) and a weight of 130–275 kg (287–606 lb) – heavier than three adult men.

▲ MOST WIDELY DISTRIBUTED PECCARY

The collared peccary or javelina (*Pecari tajacu*) extends from northern Argentina through Central America and Mexico into the US states of Texas and Arizona. It is also native to Caribbean islands such as Trinidad, Cuba and Puerto Rico. Weighing as little as 14 kg (30 lb 13 oz), it is also the **lightest peccary**.

▼ LARGEST HELL PIG

Known as hell or terminator pigs, entelodonts were a now-extinct taxonomic family of pig-like omnivores that were alive during the early Miocene epoch. The largest species – *Daeodon shoshonensis*, aka *Dinohyus hollandi* – stood 1.8–2.0 m (5 ft 10 in–6 ft 6 in) at the shoulder, taller than an average human male (see below). Its 90-cm-long (35.4-in) skull held a brain no larger than an orange.

Newest wild boar

The Central Asian wild boar (*S. scrofa davidi*) was not recognized as a separate subspecies of wild boar until 1981. Relatively small and light brown in colour, with a long mane, it has a distribution range extending from Pakistan and north-western India to south-eastern Iran.

Smallest pig

The mature male pygmy hog (*Porcula salvania*) measures 61–71 cm (24–28 in) long; females grow to 55–62 cm (21–24 in). Indigenous to the Terai region of India, Nepal and Bhutan, since 1996 it has been listed as "Critically Endangered" by the International Union for Conservation of Nature (IUCN). Only isolated populations survive in Assam, India, and wildlife sanctuaries.

This species is the only known host of an ectoparasitic (i.e., existing on the outside) sucking louse, making the pygmy hog-sucking louse (*Haematopinus oliveri*) the **rarest porcine ectoparasite**. Only around 150 pygmy hogs still exist, meaning that both they and the pygmy hog-sucking louse are listed as "Critically Endangered".

▲ LARGEST PIG
Reared on a diet of sorghum molasses, banana peels and slop, the Poland-China hog Big Bill grew to 2,552 lb (1,157 kg) – twice the weight of an adult male polar bear. In 1933, Big Bill had to be put down after breaking his leg. Stuffed and mounted, he was placed on display at travelling carnivals before vanishing. His current whereabouts are a mystery.

▲ LARGEST BABIRUSA
The babirusa, or "deer-pig", is notable for its curved canine tusks. All members of the *Babyrousa* genus were considered a single species until they were divided up in 2002. A native of Indonesia's Togian Archipelago – where it is found on the small islands of Malenge, Batudaka, Togian and Talatakoh – the Malenge or Togian babirusa (*B. togeanensis*) can tip the scales at 90 kg (198 lb).

Smallest African river hog
The brightly furred red river hog (*Potamochoerus porcus*) is native to rainforests and swamps in central and western Africa, especially Guinea and the Congo. Adult males weigh 45–120 kg (99–264 lb), measure 100–145 cm (39–57 in) long and stand 55–80 cm (21–31 in) at the shoulder. The red river hog is also notable for its unexpectedly mellifluous and tuneful vocalizations.

Oldest pig ever
Born on 17 Jul 1991, a pot-bellied pig (*S. scrofa domesticus*) named Ernestine was aged 23 years 76 days when she passed away on 1 Oct 2014. She lived with her owners Jude and Dan King in Calgary, Alberta, Canada.

Rarest wild boar
The Visayan warty pig (*S. cebifrons*) is known with certainty to exist only on Negros and Panay, two of the Visayan Islands in the Philippines. Its fragmented population has decreased by around 80% in recent years, and the species has disappeared from around 95% of its former distribution range. The IUCN categorizes the Visayan warty pig as "Critically Endangered".

Highest jump by a pig
Pigs might not fly, but a pot-bellied pig called Kotetsu did leap 70 cm (2 ft 3.5 in) into the air at the Mokumoku Tedsukuri Farm in Mie, Japan, on 22 Aug 2004. The 18-month-old Kotetsu had been trained by Makoto Ieki (JPN).

The **longest dive by a pig** is 3.31 m (10 ft 10 in), by Miss Piggy, owned by Tom Vandeleur (AUS). She leapt into a 86.5-cm-deep (34-in) pool at the Royal Darwin Show in Darwin, Australia, on 22 Jul 2005.

A pig's squeal can be as loud as 115 decibels

The collective name for a group of pigs is a "drift" or "drove"

2 billion

Approximate number of domestic pigs in the world today

▲ LARGEST WARTHOG

The common warthog (*Phacochoerus africanus*) is native to much of sub-Saharan Africa, including Kenya, Tanzania, Nigeria and South Africa. Adult males weigh up to 150 kg (330 lb), with females as much as 15% lighter, and boast a head-and-body length of up to 1.5 m (4 ft 11 in). Although a fierce fighter – especially during mating season – the warthog's primary method of defence against predators such as lions and crocodiles is a hurried exit.

▲ HAIRIEST DOMESTIC PIG

The Mangalitsa (aka Mangalitza or Mangalica) breed of domestic pig (*S. scrofa*) has a long, hairy coat that resembles a sheep's fleece. Originating in Hungary in the 1830s, it is a four-way crossbreed of the European wild boar, the Serbian Šumadija breed and two domestic pigs. It comes in three types – blonde, red and swallow-bellied – and is prized for its succulent meat. The only other pig known to have similar-length hair, the Lincolnshire Curly Coat, is now extinct.

▶ SMALLEST DOMESTIC PIG

With a name that means "fat and round" in Maori, the kunekune pig comes from New Zealand, where it is thought to have arrived from Asia via 19th-century trading ships and whalers. Adults stand as little as 48 cm (18.8 in) at the shoulder and can weigh a mere 60 kg (132 lb). They were widely hunted, and by the late 1970s the numbers of purebred kunekune had dropped to as low as 50. A breeding programme helped to save the species from extinction.

The prehistoric wild pig *Kubanochoerus* possessed a long single brow-horn in the male, just like a unicorn

19

Species of wild pig alive today

Big Major Cay in The Bahamas is home to wild pigs who greet tourists by swimming out to visiting boats

Adult domestic pigs can reach speeds of 11 mph (17.7 km/h)

Most cloned pigs born in one litter

On 5 Mar 2000, five piglets named Millie, Christa, Alexis, Carrel and Dotcom were born as a result of a cloning procedure known as nuclear transfer. They were created by PPL Therapeutics Plc – the company that created Dolly the cloned sheep in 1996 – in Blacksburg, Virginia, USA.

First bioluminescent pigs

In 2005, a team from Taiwan University's Department of Animal Science and Technology added DNA from bioluminescent jellyfish to approximately 265 pig embryos, which were then implanted into eight sows. Three male bioluminescent piglets were born. Their skin and internal organs have a greenish tinge, which becomes a torch-like glow if blue light is shone on them in the dark. Stem cells taken from them will be used to trace human diseases, as the green-glowing protein that the pigs produce can be readily observed without the need for biopsies or invasive tests.

First documented animal execution

In the early medieval period, animals such as dogs, cows, horses and pigs could be brought before a judge if suspected of a capital offence. In 1266, a pig was tried and burned for the crime of eating a child. The execution took place in Fontenay-aux-Roses, France, overseen by the monks of St Genevieve.

Reptiles

Since *GWR 2017* came out, we've visited the record-breaking Reptile Gardens in South Dakota, USA. Here are some of the staff, along with a few of the inhabitants.

▼ YEMEN VEILED CHAMELEON

Confined to Yemen and Saudi Arabia, this lizard (*Chamaeleo calyptratus calcarifer*) sometimes grows to just 43 cm (1 ft 4.9 in) long, making it the **smallest veiled chameleon subspecies**. Above, Virginia from Reptile Gardens provides a perch for one member of this colourful family.

▲ KING COBRA

Also known as the hamadryad (*Ophiophagus hannah*), this serpent averages 3–4 m (9 ft 10 in–13 ft 1 in) long, making it the **longest venomous snake**. Terry from Reptile Gardens is seen here confidently handling one lengthy specimen, but it's far from the longest ever. That honour goes to a king cobra captured in Apr 1937 near Port Dickson in Negeri Sembilan, Malaysia, and displayed at London Zoo, UK; by autumn 1939, it had grown to 5.71 m (18 ft 8 in).

LARGEST REPTILE ZOO

As of 28 Feb 2017, Reptile Gardens, located outside Rapid City in South Dakota, housed more than 225 different reptilian species and subspecies – more than any other zoo or wildlife park.

▶ FRESHWATER CROCODILE

Above, Lance carefully handles a young *Crocodylus johnstoni* specimen. Native to Australia, this species is the **fastest crocodile on land**. It can reach speeds of 17 km/h (10.56 mph) at full gallop – a mode of terrestrial locomotion of which only a few crocodile species are capable.

▲ SAVANNAH MONITOR

Chelsea is shown monitoring a monitor. A medium-sized lizard native to much of sub-Saharan Africa, this species (*Varanus exanthematicus*) is a popular pet. According to CITES (the Convention on International Trade in Endangered Species of Wild Fauna and Flora), the USA is the **largest importer of savannah monitors**, with 642,500 specimens to 2010. The species' global population is not currently considered to be at risk.

In the wild, Galápagos giant tortoises may live for a century or more. The **oldest tortoise** recorded, however, was a Madagascar radiated tortoise (*Astrochelys radiata*) that lived for 188 years.

▲ GALÁPAGOS GIANT TORTOISE

Seen here with a member of the mighty reptilian species *Chelonoidis nigra* is Matt. He is proudly displaying Reptile Gardens' GWR certificate for being the **largest reptile zoo**.

The **largest tortoise ever** was a Galápagos giant tortoise named Goliath. He was 135.8 cm (4 ft 5 in) long, 102 cm (3 ft 4 in) wide, 68.5 cm (2 ft 3 in) high and weighed 417 kg (920 lb). Goliath lived at the Life Fellowship Bird Sanctuary in Seffner, Florida, USA, from 1960 to 2002.

◀ *BRACHYLOPHUS BULABULA*

Until 2008, only two species of iguana were known to exist in the Fijian islands. But that year, a research paper revealed a third species, found in the central regions of Fiji. Still lacking a common name, the **newest Fijian iguana** was formally titled *Brachylophus bulabula* ("bulabula" is the Fijian word for "healthy" or "flourishing"). Katherine holds a specimen here.

Members of this species (*Python bivittatus*) commonly grow to 3.7 m (12 ft 1 in), although the **longest Burmese python** – a female named Baby – reached a length of 5.74 m (18 ft 10 in). She lived at Serpent Safari in Gurnee, Illinois, USA, for 27 years. Here, Clint displays an albino variant of the species.

▶ **MEXICAN BEADED LIZARD**

A black-and-yellow forest-dwelling species, *Heloderma horridum* can grow to a length of 90 cm (2 ft 11.4 in). One specimen lived in captivity for 33 years 11 months, making it the **longest-lived venomous lizard**. Right, Kyle holds a specimen from Reptile Gardens.

◄ RETICULATED PYTHON
Kathy displays an albino member of this species here. Native to south-east Asia, Indonesia and the Philippines, *Python reticulatus* regularly grows to more than 6.25 m (20 ft 6 in). The **longest snake** ever documented was a reticulated python that measured 10 m (32 ft 9.7 in).

The term "reticulated" means "net-like". It refers to the pattern of the snake's skin.

► GILA MONSTER
Heloderma suspectum is native to the south-western USA and north-western Mexico. Just 0.4 mg/kg of its venom has proved lethal in mice, making it the **most venomous lizard**. Teresa (right) is no doubt aware that humans rarely die from a gila monster bite, as only relatively small amounts of venom are injected.

▲ RED-FOOTED TORTOISE
Chelonoidis carbonaria is found in northern South America. The **largest red-footed tortoise** was 60 cm (1 ft 11.6 in) long and weighed more than 28 kg (61 lb 11.6 oz). Diet availability and longevity are two factors that promote growth. Above, Linda holds aloft a more modestly sized specimen.

Turtles

A turtle shell is actually made up of 50 bones. Ribs and vertebrae fuse together outside the turtle's body to form a tough, made-to-measure body armour.

Earliest turtle with only a partial shell

Formally described and named in 2008, *Odontochelys semitestacea* existed around 220 million years ago during the late Triassic period, in what is now south-western China. Unlike modern-day turtles it had teeth, and instead of a dorsal (upper) shell or carapace it sported neural plates and broadened ribs.

The first recorded specimen of *Archelon ischyros* was obtained in 1895 from the Pierre Shale of South Dakota, USA. It was formally described by Dr G R Wieland (below, with the specimen).

Earliest turtle with a complete shell

Proganochelys first appeared on Earth around 210 million years ago, during the late Triassic period, just after the evolution of dinosaurs and mammals. It possessed a complete shell, with both a dorsal carapace and a ventral plastron (lower shell). An omnivore with no teeth, it measured about 60 cm (2 ft) in length.

◀ **LARGEST SEA TURTLE EVER**

Archelon ischyros lived around 70–80 million years ago, during the late Cretaceous period, and occupied the seas around what is now North America. The largest specimen on record measured more than 4 m (13 ft 1.4 in) long and 4.9 m (16 ft 0.9 in) wide from flipper to flipper. It is estimated to have weighed more than 2,200 kg (4,850 lb) – about the same as a rhinoceros. Instead of a solid shell, *Archelon* had a leathery or bony carapace supported by a skeletal framework.

◄ SMALLEST TURTLE FAMILY

Three taxonomic families of turtle each contain only a single living species. They are: Carettochelyidae, which contains the pig-nosed or Fly River turtle (*Carettochelys insculpta*, left); Dermatemydidae, containing the hickatee or Central American river turtle (*Dermatemys mawii*); and Dermochelyidae, which contains the leatherback sea turtle (*Dermochelys coriacea*).

Earliest fossil sea turtle

Initially unearthed during the 1940s at Villa de Leyva in Colombia, fossils of the 2-m-long (6-ft 6-in) species *Desmatochelys padillai* date from the early Cretaceous period, more than 120 million years ago.

Largest freshwater turtle ever

The first-known remains of *Carbonemys cofrinii* were discovered in a coal mine in Colombia in 2005, but the species was not officially named and described until 2012. It lived 60 million years ago during the Palaeocene epoch. *C. cofrinii*'s shell was 1.72 m (5 ft 7.7 in) long, its skull was the size of an American football and its total length was nearly 2.5 m (8 ft 2.4 in) – slightly smaller than a Smart car.

▲ LAZIEST FRESHWATER TURTLE

Found in large lowland rivers such as the Mekong in Cambodia, Cantor's giant softshell turtle (*Pelochelys cantorii*) spends 95% of its life motionless, buried in sand on the river bottom waiting for prey such as fish and molluscs to approach. Twice a day, it comes up to the surface of the water to breathe. Its primarily passive existence is a contrast to the far more active loggerhead turtle (see right), although both species spend long periods underwater.

Longest dive by a marine vertebrate

In Feb 2003, an adult female loggerhead turtle (*Caretta caretta*) dived for 10 hr 14 min in the Mediterranean Sea off the coast of Tunisia. The marathon underwater swim was recorded by researchers led by Dr Annette Broderick of the University of Exeter, UK. Loggerhead turtles are able to slow down their internal systems, reducing the need for oxygen and enabling them to survive underwater for hours on one breath.

Q: How old was Tu'i Malila, the **oldest recorded chelonian**, when he died in 1965?

A: 188

Longest reptile migration

From 2006, satellites tracked a tagged leatherback turtle (*D. coriacea*) for two years as it made a 20,558-km (12,774-mi) journey from its nesting site on the beaches of Papua, Indonesia, to feeding grounds off the coast of the US state of Oregon. The journey took the intrepid turtle 647 days to complete.

The leatherback is also the **fastest chelonian in water**, with a speed of up to 35 km/h (22 mph) recorded for one specimen.

Largest congregation of turtles

Every February, turtles emerge from the sea after dark to the same 10-km (6.2-mi) stretch of beach at Gahirmatha in Odisha, eastern India. There, they lay more than 50 million eggs in the sand, and are back in the sea by dawn. In 1991, approximately 610,000 specimens of olive ridley turtles (*Lepidochelys olivacea*) were counted nesting on the beach.

Rarest turtle

Once native to the Yangtze River and across China, the Yangtze giant softshell turtle (*Rafetus swinhoei*) is currently only represented by three living specimens. A fourth died in Jan 2016 (see p.97). One of the surviving turtles inhabits a lake in northern Vietnam, where it was discovered in 2008; the other two, a male and female, are in captivity in China's Suzhou Zoo. Efforts to breed young turtles have so far failed. Not surprisingly, the Yangtze giant softshell turtle is categorized as "Critically Endangered" by the IUCN.

▲ **LARGEST CHELONIAN**
On 23 Sep 1988, the body of a male leatherback turtle (*D. coriacea*) washed up on the beach at Harlech in Gwynedd, UK. It measured 2.91 m (9 ft 6.5 in) along the carapace, and 2.77 m (9 ft 1 in) across the front flippers. At 914 kg (2,019 lb 6 oz), the leatherback leviathan weighed twice as much as a grand piano. On 16 Feb 1990, the turtle was put on display at the National Museum Wales in Cardiff, UK.

▲ **SMALLEST SEA TURTLE**
Native to the Gulf of Mexico and warm stretches of the Atlantic Ocean, Kemp's ridley sea turtle (*Lepidochelys kempii*) exhibits a maximum carapace length of 75 cm (29.5 in) and a weight of 50 kg (110 lb). Its carapace width is almost the same as its length, giving it a circular appearance. The olive or Pacific ridley turtle (*L. olivacea*), found in the Pacific and Indian oceans, is slightly heavier than its close relation.

Turtles have no teeth

It has been estimated that only one newly hatched sea turtle in every thousand survives to adulthood

Green sea turtles can stay underwater without breathing nasally for up to five hours

A turtle's shell has evolved from its ribcage and part of its backbone

A group of turtles is variously known as a nest, a bale, a dole or a turn

North America's stinkpot turtle earned its name from the foul smell released from scent glands around its shell's edge, probably to deter predators

Mock turtle soup is a turtle-free dish dating back to 18th-century England. It inspired the character of the Mock Turtle in Lewis Carroll's novel *Alice's Adventures in Wonderland* (1865).

▲ LARGEST SNAPPING TURTLE

Members of the Chelydridae family, snapping turtles are notable for their large heads and powerful hooked jaws. The alligator snapping turtle (*Macrochelys temminckii*, below) has a plated shell and a powerful bite, just like its namesake. Native to fresh water in the south-eastern USA, the turtle weighs on average 80 kg (176 lb), but can come in at more than 100 kg (220 lb). One specimen found in Kansas in 1937 had a reported weight of 183 kg (403 lb).

Rarest sea turtle

Numbers of Kemp's ridley sea turtle (*L. kempii*) have suffered owing to pollution, habitat loss and entanglement in shrimp nets. They are also a popular food in Mexico. A 2014 estimate of nest numbers placed them at 118, but during that year 10,594 hatchlings were released by wildlife officials along the coast of the US state of Texas. The sea turtle occurs in the Gulf of Mexico and warmer stretches of the Atlantic Ocean, but has been spotted as far north as New Jersey, USA. It is categorized as "Critically Endangered" by the IUCN.

▶ LARGEST LIVING FRESHWATER TURTLE

The Yangtze giant softshell turtle (*R. swinhoei*) measures more than 1 m (3 ft 3 in) long and up to 0.7 m (2 ft 3.5 in) wide. The heaviest recorded specimen tipped the scales at 250 kg (551 lb). Claims that Cantor's giant softshell turtle (*Pelochelys cantorii*, see p.94) is a larger freshwater turtle are debatable, as it seems likely that this species is a composite of several separate undifferentiated species.

On 19 Jan 2016, the Yangtze giant softshell turtle Cu Rùa ("Great Grandfather Turtle") died in Hanoi, Vietnam. Sightings of the venerable turtle had been thought to bring good luck.

▲ DEEPEST DIVE BY A CHELONIAN

Unusually for turtles, the leatherback spends most of its time in the open ocean, where it dives for jellyfish to eat. Broad shoulders and a tapered shell make it a powerful, streamlined swimmer. In May 1987, a leatherback fitted with a recording device was measured by Dr Scott Eckert (USA) as reaching a depth of 1,200 m (3,937 ft) off the US Virgin Islands in the West Indies.

Whales

Taxonomically, there is no such thing as a whale: whales are a diverse group of mammals within the infraorder Cetacea

▲ SMALLEST WHALE
Whales are generally considered to be the larger members of the Cetacea infraorder (which also includes dolphins and porpoises), although not all whales are enormous. The smallest species commonly understood to be a whale is the dwarf sperm whale (*Kogia sima*), at up to 2.72 m (8 ft 11 in) long and weighing 272 kg (600 lb).

Longest basilosaurid

Basilosaurids were prehistoric whales that existed 34–40 million years ago, during the late Mid- to early Late Eocene epoch. Most were characterized by lengthy, serpentine or eel-like bodies, and some grew to immense sizes. The longest basilosaurid species presently known from fossils is *Basilosaurus cetoides*, which grew to 18 m (59 ft) and possibly longer. Its great length was due to a marked elongation of the central portion (centrum) of the thoracic and anterior caudal vertebrae in its backbone.

Largest mouth

The blue whale might be the world's **largest animal** (see opposite) but it doesn't have the biggest mouth. That honour belongs to the bowhead whale (*Balaena mysticetus*), which has a mouth measuring 5 m (16 ft 4 in) long, 4 m (13 ft 1 in) high and 2.5 m (8 ft 2 in) wide. Its tongue weighs approximately 1 tonne (2,200 lb) – about the same as a dairy cow.

▲ LONGEST WHALE TOOTH
The single-spiralled ivory tusk of the male narwhal (*Monodon monoceros*) attains an average of around 2 m (6 ft 6 in) long. Occasionally, however, specimens have been found that exceed 3 m (9 ft 10 in) and weigh up to 10 kg (22 lb), with a maximum girth of approximately 23 cm (9 in). Very rarely, the narwhal grows a pair of tusks.

Q: What is unusual about the way in which sperm whales sleep?

A: They float "standing up"

Most common baleen whale

Owing to its relatively small size, low oil yield and a distribution mainly in the southern hemisphere, the Antarctic or southern minke whale (*Balaenoptera* [aka *Rorqualus*] *bonaerensis*) was generally ignored by the whaling industry during the pre-modern age, so its numbers have remained high. In 2006, a scientific report detailing three completed circumpolar sets of Antarctic minke whale surveys, spanning 1978–79 to 2003–04, estimated that it numbered in the hundreds of thousands – far more than the number estimated for any other baleen whale.

The **largest taxonomic family of baleen whales** is Balaenopteridae, containing the rorquals, which consists of nine currently recognized species. These include the blue whale, the sei whale (*Balaenoptera* [aka *Rorqualus*] *borealis*) and the humpback whale (*Megaptera novaeangliae*). Like all baleen whales, rorquals feed mainly on tiny marine organisms that they strain from seawater via large comb- or sieve-like baleen plates, but some will also gulp down larger fishes.

Adult male short-finned pilot whales (*Globicephala macrorhynchus*) have a maximum recorded body length of 7.2 m (23 ft 7.4 in), the **largest pilot whale**. Adult females grow to 5.5 m (18 ft). The species inhabits the Pacific Ocean's warm temperate and tropical waters.

▲ LARGEST TOOTHED MAMMAL
Mature male sperm whales (*Physeter macrocephalus*, see p.100) can grow to 20.5 m (67 ft 3 in) long, but average 16 m (52 ft 5 in). The species only has functional teeth in the lower jaw (there are 18 to 26 on each side) and they fit into slots in the upper jaw. Each lower-jaw tooth can weigh 1 kg (2 lb 3 oz).

◀ LARGEST ANIMAL
The blue whale (*Balaenoptera musculus*) can weigh 160 tonnes (352,000 lb), with an average length of 24 m (80 ft). A specimen caught in the Antarctic Ocean on 20 Mar 1947 was said to weigh 190 tonnes (418,878 lb) with a length of 27.6 m (90 ft 6 in). The **longest animal**, however, is the bootlace worm (*Lineus longissimus*), found in the shallow waters of the North Sea: one such worm washed ashore in 1864 exceeded 55 m (180 ft).

The nose of a blue whale measures **5 m (16 ft 4.8 in)** long

A blue whale's heartbeat is loud enough to be heard **3 km (1.86 mi)** away

The tongue of a blue whale weighs the same as an adult bull elephant

Largest beaked whale

Baird's beaked whale (*Berardius bairdii*) is one of three species categorized as giant beaked whales. Native to cold temperate waters in the North Pacific, it attains a maximum confirmed length of 13 m (42 ft 7.8 in) and weighs up to 14 tonnes (30,864 lb).

The **smallest species of beaked whale** is the pygmy or Peruvian beaked whale (*Mesoplodon peruvianus*). It measures some 4 m (13 ft) long when adult and is around 1.6 m (5 ft 3 in) long when newborn. It has been recorded in eastern tropical Pacific waters stretching south from California in the USA and Baja California in Mexico to Peru and Chile in north-western South America.

As of Oct 2016, the **newest species of beaked whale** was a recently recognized species from Japan, known colloquially by local Japanese fishermen as the *karasu* but still awaiting formal scientific description and naming. Much smaller and darker in colour than its closest relatives, the giant beaked whales (genus *Berardius*), the *karasu* inhabits shallow waters off Japan and the Korean Peninsula and also in the Bering Sea off Alaska.

A sperm whale's upper teeth do not emerge on its upper jaw. Indeed, these creatures often simply swallow their food, without biting. Sperm whales with no teeth at all are still able to survive.

◀ LARGEST JAW

The Natural History Museum in London, UK, owns a 5-m-long (16-ft 4.8-in) jaw from a sperm whale, or cachalot. That's almost the same as the length of five baseball bats laid end to end. The massive lower jaw belonged to a male whale that had been nearly 25.6 m (84 ft) long.

◀ GREATEST SIZE DIFFERENCE BETWEEN PREDATOR AND PREY

Blue whales are the **largest mammals** and the **largest animals** (see p.99). Their prey is minuscule, however: they feed on krill, tiny shrimp-like crustaceans around 50 mm (2 in) long. To feed, a blue whale gulps in vast quantities of krill-filled seawater. It expels the water by lifting the world's **heaviest tongue** (typically weighing 4 tonnes, or 8,818 lb) to the roof of its mouth, leaving the krill trapped in the strands of baleen (bristle-like protein) that hang from its upper jaw. Then they are swallowed.

100%

▶ GREATEST WEIGHT LOSS IN AN ANIMAL

During her seven-month lactation period, a 120-tonne (264,555-lb) female blue whale can lose 25% of her weight while nursing her calf. Blue whale calves weigh around 2,500 kg (5,511 lb 9 oz) at birth, but thereafter add some 80–100 kg (176–220 lb) per day during the lactation period. The mother eats very little during these seven months, relying almost entirely on her body reserves for energy.

▲ LARGEST TAIL
In absolute terms, the tail of the humpback whale (*Megaptera novaeangliae*) is the largest in the animal kingdom. Comprising two lobes (or "flukes"), a fully grown tail is as wide as a giraffe is tall, with one measured specimen reaching 17 ft 4 in (5.28 m), according to research by Nancy Stevick of WhaleNet.org.

The **deepest dive by a mammal** was made by a Cuvier's beaked whale (*Ziphius cavirostris*) off the coast of southern California, USA, in 2013. During a three-month study of eight individuals, marine scientists used satellite-linked tags to record the whales' dives, the deepest of which reached 2,992 m (9,816 ft) – equivalent to more than three-and-a-half times the height of the Burj Khalifa, the world's **tallest building** (see pp.50–54).

Shepherd's beaked whale (*Tasmacetus shepherdi*) has been recorded off New Zealand, Australia and Argentina. With as many as 27 pairs of functional teeth in each jaw, plus a pair of short tusks at the tip of the lower jaw in males, it has the **most teeth for a beaked whale species**. All other beaked whales possess only a handful of teeth at most. Indeed, the paucity of teeth is a characteristic feature of these whales.

▲ LARGEST MAMMAL TO EXPLODE
In 2004, a bull sperm whale 17 m (55 ft 9 in) long and weighing 50 tonnes (110,230 lb) died after becoming beached in south-west Chinese Taipei. It was placed on the back of a truck and taken away (below), but as the carcass decomposed, powerful internal gases gathered within it. On 26 Jan, the deceased cetacean exploded while the truck was driving through the city of Tainan, splattering nearby shop fronts, vehicles and pedestrians with blood and entrails (above).

Pets

The ancient Egyptians kept a variety of pets as well as dogs and cats, including baboons, falcons, gazelles, lions, mongooses and hippopotamuses.

Fastest 100 m on a skateboard by a dog
On 16 Sep 2013, Jumpy the dog skateboarded 100 m (328 ft) in 19.65 sec on the set of *Officially Amazing* in Los Angeles, California, USA.

Largest gathering of pets
A troupe of 4,616 pets went for a walk with their owners at the Feria de las Flores in Medellín, Colombia, on 7 Aug 2007.

Most wins of the World's Ugliest Dog contest
Chi-Chi, a rare African sand dog, is a seven-time winner of the World's Ugliest Dog Contest at the Sonoma-Marin Fair in Petaluma, California, USA. The wins came in 1978, 1982–84, 1986–87 and 1991. The family tradition continued with Chi-Chi's grandson, Rascal, who took the title in 2002.

Highest jump by a miniature horse
On 15 Mar 2015, Castrawes Paleface Orion – owned by Robert Barnes – leapt 1.08 m (3 ft 6.5 in) in Tamworth, New South Wales, Australia.

Farthest jump by a guinea pig
On 6 Apr 2012, a guinea pig named Truffles cleared a gap of 48 cm (1 ft 6.8 in) in Rosyth, Fife, UK.

Tallest horse ever
Foaled in 1846, a shire gelding named Sampson (later renamed Mammoth), bred by Thomas Cleaver of Toddington Mills, Bedfordshire, UK, measured 21 hands 2.5 in (2.19 m; 7 ft 2.2 in) in 1850.

The **tallest living horse** is Big Jake, a nine-year-old Belgian gelding who measured 20 hands 2.75 in (2.10 m; 6 ft 10.75 in), without shoes, at Smokey Hollow Farms in Poynette, Wisconsin, USA, on 19 Jan 2010.

Tallest goat
Mostyn Moorcock, a British Saanen who died in 1977, reached a shoulder height of 3 ft 8 in (1.11 m) and an overall length of 5 ft 6 in (1.67 m). His owner was Pat Robinson of the UK.

▲ **OLDEST COCKATIEL**
Sunshine the pied cockatiel was aged 32 years as of 27 Jan 2016. The record-breaking bird lives with his owner Vickie Aranda in Albuquerque, New Mexico, USA. He was first purchased in Colorado in 1983, but has been moving with Vickie around the country ever since. Sunshine is rather particular when it comes to his food: he will not eat vegetables, but loves cheese and spaghetti noodles.

Shortest cow

Manikyam, owned by Akshay N V, measured 61.1 cm (2 ft) from the hoof to the withers on 21 Jun 2014 in Kerala, India. The term "withers" refers to the ridge between the shoulder blades.

Shortest donkey

KneeHi measured 64.2 cm (2 ft 1.2 in) to the withers at Best Friends Farm in Gainesville, Florida, USA, on 26 Jul 2011. A registered miniature Mediterranean donkey, KneeHi is owned by James, Frankie and Ryan Lee.

Longest fur on a cat

A cat named Sophie Smith had fur 25.68 cm (10.11 in) long, as measured in Oceanside, California, USA, on 9 Nov 2013. She belongs to Jami Smith.

Longest fur on a rabbit

On 17 Aug 2014, the fur on Franchesca, an Angora rabbit, was verified at 36.5 cm (1 ft 2.37 in) long. Franchesca lives with her owner, Betty Chu, in Morgan Hill, California, USA.

Longest tongue on a dog (current)

Mochi, a female St Bernard owned by Carla and Craig Rickert, has a tongue that measured 18.5 cm (7.3 in) in Sioux Falls, South Dakota, USA, on 25 Aug 2016.

The **longest tongue on a dog ever** is 43 cm (1 ft 5 in) and belonged to Brandy, a boxer who lived with her owner John Scheid in St Clair Shores, Michigan, USA, until Sep 2002.

Oldest chinchilla

Radar (b. 1 Feb 1985), owned by Christina Anthony, was 29 years 229 days old when he died in Acton, California, USA, on 18 Sep 2014.

▼ OLDEST BEARDED DRAGON EVER

Born on 1 Jun 1997, Sebastian the bearded dragon was aged 18 years 237 days as of 24 Jan 2016, when he passed away. His owner, Lee-Anne Burgess of Middlesex, UK, brought Sebastian home on Christmas Eve in 1997. The life expectancy for a bearded dragon in captivity is usually 7–14 years, although in the wild they are more likely to live for 5–8 years.

The bearded dragon's throat is covered in spine-like pouches. It puffs them out to scare off predators, or when it feels that its territory is being threatened, and (in males) as part of its courtship ritual.

A: 2.7 million, according to the American Society for the Prevention of Cruelty to Animals (ASPCA)

► **TALLEST DOMESTIC CAT (LIVING)**

Arcturus Aldebaran Powers is 48.4 cm (1 ft 7 in) tall to the shoulders, as verified in Ann Arbor, Michigan, USA, on 3 Nov 2016.

Remarkably, his owners, William and Lauren Powers, own another record-breaking feline. Their silver Maine Coon named Cygnus has the **longest tail on a domestic cat (living)**. It measured 44.6 cm (1 ft 5.5 in) in Ferndale, Michigan, USA, on 28 Aug 2016.

Only 25% of Americans *chose* to have a cat as a pet; the other 75% were *adopted* by a cat

Cats are "**obligate carnivores**" – they must eat meat to survive

Guinea pigs have **three** toes on their **back** paws and **four** on their **front** paws

Nearly a third of all Dalmatian dogs are deaf

TOP FIVE PETS IN THE USA
(in millions)

1.
Freshwater fish: 95.5

2.
Cats: 85.8

3.
Dogs: 77.8

4.
Birds: 14.3

5.
Small animals: 12.4

Oldest donkey

A donkey named Suzy reached 54 years old in 2002. She was owned by Beth Augusta Menczer and lived in Glenwood, New Mexico, USA.

Oldest rabbit

A wild rabbit named Flopsy was caught on 6 Aug 1964 and died 18 years 10 months 3 weeks later at the home of L B Walker of Longford in Tasmania, Australia.

▲ LARGEST DOG YOGA CLASS

Link Asset Management Ltd (HKG) assembled 270 canine participants and their owners for a yoga class on 17 Jan 2016 in Stanley Plaza, Hong Kong, China. Part of the Paws by the Sea event, the proceeds of which went to the Hong Kong Guide Dogs Association, the class was overseen by "doga" (dog yoga) instructor Suzette Ackermann (HKG).

On 28 Sep 2014, at the same venue, Link Asset Management Ltd set a new record for the **most dogs balancing a treat on their nose**. A total of 109 animals proved their canine dexterity.

▶ FASTEST 10 M ON A WALKING GLOBE BY A DOG

A dog named Sailor covered a distance of 10 m (32 ft) on a walking globe in 33.22 sec on 5 Feb 2016. The event took place in the gymnasium at Hawthorn Middle School South in Vernon Hills, Illinois, USA.

On the same occasion, the well-balanced Sailor also performed the **fastest backwards 10 m on a walking globe by a dog**, in a time of 17.06 sec.

▼ TALLEST LIVING DOG

When measured on 13 Sep 2016, in Leigh-on-Sea, Essex, UK, Freddy the Great Dane was found to be 1.035 m (3 ft 4.75 in) tall. Freddy's owner is Claire Stoneman (pictured). Ironically, when he was born, Freddy was the smallest puppy in the litter, but then underwent an unexpected growth spurt. Unfortunately for Claire, Freddy has a soft spot for leather sofas: he'd chomped through 14 of them within 18 months of arriving at her home!

It costs around £4,000 ($5,090) a year to feed Freddy. But as a young pup, "Freddy was such a poor eater," remembers Claire, "I tried everything. I suspect I rather spoiled him!"

Animals Round-Up

An ant colony trapped inside a Polish nuclear bunker has formed its own society with no queen or males.

IN THE NEWS...

Great white shark

On 15 Apr 2012, a great white shark nearly 20 ft (6.09 m) long and weighing at least 2,000 lb (907 kg) was caught in the Sea of Cortez in Mexico. Great whites are the **largest predatory fish**: adults average 14–15 ft (4.3–4.6 m) in length, with females usually larger than males, although there is evidence of some exceeding 20 ft.

Masai giraffe

The Wild Nature Institute's ongoing Project GIRAFFE (short for Giraffe Facing Fragmentation Effects) is the **largest giraffe research project**, monitoring more than 2,100 specimens in an area of 4,000 km² (1,544 sq mi). It focuses on the possible effects of environmental fragmentation – i.e., habitat decrease or loss – upon the Masai giraffes (*Giraffa tippelskirchi*) of Tanzania's Tarangire National Park.

▼ FIRST THREE-PIECE SUIT DESIGNED FOR A HORSE

To celebrate the opening of the Cheltenham Festival in Gloucestershire, UK, on 15 Mar 2016, fashion designer Emma Sandham-King (UK) designed and made a Harris Tweed suit for Morestead, a chestnut gelding racehorse. The three-piece suit, complete with shirt, tie and flat cap, took four weeks to make and required more than 18 m (59 ft) of hand-woven tweed – enough for 10 regular human-sized suits.

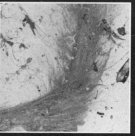

▲ **FIRST DINOSAUR TAIL PRESERVED IN AMBER**

In 2015, palaeontologist Dr Lida Xing from Beijing's China University of Geosciences made a startling discovery while browsing an amber market in Kachin State, Burma. Preserved inside one lump of amber, dated to the mid-Cretaceous period 99 million years ago, was a finely feathered tail. Tomographic scans of the feathers and accompanying eight vetebrae suggested that the tail had belonged not to a bird but to a dinosaur, most likely a coelurosaur (pictured above).

The **tallest giraffe** ever documented was a Masai bull named George, who was received by Chester Zoo, UK, on 8 Jan 1959. Measuring c. 19 ft (5.8 m) in height, George was so tall that he had to duck his head to get in and out of the giraffe house!

Dinosaurs

Researchers from the Natural History Museum in London, UK, constructed a detailed dinosaur family tree that suggests the creatures may have evolved up to 10 million years earlier than the current **oldest-dated dinosaur**, a *Nyasasaurus* approximately 240 million years old.

Apes

The **largest primate**, *Gigantopithecus blacki*, stood 3 m (9 ft 10 in) tall and weighed around 1,580 kg (3,483 lb). Research in 2016 suggested that the ape died out 100,000 years ago owing to a lack of food, as forests turned into savannahs.

Nile crocodile

In May 2016, DNA tests confirmed that three crocodiles found in swamps in Florida, USA, were man-eating Nile crocodiles. It is not known for certain how they got there – one possibility is that they were smuggled into the country by unlicensed collectors.

The Nile crocodile (*Crocodylus niloticus*) is one of 12 species contained within *Crocodylus* – the **largest crocodile genus**. Other species include the recently recognized desert crocodile (*C. suchus*) and the mugger crocodile (*C. palustris*).

▼ RAREST WILD BUFFALO

The tamaraw (*Bubalus mindorensis*) is confined entirely to the Philippine island of Mindoro. Thanks to habitat destruction caused by logging and human habitation, the tamaraw's range has shrunk to a few grassy plains in the mountainous interior of the island. As of 2016, it is believed to number around 430 individuals, and is categorized as "Critically Endangered" by the IUCN.

Moose

In Nov 2016, two hikers in Unalakleet, Alaska, USA, stumbled across two pairs of bull moose antlers protruding through an 8-in (20.32-cm) layer of ice over open water. It is thought that the two bulls had locked antlers while fighting before drowning together in water that later iced over.

The Alaskan moose (*Alces alces gigas*) is the **largest deer**. A bull standing 7 ft 8 in (2.34 m) tall and weighing an estimated 1,800 lb (816 kg) was shot in the Yukon Territory of Canada in Sep 1897.

Dog

Jiff the Pomeranian, aka Jiffpom (USA), was recognized as the **most followed dog on Instagram**, with 4.8 million fans as of 3 May 2017. In his social media accounts, Jiffpom describes himself as a "movie actor/model" and fills his Instagram feed with snapshots of himself wearing various outfits, chilling out at home, and attending movie premieres, award ceremonies, TV studios and fashion shows.

▲ FIRST WARM-HEARTED FISH

The opah or moonfish (*Lampris guttatus*) has a unique metabolic condition, discovered in 2015, which enables it to maintain its body temperature at a level constantly above that of the surrounding seawater. A large, disc-shaped marine species related to the oarfish and ribbonfish, the opah is found in temperate and tropical waters of most oceans.

▲ MOST EXPENSIVE DODO SKELETON SOLD AT AUCTION

On 22 Nov 2016, a near-complete skeleton of a dodo (*Raphus cucullatus*) sold to a private collector for £346,300 ($428,931), with buyer's premium, at the Summers Place "Evolution" auction in Billingshurst, West Sussex, UK. The skeleton is believed to be one of only 13 such skeletons in existence; the others are all held by museums.

▼ LARGEST SPECIES OF PANGOLIN

In 2016, the 182 nations of the Convention on International Trade in Endangered Species (CITES) agreed a total ban on the international trade of pangolins. Measuring 2 m (6 ft 6 in) long and weighing 70 lb (32 kg), the giant pangolin (*Smutsia gigantea*) can be found from Senegal to Angola in Africa. It is entirely terrestrial on account of its size, while many other pangolins are at least partly arboreal.

Caribou

A study published by the University of Manitoba in Feb 2016 suggested that there may be a type of caribou in the Sahtu region of Canada's Northwest Territories as yet unrecognized by science. The search is now on for the mysterious caribou, known by the indigenous Dene people as "fast runners".

The **longest terrestrial animal migration** is made by Grant's caribou (*Rangifer tarandus granti*) of Alaska and the Yukon Territory of North America. It travels up to 4,800 km (2,982 mi) each year (see p.64 for more details).

▲ FIRST AMPHIBIOUS CENTIPEDE

Formerly described in the scientific journal *ZooKeys* in May 2016, *Scolopendra cataracta* is a venomous and carnivorous centipede measuring up to 20 cm (7.87 in) in length. It is native to south-east Asia. The centipede is adapted for an amphibious existence, and can swim like an eel through the water by horizontally undulating its body.

Trogons are brightly coloured birds native to tropical and subtropical Africa, south-east Asia and Latin America. Most are only 23–40 cm (9–15.7 in) long, but the male resplendent quetzal (*Pharomachrus mocinno*, recently photographed in Costa Rica, right) can measure up to 1.05 m (3 ft 5.3 in). This is due to the two long tail-covert plumes it grows to attract females in the breeding season.

Monitor lizard

In Feb 2016, researchers from the University of Turku in Finland announced the discovery of the newest monitor lizard on the remote Pacific island of Mussau. Dubbed *Varanus semotus*, the lizard's body measured more than 1 m (3 ft 3 in) in length, sporting a predominantly black body with orange and yellow markings and a blue tail. Genetic analysis has revealed that *Varanus semotus* has been isolated from other species of monitor lizard on Mussau for millions of years.

Sumatran rhino

On 12 Mar 2016, a Sumatran rhinoceros (*Dicerorhinus sumatrensis*) was discovered in Kalimantan in Indonesian Borneo. It had been thought to be extinct in the region. Sadly, the rhino died only weeks later, succumbing to an infection caused by an old snare injury.

With a maximum head-to-body length of 3.18 m (10 ft 5 in), tail length of 70 cm (2 ft 3 in) and shoulder height of 1.45 m (4 ft 9 in), the Sumatran rhinoceros is the **smallest rhinoceros**.

▲ **OLDEST BREEDING SEA BIRD**
In Dec 2016, a female Laysan albatross (*Phoebastria immutabilis*) named Wisdom laid an egg and was observed incubating it aged 66 years. Wisdom has been monitored by conservationists for many years, returning to Midway Atoll national wildlife refuge in the Pacific Ocean every year. This latest egg is known to be Wisdom's 41st, and she has hatched at least nine chicks since 2006.

The resplendent quetzal is the national bird of Guatemala. It appears on the national flag and coat of arms, and is also the name of the local currency (abbreviated to GTQ).

Fastest...

Whether a product of the natural or the man-made world, speed retains the same power to thrill. From tanks to roller-coasters, biplanes to spaceships, the story of speed records is also the story of human development – how we have pushed the boundaries of technological possibilities in order to defy nature and travel faster than ever before.

0-100 km/h

Human (running) 37.57 km/h

On 16 Aug 2009, Usain Bolt (JAM) won the World Championships 100 m in 9.58 sec in Berlin, Germany. His average speed was 37.57 km/h (23.34 mph), with a peak speed nearer 44 km/h (27.34 mph).

Land animal (long distances) 56 km/h

The pronghorn (*Antilocapra americana*) is an antelope-like ungulate found in the USA, Canada and Mexico. It has been observed moving at 56 km/h (34.7 mph) over 6 km (3.7 mi).

Greyhound 67.2 km/h

On 5 Mar 1994, a greyhound named Star Title was timed at 67.2 km/h (41.7 mph) on a straight track at Wyong in New South Wales, Australia. It blitzed the 400-yd (1,200-ft; 365.7-m) course in 19.57 sec.

Tank 82.23 km/h

A production standard S 2000 Scorpion Peacekeeper tank developed by Repaircraft PLC (UK) achieved a speed of 82.23 km/h (51.10 mph) at the QinetiQ test track in Chertsey, Surrey, UK, on 26 Mar 2002. Powered by an RS 2133 high-speed diesel engine, the tank was fitted with appliqué hull armour, ballistic skirts and a replaceable rubber pad track.

Monowheel motorcycle 98.464 km/h

Riding *WarHorse*, Kevin Scott and the UK Monowheel Team (all UK) achieved a speed of 98.464 km/h (61.18 mph) at Elvington airfield in North Yorkshire, UK, on 20 Sep 2015. It took four engineers two years to build the carbon-fibre-framed vehicle.

100–300 km/h

Land mammal (short distances) 104.4 km/h

During research conducted in 1965, an adult female cheetah (*Acinonyx jubatus*) reached a speed of 29 m/s (104.4 km/h; 64.8 mph) over a distance of 220 yards (201.1 m; 660 ft).

Bird (in level flight) 127 km/h

In a report published by researchers working in the sub-Antarctic, the mean estimated ground speed recorded for a satellite-tagged grey-headed albatross (*Thalassarche chrysostoma*) was 127 km/h (78.9 mph). This speed was sustained for more than 8 hr while the albatross made for its nest at Bird Island, South Georgia, in the middle of an Antarctic storm.

Human-powered vehicle 139.45 km/h

Riding his Team AeroVelo's *Eta* bike at the World Human Powered Speed Challenge, Todd Reichert (CAN) achieved a speed of 139.45 km/h (86.65 mph) on 19 Sep 2015. It was the third time in three days that the fearless Canadian had set a new record during the event, which was held near Battle Mountain in Nevada, USA.

Roller-coaster 240 km/h

Formula Rossa at Ferrari World in Abu Dhabi, UAE, can accelerate to 240 km/h (149.1 mph). Even when travelling upward, it covers 52 m (170 ft) in 4.9 sec. It opened to the public on 4 Nov 2010.

Tennis serve 263 km/h

On 9 May 2012, Samuel Groth (AUS) served an ace recorded at 263 km/h (163.4 mph) during an ATP Challenger event in Busan, South Korea. It came during Groth's second-round tie against Uladzimir Ignatik (BLR). The Aussie pro also hit serves of 255.7 km/h (158.8 mph) and 253.5 km/h (157.5 mph) during the match – both of which surpassed Ivo Karlovic's (HRV) previous record of 251 km/h (156 mph). Although he gained a world record, Groth lost the match 6–4, 6–3.

Images not to scale

300–1,000 km/h

Bird (in a dive)
389.46 km/h

The peregrine falcon (*Falco peregrinus*) has reached an estimated terminal velocity of 300 km/h (186.4 mph) in a diving stoop. No animal is capable of reaching a faster speed than the falcon in full flight.

Surface wind speed (high altitude)
371 km/h

On 12 Apr 1934, Mount Washington (elev. 1,916 m; 6,286 ft) in New Hampshire, USA, experienced a surface wind speed of 371 km/h (230 mph).

Quad bike
315.74 km/h

Terry Wilmeth (USA) reached an average speed of 315.74 km/h (196.19 mph) over two runs at Madras Airport in Oregon, USA, on 15 Jun 2008. His ALSR Rocket Raptor version 6.0 was a modified Yamaha Raptor 700 with a hybrid rocket thruster.

Boat
511.09 km/h

The world water-speed record is 275.97 knots (511.09 km/h; 317.58 mph), by Ken Warby (AUS) in the jet-powered hydroplane *Spirit of Australia* on Blowering Dam Lake, New South Wales, Australia, on 8 Oct 1978.

Biplane
520 km/h

In 1941, the Fiat CR.42DB attained a speed of 520 km/h (323 mph). The Italian biplane was powered by a 753-kW (1,010-hp) Daimler-Benz DB 601A engine. Despite its speed, only a single prototype was ever constructed, as biplanes were eclipsed by new monoplanes.

Maglev train
603 km/h

The L0 (A07) series is a magnetically levitated (maglev) train series operated by the Central Japan Railway Company. On 21 Apr 2015, the L0 achieved a speed of 603 km/h (374.68 mph) on the Yamanashi Maglev Line, a test track in Yamanashi, Japan.

1,000–20,000 km/h

Car (land-speed record)
1,227.985 km/h

Andy Green (UK) drove *Thrust SSC* at 1,227.985 km/h (763.035 mph; Mach 1.020) on 15 Oct 1997 in the Black Rock Desert in Nevada, USA. Powered by two Rolls-Royce jet engines, *Thrust SSC* was the **first car to break the sound barrier.**

Human (in freefall)
1,357.6 km/h

Felix Baumgartner (AUT) fell from the edge of space to Earth at 1,357.6 km/h (843.5 mph) during the Red Bull Stratos mission above New Mexico, USA, on 14 Oct 2012.

Airliner
2,587 km/h

First flown in the former USSR on 31 Dec 1968, the Tupolev Tu-144 was reported to have reached Mach 2.4 (2,587 km/h; 1,607 mph), although its normal cruising speed was Mach 2.2. Following two crashes, the aircraft was withdrawn from service in 1978.

Manned aircraft
3,529.56 km/h

The highest recorded speed in a manned aircraft capable of taking off and landing under its own power is 3,529.56 km/h (2,193.17 mph). It was achieved by Captain Eldon Joersz and Major George Morgan Jr (both USA) in a Lockheed SR-71A "Blackbird" near Beale Air Force Base in California, USA, on 28 Jul 1976.

Aircraft (rocket-powered)
7,274 km/h

On 3 Oct 1967, USAF test pilot "Pete" Knight reached Mach 6.7 (7,274 km/h; 4,520 mph) over California, USA. Knight was flying the experimental X-15A-2 aircraft, which was launched in mid-air from beneath a B-52 bomber.

Images not to scale

> 20,000 km/h

Human (absolute)
39,897 km/h

On 26 May 1969, the command module of *Apollo 10* reached 39,897 km/h (24,790.8 mph) on its trans-Earth return flight. It carried a three-man crew of American astronauts: Col Thomas Stafford, Cdr Eugene Cernan and Cdr John Young.

Atmospheric entry into Earth's atmosphere
46,660 km/h

On 15 Jan 2006, NASA's *Stardust* spacecraft successfully returned to Earth after a seven-year mission to collect samples of comet Wild 2. It entered Earth's atmosphere at a velocity of 46,660 km/h (28,993 mph).

Planet
172,248 km/h

Mercury orbits the Sun at an average distance of 57.9 million km (35.9 million mi), and has an orbital period of 87.9686 days. Its average orbit speed – 172,248 km/h (107,030 mph) – is almost twice as fast as that of Earth.

Approaching galaxy
1,508,400 km/h

Although the universe is expanding, there are a small number of galaxies that are coming closer to our own. M86, a lenticular (lens-shaped) galaxy situated around 52 million light years away in the Virgo Cluster, is moving towards our Milky Way at a speed of 419 km/sec (260 ml/sec).

Star
2,400,000 km/h

On 8 Feb 2005, astronomers from the Harvard-Smithsonian Center for Astrophysics in Massachusetts, USA, announced the discovery of a star, SDSS J090745.0+024507, which is travelling at 2.4 million km/h (1.5 million mph).

Speed possible
1,079,252,848.8 km/h

The fastest speed possible in the universe is the speed of light. This is achieved only by light itself and other forms of electromagnetic radiation such as radio waves. When travelling through a vacuum, the speed of light peaks at 299,792.458 m/sec (983,571,056 ft/sec).

Images not to scale

Superhumans

Diver Aleix Segura Vendrell (ESP) can hold his breath for longer than an average episode of *The Big Bang Theory*.

▲ LONGEST FINGERNAILS ON A PAIR OF HANDS (FEMALE)

Ayanna Williams of Houston in Texas, USA, has been growing her nails for more than 20 years; as of 7 Feb 2017, they had a combined total length of 576.4 cm (18 ft 10.9 in). The nails on her left hand are longer than her right, measuring a total of 326.5 cm (10 ft 8.5 in) compared with 249.8 cm (8 ft 2.3 in). It takes Ayanna up to 20 hr – and two bottles of nail polish – to paint her tremendous talons. In order to protect them, she avoids washing dishes and sleeps with them resting on a pillow. Ayanna became the record holder after Chris "The Dutchess" Walton (USA) cut her own nails, which had grown to a total length of 731.4 cm (23 ft 11 in).

Contents

Ayanna's longest individual nail is on her left thumb, and measures 68 cm (2 ft 2.7 in). This is longer than the **shortest man ever**, Chandra Bahadur Dangi, at 54.6 cm (1 ft 9.5 in; see p.134).

Robert Wadlow

The year 2018 marks the centenary of the birth of Guinness World Records' most iconic record holder, Robert Pershing Wadlow. He was the tallest man ever, measuring 8 ft 11.1 in (272 cm) at the time of his death in 1940. Robert's height was caused by an overactive pituitary gland, which produced abnormally high levels of growth hormones. Known as the "Alton Giant" or the "Giant of Illinois", Robert was a humble and gentle man who endeavoured to lead as ordinary a life as possible, despite his extraordinary appearance. Photographs of him still amaze and astound. His record may well never be beaten; his legacy endures to this day.

10 YEARS OLD
195.5 cm (6 ft 5 in)

Born in Alton, Illinois, USA, on 22 Feb 1918, Robert weighed an unremarkable 8 lb 6 oz (3.8 kg) at birth. But by the age of eight he had already outgrown his father Harold, who measured 182 cm (5 ft 11.5 in). A special desk had to be built for Robert at elementary school. Word of the "Alton Giant" started to spread beyond his home town.

Inevitably, Robert's incredible size brought him a great deal of public attention, whether in the street or being interviewed by members of the press (left). Although he agreed to tour with the Ringling Bros. Circus in 1937, Robert insisted on short, dignified appearances, and would only wear a business suit on stage.

13 YEARS OLD
224 cm (7 ft 4 in)

As he entered his teens, Robert's extraordinary growth showed no sign of slowing – as can be seen in family photographs featuring his father and brother Eugene (left in picture). When Robert joined the Boy Scouts, a special uniform had to be made to fit his 7-ft 4-in frame, fashioned from 14 yards (12.8 m; 42 ft) of material measuring 3 ft (0.9 m) in width.

18 YEARS OLD
252.7 cm (8 ft 3.5 in)

Robert graduated from high school in 1936 and enrolled in college. His size posed challenges – not least clothing! Robert also had the **largest feet ever**. His shoes were a US size 37AA (UK size 36, roughly a European size 75) – equivalent to 47 cm (18.5 in) long. His shoes could cost as much as $100, equal to $1,500 (£1,026) in today's money.

ROBERT WADLOW – AN EXTRAORDINARY LIFE

Age (years)	Height	Weight (where known)
5	5 ft 4 in (162.5 cm)	105 lb (48 kg)
8	6 ft (182.8 cm)	169 lb (77 kg)
9	6 ft 2.25 in (188.5 cm)	180 lb (82 kg)
10	6 ft 5 in (195.5 cm)	210 lb (95.6 kg)
11	6 ft 7 in (200.6 cm)	--
12	6 ft 10.5 in (209.5 cm)	--
14	7 ft 5 in (226.0 cm)	301 lb (137 kg)
15	7 ft 8 in (233.6 cm)	355 lb (161 kg)
16	7 ft 10.24 in (239.3 cm)	374 lb (170 kg)
17	8 ft 0.38 in (244.8 cm)	315 lb (143 kg)*
18	8 ft 3.5 in (252.7 cm)	--
19	8 ft 5.5 in (257.8 cm)	480 lb (218 kg)
20	8 ft 6.75 in (260.9 cm)	--
21	8 ft 8.25 in (264.7 cm)	491 lb (223 kg)
22	8 ft 11.1 in (272.0 cm)	439 lb (199 kg)

*weight loss owing to ill health

21 YEARS OLD
264.7 cm (8 ft 8.25 in)

Together with his father Harold, Robert embarked on a busy schedule of tours and personal appearances, visiting 800 towns in 41 states. He went to Hollywood and was photographed with movie stars such as Mary Pickford. However, Robert's immense size was taking its toll on his body. He needed leg braces to walk, and had little feeling in his feet.

22 YEARS OLD
272 cm (8 ft 11.1 in)

Robert died on 15 Jul 1940 in Manistee, Michigan, USA, as a result of a septic blister on his ankle caused by a poorly fitted brace. He was buried in Oakwood Cemetery, Alton, in a coffin 3.28 m (10 ft 9 in) long, 81 cm (32 in) wide and 76 cm (30 in) deep. His funeral drew 27,000 people wishing to say farewell to Alton's gentle giant.

272 cm —
250 cm —
225 cm —
100 cm —
75 cm —
50 cm —
25 cm —
0 —

LASTING LEGACY

Nearly century after his birth, Robert's life continues to exert a fascination over people. He is the subject of songs by The Handsome Family ("The Giant of Illinois") and Sufjan Stevens ("The Tallest Man, the Broadest Shoulders").

In 2010, the Wadlow exhibit at Ripley's Believe It or Not! in New York City, USA, was visited by the world's **shortest living man**, Khagendra Thapa Magar (NPL). Khagendra measures 67.08 cm (2 ft 2.41 in) tall – just 20 cm (7.87 in) more than the length of one of Robert's shoes!

In Jul 2016, the "World's Biggest LEGO® Brick Show" at Galeria Kazimierz in Krakow, Poland, displayed a LEGO statue of Robert, complete with cane. Other statues can be found in Alton, Niagara Falls and Farmington Hills, Michigan, USA.

Big Boy Day

SEE HIM *in person!*

ROBERT WADLOW

THE BIGGEST MAN IN THE WORLD

8 ft. 8¼ in. Tall

IN HIS STOCKING FEET

WEARS SIZE 37 PETERS SHOE

21 YEARS OLD

This is an honest-to-goodness photo of Robert and his dad this dad is six feet tall". When Robert was born February 22, 1918, he weighed 8½ pounds. At 6 months he weighed 30 pounds, and today he weighs 491 pounds . . . and towers above any other living man.

COME SEE HIM! - - - MEET HIM! - - - TALK TO HIM!

REMEMBER THE DATE . . . THURSDAY, MAY 4th

HE WILL BE IN OUR STORE FROM 2:30 P.M. to 4:00 P.M.

THOMAS SMITH

DUANE, KENTUCKY

In 1937, Robert did promotional work for the International Shoe Company (above), the makers of "Peter's Shoes". In return, the shoe company provided Robert with super-sized footwear for free.

126 **ROBERT WADLOW**

Oldest People

According to the World Health Organization, the population of people aged 80 or over will be 395 million by 2050, some four times the level in 2000.

Highest combined age for a parent and child (ever)
Sarah Knauss (USA, 1880–1999) and her 96-year-old daughter Kathryn "Kitty" Knauss Sullivan (USA, 1903–2005) had a combined age of 215 years 140 days when Sarah passed away. She was 119 years 97 days old at the time, while Kathryn was aged 96 years 43 days.

OLDEST...

Olympic gymnast (female)
At the age of 41 years 56 days, Oksana Chusovitina (UZB) competed at the 2016 Olympic Games, in Rio de Janeiro, Brazil, on 14 Aug. She finished seventh in the women's vault final.

Professional soccer player to score a competitive league goal
Kazuyoshi Miura (JPN, b. 26 Feb 1967) netted aged 50 years 14 days playing for Yokohama FC at Nippatsu Mitsuzawa Stadium in Yokohama, Japan, on 12 Mar 2017.

Match-winner on the ITF circuit
Aged 69 years 85 days old, tennis player Gail Falkenberg (USA, b. 16 Jan 1947) defeated an opponent 47 years her junior. On 10 Apr 2016, she beat 22-year-old Rosalyn Small (USA, b. 22 Jun 1993) 6–0, 6–1 on clay in the first qualifying round of an International Tennis Federation (ITF) Futures tournament in Pelham, Alabama, USA.

▲ **OLDEST COMPETITIVE DARTS PLAYER**
As of 18 Jul 2016, George Harness (UK, b. 7 Aug 1917) was still playing in darts competitions in the Old Leakes and District Darts League in Boston, UK, at the age of 98 years 346 days. George started playing darts in 1938. During his long career, he even played against British darts legend Eric Bristow – but lost.

▲ **LARGEST GATHERING OF CENTENARIANS**

On 4 Nov 2016, a group of 45 individuals aged 100 or more assembled at Parliament House in Brisbane, Queensland, Australia, in an event organized by Queensland Community Care Network (AUS). They were attending an early Christmas luncheon hosted by the Honourable Annastacia Palaszczuk – Queensland's state premier and patron of the care home's 100+ Club.

Astronaut

John Glenn Jr (USA, 18 Jul 1921–8 Dec 2016) was 77 years 103 days old when he was launched into space as part of the crew of *Discovery STS-95* on 29 Oct 1998. The mission lasted nine days, and Glenn landed back on Earth on 7 Nov 1998.

Peggy Whitson (USA, b. 9 Feb 1960) became the **oldest female astronaut** aged 56 years 282 days. The NASA astronaut was on board a Soyuz MS-03 spacecraft that set off for the *International Space Station* (*ISS*) from the Baikonur Cosmodrome in Kazakhstan at 2:20 a.m. local time on 18 Nov 2016 and went into orbit 8 min later.

On 30 Mar 2017 at 15:51 GMT, Whitson equalled the 50-hr 40-min record for the **most accumulated time on spacewalks by a woman**, previously achieved by fellow NASA astronaut Sunita Williams. The spacewalk formally began at 11:29 GMT and lasted 7 hr 4 min. Upon completion, it gave Whitson a record-breaking cumulative spacewalk time of 53 hr 22 min.

It was Whitson's eighth spacewalk – itself a record for the **most spacewalks by a woman**.

▲ **OLDEST ACTIVE SOCCER REFEREE**

Peter Pak-Ngo Pang (USA, b. IDN, 4 Nov 1932) was still regularly refereeing at soccer matches in the adult men's league in San José, California, USA, at the age of 83 years 137 days. Peter's record-breaking achievement was verified on 20 Mar 2016, when he officiated a game between Agave and Moctezuma, played in San José.

Graduate

On 19 Mar 2016, at the age of 96 years 200 days, Shigemi Hirata (JPN, b. 1 Sep 1919) received a Bachelor of Arts degree from the Kyoto University of Art and Design, in Kyoto, Japan.

Person to receive their first tattoo

Aged exactly 104 years, Jack Reynolds (UK, b. 6 Apr 1912) was tattooed in Chesterfield, UK, on 6 Apr 2016. The design of the tattoo – a script reading "Jacko 6.4.1912" – was by Jack himself.

▲ OLDEST ATHLETES

Robert Marchand (FRA, b. 26 Nov 1911) is the **oldest competitive cyclist**. On 4 Jan 2017, aged 105 years 39 days, he rode 22.547 km (14.01 mi) in the Best Hour Performance in the Men's "Master aged 105 years and above" category at the Vélodrome National de Saint-Quentin-en-Yvelines, France.

The **oldest competitive canoeist** is Avis Noott (UK, b. 24 Jun 1938). On 6 Mar 2016, aged 77 years 256 days old, she rowed in a race in Dulverton, UK.

The aggregate age of the **oldest married couple to run a marathon** is 163 years 360 days, by Masatsugu Uchida, aged 83 years 272 days, and his wife Ryoko Uchida (both JPN), aged 80 years 88 days. They ran in the Shimada Oigawa Marathon in Shimada, Shizuoka, Japan, on 30 Oct 2016.

1. Violet Brown (JAM) 10 Mar 1900 117 years 47 days	**2. Nabi Tajima** (JPN) 4 Aug 1900 116 years 265 days	**3. Chiyo Miyako** (JPN) 2 May 1901 115 years 359 days	**4. Ana Vela-Rubio** (ESP) 29 Oct 1901 115 years 179 days	**5. Marie-Josephine Gaudette** (ITA/USA) 25 Mar 1902 115 years 32 days

▶ OLDEST COMIC-BOOK ARTIST AND OLDEST ARTIST TO ILLUSTRATE A COMIC-BOOK COVER

Ken Bald (USA, b. 1 Aug 1920, near right) drew the cover of *Contest of Champions* #2 (Classic Variant, 2015) aged 95 years 95 days, as verified on 4 Nov 2015. GWR caught up with Ken recently:

GWR: Do you have a favourite cover that you've illustrated?
A: My first favourite cover is *Namora* #1, which came out in the late 1940s. My second favourite cover is *Millie the Model* #9. And my third favourite cover is what I did for Marvel back in 2015 – the *Contest of Champions*. This great cover not only allowed me to have the opportunity to do a widely distributed comic-book cover when I was 95 years old, but it also gave me an opportunity to bring back three of my Golden Age characters, plus let me illustrate the same three characters the way they are being drawn today.

GWR: How does it feel to have a second Guinness World Records title under your belt?
A: Both records have been a great thrill for me. Seeing my best friend, Stan Lee [above far right], and I in the same *Guinness World Records* book would definitely be one of the real highlights of my career. Stan and I pretty much started out in comics together, and after all these years – we're talking over 70 years – that we'd end up together, again, towards the end of our careers, is really amazing.

Twins ever

Kin Narita and Gin Kanie (both JPN, b. 1 Aug 1892) were the oldest authenticated female twins. Kin died of heart failure on 23 Jan 2000 at the age of 107 years 175 days.

The **oldest male twins** ever authenticated were Glen and Dale Moyer (USA, b. 20 Jun 1895), both of whom reached 105. Glen passed away on 16 Apr 2001, aged 105 years 300 days.

▶ LONGEST CAREER AS A BAND MEMBER

John Gannon (IRL, b. 27 May 1918) has been a registered member of the St James's Brass and Reed Band (est. 1800) since 22 Mar 1936. As of 22 Mar 2017, he had enjoyed 81 years of continuous active service with the band. John became a life member of the band in 1961, after 25 years' service, at which time he became exempt from paying subs.

As we go to press, 19 of the 20 oldest people in the world are women. And of those, nine are Japanese.

Source: Gerontology Research Group (www.grg.org)

6. Giuseppina Projetto-Frau
(ITA) 30 May 1902
114 years 331 days

7. Kane Tanaka
(JPN) 2 Jan 1903
114 years 114 days

8. Maria-Giuseppa Robucci-Nargiso
(ITA) 20 Mar 1903
114 years 37 days

9. Iso Nakamura
(JPN) 23 Apr 1903
114 years 3 days

10. Tae Ito
(JPN) 11 Jul 1903
113 years 289 days

OLDEST BILLIONAIRE

Billionaire movie producer Sir Run Run Shaw (CHN, left) died on 7 Jan 2014, reportedly aged 106. His precise birth date is not known. Based on an unconfirmed month and year of birth of Nov 1907, he would have been at least 106 years 38 days old at the time of his passing.

David Rockefeller Sr (USA, b. 12 Jun 1915, right) had a net worth of $3.3 bn (£2.6 bn) upon his death on 20 Mar 2017, aged 101 years 281 days old. He is the **oldest verified billionaire**.

Person ever

The greatest confirmed age to which any human has ever lived is 122 years 164 days, by Jeanne Louise Calment (FRA). Born on 21 Feb 1875, she died at a nursing home in Arles, France, on 4 Aug 1997. Asked on her 120th birthday what she expected of the future, she replied, "a very short one".

The **oldest man ever** was Jiroemon Kimura (JPN), who was born on 19 Apr 1897 and passed away on 12 Jun 2013, aged 116 years 54 days.

OLDEST LIVING PEOPLE

The **oldest living person** is Violet Brown (JAM, b. 10 Mar 1900), who was 117 years 47 days old as of 26 Apr 2017. She is the last living verified subject of Queen Victoria. Violet became the record holder when Italy's Emma Martina Luigia Morano passed away on 15 Apr 2017, aged 117 years 137 days.

The **oldest living man** is Israel Kristal (ISR), who was born on 15 Sep 1903 in the village of Malenie, near Żarnów in the Russian Empire (now Poland). He was aged 113 years 223 days as of 26 Apr 2017.

In Oct 2016, Israel Kristal had his bar mitzvah – 100 years late! He had not been able to have his coming-of-age ceremony at the usual age – 13 – as life was disrupted at the time by World War I.

Anatomy

Humans glow. Our bodies emit tiny amounts of light, a thousand times weaker than the human eye can perceive.

▼ TALLEST ACTOR

Neil Fingleton (UK, below, with *GWR* Editor-in-Chief Craig Glenday in 2008) measured 232.5 cm (7 ft 7.53 in). He swapped the basketball court for the movie set, appearing in *X-Men: First Class* (USA/UK, 2011), *47 Ronin* (USA, 2013) and *Jupiter Ascending* (USA/AUS, 2015). Neil also featured in TV series *Doctor Who* and *Game of Thrones*, playing the wildling giant Mag the Mighty (below right) in the latter. Sadly, Neil died on 25 Feb 2017.

Most fingers and toes (polydactylism) at birth

India's Akshat Saxena was born with 14 fingers (seven on each hand) and 20 toes (10 on each foot), as confirmed by doctors on 20 Mar 2010. Akshat subsequently underwent a successful operation to reduce his number of fingers and toes to 10 apiece.

Longest fingernails on one hand (ever)

The fingernails on the left hand of Shridhar Chillal (IND) reached an aggregate length of 909.6 cm (29 ft 10.11 in), as measured in Pune, Maharashtra, India, on 17 Nov 2014. The longest nail was on the thumb and measured 197.8 cm (6 ft 5.8 in).

The **longest fingernails on a pair of hands (male, ever)** belonged to Melvin Boothe (USA). Boothe's nails had a combined length of 9.85 m (32 ft 3.8 in) when measured in Troy, Michigan, USA, on 30 May 2009.

The **longest fingernails on a pair of hands (female, ever)** belonged to Lee Redmond (USA). She began to grow her nails in 1979 and carefully manicured them to reach a length of 8.65 m (28 ft 4.5 in) by 23 Feb 2008. Sadly, Lee lost her nails in a car accident in 2009. For the woman who currently has the longest nails, see p.119.

Q: Hypertrichosis is an abnormal amount of what on the human body?

A: Hair

▲ SHORTEST LIVING PEOPLE (MOBILE)

Jyoti Amge (IND, above left) measured 62.8 cm (2 ft 0.7 in) tall on 16 Dec 2011 – her 18th birthday. She had previously been the shortest female teenager.

Khagendra Thapa Magar (NPL, above right) – previously the shortest male teenager – measured 67.08 cm (2 ft 2.4 in) tall on 14 Oct 2010.

Tallest athlete to compete at a Paralympic Games

Measuring 2.46 m (8 ft 0.85 in), Morteza Mehrzad Selakjani was a member of Iran's sitting volleyball team at the Rio Paralympic Games in Brazil on 7–18 Sep 2016. He helped his team to the gold medal, top-scoring in the final with 28 points. Even when sitting down, Selakjani's right hand can strike the ball from a height of 6 ft 4 in (1.93 m).

Tallest living man

Sultan Kösen (TUR, b. 10 Dec 1982) measured 251 cm (8 ft 2.8 in) in Ankara, Turkey, on 8 Feb 2011. He also boasts the **widest hand-span**: 12 in (30.48 cm), as measured in the Guinness World Records office in London, UK, on 7 May 2010.

The **tallest living woman** is Siddiqa Parveen (IND). Initial reports put her height at 249 cm (8 ft 2 in) – unfortunately, because of ill health and Ms Parveen's inability to stand upright, it is impossible to ascertain her exact stature. Dr Debashis Saha, who performed the examination on Ms Parveen, estimates her standing height to be at least 233.6 cm (7 ft 8 in).

LONGEST HUMAN HAIRS

Hairs are fine, thread-like strands of protein (largely keratin, which is also a part of fingernails and toenails) that grow on every part of the body apart from areas such as the soles, the palms and the lips.

Back: 13 cm (5.1 in) – Craig Bedford (UK), 9 Nov 2012

Abdomen: 16.77 cm (6.6 in) – Elaine Martin (USA), 25 Jan 2013

Nipple: 17 cm (6.69 in) – Daniele Tuveri (ITA), 13 Mar 2013

Ear: 18.1 cm (7.12 in) – Anthony Victor (IND), 26 Aug 2007

Arm: 18.9 cm (7.44 in) – Kenzo Tsuji (JPN), 22 Oct 2012

Eyebrow: 19.1 cm (7.5 in) – Zheng Shusen (CHN), 6 Jan 2016

Leg: 22.46 cm (8.84 in) – Jason Allen (USA), 25 May 2015

Chest: 23.5 cm (9.25 in) – Zhao Jingtao (CHN), 13 Sep 2014

Tallest twins (male)

Identical twins Michael and James Lanier (both USA) of Troy, Michigan, both stand 2.235 m (7 ft 4 in) tall. They played basketball at the University of Denver and UCLA, respectively. Their sister Jennifer is 1.57 m (5 ft 2 in) tall.

The **tallest twins (female)** are Ann and Claire Recht (both USA). They were measured on 10 Jan 2007 and found to have an average overall height of 2.01 m (6 ft 7 in). Both sisters are volleyball players.

Tallest married couple (ever)

Anna Haining Swan (CAN, 1846–88) was said to be 246.38 cm (8 ft 1 in) tall but, in fact, measured 241.3 cm (7 ft 11 in). On 17 Jun 1871, she married Martin van Buren Bates (USA, 1837–1919), who stood 236.22 cm (7 ft 9 in). The lofty couple's combined height was 477.52 cm (15 ft 8 in).

Shortest woman (ever)

Pauline Musters, known as Princess Pauline (NLD), measured 30 cm (1 ft) at birth. When she died at the age of 19 in 1895, her post-mortem examination confirmed her height as 61 cm (2 ft).

Chandra Bahadur Dangi (NPL), the **shortest man ever**, measured 54.6 cm (1 ft 9.49 in), as verified in Kathmandu, Nepal, on 26 Feb 2012.

▲ **LONGEST EYELASH**
Shanghai-born You Jianxia (CHN) has a profusion of long and luxurious eyelashes, the longest of which grows on her left upper lid and measures 12.40 cm (4.88 in) in length. It was measured in Changzhou, Jiangsu Province, China, on 28 Jun 2016. This beat the previous longest eyelash, which was found on the left upper lid of Gillian Criminisi (CAN) and was measured at 8.07 cm (3.17 in) long on 13 May 2016.

▲ **TALLEST HIGH TOP FADE**
Model Benny Harlem (USA) became an internet sensation thanks to photographs of himself and daughter Jaxyn on Instagram. His high top fade is 20.5 in (52 cm) tall, as measured in Los Angeles, California, USA, on 6 Nov 2016. Benny's hair – which he refers to as his "crown" – can take more than two hours to style and get in shape.

▲ **OLDEST BODYBUILDER**
On 7 Sep 2015, Jim Arrington (USA, b. 1 Sep 1932) competed at a professional bodybuilding competition at Muscle Beach in Venice, California, USA, aged 83 years 6 days. He came fourth among contestants aged over 60. Jim has been bodybuilding for more than 40 years, and says he feeds off the inspiration of going to the gym.

Shortest twins
Matyus and Béla Matina (b. 1903–c. 1935) of Budapest, Hungary, who later became American citizens, both measured 76 cm (2 ft 6 in).

Most variable stature
Adam Rainer (AUT, 1899–1950) is the only person in medical history to have been both a dwarf and a giant. At the age of 21 he measured just 118 cm (3 ft 10.5 in), but then started to grow rapidly. By 1931, he had nearly doubled in height to 218 cm (7 ft 1.75 in). He grew so weak as a result of his growth spurt that he became bedridden and was to remain so. At the time of his death, he measured 234 cm (7 ft 8 in).

▲ SHORTEST MARRIED COUPLE

Paulo Gabriel da Silva Barros and Katyucia Hoshino (both BRA) measure a combined height of 181.41 cm (5 ft 11.42 in). Their heights were verified in Itapeva, São Paulo, Brazil, on 3 Nov 2016. Paulo and Katyucia met on a social media platform on 20 Dec 2008 and tied the knot on 17 Sep 2016. On GWR Day 2016, the happy couple travelled to the offices of Guinness World Records in London, UK, where they took part in a special Facebook Live event.

A study of OECD (Organization for Economic Cooperation and Development) countries in 2014 found that Mexico had an obesity rate of 32%. Among industrialized nations, only the USA (36.5%) had a higher rate.

▶ HEAVIEST LIVING MAN

In Nov 2016, Juan Pedro Franco Salas (MEX) left his bedroom for the first time in six years to be hospitalized for life-saving treatment. On 18 Dec, he was weighed at 594.8 kg (1,311 lb 4.9 oz; 93 st 9 lb). Juan Pedro suffers from morbid obesity, and by the age of six weighed the same as the average adult man (63.5 kg; 140 lb). Doctors diagnosed him with type-2 diabetes, thyroid dysfunction, hypertension and liquid in his lungs. It is hoped that weight-loss surgery will enable him to walk unaided once again.

Body art

A tattoo machine pierces the skin up to 3,000 times per minute, penetrating to a depth of around 1 mm.

▲ **MOST BONES TATTOOED ON THE BODY**

As of 27 Apr 2011, "Rico", aka Rick Genest (CAN), had 139 bone tattoos on his body. The count was verified on the set of *Lo Show dei Record* in Milan, Italy. Rick is tattooed in the style of a corpse across much of his body, hence another moniker: "Zombie Boy". He created most of the designs with Montreal tattoo artist Frank Lewis.

BODY MODIFICATIONS

Most body modifications

Rolf Buchholz (DEU) had undergone a total of 516 body mods as of 14 Mar 2017. They include 481 piercings, two subdermal "horn" implants and five magnetic implants in the fingertips of his right hand.

The record for **most body modifications (female)** is held by María José Cristerna (MEX). María's 49 body alterations include transdermal implants on her forehead, chest and arms, and multiple piercings in her eyebrows, lips, nose, tongue, earlobes and belly button. As of 8 Feb 2011, her tattoos covered 96% of her body, making her the **most tattooed woman**.

Victor Hugo Peralta (URY) and his wife Gabriela (ARG) have the **most body modifications for a married couple** – 84 – as verified for *Lo Show dei Record* in Milan, Italy, on 7 Jul 2014. Together, they have 50 piercings, eight microdermals, 14 body implants, five dental implants, four ear expanders, two ear bolts and one forked tongue.

Most piercings in a lifetime (female)

Elaine Davidson (BRA/UK) had been pierced 4,225 times as of 8 Jun 2006. She enhances her exotic looks with tattoos, bright make-up and feathers and streamers for her hair.

Most piercings on the face

Axel Rosales from Villa María, Argentina, had 280 facial piercings as of 17 Feb 2012.

As of 5 Jan 2017, the record for the **most piercings in the tongue** was 20, by Francesco Vacca from Belleville, New Jersey, USA.

▲ LONGEST TATTOO SESSION (MULTIPLE PEOPLE)

"Alle Tattoo", aka Alessandro Bonacorsi (ITA), carried out a 57-hr 25-min 30-sec tattooing session in Limidi di Soliera, Italy, on 3 Jan 2017. He completed 28 tattoos in all, including representations of a Minion (above left) and the Hindu god Ganesha (above centre), as well as abstract patterns (above right). For another of Alessandro's world records, see p.141.

▼ MOST FLESH TUNNELS IN THE FACE

A flesh tunnel is a hollow, tube-shaped piece of body jewellery. Joel Miggler (DEU) has had his face decorated with 11 flesh tunnels, as verified in Küssaberg, Germany, on 27 Nov 2014. Joel's face adornments range in size from 3 mm to 34 mm (0.1–1.3 in).

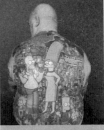

▲ MOST TATTOOS OF CHARACTERS FROM A SINGLE ANIMATED SERIES

Australia's Michael Baxter has had himself adorned with tattoos of 203 different characters from *The Simpsons*. The count was verified in Bacchus Marsh, Victoria, Australia, on 3 Dec 2014. It took some 12 months for the tattoos to be completed, requiring around 130 hr of needle time. The tattoo artist was Jade Baxter-Smith.

Q: Tattoos were officially banned in New York City from 1961 to 1997. Why?

A: Because of fears that tattooing could spread the hepatitis B virus

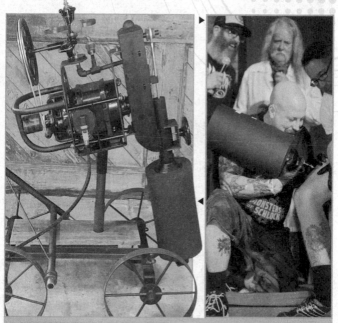

▲ LARGEST TATTOO MACHINE

Ray Webb of NeoTat (USA), and Burnaby Q Orbax and Sweet Pepper Klopek (both CAN) created a tattoo machine 4 ft 3 in (1.29 m) tall, 2 ft 9 in (0.83 m) deep, 1 ft 0.59 in (0.32 m) wide and weighing 152 lb (68.94 kg). A scaled-up version of a NeoTat tattoo machine, it was measured on 30 Aug 2015 at the Hell City Tattoo Festival in Phoenix, Arizona, USA. Orbax used the contraption to tattoo Pepper's leg (above right).

◄ MOST BODIES PAINTED

On 31 Jul 2015, a total of 497 individuals were daubed in bright colours in an event organized by PLAY (POL) at Woodstock Festival Poland. The colourful cover-up took place at the 21st instalment of this annual free festival. Why choose body paint? The organizers felt that it tied in with the festival's values of fun and self-expression.

HISTORY OF BODY ART...

5000 BCE
Henna body painting emerges in India

3200 BCE
Ötzi the iceman is tattooed – his 61 designs represent the **oldest existing tattoos**

3000 BCE
Nose and tongue piercing becomes widespread

c. 1000 BCE
The practice of Chinese foot binding is introduced

▶ LONGEST TATTOO SESSION (TEAM OF TWO)

Giuseppe Colibazzi tattooed Danny Galassi (both ITA) for a duration of 52 hr 56 min at the Tattoo Fantasy parlour in Civitanova Marche, Italy, from 17 to 19 Jul 2016. Colibazzi has more than 30 years of experience in the tattooing business and has been streaming tattoo sessions live on his website for many years.

▼ MOST TATTOOED SENIOR CITIZENS

Since getting her first tattoo of a butterfly in 2006, the **most tattooed female senior citizen**, Charlotte Guttenberg (USA), has spent more than 1,000 hr covering 91.5% of her body, as confirmed on 3 Jun 2015.

The **most tattooed male senior citizen**, Charles "Chuck" Helmke (USA), received his first tattoo in 1959. As of 2 Aug 2016, he had covered 93.75% of his body. Life-partners Chuck and Charlotte first met... at a tattoo studio.

200 CE
The Paracas of
South America
practise cranial
deformation

1300
Marco Polo
first describes
neck elongation in
Burma

c. 1850
Extreme corsetting is
introduced to create
"wasp" waists

2017
Cosmetic plastic
surgery and sunbed
tanning are common

Largest flesh tunnel in the earlobe

Kalawelo Kaiwi (USA) had a 10.5-cm (4.13-in) flesh
tunnel inserted in each of his earlobes, as confirmed
at the Hilo Natural Health Clinic in Hawaii, USA, on
14 Apr 2014.

TATTOOS

Most people to form a tattooed sentence

Alessandro Bonacorsi (ITA) inked the words "Step
by step together for a world of peace happiness family
passion art love tattoo and music" on 77 people in Limidi
di Soliera, Modena, Italy, on 10 Oct 2015. Each person
received a tattoo of one letter of the sentence.

Oldest person to have their first tattoo

Jack Reynolds (UK, b. 6 Apr 1912) was tattooed on
his 104th birthday in Chesterfield, UK.

Most tattoos of the same cartoon character

Lee Weir (NZ) must really love *The Simpsons*... He
has 41 tattoos of Homer Simpson on his body, as
verified on 5 Jun 2014 in Auckland, New Zealand.
They include Homer as a jack-in-the-box, as the
Grim Reaper, as the Hulk and as a doughnut.
See also Michael Baxter (see p.138).

Most people to receive henna tattoos simultaneously

A total of 1,200 people received henna tattoos in an
event organized by Charotar Education Society (IND)
in Anand, Gujarat, India, on 28 Jul 2015.

▶ SMALLEST WAIST FOR A LIVING PERSON

Cathie Jung (USA), who stands 5 ft 8 in (1.7 m) tall,
has a corseted waist measuring 15 in (38.1 cm).
Uncorseted, it measures 21 in (53.3 cm).
Inspired by her enthusiasm for Victorian
clothes, Cathie began wearing a 6-in-thick
(15.2-cm) training belt to gradually reduce her
then 26-in (66-cm) waist. She has never had
surgery to define her waist.

Transhumanism

The term "transhumanism" describes the use of science and technology to overcome human limitations and enhance our physical and mental capacities.

FIRST...

Camera implant

Wafaa Bilal, an Iraqi-born photographer and professor at New York University, USA, had a camera implanted for an art project ("3rdi") in Nov 2010. As if he literally had eyes in the back of his head, Wafaa's rear-facing camera was attached to a titanium plate inserted under his scalp. The camera took snapshots at 1-min intervals and the pictures were then uploaded to the internet. The images were also displayed live as a digital art installation in a museum in Qatar.

Biohacker with earthquake-sensing technology

"Biohacking" describes the act of implanting cybernetic devices into the human body to enhance its abilities. In 2013, artist and dancer Moon Ribas (ESP) had her left arm fitted with an implant that receives data about earthquakes anywhere on Earth in real time. It does so via a bespoke smartphone app that connects with geological monitors worldwide, detecting seismic activity as low as 1 on the Richter scale. The intensity of the vibrations that Ribas experiences depends on the strength of the quake. She also performs a stage show in which she moves her body to interpret the tremors she is experiencing.

◀ FIRST IMPLANTED ANTENNA

In 2004, Neil Harbisson (UK) had an antenna fitted into the back of his skull. He was born with a rare form of colour blindness and cannot perceive any colours other than black and white. The antenna is attached to a camera that hangs in front of his eyes and converts colour – in the form of light waves – into sound waves that he can hear as musical notes. The colour spectrum he can now hear runs from low notes, which appear as dark red to him, to high notes, which register as purple. Neil is the **first officially recognized cyborg**.

Biomonitoring computer implant

Software developer Tim Cannon (USA) is a biohacking pioneer and co-founder of Grindhouse Wetware, which designs biohacking technologies. In 2013, he became the first person to be implanted with the Grindhouse "Circadia" body sensor, inserted under the skin of his forearm. The device sent his pulse and body temperature wirelessly to a smartphone at regular intervals. The Circadia featured wireless charging and LED status lights that shone through the skin and remained in place for three months.

Fully integrated prosthetic arm

In Jan 2013, a Swedish truck driver became the first recipient of a prosthetic arm implanted into existing bone and controlled directly by existing nerves – despite losing the limb more than a decade previously. Researchers at Chalmers University of Technology in Gothenburg, Sweden, first inserted a permanent titanium implant into the bone marrow of the man's upper arm. They then attached a prosthetic arm controlled by electrodes also implanted into the upper limb. These gave greater control and reliability over sensors that typically sit on the surface of the skin.

Person with an ear implanted in their arm

Stelarc (AUS, b. CYP), a performance artist and academic at Curtin University in Perth, Australia, has had a "third ear" – an ear-shaped implant under the skin of his left forearm – since 2007. The project took a decade to research and fund, but Stelarc eventually found three plastic surgeons who created the ear from the artist's own cells and a biocompatible frame. The cells grew around the structure until it became a living body part with its own blood supply. It cannot hear, however.

Earphone implants

In 2013, Rich Lee (USA) had speakers implanted in his tragus (part of the outer ear), enabling him to listen to music and take phone calls using an electromagnetic coil worn around his neck. Lee plans to modify his implants to give him powers of echolocation similar to those of a bat.

3D-printed bionic ear

In May 2013, nanotechnology scientists at Princeton University in New Jersey, USA, in collaboration with Johns Hopkins University (USA), created a 3D-printed artificial ear that can pick up radio frequencies. It was printed from a hydrogel, a material used as a framework for tissue engineering, using a commercially available 3D printer. The ear was found to receive signals across a frequency range up to 5 GHz.

▲ **FIRST 3D-PRINTED PROSTHETIC USED AT THE PARALYMPICS**
German cyclist Denise Schindler competed in the 2016 Rio Paralympics with a 3D-printed polycarbonate prosthetic right leg. She was the first athlete to use a 3D-printed limb at the Games, winning a silver in the time trial and a bronze in the road race. Her leg weighed just 812 g (1 lb 12.6 oz) and took only 48 hr to complete from initial body scans to the finished product.

History of prosthetics

10th–8th century BCE
The mummy of a noblewoman dated to 950–710 BCE has a wood-and-leather replacement for one of her toes, the **oldest prosthesis** currently known

5th century BCE
Herodotus writes about a wooden foot made for a soldier amputee

c. 200 BCE
Roman general Marcus Sergius replaces his lost right hand with one made from iron to help him hold his shield

c. 1540
Ambroise Paré, a French military surgeon, creates "Le Petit Lorrain", a mechanical spring-operated hand, and a leg with a lockable knee joint

1861
James Hanger, a Confederate soldier in the American Civil War, loses his leg in the conflict and later designs and patents the "Hanger Limb", which is hinged at the knee and ankle

1880s
The first glass contact lenses are developed, by glassblower F A Muller in Germany, and – at around the same time – by physician Adolf E Fick (DEU) and French optician Edouard Kalt

2008
Touch Bionics (UK) launch the i-limb hand, the **first commercially available bionic hand**

1982
Graeme Clark (AUS) invents the cochlear implant, arguably the first body part that could be described as "bionic" (i.e., an electronic or mechanical aid incorporated into the body)

Commercially available bio-compass

The North Sense (below) is a small compass attached to a person's chest that vibrates whenever the user faces magnetic north. The product was created by the biohacking group Cyborg Nest and is designed to help people navigate without having to read an external compass. Instead, the wearer "feels" the bearing within his or her body, like a sixth sense. The North Sense, which is held in place by permanent metal bar piercings, went on sale in Jun 2016. One of Cyborg Nest's co-founders, Neil Harbisson, has a record-breaking implant of his own (see p.142).

100%

Some Cybathlon entrants use exoskeletons, robotic limbs and electric wheelchairs. Others use technology to stimulate paralysed muscles, enabling them to race recumbent bikes.

► FIRST PROSTHETIC LIMB BASED ON A VIDEOGAME

Conceived in Apr 2015 and completed on 1 Jun 2016, the "Jensen arm" created by the UK company Open Bionics is the first functional artificial limb based on a videogame. Owned and worn by gamer Daniel Melville (UK), it is a copy of the one worn by Adam Jensen in *Deus Ex*, a cyberpunk videogame series set in a futuristic era of transhumanist body upgrades. The 3D-printed limb took around one month to make, from rendering to being made wearable.

► MOST MIND-CONTROLLED PROSTHETIC LIMBS

In Dec 2014, Leslie Baugh (USA), who lost his arms in an accident, became the first person to manipulate two nerve-controlled bionic arms. The arms were developed by Johns Hopkins University in Maryland, USA. Baugh underwent surgery in which the nerves that had controlled his limbs were redirected to work with the prosthetic arms. He then trained his mind to work with the limbs until he could move each arm independently.

◄ FIRST COMPETITION FOR BIONIC ATHLETES

On 8 Oct 2016, the Swiss Federal Institute of Technology in Zurich hosted the inaugural Cybathlon, the first "Bionic Olympics" and the only competition for people using assisted bionic prosthetics. It featured races involving a variety of activities, from doing laundry to overcoming a range of obstacles, and attracted 66 teams and 400 competitors from various countries. Unlike Paralympians, Cybathlon entrants use powered prosthetics.

▲ FIRST BIONIC CAMERA- EQUIPPED FALSE EYE

In 2009, Rob Spence (CAN) developed a bionic eye to replace the eyeball he lost as a child. Known as "Eyeborg", it uses a tiny digital camera inside a false eye that can record and wirelessly transmit live video. One version of the eye features a red LED light to resemble the one worn by the titular cyborg in the 1984 movie *The Terminator*.

▲ FARTHEST DISTANCE TRAVELLED USING A POWERED EXOSKELETON

In 2005, Monty Reed (USA) completed the 3.4-mi (5.47-km) Seattle St Patrick's Day Dash fun run in his "Lifesuit" exoskeleton in 95 min. His average speed was slightly more than 2 mph (3.2 km/h). Reed designed and built the powered robotic suit, which he conceived of in 1987 after breaking his back serving as a US Army Ranger.

▲ FIRST PROSTHETIC TATTOO GUN ARM

In 2016, artist and engineer J L Gonzal created a prosthetic limb for Lyon-based tattoo artist J C Sheitan Tenet (both FRA, above) complete with a removable tattoo gun. Gonzal used parts from an old mechanical typewriter and a gramophone to give the lightweight prosthetic a steampunk-inspired look. Tenet, who lost his lower right arm as a child, uses the gun primarily for shading his designs.

Fitness Fanatics

Paddy Doyle (UK) completed 1,500,230 documented push-ups in a single calendar year – that's more than 4,100 a day.

BURPEES

Most burpees in...	Record	Holder	Location	Date
1 min	47	Mario Silvestri (ITA)	Venafro, Italy	19 Mar 2016
1 min (female)	37	Wendy Ida (USA)	Lakewood, USA	2 Jul 2012
1 min with backflip	25	Joshua Romeo (USA)	Coral Gables, USA	12 Dec 2015
1 hr	1,840	Paddy Doyle (UK)	Birmingham, UK	4 Feb 1994
1 hr (female – see below)	1,272	Eva Clarke (AUS)	Dubai, UAE	9 Jan 2015
1 hr, chest to ground	920	Eva Clarke (AUS)	Dubai, UAE	14 Nov 2016
12 hr	8,718	Eva Clarke (AUS)	Dubai, UAE	9 Jan 2015
12 hr (male)	6,800	Lee Ryan (UK)	Dubai, UAE	9 Jan 2015
24 hr	12,003	Eva Clarke (AUS)	Dubai, UAE	10 Jan 2015
24 hr (male)	10,110	Lee Ryan (UK)	Dubai, UAE	10 Jan 2015

▲ **MOST BURPEES IN ONE HOUR (FEMALE)**
From ultramarathons to CrossFit or Brazilian jiu-jitsu, former soldier Eva Clarke (AUS) loves challenging herself to reach new physical heights. On 9 Jan 2015, she did 1,272 burpees in an hour at Dubai Autodrome in the UAE.

PULL-UPS & CHIN-UPS

Most pull-ups in...	Record	Holder	Location	Date
1 min	50	Michael Eckert (USA)	Iwakuni, Japan	11 Oct 2015
1 min with claps	30	Blake Augustine (USA)	Neosho, USA	19 Dec 2015
1 min (rear – bar behind head)	23	Jamshid Turaev (UZB)	Limassol, Cyprus	16 May 2015
1 min with two fingers (see below)	19	Jamshid Turaev (UZB)	Limassol, Cyprus	19 Mar 2016
1 min with 40-lb pack	=29	Ron Cooper (USA)	Allston, USA	20 Jul 2016
	=29	Adam Sandel (USA)	Allston, USA	20 Jul 2016
1 min with 60-lb pack	23	Ron Cooper (USA)	Marblehead, USA	23 Jul 2016
1 hr	1,009	Stephen Hyland (UK)	Stoneleigh, UK	1 Aug 2010
1 hr (female)	725	Eva Clarke (AUS)	Abu Dhabi, UAE	10 Mar 2016
6 hr	3,515	Andrew Shapiro (USA)	Great Falls, USA	14 May 2016
12 hr	5,742	Andrew Shapiro (USA)	Great Falls, USA	14 May 2016
12 hr (female)	2,740	Eva Clarke (AUS)	Abu Dhabi, UAE	11 Mar 2016
24 hr	7,306	Andrew Shapiro (USA)	Great Falls, USA	14 May 2016

Fastest explosive pull-ups...	Record	Holder	Location	Date
Ascending 4 m	8.23 sec	Tazio Gavioli (ITA)	Beijing, China	7 Dec 2012
Ascending 7 m	19.5 sec	Tazio Gavioli (ITA)	Beijing, China	12 Jan 2016

Most chin-ups in...	Record	Holder	Location	Date
1 min	57	Guy Schott (USA)	Santa Rosa, USA	20 Dec 2008
1 hr	993	Stephen Hyland (UK)	Stoneleigh, UK	16 Nov 2011
8 hr	3,733	Stephen Hyland (UK)	Stoneleigh, UK	24 Jun 2007
12 hr	4,040	Joonas Mäkipelto (FIN)	Helsinki, Finland	28 Oct 2016
24 hr	5,050	Joonas Mäkipelto (FIN)	Lempäälä, Finland	6–7 Feb 2016
Human flag position (consecutive)	25	Zheng Daxuan (CHN)	Beijing, China	8 Jan 2016

▶ **MOST TWO-FINGER PULL-UPS IN ONE MINUTE**

On 19 Mar 2016, Jamshid Turaev (UZB) pulled himself up by his middle fingers 19 times in one minute at a fitness club in Limassol, Cyprus. Turaev, who had been practising for this record attempt for five years, managed 25 in the allotted time, but six pull-ups were discounted for breaching the record guidelines.

SQUATS, SQUAT THRUSTS & PISTOL SQUATS

Most squats in...	Record	Holder	Location	Date
1 min (single leg)	47	Silvio Sabba (ITA)	Milan, Italy	2 Jan 2012
1 min with 40-lb pack	59	Silvio Sabba (ITA)	Milan, Italy	6 Sep 2016
1 min with 60-lb pack	47	Silvio Sabba (ITA)	Milan, Italy	21 Jul 2016
1 min with 80-lb pack	42	Silvio Sabba (ITA)	Milan, Italy	24 Jul 2016
1 min with 100-lb pack	38	Paddy Doyle (UK)	Birmingham, UK	30 Dec 2012
1 hr	4,708	Paddy Doyle (UK)	Birmingham, UK	8 Nov 2007

Most squat thrusts in...	Record	Holder	Location	Date
1 min	70	Craig De-Vulgt (UK)	Margam, UK	24 Jun 2007
1 min with 40-lb pack	21	Paddy Doyle (UK)	Birmingham, UK	28 Mar 2011
1 hr (alternating legs)	2,504	Paddy Doyle (UK)	London, UK	3 Sep 1992

Most pistol squats in...	Record	Holder	Location	Date
1 min on a bed of nails	30	Silvio Sabba (ITA)	London, UK	6 Mar 2015
1 min on a scaffold pole	30	Silvio Sabba (ITA)	Milan, Italy	10 Oct 2013
1 min barefoot on three axe blades	29	Silvio Sabba (ITA)	Milan, Italy	4 Jul 2016
1 min on an American football	23	Silvio Sabba (ITA)	Milan, Italy	21 Jul 2015
1 min on a balance board (see p.150)	22	Silvio Sabba (ITA)	Milan, Italy	10 Jun 2016
1 min on a steel wire rope	20	Silvio Sabba (ITA)	Milan, Italy	5 May 2015
1 min on another person's hands	18	Silvio Sabba (ITA)	Milan, Italy	21 Jun 2016

TREADMILL

Greatest distance in...	Record	Holder	Location	Date
12 hr	143.84 km	Ronnie Delzer (USA)	The Woodlands, USA	20 Aug 2016
12 hr (female)	128.62 km	Bernadette Benson (AUS)	Perth, Australia	28 May 2016
24 hr	260.40 km	Dave Proctor (CAN)	Calgary, Canada	28 May 2016
24 hr (female)	247.20 km	Edit Bérces (HUN)	Budapest, Hungary	9 Mar 2004
48 hr	405.22 km	Tony Mangan (IRE)	Longford, Ireland	24 Aug 2008
48 hr (female)	322.93 km	Kristina Paltén (SWE)	Stockholm, Sweden	5 Nov 2014
48 hr (team of 12)	868.64 km	Porsche Human Performance (UK)	Goodwood, UK	5 Jul 2009
1 week	833.05 km	Sharon Gayter (UK)	Middlesbrough, UK	21 Dec 2011
1 week (male)	827.16 km	Márcio Villar do Amaral (BRA)	Rio de Janeiro, Brazil	4 Jul 2015

Fastest time to run...	Record	Holder	Location	Date
50 km (female)	3 hr 55 min 28 sec	Gemma Carter (UK)	London, UK	6 Mar 2015
50 mi (male)	7 hr 1 min	Ian Griffiths (UK)	Goudhurst, UK	7 Nov 2001
100 km	6 hr 21 min 40 sec	Phil Anthony (UK)	Canterbury, UK	3 Dec 2014
100 km (female)	8 hr 30 min 34 sec	Arielle Fitzgerald (CAN)	Calgary, Canada	28 May 2016
100 km (team of 12)	5 hr 1 min 20 sec	High Performance Running (BEL)	Lokeren, Belgium	14 Dec 2013
100 mi	13 hr 42 min 33 sec	Suresh Joachim (AUS)	Mississauga, Canada	28 Nov 2004
100 mi (female)	14 hr 15 min 8 sec	Edit Bérces (HUN)	Budapest, Hungary	9 Mar 2004
100 mi (team of 12)	8 hr 23 min	Radley College (UK)	Abingdon, UK	13 Feb 2011

All records current as of 21 Dec 2016

▲ MOST HANDSTAND PUSH-UPS IN ONE MINUTE

On 23 Oct 2015, Armenian athlete Manvel Mamoyan managed 27 handstand push-ups in 60 sec in Yerevan, Armenia. For his push-ups to qualify, the angle of Mamoyan's elbow had to reach 90° or less before he fully straightened his arms.

▲ MOST PUSH-UPS ON BACK OF HANDS CARRYING 40-LB PACK IN ONE HOUR

On 13 May 2008, endurance athlete Paddy Doyle (UK) did 663 push-ups on the back of his hands in 1 hr, while carrying the equivalent of a four-year-old child on his back! It took place at Stamina's Boxing Martial Arts Club in Birmingham, UK.

▼ MOST PISTOL SQUATS IN ONE MINUTE ON A BALANCE BOARD

Serial record-breaker Silvio Sabba (ITA) has achieved pistol-squat records on a variety of objects, from axe blades to American footballs. On 10 Jun 2016, Sabba managed 22 pistol squats on a balance board in one minute in Milan, Italy. He narrowly beat his own record – set the previous year, also in Milan – by one.

▲ LONGEST DURATION HOPPING ON A TREADMILL

Seven-time World Jump Rope champion Peter Nestler (USA) hopped on one leg on a treadmill for 8 min 6.5 sec in Tulsa, Oklahoma, USA, on 6 Sep 2014. The treadmill was kept at a constant speed of 6.5 km/h (4 mph). Peter learnt his skill while training for a hopping marathon.

PUSH-UPS

Most push-ups...	Record	Holder	Location	Date
Consecutively, one finger	124	Paul Lynch (UK)	London, UK	21 Apr 1992
Consecutively, 90°	16	Willy Weldens (FRA)	Paris, France	9 Nov 2014
In 30 sec, one finger	41	Xie Guizhong (CHN)	Beijing, China	8 Dec 2011
In 5 hr, one arm	8,794	Paddy Doyle (UK)	Birmingham, UK	12 Feb 1996
In 12 hr	19,325	Paddy Doyle (UK)	Birmingham, UK	1 May 1989
In 24 hr	46,001	Charles Servizio (USA)	Fontana, USA	25 Apr 1993
In 24 hr, knuckles	9,241	Eva Clarke (AUS)	Abu Dhabi, UAE	1 Feb 2014

Most push-ups in 1 min	Record	Holder	Location	Date
Back of hands	132	Abdul Latif Mahmoud Saadiq (QAT)	Doha, Qatar	20 Nov 2009
Explosive, full body	82	Stephen Buttler (UK)	Morda, UK	17 Nov 2011
Plyometric (pushing up on to a 1-m-tall platform)	9	Ahmed Valentino Kerigo (NOR)	Beijing, China	11 Jan 2016
Handstand (see opposite)	27	Manvel Mamoyan (ARM)	Yerevan, Armenia	23 Oct 2015
Planche (without feet touching the ground)	36	Temur Dadiani* (GEO) *Double leg amputee	Tbilisi, Georgia	3 Aug 2014
Aztec (touching feet with hands on each push-up)	50	Jason Shen (USA)	Palo Alto, USA	18 Jan 2014
On medicine balls	68	Mohammad Hassaan Butt (PAK)	Karachi, Pakistan	7 Jun 2015
Claps	90	Stephen Buttler (UK)	Morda, UK	17 Nov 2011
Knuckles	85	Roman Dossenbach (CHE)	Basel, Switzerland	21 Dec 2016
Two fingers/two arms	52	Aryan Grover (IND)	Jaipur, India	26 Aug 2015
40-lb pack	77	David Wileman (UK)	Mansfield, UK	27 Nov 2013
40-lb pack, claps	55	Stephen Buttler (UK)	Morda, UK	17 Nov 2011
40-lb pack, knuckles	26	Irfan Mehsood (PAK)	Khyber Pakhtunkhwa, Pakistan	5 Sep 2016
40-lb pack, one arm	33	Hiroyuki Gondou (JPN)	Yamato, Japan	10 May 2014
40-lb pack, one leg raised	31	Irfan Mehsood (PAK)	Khyber Pakhtunkhwa, Pakistan	21 Jul 2016
60-lb pack	57	Ron Cooper (USA)	Marblehead, USA	11 Feb 2016
60-lb pack, one arm	22	Paddy Doyle (UK)	Birmingham, UK	18 Jul 2011
60-lb pack, back of hands	38	Paddy Doyle (UK)	Birmingham, UK	18 Jul 2011
80-lb pack	51	Rohtash Choudhary (IND)	Faridabad, India	21 Jun 2016
80-lb pack, one arm	21	Paddy Doyle (UK)	Birmingham, UK	8 Sep 2011
80-lb pack, back of hands	37	Paddy Doyle (UK)	Birmingham, UK	8 Jan 2012
80-lb pack, one leg raised	21	Irfan Mehsood (PAK)	Khyber Pakhtunkhwa, Pakistan	5 Sep 2016
100-lb pack	38	Ron Cooper (USA)	Marblehead, USA	2 Dec 2016
100-lb pack, back of hands	26	Paddy Doyle (UK)	Birmingham, UK	8 Jan 2012

Most push-ups in 1 hr	Record	Holder	Location	Date
Two arms	2,392	Roman Dossenbach (CHE)	Basel, Switzerland	29 Nov 2016
Back of hands	1,940	Paddy Doyle (UK)	Birmingham, UK	8 Nov 2007
One arm	1,868	Paddy Doyle (UK)	Birmingham, UK	27 Nov 1993
One arm, back of hands	1,025	Doug Pruden (CAN)	Edmonton, Canada	8 Nov 2008
Knuckles	2,175	Syed Taj Muhammad (PAK)	Karachi, Pakistan	20 Mar 2016
Knuckles (female)	1,206	Eva Clarke (AUS)	Abu Dhabi, UAE	31 Jan 2014
40-lb pack, back of hands (see opposite)	663	Paddy Doyle (UK)	Birmingham, UK	13 May 2008

Feats of Strength

The North Korean weightlifting team attributes its success to a diet of kimchi (fermented cabbage) and cold noodles.

BARBELLS

Most weight lifted by...	Record	Holder	Location	Date
Arm curl (1 hr)	50,320 kg	Eamonn Keane (IRL, see opposite)	Louisburgh, Ireland	31 May 2012
Arm curl (1 min)	3,600 kg	Eamonn Keane (IRL)	Louisburgh, Ireland	18 Nov 2012
Bench press (single lift)	401.5 kg	Blaine Sumner (USA)	Columbus, USA	5 Mar 2016
Bench press (1 hr, single arm)	10,458.42 kg	Dariusz Slowik (CAN)	Hornslet, Denmark	2 Jun 2016
Bench press (1 hr, both arms)	138,480 kg	Eamonn Keane (IRL)	Marina del Rey, USA	22 Jul 2003
Bench press (1 min)	6,960 kg	Eamonn Keane (IRL)	Louisburgh, Ireland	18 Nov 2012
Powerlift bench press (12 hr)	815,434 kg	Glen Tenove (USA)	Irvine, USA	17 Dec 1994
Press, standing (1 hr)	68,500 kg	Eamonn Keane (IRL)	Louisburgh, Ireland	8 Dec 2012
Press, standing (1 min)	4,000 kg	Eamonn Keane (IRL)	Louisburgh, Ireland	8 Dec 2012
Rows (1 hr)	126,720 kg	Eamonn Keane (IRL)	Louisburgh, Ireland	18 Nov 2012
Rows (1 min)	4,700 kg	Eamonn Keane (IRL)	Louisburgh, Ireland	8 Dec 2012
Standing upright row (1 min)	4,440 kg	Eamonn Keane (IRL)	Louisburgh, Ireland	18 Nov 2012
Deadlift (strongman, single lift)	500 kg	Eddie Hall (UK)	Leeds, UK	9 Jul 2016
Deadlift (tyre, single lift)	524 kg	Žydrūnas Savickas (LTU)	Columbus, USA	1 Mar 2014
Deadlift (one finger)	121.70 kg	Benik Israelyan (ARM)	Yerevan, Armenia	12 Feb 2012
Deadlift (little finger)	110 kg	Suren Aghabekyan (ARM)	Yerevan, Armenia	23 Mar 2013
Deadlift (24 hr)	475,065 kg	Ian Atkinson (UK)	Warrington, UK	16 Nov 2002
Deadlift (1 hr)	115,360 kg	Eamonn Keane (IRL)	Louisburgh, Ireland	14 Jul 2013
Deadlift (1 min)	5,520 kg	Eamonn Keane (IRL)	Louisburgh, Ireland	18 Nov 2012
Sumo deadlift (1 hr, male)	54,464 kg	Nick Mallory (UK)	Hemel Hempstead, UK	21 Mar 2011
Sumo deadlift (1 hr, female)	47,552.9 kg	Thienna Ho (USA)	San Francisco, USA	14 Aug 2010
Sumo deadlift (1 min)	9,130 kg	Greg Austin Doucette (CAN)	Halifax, Canada	9 Aug 2015
Squat lifts (24 hr)	459,648 kg	Shaun Jones (UK)	Norwich, UK	23 Mar 2010
Squat lifts (1 hr)	57,717.36 kg	Walter Urban (CAN)	New York City, USA	16 Sep 2011
Squat lifts (1 min)	5,035.42 kg	Joshua Spaeth (USA)	Kennewick, USA	15 Aug 2015

DUMBBELLS

Most weight lifted by...	Record	Holder	Location	Date
Front raises (1 hr)	18,830 kg	Eamonn Keane (IRL)	Louisburgh, Ireland	12 Oct 2011
Front raises (1 min)	1,215 kg	Eamonn Keane (IRL)	Louisburgh, Ireland	16 Oct 2013
Rows, two arms (1 hr)	32,730 kg	Eamonn Keane (IRL)	Castlebar, Ireland	30 Mar 2010
Rows, one arm (1 min)	1,975.85 kg	Robert Natoli (USA)	Liverpool, USA	22 Mar 2014
Standing dumbbell press (1 min, female)	910 kg	Kristin Rhodes (USA)	Beijing, China	4 Dec 2012
Incline dumbbell flyes (1 hr)	40,600 kg	Eamonn Keane (IRL)	Louisburgh, Ireland	28 Sep 2011
Incline dumbbell flyes (1 min)	2,160 kg	Eamonn Keane (IRL)	Louisburgh, Ireland	16 Oct 2013
Lateral raises (1 hr)	19,600 kg	Eamonn Keane (IRL)	Louisburgh, Ireland	1 Feb 2011
Lateral raises (1 min)	1,575 kg	Eamonn Keane (IRL)	Louisburgh, Ireland	16 Oct 2013
Rear lateral raises (1 hr)	32,500 kg	Eamonn Keane (IRL)	Louisburgh, Ireland	6 Oct 2010
Rear lateral raises (1 min)	1,845 kg	Eamonn Keane (IRL)	Louisburgh, Ireland	16 Oct 2013

At the top of this page, strongman Eamonn Keane (centre) receives 12 of his GWR certificates from Guinness World Records staff. When he's not weightlifting, Eamonn is a primary school teacher!

▶ FASTEST POWER STAIRS (3 X 225 KG)

Žydrūnas "Big Z" Savickas (LTU) carried three 225-kg (496-lb) weights separately up five steps (known as "power stairs") in just 31.60 sec on the set of *Lo Show dei Record* in Milan, Italy, on 26 Jun 2014. Each weight was equivalent to that of half a grand piano.

KETTLEBELLS

Most weight lifted by...	Record	Holder	Location	Date
Long cycle (1 hr)	33,184 kg	Anatoly Ezhov (BLR)	Zagreb, Croatia	21 Sep 2014
Military press (1 hr, male)	51,030 kg	Anatoly Ezhov (BLR)	Tel Aviv, Israel	7 Jun 2015
Military press (1 hr, female)	26,441.8 kg	Larisa Strucheva (RUS)	Arkhangelsk, Russia	7 Feb 2016
Snatch (1 hr, male)	34,160 kg	Evgeny Nazarevich (BLR)	Grodno, Belarus	13 Apr 2015
Snatch (1 hr, female)	14,430.3 kg	Anna Lewandowska (POL)	Grodno, Belarus	17 Oct 2015
Jerk (1 hr)	53,424 kg	Anatoly Ezhov (BLR)	Tashkent, Uzbekistan	15 Jun 2014
Swing (1 hr)	21,224 kg	Jason Peter Gee (USA)	Brighton, USA	6 Jun 2015
Swing (1 hr, female)	20,816 kg	Eszter Füleki (HUN)	Gyöngyös, Hungary	17 Sep 2016

HEAVIEST WEIGHT PULLED BY...

Body part/method	Object	Record	Holder	Location	Date
Tongue (female)	Woman	113 kg	Elaine Davidson (UK)	London, UK	16 Sep 2012
Tongue (male)	Woman	132 kg	Gordo Gamsby (AUS)	London, UK	16 Sep 2012
Eye sockets	Rickshaw with three women	411.65 kg	Space Cowboy, aka Chayne Hultgren (AUS)	Milan, Italy	25 Apr 2009
Ears (pierced)	Cessna aircraft	677.8 kg	Johnny Strange (UK)	North Weald, UK	12 May 2014
Hook through nasal cavity and mouth	Car	983.1 kg	Ryan Stock (CAN)	Istanbul, Turkey	5 Jun 2013
Eyelids	Car	1,500 kg	Dong Changsheng (CHN)	Changchun, China	26 Sep 2006
Ears (earrings)	Car	1,562 kg	Gao Lin (CHN)	Beijing, China	19 Dec 2006
Swallowed sword	Car	1,696.44 kg	Ryan Stock (CAN)	Las Vegas, USA	28 Oct 2008
Ears (clamped, female)	Van	1,700 kg	Asha Rani (IND)	Leicester, UK	20 Jun 2013
Beard	Car	2,205 kg	Kapil Gehlot (IND)	Jodhpur, India	21 Jun 2012
	Train	2,753.1 kg	Ismael Rivas Falcon (ESP)	Madrid, Spain	15 Nov 2001
In high heels	Truck	6,586.16 kg	Lia Grimanis (CAN)	Toronto, Canada	11 Jun 2014
Hair (male)	Bus	9,585.4 kg	He Yi Qun (CHN)	Jiangyin, China	13 Jan 2015
Hair (female)	Double-decker bus	12,216 kg	Asha Rani (IND)	Milan, Italy	7 Jul 2014
Arm-wrestling move	Fire truck	14,470 kg	Kevin Fast (CAN)	Cobourg, Canada	13 Apr 2016
Teeth	Bus with 12 passengers	13,713.6 kg	Igor Zaripov (RUS)	Jiangyin, China	7 Jan 2015
	Two trains	260.8 tonnes	Velu Rathakrishnan (MYS)	Kuala Lumpur, Malaysia	18 Oct 2003
	Tanker	576 tonnes	Omar Hanapiev (RUS)	Makhachkala, Russia	9 Nov 2001

◄ HEAVIEST HOUSE PULLED

Multiple record holder Reverend Kevin Fast (CAN) pulled a house weighing 35.9 tonnes (79,145 lb) a distance of 11.95 m (39 ft 2.4 in) in Cobourg, Ontario, Canada, on 18 Sep 2010. The feat, part of a fundraising charity event, took him 1 min 1 sec. The power-lifting pastor claims that the secret to his success is poutine: deep-fried potato pieces coated in cheese and smothered in gravy.

HEAVIEST WEIGHT LIFTED BY...

Body part/method	Record	Holder	Location	Date
Hook through the forehead	4.5 kg	Burnaby Q Orbax (CAN)	Milan, Italy	21 Jul 2014
Eye socket (female)	6 kg	Asha Rani (IND)	Mahilpur, India	1 Feb 2013
Hooks through the cheeks	6.89 kg	Sweet Pepper Klopek (CAN)	Saint John, Canada	18 Jul 2016
Fingernail	9.98 kg	Alagu Prathap (IND)	Tamil Nadu, India	18 Sep 2016
Tongue	12.5 kg	Thomas Blackthorne (UK)	Mexico City, Mexico	1 Aug 2008
Mental floss (mouth and nose)	15.8 kg	Christopher Snipp (UK)	Gravesend, UK	11 May 2013
Ears (pierced, lifted and spun)	16 kg	Lizardman, aka Erik Sprague (USA)	Milan, Italy	19 Jun 2014
Eye socket (male)	16.2 kg	Manjit Singh (IND)	Leicester, UK	12 Sep 2013
Ears (pierced)	21.63 kg	Johnny Strange (UK, below)	Blackpool, UK	21 Aug 2016
Both eye sockets (female)	22.95 kg	Ellen "Pinkie" Pell (USA)	Chattanooga, USA	2 Apr 2016
Toes	23 kg	Guy Phillips (UK)	Horning, UK	28 May 2011
Both eye sockets (male)	24 kg	Manjit Singh (IND)	Leicester, UK	15 Nov 2012
Nipples	32.6 kg	The Baron, aka Mika Nieminen (FIN)	London, UK	19 Jul 2013
Two ears (clamped)	34.9 kg	Asha Rani (IND)	Rampur, India	18 Jul 2014
Hooks through the forearms	45.18 kg	Burnaby Q Orbax (CAN)	Saint John, Canada	17 Jul 2015
Shoulder blades	51.4 kg	Feng Yixi (CHN)	Beijing, China	8 Dec 2012
Hair (female)	55.6 kg	Asha Rani (IND)	Rampur, India	18 Jul 2014
Beard	63.80 kg	Antanas Kontrimas (LTU)	Istanbul, Turkey	26 Jun 2013
Little fingers	67.5 kg	Kristian Holm (NOR)	Herefoss, Norway	13 Nov 2008
Hair (male)	81.5 kg	Abdurakhman Abdulazizov (RUS)	Zubutli-Miatli, Russia	16 Nov 2013
One ear (clamped)	82.6 kg	Rakesh Kumar (IND)	Istanbul, Turkey	25 Jul 2013
Teeth	281.5 kg	Walter Arfeuille (BEL)	Paris, France	31 Mar 1990
Neck	453.59 kg	Eric Todd (USA)	Turney, USA	19 Oct 2013
Breath (lift bag)	=1,990.25 kg	Brian Jackson (USA)	Jiangyin, China	12 Jan 2015
	=1,990.25 kg	Ding Zhaohai (CHN)	Jiangyin, China	12 Jan 2015

▶ **HEAVIEST WEIGHT LIFTED BY PIERCED EARS**

On 21 Aug 2016, daredevil performer Johnny Strange (UK) lifted a beer keg weighing 21.63 kg (47 lb 10 oz) by his pierced ears at Norbreck Castle Hotel in Blackpool, UK. He beat his own record by 6.73 kg (14 lb 13 oz). No wonder Johnny's known as "the man with ears of steel".

MISCELLANEOUS

Object lifted	Record	Holder	Location	Date
Line of bricks held at chest height	102.73 kg (20 bricks)	Fred Burton (UK)	Cheadle, UK	5 Jun 1998
Log (150-kg log, 1 min)	900 kg	Žydrūnas Savickas (LTU)	Milan, Italy	3 Jul 2014
Hay bale (Force Basque, 45-kg bale raised to 7 m by pulley, 2 min)	990 kg	Inaki Berceau Sein (ESP)	Milan, Italy	25 Apr 2009
Anvil (18 kg minimum, 90 sec)	1,584 kg	Alain Bidart (FRA)	Soulac-sur-Mer, France	17 Aug 2005
Stone (Force Basque, 100-kg stone, 1 min)	2,200 kg	Izeta II, aka Jose Ramón Iruretagoiena (ESP)	Madrid, Spain	16 Feb 2008
Greatest weight lifted (single lift, two cars plus drivers and platform)	2,422.18 kg	Gregg Ernst (CAN)	Bridgewater, Canada	28 Jul 1993
Stone (50.2-kg atlas stone, 1 hr)	13,805 kg	Nick Mallory (UK)	Hemel Hempstead, UK	28 Oct 2011
Beer keg (62.5-kg keg, 6 hr)	56,375 kg	Tom Gaskin (UK)	Newry, UK	26 Oct 1996

▲ **MOST WEIGHTED SQUATS LIFTED IN TWO MINUTES (130-KG BAR – FEMALE)**
Maria Strik (NLD) achieved 29 squats lifting a 130-kg (286-lb 9.6-oz) bar in two min. She set the record on *Lo Show dei Record* in Rome, Italy, on 4 Apr 2012 during a challenge against Anett von der Weppen (DEU) and Nina Geria (UKR).

▲ **MOST PEOPLE LIFTED AND THROWN IN TWO MINUTES (FEMALE)**
On 19 Dec 2008, Aneta Florczyk (POL) lifted and threw 12 male volunteers on the set of *Guinness World Records* in Madrid, Spain. She broke the record of 10, achieved minutes earlier by Irene Gutierrez (ESP). Aneta rose to fame when a video of her rolling up a frying pan with her bare hands went viral.

Fastest 100m

How far is 100 m (328 ft)? Around five times the length of a bowling lane. Or 150 times the length of a footstep. Or 80,000 times as long as a grain of sand!

Bum walk

Powered primarily by his *gluteus maximus*, Miki Sakabe (JPN) finished a 100-m course in 11 min 59 sec at Fukagawa City Athletic Stadium in Hokkaido, Japan, on 25 Oct 2009.

While blowing a stamp

On 3 Oct 2010, Christian Schäfer (DEU) blew a stamp down a 100-m course in 3 min 3 sec, at ASV Dachau in Dachau, Germany.

In a bath tub

Tony Bain (NZ) paddled a 100-m course in a floating bath tub in 1 min 26.41 sec on the set of *Officially Amazing* in Cardiff, UK, on 17 Aug 2013.

On a tightrope

Aisikaier Wubulikasimu (CHN) completed a 100-m walk along a tightrope in 38.86 sec in Wenzhou City, Zhejiang Province, China, on 6 Jun 2013.

The **fastest backwards 100 m tightrope walk** took 1 min 4.57 sec and was performed by Maurizio Zavatta (ITA) in Kaifeng, Henan Province, China, on 20 May 2014.

In a pedal-powered boat (individual)

On 13 Oct 2013, Giuseppe Cianti (ITA) propelled a pedalo down a 100-m course in 38.7 sec at the Marina di Scilla in Reggio Calabria, Italy.

▶ **FASTEST 100 M HURDLES WEARING FLIPPERS**

On 13 Sep 2008, Christopher Irmscher (DEU) donned swim fins (aka flippers) to flap his way down a 100-m hurdle track in 14.82 sec in Cologne, Germany, for *Guinness World Records – Die Größten Weltrekorde*.

Two years later, Veronica Torr (NZ) achieved the **fastest 100 m hurdles wearing swim fins (female)** in 18.523 sec, on the set of *Zheng Da Zong Yi – Guinness World Records Special* in Beijing, China, on 8 Dec 2010.

Moonwalking

China's Luo Lantu performed a 100-m moonwalk in 32.06 sec in Beijing, China, on 8 Dec 2010. The record was filmed for *Zheng Da Zong Yi – Guinness World Records Special*.

While pulling a light aircraft

It took Montystar Agarwal (IND) just 29.84 sec to drag a Cessna aircraft 100 m on the set of *Guinness World Records – Ab India Todega* in Baramati, Maharashtra, India, on 23 Feb 2011.

Montystar (see right) wore a harness to tug the Cessna aeroplane 100 m. The plane weighed at least 500 kg (1,100 lb) – or approximately the same weight as an adult polar bear.

Zorbing

Cricket legend Andrew Flintoff (UK) zorbed his way along a 100-m course in 26.59 sec for *BT Sport Relief Challenges: Flintoff's Record Breakers*. Fittingly, the record attempt was staged at the KIA Oval cricket ground in London, UK, on 19 Mar 2012.

On trampolines

On 26 Feb 2009, Steve Jones (UK) bounced his way across 100 m on a series of trampolines in 24.11 sec on the set of *Guinness World Records – Smashed* in Crowthorne, UK.

In clogs

On 3 Mar 2016, Australian rugby union star Drew Mitchell ran 100 m in clogs in 14.43 sec on the set of *Sky Sports Rugby* in Toulon, France. It was one of four records set by the fleet-footed Wallaby winger – all in the same day! Mitchell ran through the pain barrier to smash the previous best of 16.27 sec, set by Andre Ortolf (DEU, see p.160) on 25 Oct 2013.

Rap jumping

The term for abseiling down a vertical wall in a standing position (feet on the wall) while facing the ground is rap jumping. The fastest 100-m rap jump took 14.09 sec and was achieved by Luis Felipe de Carvalho Leal (BRA) on the RB1 building in Rio de Janeiro, Brazil, on 23 Oct 2011.

◀ ON CRUTCHES (INVERTED)

On 6 Mar 2014, in a remarkable demonstration of strength, stamina and balance, Tameru Zegeye (ETH) raced down a 100-m track upside down and on forearm crutches in 57.00 sec in Fürth, Bavaria, Germany. Tameru was born with deformed feet and cannot use his legs, but has developed prodigious upper-body strength and is now a circus performer.

▲ ON A SPACE HOPPER (FEMALE)

On 26 Sep 2004, Dee McDougall (UK) bounced her way through a 100-m race in a time of 39.88 sec at the University of St Andrews in Fife, UK.

The record for the **fastest time to travel 100 m on a spacehopper** is 30.2 sec, by Ashrita Furman (USA) at Flushing Meadows Park in New York City, USA, on 16 Nov 2004.

Q: Which is faster, Usain Bolt or a domestic cat?

A: A cat. Bolt hit 27.78 mph (44.71 km/h) during his world-record
100 m in 2009, but a cat can reach 29.8 mph (47.9 km/h).

▲ IN AN EGG AND SPOON RACE
At an event to mark the launch of *GWR 2014*, Australia's Sally Pearson ran a 100-m egg and spoon race in 16.59 sec in Sydney, New South Wales, on 23 Sep 2013. She already had experience at this distance: Sally is an Olympic hurdler and her speciality is the 100 m hurdles event – in fact, she was the 2012 Olympic champion!

▲ IN A PUMPKIN
Dmitri Galitzine (UK) paddled a 600-lb (272.15-kg) pumpkin for a distance of 100 m in 2 min 0.3 sec at Trafalgar Wharf in Portchester, Hampshire, UK, on 23 May 2013. In accordance with GWR's guidelines, Dmitri used a standard, commercially available kayak paddle. Aside from hollowing it out, he did not modify the pumpkin in any way.

In a wheelbarrow race
Otis Gowa (AUS) propelled a wheelbarrow down a 100-m track in 14 sec at Davies Park in Mareeba, Queensland, Australia, on 15 May 2005.

By a pantomime horse (men)
Shane Crawford and Adrian Mott (both AUS) ran 100 m in 12.045 sec wearing a pantomime horse costume on *The Footy Show* in Melbourne, Victoria, Australia, on 30 Jul 2009.

Samantha Kavanagh and Melissa Archer (both UK) ran the **fastest 100 m by a pantomime horse (women)** – 18.13 sec – at an event organized by the advertising agency Claydon Heeley Jones Mason at Harrow School, Harrow-on-the-Hill, Middlesex, UK, on 18 Aug 2005.

◄ IN HIGH HEELS (FEMALE)
On 2 May 2015, Denmark's Majken Sichlau raced down a 100-m track in 13.557 sec wearing 9.5-cm-high (3.7-in) heels. Majken's sprint took place at the Tårnby Games 2015 at Tårnby Stadium in Copenhagen, Denmark.

◀ IN HIGH-HEELED ROLLER SKATES

On 21 Aug 2013, Marawa Ibrahim (AUS) glided across a distance of 100 m on her high-heeled roller skates in 26.10 sec in Regent's Park, London, UK.

Four years later, on 1 Feb 2017, the multi-talented Marawa recorded the **fastest 100 m hula hooping** – 17.87 sec – in Sheep Meadow, Central Park, New York City, USA. The feat was filmed for a Guinness World Records Facebook Live event.

On stilts

It took Liang Shaolun (CHN) just 11.86 sec to cover 100 m on stilts on 17 Aug 2013 at the Asia-Pacific Experimental School of Beijing Normal University in China.

Backwards downhill skiing

On 27 Apr 2009, Andy Bennett (UK) reverse-skiied 100 m in 9.48 sec. The record-breaking feat took place at the Snozone indoor snow slope in Milton Keynes, UK.

▲ IN A CHAIR

André Ortolf (DEU) covered 100 m in 31.92 sec in a six-wheeled swivel chair in Augsburg, Germany, on 15 Aug 2014. Earlier that year, he had run the **fastest 100 m in ski boots**, but Max Willcocks (UK) now holds this record, with a time of 14.09 sec.

André was also in the team that ran the **fastest 4 x 100 m relay in firemen's uniform** (59.58 sec), again in Augsburg, on 30 Jun 2016. His team-mates were Markus Eppler, Peter Mayer and Anselm Brieger (all DEU).

▲ ON ALL FOURS

On 6 Nov 2015, Kenichi Ito (JPN) scuttled across 100 m on his hands and feet in a time of 15.71 sec at Komazawa Olympic Park Athletic Field in Setagaya, Tokyo, Japan. He had broken the record on four separate occasions previously. Kenichi spent nearly 10 years developing his trademark means of propulsion, which is based largely on the way African patas monkeys move around.

▶ ON A SLACKLINE

France's Lucas Milliard took just 1 min 59.73 sec to navigate a 100-m-long slackline at an event staged by Hailuogou National Glacier Forest Park and Huway.com in Luding, Sichuan, China, on 12 Jun 2016.

The **fastest time to walk 100 m backwards on a slackline** is 6 min 1 sec by Théo Sanson (FRA). The event was staged by Wind Team (CHN) in the Yuntai Mountain area of Henan Province in China on 6 Nov 2016.

For Lucas's vertiginous record attempt, the slackline was suspended approximately 70 m (230 ft) above the ground, between two piers of Hailuogou Valley Bridge.

Circus Performers

World Circus Day is celebrated on the third Saturday of April each year. It was established in 2010 by HSH Princess Stéphanie of Monaco.

The Nock family has a long history as performers. They formed Switzerland's first circus in 1840. In 1954, they performed for Queen Elizabeth II, who dubbed them the "Nerveless Nocks".

Highest annual earnings for a magician (current year)

According to Forbes' annual list of the highest-earning celebrities, magician and illusionist David Copperfield (USA) earned an estimated $64 m (£43.8 m) between 1 Jun 2015 and 1 Jun 2016. Most of this income comes from his long-running show based in Las Vegas, Nevada, USA.

Longest duration juggling with three basketballs

Morimori (aka Shun Ishimori, JPN) juggled a trio of basketballs for 1 hr 37 sec in Sendai, Miyagi, Japan, on 7 Oct 2016.

Farthest distance travelled on a unicycle while juggling three objects

On 9 Aug 2015, Ole-Jacob Hovengen (NOR) unicycled 6,400 m (20,997 ft 4 in) while juggling in Drammen, Norway.

◄ MOST SOMERSAULTS ON A WHEEL OF DEATH IN ONE MINUTE

On 12 Feb 2016, Annaliese Nock (USA) completed four somersaults on a wheel of death in 60 sec at Circus Sarasota in Sarasota, Florida, USA. She is an eighth-generation circus performer and executed the feat with her father, Bello Nock (USA, also pictured left). Bello is himself a GWR record holder: on 10 Nov 2010, he achieved the **greatest distance for an unsupported tightrope walk** (130 m; 429 ft). Bello's cousin Freddy Nock (CHE) is another high achiever, whose records include the **longest walk on a cable-car cable** (995 m; 3,624 ft) on 30 Aug 2009 and **longest tightrope crossed by bicycle** (85 m; 278 ft 10 in), on 7 Sep 2015.

Q: "Circus" is a Latin word. What does it mean?

A: "Circle" or "ring"

FASTEST...

150 m blindfold tightrope walk

Maurizio Zavatta (ITA) crossed a 150-m (492-ft) tightrope while blindfolded in 4 min 55.12 sec for *CCTV – Guinness World Records Special* in Wulong, Chongqing, China, on 15 Nov 2016. GWR guidelines stipulate that the tightrope must be at least 10 m (32 ft 9.7 in) above the ground.

He performed the perilous walk at a height of 212.8 m (698 ft 1.9 in), thereby securing the record for the **highest blindfold tightrope walk** too.

Time to travel 20 m in a contortion roll

On 11 Mar 2013, contortionist Leilani Franco (UK/PHL) propelled herself 20 m (65 ft) in a chest-down roll in 17.47 sec at the Royal Festival Hall in London, UK.

MOST...

Blow torches extinguished with the tongue in one minute

The Space Cowboy put out 48 blow torches with his tongue in Byron Bay, New South Wales, Australia, on 13 May 2016.

Bullwhip cracks in one minute

In just 60 sec, Jack Lepiarz (USA) produced 278 cracks of a whip in Carver, Massachusetts, USA, on 16 Oct 2016.

Hula hoops spun simultaneously on multiple body parts

On 16 Apr 2016, Germany's Dunja Kuhn kept 43 hula hoops spinning using various parts of her body on *The Saturday Show* in London, UK.

The **most hula hoops spun simultaneously** is 200, by Marawa Ibrahim (AUS) in Los Angeles, California, USA, on 25 Nov 2015.

Long-time GWR record-breaker Ashrita Furman (USA) performed the **most revolutions with a 2-kg hula hoop in one minute**. He completed 142 revolutions on the show *¡Despierta América!* in New York City, USA, on 22 Jul 2016.

▲ **MOST JUGGLING CATCHES (CHAINSAW AND TWO BALLS)**

The Space Cowboy (aka Chayne Hultgren, AUS) completed 162 catches of a running chainsaw and two balls that he juggled in Byron Bay, New South Wales, Australia, on 13 May 2016. Hultgren achieved his record using a petrol chainsaw and a pair of standard juggling balls.

Most swords swallowed...

...by a male: 24
(The Space Cowboy, AUS)

...while juggling: 18
(The Space Cowboy)

...by a female: 13
(Natasha Veruschka, USA)

...and twisted: 13
(Franz Huber, DEU)

...while hanging upside down: 5
(Franz Huber)

...underwater: 4
(The Space Cowboy)

...on a unicycle: 3
(The Space Cowboy)

Heaviest object sword-swallowed:
DeWALT D25980 demolition hammer weighing 38 kg (83 lb 12.4 oz) – including the bit – by Thomas Blackthorne (UK)

Heaviest vehicle pulled with a swallowed sword:
2002 Audi A4 weighing 1,696.44 kg (3,740 lb), by Ryan Stock (CAN)

Most people swallowing the same object:
4, for bar stool "swallowed" by Thomas Blackthorne, Space Cowboy, Captain Frodo (NOR) and Gordo Gamsby (AUS)

Rat traps released on the tongue in one minute

Casey Severn (USA) set off 13 rat traps on his tongue in 60 sec at the Baltimore Tattoo Arts Convention in Baltimore, Maryland, USA, on 16 Apr 2016.

Juggling catches of five balls in one minute

Michael Ferreri (ESP) made 388 catches of five balls in 60 sec at the Festival du Cirque de Namur in Belgium, on 10 Nov 2016.

Juggling head rolls in one minute using three balls

On 27 Feb 2016, David Rush (USA) executed 194 juggling head rolls in 60 sec in Garden City, Idaho, USA. For the purposes of this record, GWR defines a "head roll" as rolling a single ball across the front of the head and catching it again while continuing to juggle in-between catches.

On 2 Apr 2016, David performed the **most juggling catches in one minute blindfolded using three balls**, with 364, at the Taco Bell Arena in Boise, Idaho, USA.

Then, on 4 Jun, David managed the **most juggling catches in one minute using three balls**, with a total of 428 in Meridian, Idaho, USA.

Juggling catches on a unicycle (blindfolded)

The Space Cowboy completed 10 consecutive juggling catches while riding a unicycle blindfolded in Byron Bay, New South Wales, Australia, on 13 May 2016.

▲ LONGEST CAREER AS A RINGMASTER

Norman Barrett (UK) first became master of ceremonies for Robert Brothers Circus in the winter of 1956–57. He has been a master of ceremonies at various circuses ever since, and celebrated his 60th career anniversary in the winter of 2016–17. In 2010, Norman became an MBE, and a year later he was inducted into the International Circus Hall of Fame.

▲ MOST SKIPS OF A ROPE BY A THREE-LEVEL HUMAN PYRAMID IN 30 SECONDS

On 7 Jan 2016, six students at Tagou Martial Arts School (CHN) formed a human pyramid and skipped a rope 32 times in half a minute without error. The coordinated display of outstanding acrobatic agility and strength took place on the set of *CCTV – Guinness World Records Special* in Beijing, China. For this record attempt, Tagou went head-to-head against Zhonghua Martial Arts School (CHN).

▲ FASTEST TIME TO WALK 10 M ON GLASS BOTTLES

It took Tang Hui (CHN) just 57.1 sec to cover a distance of 10 m (32 ft 9.7 in) on the tops of a row of glass bottles on the set of *CCTV – Guinness World Records Special* in Beijing, China, on 12 Jan 2016. It's no easy feat to go the distance without touching the floor, and she only achieved the record on her third and final attempt.

▲ MOST BOTTLE CAPS REMOVED WITH A WHIP IN ONE MINUTE

Adam Winrich (USA) whipped 12 caps from their bottles in 60 sec on the set of *CCTV – Guinness World Records Special* in Beijing, China, on 12 Jan 2016. He has also achieved the **most bottles caught with a whip in one minute** (18) and **most candles extinguished with a whip in one minute** (102).

▲ FARTHEST DISTANCE TO LIMBO UNDER 12-INCH BARS

On 14 Jan 2016, Shemika Charles (TTO) limboed for 10 ft 2 in (3.1 m) below 12-in-high (30.48-cm) bars on *CCTV – Guinness World Records Special* in Beijing, China.

The super-supple Shemika also holds the record for the **lowest limbo for a female** – an astonishing 8.5 in (21.59 cm), which she achieved on the set of *Live! with Regis and Kelly* in New York City, USA, on 16 Sep 2010.

▶ MOST JENGA BLOCKS REMOVED USING A WHIP IN ONE MINUTE

On 27 Sep 2016, April Choi (USA) whipped away four blocks from a Jenga column in 60 sec in Peoria, Illinois, USA. It proved to be an auspicious date for April... On the same day, she achieved the **most stock whip cracks on a slackline in one minute**, with 127, at Bradley Park in Peoria. For this record, only audible volley cracks count towards the total.

Why do whips "crack"? In 2002, Alain Goriely and Tyler McMillen of the University of Arizona found that the loop of the whip speeds up as it travels along its length. It "cracks" as it breaks the sound barrier.

Superhumans Round-Up

The messages from your brain travel along the nerves in your body at speeds of around 200 mph (322 km/h).

Longest bout of yawning
In 1888, Dr Edward W Lee reported on the case of a 15-year-old girl who yawned continuously for five weeks. The case was published in the *Memphis Journal of the Medical Sciences*.

Most prolific mother
The greatest officially recorded number of children born to one mother is 69, to Valentina Vassilyev, a peasant who lived in Shuya, Russia, during the 18th century. In 27 confinements, she gave birth to 16 pairs of twins, seven sets of triplets and four sets of quadruplets.

Most consecutive generations of twins
Three families share this record. Within the Rollings family (UK) there have been four consecutive generations of twins, born from 1916 to 2002. The Taylor family (USA) registered the same count from 1919 to 2002, while the Sims family (UK) saw four successive generations of twins born between 1931 and 2013.

▼ OLDEST DRAG QUEEN
As of 15 Aug 2016, Walter "Darcelle XV" Cole (USA, b. 16 Nov 1930) remained an active drag queen performer at the age of 85 years 273 days. He is the owner and operator of Darcelle XV Showplace in Portland, Oregon. The club hosts the longest-running drag show on the west coast of the USA.

Most Pi places memorized

India's Rajveer Meena memorized Pi to an astonishing 70,000 decimal places, as demonstrated at VIT University in Vellore, Tamil Nadu, India, on 21 Mar 2015. Rajveer wore a blindfold throughout the entire recall, which took nearly 10 hr to complete.

Longest sequence of binary numbers memorized in one minute

On 3 Apr 2015, Aravind Pasupathy (IND) memorized a sequence of 270 binary numbers in 60 sec at the Kasthuri Sreenivasan Trust in Coimbatore, India.

Longest time to hold the breath voluntarily (male)

Spain's Aleix Segura Vendrell held his breath for a lung-bursting 24 min 3.45 sec in Barcelona, Spain, on 28 Feb 2016. Aleix is a professional freediver.

Longest time to restrain two aircraft

Chad Netherland (USA) successfully prevented the take-off of two Cessna light aircraft pulling in opposite directions for 1 min 0.6 sec at Richard I Bong Airport in Superior, Wisconsin, USA, on 7 Jul 2007.

Most operations endured

From 22 Jul 1954 to the end of 1994, Charles Jensen (USA) underwent a total of 970 operations to remove a number of tumours associated with basal cell nevus syndrome.

▲ LONGEST-LASTING HIP REPLACEMENT

As of 23 Mar 2016, the hip replacement belonging to Norman Sharp (UK) had lasted 68 years 116 days. In 1925, at just five years old, Norman was admitted to hospital with septic arthritis. He spent five years in the Royal National Orthopaedic Hospital (RNOH) having his hips fused and learning to walk again. It was another 18 years before he was fitted with his left hip replacement on 1 Dec 1948. He then had his right hip replaced on 22 Dec 1948. Norman is shown above, along with an x-ray of his record-breaking left hip.

▶ LARGEST FEET ON A LIVING PERSON

Jeison Orlando Rodríguez Hernández of Venezuela has a 40.1-cm-long (1-ft 3.79-in) right foot and a 39.6-cm (1-ft 3.59-in) left foot, as measured in Maracay, Aragua, Venezuela, on 6 Oct 2014. Jeison – a keen basketball player – stands 221 cm (7 ft 3 in) tall and is 21 years old. He lives in Maracay with his family and has spent much of his life barefoot. He needs specially large shoes – US size 26 – that are hand-made for him in Germany.

The **largest feet ever** belonged to the "Alton Giant", Robert Wadlow – find out more on pp.122–26.

▲ **LOUDEST CROWD ROAR AT AN INDOOR SPORTS EVENT**
Fans of the Kansas Jayhawks (USA) combined to create a roar that measured 130.4 dBA at the men's basketball game vs West Virginia in Lawrence, Kansas, USA, on 13 Feb 2017. The successful record attempt actually took place before the game tipped off. A tense match followed, ultimately resulting in Kansas forcing a win in overtime.

▲ **WIDEST MOUTH**
The mouth of Angola's Francisco Domingo Joaquim – aka "Chiquinho" – measures 17 cm (6.69 in) when unstretched, although at full stretch he can fit a 330-ml (11-US-fl-oz) soda can sideways into his massive maw. Chiquinho was discovered at a marketplace in Angola and invited by Guinness World Records to be measured on the set of *Lo Show dei Record* in Rome, Italy, on 18 Mar 2010.

Highest percentage of burns to the body survived
Tony Yarijanian (USA) survived third-degree burns to approximately 90% of his body after being caught in an explosion in California, USA, on 15 Feb 2004. Tony was in a coma for three months altogether, and had 25 operations and 60 blood transfusions.

Longest survival without a pulse
Julie Mills (UK) was at the point of death owing to severe heart failure and viral myocarditis when, on 14 Aug 1998, cardiac surgeons at the John Radcliffe Hospital in Oxford, UK, used a non-pulsatile blood pump (AB180) to support her for one week. For three days during that period, Julie had no pulse. The device, which was implanted by Consultant Cardiac Surgeon Stephen Westaby, was the fourth one to be used since it was developed in the USA. This operation marked the first case in which the patient survived the procedure.

Longest survival with heart outside body
Christopher Wall (USA, b. 19 Aug 1975) is the longest-lived known survivor of the congenital birth defect *ectopia cordis*, in which the heart lies outside the body. Most patients do not live beyond 48 hr.

Youngest recipient of two donor hearts
In 1992, at the age of 2, Sophie Parker (UK) had an operation at Harefield Hospital in London, UK, to give her a donor heart to complement her weak natural heart. By Mar 1998, Sophie's natural heart was no longer working properly, so she had a second donor heart transplant to aid her first donor heart.

Longest time to undergo kidney dialysis

Muris Mujičić (HRV) had kidney dialysis (also known as haemodialysis) for 41 years 112 days in Rijeka, Croatia, between 15 May 1974 and 4 Sep 2015. During that time, Muris also had two unsuccessful kidney transplants.

Most mammograms performed in 24 hours

Super Farmacia Rebeca and Servicios Preventivos de Salud (both PRI) carried out 352 mammograms in 24 hr in Isabela, Puerto Rico, on 30 Sep 2016.

Most blood plasma donated

As of 11 May 2015, Terry Price (USA) had donated 894.206 litres (236.2 US gal) of blood plasma at BioLife Plasma Services in Denton, Texas, USA.

▲ MOST FINGER SNAPS IN A MINUTE (ONE HAND)

Satoyuki Fujimura (JPN) performed 296 finger snaps in 60 sec on the set of *Tantei! Knight Scoop* in Osaka, Japan, on 23 Dec 2016. Satoyuki is a university student from Osaka and learned the trick from his mother when he was 15 years old.

The **most tap-dancing taps in one minute** is 1,163 and was achieved by Anthony Morigerato (USA) – a professional tap dancer – at Eleanor's School of Dance in Albany, New York, USA, on 23 Jun 2011.

▲ MOST HEADS SHAVED SIMULTANEOUSLY

On 12 Mar 2016, the Canadian Cancer Society and the Calgary Fire Department combined forces to shave the heads of 329 people at the same time at the Fire Training Academy in Calgary, Alberta, Canada. The attempt took place at an event to raise money to fight cancer and increase awareness about workplace carcinogens. More than $140,000 (£97,829) was donated.

▲ LONGEST-SURVIVING HEART-TRANSPLANT PATIENT

John McCafferty (UK, b. 28 Jul 1942) underwent an orthotopic cardiac transplant during the night of 20–21 Oct 1982 at Harefield Hospital, Middlesex, UK. He was told at the time that he could expect to live for a further five years or so. In fact, he survived for a further 33 years 111 days, eventually passing away on 9 Feb 2016. John is shown (near left) with his surgeon, Sir Magdi Yacoub.

▶ NEWEST HUMAN ORGAN

The mesentery, which connects the stomach to the intestines and holds the lower digestive system in place, is the latest structure in the human body to be classified as an organ, bringing the total number to 79. Research by Irish surgeon Prof J Calvin Coffey, FRCSI (above), and D Peter O'Leary, PhD, published in *The Lancet Gastroenterology & Hepatology* in Nov 2016, confirmed the mesentery as a discrete piece of tissue that has its own functions, although further research is required to identify the precise role that the organ plays.

▶ MOST PEOPLE TO SIGN UP AS ORGAN DONORS IN ONE HOUR

On 6 Sep 2016, a total of 6,697 people registered as organ donors in Dindigul, Tamil Nadu, India. The event was organized by the Indian Medical Association Dindigul district, Rotary International District 3000 and PSNA College of Engineering and Technology (all IND) to highlight the importance of organ donation and how it can impact on lives.

Longest...

We often make assumptions about the world we live in, only to find that the reality is quite different. The longest animal couldn't be a worm... could it? Is it possible for a train to be heavier than more than 800 blue whales? And was there really once a traffic jam of 18 million cars? Read on to find out!

1 cm–1 m

Human tooth extracted
3.2 cm

A 3.2-cm-long (1.26-in) tooth was removed from Loo Hui Jing (SGP) in Singapore on 6 Apr 2009 by Dr. Ng Lay Choo at the Eli Dental Surgery.

Tongue
10.1 cm

Nick Stoeberl (USA) has a tongue measuring 10.1 cm (3.97 in) from the tip to the middle of the closed top lip, as verified in Salinas, California, USA, on 27 Nov 2012.

Ear hair
18.1 cm

Anthony Victor (IND) has hair sprouting from the centre of his outer ears (middle of the pinna) that measures 18.1 cm (7.12 in) at its longest point.

Insect
62.4 cm

Discovered in 2014, the stick insect *Phryganistria chinensis* is 62.4 cm (24.5 in) long. A specimen is housed in the collections of the Insect Museum of West China, based in Chengdu, Sichuan Province.

100%

LONGEST HUMAN TOOTH EXTRACTED

Our line-up of the world's longest things begins here, with a 3.2-cm-long (1.26-in) tooth. By the end of our survey, you'll read about a train longer than the Las Vegas Strip, a traffic jam twice the length of the Panama Canal and a river longer than all of them.

Fingernails (average)
98.5 cm

Melvin Boothe (USA) had fingernails with an average length of 98.5 cm (38.77 in), when measured in Troy, Michigan, USA, on 30 May 2009. Sadly, Melvin passed away in Dec 2009. The **longest fingernails ever (average, female)** belonged to Lee Redmond (USA). Her nails averaged 86.5 cm (34.05 in) when measured for *Lo Show dei Record* in Madrid, Spain, on 23 Feb 2008.

1–50 m

Bean
1.3 m

Harry Hurley of North Carolina, USA, grew a *Vigna unguiculata sesquipedalis* that was 1.3 m (4 ft 3 in) long when measured on 13 Sep 1997 at the North Carolina State Farmers Market.

Hair (female)
5.627 m

Xie Qiuping (CHN) has been growing her hair since 1973, when last was aged 13. When last measured, on 8 May 2004, her tresses were 5.627 m (18 ft 5.54 in) long.

Fish
7.6 m

The longest of the bony or "true" fishes is the oarfish (*Regalecus glesne*), also called the "King of the Herrings", which has a worldwide distribution. In c. 1885, a 25-ft-long (7.6-m) example weighing 600 lb (272 kg) was caught by fishermen off Pemaquid Point in Maine, USA. Another oarfish, seen swimming off Asbury Park, New Jersey, USA, on 18 Jul 1963 was estimated to have measured 50 ft (15.2 m) long. It was observed by a team of scientists from the Sandy Hook Marine Laboratory.

Snake
10 m

The reticulated python (*Python reticulatus*) of south-east Asia, Indonesia and the Philippines regularly exceeds 6.25 m (20 ft 6 in). The longest specimen recorded measured 10 m (32 ft 9.7 in); it was shot in Celebes (now Sulawesi), Indonesia, in 1912.

Bicycle
41.42 m

At 41.42 m (135 ft 10.7 in), or approximately twice the length of a bowling lane, the longest bicycle was built by energy company Santos and University of South Australia (both AUS). It was measured and ridden in Adelaide, Australia, on 17 Jan 2015.

50 m – 5 km

Animal
55 m

The bootlace worm (*Lineus longissimus*) is a species of nemertean or ribbon worm that inhabits shallow waters of the North Sea. In 1864, following a storm at St Andrews in Fife, UK, a specimen measuring at least 55 m (180 ft) – longer than an Olympic-sized swimming pool – washed ashore.

Ship
399 m

The Maersk Triple E class (DNK) container ships are 399 m (1,309 ft) long – more than five-and-a-half times longer than a 747 jumbo jet. The lead vessel is the *MV Mærsk Mc-Kinney Møller*, which was launched at the Daewoo Shipbuilding & Marine Engineering shipyard in Okpo, Geoje, South Korea, on 24 Feb 2013.

Wedding dress train
2,599 m

On 20 Aug 2015, Shillanshan (CHN) unveiled a wedding dress with a train 2,599 m (8,526 ft 10 in) long in Xiamen, Fujian, China. It's more than 20 times longer than an American football field.

Hot dog
203.80 m

At 203.80 m (668 ft 7.6 in), the longest hot dog was made by Novex S A (Paraguay) at Expoferia 2011 in Mariano Roque Alonso, Paraguay, on 15 Jul 2011.

Sofa
1,006.61 m

Mnogo Mebeli (RUS) constructed a sofa measuring 1,006.61 m (3,302 ft 6 in) in Saratov, Russia, on 25 Jul 2014.

5–200 km

Train
7.353 km

At 7.353 km (4,568 mi), the longest train consisted of 682 ore cars pushed by eight diesel-electric locomotives. Assembled by BHP Iron Ore, it travelled 275 km (171 mi) across Australia on 21 Jun 2001. It was also the **heaviest train**, weighing 99,732.1 tonnes (109,935.8 tons).

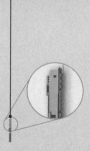

Paper-clip chain
37.41 km

On 16 Dec 2011, employees of Lyreco Deutschland GmbH (DEU) completed a 37.41-km-long (23.25-mi) paper-clip chain in an event at the InterContinental Berlin hotel in Germany.

Rail tunnel
57 km

On 15 Oct 2010, engineers working 2,000 m (6,560 ft) beneath the Swiss Alps drilled through the last remaining rock blocking the creation of the world's longest rail tunnel. The 57-km (35.42-mi) Gotthard Base Tunnel took 14 years to build, at a cost of 12.2 bn Swiss francs ($12.2 bn; £8.4 bn). The opening ceremony was on 1 Jun 2016. Full service began on 11 Dec 2016, with the tunnel set to accommodate 300 trains a day.

Bridge
164 km

The Danyang-Kunshan Grand Bridge on the Jinghu High-Speed Railway (aka the Beijing-Shanghai High-Speed Railway) is 164 km (102 mi) long. This line, which opened in Jun 2011, also crosses the 114-km (70.8-mi) Langfang-Qingxian viaduct, the second-longest bridge in the world.

Traffic jam
176 km

The longest gridlock ever reported stretched 176 km (109 mi) northwards from Lyon towards Paris, France, on 16 Feb 1980.

The **longest traffic jam by number of vehicles** comprised 18 million cars, crawling bumper-to-bumper on the East-West German border on 12 Apr 1990.

> 200 km

Canyon
446 km

The Grand Canyon was created over millions of years by the Colorado River in north-central Arizona, USA. It extends 446 km (277 mi) from Marble Gorge to the Grand Wash Cliffs – more than the length of London's Underground network. The canyon is 1.6 km (1 mi) deep, while its width ranges from 0.5–29 km (0.31–18 mi).

Human chain
1,050 km

On 11 Dec 2004, more than 5 million people joined hands to form a human chain 1,050 km (652.4 mi) long, from Teknaf to Tentulia in Bangladesh. The event was staged as part of a protest to press for fresh polls in an election.

Power line
2,500 km

The longest High Voltage Direct Current (HVDC) power line is the Rio Madeira link in Brazil, which runs for more than 2,500 km (1,550 mi) between Porto Velho and São Paulo. The line transfers hydroelectric power from the Itaipu Dam to São Paulo across large sections of Amazonian rainforest.

Wall
3,460 km

The Great Wall of China has a main-line length of 3,460 km (2,150 mi) – more than three times the length of Britain. It includes an additional 3,530 km (2,193 mi) of branches and spurs.

River
6,695 km

The main source of the Nile river is Lake Victoria in east Central Africa. From its farthest tributary in Burundi, the Nile runs for a distance of 6,695 km (4,160 mi). That's longer than the Mississippi, Rhine, Seine and Thames rivers combined!

SUPERHEROES

![Batman collection photo]

LARGEST BATMAN COLLECTION
As of 11 Apr 2015, Brad Ladner of Roswell, Georgia, USA, had 8,226 unique pieces of Batman-related memorabilia. Brad started his world-beating collection back in 1988, when the book *Batman: A Death in the Family* hit the shelves. If he had a superpower, Brad would opt for one that Batman *doesn't* possess: invisibility.

CONTENTS

Brad keeps his Dark Knight collection in his basement "bat museum". Among his favourite items are a copy of *Batman* Vol.1 #11 from 1942 and a 1966 utility belt made by the Ideal Toy Company.

Superheroes Timeline

There are plenty of "superhumans" in GWR 2018 – including many ordinary people who have done extraordinary things. Below, however, we present a chronology of classic superheroes, ordered in terms of their first appearance – whether that be in a comic book, a movie or elsewhere – and shown in their original costumes.

1936–40

1936
The Phantom

Created by Lee Falk (USA), the **first superhero** was The Phantom, who debuted in his own newspaper comic strip on 17 Feb 1936. It recounted the adventures of Kit Walker, who donned a mask and purple outfit to become The Phantom – aka "the ghost who walks". The character's whited-out eyes, with no visible pupils, became a feature of many later superheroes, including Batman, Green Lantern and Green Arrow.

1938
Superman

The "Man of Steel" first appeared in Action Comics #1, now the **most valuable comic**. Superman was the **first superhero with superpowers**: out-of-this-world abilities that enabled him to run faster than an express train and leap tall buildings in a single bound. In later issues, he demonstrated X-ray vision, super strength and the ability to fly.

1939
Batman

The creation of artist Bob Kane and writer Bill Finger (both USA), the "Caped Crusader" debuted in Detective Comics #27. Kane's early drafts for Batman's costume involved a bright red tunic, wings and a black eye mask; Finger made some key suggestions to transform the outfit into something altogether more threatening.

1939
Captain Marvel

There are a number of Captain Marvels in the Marvel Universe, but the one seen here debuted in Whiz Comics #2 (cover-dated Feb 1940) and is now owned by DC. He proved so popular in the 1940s that sales of his comic books outsold those featuring Superman. He's also known as "Shazam", after the cry that changes the boy Billy Batson into the mighty Captain Marvel.

1940
The Comet

Jan 1940 saw the debut of The Comet in Pep Comics #1. In issue #17, he became the **first superhero to die**, although the character would go on to be revived several times from the 1960s onwards.

1940
The Flash

Created by artist Harry Lampert and writer Gardner Fox, the "Scarlet Speedster" originally appeared in *Flash Comics* #1 (cover-dated Jan 1940). Initially, his alter ego was Jay Garrick, although the character has been through several incarnations.

1940
Fantomah/Woman in Red

Two comic-book characters have a claim to being the **first female superhero.** Fantomah (above) was the first female superhero with superhuman powers to appear in print, in *Jungle Comics* #2 (Feb 1940). The first masked and costumed superheroine (and of "natural" birth), however, was the Woman in Red (right), created by Richard Hughes and George Mandel for *Thrilling Comics* #2 (Mar 1940).

1940
Justice Society of America

The **first superhero team,** the JSA were initially seen on the cover of *All Star Comics* #3 (winter issue 1940–41). The founding members, shown left to right above, were: The Atom, Doctor Fate, Green Lantern, Hawkman, The Flash, The Sandman, Hourman (then known as Hour-Man) and The Spectre.

1941
Captain America

Created by artists Joe Simon and Jack Kirby, this star-spangled superhero debuted in *Captain America Comics* #1, cover-dated Mar 1941. Cap's signature round shield (inset) replaced the triangular version in issue #2.

1941
Aquaman

DC's waterborne wonder was created by Paul Norris and Mort Weisinger and debuted in *More Fun Comics* #73 from Nov 1941. He went on to become one of the founders of the Justice League of America.

1941
Wonder Woman

DC Comics' Amazonian heroine burst on to the scene in *All Star Comics* #8 (cover-dated Dec 1941), although she didn't get her own comic book until summer 1942.

1959
Supergirl

Superman's success inspired DC to devise a female counterpart – namely his cousin, Kara Zor-El. Created by Otto Binder (writer) and Al Plastino (art), she first appeared in *Action Comics* #252 in May 1959.

1960
The Justice League

Also known as the Justice League of America (JLA), this supergroup of DC stars debuted in Oct-Nov 1960. Batman and Superman, although part of the original line-up, seldom appeared in the group's adventures, while Martian Manhunter (below, far right) ended his initial stint with the JLA in 1968. The quintet below appeared on the cover of their first issue.

1961
Fantastic Four

Stan Lee and Jack Kirby's first co-production, *The Fantastic Four* #1 hit the shelves in Nov 1961. They were Marvel's first superteam and contributed to the company's meteoric rise in the 1960s.

1962
The Hulk

Gamma radiation turned Doctor Robert Bruce Banner into a rampaging Green Goliath, and one of Marvel's most enduring characters. *The Incredible Hulk* debuted in May 1962.

1962-74

1962
Spider-Man

Marvel's iconic web-slinger made his debut in *Amazing Fantasy* #15 (Aug 1962), while *The Amazing Spider-Man* appeared in Mar 1963. The character was devised by Stan Lee and artist Steve Ditko.

1963
Ironman

Tales of Suspense #39 (Mar 1963) saw the appearance of Tony Stark's super-powered alter ego. The six films to date starring Robert Downey Jr (USA) as the man in the iron suit have made him the **most successful superhero actor.**

1963
The X-Men

The X-Men #1 was published on 10 Sep 1963, but the denizens of Professor X's School for Gifted Youngsters were originally to be known as "The Mutants". Marvel's publisher, Martin Goodman, thought the name might puzzle readers, so Stan Lee changed it.

1971
Swamp Thing

Created by Len Wein (writer) and Bernie Wrightson (art), DC's unsettling character was first seen in *House of Secrets* #92 (Jul 1971) before getting his own comic the following year.

1974
Wolverine

First glimpsed in the last panel of *The Incredible Hulk* #180 (Oct 1974), the clawed Canadian was recruited as another of Professor X's gifted youngsters in 1975's *Giant-Size X-Men #1*.

KABOOM!

1984
Teenage Mutant Ninja Turtles

In May 1984, "heroes in a half shell" Michelangelo, Leonardo, Donatello and Raphael got their own comic, published by Mirage Studios. An animated TV series followed in 1987. The quartet was initially created (by Kevin Eastman and Peter Laird) as a satire of four hit comics of the time: *Ronin*, *Cerebus*, *Daredevil* and *New Mutants*.

1991
Deadpool

On the subject of *New Mutants*, #98 (Feb 1991) saw the appearance of the "Merc with a mouth". Initially a villain, Deadpool morphed into an ambiguous antihero, and in 1993 got his own miniseries. *The Circle Chase*. The 2016 movie *Deadpool* (USA) is the **highest-grossing R-rated movie**.

1993
Hellboy

Mike Mignola's demonic superhero debuted – in prototype form – on the cover of Italian fanzine *Dime Press* #4 (Mar 1993) before emerging as a fully formed character in *San Diego Comic-Con Comics* #2 (Aug 1993).

1993
Mighty Morphin Power Rangers

The hit 1993 TV series gave rise to a number of Power Rangers comics published by Hamilton from Nov 1994. Marvel Comics subsequently published two series of their own. Mar 2016 saw a comic-book reboot by Boom! Studios, which referenced the original series.

2004
The Incredibles

Produced by Pixar, the *Incredibles* (USA) movie premiered on 27 Oct 2004 and gave the company what was then its highest opening-weekend gross. Five years later, Boom! Studios began publishing a comic-book miniseries based on the film. A sequel to the original movie is due to appear in Jun 2018.

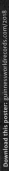

FIRST COMIC-STRIP SUPERHERO

The Phantom, aka "the ghost who walks", was created by US cartoonist Lee Falk and first made an appearance in Feb 1936 (two years before Superman). The *Phantom* newspaper strip featured the adventures of Kit Walker, who sported a mask and a figure-hugging purple outfit as the eponymous superhero. The character continues to fight crime in newspaper strips today.

Most valuable comic

Action Comics #1, published on 18 Apr 1938 (but cover-dated June), was valued at $8,140,000 (£6,490,920) by the Nostomania comic-book price guide in Jan 2017. For the **most expensive comic book** – i.e., the highest price paid for one – see p.186.

Action Comics #1 marked the debut appearance of Superman, the **first superhero with superpowers**, created by writer Jerry Siegel (USA) and artist Joe Shuster (CAN/USA).

First superhero to die

Crime-fighting vigilante The Comet, aka John Dickering, was drawn by Jack Cole (USA) for *Pep Comics*. He first appeared in Jan 1940 and was shot and killed (by the henchmen of his nemesis, Big Boy Malone) 17 issues later in Jul 1941.

FIRST FEMALE CHARACTER TO STAR IN HER OWN COMIC BOOK

Sheena, Queen of the Jungle debuted in the first issue of the comic *Wags*, published in the UK in 1937; her US debut came in the first issue of *Jumbo Comics* in Sep 1938. In spring 1942 came the first issue of *Sheena, Queen of the Jungle*. The debut issue of *Wonder Woman* also appeared in 1942, but not until the summer.

FIRST FEMALE SUPERHERO

The first female character to appear in print as a superhero was Fantomah (above), a shape-shifting ancient Egyptian princess with supernatural powers. Created by Barclay Flagg (aka Fletcher Hanks, USA), she debuted in *Jungle Comics* #2 in Feb 1940.

The first superheroine to wear a mask and costume, however, was the Woman in Red (below), created by Richard Hughes and George Mandel (both USA) for *Thrilling Comics* #2, published in Mar 1940. She was the alter ego of policewoman Peggy Allen.

Longest time between a superhero's death and revival

There were 37 real-time years between the death of Captain America's sidekick Bucky Barnes in *Avengers* vol. 1 #56 (1968) and his return in *Captain America* vol. 5 #1 (2005). Ed Brubaker revised Bucky's history in 2005 to reintroduce him as Winter Soldier.

Best-selling videogame based on a comic

According to VGChartz, *Batman: Arkham City* (Rocksteady, 2011) had sold more than 11.13 million copies as of 27 Apr 2016.

Largest superhero wardrobe

Including variants on designs, Marvel's Iron Man has 58 different sets of armour, starting with the Model 1 and ending with the Model 52. The latter can transform from a car to armour and back again with the push of a button on the car's dashboard.

MOST EXPENSIVE COMIC

On 24 Aug 2014, a 1938 copy of *Action Comics* #1 – which saw the debut of Superman – sold for $3,207,852 (£1,935,080) to Metropolis Collectibles (USA) in an online auction.

The **most expensive Silver Age comic book** ever sold is a 1962 issue of *Amazing Fantasy* #15, featuring Spider-Man's debut. It was bought anonymously in an online auction for $1.1 m (£676,578) on 8 Mar 2011. The term "Silver Age" denotes publication between 1956 and c. 1970.

MOST PROLIFIC CREATOR OF COMIC-BOOK CHARACTERS

From the introduction of the Destroyer in Aug 1941 to Stripperella in 2011 (and beyond), Stan Lee (USA) has introduced at least 343 characters to the world through comic books. This total includes "Stan the Man"'s collaborations with co-creators such as artists Jack Kirby and Steve Ditko (both USA).

MOST...

Movies adapted from the work of a comic-book creator

With the inclusion of 2016's *Doctor Strange* (USA), the comic-book creations and co-creations of Stan Lee (USA) had been adapted into Hollywood films 29 times as of 31 Jan 2017.

Comics published by one author

Known as "The King of Manga", Shotaro Ishinomori (JPN) published 770 comic-book titles (included in 500 volumes).

Covers for a superhero comic book

Marvel's *The Amazing Spider-Man* #666 – the prologue to Dan Slott's "Spider Island" story arc – was sold with 145 variant covers. Most of the variants for this issue had covers dedicated to individual comic-book retailers.

The **most expensive comic-book cover sold at auction** was a special edition of *Tintin in America*. It sold for €1.3 m (£1 m; $1.6 m) to an anonymous bidder at an event held by the Paris-based auction house Artcurial in Jun 2012. The ink-and-gouache artwork was created in 1932 by Tintin creator Hergé, aka Georges Remi (BEL).

An unknown collector paid €312,500 (£279,569; $425,884) for a hand-drawn page from the 1963 Tintin book *The Castafiore Emerald* on 10 May 2009 – the **most expensive page of comic art sold at auction**.

MOST CONSECUTIVE COMIC-BOOK ISSUES DRAWN AND WRITTEN

Comic fans might think of Stan Lee or Brian Michael Bendis as contenders for having enjoyed the longest continuous run writing a character or team comic book. However, the record holder is actually Canadian Dave Sim, creator of the indie comic *Cerebus*. From Dec 1977 until Mar 2004, Sim wrote and drew the adventures of the titular aardvark Cerebus for a total of 300 consecutive issues.

Eisner Comic Award wins for...

• **Best Writer:** Alan Moore (UK) has been voted Best Writer nine times at the Eisner Comic Awards, for a number of key works. They include: *Watchmen* (1988), *Batman: The Killing Joke* (1989), *From Hell* (1995–97), *Supreme* (1997) and *The League of Extraordinary Gentlemen* (2000–01 and 2004).

• **Best Artist/Penciller:** P Craig Russell and Steve Rude (both USA) have each won four times.

• **Best Colouring:** Dave Stewart (USA) has picked up nine Eisner Awards, in 2003, 2005, 2007–11, 2013 and 2015. He has won for his work on, among others, *Hellboy*, *Captain America*, *Daredevil*, *Batwoman* and *X-Men*, colouring for Dark Horse, DC and Marvel.

• **Best Cover Artist:** Comic-book artist James Jean (USA, b. TPE) won six times consecutively between 2004 and 2009, in part for his work on the DC/Vertigo title *Fables*.

• **In one category:** US comic-book letterer Todd Klein has won the Best Letterer award 16 times, most recently in 2011.

• **Best New Series:** Brian K Vaughan (USA) has written four titles that have won Best New Series gongs: *Ex Machina* in 2005; *Buffy the Vampire Slayer* Season Eight in 2008; *Saga* in 2013; and *Paper Girls* in 2016.

• **Best Anthology:** *Dark Horse Presents*, which has been published by Dark Horse Comics since 1986, has picked up five Best Anthology awards, winning in 1992, 1994 and 2012–14.

MOST VIDEOGAMES BASED ON A JAPANESE SUPERHERO COMIC

Akira Toriyama's *Dragon Ball* series stars Son Goku, a monkey-tailed boy with superhuman strength and top martial arts skills. The series included 146 titles between 1986 and 2016, across a vast selection of platforms from Super Cassette Vision to PlayStation and Xbox One. Toriyama's original *Dragon Ball* manga was serialized in 1984–95 in *Weekly Shōnen Jump*.

BEST-SELLING SINGLE EDITION OF A COMIC

X-Men #1 (Marvel Comics, 1991) enjoyed sales of 8.1 million copies. It was created by Chris Claremont (UK) and Jim Lee (USA, b. KOR). Lee drew four variant covers: 1A, 1B, 1C and 1D. These fitted together to form a larger image, used as the gatefold cover to 1E, which appeared a month later.

Why is there a hyphen in "Spider-Man"? Stan Lee introduced it to distinguish the name of the character from DC Comics' Superman.

LARGEST PUBLISHER OF COMICS (CURRENT)

Marvel (USA) had a larger market share than any comic publisher at the end of 2015, claiming 41.82% in terms of units sold, according to global comic-book wholesaler Diamond Comic Distributors. The second-largest comic publisher of that year was DC (USA), with a 27.35% market share.

SUPERHEROES
ON SCREEN

First superhero on television
Superman was the first comic-book superhero to appear in his own television series. *Adventures of Superman*, which began in 1952, starred George Reeves as the Man of Steel and was sponsored by cereal company Kellogg's.

Most-portrayed superhero on television
The character of Superman has featured in four live-action TV series and been played by five different US actors: George Reeves (*Adventures of Superman*, syndicated, 1952–58); John Newton and Gerard Christopher (*Superboy*, syndicated, 1988–92); Dean Cain (*Lois & Clark: The New Adventures of Superman*, ABC, 1993–97); and Tom Welling (*Smallville*, Warner Bros., later CW, 2001–11). A sixth actor, John Rockwell (USA), played the character in *The Adventures of Superboy* (1961), an untransmitted pilot for a series that was never aired. The character of Superman has also appeared in numerous films, cinema serials and animated TV series over the years.

Highest-grossing superhero actor
The six films to date starring Robert Downey Jr (USA) as Tony Stark, aka Iron Man, have earned $6.5 bn (£5 bn) at the box office – more than that for any other actor playing a superhero. See p.193 for a costing of Iron Man's suit.

Highest-grossing movie superhero
According to The-Numbers.com, Batman tops the worldwide box-office grosses, with films totalling $4.573 bn (£3.61 bn), as of 14 Dec 2016. The Dark Knight's closest competitor is Spider-Man, whose five films have brought in $3.963 bn (£3.12 bn) as of the same date.

In 2008, a British teenager changed his name to "Captain Fantastic Faster Than Superman Spiderman Batman Wolverine Hulk And The Flash Combined"!

HIGHEST-GROSSING R-RATED MOVIE

No other R-rated movie has earned more at the worldwide box office than Marvel's risqué superhero film *Deadpool* (USA, 2016), starring Ryan Reynolds. By 8 Dec 2016, it had grossed $783,770,709 (£553,444,000), according to The-Numbers.com.

FIRST SUPERHERO MOVIE

It is possible to credit the earliest cinematic superhero if the term "superhero" is narrowly defined. Not until *Adventures of Captain Marvel* (USA) in Mar 1941 had moviegoers seen an ordinary man, Billy Batson (played by Frank Coghlan Jr), change into a costumed hero with superhuman powers (Captain Marvel, played by Tom Tyler, above).

Longest runtime for a superhero film
The Dark Knight Rises (USA/UK, 2012) claims the record for longest runtime
at 164 min. Close behind is another film featuring the caped crusader:
Batman v Superman: Dawn of Justice (USA, 2016) clocks in at 151 min.

Highest-grossing movie reboot
Of the movies that have been "rebooted" – i.e., had their continuity discarded and
started anew – *The Amazing Spider-Man* (USA, 2012) is the most successful,
grossing $757,890,267 (£471,460,000) according to The-Numbers.com,
as of 4 Nov 2016.

Most-watched superhero movie trailer
The online trailer for Marvel's *Avengers: Age of Ultron* (USA) film – which was
released at cinemas in Apr/May 2015 – had 79,919,212 views as of 15 Dec 2016.

Highest death toll in a superhero movie
There were a total of 83,871 on-screen fatalities in Marvel's *Guardians of the
Galaxy* (USA, 2014). The mammoth death toll is boosted by the inclusion of
the entire Nova Corps on the casualty list.

   Man of Steel (USA/CAN/UK, 2013) sees massive loss of life in Metropolis and
Smallville, but also the death of every living thing on the planet Krypton (its
destruction also features in *Superman* [USA/UK, 1978]). If Krypton is comparable
to Earth in terms of variety and abundance of life, then the individual death toll
of that film is incalculable – but could be equivalent to 1 trillion species.

Highest box-office film gross for a composer

The 94 movies scored by Hans Zimmer (DEU) – including superhero spectaculars such as *Batman v Superman: Dawn of Justice* (USA, 2016), *The Amazing Spider-Man 2* (USA, 2014) and *The Dark Knight Rises* (USA/UK, 2012) – had topped $26.3 bn (£21.1 bn) at the global box office as of 1 Mar 2017, according to The-Numbers.com.

Longest score for a superhero film

Including the 28-min 16-sec piece "Man of Steel: Hans' Original Sketchbook", the score for the film *Man of Steel* (USA, 2013), composed by Hans Zimmer, enjoys an overall running time of 118 min.

Helmet with projected head-up display
$54,100,000

Shoulder-mounted guns **$400,000**

Arc nuclear power source **$36,000,000**

Wrist-mounted missile launchers **$1,500,000**

Hand-mounted stabilizing jets **$2,000,000**

Hip-mounted battery packs **$2,000**

Gold-titanium exoskeleton **$10,000,000**

Boot-mounted jets **$3,800,000**

In the real world, the suit Tony Stark wears in *Iron Man 3* (USA, 2013) would set you back well over $100 m (£80.2 m), according to mashable.com. And that's before paying for the mind-control technology to operate it!

193

HIGHEST-GROSSING ANIMATED SUPERHERO MOVIE

Big Hero 6 (2014) earned a huge $652,127,828 (£424,129,000) at the global box office, topping Pixar's 2004 movie *The Incredibles* ($614,726,752; £328,748,000). The film sees boy genius Hiro transform himself, health-care robot Baymax and a gang of nerdy kids into high-tech superheroes to save their home city of San Fransokyo.

In the list of the 100 most successful movies, 17% feature superheroes. *The Avengers* sits at No.5 in the list, as of Nov 2016.

HIGHEST-GROSSING SUPERHERO MOVIE

The most successful superhero movie at the international box office is Marvel's *The Avengers* (USA, 2012), which took $1,519,479,547 (£943,278,000) in its 22 weeks on general release between 4 May and 4 Oct 2012. The film, directed by Joss Whedon (USA), accounted for 52% of all domestic box-office takings in the USA for the month of May.

MOST OFFICIAL SUPERHERO COSTUMES IN A VIDEOGAME

As of 14 Mar 2017, US-based developer Gazillion Entertainment had released 462 superhero costumes for its Massively Multiplayer Online Role-Playing Game (MMORPG) *Marvel Heroes 2016*, with each outfit officially adapted from either a comic book or movie source. The full list includes 24 outfits for Iron Man, 21 for Spider-Man and 11 each for Storm and Jean Grey. The MMORPG was first released in 2013, before its rebrand in Jan 2016.

First text adventure with a licensed superhero

Questprobe featuring The Hulk was released in 1984 across seven platforms. Two sequels followed – one featuring Spider-Man, a second with Human Torch and The Thing – before developers Adventure International went bust.

First superhero created for a videogame

Released in 1986 for the ZX Spectrum, *Redhawk* let players transform into the mighty hero using the magic word "Kwah!" Typed commands triggered actions that appeared in an animated comic strip at the top of the screen.

First superhero first-person shooter

X-Men: The Ravages of Apocalypse was released for the PC in 1997. Players took the role of a cyborg created by Magneto, hunting down evil cloned versions of the X-Men. Published by Marvel, the game was a conversion of id Software's *Quake* (1996), and required that game to run.

MOST PROLIFIC COMIC-BOOK TEAM IN VIDEOGAMES

From DC Comics' *Justice League of America* to Marvel's *Avengers*, superhero teams have long been a popular comic-book staple. But none has headlined more videogames than the X-Men. As of 1 Mar 2017, Charles Xavier's super-mutants have starred in 27 of their own videogames, with a further five solo games fronted by their iconic linchpin Wolverine. Only Spider-Man and Batman have enjoyed more dedicated games.

FIRST OFFICIAL SUPERHERO VIDEOGAME

Designed by John Dunn (USA), *Superman* was initially released for the Atari 2600 in Dec 1978 to coincide with the film of the same name. Players had to capture Lex Luthor before returning to the *Daily Planet* as quickly as possible. *Superman* was the first game written for the Atari 4K ROMs.

The first Batman videogame (see opposite) set players the task of hunting through isometric rooms (above left) to locate the superhero's partner Robin, solving puzzles and picking up items along the way.

First Batman videogame

The Dark Knight made his videogame debut in 1986's *Batman* (see opposite), published by Ocean Software for the ZX Spectrum, MSX and Amstrad CPC. The devious isometric platformer was created by just two people: programmer Jon Ritman and artist Bernie Drummond.

The **first Batman villain introduced in a videogame** is Sin Tzu. The evil warlord, created by writer Flint Dille and artist Jim Lee, first appeared in Ubisoft's *Batman: Rise of Sin Tzu* in 2003. Tzu has rarely appeared in the comic series since.

First videogame set in the Marvel Cinematic Universe (MCU)

As of 4 Jan 2016, there had been 14 movies released as part of the Marvel Cinematic Universe. The first videogame was SEGA's *Iron Man*, released in 2008.

Longest-running superhero MMO ever

NCSOFT's MMO *City of Heroes* ran for 8 years 300 days before closing services on 30 Nov 2012.

The **longest-running superhero MMO (current)** is *Champions Online*. Based on a table-top game and developed by Cryptic Studios (USA), it had run for 7 years 194 days as of 14 Mar 2017.

Fastest completion of *Batman: Arkham City*

"DarkAtrax" (CAN) completed Rocksteady's action-adventure on the PC in 1 hr 21 min 31 sec on 22 Dec 2016. "DarkAtrax" finished the game on the "Easy" setting without using Catwoman, a playable character who extends the run. Speedrun.com verified the record on 24 Dec 2016.

MOST COMIC-BOOK CHARACTERS IN A VIDEOGAME
Scribblenauts Unmasked: A DC Comics Adventure (5th Cell, 2013) features 1,718 characters from the DC Universe, including superheroes, super-villains and normal humans such as Lois Lane and Alfred Pennyworth. *Scribblenauts* allows players to jot down their favourite characters in Max's notebook and summon them into the game world.

MOST PROLIFIC VIDEOGAME SUPERHERO

From his 1982 debut *Spider-Man* on the Atari 2600 to Gameloft's endless runner *Spider-Man Unlimited* (2014), Marvel's Spider-Man had headlined 37 videogames across 32 formats as of 8 Feb 2017. The web-slinger has also appeared in almost 20 "non-solo" titles, such as *Marvel Super Hero Squad* (2009) and even as a boss battle in the 1989 ninja title *The Revenge of Shinobi*.

Lowest-rated superhero videogame

Voted "Worst Game Ever" by GameTrailers.com and "Worst Comic Book Game of All Time" by GameSpy, *Superman: The New Superman Adventures* (Titus Software, 1999) for the Nintendo 64 was critical Kryptonite. As of 13 Feb 2017, it had a GameRankings rating of just 22.9%.

The **most critically acclaimed superhero videogame** was *Batman: Arkham City* (Rocksteady, 2011) for the PlayStation 3, which boasted a GameRankings rating of 95.94%.

Fastest completion of *LEGO Marvel Super Heroes*

Playing on the Xbox, "Shadowsmith97" (USA) completed the 2013 action-adventure in 4 hr 40 min 4 sec on 21 Nov 2015, more than 20 min faster than the second-quickest time. The same player also achieved the **fastest time for the game in co-op mode** – 3 hr 57 min 29 sec – playing alongside "xKingofCTownx".

Most voice-acting appearances in superhero videogames

Veteran voice actor Fred Tatasciore (USA) had performed in 53 separate superhero releases as of 23 Mar 2017. He specializes in heavyweight heroes and villains such as The Hulk, Bane, The Thing and Dr Doom. His credits include *LEGO Marvel's Avengers*, *Viewtiful Joe 2* and multiple Spider-Man and X-Men titles.

Most videogame performances as a single superhero
Steve Blum (USA) first starred as Marvel's Wolverine in Activision's action-RPG *X-Men Legends* in 2004. As of 8 Feb 2017, Blum had portrayed the gravel-voiced antihero 15 times in all.

Most videogame performances as a single superhero (female)
DC Comics' Harley Quinn (aka Harleen Quinzel) is a villainess who often features in Batman and Superman storylines. Tara Strong (CAN) had voiced her in 10 games as of 8 Feb 2017.

With his LEGO and *Arkham* (right) titles, Batman has amassed total videogame sales of 55.44 million, according to VGChartz.

BEST-SELLING SUPERHERO VIDEOGAME

LEGO® Batman: The Videogame (Traveller's Tales, 2008) had sold 13.45 million copies across all platforms as of 17 Mar 2017, according to VGChartz. This also makes it the **best-selling Batman videogame** and the **best-selling videogame based on a DC Comics character**. The first Traveller's Tales LEGO game with an original storyline, it pitted Batman against gangs of super-villains led by Penguin, Joker and the Riddler. Two sequels followed: *DC Super Heroes* (2012) and *Beyond Gotham* (2014).

LARGEST GATHERING OF PEOPLE DRESSED AS COMIC-BOOK CHARACTERS

On 25 Sep 2015, a group of 1,784 participants dressed up as familiar comic-book characters at the Salt Lake Comic Con in Utah, USA. Only characters that had originated in comics (rather than on TV or in movies) were eligible for this record; an elite group of local comic-book experts were on hand to make sure that the guidelines were being followed.

SUPERHEROES

COSPLAY

Fastest half marathon in a superhero costume
On Sunday, 2 Oct 2016, Michael Kallenberg (UK) ran the Cardiff Half Marathon in Wales, UK, in 1 hr 9 min 33 sec dressed as Robin. Batman (aka Carwyn Jones) finished behind him in 1 hr 10 min 45 sec.

Longest-running dedicated cosplay event
The World Cosplay Summit has run annually in Nagoya, Japan, for 13 years as of the 2016 event, held from 30 Jul to 7 Aug. Competitors star as characters from Japanese videogames, anime, manga and tokusatsu.

The finale of the summit is the World Cosplay Championship. The record for **most World Cosplay Championship victories** is three, shared by two teams. The Italians were Grand Champions in 2005, 2010 and 2013, with Brazil winning in 2006, 2008 and 2011. Perennial hosts Japan have won twice, while the winner in 2016 was Indonesia.

The **most countries at a dedicated cosplay tournament** is 30, at the 2016 World Cosplay Championship, staged on 6–7 Aug in Nagoya. The participants included China, Australia, India, Kuwait, Denmark and Mexico.

MOST PEOPLE DRESSED AS...

Dragon Ball characters
On 1 Nov 2012, Editorial Planeta (ESP) arranged for 307 people to dress as characters from the manga series *Dragon Ball* at the Saló del Manga comic festival in Barcelona, Spain.

Spider-Man
Recruitment company Charterhouse (AUS) assembled 438 individuals dressed as the famous web-slinger in Sydney, New South Wales, Australia, on 28 Jul 2015.

Ben 10
On 25 Mar 2016, a group of 475 participants became cartoon hero Ben 10 for a day at Red Sea Mall in Jeddah, Saudi Arabia. The event was organized by Rainbow Flavoured Milk (SAU).

Batman
A total of 542 individuals donned the famous caped crusader's attire in Calgary, Alberta, Canada, on 18 Sep 2014. The mass costuming was staged by Nexen Energy (CAN).

Thomas modelled this suit on one that appears in *Avengers: Age of Ultron* (USA, 2015). Tony Stark builds it to help him fight the Hulk.

LARGEST COSPLAY COSTUME (SINGLE PERSON)
Designed and built by Thomas DePetrillo (USA), the Iron Man Hulkbuster is 9 ft 6 in (2.89 m) tall, has a shoulder width of 6 ft 4 in (1.93 m) and weighs 106 lb (48.08 kg). It takes Thomas 20 min to don the suit, which (with helmet fitted) is some 7 in (17.7 cm) taller than the **tallest man ever,** Robert Wadlow.

FASTEST MARATHON IN A SUPERHERO COSTUME

On 24 Apr 2016, Matt Gunby (UK) completed the Virgin Money London Marathon in 2 hr 27 min 43 sec, dressed as Wonder Woman.

The **fastest marathon dressed as a superhero (female)** is 2 hr 48 min 51 sec, by Camille Herron (USA), as Spider-Man, at the 2012 Route 66 Marathon in Tulsa, Oklahoma, USA, on 18 Nov 2012.

LARGEST GATHERING OF PEOPLE DRESSED AS SUPERMAN

On 27 Jul 2013, the Kendal Calling festival in Lowther Deer Park, Cumbria, UK, welcomed 867 Men (and Women and Children) of Steel in an event organized by Escapade (UK). The record attempt was staged to coincide with the launch of the movie *Man of Steel* (USA/CAN/UK, 2013) and to help raise awareness for the "Help for Heroes" charity.

MOST FUNCTIONAL GADGETS IN A COSPLAY SUIT

A Batsuit created by creature special-effects expert Julian Checkley (UK) incorporates 23 functional gadgets. These include a fireball launcher, tracking device, folding batarang, smoke bombs and Batman's signature grapnel gun. The costume, which was designed and built in 2016, is based on the suit in the videogame *Batman: Arkham Origins* (Warner Bros., 2013).

Julian's Batsuit was 3D-printed then cast in a pliable urethane rubber. He spent three months loading up his creation with gadgets.

The Hulk

On 13 Jul 2012, a total of 574 people turned green at the Muckno Mania Festival in Castleblayney, Ireland.

Ninja Turtles

The Nickelodeon Suites Resort brought together 1,394 Ninja Turtles in Orlando, Florida, USA, on 9 Aug 2014.

Superheroes (single venue)

As part of the promotion for the DreamWorks movie *Megamind* (USA, 2010), a group of 1,580 participants decked themselves out as various superheroes on 2 Oct 2010 in Los Angeles, California, USA. The event was organized by Paramount Pictures (USA).

MOST PEOPLE DRESSED AS SUPERHEROES IN 24 HOURS (MULTIPLE VENUES)

On 18 Apr 2015, over the course of 24 hr, a total of 2,003 people dressed up as superheroes across 14 different locations around the world, in an event arranged by DC Comics (USA). All of the characters portrayed were chosen from the pantheon of DC's costumed crimefighters. The event kicked off in Queensland, Australia, and came to a close in Los Angeles, California, USA.

KAPOW!

Comic-book expert Rob Cave presents his rundown of superhero superlatives. Watch the forces of good and evil face off against one another as they vie to become intergalactic record-breakers, putting the puny efforts of mere mortals firmly in their place...

FASTEST

SUPERHERO: DC's The Flash has access to the Speed Force, an extra-dimensional energy that allows him to move at incredible speeds. He has appeared in several incarnations, with the fastest being Wally West (top left). Rival Marvel speedster Quicksilver used the Terrigen Mists to travel faster than time in the limited series *Son of M*, but could not sustain this ability.

SUPERVILLAIN: Hunter Zolomon, aka Zoom (bottom left), was even faster than The Flash. In *Flash Vol. 2* #199, Wally West struggles to even see Zoom as he runs, let alone match him for pace!

STRONGEST

SUPERHERO: Thor, Hercules and The Incredible Hulk are all mighty contenders for this title, but it's Superman (above left) who comes out on top. Thanks to an overcharged solar battery, he was able to lift 200 quintillion tons in *All-Star Superman* #1. And in three heavyweight battles against Hulk ("the Strongest one there is"), Superman was the clear winner in at least two of the bouts.

SUPERVILLAIN: Prehistoric Kryptonian monster Doomsday (above right) beat up Superman seemingly to the point of death, and kept the Justice League at bay with his strength. He can't be beaten the same way twice.

Largest superhero

A number of heroes – including Mr Fantastic, Plastic Man and Elongated Man – have the ability to reshape their bodies but cannot significantly alter their mass. Thom Kallor, aka Star Boy/Starman, has the power to increase the density and mass of an object, while original Ant-Man Hank Pym grew beyond the Macroverse and into the Overspace, "a point above and apart from all other realities", in *The Mighty Avengers Vol. 1* #30.

However, discounting characters who can change their size, the largest superhero is Mogo, a sentient planet and member of the Green Lantern Corps. Introduced in *Green Lantern Vol. 2* #188, Mogo is sufficiently massive that it possesses its own gravitational field.

Smallest superhero

Several superheroes, including Ant-Man Hank Pym, The Wasp (aka Janet van Dyne) and The Atom (aka Ray Palmer) have developed the ability to shrink in size to the sub-atomic level. However, Arcturus Rann and his fellow Micronauts were born and live in the Microverse, a space only accessible by shrinking below the sub-atomic level.

Smartest superhero

Michael Holt, aka Mr Terrific, holds 14 PhDs but estimates in *Infinite Crisis* #5 that he is only the third smartest person on Earth in the DC Universe. Hank Pym discovered Pym particles and was dubbed "Earth's Scientist Supreme" by the cosmic entity Eternity in *The Mighty Avengers Vol. 1* #30. However, Reed Richards of the Fantastic Four has displayed intelligence beyond his scientific exploits. Aware of his own limitations, Richards regularly solicits the expertise of others – including his own children Franklin and Valeria – enabling him to solve seemingly intractable problems such as the ruthless Interdimensional Council of Reeds.

Smartest supervillain

The extra-terrestrial/android villain Braniac might possess a 12th-level intellect, but he has been outsmarted and defeated by Superman on various occasions. Adrian Veidt, aka Ozymandias, is dubbed "the smartest man on the planet" in *Watchmen.* He successfully fools the governments of the world – and Doctor Manhattan – with his deadly scheme involving a fictional alien threat of his own manufacture.

MOST POWERFUL

SUPERHERO: "Supreme super-hero" Doctor Manhattan of Alan Moore's *Watchmen* (above) is the product of an accident during a nuclear physics experiment. He can manipulate matter on an atomic level and view reality from a perspective outside of linear time.

SUPERVILLAIN: The Anti-Monitor (right) is an omnipotent and omniscient being from the planet of Qward in the anti-matter universe. In *Crisis on Infinite Earths,* he consumes stars to power himself, killing thousands of universes and many of their heroes.

RICHEST

SUPERHERO: T'Challa, aka the Black Panther (above), is the absolute monarch of the small African kingdom of Wakanda, a nation that has become wealthy thanks to the selling-off of some of its deposits of the extra-terrestrial metal vibranium. Thanks to careful reinvestment of the profits, T'Challa has helped ensure that Wakanda's national reserve runs to trillions of dollars.

SUPERVILLAIN: Fantastic Four nemesis Dr Victor Von Doom (right) is both a brilliant inventor and the absolute ruler of Latveria. While he has been deposed a number of times, he inevitably ends up back in power, with the economic resources of his homeland once again at his disposal.

Least powerful superhero

Created by Mark Millar and John Romita Jr in *Kick-Ass* #1, Dave Lizewski, aka Kick-Ass, is an ordinary teenager who dons a wetsuit to take on the forces of evil. Lacking training, gadgets and a certain amount of common sense, Lizewski learns the realities of crime-fighting the hard way, but refuses to let his mishaps and injuries deter him.

First mutant

The X-Men mutant adversary Apocalypse was born around 5,000 years ago, earning himself the title "the one that came first". However, in *X-Necrosha* #1, mutant and psychic vampire Selene Gallio, aka the Black Queen, is seemingly 17,000 years old. She has also been shown as having links to the Hyborian age before recorded civilization.

Slowest supervillain

A simple bank robber, Turtle Man planned to commit the perfect crime by breaking into a high-security bank vault and hiding there, hoping to slip out again later when the bank staff were off-guard. His plot was foiled by the Barry Allen incarnation of super-speedy superhero The Flash. In comparison, Turtle Man was called "The Slowest Man on Earth".

Most generic superhero

Making his debut in Marvel's tongue-in-cheek *Generic Comic Book* #1, Super-Hero gained his strength and heightened senses from his collection of glow-in-the-dark items. As the disclaimer on the cover put it: "THIS COMIC CONTAINS: One neurotic Super-Hero type with a variety of personal problems", along with "one bad-guy bent on world domination through arcane means".

Youngest superhero

The tradition of teenage superheroes in comics stretches back at least to the debut of Dick Grayson in *Detective Comics* #38 (1940), but there are super-youngsters who started their careers earlier than the Boy Wonder. Franklin Richards was just four-and-a-half when he joined child superheroes Power Pack in *Power Pack* #17. Yet this is positively elderly compared to Winter Moran, who in *Miracleman* #9 saves the world at birth! She inherits her father Miracleman's powers, which she received via technology belonging to the alien Qys. This is enough to convince the Qys and their traditional rivals, the Warpsmiths, of humanity's ascension to an "intelligent-class" world, and they decide not to destroy Earth.

MOST UNBEATABLE SUPERHERO

Even the strongest superheroes taste defeat at some point in their career. But not Doreen Green, aka Squirrel Girl (right). First appearing in *Marvel Super-Heroes Vol. 2* #8, she graduated to *The Unbeatable Squirrel Girl Beats Up the Marvel Universe!*, in which Doreen and/or her misguided duplicate Allene beat up, take down or equitably resolve conflicts against all-comers.

MOST EXPENSIVE COSTUME FROM A TV SERIES
The Superman suit from the 1955 series of *Adventures of Superman* (USA) sold for $180,000 (£118,682) at a Profiles in History auction in Los Angeles, California, USA, on 30 Sep 2015. Until 1955, the show was filmed in black and white. In those years, the Superman outfit was coloured brown and white, to sharpen its definition for TV screens.

SUPERHEROES
ROUND-UP

First superhero team
The founding members of the Justice Society of America were the Atom, Doctor Fate, the Flash, Green Lantern, Hawkman, Hourman (Hour-man at that point), the Sandman and the Spectre, as seen seated around a table on the cover of *All Star Comics* #3, dated for the winter of 1940. Although he is also mentioned on the cover, Johnny Thunder is not depicted and did not become a member until issue #6. In later issues, the heroes would collaborate in order to defeat more powerful foes than they could alone, an idea that served as the template for every later superhero team, from the Justice League to The Avengers and The X-Men.

Highest-grossing PG-13-rated superhero movie
In *The Avengers* (2012), multiple Marvel superheroes, including Iron Man, Thor and Captain America, united to save the world from Loki. According to The-Numbers. com, the film had earned $1,519,479,547 (£943,278,000) by 14 Dec 2016.

When combined with *Avengers: Age of Ultron* (2015), the Avengers series averages an incredible $1,462,092,708 (£936.1 m) per movie – the **highest average gross for a movie series**.

Highest-grossing PG-rated superhero movie
Initially a Marvel property, *Big Hero 6* (USA, 2014) was developed by Disney Animation Studios. The anime-inspired movie had earned $652,127,828 (£424,129,000) as of 14 Dec 2016, according to The-Numbers.com.

LARGEST *2000 AD* COLLECTION

Robert Stewart (UK) owns 10,018 items of *2000 AD* memorabilia, as verified in Sunderland, UK, on 25 Mar 2016. He has been collecting *2000 AD* comics since 1977, but stepped up his collection in the late 1980s. His first piece of additional memorabilia was a Judge Death T-shirt, which his mother eventually threw out. Robert's favourite item is a Judge Dredd pinball machine.

LARGEST *SWAMP THING* COLLECTION

John Boylan (USA) owns 797 unique pieces of Swamp Thing memorabilia, as verified in Sioux Falls, South Dakota, USA, on 21 Mar 2015. John's hoard includes comics, advertisements, movie posters, figurines, clothing and even some original production art. His favourite items include a *Swamp Thing* TV crew member jacket, a *Swamp Thing* promotional watch and a sleeping bag.

Most common character in the Marvel Cinematic Universe

Nick Fury, portrayed by Samuel L Jackson (USA), has appeared in seven Marvel Cinematic Universe (MCU) films. They are *Iron Man* (2008), *Iron Man 2* (2010), *Thor* (2011), *Captain America: The First Avenger* (2011), *The Avengers* (2012), *Captain America: The Winter Soldier* (2014) and *Avengers: Age of Ultron* (2015). Jackson also played Fury in two episodes of the TV series *Agents of S.H.I.E.L.D.* (ABC, 2013–present).

Longest gap between character appearances in Marvel Cinematic Universe movies

The character of Thaddeus "Thunderbolt" Ross, played by William Hurt (USA), made his screen debut in *The Incredible Hulk* (USA, 2008). His second outing was not for another 7 years 328 days, however, in *Captain America: Civil War* (USA, 2016).

Most property damage in a superhero movie

The cost of the damage to the city of Metropolis (plus a Wayne Enterprises satellite) during Superman's climactic battle with General Zod in *Man of Steel* (USA/CAN/UK, 2013) has been put at $750 bn (£610 bn). The film sees an entire alien world (Krypton) destroyed too, an event that also features in *Superman* (USA/UK/PAN/CHE, 1978), starring Christopher Reeve.

LARGEST COMIC-BOOK COLLECTION

Bob Bretall (USA) has an unmatched 101,822 unique comic books in his collection in Mission Viejo, California, USA. His achievement was verified on 6 Aug 2015. Bob mainly keeps his collection in his three-car garage, although he also has a "comic room" with selected comic books and other associated items of memorabilia.

At the same sale, the Batsuit from *The Dark Knight Rises* sold for £192,000 ($248,857), while Bane's outfit fetched £96,000 ($124,428).

MOST EXPENSIVE BATPOD SOLD AT AUCTION

A Batpod motorcycle from *The Dark Knight Rises* (USA, 2012) sold at the 2016 Prop Store Live Auction (UK) on 27 Sep 2016 for £312,000 ($404,393).

But it's not the **most expensive Batman memorabilia sold at auction**. On 19 Jan 2013, a Batmobile (above right) used in the 1960s *Batman* TV show sold at the Barrett-Jackson car auction in Scottsdale, Arizona, USA, for $4,620,000 (£2,897,770), inclusive of the seller's premium.

Most prolific TV, film and theatre stuntman

Roy Alon (UK, 1942–2006) worked on 937 TV, film and theatre productions as either a stunt co-ordinator, performer or 2nd Unit Director. These comprise 148 films (including all four of the Christopher Reeve Superman movies and most of the James Bond series), 739 TV shows, 13 theatre productions and 37 adverts.

Shortest stuntman

Kiran Shah (UK, b. KEN) stood 126.3 cm (4 ft 1.7 in) when measured on 20 Oct 2003. He has appeared in 52 movies since 1976 and performed stunts in 31 of them, including being perspective stunt double (for long shots during action scenes) for Elijah Wood in *the Lord of the Rings* trilogy (NZ/USA, 2001–03).

LARGEST SUPERMAN COLLECTION

Marco Zorzin (BRA) had gathered 1,518 individual items related to the Man of Steel as of 14 Feb 2016. Marco is such a huge fan of Kal-El, the last Kryptonian, that he has officially changed his middle name to "Superman". His super-collection includes all the *Superman* films starring Christopher Reeve on VHS tape, along with a themed thermos flask, lunch box, baseball cap, wrist watch, headphones and an inflatable punch bag.

MOST ADAPTED SUPERHERO IN LIVE-ACTION MOVIES

Excluding animated series, Batman has starred in 10 full-length movies. The run began with *Batman* (USA, 1966), a movie version of the TV show starring Adam West. The Caped Crusader was subsequently portrayed by Michael Keaton, Val Kilmer, George Clooney and Christian Bale. For *Justice League* (USA, 2017, above), Batman is played by Ben Affleck, who also starred in *Batman v Superman: Dawn of Justice* (USA, 2016).

Eric's favourite items are four unreleased prototypes of X-Men statues and figures that never went into production.

LARGEST X-MEN COLLECTION

As of 28 Jun 2012, Eric Jaskolka's (USA) hoard of X-Men memorabilia ran to 15,400 individual items when counted in West Des Moines, Iowa, USA. Eric began his collection in 1989, initially concentrating just on comic books and branching into X-Men toys two years later.

Heaviest...

The heaviest man was 63 times heavier than the heaviest baby, although only half the weight of the heaviest carnivore on land. But is the heaviest bell heavier than the heaviest tank? And can anything on Earth outweigh a blue whale? GWR has the answers.

0–100 kg

Apple
1.849 kg

Chisato Iwasaki (JPN) grew an apple weighing 1.849 kg (4 lb 1 oz) at his apple farm in Hirosaki City, Japan, on 24 Oct 2005.

Object removed from the stomach
4.5 kg

"Trichobezoar" is the medical name for a hairball, which occurs as a result of trichophagia – eating one's own hair. The largest trichobezoar surgically removed from a human was a hairball weighing 4.5 kg (10 lb), found in the stomach of an unnamed 18-year-old woman treated at Rush University Medical Center in Chicago, Illinois, USA, in Nov 2007. The excised trichobezoar measured 37.5 x 17.5 x 17.5 cm (15 x 7 x 7 in).

Birth
9.98 kg

Giantess Anna Bates (née Swan, CAN) measured 7 ft 11 in (241.3 cm). On 19 Jan 1879, she gave birth to a boy weighing 22 lb (9.98 kg) and measuring 28 in (71.12 cm) at her home in Seville, Ohio, USA.

Flying bird
18.1 kg

The kori bustard (*Ardeotis kori*) is found in South and East Africa. The heaviest recorded specimen was a male that weighed 40 lb (18.1 kg). It was shot in South Africa by big-game hunter H T Glynn in 1936. He later presented its head and neck to the British Museum in London, UK.

Mantle of bees
63.7 kg

Ruan Liangming (CHN) wore a 63.7-kg (140-lb 6.95-oz) mantle of bees in Fengxin County, Yichun City, Jiangxi Province, China, on 15 May 2014. An estimated 637,000 bees made up the mantle, including 60 queens.

Images not to scale

Tortoise
417 kg

A Galápagos tortoise (*Chelonoidis nigra*) named Goliath measured 135.8 cm (4 ft 5 in) long, 102 cm (3 ft 4 in) wide, 68.5 cm (2 ft 3 in) high, and weighed 417 kg (920 lb) at his heaviest. Goliath lived at the Life Fellowship Bird Sanctuary in Seffner, Florida, USA, from 1960 to 2002.

Sportswoman
203.21 kg

Sumo wrestler Sharran Alexander (UK) weighed 203.21 kg (448 lb) on 15 Dec 2011.

Man (ever)
635 kg

Jon Brower Minnoch (USA, 1941–83) had suffered from obesity since childhood. He was 6 ft 1 in (185 cm) tall and weighed 392 kg (178 kg: 28 st) in 1963, rising to 700 lb (317 kg: 50 st) in 1966 and 975 lb (442 kg: 69 st 9 lb) in Sep 1976. In Mar 1978, Minnoch was admitted to University Hospital in Seattle, USA, where consultant endocrinologist Dr Robert Schwartz calculated that he must have weighed more than 1,400 lb (635 kg: 100 st). Much of this was water accumulation owing to his congestive heart failure.

Rideable bicycle
860 kg

Jeff Peeters (BEL) built a bicycle weighing 860 kg (1,895 lb 15.6 oz) and rode it in Mechelen, Belgium, on 19 Aug 2015. The vehicle was built entirely from reused materials.

Carnivore on land
900 kg

In 1960, a polar bear weighing some 900 kg (1,984 lb) was identified at a frozen ice pack in the Chukchi Sea, west of Kotzebue in Alaska, USA. Its size was estimated at 3.5 m (11 ft 5 in) over the body contours from nose to tail, 1.5 m (4 ft 11 in) around the body and 43 cm (16.9 in) around the paws.

Pumpkin
1,190.49 kg

Belgium's Mathias Willemijns grew a pumpkin that weighed 1,190.49 kg (2,624 lb 9 oz), as authenticated by the Great Pumpkin Commonwealth (GPC) in Ludwigsburg, Germany, on 9 Oct 2016.

Doughnut
1,695 kg

On 21 Jan 1993, a 1.69-tonne (3,739-lb) filled doughnut was served up by representatives from Hemstrought's Bakeries, Donato's Bakery and the radio station WKLL-FM (all USA) in Utica, New York, USA.

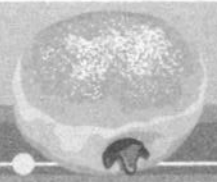

Bony fish
2,000 kg

Specimens of the sunfish (*Mola mola*) have been recorded weighing around 2 tonnes (4,400 lb) and measuring 3 m (10 ft) between the tips of the fins.

Rideable motorcycle
4,749 kg

The *Panzerbike*, constructed by Tilo and Wilfried Niebel of Harzer Bike Schmiede in Zilly, Germany, weighed 4.749 tonnes (10,470 lb) on 23 Nov 2007.

Wedding cake
6,818 kg

The world's largest wedding cake weighed 6.818 tonnes (15,032 lb) and was made by chefs at the Mohegan Sun hotel and casino in Uncasville, Connecticut, USA. It was displayed at their New England bridal showcase on 8 Feb 2004.

7,000–600,000 kg

Cartilaginous fish
21,500 kg

A scientifically recorded whale shark (*Rhincodon typus*) caught off Baba Island, near Karachi, Pakistan, on 11 Nov 1949, weighed 21.5 tonnes (47,400 lb). At 12.65 m (41 ft 6 in) long, it was also the **largest fish**. Cartilaginous fish have skeletons made of cartilage, rather than the hard bone of many other fish species.

Tank (present day)
63,000 kg

The M1A2 Abrams main battle tank, produced by General Dynamics Land Systems (USA), has a combat weight of 63 tonnes (138,900 lb), making it the heaviest tank currently in operational service. It is equipped with one 120-mm gun and has a top speed of 68 km/h (42 mph).

Bell still in use
92,000 kg

The Mingun bell weighs 92 tonnes (202,825 lb) and has a diameter of 5.09 m (16 ft 8 in) at the lip. Located near Mandalay in Burma, the bell is struck by a teak boom from the outside. It was cast at Mingun late in the reign of King Bodawpaya (1782–1819).

Animal
190,000 kg

The blue whale (*Balaenoptera musculus*) weighs up to 160 tonnes (352,000 lb) and has an average length of around 24 m (80 ft). A huge specimen caught in the Southern Ocean, Antarctica, on 20 Mar 1947 weighed 190 tonnes (418,878 lb) with a recorded length of 27.6 m (90 ft 6 in).

Aircraft (ever)
640,000 kg

The aircraft with the highest standard maximum take-off weight is the Antonov An-225 "Mriya" (Dream). Originally it weighed 600 tonnes (1.32 million lb), but between 2000 and 2001 its floor was strengthened, which resulted in an increased maximum take-off weight of 640 tonnes (1.41 million lb). Only two of these behemoths were ever built.

> 600,000 kg

Rocket
2,965,000 kg

Saturn V (USA) was the largest rocket, although not the most powerful. It was 110.6 m (363 ft) high with the *Apollo* spacecraft on top and weighed 2,965 tonnes (6.5 million lb) on the launchpad. Saturn V had a lift-off thrust of 3,447 tonnes (7.6 million lb). The first Saturn V was launched in 1967 and the 13th, and last, took off in 1973.

Land vehicle
14,196,000 kg

According to Off-Highway Research, the heaviest machine capable of moving under its own power is the 14,196-tonne (31.3-million-lb) Bagger 293 bucket-wheel excavator, an earth-moving machine made by TAKRAF of Leipzig, Germany. Employed in an open-cast coal mine in the German state of North Rhine-Westphalia, it is 220 m (722 ft) long and 94.5 m (310 ft) tall at its apex. It is capable of shifting 240,000 m³ (8.475 million cu ft) of earth per day.

Submarine
26,500,000 kg

On 23 Sep 1980, NATO announced the launch of the first of Russia's Akula-class submarines (designated "Typhoon" by NATO) at a secret covered shipyard on the White Sea. The vessels were reported to have a dived displacement of 26,500 tonnes (58.422 million lb) and measure 171.5 m (562 ft 8 in) overall. For more information, see p.473.

Building
703,500,000 kg

The Palace of the Parliament in Bucharest, Romania, is considered to be the heaviest building in the world. It contains 700,000 tonnes (771,617.9 tons) of steel and bronze combined with 1 million m³ (35.3 million cu ft) of marble, 3,500 tonnes (7.7 million lb) of crystal glass and 900,000 m³ (31.7 million cu ft) of wood.

Black hole
7.9 × 10⁴⁰ kg

In 2009, astronomers using NASA's *Swift* gamma-ray space telescope measured the mass of the supermassive black hole at the centre of the quasar S5 0014+81, based on its extreme luminosity. The resulting mass of around 40 billion solar masses makes this black hole approximately 10,000 times more massive than the supermassive black hole at the centre of the Milky Way galaxy.

Recordmania

There's no telling where a passion for collecting can take you. GWR has recognized collections of **toothpaste tubes** (2,037), **airline sick bags** (6,290) and **toe-nail clippings** (from 24,999 individuals).

▲ LARGEST COLLECTION OF TEDDY BEARS

As of 31 Dec 2012, Jackie Miley (USA) had 8,026 teddy bears, each unique. Jackie lives in Hill City, South Dakota, USA, a town whose population numbers little more than a tenth of Jackie's toy bear collection! Most of the items in her record-breaking hoard make their home in Teddy Bear Town, a small house located on Main Street in Hill City.

Contents

People from every US state and 29 other countries have donated bears to Jackie. She grew up in foster homes and never had teddies of her own as a child. But, she admits, "I'm making up for it now!"

Big Stuff

The **largest teapot (opposite)** contained enough tea to fill 30 beer barrels, or nearly 10 bathtubs!

Tallest floating slide
On 18 Jun 2016, Baysports (IRL) presented a 6.52-m-tall (21-ft 4.7-in) inflatable water slide in Athlone, County Roscommon, Ireland. The slide is part of the Baysports Boat Training and Water Sports Centre.

▲ LARGEST BOBBLEHEAD
Applied Underwriters (USA) displayed a 15-ft 4.75-in-tall (4.69-m) bobblehead in Orlando, Florida, USA, on 8 Apr 2016. Created by scenic prop shop Dino Rentos Studios, it takes the form of a scaled-up version of a St Bernard dog, the company's mascot. The head bobs when a leash attached to the neck is pulled.

LARGEST...

Badminton racket
M Dileef (IND) created a badminton racket 16.89 m (55 ft 4.9 in) long, as verified in Kozhikode, Kerala, India, on 1 Apr 2016. The outsized implement was more than 24 times the size of a conventional badminton racket.

Bar of soap
On 11 Dec 2015, Jinan Rujia Co., Ltd (CHN) presented a soap bar weighing 14.45 tonnes (31,856 lb) – around twice the weight of an African elephant – in Jinan, Shandong, China. It had taken three months to produce.

Business card
On 14 Nov 2016, a 45-sq-ft (4.18-m²) business card – as big as a king-size bed – was unveiled by Santosh Kumar Rai (IND) in Chhattisgarh, India. It was a replica of Rai's existing business card.

Envelope
Bhanu and Aaditya Pratap Singh (both IND) exhibited a 23.93-m-long (78-ft 6-in), 13.5-m-wide (44-ft 3-in) envelope in Chhattisgarh, India, on 24 Nov 2015.

▲ **LARGEST SANDAL**
Appointed by the Municipio de Sahuayo (MEX), a group of artisans created a giant *huarache* – a type of traditional Mexican sandal – measuring 7.45 m (24 ft 5.3 in) long and 3.09 m (10 ft 1.6 in) wide. Its size was verified in Sahuayo, Michoacán, Mexico, on 24 Nov 2016. The sandal incorporated around 80 m² (861.1 sq ft) of leather.

▲ **LARGEST TEAPOT**
Measuring 4 m (13 ft 1 in) tall and 2.58 m (8 ft 5 in) in diameter at the widest part of its "belly", this giant iron teapot was created by Sultan Tea (MAR) and unveiled in Meknes, Morocco, on 27 Apr 2016. It weighs around 1,200 kg (2,645 lb). For its inauguration, 1,500 litres (396.25 US gal) of tea was prepared, using 3 kg (6 lb 9 oz) of mint.

Horseshoe
Abhishek Mazumder (IND) created a steel horseshoe 2.36 m (7 ft 8.9 in) wide and 2.47 m (8 ft 1.2 in) high, as confirmed in Mumbai, India, on 20 Nov 2016.

Hurdy-gurdy
The "Bosch Hurdy-Gurdy" instrument made by Steven Jobe (USA) measured 3.04 m (9 ft 11.6 in) long in Warren, Rhode Island, USA, on 2 Jun 2016.

Key
On 15 May 2016, Ard Canaan Restaurant (QAT) presented a 7.76-m-long (25-ft 5.5-in), 2.8-m-wide (9-ft 2.2-in) key in Doha, Qatar.

Monopoly board
Studentenvereniging Ceres (NLD) produced a 900.228-m² (9,689.97-sq-ft) Monopoly board in Wageningen, Netherlands, on 30 Nov 2016. The scaled-up board game was nearly 3,500 times larger than the standard size.

Ouija board
Blair Murphy and Team Grand Midway (USA) unveiled a 121.01-m² (1,302.54-sq-ft) Ouija board – about half the size of a tennis court – in Windber, Pennsylvania, USA, on 28 Oct 2016.

Screwdriver
Engineering student Aaditya Pratap Singh (IND) unveiled a 20-ft 9-in-long (6.32-m) screwdriver in Raipur, India, on 16 Jun 2016.

Puppet/marionette
The mascot for Ottawa's annual Italian Festival was 17.82 m (58 ft 5.5 in) tall. It was presented by the Villa Marconi Long-Term Care Center in Ottawa, Canada, on 6 Sep 2008.

Rag doll
Created by Fundación Mundo Mejor (COL), the largest rag doll measures 6.5 m (21 ft 4 in) tall. It was made for the Feria Nacional de la Niñez y su Mundo in Palmira, Valle del Cauca, Colombia, on 4 Apr 2014.

Rubik's Cube
Tony Fisher (UK) built a cube with sides measuring 1.57 m (5 ft 1.8 in), as verified in Ipswich, Suffolk, UK, on 5 Apr 2016. (See also p.257.)

Teddy bear
Constructed by Dana Warren (USA), the largest stitched teddy bear measured 55 ft 4 in (16.86 m) long. It was completed on 6 Jun 2008 and displayed at Exploration Place in Wichita, Kansas, USA.

◀ LARGEST PACK OF PLAYING CARDS

On 14 May 2016, Sweden's Claes Blixt (front) presented a pack of playing cards that measured 158.4 x 104.4 cm (5 ft 2.3 in x 3 ft 5.1 in) in Tranemo, Sweden. In total, the outsized pack – which comprised 55 playing cards altogether – weighed 200 kg (440 lb 14 oz), around the same as four real-life queens.

To prove it was genuinely rideable – and by human pedal-power alone – Jeff rode his bike down a street in Mechelen for 100 m (328 ft), as stipulated in GWR's guidelines.

▼ HEAVIEST BICYCLE

Jeff Peeters (BEL) built a bike weighing 860 kg (1,895 lb 15 oz), then rode it in Mechelen, Belgium, on 19 Aug 2015. Jeff, who has an extensive history of creating mechanical contraptions, recycled materials to make the record-breaking bicycle. Its hefty tyres once belonged to a tractor.

Rocking horse
Created by Gao Ming (CHN), the largest rocking horse measured 12.727 x 4.532 x 8.203 m (41 ft 9 in x 14 ft 10.4 in x 26 ft 10.9 in), as confirmed in Linyi, Shandong Province, China, on 7 Jul 2014.

Spinning top
A team from the Mizushima plant of Kawasaki Steel Works in Okayama, Japan, made a top 2 m (6 ft 6.75 in) tall, 2.6 m (8 ft 6.25 in) wide and weighing 360 kg (793 lb 10 oz). They spun it for 1 hr 21 min 35 sec on 3 Nov 1986.

Yo-yo
On 15 Sep 2012, Beth Johnson (USA) demonstrated a yo-yo 11 ft 10.75 in (3.62 m) in diameter and weighing 4,620 lb (2,095.6 kg) in Cincinnati, Ohio, USA. The disc plunged 120 ft (36.5 m) on a rope attached to a 150,000-lb (68-tonne) crane before rebounding.

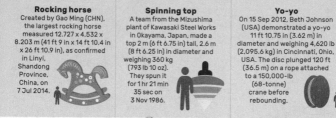

▲ LARGEST STAND-UP PADDLE SURFING BOARD

On 25 Sep 2016, Tropical (ESP) unveiled a 14.85-m-long (48-ft 8.6-in) stand-up paddle (SUP) surfboard in Playa de Las Canteras, Las Palmas de Gran Canaria, Spain. A group of 25 participants paddled it for a distance of 2 km (1.24 mi) in 40 min. Eight days earlier, at the same location, Tropical had presented the **largest inflatable lilo** (right), measuring 73.95 m² (796 sq ft).

LEGO®

• **Mammoth:** A LEGO brick mammoth 2.47 m (8 ft 1 in) tall, 3.8 m (12 ft 5 in) long and 1.3 m (4 ft 3 in) wide was built by Bright Bricks (UK) at BRICKLIVE, Birmingham, UK, on 1 Nov 2015.
• **Sculpture of a stadium:** On 12 May 2005, LEGOLAND Deutschland Resort (DEU) unveiled a 1:50-scale model of the Allianz Arena soccer stadium in Munich, Germany, made from more than 1 million LEGO bricks. Presented in Günzburg, Germany, it stood 5 m (16 ft 4 in) long, 4.5 m (14 ft 9 in) wide and 1 m (3 ft 3 in) tall.
• **Ship (supported):** Denmark's DFDS built a 12.035-m-long (39-ft 5.8-in) model ship out of LEGO bricks, as confirmed in Copenhagen, Denmark, on 17 Aug 2016.
• **Sculpture (number of bricks):** Land Rover (UK) built a model of London's Tower Bridge comprising 5,805,846 LEGO bricks, as confirmed on 28 Sep 2016. Measuring 44 m (144 ft 4.28 in) wide and 13 m (42 ft 7.81 in) tall, it stood at Packington Hall in Solihull, UK.

▶ LARGEST PRAM

Jamie Roberts and president of Kolcraft Tom Koltun (both USA) unveiled a pram with an enclosure length of 4 ft 6.3 in (1.38 m) in Chicago, Illinois, USA, on 19 Sep 2016. A scaled-up version of the Contours Bliss stroller, it allows adults to test how the pram feels before buying it! Kolcraft manufactures products for babies.

▲ LARGEST COVERED WAGON

At 40 ft (12.2 m) long, 12 ft (3.65 m) wide and 25 ft (7.6 m) tall, this scaled-up covered wagon was hand-built from Illinois oak and steel by David Bentley (USA) in 2001. Six years later, the Abraham Lincoln Tourism Bureau of Logan County, Illinois, bought the wagon for $10,000 (£6,147) and moved it from outside Bentley's home in Pawnee, Illinois, to Route 66 in Lincoln, Illinois. A 12-ft (3.6-m) fibreglass Abraham Lincoln sits on the seat. In the picture above, he is joined by Tina Rusk, from the local council's marketing department.

The power to fire the darts comes from a 3,000-lb-per-sq-in (psi) paintball tank inside the gun.

▶ LARGEST NERF GUN

Mark Rober (USA) constructed a 6-ft-long (1.82-m) Nerf gun, as verified in Sunnyvale, California, USA, on 22 Jun 2016. He also created scaled-up foam darts from pool noodles (foam floats) and sink plungers, which are ejected at a speed of around 40 mph (64.3 km/h).

Collections

From Queen Elizabeth II to former US president Franklin D Roosevelt, so many world leaders have been keen stamp collectors that it is known as the "hobby of kings".

Lip balms
As of 29 Nov 2015, Jace Hoffman of Marietta, Georgia, USA, had 553 lip balms.

The Little Mermaid memorabilia
Jacqueline Granda (ECU) had assembled 874 separate items related to the Disney animation *The Little Mermaid* in Quito, Ecuador, by 16 Jan 2016.

Journey to the West memorabilia
There were 1,508 individual *Journey to the West*-themed items in the collection of actor Liu Xiao Ling Tong (CHN) as of 30 Jan 2016. They are stored in Huai'an, Jiangsu, China.

The Legend of Zelda memorabilia
As of 14 Jul 2016, Anne Martha Harnes (NOR) owned 1,816 pieces of memorabilia relating to videogame series *The Legend of Zelda*, as verified in Molde, Norway.

Police hats
Andreas Skala (DEU) had assembled a collection of 2,534 unique police hats as of 31 Dec 2015. The hoard of headwear was counted and confirmed in Hennigsdorf, Germany.

Tomb Raider memorabilia
Spain's Rodrigo Martín Santos had amassed 3,050 distinct pieces of *Tomb Raider* memorabilia as of 26 Sep 2016 in Madrid, Spain.

Candy wrappers
As of 23 Dec 2015, the most extensive collection of candy wrappers numbered 5,065 items. It belongs to Milan Lukich Valdivia of Tacna, Peru. He began collecting around 32 years ago.

Crocodile-related items
By 2 Sep 2015, Andrew Gray (UK) had snapped up 6,739 crocodile-themed objects in Burton Latimer, Northamptonshire, UK.

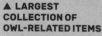

▲ LARGEST COLLECTION OF OWL-RELATED ITEMS
As of 4 Aug 2016, Yaakov Chai of Tel Aviv, Israel, owned 19,100 owl-related objects. Sadly, Yaakov passed away before the collection was verified. Friends and loved ones subsequently donated more owls, bringing the total to 20,239.

Espionage-related items
Author and military intelligence historian H Keith Melton (USA) owns more than 7,000 spy-related objects, including cameras, concealment devices and various other items of espionage gadgetry. So secret is the collection that we cannot reveal its location!

Mickey Mouse memorabilia
By 29 Apr 2016, Janet Esteves (USA) had collected 10,210 unique items of Mickey Mouse memorabilia, as verified in Katy, Texas, USA.

Winnie the Pooh memorabilia
Deb Hoffmann of Waukesha, Wisconsin, USA, had accumulated 13,213 objects with a Winnie the Pooh theme as of 18 Oct 2015.

Cow-related items
By 9 Jun 2015, Ruth Klossner (USA) owned 15,144 items related to cows, as verified in Lafayette, Minnesota, USA.

Banana-related memorabilia
Ken Bannister (USA), owner of the International Banana Club Museum in Altadena, California, USA, has collected 17,000 banana-related articles since 1972. They are all on display in his museum.

Pokémon memorabilia
As verified on 10 Aug 2016, Lisa Courtney of Welwyn Garden City, UK, has put together 17,127 items that relate to Pokémon.

First screened in 1973, The Wombles was a UK children's TV show that promoted the idea of recycling. Gill clearly got the message: she is now an environmental scientist working on sustainable living.

▼ WOMBLES MEMORABILIA
Gill Seyfang (UK) had amassed 1,703 individual items of Wombles memorabilia by 7 Aug 2016, as verified in Norwich, Norfolk, UK. Gill is particularly fond of her original Womble-themed 1970s bathroom toiletry sets with shaped soaps, bubble bath and talcum powder, which have survived intact for more than 40 years.

Q: US actor Nicolas Cage is a big collector. Of what?

A: Comic books. He reportedly spent $1 million on them at 2016's Amazing Las Vegas Comic Con.

▼ MONOPOLY SETS

As featured on BBC TV's *The One Show*, Neil Scallan (UK) owned 1,677 separate Monopoly board games as of 27 Jul 2016. All of the items are officially released sets and still sealed. Neil divides the storage of his collection between Hayes in Middlesex and Crawley in West Sussex, UK.

Paw prints

RedPepper Agency and Area Metropolitana del Valle de Aburrá (both COL) took 22,429 prints from various animals as part of the Huellatón campaign, to raise awareness of the harmful effects that fireworks have on animals. The count took place in Medellín, Colombia, on 4 Oct 2015.

◄ DOCTOR WHO MEMORABILIA

Lily Connors (UK) had assembled a total of 6,641 different *Doctor Who*-related items as of 20 Jun 2016. Her collection was counted in Pontypridd, UK. It's a terrific achievement, but Lily wants to go further: her dream is to be an extra in an episode of *Doctor Who* and to own a full-sized Dalek.

Record-breaking runs in this family: Lily's brother Thomas holds multiple GWR records for basketball tricks, including **longest time spinning three basketballs** (7.5 sec) and **most backward free throws in one minute** (nine).

ALL-TIME LARGEST COLLECTIONS

1. Matchbook covers: 3,159,119 – Ed Brassard (USA)

2. Human teeth: 2,000,744 – Brother Giovanni Battista Orsenigo (ITA)

3. Books: 1,500,000 – John Q Benham (USA)

4. Matchbox labels: 1,054,221 – Steven Smith (UK)

5. Beer labels: 548,567 – Hendrik Thomann (DEU)

6. Buttons: 439,900 – Dalton Stevens (USA)

7. Scratchcards: 319,011 – Darren Haake (AUS)

8. Ball-point pens: 285,150 – Angelika Unverhau (DEU)

9. Cigar bands: 211,104 – Alfred Manthe (DEU)

10. Bus tickets: 200,000 – Ladislav Šejnoha (CZE)

11. Racing pigeon rings: 164,023 – Christian Hennek (DEU)

12. Train tickets: 163,235 – Frank Helker (DEU)

13. Beer mats: 152,860 – Leo Pisker (AUT)

14=. Magic artefacts: 150,000 – David Copperfield (USA)

14=. Paper and plastic bags: 150,000 – Heinz Schmidt-Bachem (DEU)

16. Cigarette packets: 143,027 – Claudio Rebecchi (ITA)

17. Napkins: 125,866 – Martina Schellenberg (DEU)

18. Nightclub flyers: 113,012 – Marco Brusadelli (ITA)

19. Four-leaf clovers: 111,060 – Edward Martin Sr (USA)

20. Bookmarks: 103,009 – Frank Divendal (NLD)

Corkscrews

Romania's Ion Chirescu has 23,965 corkscrews, as confirmed in Bucharest on 18 Jun 2015.

Ion also owns the **largest collection of irons**, from different countries and periods. It comprised 30,071 items as of 3 Aug 2016.

Model cars

By 9 Jun 2016, Nabil Karam (LBN) owned 37,777 model cars, as verified in Zouk Mosbeh, Lebanon.

Coins from the same year

Samirbhai Patel (AUS) has 51,504 Australian five-cent pieces, all from 2006. His collection was confirmed on 22 Aug 2015 in Perth, Australia.

Wendy's first snow globe – given to her by her husband – has a grey cat on the outside and a mouse inside.

▼ **SNOW GLOBES**

Wendy Suen (CAN/CHN, b. HKG) has collected 4,059 individual snow globes, as verified on 27 Nov 2016 in Shanghai, China. She started her collection in 2000 and this is the second time she has surpassed her own record, having increased her hoard substantially since she first achieved the feat with 904 snow globes in 2005.

Big Food

The patty in a fast-food hamburger may contain the meat from up to 100 different cows.

Largest sushi mosaic

On 18 Sep 2016, a 56.50-m² (608.16-sq-ft) mosaic of sushi was created by Leonardo Figueroa Aguilar, Salten Aqua AS, Rå:Bra Sushi, Du Verden Restaurant, Svolvær, AMJ Gruppen Bodø, Glimt, Køltzow and Sparebank1 Nord-Norge (all NOR). It was displayed in Aspyrma Stadion, Bodo, Norway.

This record-breaking drink contained the same volume of liquid as around 60 bathtubs.

HEAVIEST...

Naan bread: Loblaw Companies Limited (CAN) presented a 32-kg (70-lb 8.7-oz) naan bread in Toronto, Ontario, Canada, on 19 Apr 2016.

Muffin: On 16 Oct 2015, Schär and NIP Food (both ITA) served up a muffin weighing 146.65 kg (323 lb) in Milan, Italy.

◀ LARGEST ICED TEA

At 2,523.9 US gal (9,554 litres), the most voluminous iced tea was made by the town of Summerville in South Carolina, USA, on 10 Jun 2016. It was brewed using 210 lb (95.2 kg) of loose-leaf tea and 1,700 lb (771.1 kg) of sugar. Organizers initially used 300 lb (136 kg) of ice to chill the tea. This failed to reduce the beverage to the temperature of 45°F (7.2°C) required by GWR's rules, however, so hundreds of pounds of extra ice were added.

World's Largest Sweet Tea Summerville SOUTH CAROLINA

Q: In 16th-century Denmark, cheese was not just a food. What else was it used as?

A: Currency

Profiterole: Italian companies Associazione Cons.erva, Etica Del Gusto, Despar, Uova Pascolo Fantoni and Crespi made a 150-kg (330-lb 11-oz) profiterole – half the weight of a grand piano – at Gemona del Friuli in Udine, Italy, on 17 Apr 2016.

Vegan cake: Skipp Communications AG and Merz AG (both CHE) created a 433.56-kg (955-lb 13.3-oz) cake that contained no animal products whatsoever. It was presented and weighed in Chur, Switzerland, on 16 Jun 2016.

Halwa: Weighing 630 kg (1,388 lb 15 oz), heavier than an adult polar bear, the largest halwa was created by Al Hosni Omani Sweets and Murshid bin Sulaiman Al Hosni (both OMN) in Muscat, Oman, on 23 Nov 2015.

Box of biscuits: Oreo (USA) and Tmall (CHN) unveiled a 904.58-kg (1,994-lb 4.1-oz) box of biscuits – around the same as 70 gold bars – at Super Brand Day in Beijing, China, on 3 May 2016.

Box of chocolate bars: Meiji Corporation (JPN) displayed a 2,044-kg (4,506-lb 3.9-oz) box of chocolate in Tokyo, Japan, on 29 Jan 2016.

Tiramisu: Weighing in at 3,015 kg (6,646 lb) – nearly 50 times heavier than the average man – the largest tiramisu was prepared by Associazione Cons.erva with Despar, Latte Blanc, Caffè Toto and Uova Pascolo (all ITA) in Gemona del Friuli, Italy, on 25 May 2015.

▲ TALLEST ICE-CREAM CONE
Hennig-Olsen Is AS and Trond L Wøien (both NOR) presented a 3.08-m-tall (10-ft 1.2-in) ice-cream cone – about half the height of an adult giraffe – at Kristiansand, Norway, on 26 Jul 2015. It comprised a 95.85-kg (211-lb 5-oz) wafer cone, 60 kg (132 lb 4 oz) of chocolate lining, 1,080 litres (285.3 US gal) of ice-cream and 40 kg (88 lb 3 oz) of jam.

Laddu: On 6 Sep 2016, PVVS Mallikharjuna Rao (IND) served up a version of this round Indian sweet weighing 29,465 kg (64,959 lb 3 oz) – about four times the weight of an African elephant – in Tapeswaram, Andhra Pradesh, India.

LARGEST SERVING OF...

Pulled pork: Sonny's BBQ (USA) presented 2,012 lb (912.62 kg) of pulled pork at Central Park in Winter Park, Florida, USA, on 12 Oct 2016.

Mashed potato: Jason Lin, Colin Stockdale, Tyler Hubeny and Evan Armstrong (all USA) presented 2,641 lb (1,197.94 kg) of mashed potato – similar to the weight of a walrus – in Binghamton, New York, USA, on 20 Jun 2015.

Heaviest gingerbread man

651 kg (1,435 lb 3 oz)

Tallest chocolate Father Christmas (hollow)

5 m (16 ft 4.85 in)

Largest candy cane

36 ft 7 in (11.15 m) long, 4 in (10.1 cm) in diameter

Heaviest Christmas dinner

9.6 kg (21 lb 2.6 oz), comprising a turkey, carrots, parsnips, broccoli and cauliflower pieces, roast potatoes, "pigs in blankets" and 25 sprouts

Heaviest Christmas pudding

3.28 tonnes (7,231 lb 2 oz)

Heaviest Yule log

2,490 kg (5,489 lb 8 oz)

▲ LONGEST PIZZA

Napoli Pizza Village (ITA) baked a pizza 1,853.88 m (6,082 ft 3.4 in) long in Naples, Italy, on 18 May 2016. In all, 250 masters of traditional Neapolitan pizza gathered from all over the world – some from as far away as Australia – for the attempt. The recipe included 2,000 kg (4,400 lb) of flour, 1,600 kg (3,527 lb 6 oz) of tomatoes, 2,000 kg of fiordilatte cheese and 200 litres (52.8 US gal) of olive oil, all from local suppliers.

Quinoa: The Comité Organizador FEGASUR 2016 and La Municipalidad Provincial San Roman (both PER) produced a 1,680.2-kg (3,704-lb 3.3-oz) serving of quinoa in Juliaca, Peru, on 18 Jun 2016. The average US car weighs about the same.

Rice pudding: On behalf of the Shree Parshwa Padmavathi Seva Trust, His Holiness Dr Vasanth Vijayji Maharaj (IND) served up 2,070 kg (4,563 lb 9 oz) of rice pudding in Krishnagiri, Tamil Nadu, India, on 31 May 2015.

Gumbo: Braud & Gallagher (USA) cooked up 5,800 lb (2,630 kg) of this signature Creole dish in Larose, Louisiana, USA, on 7 Nov 2015. That's almost six times the weight of one of the American alligators found in the area.

▲ LARGEST DISPLAY OF CHEESE VARIETIES

Brigitta Bonino (CHE) produced a display of 590 varieties of cheese in Thörishaus, Bern, Switzerland, on 21 May 2016. The display consisted entirely of Swiss cheeses. Brigitta owns a cheese shop called Chäsi Thörishaus, and she attempted the record in celebration of its 25th anniversary.

The **largest cheese platter** weighed 1,531.27 kg (3,375 lb 13.9 oz) and was prepared by Bel Leerdammer (NLD) in Leerdam, Utrecht, Netherlands, on 11 Sep 2015.

Grilled chicken: On 27 Feb 2016, Simplemente Parrilla La Balanza (URY) grilled 6,487.9 kg (14,303 lb 6 oz) of chicken in Maldonado, Uruguay – half the weight of a London double-decker bus.

Roast pork: Fundación Produce Yucatán, A C (MEX) served up 6,626.15 kg (14,608 lb 2.5 oz) of pork in Mérida, Yucatán, Mexico, on 6 Mar 2016. This is more than three times the weight of an adult great white shark.

▲ LARGEST GLASS OF SPRITZ

At 1,000.25 litres (264.23 US gal), this outsized sparkling drink was prepared by Costa Crociere (ITA) on 10 May 2016. The attempt took place during the trade event Protagonisti del Mare, on board the *Costa Favolosa* cruise ship en route from Barcelona in Spain to Marseille in France.

The **largest glass of mojito** measured 3,519 litres (929.6 US gal) – about the same volume as 60 beer kegs – and was achieved by 4-Jack's Bar & Bistro (DOM) in Punta Cana, Dominican Republic, on 16 Apr 2016.

▲ MOST BUILDINGS IN A GINGERBREAD VILLAGE

There are 1,102 buildings in the gingerbread village shown above, which was constructed by Jon Lovitch (USA). It was displayed at the New York Hall of Science in Corona, New York City, USA, on 17 Nov 2015.

The **largest gingerbread village by area** measured 45.29 m² (487.49 sq ft). It was unveiled by El Dorado Royale by Karisma (MEX) in Playa del Carmen, Quintana Roo, Mexico, on 11 Dec 2015. Based on actual buildings in towns on the Yucatán Peninsula, it comprised 216 buildings spread over 27 blocks, and was completed by 16 chefs.

◀ LARGEST TIN OF CAVIAR

On 28 Dec 2016, AmStur Caviar of Dubai (UAE) unveiled a tin of caviar weighing 17.82 kg (39 lb 4.58 oz) at Dubai's Burj Al Arab Jumeirah hotel. Named "The Mashenomak", after a spirit monster fish of Native American legend, the entire tin of Empress organic caviar was devoured by the hotel guests, who ate from specially engraved mother-of-pearl spoons.

▲ LARGEST PRETZEL

Parent company Industrias La Constancia and its brand Pilsener (both SLV) produced a 783.81-kg (1,728-lb) pretzel on 25 Oct 2015 at CIFCO in San Salvador, El Salvador. That makes the gigantic baked snack more than 4,600 times heavier than an ordinary 170-g (6-oz) pretzel, or the same weight as the heart of a blue whale. The pretzel measured 8.93 m (29 ft 3 in) long by 4.06 m (13 ft 3 in) wide.

▼ LARGEST BUTTER SCULPTURE

On 26 Sep 2015, Lactalis American Group, Inc. (USA) presented a 2,370-lb (1,075-kg) butter sculpture in New York City, USA. Made from Président butter and constructed without any internal or external supports, the sculpture was modelled after the Parisian skyline. It featured famous landmarks of the city such as the Eiffel Tower, Notre Dame and the Arc de Triomphe.

Fun with Food

Never take on a bird in a chili-eating contest: only mammals feel the fiery heat of peppers such as the Carolina Reaper.

▲ TALLEST PANCAKE STACK

Center Parcs Sherwood Forest (UK) put together a 101.8-cm-tall (3-ft 4-in) pancake stack in Rufford, Newark, UK, on 8 Feb 2016. The pile comprised 213 pancakes, which were made and stacked by James Haywood and Dave Nicholls (both UK).

Largest dirt cake
On 31 Jul 2016, the Bangalore Baking Buddies (IND) made a dirt cake weighing 1,078 kg (2,376 lb 9.33 oz) at the Park hotel in Bangalore, Karnataka, India. It took more than 10 hr to make and included 550 kg (1,212 lb) of crushed cookies. It was later distributed to local schools.

Largest hamburger
Black Bear Casino Resort (USA) made a 2,014-lb (913.54-kg) hamburger in Carlton, Minnesota, USA, on 2 Sep 2012. Its topping included 52 lb 8 oz (23.81 kg) of tomatoes, 50 lb (22.68 kg) of lettuce, 60 lb (27.22 kg) of onions, 40 lb (18.14 kg) of cheese and 16 lb 8 oz (7.48 kg) of bacon.

Largest serving of beshbarmak
A dish of chopped meat and noodles, beshbarmak means "five fingers" (it would traditionally be eaten by hand). On 6 Jul 2015, the Kazakh Geographic Society (KAZ) made a beshbarmak weighing 736.5 kg (1,623 lb 11.27 oz) – heavier than a dromedary – in Astana, Kazakhstan.

▲ MOST CAROLINA REAPER CHILIS EATEN IN ONE MINUTE
On 13 Nov 2016, Gregory Foster (USA) ate 120 g (4.23 oz)of Carolina Reaper chilis. Foster was one of nine contestants in an event organized by PuckerButt Pepper Company at the Arizona Hot Sauce Expo in Tempe, Arizona, USA.

Takeru's trademark move is the "Kobayashi shake". He wriggles while eating to settle the food in his gut.

▲ MOST HAMBURGERS EATEN IN 3 MINUTES

Competitive eater Takeru Kobayashi (JPN) munched his way through 12 hamburgers in 3 min on the set of *Lo Show dei Record* in Milan, Italy, on 11 Jul 2014. Each meat patty weighed 113 g (4 oz), pre-cooked, while the bun weighed in at 50 g (1.76 oz). Takeru's other feats include the **most hot dogs eaten in three minutes** – six, on 25 Aug 2009 – and the **most meatballs eaten in one minute** – 29, on 8 Mar 2010.

Largest burrito

On 3 Nov 2010, CANIRAC La Paz created a burrito weighing 5,799.44 kg (12,785 lb 9 oz) in La Paz, Baja California Sur, Mexico. Filled with fish, onion and refried beans, it was made from a single flour tortilla that weighed more than 2,000 kg (4,409 lb) and measured 2.4 km (1.49 mi) long.

▼ MOST CANDLES ON A CAKE

On 27 Aug 2016, Ashrita Furman and the Sri Chinmoy Centre (both USA) decorated a cake with 72,585 candles in New York City, USA. The cake was in honour of meditation teacher Sri Chinmoy, on what would have been his 85th birthday. It topped the previous mark of 50,151 candles, set by Mike's Hard Lemonade in Los Angeles, California, USA, on 13 Apr 2016.

Q: What is the most popular pizza topping in the USA?

A: Pepperoni.

Largest commercially available pizza

"The Giant Sicilian" has an area of 20 sq ft (1.87 m²) and is sold at Big Mama's and Papa's Pizzeria in Los Angeles, California, USA. It can be made with any topping, and is delivered in its own giant-sized box.

Longest tamale

The Municipalidad Distrital de San Luis de Shuaro (PER) made a tamale measuring 39.55 m (129 ft 9 in) in San Luis de Shuaro, Chanchamayo, Junín, Peru, on 21 Jun 2016 – longer than a blue whale.

Longest relay of people feeding each other

On 11 Dec 2016, a total of 1,101 people flocked to the Tsugaru fresh apple market in the town of Itayanagi in Kitatsugaru, Aomori, Japan, and fed each other fresh apples. Itayanagi has been the home of Japanese apple production since 1875, and produces around 26,000 tons (23,586 tonnes) of fruit every year.

Tallest cake pyramid

On 11 Nov 2016, Stratford University constructed a cake pyramid measuring 2.79 m (9 ft 2 in) tall at Potomac Mills mall in Woodbridge, Virginia, USA. It contained more than 8,000 lb (3,628.7 kg) of sheet cake (flat, rectangular cakes) and had no internal support. The pyramid was made in honour of the institution's 40th anniversary.

Largest chocolate-tasting event

Fundación Nuestra Tierra hosted a chocolate-tasting event at the Expoferia Internacional del Chocolate 2016 in Caracas, Venezuela. A total of 419 people tried three brands of artisanal Venezuelan chocolate on 1 Oct 2016.

▲ TALLEST MARZIPAN STRUCTURE

To commemorate the 400th anniversary of the death of author Miguel de Cervantes (ESP), the city of Toledo in Spain manufactured a marzipan statue of his legendary comic hero Don Quixote. Unveiled on 23 Apr 2016, the statue measured 3.59 m (11 ft 9 in). It took 300 hr to make, and used 770 lb (349 kg) of almonds.

▶ MOST SAUSAGES PRODUCED IN ONE MINUTE

On 20 Jul 2016, Tim Brown (UK) produced 60 sausages in 60 sec in Moodiesburn, North Lanarkshire, UK. Family butcher Brown teamed up with sausage-casing producer Devro to take a tilt at the record, which had previously stood at 44. Witnesses described Brown's sausages as "delicious".

MOST EATEN IN ONE MINUTE...

Apple sauce:
1,163 g (2 lb 9 oz)
André Ortolf (DEU),
7 Oct 2016

Marshmallows:
25
Anthony Falzon
(MLT), 25 Mar
2013

Gyoza
dumplings: 10
Pete Czerwinski
(CAN), 16 May
2016

Baby food:
590 g (20.81 oz)
Abdulrahman
Abood Eid (KWT),
16 Mar 2013

Sponge cakes:
16
Patrick
Bertoletti (USA),
26 Jun 2013

◄ MOST BAKED BEANS EATEN WITH CHOPSTICKS IN ONE MINUTE

On 1 Jul 2015, Mr Cherry, aka Cherry Yoshitake (JPN), ate 71 baked beans in 60 sec – one bean at a time – using chopsticks. The record took place on the set of *Officially Amazing* at RAF Bentwaters in Suffolk, UK. He saw off two challengers – "Sizzling" Steve Kish and US Ray (aka Ray Butler) – who ate 65 and 36 baked beans respectively.

Most people eating breakfast in bed

On 16 Aug 2015, a total of 418 guests at the Sheraton Langfang Chaobai River Hotel in Langfang, Hebei, China, dined in bed. This beat the previous record of 388, set by the Pudong Shangri-La in East Shanghai, China.

Fastest time to make an omelette

Cookery TV show *Saturday Kitchen* (UK) challenges chefs to make a three-egg omelette in the fastest possible time. On 2 May 2015, Theo Randall (UK) set a mark of 14.76 sec live on set at Cactus Studios in London, UK.

Fastest time to drink a pint of milk

On 26 Jul 2015, James McMillan (NZ) drank a pint of milk in 3.97 sec in Christchurch, New Zealand. The calcium-rich record was set on the GWR Challengers website.

On 17 May 2016, Dennis "The Menace" Bermudez (USA) achieved the **fastest time to drink one litre of lemon juice through a straw** – 22.75 sec, in New York City, USA.

◄ FASTEST TIME TO DRINK A BOTTLE OF KETCHUP

On 17 Feb 2012, German TV reporter Benedikt Weber downed a bottle of ketchup in 32.37 sec, for the infotainment programme *Galileo*, at Chong's Diner in Nuremberg, Germany. During the attempt, Weber used a drinking straw measuring 0.60 cm (0.23 in) in diameter.

Creme Eggs: 6
Pete Czerwinski
(CAN), 11 Apr 2014

Ferrero Rocher: 9
Pete Czerwinski
(CAN), 4 Jan 2012
Patrick Bertoletti
(USA), 14 Jan 2012

Grapes: 73
Dinesh Shivnath
Upadhyaya (IND),
7 Jun 2014

Hamburgers: 5
Ricardo Francisco,
aka Rix Terabite
(PHL), 27 Aug 2016

Jaffa Cakes: 17
Pete Czerwinski
(CAN),
9 Jan 2013

Most drink cans balanced on the head

John Evans (UK) balanced 429 drink cans on his head at Ilkeston School in Derbyshire, UK, on 5 Jun 2007. The cans weighed 173 kg (381 lb 6 oz) – the same as two average-sized adult men.

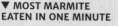

▼ MOST MARMITE EATEN IN ONE MINUTE

On 7 Sep 2016, André Ortolf (DEU) ate 252 g (8.8 oz) of Marmite in Augsburg, Germany. He beat the previous record of 218 g (7.6 oz), set by his hero Ashrita Furman (USA) on 16 May 2012.

Record-hungry André also achieved the **most mashed potato eaten in 30 sec**, wolfing down 598 g (21.09 oz) in Augsburg on 17 Jun 2016.

Mass Participation

GWR's smallest mass participation record is for the **most people crammed into a swimming cap (4)**, set by Team Badekappe in Mainz, Germany, in 2015.

Largest gathering of dancing dragons
Dance troupe Persatuan Tarian Naga Dan Singa Qi Ling Malaysia assembled 99 dancing dragons (steered by 990 dancers) in Shah Alam, Malaysia, on 15 Nov 2015.

Largest gathering of Lottery millionaires
The National Lottery (UK) brought together 110 of these extremely lucky people in London, UK, on 7 Oct 2015. Their combined winnings came to £646 m ($980.4 m)!

Most people on one scale
On 8 Jan 2016, public-health campaign Scale Back Alabama (USA) persuaded 157 Alabamians to check their collective weight on a truck weigh-station scale in Montgomery, Alabama. The participants weighed in at a total of 30,400 lb (13,789 kg), or roughly 193 lb (87 kg) each.

Most people dressed as ninjas
On 17 Apr 2016, a group of 268 ninjas stood out in the open long enough not only to be seen but also counted. The ninjas were lured to Jyosei Elementary School in Hikone, Shiga, Japan, by Kuniko Teramura and friends (all JPN).

▼ MOST PEOPLE CRAMMED IN A VW CAMPERVAN (CLASSIC MODEL)
To count everyone involved in a mass participation record, we usually employ checkpoints, lots of stewards and football-pitch-sized holding areas. This record, however, achieved by Comfort Insurance (UK) in Malvern, UK, on 5 Sep 2015, was far easier to adjudicate. A handful of stewards simply stood by and counted as all 50 campervan passengers climbed out.

Largest gathering of organ transplant recipients

The Donate Life Run/Walk (USA), a charity event held on the campus of California State University in Fullerton, USA, attracted 314 organ transplant recipients on 30 Apr 2016.

Most people dressed as dogs

Farm insurance firm NFU Mutual (UK) hosted a gathering of 439 people in one-piece dog costumes to promote the Guide Dogs for the Blind Association (UK). The charity attempt took place in Stratford-upon-Avon, UK, on 20 Apr 2016.

Most people playing Monopoly

To mark World Monopoly Day on 19 Mar 2016, Universal Studios in Singapore organized for 605 people to play the board game simultaneously.

Most people dressed as penguins

For Guinness World Records Day on 12 Nov 2015, Richard House Children's Hospice (UK) brought together 624 people dressed as penguins at The Scoop in London, UK.

▲ LARGEST GATHERING OF PEOPLE DRESSED AS *DOCTOR WHO* CHARACTERS

Science fiction TV channel Syfy Latinoamérica (USA) scoured the halls of La Mole Comic-Con in Mexico City, Mexico, to bring together an army of 492 Cybermen, Daleks, companions, Oods, Weeping Angels and, of course, various regenerations of the famous Time Lord. The attempt took place on 19 Mar 2016 and the 12th Doctor himself, Peter Capaldi (top), was on hand to accept the certificate.

▲ LARGEST GATHERING OF PEOPLE DRESSED AS FRUIT

On 18 Jul 2015, eccentric DJ duo Dada Life (Olle Cornéer and Stefan Engblom, both SWE) persuaded 629 attendees of their Citizens of Dada Land event in San Bernardino, California, USA, to show up dressed as bananas. The duo are known for their playful live events; in 2013, they and their audience broke the record for the **largest pillow fight** (with 3,813 participants) – a record that stood for just under a year.

AT CHRISTMAS

Largest gathering of...

Snowmen
398
Buttercrane Shopping
Centre (UK), 17 Nov 2016

Angels
1,275
Misericordia Health
Centre Foundation
(CAN), 1 Dec 2015

Santa's elves
1,762
Siam Paragon Development
Company Limited (THA),
25 Nov 2014

**Christmas
jumpers**
3,473
Kansas Athletics
(USA), 19 Dec 2015

Santas
18,112
Thrissur Archdiocese
(IND), 27 Dec 2014

Carol singers
25,272
Godswill Akpabio
Unity Choir (NGA),
13 Dec 2014

Most people keeping a football aloft
Italian sporting goods manufacturer Diadora recruited 1,406 youth soccer players with a knack for keepie-uppies for an event held to mark the launch of their new football boots. The attempt was made at Diadora's headquarters in Caerano di San Marco, Italy, on 7 May 2016.

Most people holding the abdominal plank position
On 6 Nov 2016, a total of 1,623 people held the abdominal plank position at the Jio Garden in the Bandra Kurla Complex, Mumbai, India.

Most people wearing antlers
On 26 Mar 2016, a group of 1,731 fans of Chinese megastar Lu Han (whose name roughly translates as "deer of the dawn") attended his concert in Beijing, China, wearing glow-in-the-dark antlers.

Most people using selfie sticks
During a pause in the 6 May 2016 baseball game between the Los Angeles Angels and the Tampa Bay Rays in Anaheim, California, USA, 2,121 people used selfie sticks to snap a picture of themselves.

Most models on a catwalk
Showcasing every fashion choice from flowing ball gowns to Darth Vader costumes, 3,651 people strutted down a catwalk set up by Culture Liverpool and very.co.uk (both UK) in Pier Head, Liverpool, UK, on 4 Jul 2015.

For a mass skipping record to count, everyone must clear the rope at least 12 times, according to GWR rules.

▲ MOST PEOPLE BRUSHING THEIR TEETH

Having been supplied with a toothbrush, toothpaste and a cup of water by My Dental Plan (IND), an astonishing 16,414 people set a new record for simultaneous tooth-scrubbing on 7 Jan 2016. The attempt was held on the sports ground of Delhi Public School (East Campus) in Karnataka, India. All participants were required to follow the World Health Organization's favoured tooth-brushing technique, which involves a minimum of a minute's brushing.

Most people singing in a round

A choir of 4,166 people performed a four-part song entitled "Forward Only Forward, My Dear Country Turkmenistan" at the opening event of the Turkmen's Ak Öÿü cultural centre in Mary, Turkmenistan, on 26 Nov 2015.

Most people wearing clogs

The playgrounds of Nantun Elementary School in Taichung, Taiwan, echoed to the sound of 5,008 clog-wearing people clad in traditional costume on 20 Jun 2015.

Most people wearing false moustaches

On 29 Nov 2015, a total of 6,471 Denver Broncos fans attended their team's American football game against the New England Patriots wearing bright orange false moustaches – the Broncos' colour – in Denver, Colorado, USA.

▲ MOST PEOPLE SKIPPING ON THE SAME ROPE

The students of Wat Lam Nao School (THA) set a new jump-rope record in Bangkok, Thailand, on 11 Jan 2016. Not one of the 300 students who took part touched the rope (which means disqualification), even though they performed more than twice the minimum number of jumps.

▲ LARGEST GATHERING OF PEOPLE DRESSED AS ELEPHANTS

Family bereavement charity 2 Wish Upon a Star (UK) gathered a herd of 385 polyester elephants in Cardiff's Principality Stadium on 13 Aug 2016. The charity was founded by Rhian Burke (UK) following the loss of her infant son, George, and her husband, Paul, within a week of each other, and has an elephant named "Gorgeous George" as its mascot. The aim of the event was to raise awareness of family bereavement services in Wales and the UK as a whole.

▲ LARGEST GATHERING OF PEOPLE WEARING HAND PUPPETS

On 14 May 2016, San Diego Zoo (USA) spokesman Dr Zoolittle performed a 2-min 45-sec reenactment of the founding of the zoo, aided by a supporting cast of 508 lion hand puppets. The lions recreated the dramatic roar that inspired zoo founder Harry Wegeforth to bring exotic animals to his town. The performance was part of a series of events organized to mark the world-famous zoo's centennial.

▲ LARGEST GATHERING OF STEAMPUNKS

Brought together by their love of Victorian clothing, brass and attaching things to hats, 228 devotees of steampunk culture attended the Steampunk New Zealand Festival in Oamaru on 4 Jun 2016. Steampunk is a science-fiction genre characterized by a re-imagining of the modern world using the gears, smoke and steam engines of the Industrial Age.

Odd Talents

When it comes to a talent for record-breaking, Ashrita Furman (USA) remains the greatest. More than 550 records broken, and counting...

Fastest time to duck tape (duct tape) a person to the wall

Ashrita Furman taped Alec Wilkinson (both USA) to a wall in 26.69 sec at the Sri Chinmoy Centre in New York City, USA, on 9 Jun 2015. It was the sixth time that Ashrita had broken this record.

Ashrita is also responsible for the **fastest time to duck tape (duct tape) yourself to a wall** – 2 min 12.63 sec, also achieved at the Sri Chinmoy Centre, on 5 Oct 2011.

Fastest sport stacking individual cycle stack

William Orrell (USA) broke the 5-sec sport stacking cycle stack barrier for the first time on 7 Jan 2017, recording a time of 4.813 sec in Columbus, Georgia, USA. William also holds the record for the **fastest sport stacking individual 3-3-3 stack**: 1.363 sec, achieved in Eatonton, Georgia, USA, on 14 Nov 2015.

On 18–19 Oct 2013, Mohammed Sahraoui (DEU) of the SST Butzbach club completed the **most sport stacking cycle stacks in 24 hours**: 4,719. The record attempt took place at the ninth Sportkongress staged in Stuttgart, Baden-Württemberg, Germany.

MOST...

Lit candles in the mouth

On 10 Jul 2016, Dinesh Shivnath Upadhyaya (IND) stuffed 17 lit candles in his mouth in his home city of Mumbai, India.

He followed up with the record for the **most blueberries stuffed into the mouth** – 70, recorded on 25 Jul 2016.

Dinesh had previously set the **fastest time to peel and eat three oranges** – 1 min 7.94 sec – on 25 Feb 2016.

▲ **HEAVIEST STACK OF BOTTLE CRATES BALANCED ON CHIN**

On 13 Jan 2016, Sun Chaoyang (CHN) balanced a 44.2-kg (97-lb 7-oz) stack of bottle crates on the set of *CCTV – Guinness World Records Special* in Beijing, China. The previous best was 42.40 kg (93 lb 7 oz), set by Ashrita Furman in 2006.

Sun also holds the record for **most bicycles balanced on the chin** – three, on 8 Dec 2011.

Bowling balls stacked vertically

Shen Xiaoshi (CHN) vertically stacked 10 bowling balls without the use of adhesive on 8 Jan 2016, in front of the audience of *CCTV – Guinness World Records Special* in Beijing, China. It took Shen more than 2 hr to complete his stack, which collapsed when he tried to add an 11th ball. He equalled the mark set by Dave Kremer (USA) in Los Angeles, California, USA, on 19 Nov 1998.

Cream-filled biscuits stacked in 30 seconds

Mr Cherry, aka Cherry Yoshitake (JPN), stacked 26 cream-filled biscuits in half a minute on the set of CBBC's *Officially Amazing* programme in Glasgow, UK, on 22 Nov 2016. He edged out rival Stephen "Sizzling Steve" Kish, who had managed 25 in the same time.

Also on *Officially Amazing*, acrobatic group Acropolis (UK) completed the **most skips over a human skipping rope in one minute**: 48, achieved on 18 Oct 2016 at Durham Cathedral in County Durham, UK.

Head spins in a wind tunnel in one minute

On 6 Dec 2016, a trio of skydiving records were attempted across Australia and broadcast on *Facebook Live*. At iFLY Indoor Skydiving Downunder in Sydney, New South Wales, Australia, Kurmet Jaadla (EST) achieved 54 head spins in 60 sec.

At iFLY Indoor Skydiving Perth in Western Australia, instructor David Hyndman (AUS) managed the **longest distance run on the wall of a vertical wind tunnel in one minute** – 227.89 m (747 ft 8 in).

Meanwhile, at iFLY Indoor Skydiving Gold Coast in Queensland, 11-year-old Amy Watson achieved the **most 360 horizontal spins in one minute (individual)**, with her mark of 44 smashing the previous best of 26.

Swim caps put on in one minute

André Ortolf (DEU) put on 26 swim caps in 60 sec in his home town of Augsburg, Germany, on 16 May 2016.

◄ FASTEST TIME TO BUILD A 171-CUP PYRAMID

On 3 Jan 2017, James Acraman (UK) returned to GWR HQ in London to take another shot at the 171-cup stacking record, having missed out by just 5 sec on a previous attempt on 1 Dec 2016. This time, watched by thousands of viewers on *Facebook Live*, James successfully completed a pyramid with an 18-cup bottom row in 1 min 26.9 sec. James has been a dedicated sport-stacker for almost eight years, and practises his skills for 1–2 hr a day.

Official sport-stacking cups are designed to help competitors stack as quickly as possible. They have inner ribs to separate them when nestled and holes in their top to prevent them sticking.

Q: Singer Justin Bieber has a talent for puzzles. Which one in particular?

A: The Rubik's Cube. He can complete one in under 2 min.

▼ MOST PARTY POPPERS POPPED IN ONE MINUTE

André Ortolf (DEU) celebrated another year of record-breaking success by popping 78 party poppers at the old fire station in Augsburg, Germany, on 9 Jan 2016. Previous holders of this party record include survival expert Edward "Bear" Grylls, cricketer Andrew Flintoff (both UK) and – of course – André's hero, Ashrita Furman (USA).

Coupé glasses stacked with a forklift
An Liqiang (CHN) stacked a total of 16 coupé glasses using a forklift on the set of *CCTV – Guinness World Records Special* in Beijing, China, on 9 Jan 2016. This tricky feat took almost an entire hour to complete.

▲ HIGHEST SUCCESSFUL BASKETBALL SHOT

On 26 Sep 2016, Brett Stanford, Derek Herron and Scott Gaunson (all AUS, pictured top right) – from the *How Ridiculous* YouTube channel – travelled to the Mauvoisin Dam in Valais, Switzerland, to regain a record they had lost to fellow sports entertainers Dude Perfect (USA). From the top of the dam, Herron took aim at a basket 180.968 m (593 ft 8 in) below him. Incredibly, it only took him three attempts to sink a successful shot.

AMAZING BODIES

Mouse traps on the tongue

Sweet Pepper Klopek (CAN) set off 58 mouse traps on his tongue in 60 sec on 16 Jul 2015

Rubber bands on face

Shripad Krishnarao Vaidya (IND) stretched 82 rubber bands over his face in 1 min on 19 Jul 2012

Passing body through a tennis racket

Thaneswar Guragai (NPL) passed through a tennis racket 38 times in 60 sec on 26 Feb 2012

Most hand claps

On 5 May 2014, Eli Bishop (USA) clapped 1,020 times in 1 min in Boston, Massachusetts, USA

Coins snatched off elbow

Dean Gould (UK) caught 328 10p pieces from the back of his forearm into the same downward palm on 6 Apr 1993

Toothpicks in a beard

Jeff Langum (USA) made a beard of 3,157 toothpicks on 3 Jul 2014 in Milan, Italy

Socks sorted with one foot in one minute

Using just one foot, Japan's Yui Okada sorted out 11 pairs of socks, picked them up and put them in a basket in one minute. The attempt took place on the set of *Grand Whiz-Kids TV* (NHK) in Shibuya, Tokyo, Japan, on 3 Jun 2012.

Skips of a rope wearing ski boots and skis in one minute

Sebastian Deeg (DEU) managed 61 skips while dressed for the slopes on the set of *ZDF Fernsehgarten* in Garmisch-Partenkirchen, Germany, on 27 Nov 2016.

▼ TALLEST HOUSE OF CARDS BUILT IN 12 HOURS

On 15–16 Mar 2016, professional cardstacker Bryan Berg (USA) built a 48-level house of cards in the shape of the Empire State Building on top of a running washing machine. The feat, which took place in Seoul, South Korea, was staged in order to publicize the stability of LG Electronics' (KOR) latest product. Bryan's completed creation measured 3.3 m (10 ft 9.9 in) and comprised 10,800 cards taken from 200 decks.

▲ MOST BALLOONS BLOWN UP IN AN HOUR

On 4 Sep 2015, Hunter Ewen (USA) blew up 910 balloons in 60 min at the Wild Basin Lodge & Event Center in Allenspark, Colorado, USA. He exploded the previous record of 671, set by Ashrita Furman (USA) on 21 Jan 2014. Each balloon had to be inflated to a diameter of 20 cm (7.87 in) or more to count towards the total. Hunter last held this record in 2011.

▶ MOST SHUTTLECOCKS CAUGHT WITH CHOPSTICKS IN ONE MINUTE

Mr Cherry (pictured) and Haruka Kuroda (both JPN) caught 23 shuttlecocks with chopsticks in 60 sec on the set of *Officially Amazing* at RAF Bentwaters in Suffolk, UK, on 8 Aug 2015. In a specially designed televised challenge, "Team Japan" destroyed the competition, beating both of their rivals – "Team USA" and "Team UK" – by a margin of 19 shuttlecocks.

Whether it's moving marbles with chopsticks, running backwards on all fours or breaking nuts with his backside, few talents are odder than Mr Cherry's – and he's got the records to prove it!

Rubik's Cube

There are 43,252,003,274,489,856,000 (43 quintillion) ways to scramble a Rubik's Cube. But any 3 x 3 cube can be solved in 20 moves or fewer.

Fastest time to complete two Rubik's Cubes simultaneously underwater
David Calvo (ESP) solved two cubes at the same time underwater in 1 min 24 sec on the set of *Lo Show dei Record* in Rome, Italy, on 1 Apr 2010.

Fewest moves to complete a Rubik's Cube
Marcel Peters (DEU) took just 19 moves to finish a Rubik's Cube at Cubelonia, held on 9–10 Jan 2016 in Cologne, Germany. In doing so, he equalled the record by Tim Wong (USA), achieved at the Irvine Fall 2015 speed-cubing event in Irvine, California, USA, on 11 Oct 2015.

The World Cube Association also monitors the record for the **fewest average moves to complete a Rubik's Cube**, which is calculated from performances over the course of three rounds in the competition final. Peters scored an average of 24.33 moves (24–25–24) to solve a 3 x 3 x 3 cube at the Schwandorf Open in Germany on 28–29 May 2016.

MOST RUBIK'S CUBES SOLVED...

Underwater
Anthony Brooks (USA) solved five Rubik's Cubes on a single breath at the Liberty Science Center in Jersey City, New Jersey, USA, on 1 Aug 2014.

Blindfolded
On 16 Nov 2013, Marcin Kowalczyk (POL) broke his own record by solving 41 out of 41 cubes in one hour while wearing a blindfold, at SLS Świerklany 2013 in Świerklany, Poland. It took 54 min 14 sec.

▼ FIRST RUBIK'S CUBE
The Rubik's Cube was invented in 1974 by Ernő Rubik, a professor of architecture in Budapest, Hungary. It resulted from his attempts to build an "impossible object" to engage his students – and once he'd made one, it took him three months to solve it! The first cubes were sold as Büvös Kocka ("Magic Cubes") and were twice as heavy as today's cubes. Around 400 million Rubik's Cubes have been sold since 1980.

▲ FASTEST ROBOT TO SOLVE A RUBIK'S CUBE

Built by Albert Beer (DEU), Sub1 Reloaded completed a Rubik's Cube in 0.637 sec in Munich, Germany, on 9 Nov 2016. It used two webcams to capture the arrangement of all six sides of the cube, then employed an algorithm to devise a solution. This was passed to a microcontroller board that orchestrated 20 moves of six stepper motors to turn the sides.

▲ MOST PEOPLE SOLVING RUBIK'S CUBES

On 4 Nov 2012, the College of Engineering, Pune (COEP) arranged for 3,248 people to try to solve Rubik's Cubes simultaneously at an arena in the college grounds in Maharashtra, India. A total of 3,267 people were brought together to take part in the attempt, although only 3,248 of them completed the Rubik's Cube within the allotted time of 30 min.

On a unicycle

India's Krishnam Raju Gadiraju completed 170 cubes in less than 90 min while unicycling in Bangalore, India, on 19 Oct 2016.

On 19 Oct 2014, Krishnam completed 2,176 cubes using only his left hand in Hyderabad, India – the **most Rubik's Cubes solved in 24 hr with one hand**. He solved his last cube with only one sec remaining! Krishnam finished with an average solve time of 33.34 sec per cube.

While running a marathon

On 3 Nov 2012, during the course of the Rock 'n' Roll Savannah Marathon in Savannah, Georgia, USA, Shane White (USA) solved 175 Rubik's Cubes.

On a bicycle

On 7 Aug 2016, 17-year-old Shreevatsh Rajkumar (IND) cycled for 7 hr 2 min 56 sec while unscrambling 751 cubes at the Abacus Montessori School in Chennai, Tamil Nadu, India.

In competition in a single year

In 2012, Sébastien Auroux (DEU) solved 2,033 out of 2,122 Rubik's Cubes in World Cube Association competitions. That's the equivalent of more than 5.5 solves every day – and the figure doesn't include any cubes that were solved outside of official events.

◄ LARGEST ORDER MAGIC CUBE

Oskar van Deventer (NLD) has created a 17 x 17 x 17 Magic Cube comprising 1,539 parts. He took 10 hr to sort and dye all the pieces, which were 3D-printed by US company Shapeways, and a further 5 hr to assemble the cube. It was presented at the New York Puzzle Party Symposium in New York City, USA, on 12 Feb 2011.

In one hour (team of nine)

The greatest number of cubes unscrambled in 60 min is 2,454 and was achieved by nine members of TEAM INDIA (all IND) in Chennai, Tamil Nadu, India, on 23 Jan 2016.

In 24 hours

On 3 Oct 2013, Eric Limeback (CAN) finished 5,800 Rubik's Cubes at Wilfrid Laurier University in Waterloo, Ontario, Canada. Impressively, Eric broke the previous record of 4,786 with 4 hr 7 min left. He completed the 5,800th cube in 23 hr 59 min 59.7 sec and recorded an average solve time of 14.89 sec per cube.

▲ FASTEST TIME TO SOLVE A RUBIK'S CUBE WHILE JUGGLING

Singapore's Teo Kai Xiang simultaneously juggled two balls and solved a Rubik's Cube in 22.25 sec on 14 Feb 2015. He used his right hand to juggle and his left to align the facets of the puzzle. The attempt took place at the National University of Singapore as part of the Rubik's Cube Competition 2015.

▲ LARGEST RUBIK'S CUBE MOSAIC

On 7 Dec 2012, this 277.18-m² (2,983.54-sq-ft) artwork of famous views in Macau, China, was unveiled at One Central Macau. Canadian design studio Cube Works, led by creative director Josh Chalom (USA), made the 68.78- x 4.03-m (225-ft 7.87-in x 13-ft 2.66-in) mosaic out of 85,626 cubes.

▶ LARGEST RUBIK'S CUBE SOLVED BY A ROBOT

On 15 Mar 2014, MultiCuber 999 built by David Gilday (UK) solved a 9 x 9 x 9 cube at The Big Bang Fair in the Birmingham NEC, UK. MultiCuber 999 is a LEGO® robot controlled by a custom-made app running on a smartphone. The number of solution possibilities ran to 278 digits and the robot finished the puzzle in 34 min 25.89 sec. David is a principal engineer at ARM, the company that designs processors used in most smartphones.

◀ LARGEST RUBIK'S CUBE

Lifelong puzzle fan Tony Fisher (UK) has created a Rubik's Cube with sides 1.57 m (5 ft 1.8 in) long, as confirmed in Ipswich, Suffolk, UK, on 5 Apr 2016. It took Tony two months to build this fully functional cube at his home. Visitors have come from as far afield as Japan to see his super-sized puzzle. Tony makes tiny cubes too (see p.258)!

▲ **SMALLEST RUBIK'S CUBE**
A mere 5.6 mm (0.22 in) wide, this minuscule cube was created by Tony Fisher (UK). But despite its diminutive size, it can be operated like a normal Rubik's Cube, albeit with the use of tweezers. The cube – which can easily be balanced on a fingertip – was produced from frosted plastic using a multi-jet modelling 3D printer.

FASTEST TIME TO SOLVE A...

CUBE	HOLDER	TIME	YEAR
3 x 3 x 3	Feliks Zemdegs (AUS)	4.73	2016
2 x 2 x 2	Maciej Czapiewski (POL)	0.49	2016
4 x 4 x 4	Feliks Zemdegs (AUS)	21.54	2015
5 x 5 x 5	Feliks Zemdegs (AUS)	41.27	2016
6 x 6 x 6	Feliks Zemdegs (AUS)	1:27.85	2017
7 x 7 x 7	Feliks Zemdegs (AUS)	2:18.13	2017
Megaminx	Yu Da-hyun (KOR)	33.17	2016
Pyraminx	Drew Brads (USA)	1.32	2015
Clock	Nathaniel Berg (SWE)	3.73	2015
Skewb	Jonatan Kłosko (POL)	1.10	2015
Square-1	Tommy Szeliga (USA)	6.84	2016
3 x 3 x 3 blindfold	Kaijun Lin (CHN)	18.50	2016
3 x 3 x 3 one hand	Feliks Zemdegs (AUS)	6.88	2015
3 x 3 x 3 with feet	Jakub Kipa (POL)	20.57	2015

Source: World Cube Association, as of 23 Mar 2017

Feliks achieved the record, but Mats won the 2016 contest. He averaged 6.83 sec in his rounds, compared with Feliks's 6.97 sec.

▲ **FASTEST TIME TO COMPLETE A RUBIK'S CUBE**
Student Feliks Zemdegs (AUS) took just 4.73 sec to solve a 3 x 3 x 3 Rubik's Cube at the POPS Open competition in Melbourne, Australia, on 11 Dec 2016. Feliks shaved one-hundredth of a second off the previous record, which had been set five weeks earlier by Mats Valk (NLD). When Feliks broke the record, Mats was sitting right next to him!

Great Balls of...

Paper, string, cling film, paint, dog hair, popcorn and more! We present a selection of extraordinary record-breaking spheres from the GWR archive.

LARGEST...

Cling-film ball

Hessle Road Network Young People's Centre (UK) put together a 470-lb (213.2-kg) ball of cling film – around half the weight of a grand piano. The record was confirmed in Hull, UK, on 14 Nov 2013.

Dog hair ball

On 7 Apr 2012, Texas Hearing and Service Dogs (USA) presented a 201-lb (91.17-kg) lump of dog hair – three times heavier than a Dalmatian. It incorporated the hair of 8,126 dogs, acquired by grooming, and was weighed in Austin, Texas, USA.

▲ LARGEST ANCIENT STONE BALLS

There are more than 1,000 perfectly spherical granitic globes scattered widely over the Diquis Delta of Costa Rica. Known locally as Las Bolas Grandes ("The Giant Balls"), they were carved from naturally spherical masses of granite by an as-yet-unidentified race of pre-Colombian people. The largest ones reach 2.5 m (8 ft 2 in) in diameter and weigh more than 16 tonnes (35,270 lb).

Inflatable beach ball

Polish supermarket chain Real created an inflatable beach ball with a diameter of 15.82 m (51 ft 10 in), which was presented and measured in Człuchów, Poland, on 8 May 2012.

Magnetic-tape ball

EMC Corporation (UK) made a ball of magnetic tape weighing 570 kg (1,256 lb), and measuring 2.125 m (6 ft 11 in) wide by 2.030 m (6 ft 8 in) tall. It was displayed at the Kings Place gallery in London, UK, on 19 Jan 2011, and comprised 6,500 tapes. Placed end to end, they would have reached from London to New York City, USA.

Matzah ball

Noah's Ark Original Deli (USA) cooked up a 267-lb (121.1-kg) matzah ball (an unleavened dumpling), as weighed in New York City, USA, on 6 Aug 2009.

Paper ball

Minnesota Pollution Control Agency (USA) made a 426-lb (193.2-kg), 10-ft 3-in-wide (3.13-m) ball of recycled paper, as measured on 5 Aug 2014.

Popcorn ball
Workers at The Popcorn Factory in Lake Forest, Illinois, USA, created a ball of popcorn weighing 3,423 lb (1,552.6 kg) on 29 Sep 2006.

Rose-quartz ball
Yang Chin-Lung (TPE) owns a ball of rose quartz with a diameter of 145.6 cm (4 ft 9 in), as certified in Tainan, Chinese Taipei, on 31 Mar 2015.

String ball
Bound by J C Payne of Valley View, Texas, USA, between 1989 and 1992, the largest ball of string measured 4.03 m (13 ft 2.6 in) in diameter.

MISCELLANEOUS

Fastest tennis ball caught
Anthony Kelly (AUS) grasped a tennis ball travelling at 119.86 mph (192.9 km/h) in Sydney, New South Wales, Australia, on 12 Nov 2015.

Most tennis balls caught in one hour
On 21 Jul 2015, Ashrita Furman (USA) caught 1,307 tennis balls in 60 min in New York City, USA. Each ball he caught was travelling at a minimum of 100 km/h (62 mph).

Fastest ping pong ball
Father and son David and Abraham Knierim (both USA) fired a ping pong ball from a vacuum launcher at 806 m/sec (2,644 ft/sec) – more than twice the speed of sound – in Wilsonville, Oregon, USA, on 24 May 2016.

It took a whole year to create this super-sized tape ball. That's not surprising when you consider that it includes some 73.2 mi (117.8 km) of tape – around the same length as Hadrian's Wall in the UK!

◄ LARGEST TAPE BALL
Weighing 2,000 lb (907.18 kg), and with a circumference of 12 ft 9 in (3.89 m), this huge ball of tape was completed in Louisville, Kentucky, USA, on 6 May 2011. The record attempt was organized by the Portland Promise Center (USA), a community- development group, and the ball was assembled by children who attend programmes run by the centre. The tapes used included duct tape, electrical tape, masking tape, gaffer tape, packing tape, foil tape and athletic tape.

A: 54,250

R Stanton Avery (USA) invented the self-adhesive label. His birthday, 13 Jan, was chosen for National Sticker Day.

▶ LARGEST BALL OF STICKERS

John Fischer and his team at StickerGiant (both USA) patiently created a 105.05-kg (231-lb 9.6-oz) ball out of more than 177,000 stickers and labels, as verified in Longmont, Colorado, USA, on 13 Jan 2016. This record was attempted for the first National Sticker Day in the USA. Dubbed "Saul", the ball was an officially declared candidate in the 2016 presidential elections, under the motto "Stick together".

Highest catch of a cricket ball

For Sky Sports Cricket, former England captain Nasser Hussain (UK, b. IND) caught a cricket ball dropped by a "Batcam" drone from 46 m (150 ft 11 in) – the equivalent of 14 storeys – at Lord's Cricket Ground in London, UK, on 30 Jun 2016.

Highest-altitude for a soccer ball to be dropped and controlled

Theo Walcott (UK) controlled a ball dropped from a height of 34 m (111 ft 6 in) at the Arsenal FC training ground in St Albans, UK, on 29 Nov 2016. The attempt was sponsored by Betfair (UK).

◀ LARGEST BALL OF HUMAN HAIR

Henry Coffer (USA), a barber from Charleston in Missouri, USA, collected hair into a giant ball that weighed 167 lb (75.7 kg) as of 8 Dec 2008. It was 4 ft (1.2 m) high and had a 14-ft (4.26-m) circumference. Over the course of 50-plus years, Henry found many uses for his hair clippings, from patching potholes to fertilizing soil.

Most balls juggled (multiplex technique): i.e., more than one ball thrown at a time:
14
Aleksandr Koblikov (UKR), 2013

Most balls bounce-juggled:
12
Alan Sulc (CZE), 2008

Most balls juggled (traditional):
11
Alex Barron (UK), 2012

Most ping-pong balls juggled by mouth:
7
Tony Fercos (USA, b. CZE), mid-1980s

Most soccer balls juggled:
5
Victor Rubilar (ARG), 2006; equalled by Marko Vermeer (NLD), 2014 Isidro Silveira (ESP), 2015

Most bowling balls juggled:
3
Milan Roskopf (SVK), 2011

▲ **LARGEST SOCCER BALL**
On 12 Feb 2013, Doha Bank (QAT) presented a 12.19-m-diameter (39-ft 11.9-in) soccer ball made out of artificial leather in Doha, Qatar. It has a circumference of 38.3 m (125 ft 8 in) and weighs approximately 960 kg (2,116 lb 7 oz). The super-sized sphere was displayed in the LuLu Hypermarket car park in Doha.

Most golf balls stacked
Don Athey of Bridgeport, Ohio, USA, stacked nine golf balls vertically – without adhesives – on 4 Oct 1998. They remained in place for 20 sec.

Largest pyramid of balls
In all, 16,206 golf balls formed the pyramid made by Cal Shipman and The First Tee of Greater Tyler (both USA) and presented at Mamie G Griffin Elementary School in Tyler, Texas, USA, on 31 Jan 2014.

▲ **LARGEST DISCO BALL**
Bestival (UK) music festival presented a mirror ball with a diameter of 10.33 m (33 ft 10 in) for the Desert Island Disco at Robin Hill Country Park on the Isle of Wight, UK, on 7 Sep 2014. The ball was made by the firm NEWSUBSTANCE, led by Mungo Denison (both UK), and formed part of the climax of the weekend. It was lit and began to rotate as Nile Rodgers and Chic emerged to perform on the main stage.

▲ LARGEST RUBBER-BAND BALL

Weighing 4,097 kg (9,032 lb) – around twice the weight of an adult rhinoceros – "Megaton" was created by Joel Waul (USA) and measured in Lauderhill, Florida, USA, on 13 Nov 2008 for GWR Day. In all, 700,000 rubber bands were used for the sphere, which Joel began making in Apr 2004. It is 2 m (6 ft 7 in) tall.

◄ LARGEST RUGBY BALL

On 15 Mar 2011, Cathay Pacific Airways Ltd presented a rugby ball 4.709 m (15 ft 5.39 in) long and 2.95 m (9 ft 8.14 in) tall for the Cathay Pacific/Credit Suisse Hong Kong Sevens in Hong Kong, China. The ball is 12.066 m (39 ft 7 in) in circumference from side to side and 9.34 m (30 ft 7.7 in) from top to bottom. It is about 20 times the size of a regular rugby ball, one of which is held (left) by GWR's Angela Wu.

How do you count paint layers? A tree surgeon took a core sample from the ball and estimated that one layer is around 0.000778 in thick, making a total of 25,506 layers in all.

▶ MOST LAYERS IN A BALL OF PAINT

As of 2 May 2017, there were some 25,506 layers of paint on a baseball owned by Michael Carmichael of Alexandria, Indiana, USA. Since first painting the ball in 1977, he and his wife Glenda had added nearly two coats of paint per day. The ball has a circumference of around 15 ft (4.57 m) at its widest.

Recordmania Round-Up

You don't always have to be a trained professional to go for a GWR record. Try using a little imagination...

▲ FASTEST SIDE-WHEELIE LAP OF THE NÜRBURGRING NORDSCHLEIFE

On 3 Nov 2016, Han Yue (CHN) completed a lap of the infamous Nürburgring Nordschleife (North Loop) in a Mini Cooper without letting his right wheels touch the ground. It took him a record 45 min 59.11 sec to negotiate the 73 twists and turns along the 20.8-km-long (12.9-mi) track, which winds its way through Rhineland-Palatinate, Germany.

Largest online photo album of people giving a thumbs-up

Between 9 Apr and 7 May 2016, Unicharm Consumer Products (CHN) collected 50,470 images of enthusiastic people giving the thumbs-up sign.

Largest spring mattress

Lijun Hou and his team (all CHN) produced a gigantic mattress measuring 20 x 18.18 m (65 ft 7 in x 59 ft 7 in), with a thickness of 0.31 m (1 ft 0.2 in). That makes it around the same size as a tennis court. The monster mattress was put on display at a public event in Harbin, Heilongjiang, China, on 15 Apr 2016.

Largest fruit sculpture

Saadeddin Co. (SAU) made a 5.95-m-tall (19-ft 6-in) sculpture from dates in Jeddah, Saudi Arabia, on 23 Nov 2016. The sculpture – around the same height as an adult giraffe – took the form of a palm tree.

Largest display of toy windmills/pinwheels

The LunEur amusement park in Rome, Italy, celebrated its reopening by displaying 576 toy windmills/pinwheels on 27 Oct 2016. LunEur is thought to be the oldest amusement park in Italy, dating back to 1953.

Largest display of origami frogs

On 1 Apr 2016, a frog-shaped mosaic of 1,578 origami frogs was created in the Kumamoto Kodomo Bunka Kaikan, a children's culture centre in Kumamoto, Japan. It was made by 238 children, their parents, volunteers and employees at the centre.

Longest backwards golf carry

On 4 Mar 2016, Lynn Ray (USA) hit a golf ball 313 yd (286.2 m) facing away from the direction of his drive. The "carry" is the distance that the ball travels in the air.

The next day, he achieved the **most golf balls hit over 300 yards in one hour**: 459.

▲ MOST BRIDAL BOUQUETS CAUGHT

Jamie "The Bouquet Slayer" Jackson of Draper, Utah, USA, goes to a lot of weddings. So many, in fact, that she has been able to become a master bouquet-catcher. Jamie has attended more than 100 weddings since 1996, and has caught 50 bridal bouquets. There have been just four divorces among the brides whose bouquets she has caught – a fact that she believes makes her a good-luck charm.

Most tandem parachute jumps in 8 hours

RedBalloon (AUS) carried out 155 tandem parachute jumps in 8 hr in Wollongong, Australia, on 17 Dec 2016.

Most cups balanced on the forehead

On 9 Jul 2016, Saar Kessel (ISR) balanced an 81-cm-high (2-ft 7.8-in) stack of 305 plastic cups on his forehead for 10 sec in Mishmar HaShiv'a, Israel.

He also recorded the **most poker chips balanced on one finger** (84).

Longest line of bird's-nest boxes

Russian television station Tricolor TV lined up 4,000 bird's-nest boxes – stretching for 1.124 km (0.698 mi) – in Ostankino Park in Moscow, Russia, on 23 Apr 2016.

Most people blowing out candles simultaneously

In all, 1,717 participants blew out candles on 21 Nov 2016 in Muscat, Oman, in an event organized by the Fellowship Fund for Employees of the Ministry of Health Muscat (OMN).

Fastest time to eat 500 g of mozzarella

Ashrita Furman (USA) continued his extraordinary record-breaking exploits by eating 500 g (1 lb 1.63 oz) of mozzarella cheese in 1 min 34 sec on 12 Apr 2016.

MOST PEOPLE IN A...

Nativity scene
Calne Town Council and the Bible Society (both UK) assembled 1,254 people into a living nativity scene in Calne, UK, on 3 Dec 2016.

Hug relay
A total of 1,290 people were brought together by Fundación Teletón México A.C. (MEX) for a hug relay in Mexico City on 10 Dec 2016.

Transforming human image
GEMS Education (UAE) assembled 2,223 participants in Dubai, UAE, on 28 Nov 2016 to form the shape of an open hand in Emirati colours. They then changed into the shape of a three-fingered salute made popular by Sheikh Mohammed bin Rashid Al Maktoum, Dubai's ruler.

Chain of people clasping wrists
Telenor Pakistan employees and Beaconhouse School System students (both PAK) clasped wrists to form a line of 2,950 people in Islamabad, Pakistan, on 29 Sep 2016.

▲ LONGEST WHIP CRACKED
On 18 Aug 2016, whip performer Nathan Griggs (AUS) coaxed an audible "crack" from a whip 329 ft 7 in (100.45 m) long during a show at Defiance Mill Park in Queensland, Australia.

On 9 Mar 2017, Nathan achieved the **most whip cracks with two whips in one minute**. With a kangaroo-leather whip in each hand, he made 697 distinct whip cracks in 60 sec – more than 11 a second – in Altona, Victoria, Australia.

◄ MOST DRINK CANS CRUSHED WITH THE ELBOW
Pakistani martial arts instructor Muhammad Rashid set a new world record (and made a sticky mess) when he crushed 77 drink cans with his elbow in one minute. This record was set in Gemona del Friuli, Italy, on 17 Apr 2016 at an event organized by Associazione Cons.erva (ITA). Rashid holds numerous in-a-minute martial arts records, including **most nunchaku hits** (350) and **most spins of a fire staff** (188).

▶ MOST DRINK CANS PLACED ON THE HEAD USING AIR SUCTION

Jamie "Canhead" Keeton (USA) has a very unusual talent. For reasons that are still not clear, the pores in his skin seem to act like suction cups, adhering to anything with which they can form an air-tight seal. Jamie demonstrated this remarkable ability in front of the audience of *CCTV – Guinness World Records Special* in Beijing, China, on 11 Jan 2016, when he successfully stuck eight aluminium drink cans to his head.

Human DNA helix

On 23 Apr 2016, the Medical University of Varna (BGR) recruited 4,000 people to assemble themselves in the shape of a DNA helix. The group-formation helix was created on South Beach in Varna, Bulgaria, on the coast of the Black Sea. Participants wore coloured T-shirts and hats to differentiate the two intertwining strands of the helix and other DNA parts.

Variety act (amateur)

On 25 Nov 2016, the finale of the Schools Spectacular (AUS) saw an ensemble of 5,322 students dance, sing and play music on stage in Sydney, Australia.

Human number

On 7 May 2016, a group of 7,511 participants combined to form the number "450", in an event organized by the Government of Orel Region and the Youth Organization Volunteers of Victory (both RUS), in Orel, Russia. The record attempt was staged to celebrate the 450th anniversary of the Orel region – hence the choice of this particular number.

▶ LARGEST SERVING OF ROCOTOS RELLENOS

Universidad San Ignacio de Loyola and Municipalidad Provincial de Arequipa (both PER) served up 542.72 kg (1,196 lb 8 oz) of rocotos rellenos at Plaza de Armas in Arequipa, Peru, on 27 Nov 2016. This dish of stuffed peppers is a Peruvian speciality.

▲ **FASTEST 50 M WALKING ON HANDS WITH A SOCCER BALL BETWEEN THE LEGS**

Zhang Shuang (CHN) covered 50 m (164 ft) in 26.09 sec walking on his hands while grasping a soccer ball between his knees. This record was set at the China West Normal University on 30 Apr 2016.

The overall record for the **fastest 50 m running on hands** currently stands at 16.93 sec. It was set by Mark Kenny (USA) way back on 19 Feb 1994.

▲ **FARTHEST DISTANCE WALKED BALANCING A BIKE ON THE CHIN**

On 13 Apr 2016, Ashrita Furman (USA) covered 20.62 m (67 ft 7 in) on foot with a vintage Raleigh Super Course on his chin.

On 29 Jun 2015, he recorded the **farthest distance walked balancing a lawnmower on the chin**: 122.92 m (403 ft 3 in).

▼ LARGEST HUMAN AIR-BED (LILO) DOMINOES

On 17 Sep 2016, Tropical (ESP) lined up 603 participants, each with an air bed at Playa de Las Canteras in Las Palmas de Gran Canaria, Spain. On a signal, they then fell over consecutively. It took 3 min 40 sec for all of the participants to topple into one another.

► MOST SPOONS BALANCED ON THE BODY

On 7 Aug 2016, Marcos Ruiz Ceballos (ESP) kept 64 stainless-steel spoons on his body for the 5 sec required by GWR guidelines. The attempt happened in Kashikojima, Japan, and took around 4 min from start to finish, with Marcos keeping very still as the spoons were placed on his chest and back by Kana Okamoto (JPN). For this record, the spoons can be placed anywhere on the body other than the face, which has its own separate record (below).

The **most spoons balanced on the face** is 31, by Dalibor Jablanovic (SRB) in 2013.

Youngest...

Starting with a 109-year-old great-great-great-grandmother and ending with a baby still in the womb, we present a selection of GWR's youngest record-breakers...

< 110 years

Great-great-great-great-grandmother
109 years 100 days

On 21 Jan 1989, Augusta Bunge (USA, b. 13 Oct 1879) learned that she had become a great-great-great-grandmother at the age of 109 years, when her great-great-great-granddaughter gave birth to a son, Christopher John Bollig.

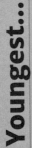

Holder of the "oldest living person" record
107 years 327 days

When the world's **oldest person** Jennie Howell (USA) died on 16 Dec 1956, Anne Marie Carsterson (USA, b. 24 Jan 1849) became not only the oldest person alive, but also the youngest person to hold that title – a record still unbeaten as of 20 Mar 2017.

US president
42 years 322 days

Theodore Roosevelt (b. 27 Oct 1858) succeeded to the US presidency on 14 Sep 1901, with the assassination of his predecessor, William McKinley.

The **youngest elected US president** was John F Kennedy (b. 29 May 1917), who was 43 years 236 days old at his inauguration on 20 Jan 1961.

Moon walker
36 years 201 days

Charlie Duke (USA, b. 3 Oct 1935) became the youngest person to land on the Moon, aged 36 years old, when he touched down on 21 Apr 1972 during the Apollo 16 mission.

Chief Scout
34 years 334 days

Edward "Bear" Grylls (UK, b. 7 Jun 1974) was 34 years old when his appointment as Chief Scout was confirmed. The announcement by the Council of the Scout Movement took place in London, UK, on 17 May 2009. Previously, the youngest Chief Scout had been Charles Maclean (UK), who was 43 when he took the role in 1959.

Head of state (current)
c.27 years

Kim Jong-un became leader of North Korea on 17 Dec 2011, following the death of his father, Kim Jong-il. Kim Jong-un's exact age has never been officially confirmed, but it is speculated that he was 27 years old upon succeeding his father – although his date of birth has been listed as 8 Jan 1982 or the same date in 1983 or 1984.

Person to row any ocean solo
20 years 219 days

Callum Gathercole (UK, b. 15 May 1995) was 20 years old when he began rowing the Atlantic Ocean east to west, from La Gomera to Antigua, in his boat *Small and Mighty*. The row lasted 58 days 15 hr 15 min, from 20 Dec 2015 to 16 Feb 2016. In keeping with the rules of the Ocean Rowing Society, GWR dates ocean rowing records from the holder's age at departure.

Billionaire (current)
19 years 236 days

As of 16 Mar 2016, Norway's Alexandra Andresen (b. 23 Jul 1996) was aged 19 years old and had an estimated wealth of $1,180,000,000 (£829,800,000; €1,062,620,000) according to Forbes. She competes in dressage professionally. Her family's fortune comes from the tobacco industry.

Professional bull rider
18 years 125 days

Brian Canter (USA, b. 25 Jun 1987) was 18 years old when he appeared in the 2005 Professional Bull Riders (PBR) World Finals. He finished in the top 50 that year, and was eighth in the rankings for 2006.

NBA player
18 years 6 days

Andrew Bynum (USA, b. 27 Oct 1987) became the youngest individual to play in an NBA game when he featured for the Los Angeles Lakers against the Denver Nuggets (both USA) on 2 Nov 2005.

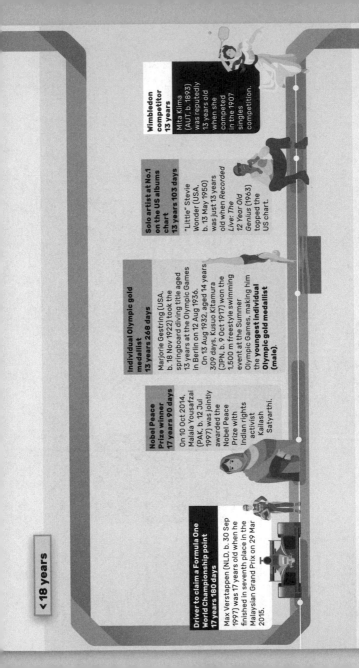

< 18 years

Driver to claim a Formula One World Championship point
17 years 180 days

Max Verstappen (NLD, b. 30 Sep 1997) was 17 years old when he finished in seventh place in the Malaysian Grand Prix on 29 Mar 2015.

Nobel Peace Prize winner
17 years 90 days

On 10 Oct 2014, Malala Yousafzai (PAK, b. 12 Jul 1997) was jointly awarded the Nobel Peace Prize with Indian rights activist Kailash Satyarthi.

Individual Olympic gold medallist
13 years 268 days

Marjorie Gestring (USA, b. 18 Nov 1922) took the springboard diving title aged 13 years at the Olympic Games in Berlin on 12 Aug 1936. On 13 Aug 1932, aged 14 years 309 days, Kusuo Kitamura (JPN, b. 9 Oct 1917) won the 1,500 m freestyle swimming event at the Summer Olympic Games, making him the **youngest individual Olympic gold medallist (male)**.

Solo artist at No.1 on the US albums chart
13 years 103 days

"Little" Stevie Wonder (USA, b. 13 May 1950) was just 13 years old when *Recorded Live: The 12 Year Old Genius* (1963) topped the US chart.

Wimbledon competitor
13 years

Mita Klima (AUT, b. 1893) was reputedly 13 years old when she competed in the 1907 singles competition.

X Games athlete
11 years 129 days

Jagger Eaton (USA, b. 21 Feb 2001) was 11 years old when he debuted at X Games 18, staged from 28 Jun to 1 Jul 2012 in Los Angeles, California, USA. He competed in the Skateboard Big Air event, finishing 12th.

Soccer referee
9 years 303 days

Aged just 9 years old, Samuel Keplinger (DEU, b. 27 Apr 1998) officiated during a 0–0 draw between SSV Bobingen and SV Reinhartshausen in Bobingen, Bavaria, Germany, on 24 Feb 2008. The game was part of a tournament for U7 boys' teams.

Pirate
8–11 years

The youngest pirate for whom there is documentary proof is John King. On 9 Nov 1716, the notorious pirate "Black Sam", aka Samuel Bellamy (UK), captured a passenger ship, the *Bonetta*. King (then aged between eight and 11 years old) and his mother were both passengers. According to a statement by Abijah Savage (the captain of the *Bonetta*) dated 30 Nov 1716, King insisted on joining the pirate crew, threatening to kill himself or hurt his mother if his wish was not granted. Eventually "Black Sam" allowed him to do so.

Movie director
7 years 340 days

Saugat Bista (NPL, b. 6 Jan 2007) is the youngest director of a professionally made film. He was 7 years old when *Love You Baba* (NPL, 2014) was released in cinemas on 12 Dec 2014.

Oscar winner
6 years 310 days

"Little Miss Miracle" Shirley Temple (USA, b. 23 Apr 1928) won a special Juvenile Award "in grateful recognition of her outstanding contribution to screen entertainment during the year 1934" on 27 Feb 1935, aged 6 years.

< 6 years

Drummer
4 years 319 days

Four-year-old Julian Pavone (USA, b. 14 May 2004) performed in his 20th concert (the minimum count that GWR guidelines stipulate for this record) on 29 Mar 2009.

Circus ringmaster
3 years

On 26 Dec 2005, aged three years old, Cranston Chipperfield (UK) became the youngest person to take the stage as master of ceremonies, at the Circus Royale in Strathclyde Country Park in Lanarkshire, UK. He is the eighth generation of ringmasters in the Chipperfield family.

Survivor of the *Titanic*
72 days

On 10 Apr 1912, Millvina Dean (UK, b. 2 Feb 1912), her parents and 18-month-old brother set off on the maiden voyage of the RMS *Titanic* cruise liner. They were travelling third class. Millvina, along with her mother and brother, survived when the "unsinkable" ship hit an iceberg on 14 Apr 1912 and began to sink. Her father, Bert, was among the 1,517 passengers who perished.

Heart-transplant recipient
1 hr

On 8 Nov 1996, one-hour-old Cheyenne Pyle (USA) became the youngest ever patient to undergo a transplant when she received a donor heart at Jackson Children's Hospital in Miami, Florida, USA.

Open-heart-surgery patient
24 weeks (antenatal)

Tucker Roussin (USA, b. 9 May 2013) had open-heart surgery while still in the womb, at just 24 weeks' gestation. The operation took place in Philadelphia, Pennsylvania, USA, in Feb 2013.

Adventures

Daredevil adventurer Erik Weihenmayer (USA) has conquered the Seven Summits and kayaked the length of the Grand Canyon. He lost his sight aged 13.

▲ LARGEST NO-GRIP WINGSUIT FORMATION (FAI-APPROVED)

On 17 Oct 2015, a team of 61 wingsuit-clad skydivers led by Taya Weiss (USA) jumped from three planes at 13,500 ft (4,114 m) before coming together at 5,500 ft (1,676 m) to form a spectacular human diamond shape (right) over Perris Valley in California, USA. To qualify for the record, the team had to fly in close formation – without holding one another – in designated flying spaces. This was checked and certified by three judges from the Fédération Aéronautique Internationale (FAI).

Contents

An early wingsuit was created by inventor and tailor Franz Reichelt. On 4 Feb 1912, he tested his home-made parachute by leaping from the Eiffel Tower in Paris, France. Tragically, he fell to his death.

Circumnavigation

Ferdinand Magellan is often credited as the first person to circumnavigate the globe, but he died – with most of the crew in his fleet – before completing the journey.

Kane Avellano used his round-the-world trip to raise funds for the children's charity UNICEF; his original donation target was £1,000 ($1,464), but he had more than doubled that figure as of Apr 2017.

First circumnavigation by amphibious car
The only circumnavigation by an amphibious vehicle was by Ben Carlin (AUS) and a series of partners in *Half-Safe*, a modified Ford GPA amphibious jeep. He left from Nova Scotia, Canada, on 19 Jul 1950 and returned to Montreal, Canada, on 8 May 1958, after a journey of 39,000 mi (62,764 km) over land and 9,600 mi (15,450 km) by sea and river.

First circumnavigation by solar-powered boat
An international crew led by Raphaël Domjan (CHE) steered the MS *Tûranor PlanetSolar* around the globe westwards from Monaco in 1 year 220 days, from 27 Sep 2010 to 4 May 2012.

Longest series of sailing circumnavigations
Jon Sanders (AUS) made three non-stop single-handed circumnavigations in his 13.9-m-long (44-ft) sloop *Parry Endeavour* in 1 year 239 days, from 25 May 1986 to 13 Mar 1988. Starting and finishing in Fremantle, Western Australia, he made one circumnavigation westwards and two eastwards. He covered 71,023 nautical mi (131,535 km; 81,732 mi), **the longest distance sailed non-stop by any vessel**.

◄ YOUNGEST PERSON TO CIRCUMNAVIGATE THE GLOBE BY MOTORCYCLE (MALE)
Kane Avellano (UK, b. 20 Jan 1993) circled the world on his Triumph Bonneville T100 motorcycle, solo and unsupported, leaving his home town – South Shields, Tyne and Wear, UK – on 31 May 2016 and arriving back there on 19 Jan 2017, one day short of his 24th birthday. In 233 days, Avellano covered 28,062 mi (45,161 km), passing through 36 countries and six continents and negotiating extremes of weather from Indian monsoons to the intense heat of Australia's deserts.

Q: Who was the fictional circumnavigator created by author Jules Verne?

A: Phileas Fogg

First non-motorized circumnavigation along the Equator

Mike Horn (ZAF) travelled along the Equator back to his starting point of Libreville, Gabon, by bicycle, dugout canoe and trimaran. His trip lasted 1 year 147 days, from 2 Jun 1999 to 27 Oct 2000.

Oldest person to circumnavigate the world by scheduled public transport

On 16 Aug 2012, Saburō Shōchi (JPN, b. 16 Aug 1906) returned to Fukuoka, Japan, having circled Earth using only public transport. He was exactly 106 years old.

FASTEST CIRCUMNAVIGATION...

By scheduled flights

On 8–10 Jan 1980, David J Springbett (UK) circumnavigated the world on scheduled flights in 44 hr 6 min. His route took him eastwards from Los Angeles in California, USA, via the UK, Bahrain, Thailand, Japan and Hawaii.

The **fastest circumnavigation by scheduled flights visiting six continents** is 63 hr 47 min, by Kirk Miller and John Burnham (both USA). Starting in Bangkok, Thailand, on 7 Sep 2016, they flew eastwards via Australia, the USA, South America, Europe and Africa before finishing on 10 Sep.

By passenger aircraft (FAI-approved)

Under Fédération Aéronautique Internationale (FAI) rules, which permit flights that exceed the length of the Tropic of Cancer or Capricorn, an Air France Concorde piloted by captains Michel Dupont and Claude Hetru (both FRA) circumnavigated the world in 31 hr 27 min 49 sec. The flight took place on 15–16 Aug 1995; a total of 80 passengers and 18 crew were also on board.

By helicopter (FAI-approved)

Edward Kasprowicz and crewman Stephen Sheik (both USA) flew an AgustaWestland Grand helicopter around the world in 11 days 7 hr 5 min, landing on 18 Aug 2008. Starting and finishing in New York City, USA, they flew east via Greenland, the UK, Italy, Russia and Canada, making more than 70 refuelling stops.

▲ **FIRST CIRCUMNAVIGATION BY MICROLIGHT**

Brian Milton (UK) flew around the world in a Pegasus Quantum 912 flexwing microlight between 22 Mar and 21 Jul 1998. The lack of a cockpit in Brian's craft made flying a challenge in extreme weather, notably crossing the Syrian desert and the interior of Iceland. He flew at an altitude of 2,000 ft (610 m) for most of the way, with an average flying speed of 65 mph (105 km/h).

▲ FASTEST CIRCUMNAVIGATION BY BALLOON (FAI-APPROVED)

On 12–23 Jul 2016, Fedor Konyukhov (RUS, inset) flew around the world alone in 268 hr 20 min in a Roziere combined hot-air and helium gas balloon. He took off from Northam in Western Australia and landed at Bonnie Rock in the same state. He beat the previous record set by US adventurer Steve Fossett by two days, despite taking a longer route.

By car

The record for the **first and fastest man and woman to have circumnavigated the Earth by car** covering six continents under the rules applicable in 1989 and 1991 embracing more than an equator's length of driving (24,901 road miles; 40,075 km), is held by Saloo Choudhury and his wife Neena Choudhury (both India). The journey took 69 days 19 hours 5 minutes from 9 Sep to 17 November 1989. The couple drove a 1989 Hindustan "Contessa Classic" starting and finishing in Delhi, India.

By powered boat

On 26 Jun 2009, *Earthrace* was granted the Union International Motonautique (UIM) record for the fastest circumnavigation by powered boat. The journey took 60 days 23 hr 49 min, beginning in Sagunto, Spain, on 27 Apr 2008 and returning there on 27 Jun.

Sailing non-stop, westwards, solo (female)

Between 20 Nov 2005 and 18 May 2006, Dee Caffari (UK) sailed her 22-m (72-ft) monohull *Aviva* back to her starting point of Portsmouth, UK, a journey that lasted 178 days 3 hr 5 min 34 sec. Caffari went on to complete the Vendée Globe round-the-world yacht race on 16 Feb 2009, making her the **first female to sail non-stop around the world in both directions**.

▲ FASTEST CIRCUMNAVIGATION SAILING MONOHULL SOLO

Armel Le Cléac'h (FRA, inset) spent 74 days 3 hr 35 min sailing around the world at an average speed of 15.43 knots (17.76 mph; 28.58 km/h), as ratified by the World Sailing Speed Record Council (WSSRC). He won the 2016/17 Vendée Globe single-handed yacht race in *Banque Populaire VIII*, reaching Les Sables d'Olonne in France on 19 Jan 2017.

▲ FASTEST CIRCUMNAVIGATION BY BICYCLE (FEMALE)

Paola Gianotti (ITA) cycled around the world in 144 days, covering a distance of 29,595 km (18,389 mi). Her journey started and finished at Ivrea in Turin, Italy, from 8 Mar to 30 Nov 2014. Along the way, Paola had to overcome a fractured veterbra sustained in a road-traffic accident.

In 2015, she became the first woman to complete the Red Bull Trans-Siberian Extreme cycle race.

▼ OLDEST WOMAN TO SAIL SINGLE-HANDEDLY AROUND THE WORLD

Jeanne Socrates (UK, b. 17 Aug 1942) was aged 70 years 325 days when she completed a solo nautical circumnavigation in her 38-ft (11.58-m) monohull *Nereida* on 8 Jul 2013. She started and finished in Victoria in British Columbia, Canada – a distance of some 25,000 nautical mi (46,300 km) – spending a total of 258 days 14 hr 16 min 36 sec at sea.

▲ FASTEST CIRCUMNAVIGATION BY BICYCLE (MALE)

Starting and finishing at Auckland Airport in New Zealand, Andrew Nicholson (NZ) completed a cycled circumnavigation of the globe in 123 days 43 min between 12 Aug and 13 Dec 2015. Andrew is a former speed skater who represented his home country at three Winter Olympics. He rode in aid of a cancer research centre at the University of Otago, New Zealand.

▲ FASTEST SAILING CIRCUMNAVIGATION

Francis Joyon (FRA) and a crew of five sailed around the world non-stop in 40 days 23 hr 30 min 30 sec on board the 120-ft (36.57-m) trimaran *IDEC* from 16 Dec 2016 to 26 Jan 2017. They covered a distance of 21,600 nautical mi (40,003 km) at an average speed of 21.96 knots (25.27 mph; 40.66 km/h). The voyage started and finished between Le Créac'h Lighthouse off the tip of Brittany, France, and Lizard Point in Cornwall, UK. The record was ratified by the World Sailing Speed Record Council (WSSRC).

In Mar 1999, *Solar Impulse 2* pilot Bertrand Piccard and Brian Jones (UK) steered the balloon *Breitling Orbiter 3* around the world – the **first circumnavigation by balloon**.

▼ FIRST CIRCUMNAVIGATION IN A SOLAR-POWERED AEROPLANE (FAI-APPROVED)

From 9 Mar 2015 to 26 Jul 2016, André Borschberg and Bertrand Piccard (both CHE, left) piloted *Solar Impulse 2* around the world powered entirely by energy from the Sun. Their journey time, starting and finishing in Abu Dhabi, UAE, was 505 days 19 hr 53 min, but for nearly 10 months of this time the team were grounded in Hawaii, USA, owing to damage to overheated batteries.

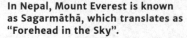

Mountaineering

In Nepal, Mount Everest is known as Sagarmāthā, which translates as "Forehead in the Sky".

> In Bhutan, climbing mountains higher than 6,000 m (19,685 ft) has been prohibited on religious grounds since 1994. For this reason, Kangkar Pünzum (see p.285) might never be climbed.

First ascent of Everest

Earth's **highest mountain** was first conquered at 11:30 a.m. on 29 May 1953, when the summit was reached by Edmund Percival Hillary (NZ) and Tenzing Norgay (IND/Tibet). The successful expedition was led by Colonel John Hunt (UK).

The **first ascent of Everest without supplementary oxygen** was completed by Reinhold Messner (ITA) and Peter Habeler (AUT) on 8 May 1978. This is regarded by some mountaineers as the first "true" ascent of Everest, since overcoming the effects of altitude (i.e., the low oxygen content of air) is the greatest challenge facing high-altitude climbers.

Fastest ascent of Everest and K2 without supplementary oxygen

Karl Unterkircher (ITA) summitted the world's two tallest mountains in 63 days, finishing at the top of K2 on 26 Jul 2004.

The **fastest ascent of Everest and K2 without supplementary oxygen (female)** is 92 days, achieved on 13 Aug 1995 by Alison Hargreaves (UK, see p.287).

The **fastest ascent of Everest and K2 by a married couple without supplementary oxygen** is 295 days, by Nives Meroi and Romano Benet (both ITA). They completed the two climbs on 17 May 2007.

◀ FIRST ASCENT OF EVEREST (FEMALE)

On 20 Oct 2016, Junko Tabei (JPN, b. 22 Sep 1939) passed away at the age of 77. The trailblazing mountaineer reached the summit of Everest on 16 May 1975 (above left). En route, she survived an avalanche that buried her expedition's camp in snow and knocked her unconscious for 6 min.

Tabei was also the **first female to climb the Seven Summits**. She achieved this by topping Puncak Jaya (or Carstensz Pyramid) in Indonesia on 28 Jun 1992, before completing both the Kosciuszko and Carstensz lists by climbing Russia's Mount Elbrus on 28 Jul 1992.

First person to climb all 8,000-m mountains

Reinhold Messner became the first person to climb the world's 14 mountains over 8,000 m (26,246 ft) when he summitted Lhotse (8,516 m; 27,939 ft), on the border of Nepal and Tibet, on 16 Oct 1986. In doing so, he also became the **first person to climb all 8,000-m mountains without supplementary oxygen**. As of 2017, only 14 other climbers have achieved this feat.

▲ OLDEST PERSON TO CLIMB MOUNT KILIMANJARO

Angela Vorobeva (RUS, b. 4 Feb 1929) summitted Mount Kilimanjaro in Tanzania aged 86 years 267 days. Her expedition left Londorossi Gate (2,360 m; 7,742 ft) on 23 Oct 2015, reaching Uhuru Peak (5,895 m; 19,340 ft) on 29 Oct.

The **oldest man to climb Mount Kilimanjaro** is Robert Wheeler (USA, b. 15 Mar 1929). He reached the summit on 2 Oct 2014, aged 85 years 201 days.

Youngest person to climb the Seven Summits

Johnny Collinson (USA, b. 29 Mar 1992) reached the peak of Vinson Massif in Antarctica on 18 Jan 2010, aged 17 years 295 days. It had taken him exactly a year to climb the highest mountain on every continent.

Jordan Romero (USA, b. 12 Jul 1996) was aged 15 years 165 days when he completed the Seven Summits on 24 Dec 2011. However, given the dangerous nature of mountaineering, Guinness World Records does not accept applications from climbers under the age of 16.

▲ FASTEST TIME TO WIN THE SNOW LEOPARD AWARD

The Snow Leopard award is presented to climbers who summit all five mountains of 7,000 m (22,965 ft) and above located in the former Soviet Union. Andrzej Bargiel (POL) did this in 29 days 17 hr 5 min on 16 Jul–14 Aug 2016. The five peaks are: Pik Imeni Ismail Samani (7,495 m; 24,590 ft); Jengish Chokusu (7,439 m; 24,406 ft); Qullai Abuali Ibni Sino (7,134 m; 23,405 ft); Pik Yevgenii Korzhenevskoy (7,105 m; 23,310 ft); and Khan Tangiri Shyngy (7,010 m; 23,000 ft).

Most Snow Leopard awards won

Boris Korshunov (RUS, b. 31 Aug 1935) won nine Snow Leopard awards (see opposite) between 1981 and 2004 – two with the original four-mountain list, and seven with the current five-mountain list. He was aged 69 when he received his ninth award in 2004, making him the **oldest person to win the Snow Leopard award**.

First climb of Saser Kangri II

A Japanese-Indian expedition summitted the north-west peak of the Indian mountain on 7 Sep 1985, but the higher south-east peak (7,518 m; 24,665 ft) wasn't reached until 24 Aug 2011, by Mark Richey, Steve Swenson and Freddie Wilkinson (all USA). Until then, Saser Kangri II had been the second-highest unclimbed mountain after Kangkar Pünzum (aka Gangkhar Puensum; 7,570 m; 24,836 ft) in Bhutan (see p.283).

▲ **MOST 6,000-M ANDES MOUNTAINS CLIMBED**

Brazilian resident Maximo Kausch (UK) is attempting to climb every one of the 6,000-m-tall (19,685-ft) mountains in the Andes. On 3 Jan 2017, he summitted Nevado del Plomo (6,070 m; 19,914 ft) – his 74th successful climb.

The **first person to climb the 12 highest Andes mountains** was Darío Bracali (ARG), ending in 2004. He disappeared on Dhaulagiri in 2008.

▲ **FIRST ASTRONAUT TO SUMMIT EVEREST**

On 20 May 2009, former NASA astronaut Scott Parazynski (USA) successfully summitted Everest, becoming the first person to travel in space and climb Earth's highest mountain. According to NASA, Parazynski participated in five space flights and spent more than 1,381 hr in space, including 47 hr during his seven space walks. Before beginning his descent down Everest, he left behind a small Moon rock that had been collected by the crew of *Apollo 11*.

EVEREST 2016

The 2016 climbing season on the Nepalese side of Everest (Apr–May) in figures:

34

Teams at base camp by the start of the season

289 Climbing permits issued, with a further 265 extended from 2015. Two permits were issued for the south-west face; all others were for the standard route.

$11,000

Cost of a climbing permit (£7,523)

$15 m

generated for the Nepali economy (£10.26 m)

11 May

First recorded summit of the season, achieved by nine Nepali climbers

23 May

Last recorded summit of the season

20+

cases of reported frostbite

5

reported deaths

▲ FASTEST TIME TO CLIMB THE SEVEN SUMMITS INCLUDING CARSTENSZ (FEMALE)

Maria Gordon (UK) climbed the Seven Summits' combined Kosciuszko and Carstensz lists in 238 days 23 hr 30 min, beginning with the ascent of Mount Kilimanjaro in Tanzania and ending atop Mount Kosciuszko in Australia on 17 Jun 2016. She beat the previous best of 295 days, set by Vanessa O'Brien (USA) in 2012–13. Gordon also skied the last degree of the North and South poles en route to the record.

First person to climb the Seven Summits

The highest mountains on each of the continents are known as the Seven Summits. Patrick Morrow (CAN) completed the Carstensz list (which recognizes Puncak Jaya in Indonesia as the highest point in Oceania, as opposed to Mount Kosciuszko in Australia) on 5 Aug 1986.

The **first person to climb the Seven Summits (Kosciuszko list)** was Richard "Dick" Bass (USA), who finished on 30 Apr 1985.

Fastest time to climb the North Face of the Eiger (solo)

On 16 Nov 2015, Ueli Steck (CHE) scaled the north face of the Eiger, in the Swiss Alps, along the Heckmair route in 2 hr 22 min 50 sec. This was his third speed record on the Eiger, after those achieved in 2007 and 2008.

Most nationalities on Everest in one season

During the spring climbing season of 2013, 661 ascents of Everest were recorded by climbers from 46 nations. The largest group by nationality was Nepali, with 362 climbers.

◀ FIRST ASCENT OF EVEREST AND K2 WITHOUT SUPPLEMENTARY OXYGEN (FEMALE)

Alison Hargreaves (UK) topped Everest on 13 May 1995 – the **first undisputed ascent of Everest without supplementary oxygen (female)** – and K2 on 13 Aug 1995, again without the use of supplementary oxygen. Tragically, she was killed while descending from K2's summit that same day.

▶ FASTEST ASCENT OF THE TOP THREE HIGHEST MOUNTAINS WITHOUT SUPPLEMENTARY OXYGEN (MALE)

Silvio Mondinelli (ITA) climbed Everest (8,848 m; 29,029 ft), Kangchenjunga (8,586 m; 28,169 ft) and K2 (8,611 m; 28,251 ft) in 3 years 64 days, finishing on 26 Jul 2004.

The **fastest ascent of the top three highest mountains without supplementary oxygen (female)** is 5 years 101 days, by Gerlinde Kaltenbrunner (AUT) on 23 Aug 2011.

▼ MOST WOMEN ON EVEREST IN ONE SEASON

The spring climbing season of 2016 saw 68 women summit Everest. The largest group by nationality was Indian, with 15 climbers, while the USA ranked second with 12 (including Vanessa Blasic, pictured below with her expedition) and China third with eight. The **most women on Everest in one day** is 22, achieved on 19 May 2013.

Climbing Mount Everest remains an extremely dangerous challenge. The deaths-to-summit ratio is around 4%, and there are thought to be more than 200 dead bodies on the mountain.

The Poles

If all of Antarctica's ice sheet melted, global sea levels would rise by around 200–210 ft (60–64 m).

FIRST...

People to reach the South Pole

A Norwegian party of five men led by Captain Roald Amundsen reached the South Pole at 11 a.m. on 14 Dec 1911. They had marched for 53 days, with dog sleds, from the Bay of Whales.

Motorized expedition to the South Pole

On 4 Jan 1958, Sir Edmund Hillary (NZ) led the New Zealand component of the Commonwealth Trans-Antarctic Expedition to the South Pole, the first party to do so in motor vehicles. The team used five modified Ferguson tractors, fitted with full tracks and an extra wheel on each side. The tracks were removable so that wheels could be used when conditions allowed. The tractors were painted red to make them easier to spot.

Surface circumnavigation via both poles

Sir Ranulph Fiennes and Charles Burton (both UK) of the British Trans-Globe Expedition travelled south from Greenwich, London, UK, on 2 Sep 1979, crossing the South Pole on 15 Dec 1980 and the North Pole on 10 Apr 1982. They returned to Greenwich on 29 Aug 1982 after a 56,000-km (34,800-mi) journey.

Robert Falcon Scott had enjoyed great success up to his final, tragic trek. He became a national hero for leading the 1901–04 National Antarctic Expedition, which went farther south than any previous trip.

▼ MOST SOUTHERLY NAVIGATION

On 26 Feb 2017, *Spirit of Enderby*, commanded by Captain Dmitry Zinchenko (RUS), reached 78°44.008'S, 163°41.434'W – the farthest south that any ship has been recorded. The expedition to the Bay of Whales in the Ross Sea of Antarctica was organized by Heritage Expeditions (NZ) and the latitude was confirmed by hand-held instruments on board the ship.

Q: How many sunrises are there at the North Pole in a year?

A: One: the Sun rises at the Spring Equinox, just before 20 Mar, stays above the horizon and sets after the Autumn Equinox, around 23 Sep

▲ FIRST COMPLETION OF THE TERRA NOVA EXPEDITION

The British Antarctic Expedition, aka the Terra Nova Expedition, was Captain Robert Falcon Scott's (UK) 1912 attempt to become the first person to reach the Geographic South Pole. He and his team perished in the attempt, but on 7 Feb 2014, Ben Saunders and Tarka L'Herpiniere (both UK) completed Scott's route, travelling the 2,890 km (1,795 mi) from Ross Island to the South Pole and back, on skis and hauling sleds that at the start weighed almost 200 kg (440 lb) each. Their 105-day journey is also the **longest polar trek**.

Person to walk to both poles

Robert Swan (UK) led a three-man expedition that reached the South Pole on 11 Jan 1986. He also led the eight-man Icewalk expedition, which reached the North Pole on 14 May 1989.

Crossing of the Arctic

The British Trans-Arctic Expedition left Point Barrow, Alaska, USA, on 21 Feb 1968 and arrived at the Seven Islands archipelago, north-east of Spitsbergen, 464 days later on 29 May 1969. This involved a haul of 4,699 km (2,920 mi) with a drift of 1,100 km (683 mi), compared with the straight-line distance of 2,674 km (1,662 mi). The team comprised Wally Herbert (leader), Major Ken Hedges, RAMC, Allan Gill and Dr Roy Koerner (glaciologist), plus 40 huskies.

This achievement also represents the **longest traverse across the Arctic Ocean**.

Person to reach the North Pole solo

On 14 May 1986, Dr Jean-Louis Étienne (FRA) reached the North Pole after 63 days, travelling solo and without dogs. He had the benefit of being resupplied several times on the journey.

Expedition to the South Pole in a wheel tractor

At 18:55 (UTC) on 22 Nov 2014, Manon Ossevoort (NLD) left Novo Runway in Antarctica in a Massey Ferguson 5610 farm wheel tractor. She went on to complete a 4,638-km (2,881.91-mi) supported and assisted round trip to the South Pole lasting 27 days 19 hr 25 min. The Antarctica 2 expedition arrived back at Novo Runway on 20 Dec 2014, having clocked 438 hr 17 min driving time at an average speed of 10.58 km/h (6.57 mph).

MISCELLANEOUS

Fastest bicycle ride to the South Pole

On 17 Jan 2014, Juan Menéndez Granados (ESP) arrived at the South Pole solo on his "fatbike" – a wide-tyred bicycle adapted for riding on snow and varied terrain – after travelling 700 mi (1,130 km) from the Hercules Inlet in 46 days. He was unsupported and unassisted, but skied and pulled his bike on his sled when unable to cycle.

Earth has multiple North and South poles. Here is a selection of those found at the South Pole.

Geographic South Pole
One of two points (along with the North Pole) at which Earth's theoretical axis of rotation intersects with its surface. At the south, it is marked with a stake that is repositioned each year, based on data from US Navy navigational satellites.

Magnetic South Pole
The point where geomagnetic field lines point up vertically, out of Earth's surface. This pole's position shifts with changes in Earth's magnetic field.

Geomagnetic South Pole
The meeting place of Earth's surface and the axis of a hypothetical dipole (bar magnet) at Earth's centre, representing the planet's geomagnetic field

Cartographic South Pole
Fixed point where all lines of longitude meet when mapped on the globe

Ceremonial South Pole
A metal globe on a fixed pole at the South Pole Station. Used for photo opportunities.

Pole of Inaccessibility
The point on Antarctica farthest from the Southern Ocean: 82°06'S 54°58'E

▲ FIRST WOMAN TO REACH THE NORTH POLE

Ann Bancroft (USA) reached the North Pole on 2 May 1986, with five other team members. They used dog sleds and had left Drep Camp on Ellesmere Island, Canada, on 8 Mar.

Bancroft is shown above (front) with Liv Arnesen (NOR), the **first woman to complete a journey to the South Pole solo, unsupported and unassisted**. Arnesen trekked solo from the Hercules Inlet on 4 Nov 1994, arriving at the pole 50 days later, on 24 Dec.

Fastest married couple to reach the South Pole (unassisted, unsupported)

Chris and Marty Fagan (USA) reached the South Pole from the Ronne Ice Shelf in 48 days, leaving on 2 Dec 2013 and arriving on 18 Jan 2014. They covered 890 km (553 mi), at an average of 18.54 km (11.52 mi) per day.

Youngest person to trek to the North Pole

Tessum Weber (CAN, b. 9 May 1989) was 20 years 340 days old when he completed a trek to the Geographic North Pole – entirely on foot – on 14 Apr 2010. Tessum was part of a four-man expedition (including his father, Richard) that had left McClintock at Cape Discovery, Nunavut, Canada, on 3 Mar 2010 and reached the pole after 41 days 18 hr, having covered a straight-line distance of 780 km (484.67 mi).

The **youngest person to trek to the South Pole** is Lewis Clarke (UK, b. 18 Nov 1997), who was 16 years 61 days old when he reached the Geographic South Pole on 18 Jan 2014. He had skied 1,123.61 km (698.18 mi), from Hercules Inlet on the Ronne Ice Shelf, in a two-man unsupported and assisted trek.

▲ MOST EXPEDITIONS TO THE SOUTH POLE BY AN INDIVIDUAL

Hannah McKeand (UK) made six expeditions to the South Pole between 4 Nov 2004 and 9 Jan 2013. The journey involves covering some 600–700 mi (965–1,126 km) – depending on the route – and 40–50 days across one of the harshest environments on the planet.

The **most polar expeditions completed by an individual** is eight, by Richard Weber (CAN). He reached the Geographic North Pole from the coast six times between 2 May 1986 and 14 Apr 2010, and the Geographic South Pole twice from the coast on 7 Jan 2009 and 29 Dec 2011.

▲ FASTEST TREK TO THE SOUTH POLE (VEHICLE-ASSISTED)

On 24 Dec 2013, Parker Liautaud (FRA/USA) and Doug Stoup (USA) reached the South Pole after skiing 563.3 km (349 mi) with sleds from the Ross Ice Shelf. The journey took 18 days 4 hr 43 min. They walked about 30 km (18 mi) a day, despite Liautaud suffering from altitude sickness. The trek also provided the opportunity to carry out research into climate change.

▲ FASTEST SOLO JOURNEY TO THE SOUTH POLE (FEMALE, UNSUPPORTED AND UNASSISTED)

Johanna Davidsson (SWE) skied her way to the Geographic South Pole from the Hercules Inlet at the edge of the Antarctic continent in 38 days 23 hr 5 min from 15 Nov to 24 Dec 2016. She did so without using kites and without resupplies, covering a straight-line distance of 1,130 km (702 mi). Davidsson kited back to Hercules Inlet in 12 days. By the end of her journey, she had covered some 2,270 km (1,410 mi).

▲ FIRST SIBLINGS TO CLIMB THE SEVEN SUMMITS AND SKI THE POLAR LAST DEGREES

Twin sisters Tashi and Nungshi Malik (IND, b. 21 Jun 1991) completed the Seven Summits (the highest peak on each continent) according to the Carstensz list and skied the last degree of the South and North poles between 2 Feb 2012 and 21 Apr 2015. The term "last degree" refers to the distance between the 89th- and 90th-degree latitudes at the poles – approximately 111 km (69 mi).

▼ FASTEST TIME TO CLIMB THE SEVEN SUMMITS AND SKI THE POLAR LAST DEGREES (MALE)

Colin O'Brady (USA) climbed all of the Seven Summits, including Carstensz Pyramid, and skied the polar last degrees (see above) in 138 days 5 hr 5 min. He embarked on his monumental adventure on 10 Jan 2016 in the South Pole, and completed it when he reached the summit of Denali in Alaska, USA, on 27 May 2016.

Ocean Rowing

Fewer people have successfully rowed an ocean than have reached the summit of Mount Everest.

ATLANTIC

First row

On 6 Jun 1896, Norwegians George Harbo and Frank Samuelsen left New York City, USA, in an 18-ft-long (5.48-m) boat and rowed to the Isles of Scilly, UK. They arrived 55 days later, on 1 Aug, having rowed 2,841 nautical mi* (5,262 km).

First row across any ocean solo (female)

Victoria "Tori" Murden (USA) arrived on the island of Guadeloupe on 3 Dec 1999, having crossed the Atlantic from Tenerife in the Canary Islands in her 7-m (23-ft) boat. During a straight-line 2,575-nautical mi (4,770-km) journey lasting 81 days 7 hr 31 min, Murden faced 80-mph (129-km/h) gusts of wind and 20-ft (6.1-m) waves.

Fastest solo row (female)

Anne Quéméré (FRA) travelled from La Gomera to Guadeloupe in 56 days 10 hr 9 min from 26 Dec 2002 to 21 Feb 2003. Quéméré covered a straight-line distance of 2,560 nautical mi (4,741 km), beating the record time set by Tori Murden in 1999.

The **fastest solo row (female, east to west, open class)** was achieved by Elaine Hopley (UK) between 14 Dec 2016 and 12 Feb 2017. Raising money for charity, Hopley rowed from La Gomera to Antigua in 59 days 19 hr 14 min.

Longest distance rowed in 24 hours

Between 23:00 GMT on 12 Jun 2015 and 23:00 GMT on 13 Jun, Tom Hudson (UK) and Pete Fletcher (AUS) rowed 116.76 nautical mi (216.24 km) on board *Macpac Challenger*. The record was set during a transatlantic row from New York City, USA, to Falmouth, UK.

Fastest row east to west (all-female, team of four)

Team Row Like a Girl – Lauren Morton, Bella Collins, Georgina Purdy and Olivia Bolesworth (all UK) – rowed from La Gomera to Antigua in 40 days 8 hr 26 min, from 20 Dec 2015 to 29 Jan 2016. They averaged a speed of 2.63 knots (4.87 km/h; 3.02 mph) on board *Mrs Nelson*.

*1 nautical mi = 1.15 mi (1.85 km)

▲ OCEAN ROWING SOCIETY INTERNATIONAL

The Ocean Rowing Society (UK) was established in 1983 by Kenneth F Crutchlow and Peter Bird, later joined by Tom Lynch (USA), Tatiana Rezvaya–Crutchlow and Chris Martin (both UK). It keeps a record of all attempts to row the oceans and major bodies of water such as the Tasman and Caribbean seas, as well as rows around Great Britain. The society also classifies, verifies and adjudicates ocean-rowing achievements.

Classic-class boat
V-shaped hull; more cover for crew; blown less by wind; relatively stable. "Classic Pair" and "Classic Four" denote the number of rowers in this class of boat.

Open-class boat
Flatter-bottomed hull; less cover for crew; blown more by wind; less stable

Mid-Pacific
Usually, a row between California and Hawaii or from South America to a mid-ocean island

► FIRST MIXED TEAM TO ROW THE ATLANTIC EAST TO WEST FROM EUROPE TO SOUTH AMERICA, MAINLAND TO MAINLAND

Luke Richmond, Susannah Cass, Jake Heath and Mel Parker (all UK) rowed from Lagos in Portugal to Pontinhas in Brazil in 54 days 10 hr 45 min on 29 Feb–23 Apr 2016.

First team to cross any ocean by kayak

Hungarian duo Levente Kovácsik and Norbert Ádám Szabó paddled the Atlantic Ocean from Huelva in Spain, via Gran Canaria, to Antigua in the West Indies in their kayak *Kele* between 21 Oct 2015 and 30 Jan 2016.

Oldest person to row any ocean (male)

Peter Smith (ATG, b. 17 May 1941) was 74 years 217 days old when he began rowing the Atlantic east to west from La Gomera in the Canary Islands to Antigua in a team of four on board *Wa'Omoni*. The row lasted 52 days 9 hr 9 min, from 20 Dec 2015 to 10 Feb 2016.

MID-PACIFIC

Fastest row east to west (Classic Pair)

Louis Bird (UK) and Erden Eruç (USA/TUR) rowed from Monterey to Hawaii, USA, in 54 days 3 hr 45 min. Their journey on board *Yves* lasted from 5 Jun to 29 Jul 2016, and had an average speed of 1.61 knots (2.98 km/h; 1.85 mph).

◄ FIRST TEAM TO ROW THE ATLANTIC EAST TO WEST FROM EUROPE TO SOUTH AMERICA, MAINLAND TO MAINLAND

Between 7 Feb and 28 Mar 2016, the five-man crew of *Ellida* – comprising Matt Bennett, Oliver Bailey, Aldo Kane, Jason Fox and Ross Johnson (all UK) – rowed 3,335 nautical mi (6,176 km) from Lagos in Portugal to Carúpano in Venezuela in 50 days 10 hr 36 min. The self-styled "rogues of ocean rowing" met while serving in the UK armed forces. They set out on their epic voyage in the hope of raising £250,000 ($353,450) for a children's charity.

Q: How many ocean rows had been successfully completed as of Mar 2017?

◀ MOST OCEAN-ROWING SPEED RECORDS HELD SIMULTANEOUSLY ON DIFFERENT OCEANS

Fiann Paul (ISL, b. POL) made the **fastest row across the Atlantic east to west** in the *Sara G* crew in 2011, and was part of the *Avalon* crew who made the **fastest row across the Indian Ocean east to west** in 2014. He set his third ocean-rowing speed record on *Danielle* in 2016 (see below).

▶ OLDEST ALL-MALE PAIR TO ROW THE MID-PACIFIC

Rick Leach (USA, b. 14 Sep 1962) and Todd Bliss (USA, b. 15 Feb 1964) had a combined age of 106 years 10 days at the start of their east-to-west row from Monterey to Diamond Head in O'ahu, Hawaii, USA, on 5 Jun 2016. They completed their crossing on 29 Jul 2016, on board *Row Aloha*. The two men met while studying at the California State University Maritime Academy in Vallejo, USA.

▲ OLDEST TEAM OF TWO TO ROW ANY OCEAN (COMBINED AGE)

Pat Hines (USA, b. 28 Jun 1954) and Liz Dycus (USA, b. 29 Aug 1957) rowed across the Mid-Pacific east to west at a combined age of 120 years 258 days. They crossed from Monterey in California, USA, to O'ahu, Hawaii, USA, on board *Roosevelt* from 5 Jun to 21 Jul 2016.

Fastest row east to west (Classic Four)

Between 5 Jun and 14 Jul 2016, Uniting Nations – Fiann Paul (ISL, b. POL see above), Thiago Silva (BRA), Cyril Derreumaux and Carlo Facchino (both USA) – crossed the Mid-Pacific in 39 days 12 hr 20 min. Their average speed was 2.21 knots (4.09 km/h; 2.54 mph) on *Danielle*.

Oldest male to row in the Mid-Pacific

Greg Vlasek (USA, b. 30 Dec 1955) was 60 years 158 days old at the start of his east-to-west row from Monterey in California, USA, to Diamond Head in O'ahu, Hawaii, USA. He rowed as part of a team of four on board *Isabel* from 5 Jun to 23 Jul 2016.

Ocean rowing's absolute firsts:

First ocean row:
George Harbo,
Frank Samuelsen
(both NOR, see p.293)
1896: A, W>E

**First person to row
an ocean solo:**
John Fairfax (UK)
1969: A, E>W

**First person to
row two oceans:**
John Fairfax (UK)
1969: A, E>W
1971–72: P, E>W

**First woman to row
an ocean:**
Sylvia Cook (UK)
1971–72: P, E>W

**First person to row
the Pacific solo:**
Peter Bird (UK)
1982–83: P, E>W

**First person to row
two oceans solo:**
Gérard d'Aboville (FRA)
1980: A, W>E
1991: P, W>E

**First woman to row
two oceans:**
Kathleen Saville (USA)
1981: A, E>W
1984–85: P, E>W

**First woman to
row an ocean solo:**
Tori Murden (USA)
1999: A, E>W

**First person to row
three oceans:**
Erden Eruç (USA/TUR)
2006: A, E>W
2007–10: P, E>W
2010: I, E>W

**First woman to
row three oceans:**
Roz Savage (UK)
2006: A, E>W
2008–10: P, E>W
2011: I, E>W

**First person to row two
oceans in one year:**
Livar Nysted (FRO)
2013: A, E>W; I, E>W

Key:
A = Atlantic
I = Indian
P = Pacific
E = East
W = West

▲ FASTEST TIME TO ROW THE ATLANTIC EAST TO WEST BY A TEAM OF FOUR

Team Latitude 35 – Jason Caldwell, Matthew Brown (both USA), Angus Collins and Alex Simpson (both UK) – rowed 2,550 nautical mi (4,722.6 km) from La Gomera in the Canary Islands to the Caribbean island of Antigua in 35 days 14 hr 3 min between 14 Dec 2016 and 19 Jan 2017. They maintained an average speed of 2.986 knots (5.53 km/h; 3.44 mph).

Fastest row east to west (Classic Pair, all-female)

Rowing team Fight the Kraken – Vicki Otmani and Megan Biging (both USA) – covered 2,090 nautical mi (3,870 km) in 57 days 16 hr 9 min between 5 Jun and 31 Jul 2016 on board *Sedna*. They travelled from Monterey, California, USA, to O'ahu, Hawaii, at an average speed of 1.51 knots (2.79 km/h; 1.73 mph).

▼ FIRST TEAM TO ROW THE SOUTH ATLANTIC OCEAN

On 4 May–23 Sep 2016, the Latvian duo of Kārlis Bardelis and Gints Barkovskis rowed 3,112 nautical mi (5,763 km) from Lüderitz in Namibia to Rio das Ostras in Brazil in 141 days 19 hr 35 min on board *Linda*. They are one of only two crews to have crossed the Atlantic with both start and finish points in the Southern Hemisphere. Amyr Khan Klink (BRA) became the **first person to row the South Atlantic Ocean** when he crossed from Namibia to Brazil on 9 Jun–18 Sep 1984.

**80 kg –
Chocolate bar**

50 kg – Nuts

▶ FIRST ALL-FEMALE CREW TO ROW THE ATLANTIC WEST TO EAST

Guin Batten, Molly Brown, Alex Holt, Mary Sutherland and Gilly Mara (all UK) rowed 2,865 nautical mi (5,306 km) from Liberty Landing Marina in New Jersey, USA, to Falmouth in Cornwall, UK, in 48 days 13 hr 49 min from 7 Jun to 26 Jul 2016 on board *Liberty*. The crew was selected during a "hell weekend" featuring power testing, an endurance task and an overnight trek.

▲ YOUNGEST PERSON TO ROW THE ATLANTIC TWICE

Shaun Pedley (UK, b. 17 Feb 1992, above left) was aged 23 years 306 days when, on 20 Dec 2015, he started his second Atlantic row from La Gomera, Spain, to Antigua.

The **youngest person to make three ocean crossings** is Angus Collins (UK, b. 21 Sep 1989, above right). He set out on his third crossing on 14 Dec 2016, aged 27 years 84 days.

Fastest row east to west (Mixed Pair, open class)

Riaan Manser and Vasti Geldenhuys (both ZAF) rowed from Monterey to O'ahu in 39 days 4 hr 46 min. They averaged a speed of 2.22 knots (4.11 km/h; 2.55 mph) between 15 Jul and 23 Aug 2016 on *Honeymoon*.

Ocean rower Kārlis Bardelis is no stranger to epic journeys. In 2013, the intrepid Latvian crossed Europe in just 60 days on a pair of inline skates.

14 – Deck hatches, cabin hatches

200 litres – Drinking water

600 packs – Professional adventure food packages (pasta, rice, potatoes, etc.)

750 – Muesli bars

FAI

The Fédération Aéronautique Internationale (FAI) is the world governing body of air sports records. The organization was founded on 14 Oct 1905 in Paris, France.

▼ LONGEST TIME IN SPACE (AGGREGATE)

By the time he landed on 12 Sep 2015, having completed a period of service on the International Space Station (ISS), cosmonaut Gennady Ivanovich Padalka had spent 878 days 11 hr 29 min 24 sec in space. His first space mission came in Aug 1998, when he was one of the last cosmonauts to stay on the ageing Mir space station. He spent 198 days preparing the station for deactivation and de-orbit, returning to Earth on 28 Feb 1999. Between 2002 and 2012, he made three visits to the newly completed ISS, including two tours as commander of the station.

Highest altitude in elliptical orbit – single astronaut

On 12 Apr 1961, Soviet pilot Yuri Gagarin reached an altitude of 327 km (203.1 mi) in Vostok 3KA (Vostok 1). He completed a single orbit of Earth, lasting 108 min from launch to landing. Gagarin landed separately from his spacecraft, having ejected with a parachute 23,000 ft (7 km) above ground. His brief journey marked one of the most significant landmarks in space flight (see p.300).

Farthest distance in freefall without a drogue

On 14 Oct 2012, after jumping from a capsule 38,969.4 m (127,852 ft) above New Mexico, USA, skydiver Felix Baumgartner (AUT) fell 36,402.6 m (119,431 ft) for a duration of 4 min 20 sec. Baumgartner then deployed his parachute and landed safely on Earth, having fallen more than four times the height of Everest, the **highest mountain**.

Greatest altitude for a solar-powered aeroplane

Swiss pilot and explorer André Borschberg set an altitude record by flying at 9,235 m (30,298 ft) in Solar Impulse 1 on 8 Jul 2010 over Payerne, Switzerland – the highest altitude achieved by a manned solar-powered aircraft.

Almost five years later, in Solar Impulse 2, Borschberg flew for 117 hr 52 min (or 4 days 21 hr 52 min) – the **longest-duration flight in a solar-powered aeroplane (solo)**. He left Nagoya in Japan on 28 Jun 2015 and landed in Hawaii, USA, on 3 Jul 2015.

Padalka is a genuine time traveller. During his long stay in orbit, he aged very slightly slower than he would have on Earth. From his perspective, he returned to an Earth that had moved forward by around 0.02 sec.

Greatest height gain in a solar-powered aeroplane
On 24 Apr 2016, en route from Kalaeloa in Hawaii to Mountain View in California, USA, Bertrand Piccard (CHE; see also p.300) gained 9,024 m (29,606 ft) flying in *Solar Impulse 2*. The **farthest distance in a solar-powered aeroplane over a course of pre-defined points** is 5,851.3 km (3,635.8 mi), also by Piccard, flying in the same craft. The record was set on a journey from New York City, USA, to Seville, Spain, ending on 23 Jun 2016.

Farthest distance in an open-class glider (out and return)
On 4 Jan 2016, Max H S Leenders (NLD) achieved an out-and-return distance of 1,251.1 km (777.4 mi) in a Schempp-Hirth Nimbus-4DM glider. The record took place in Douglas, Northern Cape, South Africa. The term "out and return" denotes a closed course with only one declared turn point.

In the same model of glider, Klaus Ohlmann (DEU; see also p.300) covered 3,009 km (1,869.7 mi) in Chapelco, Argentina, on 21 Jan 2003, the **farthest distance flown in a glider (three turn points)**. The "three turn points" category for gliding designates a course with not more than three turn points, and a declared start and finish point. Turn points may include the start and/or finish points of the route.

Farthest flight by an unmanned aircraft
The longest flight by a full-scale unmanned conventional aircraft is 13,219.86 km (8,214.44 mi), by the USAF Northrop Grumman Global Hawk *Southern Cross II*. The plane took off from Edwards Air Force Base in California on 22 Apr 2001 and landed at RAAF Base Edinburgh in Adelaide, South Australia, 30 hr 23 min later on 23 Apr. The Global Hawk is a high-altitude, long-endurance spy plane.

Farthest non-stop flight by any aircraft
Steve Fossett (USA; see also p.301) covered 41,467.53 km (25,766.68 mi) in the *Virgin Atlantic GlobalFlyer*, taking off from the Kennedy Space Centre in Florida, USA, on 8 Feb 2006 and setting his distance record over Shannon, Ireland, on 11 Feb 2006.

▲ FAI
Located in the "Olympic Capital" of Lausanne, Switzerland, the FAI (also known as the World Air Sports Federation) is a non-governmental and non-profit-making organization that seeks to expand aeronautical and astronautical activities worldwide. The FAI ratifies international records and coordinates the organization of international competitions. All the records that appear on these pages are FAI-approved.

Milestones in aviation

21 Nov 1783
First manned balloon flight
Jean-François Pilâtre de Rozier
and the Marquis d'Arlandes
(both FRA); Paris, France

2 Jul 1900
First flight in a rigid airship
Count Ferdinand Adolf August
von Zeppelin (DEU); Lake
Constance, Germany

17 Dec 1903
First powered flight
Orville Wright (USA); Kitty Hawk,
North Carolina, USA

13 Nov 1907
First helicopter flight
Paul Cornu (FRA);
Calvados, Normandy, France

14 Oct 1947
**First human to break
the sound barrier**
Chuck Yeager (USA);
Mojave Desert, USA

12 Apr 1961
First manned space flight
Yuri Gagarin (USSR, now RUS);
from Kazakhstan (then
part of USSR)

21 Jan 1976
**First scheduled supersonic
passenger flight**
Concorde; London–Bahrain and
Paris–Rio de Janeiro routes

Highest altitude by an airship

On 17 Aug 2006, Stanislaw Fuodoroff (RUS) flew the
thermal airship Augur AU-35 *Snow Goose* to a height
of 8,180 m (26,837 ft) over Moscow, Russia.

Longest-duration flight in a balloon

The FAI endurance record for a manned balloon
flight is 19 days 21 hr 47 min, by Brian Jones (UK) and
Bertrand Piccard, set on a round-the-world trip on
1–21 Mar 1999. They took off in the *Breitling Orbiter 3*
from Château-d'Œx in Switzerland and landed in
western Egypt.

From 19 Jun to 2 Jul 2002, Steve Fossett made
the **first circumnavigation by balloon (solo)** in his
140-ft-tall (42.6-m) mixed-gas balloon *Bud Light Spirit
of Freedom*. He took off from Northam in Western
Australia and landed at Eromanga in Queensland,
Australia, having covered 20,627 mi (33,195 km).

▲ **FASTEST SPEED IN A GLIDER
(OUT AND RETURN)**

Klaus Ohlmann (DEU) reached 306.8 km/h (190.6 mph)
over an out-and-return course of 500 km (310 mi)
on 22 Dec 2006 at Zapala in Argentina. He flew a
Schempp-Hirth Nimbus-4DM. He also flew the
greatest free distance in a glider: 2,256.9 km
(1,402.3 mi), at El Calafate in Argentina on 12 Jan
2010. This category incorporates a course with a
declared start point and finish point, and no turns.

▲ FASTEST SPEED IN AN AIRSHIP

Steve Fossett (USA, above left) and his co-pilot Hans-Paul Ströhle (DEU) achieved a speed of 115 km/h (71.45 mph) in a Zeppelin Luftschifftechnik LZ N07-100 airship on 27 Oct 2004 over Friedrichshafen, Germany.

Fossett went on to make the **first circumnavigation by an aircraft without refuelling (solo)**, in 67 hr 1 min, from 1 to 3 Mar 2005 in the *Virgin Atlantic GlobalFlyer* (below, left and right). He started and finished at Salina in Kansas, USA. The aircraft, constructed by Scaled Composites, was powered by a single turbofan jet engine.

◄ LONGEST INDOOR FORMATION "4-WAY" SKYDIVE SEQUENCE

On 23 Oct 2015, the NMP Pch HayaBusa team – Belgians Andy Grauwels, David Grauwels, Jeroen Nollet and Dennis Praet – completed a sequence of 43 formations in the Hurricane Factory, the only wind tunnel in Prague, Czech Republic. The four skydivers achieved the record during the first-ever FAI Indoor Skydiving World Championships.

▶ FARTHEST STRAIGHT DISTANCE TO A DECLARED GOAL IN A HANG GLIDER

On 13 Oct 2016, Brazilians André Wolf (pictured) and Glauco Pinto flew alongside each other in separate hang gliders for a straight declared distance of 603 km (374.687 mi) from Tacima to Paraíba in north-eastern Brazil. Wolf flew in a Moyes Delta Gliders Litespeed RX 3.5, while Pinto opted for an Icaro 2000 Laminar 14.

Wingsuit competitors who take part in "performance flight" contests are scored in three rounds. Each round features three different types of jump: one for distance, one for speed and one for duration.

▼ LONGEST-DURATION GLIDE IN A WINGSUIT

On 6 Nov 2016, Chris Geiler (AUS) sustained a flight for 95.7 sec during the first FAI World Wingsuit Performance Flying Championships in Florida, USA. Athletes are flown to an altitude of around 4,000 m (13,123 ft) then exit the plane. Their competition zone is between the altitudes of 3,000 m and 2,000 m (9,842–6,561 ft). They strive to fly farther, faster or for longer than each other within this 1,000-m (3,280-ft) "window".

Adventures Round-Up

John o'Groats isn't actually the northernmost point on the mainland of Great Britain. Dunnet Head is around 18 km (11 mi) farther on, to the west.

Longest human-powered flight (distance)
Kanellos Kanellopoulos (GRC) pedalled his *Daedalus 88* aircraft 115.11 km (71.52 mi) on 23 Apr 1988. He flew from Heraklion, Crete, to the Greek island of Santorini in 3 hr 54 min 59 sec before a gust of wind broke the plane's tail and it crashed into the sea a few feet from the shore.

Longest journey by cycle rickshaw/pedicab (male)
From 27 Sep to 16 Oct 2015, Scott Thompson (UK) raised money for four Indonesian charities by cycling from Banda Aceh in Aceh, Indonesia, to Bumi Serpong Damai in Tangerang, Indonesia – a distance of 2,597.2 km (1,613.82 mi).

The **longest journey by cycle rickshaw/pedicab (female)** is 1,672 km (1,039 mi), by Crystal Davis (AUS) in 2015. She cycled from Port Douglas to Hervey Bay in Queensland, Australia, on 17 Oct–12 Dec.

▼ HIGHEST-ALTITUDE SCUBA DIVE
On 21 Feb 2016, Ernő Tósoki (HUN) scuba dived into a permanent lake on the eastern flank of active volcano Ojos del Salado, on the border of Chile and Argentina, at an altitude of 6,382 m (20,938 ft). Tósoki and partner Patricia Nagy (HUN) had to carry 100 kg (220 lb) of equipment up the volcano between them. The combination of mountaineering and scuba diving made for a daunting physical challenge, and Tósoki spent five years training for the feat.

▲ FASTEST TIME TO VISIT ALL SOVEREIGN COUNTRIES (FEMALE)

From 24 Jul 2015 to 2 Feb 2017, Cassandra De Pecol (USA) visited all of the 195 sovereign countries required by the GWR guidelines in a whistlestop tour lasting 1 year 193 days. Highlights included Paro Taktsang in Bhutan (above) and Yemen (top right). A trip to Antarctica in Feb 2017 (right) ensured that Cassandra had also visited every continent.

Longest journey by motorcycle in a single country (individual)

From 19 Sep 2014 to 29 Aug 2015, Danell Lynn (USA) rode her Triumph Bonneville 48,600 mi (78,214 km) across the USA. Starting out from Phoenix, Arizona, Danell went on to visit every one of the 48 contiguous US states.

Fastest journey from Land's End to John o'Groats by elliptical cycle

On 26–31 May 2016, Idai Makaya (UK) travelled between the southernmost and northernmost points of the UK in 5 days 4 min. Idai beat the existing time of 6 days 10 hr, set by Glen Burmeister (UK) in 2014.

Longest journey on a pocketbike (minimoto)

On 5–17 Sep 2016, Sigríður Ýr Unnarsdóttir (ISL), Michael Reid and Chris Fabre (both USA) rode 2,504.77 km (1,556.39 mi) from Middletown in Ohio, USA, to Ruidoso in New Mexico, USA.

Longest journey on a telescopic handler

Leo Tergujeff (FIN) drove a Merlo P 25.6 telescopic handler (also known as a cherry picker in the USA) 4,296 km (2,669.41 mi) from Italy to Finland on 28 Apr–2 Jun 2014. He travelled through Slovenia, Hungary, the Czech Republic, Germany and Sweden.

▲ DEEPEST UNDERGROUND BALLOON FLIGHT

On 18 Sep 2014, Austria's Ivan Trifonov guided a balloon through the mouth of the Mamet Cave at Obrovac, Croatia, and descended to a depth of 206 m (675 ft 10 in). From take-off to landing, the flight – which was made in a specially designed balloon – lasted 26 min.

Ivan is also responsible for the **first balloon flight over the North Pole** – in 1996 – and, in 2000, the **first balloon flight over the South Pole**.

◄ LONGEST JOURNEY BY TRACTOR

From 8 May to 23 Oct 2016, Hubert Berger (DEU) travelled around Europe in his 1970 Eicher Tiger II tractor, covering a total distance of 25,378.4 km (15,769.38 mi). He drove to 36 countries in all, beating the previous record of 21,199 km (13,172 mi) set by Vasilii Hazkevich (RUS) in 2005. "I am an adventurer by creed," Berger declared, "[trying] to escape the everyday madness with my tractor."

Longest journey by car in a single country

On 11 Mar–14 Apr 2016, K Raju, Jayanth Varma Kunaparaju, Purushotham and Arun Kumar (all IND) toured India, covering a distance of 36,060.1 km (22,406.7 mi). Their epic journey was undertaken to raise awareness of Swachh Bharat Abhiyan ("Clean India Mission"), a government initiative to clean towns and cities across the country.

On 8 May–25 Jul 2016, Sushil Reddy (IND) completed the **longest journey on a motorized bicycle** – 7,423.88 km (4,612.98 mi), starting and finishing in Mumbai, India. His bike was solar-powered.

Longest journey by electric vehicle (non-solar)

From 29 Jul to 28 Aug 2016, Nic Megert and Anton Julmy (both CHE) drove a Tesla Model S across Europe for 22,339.7 km (13,881.2 mi), starting and finishing in Bern, Switzerland. Driving around 800 km (497 mi) per day, they beat the previous farthest distance of 19,607.96 km (12,183.82 mi), which was set by Norman Hajjar (USA) in 2014.

The **longest journey by solar electric vehicle** is 29,753 km (18,487 mi), achieved by the SolarCar Project Hochschule Bochum (DEU) from 26 Oct 2011 to 15 Dec 2012.

Fastest journey from Land's End to John o'Groats on foot by a mixed-gender team

Team FFJogle2016 (UK) travelled the length of the UK in a time of 4 days 18 hr 2 min on 23–27 Mar 2016. The 12-person team of charity runners was split into a night- and day-shift team, known as Nightswatch and Days of Thunder respectively.

▶ GREATEST DISTANCE CYCLED IN A YEAR

On 5 Apr 2017, day 326 of a year-long record attempt sanctioned by the UltraMarathon Cycling Association, Amanda Coker (USA) beat the 76,076-mi (122,432.4-km) record set by Kurt Searvogel (USA) on 9 Jan 2016. By the end of day 326, Amanda had clocked up 76,233.9 mi (122,686.56 km). Incredibly, with 39 days to go, her logs showed daily average mileage *increasing* to 233.8 mi (376.2 km) per day.

◄ MOST COUNTRIES VISITED BY BICYCLE IN 24 HOURS (TEAM)

On 2 Oct 2016, pilots James van der Hoorn (far left) and Thomas Reynolds (near left, both UK) cycled through seven countries in 24 hr for charity, visiting Croatia, Slovenia, Hungary, Austria, Slovakia, the Czech Republic and Poland.

On 9 Aug 2010, Van der Hoorn and Iain Macleod (UK) achieved the **most countries visited by fixed-wing aircraft in 24 hours**: 11.

Fastest time to cycle around Australia
Reid Anderton (AUS) cycled 14,178 km (8,809.8 mi) in 37 days 1 hr 18 min from 10 Mar to 15 Apr 2013.

Longest journey by amphibious cycle
From 22 Nov 2014 to 29 Jan 2015, Ebrahim Hemmatnia (NLD/IRN) cycled 2,371 km (1,280.2 nautical mi) across the Atlantic Ocean.

Longest journey kite surfing (female)
Anke Brandt (DEU) kite-surfed 489.62 km (264.37 nautical mi) from Amwaj Marina to Al Dar Island in Bahrain on 17–19 Apr 2016.

The **longest journey kite surfing (male)** is 862 km (465 nautical mi), by Francisco Lufinha (PRT) on 5–7 Jul 2015.

First solo row across the Black Sea
On 12 Jun–11 Jul 2016, Scott Butler (UK) spent 29 days 6 hr 2 min rowing 1,207 km (651 nautical mi) from Burgas in Bulgaria to Batumi, Georgia.

◄ HIGHEST SKYDIVE WITHOUT A PARACHUTE

On 30 Jul 2016, Luke Aikins (USA) leapt 25,000 ft (7,620 m) from a plane without a parachute or wingsuit in a stunt he named "Heaven Sent". He landed safely in a 100-sq-foot (9.2-m²) net in Simi Valley in southern California, USA. Aikins spent a year-and-a-half preparing for his 3-min jump, and used a GPS unit to guide him to the net. The stunt was broadcast live by Fox television.

▲ LONGEST BAREFOOT JOURNEY

From 1 May to 12 Aug 2016, Eamonn Keaveney (IRL) walked a distance of 2,080.14 km (1,292.54 mi) barefoot. His aim was to raise funds and awareness for Pieta House, a suicide-prevention crisis centre. Beginning his journey in Claremorris, County Mayo, Ireland, primary school teacher Eamonn completed a shoeless circumnavigation of the country, braving rain, thorns, traffic and sore feet before returning to his starting point 103 days later.

Fastest time to sail across the English Channel by monohull

On 24 Nov 2016, Phil Sharp (UK) set off from Cowes on the Isle of Wight, UK, at 06:38:27 UTC (Coordinated Universal Time) and sailed the English Channel non-stop and single-handed in 9 hr 3 min 6 sec, crossing the finishing line in Dinard, France, at 15:41:33 UTC. He averaged a speed of 15.25 knots (17.54 mph; 28.24 km/h) in his 40-ft (12.19-m) race yacht *Imerys*. Sharp beat the time of 12 hr 1 min 31 sec set by Jean Luc Van Den Heede (FRA) in Nov 2004. The speed record was verified by the World Sailing Speed Record Council.

► GREATEST DISTANCE SAILED IN 24 HOURS BY MONOHULL (SINGLE-HANDED)

Between 7 a.m. (UTC) on 15 Jan and 7 a.m. on 16 Jan 2017, Alex Thomson (UK) covered 536.81 nautical mi (994.17 km) in his 60-ft-long (18.28-m) monohull *Hugo Boss*. Thomson, who was chasing after race leader Armel Le Cléac'h during the Vendée Globe round-the-world yacht race, clocked an average speed of 22.36 knots (25.73 mph; 41.41 km/h). Despite his record pace, he finished second.

Alex Thomson's record run was even more impressive for the fact that he achieved it in variable wind conditions off the coast of Spain, and that his starboard foil had smashed earlier in the race.

Highest...

Vertigo sufferers, look away now! Here we celebrate all things vertical and vertiginous, from bouncing pogo-stick riders and super-springing sharks to towering ocean waves and homes beyond the stratosphere. Have you got a head for heights?

0–3 m

Standing jump
1.616 m

On 13 May 2016, Evan Ungar (CAN) leapt from a standing position on to a platform measuring 1.616 m (5 ft 3.6 in) high. Fitness director Ungar achieved the record in front of a 100-strong crowd at One Health Clubs in Oakville, Ontario, Canada.

Jump by a dog
1.727 m

Cinderella May a Holly Grey, owned by Kate Long and Kathleen Conroy of Miami, Florida, USA, jumped 5 ft 8 in (1.727 m) at the Purina Incredible Dog Challenge National Finals in Missouri, USA, on 7 Oct 2006.

High Jump (female)
2.09 m

Stefka Kostadinova (BGR) cleared a high jump of 2.09 m (6 ft 10.28 in) at the 1987 World Championships in Athletics in Rome, Italy, on 30 Aug. She set seven career indoor and outdoor high jump world records.

Air on a skateboard (half-pipe)
2.35 m

Jocke Olsson (SWE) achieved a height of 2.35 m (7 ft 8 in) on the set of *L'Eté De Tous Les Records* on 6 Jul 2005. This was equalled by Terence Bougdour (FRA) on the same show on 27 Jul 2005.

High jump
2.45 m

On 27 Jul 1993, Cuba's Javier Sotomayor leapt 2.45 m (8 ft 0.45 in) in Salamanca, Spain. No one else has ever jumped above 8 ft (2.44 m). Sotomayor also recorded the **highest high jump (indoors)** – 2.43 m (7 ft 11.6 in), in Budapest, Hungary, on 4 Mar 1989.

Pole vault (male, indoors)
6.16 m

On 15 Feb 2014, Renaud Lavillenie (FRA) vaulted a height of 6.16 m (20 ft 2.5 in) during the Pole Vault Stars meeting in Donetsk, Ukraine. The previous record of 6.15 m (20 ft 2.12 in), set by Sergei Bubka (UKR), had stood for almost 21 years.

Leaping shark
6 m

The shortfin mako (*Isurus oxyrinchus*) is capable of leaping up to 6 m (19 ft 8 in) out of the water, even directly into fishermen's boats. This is due in part to the mako's great speed: at 56 km/h (34.8 mph), it is also the **fastest shark**.

Pole vault (female, outdoors)
5.06 m

Russia's Yelena Isinbayeva successfully cleared a height of 5.06 m (16 ft 7 in) in Zurich, Switzerland, on 28 Aug 2009. It was the 17th time she had broken the outdoor world record since 2003.

Popping toaster
4.57 m

In 2012, Matthew Lucci (USA) designed a toaster capable of ejecting a slice of toasted bread to a height of 15 ft (4.57 m). The previous best was 2.6 m (8 ft 6 in), achieved in 2008.

Jump on a pogo stick
3.36 m

On 15 Oct 2016, Biff Hutchison (USA) leapt 3.36 m (11 ft 0.2 in) on a pogo stick in Burley, Idaho, USA. He had first broken the record in 2013 at Pogopalooza 10, where he jumped 2.93 m (9 ft 7.3 in).

Pancake toss
9.47 m

On 13 Nov 2010, Dominic Cuzzacrea (USA) tossed a pancake to a height of 9.47 m (31 ft 1 in) at the Walden Galleria mall in Cheektowaga in New York, USA. Cuzzacrea also holds the record for **fastest marathon flipping a pancake** – 3 hr 2 min 27 sec, on 24 Oct 1999.

Shallow dive
11.56 m

Professor Splash, aka Darren Taylor (USA), dived from 11.56 m (37 ft 11 in) into 30 cm (12 in) of water on *CCTV – Guinness World Records Special* in Xiamen, China, on 9 Sep 2014.

Significant wave measured by a buoy
19 m

In Dec 2016, scientists from the World Meteorological Organization ratified a 19-m (62-ft 4-in) wave measured in the North Atlantic Ocean between Iceland and the UK on 4 Feb 2013.

Fall survived down a lift shaft
70 m

Stuart Jones (NZ) survived a fall of 23 storeys – 70 m (229 ft) – down a lift shaft at the Midland Park building in Wellington, New Zealand, in May 1998.

Tightrope cycled across
72.5 m

On 28 Aug 2010, Nik Wallenda (USA) cycled more than 100 ft (30 m) across a 238-ft-high (72.5-m) tightrope between the Royal Towers of the Atlantis Paradise Island hotel in Nassau, The Bahamas.

100–10,000 m

Mountain
8,848 m

Indian and Chinese surveys have confirmed the official height of Mount Everest in the Himalayas to be 8,848 m (29,029 ft). Named after Colonel Sir George Everest, Surveyor-General of India, its peak is the highest point on Earth.

BASE jump exit point
7,700 m

On 5 Oct 2016, Russia's Valery Rozov leapt from a height of around 7,700 m (25,262 ft) from Cho Oyu – the sixth-highest mountain in the Himalayas, located on the China/Nepal border. He fell for around 90 sec before opening his parachute, landing on a glacier approximately 2 min later.

Mountain unclimbed
7,570 m

At 7,570 m (24,835 ft), Kangkar Pünzum in Bhutan is ranked as the world's 40th highest peak, and the highest mountain yet to be climbed. Several failed attempts were made in the 1980s, before a climbing ban was issued in 1994.

Railway line
4,000 m

The Qinghai-Tibet railway in China operates largely at 4,000 m (13,123 ft) above sea level, with a highest point of 5,072 m (16,640 ft). Inaugurated in 2006, the line measures 1,956 km (1,215 mi). Passenger cabins are pressurized and have oxygen masks.

Capital
3,631 m

La Paz, the administrative capital of Bolivia, stands at an altitude of 3,631 m (11,913 ft) above sea level. Bolivia's legal capital Sucre stands at 2,810 m (9,219 ft), which places it below the Ecuadorian capital of Quito at 2,850 m (9,350 ft).

> 10,000 m

**Home
330,000 m**

The *International
Space Station*
(ISS) orbits
330,000–410,000 m
(205–255 mi) above
Earth. It normally has
six occupants at any
one time.

**Freefall parachute
jump
41,422 m**

On 24 Oct 2014,
Alan Eustace (USA)
was released from
a helium-filled
balloon at a height of
41,422 m (135,898 ft)
above Roswell in New
Mexico, USA.

**Stratospheric clouds
25,000 m**

Composed of ice crystals,
super-cooled water and nitric
acid, polar stratospheric
or nacreous clouds form at
altitudes of 21,000–25,000 m
(68,897–82,020 ft).

**Flight by a hot-air
balloon
21,027 m**

On 26 Nov 2005,
Dr Vijaypat
Singhania (IND)
achieved an
altitude of 21,027 m
(68,986 ft) in a
Cameron Z-1600
hot-air balloon over
Mumbai, India.

**Flight in a glider
15,460 m**

Steve Fossett (USA)
piloted a glider at an
altitude of 15,460 m
(50,721 ft) over El
Calafate in Argentina
on 29 Aug 2006.
The adventurer and
multiple record holder
disappeared the next
year while flying a
light aircraft over the
Great Basin Desert
between Nevada and
California, USA.

**Flying bird
11,300 m**

On 29 Nov 1973, a
Rüppell's vulture
(*Gyps rueppelli*)
collided with a
commercial aircraft
at 37,073 ft over
Abidjan in the Ivory
Coast. The high-flier
is rarely seen above
6,000 m (19,685 ft).

Society

There are 22 countries in which voting is mandatory, including Brazil, Thailand and Egypt. In Australia, failure to vote carries a fine of AUS$20 ($15.34; £12.33).

▲ MOST EXPENSIVE ELECTION

The 2016 US presidential election was the biggest political news story of recent times, not just in the USA but globally. According to the Center for Responsive Politics, the total cost of the elections reached an incredible $6.6 bn (£5.3 bn). When adjusted for inflation, that sum represents $86.5 m (£69.5 m) more than the previous presidential cycle in 2012.

As part of their election campaigns, nominees Donald Trump (Republican) and Hillary Clinton (Democrat) engaged in the **most watched televised presidential debate** (pictured), which was seen by 84 million viewers in the USA alone. Held on 26 Sep 2016, the debate – the first of three – beat the mark of 80.6 million set by Jimmy Carter and Ronald Reagan in 1980.

Upon winning the election, Trump and his Inaugural Committee raised a record $90 m (£73.19 m) to cover the costs of his commencement ceremony – the **most expensive presidential inauguration** – which took place at the US Capitol in Washington, DC, on 20 Jan 2017 (see p.316).

Contents

Trump won the US election by securing 304 Electoral College seats compared with Clinton's 227. However, Clinton won the "popular vote", with 65,853,625 votes compared with Trump's 62,985,106.

Politics & Superpowers

Franklin D Roosevelt is the only US president to have served four terms (1933–45). The United States Constitution now limits all US presidents to two terms only.

▼ LONGEST-REIGNING LIVING MONARCH

Her Majesty Queen Elizabeth II ascended to the throne of Great Britain on 6 Feb 1952 and had reigned uninterrupted for 65 years 57 days as of 4 Apr 2017. The Queen's role is nominal and ceremonial, exercising no political powers.

Alongside the UK, more than 139 million people in 15 Commonwealth states, including Australia and Canada, recognize the Queen as their monarch – the **most countries governed by the same head of state simultaneously**.

First political hacktivism

"Hacktivism" describes protests that use computer networks to try to achieve a political goal. The first recorded instance of this occurred in Oct 1989, when computers owned by NASA and the US Department of Energy were penetrated by the "Worms Against Nuclear Killers" cyber worm.

Most sentences commuted by a US president

By the time he left office on 20 Jan 2017, Barack Obama had granted clemency to 1,715 prisoners. He commuted 330 federal inmates on his final full day in office, 19 Jan 2017. Obama tweeted: "America is a nation of second chances, and 1,715 people deserved that shot."

Most expensive presidential inauguration

President Donald Trump's Inaugural Committee raised $90 m (£73.19 m) to cover the costs of his inauguration on 20 Jan 2017 – more than double that raised by President Obama in 2013. Donations included $1 m (£813,445) from Boeing, Dow Chemical and the Bank of America.

Largest parliament (legislative body)

China's National People's Congress (NPC) has 2,987 members, who meet annually in the Great Hall of the People in Beijing. Members are elected for five-year terms by municipal, regional and provincial "people's congresses", as well as by the People's Liberation Army (PLA).

The Queen has a second "official" birthday in June. She follows in a tradition started in 1748 by George II, who felt that his November birthday would be too cold for a parade and so set up a second in summer.

◀ LARGEST ILLEGAL RELEASE OF CLASSIFIED DOCUMENTS

In Apr 2016, a collection of documents from the internal database of Panamanian law firm Mossack Fonseca was released, revealing the secret offshore holdings of 140 politicians, public officials and athletes. The leak, which had more than 11 million records dating back 40 years, is roughly 1,500 times as big as the data dumped in 2010 by WikiLeaks.

Longest-serving non-royal head of state (ever)

On 25 Nov 2016, Fidel Alejandro Castro Ruz, aka Fidel Castro (CUB, b. 13 Aug 1926), died. He held the top political position in Cuba, first as prime minister (1959–76) and then as president (1976–2008), for 49 years 3 days.

In 2006, Fabián Escalante, a bodyguard assigned to protect Fidel Castro, announced that there had been 638 attempts on Castro's life – the **most failed assassinations**.

Longest time in power for a political party

Founded in 1929, and elected that year, Mexico's Institutional Revolutionary Party (PRI) remained in power until 2000 – a period of 71 years. It was originally called the National Revolutionary Party before changing to the Party of the Mexican Revolution in 1938, and again in 1946 to its current name.

Shortest presidency

Pedro Lascuráin ruled Mexico for 1 hr on 19 Feb 1913. Lascuráin was the legal successor to President Madero, who was deposed and later murdered. The vice president of Mexico was under arrest at the time, so Lascuráin was sworn in, appointed General Victoriano Huerta as his successor, then resigned.

▲ YOUNGEST CABINET MEMBER

At the age of 22, Shamma bint Suhail bin Faris Al Mazrui was appointed as the UAE's Minister of State for Youth Affairs in Sheikh Mohammed bin Rashid Al Maktoum's new cabinet, announced in Feb 2016. She also holds the role of President of the Youth Council. Sheikh Mohammed tweeted: "Youth represents some half of our Arab societies, so it is only logical to give them a voice and role in governing the nation."

FEMALE HEADS OF GOVERNMENT

Women appointed or elected as head of a government:

 Germany:
Angela Merkel

 Bangladesh:
Sheikh Hasina

 Norway:
Erna Solberg

 Namibia:
Saara Kuugongelwa

 Poland:
Beata Szydło

 Myanmar:
Aung San Suu Kyi

 UK:
Theresa May

FEMALE HEADS OF STATE

Women appointed or elected as head of state in a presidential system:

 Liberia:
Ellen Johnson Sirleaf

 Switzerland:
Doris Leuthard

 Lithuania:
Dalia Grybauskaitė

 Chile:
Michelle Bachelet

 Malta:
Marie-Louise Coleiro Preca

 Croatia:
Kolinda Grabar-Kitarović

 Mauritius:
Ameenah Gurib

 Nepal:
Bidhya Devi Bhandari

 Marshall Islands:
Hilda Heine

 Chinese Taipei:
Tsai Ing-wen

Estonia:
Kersti Kaljulaid

All details correct as of 23 Mar 2017

▲ YOUNGEST CURRENT UK MP
Mhairi Black (UK, b. 12 Sep 1994) was elected as Member of Parliament for Paisley and Renfrewshire South in 2015, aged just 20 years 237 days. Representing the Scottish National Party, Black received 23,548 votes – a +32.9% swing in a seat that had previously been held by Labour.

Richest prime minister

According to Forbes, Silvio Berlusconi of Italy had an estimated fortune of $11 bn (£6 bn) in 2005. It is rumoured that Vladimir Putin, the former prime minister and current president of Russia, has an estimated net worth of $70 bn (£56.9 bn), but Forbes has been unable to substantiate this.

Tallest world leader

Filip Vujanović became president of Montenegro in May 2003. At 6 ft 5 in (196 cm), he was the tallest president as of 2016. Formerly prime minister of Montenegro, he was elected president when the country gained its independence. He was re-elected in 2008 and 2013.

The **shortest world leader** was Benito Juárez, who served as president of Mexico from 1858 to 1872 and stood 4 ft 6 in (137 cm) tall.

YOUNGEST...

Head of state (current)

Kim Jong-un became leader of North Korea on 17 Dec 2011, following the death of his father Kim Jong-il. Jong-un's exact age has never been confirmed, but he is thought to have been 27 years old at the time of his succession.

"Baby of the House"

The term "Baby of the House" is the unofficial title given to the youngest member of a parliamentary body. In 2010, Anton Abele (SWE, b. 10 Jan 1992) was elected to stand for Stockholm county aged 18 years 277 days.

▲ MOST WOMEN PRIME MINISTERS

Including *acting* officials, Norway has had three female Prime Ministers: Gro Harlem Brundtland held the title three times (4 Feb 1981–4 Oct 1981, 9 May 1986–16 Oct 1989, and 3 Nov 1990–25 Oct 1996). Anne Enger Lahnstein was appointed acting PM to cover Kjell Magne Bondevik's sick leave (30 Aug 1998–23 Sep 1998). And Erna Solberg (pictured) was elected on 16 Oct 2013 and remains the PM as of 8 May 2017.

▲ LONGEST-SERVING PRESIDENT (CURRENT)

Teodoro Obiang Nguema Mbasogo (b. 5 Jun 1942) has been president of Equatorial Guinea since 1979, when he ousted his uncle and took control of the oil-rich Central African nation. Mbasogo (pictured inset on a 1982 visit to Spain) has maintained power through elections that opponents claim are controlled. On 24 Apr 2016, he extended his 37-year rule after securing 90% of the vote in an election.

Reigning monarch

Rukirabasaija Oyo Nyimba Kabamba Iguru Rukidi IV, aka King Oyo (b. 16 Apr 1992), was three years old when he came to power in the Ugandan kingdom of Toro in 1995. He now rules over 3% of Uganda's 33-million-strong population. His influence is largely symbolic, as the country is governed by an elected president.

▲ LARGEST POLITICAL PARTY MEMBERSHIP

The Bharatiya Janata Party (BJP) in India claimed 100 million members as of Jul 2015. It was established as a political party in 1980, arising from the Bharatiya Jana Sangh (founded in 1951). Under the leadership of prime minister Narendra Modi, the right-wing political party has outgrown the Chinese Communist Party, which claimed around 86 million members as of the same date.

▲ MOST *TIME* MAGAZINE COVERS (FEMALE)

Hillary Clinton had appeared on a total of 23 covers of *Time* magazine as of Dec 2016. The former First Lady and Democratic presidential candidate made her first appearance on the issue dated 14 Sep 1992, and her most recent on 15 Feb 2016 (above right).

Since its first publication on 3 Mar 1923, the **most *Time* magazine covers** is 55 – a record held by the 37th president of the USA, Richard Milhous Nixon (above left).

▲ MOST APPLICATIONS RECEIVED FOR POLITICAL ASYLUM BY ONE COUNTRY

According to the Pew Research Center (USA), Germany received 442,000 applications for asylum in 2015. The number of asylum seekers applying to the 28-member European Union was 1.3 million. Around half of all refugees could trace their origins to one of three countries – Syria, Afghanistan or Iraq – where external and civil wars (see below) have displaced thousands of people from their homes.

▲ MOST FOLLOWERS ON TWITTER FOR A POLITICIAN

As of 25 Jan 2017, former US president Barack Obama (USA, @BarackObama) had 83,313,483 followers on the social media platform. Obama ranked third on Twitter overall, behind pop stars Katy Perry (95 million followers) and Justin Bieber (91 million).

◀ COUNTRY RANKED MOST AT PEACE

According to the 2016 Global Peace Index, Iceland was the country most at peace, with a score of 1.192, ahead of Denmark with 1.246. Iceland retained the top spot, which it has held every year since 2011. The index takes into account factors such as domestic and international conflict, safety and security in society, and militarization.

◀ COUNTRY RANKED LEAST AT PEACE

According to the Global Peace Index 2016, published by the Institute for Economics and Peace, the country least at peace is Syria, with a score of 3.806. The Middle East country has been engulfed in civil war since 2011, leading to the devastation of cities such as Aleppo (inset). The Syrian Observatory for Human Rights estimated that 313,000 people had died in the war as of Jan 2017.

Money & Economics

According to Oxfam, the wealth of the richest 1% of the world's population is now equal to the wealth of the remaining 99% combined.

Fastest-rising brand

According to Interbrand, Facebook (USA) experienced an increase of 48% in revenue growth in 2016. It has grown more than any company, from a revenue of $5.09 bn (£3.14 bn) for the fiscal (financial) year ending 12 Dec 2012 to $17.93 bn (£12.09 bn) for the fiscal year 2015.

Most innovative economy

The 2016 Global Innovation Index gives Switzerland a score of 66.28. The index is compiled by the World Intellectual Property Organization, Cornell University (USA) and the graduate business school Institut Européen d'Administration des Affaires. Nations are rated via 82 indicators to assess how creative and progressive their economic policies are.

In 2010, billionaires Warren Buffett and Bill and Melinda Gates created the Giving Pledge. It encourages the world's richest people to promise to donate more than half of their wealth to charity.

Most equal society

Although Scandinavian societies such as Denmark, Norway and Sweden are commonly cited as the most equal societies in the world, on the most recent comparable figures from the World Bank (for 2015), Ukraine emerged as the country where the gap between rich and poor is at its smallest. Ukraine scores 0.25 when measured via the Gini coefficient – the most commonly used means of evaluating income inequality. A score of "1" registers maximum inequality (where one individual takes all the income); a score of "0" shows perfect equality (where all citizens have the same income).

According to the same source, as of 2015 South Africa had a Gini coefficient of 0.65, making it the **most unequal society**.

Smallest gender gap

The World Economic Forum's 2015 Global Gender Gap Index rates gender inequality from "0" (no inequality) to "1" (absolute equality). Based on this index, Iceland has less gender inequality than any nation, with a rating of 0.881. This figure is based on four indicators relating to the treatment of women: economic participation and opportunity; educational attainment; health and survival; and political empowerment. For the **largest gender gap**, see p.324.

▲ HIGHEST HEALTH-CARE EXPENDITURE

According to the World Health Organization, the USA's health-care spending represents 17.1% of its gross domestic product (GDP, or the goods and services produced by a country). This comes from private and public sectors.

Timor-Leste was the country with the **lowest health-care expenditure** relative to GDP, standing at only 1.5%, according to the same source.

Largest company by assets

According to Forbes, in 2016 the Industrial and Commercial Bank of China (ICBC) had book assets worth $3.42 trn (£2.38 trn). This figure reflects how the bank's assets are valued in its own books, or financial statements.

In 2015, Walmart Stores (USA) remained the **largest company by sales** for the third year running, with $482.1 bn (£325.1 bn) of net revenue generated that year.

◄ LARGEST ECONOMY

According to the International Monetary Fund World Economic Outlook, the USA has the world's greatest GDP, with an estimated $18.561 trn (£15.219 trn) as of Oct 2016. That figure represents 24.7% of global GDP. China was in second place with an estimated $11.391 trn (£9.340 trn), and Japan placed third with a GDP of $4.730 trn (£3.878 trn). Between them, these three countries are responsible for around 46% of the world's GDP.

▲ HIGHEST COST OF LIVING

According to a survey conducted by Numbeo.com in 2017, Bermuda has the highest cost of living, with a score of 146.19. Relative to New York City, USA, groceries are an estimated 39.55% more expensive in Bermuda and restaurants are a hefty 51.39% pricier, while rents are 4.76% greater. In terms of the average salary, however, Bermudians' purchasing power was put at 8.35% less than that of New York's citizens.

▲ GREATEST ECONOMIC FREEDOM

As of 2016, Hong Kong retains the world's most liberated economy – rated by the Heritage Foundation at 88.6. This represents a one-point drop since 2015. The ranking reflects factors such as efficient regulation, anti-corruption measures, transparency of government and encouragement of entrepreneurship. Singapore is close behind, with 87.8.

Largest advertising agency by revenue

The Ad Age Agency Report of 2016 ranks British firm WPP as the biggest advertising agency, with earnings of $18.693 bn (£12.608 bn) in 2015. WPP has 179,000 staff in 111 countries.

◀ HIGHEST SPENDING ON DEFENCE AS A PERCENTAGE OF GDP

Both Afghanistan (left) and Oman spent 16.4% of their GDP on defence in 2015, according to The Economist. Saudi Arabia was ranked in third place, with 13%.

In terms of the overall highest defence budget, the USA spent $596 bn (£401 bn) in 2015, according to data from the Stockholm International Peace Research Institute (SIPRI). This was up from $587 bn (£377 bn) in 2014.

The Top 10 companies according to Interbrand's 2016 Best Global Brands report*

$178.119 bn
In the first three months of their 2017 fiscal year, Apple sold 78.29 million iPhones

$133.252 bn Google
There are an average of 60,000 Google searches per second

Coca-Cola **$73.102 bn**
Nearly 22,000 Coca-Cola-owned beverages are drunk each second

$72.795 bn Microsoft
If you had bought $1,000 worth of shares in Microsoft in 1986, they would be worth around $740,000 today

$53.58 bn
Japanese car giant Toyota spends more than $1 million on research and development every hour

$52.5 bn IBM
Also known as "Big Blue", IBM is one of the largest global employers, with around 380,000 workers

$51.808 bn SAMSUNG
In 2016, Samsung was granted more US patents (8,551) than any other company, according to data journalism service Sqoop

$50.338 bn amazon
On 12 Jul 2016 – "Amazon Prime Day" – the company shipped an estimated 636 items per second

$43.49 bn Mercedes-Benz
The luxury car manufacturer saw sales of 2.23 million units in 2016 – the first time they had topped 2 million

$43.13 bn
General Electric technology generates around one-third of the world's electricity

▲ **LARGEST GENDER GAP (COUNTRY)**
Yemen has the greatest gender inequality of any country, according to the World Economic Forum's 2015 Global Gender Gap Index, with a rating of 0.484. Out of 145 nations, it is ranked 145th for economic participation and opportunity; 142nd for educational attainment; 123rd for health and survival; and 140th for political empowerment.

HIGHEST...

Expenditure
The US government spends more than any other country, according to the CIA World Factbook – an estimated $3.893 trn (£3.163 trn) in 2016, or 17% of all expenditure worldwide.

The USA also has the **highest revenue** – approximately $3.363 trn (£2.733 trn) in 2016, according to the same source. This is mostly generated from taxes and duties.

▲ **LARGEST BANK (OVERALL)**
The Industrial and Commercial Bank of China (ICBC) is a government-owned bank, founded as a limited company in 1984. According to Forbes, the bank had an asset value of $3.616 trn (£2.521 trn) in 2016. This figure reflects the market value of its assets. ICBC has 490 million retail customers and 5,320 corporate customers, with branches in Asia, Europe, America and Oceania.

*Interbrand's brand valuation report assesses companies according to specific criteria. These include financial performance, brand growth and the influence that the brand name itself has on a purchase.

The poorest people are those of Burundi, according to the most recent available World Bank figures, with a GDP per capita of $277.10 (£186.90).

Excluding the tiny principalities of Monaco and Liechtenstein, the **richest people** live in Luxembourg, according to the International Monetary Fund (IMF), which had a GDP of $105,829 (£86,777) per capita as of Oct 2016.

Education expenditure

The latest available figures from *The Economist* indicate that Lithuania spends around 18% of its GDP on education. Cuba is in second place, with just over 12%. The same source ranks South Sudan as the country with the **lowest education expenditure**: around 0.8% of GDP.

Annual earnings for a CEO (current)

According to Forbes, from 1 Jun 2015 to 1 Jun 2016 John Hammergren (USA) was the highest-paid Chief Executive Officer (CEO), with $131.19 m (£89.79 m) in compensation. He is chairman, president and CEO of health-care specialists McKesson Corporation (USA).

Economic growth

Based on World Bank data, Ireland enjoyed a growth rate of 26% in 2015, partly owing to a substantial increase in foreign investment.

Yemen had the **lowest economic growth** during 2015. Its GDP shrank by 28.1% that year, according to the same report.

▲ **LOWEST COST OF LIVING**
Numbeo.com, a user-generated global database, gave Egypt a rating of 22.36 on its Cost of Living Index as of Dec 2016, lower than any other country. Nations are ranked by the relative cost of maintaining a typical international lifestyle. The prices in New York City are used as a base, with the USA having a score of 100. Every other country is then rated in comparison to this figure.

Had it not been for a $150-m cash injection from Microsoft in 1997, Apple might have folded. Under CEO Steve Jobs, however, it became profitable again. By 2011, Apple had more cash than the US Treasury.

▲ **LARGEST COMPANY BY PROFIT**
US tech giant Apple is the largest company in the world, with $53.7 bn (£37.4 bn) of annual profits as of 22 Apr 2016. For the second year in a row, Apple also led the Fortune 500 list of the 10 most profitable companies.

Crime & Punishment

Market analysts predict that by 2019 the cost of global cyber crime will exceed $2.1 tr (£1.4 tr).

The Dubai police's garage is filled with high-performance cars. Beside the Veyron, they have used a Lamborghini Aventador, a McLaren MP4-12C, an Aston Martin One-77 and two Ferrari FFs!

First stalker of a celebrity

Edward Jones (UK) stalked Queen Victoria from 1838 until 1841, repeatedly entering Buckingham Palace to spy on her and steal her underwear. Forced into service in the Royal Navy, "the boy Jones" eventually moved to Australia, where he became the town crier of Perth.

Longest serving executioner

William Calcraft (UK) served as public executioner for 45 years between 1829 and 1874. He officiated at nearly every outdoor and indoor hanging at Newgate Prison in London, UK.

Most profitable sea pirate

Born in England in 1689, Samuel Bellamy found lasting notoriety as the pirate "Black Sam". In just two years, 1715–17, he commandeered more than 50 ships in the Caribbean and Atlantic and amassed a fortune worth more than £105 m ($135 m) in today's money. Having seized the slave ship Whydah, Bellamy perished when it sank on its way back to port on 26 Apr 1717.

◀ FASTEST POLICE CAR IN SERVICE

To keep up with the sports cars of their wealthy citizens, in Apr 2016 police in Dubai decided to invest $1.6 m (£1.09 m) in one of the most powerful production cars on the planet: a Bugatti Veyron. With a blistering top speed of 407 km/h (253 mph), its 1,000-hp (746-kW), 16-cylinder engine launches the car from 0 to 60 mph (0–96.5 km/h) in just 2.5 sec. This is even quicker than the Lamborghini Gallardo, which has been used by the Italian police.

Highest cost of piracy on the high seas in a year

The World Bank estimated the economic cost of piracy off the coast of the east African country of Somalia to be approximately $18 bn (£14.4 bn) in 2013. This exceeded the previous record total of $7–11 bn (£5.6–8.8 bn), set in 2011.

Rather than lose ships and crews, commercial shipping companies and their insurers often pay ransoms. In 2010, a total of $238 m (£153.8 m) was paid out in this fashion – **the highest ransoms paid to pirates in a year**. The average cost of each incident was $5.4 m (£3.49 m).

Highest hijack ransom

The Greek-flagged *M/T Irene SL*, a Very Large Crude Carrier (VLCC) transporting two million barrels of oil, was hijacked by Somali pirates on 9 Feb 2011 off the coast of Oman. After her 25-man crew was held captive for 58 days, a ransom of $13.5 m (£8.3 m) was paid to secure the ship's safe return.

Largest diamond heist

In Feb 2003, a group of thieves robbed the vault of the Antwerp World Diamond Centre, escaping with more than $100 m (£82 m) in diamonds, gems and other jewellery. The Italian gang, led by mastermind Leonardo Notarbartolo, was later apprehended. The vast majority of the diamonds, however, have never been recovered.

▲ HIGHEST RATE OF MURDER PER CAPITA

Honduras endured 90.4 murders per 100,000 citizens in 2012, according to a global study published by the United Nations. Nigeria reported the highest absolute number of murders – 33,817 – though owing to its larger population this worked out at "only" 20 per 100,000 people.

Robert Levinson has only been sighted rarely since his 2007 abduction. In 2013, his family released photos they had received of an unkempt Levinson dressed in an orange jumpsuit.

◀ LONGEST-HELD HOSTAGE

Ex-FBI investigator Robert Levinson (USA) was abducted on the Iranian island of Kish on 9 Mar 2007. Although he claimed to be tracking cigarette smugglers for the tobacco industry, it later emerged that Levinson had been working for the CIA. His whereabouts remain a mystery, despite a $5-m (£3.37-m) reward. As of 6 Nov 2016, he had been missing for 9 years 242 days.

440,095 deaths by firearms on US soil between 2001 and 2014

3,412 deaths of US citizens – home and abroad – as a result of terrorism during the same period

Sources: CDC, CNN

Number of terrorist attacks (2006–15)

2006: 14,371
2007: 14,414
2008: 11,662
2009: 10,969
2010: 11,604
2011: 10,283
2012: 6,771
2013: 9,964
2014: 13,482
2015: 11,774

Highest crime rates per capita (figures per 100,000 people), according to the UN Office on Drugs and Crime Report 2014

Car theft: 502.8 Uruguay

Burglary (theft from property after forced entry): **1,506.7 Netherlands**

Robbery (theft of property from an individual): **1,529.3 Belgium**

Assault (non-fatal physical attack on an individual): **1,324.7 Grenada**

▲ MOST LIFE SENTENCES
On 19 Apr 1995, a federal building was bombed in Oklahoma City, Oklahoma, USA, killing 168 people. At a federal trial in 1997, Terry Lynn Nichols (USA) was sentenced to life imprisonment without parole for his role in the planning and preparation of the bombing. In 2004, Nichols was convicted on 161 counts of first-degree murder, for which he was sentenced to 161 consecutive life sentences.

Richest insurgency group
Designated a terrorist organization by the United Nations, Daesh, aka the Islamic State of Iraq and Syria (ISIS), had a net worth estimated at $2 bn (£1.64 bn) by Forbes in 2014. Much of the group's money comes from the illegal sale of oil, as well as smuggling, extortion and robbery. When it took control of the Iraqi city of Mosul in 2014, ISIS seized funds from the city's bank worth more than $300 m (£256 m).

▲ HIGHEST KIDNAP RANSOM (MODERN ERA)

Hong Kong gangster Cheung Tze-keung (known as "Big Spender" for his lavish lifestyle) received a total of $206 m (£131.8 m) for the safe return of two businessmen: Walter Kwok and Victor Li, kidnapped in 1997 and 1996 respectively. It was part of an audacious plan to kidnap the 10 richest tycoons in Hong Kong. But when a third abduction failed, Cheung was caught and executed in China on 5 Dec 1998.

Most kidnaps per country (per capita)

According to data collected by the United Nations Office on Drugs and Crime for 2014, Lebanon experienced 18.371 kidnappings for every 100,000 citizens. Belgium was second with 9.959 and Luxembourg third with 9.343.

Smallest prison

With a population of around 600 people, the island of Sark is the smallest of the UK's four main Channel Islands. Its prison, built in 1856, has a maximum capacity of two inmates.

Largest DNA database

The National DNA Index System (NDIS) was created by the FBI in 1994. As of Apr 2016, it contained 12.2 million offender profiles (genetic profiles of known criminals), 2.6 million arrestee profiles and 684,000 forensic profiles (pieces of crime-scene evidence).

◀ MOST JOURNALISTS IN JAIL (YEAR)

As of 1 Dec 2016, there were 259 journalists in prison as a result of their work, according to non-profit organization Committee to Protect Journalists (CPJ). This made 2016 the worst year for media imprisonment since the CPJ began monitoring in 1990. Pictured are protestors campaigning against Turkey's record for press imprisonment in 2016.

▲ MOST PRISON INMATES BY COUNTRY

According to the International Centre for Prison Studies, the prison population of the USA numbered 2,217,947 as of Jul 2016. China had the second largest prison population, with 1,649,804, albeit taken from a much bigger population. The USA had 693 inmates per 100,000 people, second only to the Seychelles, where 799 people per 100,000 were behind bars.

Most criminals positively identified from the composites of one artist

Between Jun 1982 and May 2016, a total of 751 criminals were positively identified and brought to justice in Texas, USA, thanks to detailed composites drawn by forensic artist Lois Gibson (USA). She honed her skills sketching tourist portraits in San Antonio, Texas, before starting work for the Houston Police Department.

▼ HIGHEST INCIDENCE OF PIRACY IN A YEAR

In 2016, the International Maritime Bureau (IMB) reported that piracy had fallen to its lowest levels since 1998, with 191 incidents of piracy on the high seas. This compares with 469 global pirate attacks in 2000, the largest total since records began. Of those attacks, 242 occurred in Southeast Asia and the Malacca Strait between Malaysia, Indonesia and Singapore. Increased police and navy patrols (shown below) helped bring about a sharp decline in incidents of piracy in the area.

The Malacca Strait links the Indian and Pacific oceans. A quarter of all traded goods passes through it.

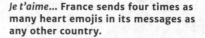

Je t'aime... **France sends four times as many heart emojis in its messages as any other country.**

First written language

Yangshao culture pottery discovered in 1962 near Xi'an in the Shaanxi Province of China bears proto-characters for the numbers 5, 7 and 8. It has been dated to 5,000–4,000 BCE.

Language with the most sounds

The remarkable language of !Xóõ (also known as Ta'a) is spoken by a small community of around 3,000 semi-nomadic people in southern Botswana and eastern Namibia. Linguists studying the language have counted 161 distinct sounds (technically known as "segments" – roughly equivalent to the sounds associated with letters or letter pairs in English). By comparison, English only has around 40.

!Xóõ's 161 distinct sounds include 130 different consonants – the **most consonants in one language**. Consonant sounds like those found in English are joined by a wide range of unvoiced stops and clicks – sounds like the "tsk" noise of disapproval used in English-speaking countries.

The Korean alphabet, known as Hangul in South Korea, was created in 1443 by King Sejong the Great. Before then, Korean texts had been composed in classical Chinese.

◄ MOST COMMON LANGUAGE ISOLATE

A "language isolate" is one that has no traceable relationships with any other languages. The third-most common language isolate is Mapudungun, spoken by the Mapuche people of South America, who number approximately 300,000. The second-most common is Basque, with 666,000 speakers concentrated in the Basque region of northern Spain. Yet neither language isolate comes anywhere close to Korean, which is spoken by an estimated 78 million people.

Most official languages for a country

Zimbabwe has 16 official languages codified into its constitution, as approved by the country's parliament on 9 May 2013. The full list of languages is: Chewa, Chibarwe, English, Kalanga, Khoisan, Nambya, Ndau, Ndebele, Shangani, Shona, sign language, Sotho, Tonga, Tswana, Venda and Xhosa. (For the **most unofficial languages for a country**, see opposite.)

Most common language sound

No known language lacks the vowel "a", as features in the English word "father".

▲ BIGGEST USER OF THE POO EMOJI

In Apr 2015, UK touch-screen keyboard developer SwiftKey announced the results of their search to find which nations used particular emojis the most. Both the skull and the birthday cake emoji were most popular in the USA, while the winking smiley appeared most frequently among UK-generated emojis. Canada proved the biggest user of the "smiling pile of poo" emoji; it accounted for 0.48% of all emojis used by Canadians.

Most popular emoji (current)

According to a joint study by the University of Michigan (USA) and the University of Peking (China), published in the *International Journal of UbiComp* in Sep 2016, the most used emoji is "Face with Tears of Joy" (aka "LOL Emoji" or "Laughing Emoji"). Of the 427 million messages examined – from 212 countries or regions – this symbol comprised 15.4% of all emoji selected through the *Kika Emoji Keyboard* app.

Biggest emoji user on Instagram (country)

In a 2015 study, researchers working for Instagram analysed the content of text comments on the photo-sharing app and found that 63% of all comments made by Finnish users contained one or more emoji. This put Finland well ahead of France with 50%, the UK with 48% and Germany with 47%. Bottom of the table was Tanzania, with just 10%.

▲ MOST GENDER-SPECIFIC LANGUAGE

For around 1,000 years, in a region of Hunan Province in southern China, *nüshu* – "women's writing" – has been used exclusively by women to communicate their feelings to other women. It is believed to have been invented by a concubine of an emperor of the Song dynasty (960–1279 CE). The last-known woman proficient in *nüshu* outside scholarly circles, Yang Huanyi, died on 20 Sep 2004 at the age of 98.

▲ FIRST BRAND WITH ITS OWN EMOJI ON TWITTER

From 18 Sep 2015 until the end of the year, typing #shareacoke into a tweet on Twitter brought up an emoji of two clinking Coke bottles. The emoji, part of a marketing campaign devised by creative agency Wieden + Kennedy, was a product of Coca-Cola's partnership with Twitter. Rival Pepsi followed suit later that year with its own paid-for emoji Twitter campaign, while 2016's #pepsimoji enabled Twitter users to add branded stickers to their photos.

◄ MOST UNOFFICIAL LANGUAGES FOR A COUNTRY

Located in the south-western Pacific Ocean, Papua New Guinea is home to speakers of 840 languages – a comprehensive list that runs from Abadi to Zimakani and includes Tok Pisin, Motu and English. Most of the island's 7 million inhabitants live in fragmented rural areas with their own regional dialects – which may explain why most of the country's languages are spoken by fewer than 1,000 people.

Least common language

According to the Ethnologue database of languages, more than 400 of the world's languages are nearly extinct, in the sense that "only a small number of elderly speakers are still living". It is thought that languages are disappearing at a rate of one every fortnight.

Among these endangered languages there are some – probably fewer than 10 – that have only one living native speaker. For example, there were 10,000 speakers of the South American Yaghan language in the late 19th century, but this number had dropped to only 70 by the 1930s. Today, the last remaining native speaker is Cristina Calderón (CHL, b. 1928).

FIRST...

Digital emoticon

The first "smiley" was written on 19 Sep 1982 by Scott Fahlman (USA) of Carnegie Mellon University in Pittsburgh, USA. In a message on a bulletin board system, he proposed the use of :-) and :-(in emails to signify the emotional context of the message and prevent misunderstandings.

◄ LONGEST NOVEL TRANSLATED INTO EMOJI

In 2009, data engineer Fred Benenson (USA) set up a project to translate the novel *Moby-Dick* by Herman Melville into emoji. The book was chosen partly because of its great length: 206,052 words. Hundreds of individuals were contracted to translate one of the book's 6,438 sentences into emoji. A vote took place to select the best versions, and these were compiled into a single work. The book was completed in 2010 and entitled *Emoji Dick*.

ENGLISH: Call me Ishmael.

EMOJI: ☎️🚣‍♂️⚓🐳👌

Most spoken languages

Ethnologue.com tracks the world's languages. Below is a top 10 of the most widely spoken languages, based on the population of first-language speakers. Each entry features the primary country, the number of countries in which that language is spoken and the total number of speakers.

1. Chinese
China (35 countries): 1.302 billion speakers

2. Spanish
Spain (31): 427 million

3. English
UK (106): 339 million

4. Arabic
Saudi Arabia (58): 267 million

5. Hindi
India (4): 260 million

6. Portuguese
Portugal (12): 202 million

7. Bengali
Bangladesh (4): 189 million

8. Russian
Russia (17): 171 million

9. Japanese
Japan (2): 128 million

10. Lahnda
Pakistan (8): 117 million

▲ MOST OFFICIAL LANGUAGES (INTERNATIONAL ORGANIZATION)

Every country joining the European Union (EU) must nominate a primary language. With the addition of Croatian in 2013, the EU now has 24 official languages, from Bulgarian to Swedish. The task of translating between these languages is shouldered by thousands of translators, a process that costs the EU around €330 m ($349 m; £287 m) a year.

Emoji password

On 15 Jun 2015, financial software company Intelligent Environments (UK) launched emoji passcode software that allowed users to access bank accounts by entering four characters from a range of 44 emojis. The code is already integrated into the company's digital banking app for Android mobile phones.

▲ MOST CONFUSING EMOJI

In an Apr 2016 study published by the University of Minnesota, USA, volunteers were asked to rank emojis on a 10-point emotional scale from positive to negative. With interpretations ranging from euphoric laughter to extreme pain, Microsoft's "smiling face with open mouth and tightly closed eyes" (above near left) gave it the largest overall spread of 4.4 points.

▲ FIRST EMOJI

The earliest pictograms known as "emoji" were designed by Shigetaka Kurita (JPN, left) in 1998–99, while devising the first mobile internet platform – known as "i-mode" – for the Japanese telecommunications company NTT DOCOMO. Inspired by symbols used in weather forecasts and manga, Kurita invented the original range of 180 expressions to provide a concise form of communication for mobile phones.

Emoji blocked on Instagram

In Apr 2015, an employee at online media company BuzzFeed noticed that searching for the eggplant (aubergine) emoji on Instagram produced zero hits. The offending emoji had been intentionally blocked because of its use as a metaphor for male genitalia, which the social networking site described as content violating its community guidelines.

▶ MOST COMMON LANGUAGE

According to online language resource Ethnologue, Chinese is listed as an official language by 35 countries and is spoken by 1.302 billion people (see opposite). With 897 million speakers, Mandarin is by far the most common variety of Chinese. Spanish can claim 427 million speakers across 31 countries, while there are 339 million English speakers in 106 countries.

Flags

At the 1936 Berlin Olympics, Haiti and Liechtenstein realized that their flags were identical. In 1937, Liechtenstein added a crown to its flag.

Most common colour in national flags

The colour red appears on 74% of all national flags. White and blue rank second and third in popularity, appearing on 71% and 50% of all national flags respectively.

Longest national flag (official aspect ratio)

Qatar's flag is the only national flag to have a width more than twice its height, based on its official height-to-width ratio of 11:28. The maroon flag with a broad white nine-pointed serrated stripe on the hoist side (see p.338) was adopted on 9 Jul 1971 – just before Qatar gained independence from Britain on 3 Sep of that year.

Smallest national flag

The Institute for Quantum Computing (CAN) created a 0.697-micrometre^2 facsimile of the Canadian flag, as measured on 6 Sep 2016 in Waterloo, Ontario, Canada. Its colour was created by oxidizing a bare silicon wafer in a tube furnace in order to grow a layer of silicon dioxide of a carefully chosen thickness. Thin film interference effects in the silicon dioxide layer give the flag a red colour. However, the flag is too small for conventional imaging techniques, so the only images of it that we are able to see are in electron-microscopy greyscale.

▼ MOST FLAGS TATTOOED ON THE BODY

Guinness Rishi (IND) adorned his body with 366 tattoos of flags between Jul 2009 and Jul 2011. He first achieved this record in May 2010, but went on to break it with an additional 61 flags, inked on to his body at KDz TATTOOs Body Art Studio in New Delhi, India. It took 3 hr 3 min altogether to complete these extra flags.

This enthusiastic fan of flags changed his name to Guinness Rishi in 1995. Prior to that date, he was known by his birth name of Har Parkash Rishi.

Q: What do the triangular shapes of Nepal's flag (see p.338) signify?

A: The Himalayan mountains

First raising of the Olympic flag

Designed in 1914 by Pierre de Coubertin (FRA), the founder of the modern Olympic Games, the Olympic flag was first raised at the 1920 Games in Antwerp, Belgium. It features five interlaced rings, representing the continents from which the Olympic athletes come. Its colours – blue, yellow, black, green and red, combined with the white background – were chosen because the national flag of every country contains at least one of them. The original flag was lost after the Antwerp Games and a replacement had to be made for the Paris Olympiad in 1924. In 1997, it was revealed that it had been stolen from the flagpole at the 1920 Games, for a dare, by US athlete Hal Haig Prieste.

The **first raising of the gold medallist's flag at an Olympic medal ceremony** took place at the 1932 Games, held in Los Angeles, California, USA.

In 2008, the swimmer Natalie du Toit (ZAF) became the **first flag-bearer at a Summer Olympic and Paralympic Games**, at the Olympiads staged in Beijing, China. The 13-time Paralympic gold medallist is one of only nine athletes to have competed at both the Olympics and Paralympics.

▲ **OLDEST CONTINUOUSLY USED NATIONAL FLAG**

A white Scandinavian cross on a red background was adopted as the official stage flag of Denmark in 1625, while the proportions of the cross were established in 1748. In Denmark it is known as the "Dannebrog" or "Danish Cloth". Aside from Greenland, all Nordic countries have the off-centre "Nordic cross" as part of their national flag.

The only non-rectangular flag is that of Nepal

The only flag to have different emblems on its obverse and reverse sides is Paraguay

The flags of Chad and Romania are identical

Rotate the Polish flag (top) to get the flags of Indonesia and Monaco

The Norwegian flag contains within it the flags of six other countries: 1: France; 2: Netherlands; 3: Poland; 4: Thailand; 5: Indonesia; and 6: Finland (not proportional)

According to the US Flag Code, the Stars and Stripes "represents a living country and is itself considered a living thing"

Contrary to popular belief, it is okay to burn the Stars and Stripes: the Boy Scouts of America set thousands of them alight every year on Flag Day (14 Jun)

Anatomy of a flag

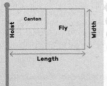

▲ TALLEST FLAGPOLE
On 23 Sep 2014, Jeddah Municipality and Abdul Latif Jameel Community Initiatives (both SAU) erected a 171-m (561-ft) flagpole in Jeddah, Saudi Arabia. The Saudi flag that flies from the pole measures 32.5 x 49.35 m (106 ft 7 in x 161 ft 10 in) – large enough to cover six tennis courts.

LARGEST…

Flag draped (laid flat)
A flag made by Moquim Al Hajiri of *Brooq Magazine* (both QAT) measured 101,978 m² (1,097,682 sq ft) in Doha, Qatar, on 16 Dec 2013. That's the equivalent of around 390 tennis courts!

The **largest flag suspended** measured 2,661.29 m² (28,645 sq ft) and was manufactured by Abina Co., Ltd (THA) in Chiang Rai, Thailand, on 30 Nov 2016. The flag was suspended from three cranes.

Car mosaic of a national flag
On 2 Dec 2009, an array of 413 cars formed a mosaic of the United Arab Emirates flag for an event organized by the Ministry of Culture, Youth and Community Development in Al Fujairah, UAE.

▲ LARGEST FLAG FLOWN
A Mexican national flag measuring 34.3 x 60 m (112 ft 6.3 in x 196 ft 10.2 in) – larger than eight tennis courts – was flown on 2 Dec 2011 at an event coordinated by the city of Piedras Negras in Coahuila, Mexico. It took 40 members of Mexico's armed forces to handle this gargantuan flag and hoist it up its 100-m (328-ft) pole.

▲ MOST COLOURS IN A NATIONAL FLAG

When considering only the flags of those countries that are members of the United Nations, the flag of South Africa, adopted on 27 Apr 1994, has more colours (excluding badges) than those of any other country: six. They symbolize unity: the red, white and blue colours are taken from the colours of the Boer Republics, while the yellow, black and green are taken from the banner of the African National Congress.

Mural of a flag

A 15,499.46-m² (166,834-sq-ft) mural of the US flag was displayed on the roof of a building in Destin, Florida, USA, on 14 Apr 2016. Slightly smaller than the area of three American football fields, the mural was created by the artist Robert Wyland (USA). The project began in Oct 2015 and was completed in Apr 2016.

▲ MOST EXPENSIVE FLAG SOLD AT AUCTION

An American Revolutionary War battle flag sold to an anonymous buyer on 14 Jun 2006 for $12,336,000 (£6,707,264), including the buyer's premium, at Sotheby's in New York City, USA. The regimental standard of the 2nd Continental Light Dragoons was captured by British cavalry officer Lt Col Banastre Tarleton at Pound Ridge in Westchester County, New York, USA, on 2 Jul 1779. Put up for auction by one of his descendants, it is the earliest surviving American flag of any kind with a field of 13 red and white stripes.

▲ MOST CHANGES TO A NATIONAL FLAG

The flag of the USA, which added a star every time a state joined the Union, has undergone 26 alterations since its adoption on 14 Jun 1777, when the Second Continental Congress passed the Flag Resolution. *The Birth of the Flag* (1911), shown above, was painted by Henry Mosler. The figure standing is Betsy Ross, who reportedly sewed the first US flag. Ross did sew flags in the Revolutionary War, but there is still debate about whether she worked on the first US flag.

▲ MOST PEOPLE DEPICTED ON A FLAG

The civil and state flag of Belize depicts two male woodcutters standing in front of a mahogany tree, symbolizing the country's logging industry. Adopted on 21 Sep 1981, when the country gained its independence from the UK, it is the only national flag that features a depiction of human beings as the central part of the design.

◀ **LARGEST FLAG FLOWN WHILE SKYDIVING**

On 10 Dec 2015, Larry Compton (USA) flew a 1,436.22-m² (15,459-sq-ft) Al Adaam – the national flag of Qatar – while skydiving at an event organized by Lekhwiya in Doha, Qatar. The flag measured 60.6 m (198 ft 9 in) long and 23.7 m (77 ft 9 in) wide, making it around three times the size of a basketball court.

MOST...

National flags displayed in one city in 24 hours

On 29 May 2000, the town of Waterloo in New York, USA, placed 25,898 American flags on display. Nearly 300 children participated in the event, which was a highlight of Waterloo's commemorative weekend, celebrating the town's historical role as the birthplace of the Memorial Day holiday.

Different flags flown simultaneously

On 12 Dec 2016, American Express Meetings & Events (USA) flew 462 unique flags at the INTER[action] showcase held at the New Orleans Morial Convention Center in Louisiana, USA.

People performing flag signals

The Scout Association of Hong Kong (CHN) united 23,321 people to make flag signals at Hong Kong Stadium on 21 Nov 2010. They used their flags to signal "HKS100" and mark the centenary of their organization.

▲ **LARGEST HUMAN NATIONAL FLAG**

On 7 Dec 2014, a total of 43,830 participants assembled to produce a gigantic image of the Indian national flag. The event was arranged by Rotary International District 3230 and News7 Tamil (both IND) at the YMCA Ground Nandanam in Chennai, India. The organizers stated that the event was intended to celebrate "unity in diversity in India".

Fashion Extremes

The global trade in knitted hats accounts for approximately $4.8 bn (£3.58 bn) every year.

▲ OLDEST MALE MODEL

On 25 Mar 2015, model and actor Wang Deshun (CHN, b. 1936) caused a stir when he strode the catwalk bare-chested at the age of 79. The show, featuring designs by Hu Sheguang, was part of China Fashion Week in Beijing. Wang – who once taught runway modelling at a fashion school – stays in shape by exercising at the gym for 3 hr a day.

Richest person in fashion

According to Forbes, Amancio Ortega (ESP), boss of Spanish fashion retailer Zara, had a personal fortune estimated at $67 bn (£45.85 bn) as of 1 Jun 2016. This makes him the second wealthiest person in the world. Ortega opened the first Zara shop in 1975; today, his Inditex group operates more than 7,000 stores.

The **richest person in fashion (female)** is Liliane Bettencourt (FRA), the major shareholder of the cosmetics company L'Oréal. Bettencourt, whose father founded L'Oréal in 1909, was worth $36.1 bn (£24.7 bn) as of 1 Jun 2016.

Most expensive fashion show

The annual Victoria's Secret Fashion Show on 30 Nov 2016 cost an estimated $20 m (£16 m). The lingerie spectacular – held at the Grand Palais in Paris, France – featured 82 outfits worn by models including Kendall Jenner and Adriana Lima, and a live performance from Lady Gaga.

Most valuable bra

Revealed at a Victoria's Secret fashion show on 13 Mar 2001, the Heavenly Star Bra was valued at $12.59 m (£8.5 m). It featured 1,200 Sri Lankan pink sapphires and an emerald-cut diamond centrepiece worth $10.6 m (£7.28 m).

Most followers on Twitter for a fashion personality

Model and reality TV star Kim Kardashian (USA) had 50.6 million followers as of 24 Mar 2017. This made her the most popular fashion personality on the social media network, and the 13th most popular overall.

First designer label

Charles Frederick Worth (1825–95) was the first designer to sign his work with a label, show garments on live models and organize seasonal collections twice a year. Born in Lincolnshire, UK, he moved to France in 1845, where his talent for design was discovered by the ladies of the court of Napoleon III. By 1871, Worth had 1,200 people in his employ.

▶ MOST TURBANS TIED IN ONE HOUR

On 24 May 2016, turban artist Santosh Raut (IND) tied *pheta* turbans for 129 people at Pune Journalists' Foundation Hall in Pune, India. *Pheta* turbans are typically worn for formal events such as weddings, and each one requires around 8 m (26 ft 3 in) of fabric to make, meaning that this record attempt used just over 1 km (1,032 m, or 3,385 ft, to be exact) of fabric.

Most Model of the Year wins at the Fashion Awards

Kate Moss (UK) has won three Model of the Year awards, in 1996, 2001 and 2006. The model has fronted campaigns for Chanel, Calvin Klein, Dior and Gucci, and designed a range for Topshop.

◀ HIGHEST ANNUAL EARNINGS FOR A MODEL (CURRENT)

Gisele Bündchen (BRA) made $30.5 m (£20.8 m) in the 12 months leading up to Jun 2016, according to Forbes. Despite retiring from catwalks in 2015, she remains the industry's top earner thanks to deals with the likes of Chanel and Carolina Herrera. Estimated career earnings of $400 m (£273.7 m) also make Gisele the richest model.

According to the latest available figures, the **highest annual earnings for a model (male, current)** is $1.5 m (£1 m), achieved by Sean O'Pry (USA) in 2013–14. O'Pry has appeared in campaigns for Versace and H&M.

Q: At which sport did model Gisele consider turning professional?

A: Volleyball

Most Designer of the Year wins at the Fashion Awards

Alexander McQueen (UK) won the Designer of the Year award four times: in 1996, 1997, 2001 and 2003. His designer label had won 10 prizes at the prestigious ceremony as of Dec 2016 – the **most wins at the Fashion Awards**.

Most American *Vogue* covers

Actress and model Lauren Hutton (USA) appeared on 26 covers from Nov 1966 to Nov 1999. This is six more than models Jean Shrimpton (UK) and Karen Graham (USA).

Oldest model to feature in *Vogue* magazine

Bo Gilbert (UK, b. 1916) modelled for the May 2016 edition of British *Vogue* aged 100, in honour of the magazine's centenary issue.

Singer Tina Turner (b. 26 Nov 1939) became the **oldest *Vogue* cover model** when she posed for German *Vogue*'s Apr 2013 issue, aged 73.

▲ OLDEST TROUSERS

In May 2014, a pair of trousers believed to be at least 3,300 years old were discovered in an ancient graveyard in the Tarim Basin of the Xinjiang region of north-west China. The trousers are made of wool with a drawstring waist and woven decorations, and are thought to have been worn by a nomadic horseman. It has been speculated that the first trousers were invented for riders to wear on horseback for protection and ease of movement.

▲ MOST EXPENSIVE SNEAKERS/ TRAINERS SOLD AT AUCTION (WORN)

A pair of size-13 Nike Air Jordan 12 basketball shoes, worn and signed by Chicago Bulls player Michael Jordan, sold for $104,765 (£63,500) in Dec 2013. The seller of the shoes was a ball boy who received them from Jordan himself after his "flu game" in 1997, so-called because Jordan scored 38 points despite being visibly ill.

SALES-TOPPING FASHION BRANDS

Best-selling activity wearable electronics brand
Fitbit (USA) had estimated sales of 19,023,200 units in 2015. (Figures retrieved on 23 Aug 2016.)

Best-selling autonomous wearable electronics company
Samsung Corp (KOR) had sales of approximately 1,705,900 units in 2014. (Figures retrieved on 17 Sep 2015.)

Best-selling smart wearable electronics brand
The Apple Watch (USA) had estimated sales of 8,719,700 units in 2015. (Figures retrieved on 23 Aug 2016.)

Largest apparel brand
Fashion outlet H&M (SWE) had estimated sales of $18,757,863,800 (£15,244,600,000) in 2016. (Figures retrieved on 16 Jan 2017.)

Largest footwear brand
Nike (USA) had estimated sales of $27,395,441,700 (£18,478,000,000) in 2015. (Figures retrieved on 27 Apr 2016.)

speedo

Largest men's swimwear brand
Speedo (UK) had estimated sales of $136,152,200 (£91,834,000) in 2015. (Figures retrieved on 27 Apr 2016.)

Largest luxury jewellery and watch retailer
Swarovski (AUT) has the most units/outlets – 525 in 2015. (Figures retrieved on 24 Oct 2016.)

Source: Euromonitor International Passport database

◀ MOST EXPENSIVE SNEAKERS/ TRAINERS SOLD AT AUCTION
On 12 Nov 2016, a pair of Nike Mag sneakers inspired by the 1989 film *Back to the Future Part II* were sold at a Michael J Fox Foundation fundraising gala in New York City, USA, for $200,000 (£158,884). The sneakers, designed by Nike's Tinker Hatfield and Tiffany Beers, came complete with LED panels and power laces, as originally sported by Fox's character Marty McFly in the hit film.

Most consecutive fashion magazine front covers
As of 2 Nov 2015, Girolamo Panzetta (ITA) had appeared on the front of every single edition of Japanese men's fashion magazine *LEON* since its launch in Sep 2001 – a total of 170 covers.

▲ LARGEST WEARABLE TURBAN
The turban belonging to Major Singh (IND), a Nihang Sikh, is made with 400 m (1,312 ft) of cloth and weighs 35 kg (77 lb). It uses more than 100 hairpins and 51 religious symbols made from metal. This style of round turban is known as a *dumaala* and is common to Nihang Sikhs, among whom there is a tradition of competing to see who can wear the largest turban.

▲ MOST EXPENSIVE SUIT (CLOTHING) SOLD AT AUCTION

On 20 Feb 2015, diamond baron Laljibhai Tulsibhai Patel (IND) bought a suit at auction for INR 43,131,311 ($693,174; £448,944) in Surat, Gujarat, India. The suit had previously been worn by Indian Prime Minister Narendra Modi (above right), whose name formed the gold pinstripe. Proceeds from the auction went to the Namami Gange fund, a project to clean the Ganges river.

Most subscribers for a fashion/beauty channel on YouTube

"Yuya", aka Mexico's Mariand Castrejón Castañeda, had 17,883,628 subscribers as of 24 Mar 2017. Also known as "lady16makeup", Yuya began her vlog in 2009.

▼ WIDEST WIG

On 27 Jan 2017, actress Drew Barrymore (USA) appeared on the set of *The Tonight Show* in New York City, USA, wearing a wig measuring 7 ft 4 in (2.23 m) wide. The humongous hairpiece was made by Kelly Hanson and Randy Carfagno Productions LLC (both USA).

Toilets

According to the United Nations, of the world's 7 billion people, 6 billion have mobile phones, while only 4.5 billion have a toilet.

First flushing toilet

Contrary to popular belief, the first flushing toilet was *not* invented by Thomas Crapper (UK, 1836–1910). The earliest known flush mechanism was designed c. 1590, about 245 years before Crapper's birth, by England's Sir John Harington – a godson of Queen Elizabeth I. Harington's invention, which he named Ajax, after "jakes", a slang word for toilet, featured a cistern that, at the turn of a handle, sent clean water into the "stool pot", which in turn opened a valve and flushed the contents down into a cesspool. The first Ajax was built in Harington's home in Kelston, Somerset, and in 1592 he had one installed for Her Majesty's use in her bedchamber at Richmond Palace.

The **first patent for a flushing toilet** was obtained in 1775 by Alexander Cumming (UK). The Scottish watchmaker and mechanic improved upon Harington's Ajax design with the invention of an S-shaped double bend in the waste pipe, which trapped water and excluded noxious sewer gases. This J-, U- or S-bend design is still in use today.

A toilet that had once belonged to J D Salinger, author of *The Catcher in the Rye*, was offered for sale on eBay in 2010 – "uncleaned and in its original condition" – with an asking price of $1,000,000!

◀ LARGEST COLLECTION OF TOILET-RELATED ITEMS

As of 19 Oct 2015, Marina and Mykola Bogdanenko of Kiev, in Ukraine, were the proud owners of 524 different toilet-themed curios. The potty pair's obsession with collecting lavatorial knick-knacks began in 1995 after they opened a "sanitary engineering" business in Kiev.

A: 40,000, according to US federal statistics

First toilet to appear on stage
The first act of André Antoine's production of Edmond de Goncourt's (both FRA) *La Fille Élisa* in Paris, France, on 24 Dec 1890 was set in a hotel room, complete with toilet and washbasin.

Although stage productions can now show a toilet on stage with impunity, the UK's Lord Chamberlain banned the sound of a lavatory being flushed off-stage in Graham Greene's *The Living Room* as recently as 1953.

In the USA, toilets were not considered suitable for depiction on movie screens either. The **first Hollywood movie to feature a toilet** was not to appear until 1960, when a flushing loo was seen in Alfred Hitchcock's (UK) slasher movie *Psycho*.

Smallest sculpture of a toilet
"Chisai Benjo" ("Small Toilet") was created in 2005 by Takahashi Kaito (JPN) of SII Nanotechnology, Inc., by etching silicon with an ion beam. The tiny toilet could only be seen when magnified 15,000 times. A scanning electron micrograph of the creation won the Most Bizarre Award at the 49th International Conference on Electron, Ion and Photon Beam Technology and Nanofabrication.

Fastest towed toilet
Brewton McCluskey (USA) achieved a speed of 83.7 km/h (52.01 mph) on a towed toilet at the South Georgia Motorsports Park in Cecil, Georgia, USA, on 4 Apr 2011. McCluskey was towed by a car driven by Brian Griffin (USA).

Fastest marathon dressed as a toilet
Marcus Mumford (UK) ran the 2014 Virgin Money London Marathon in a time of 2 hr 57 min 28 sec while dressed as a toilet.

Fastest time to pass through a toilet seat three times
At the GWR Live! Roadshow at Forum Bornova in Izmir, Turkey, on 25 May 2010, İlker Çevik (TUR) wriggled his body through a toilet seat three times in just 28.14 sec.

The following year, on 8 Apr 2011, the flexible Turk appeared on *Lo Show dei Record* in Milan, Italy, where he broke the record for the **most times to pass through a toilet seat in one minute**, achieving nine complete passes.

▲ MOST EXPENSIVE TOILET SYSTEM
When the space shuttle *Endeavour* launched into orbit on 13 Jan 1993, it carried a new unisex toilet facility. Housed on the shuttle's mid-deck, the $23.4-m (£15.1-m) facility was described by NASA as a "complete sewage collection and treatment plant... contained in a space one half the size of a telephone booth".

There are **35 toilets** in the White House

One in three people do not have access to a proper toilet

Over or under?
Toilet-paper manufacturer Cottonelle asked if consumers hung their rolls with the first sheet over or under the roll. The results:

72% **28%**

The average person spends 270 days of their life on the toilet

4,000: rolls of toilet paper you'll get through in a lifetime: a stack higher than the Empire State Building

x1 = 400 rolls

27,000 trees are chopped down every day to make toilet paper

▼ **MOST EXPENSIVE BATHROOM**
Jeweller Lam Sai-wing (CHN) built a HK$27-m (£2.4-m; $3.5-m) washroom in his Hong Kong shop made entirely out of gold and precious jewels. The toilet bowls, wash basins, toilet brushes, toilet paper holders, mirror frames, wall-mounted chandeliers, wall tiles and doors were all made out of solid 24-carat gold. Sadly, much of Lam's throne room was melted down after his death in 2008.

Most wooden toilet seats broken with the head in a minute
Kevin Shelley (USA) smashed 46 wooden toilet seats in half in 60 sec with his head on the set of *Guinness World Records - Die größten Weltrekorde* in Cologne, Germany, on 1 Sep 2007.

Largest toilet roll
On 26 Aug 2011 – known to papyrophiles (paper lovers) as National Toilet Paper Day – Charmin/ Procter & Gamble (USA) unveiled a roll of toilet paper that measured 2.97 m (9 ft 8.9 in) in diameter – wider than a school bus. The roll was displayed at the company's headquarters in Cincinnati, Ohio, USA, and had enough paper to make 95,000 regular rolls. It was estimated by Procter & Gamble plant manager Darrick Johnson that the tissue could cover more than 1 million sq ft (92,900 m²), sufficient to paper over 16 FIFA-sanctioned soccer pitches.

Tallest toilet roll pyramid
Ivan Zarif Neto, Rafael Migani Monteiro and Fernando Gama (all BRA) stacked 23,821 toilet rolls into a pyramid shape that stood 4.1 m (13 ft 5 in) tall in São Paulo, Brazil, on 20 Nov 2012.

▲ FIRST TOILET THEME PARK

A theme park dedicated to the toilet opened in Suwon, South Korea, in Jul 2012. The Restroom Cultural Park surrounds the toilet-shaped home that once belonged to Sim Jae-duck (see p.350).

As of 27 Nov 2012, the free-to-enter park was attracting an average of 10,000 visitors per month. Among the exhibits are poo sculptures (above), traditional Korean squat toilets, European bedpans and Marcel Duchamp's famous porcelain urinal sculpture *Fountain*, originally created in 1917.

As of 8 Dec 2016, the park had a 4/5 rating on the travel site TripAdvisor.

Fastest time to topple 10 portable toilets

It took Philipp Reiche (DEU) just 11.30 sec to topple 10 portable toilets – each measuring a minimum of 2 m (6 ft 6 in) tall and 1 m (3 ft 3 in) wide – at Europa-Park in Rust, Germany, on 22 Jun 2013. The attempt was filmed for the TV show *Wir holen den Rekord nach Deutschland*.

▲ TALLEST HOUSE SHAPED LIKE A TOILET

This giant 7.5-m-high (24-ft 7-in) toilet-shaped house was built as the home of "Mr Toilet", aka Sim Jae-duck (1939–2009) – a former mayor of Suwon, South Korea, and founder of the World Toilet Association. The 4,500-sq-ft (418-m²) property was designed by architect Go Gi-woong and completed on 11 Nov 2007 – in time for the first general assembly of the World Toilet Association and Sim's election to the role of president.

▲ TOILET WITH THE MOST FUNCTIONS

With a list price of $10,200 (£8,185), the Toto Neorest is a technologically advanced toilet that features 10 functions above and beyond those of the average lavatory. These include a lid that lifts automatically, a temperature-controlled seat and foot warmer, user washing and drying, air freshening and auto-cleansing. The Neorest can be operated using a remote control, although it can also be flushed manually in the event of a power cut.

▼ FASTEST TOILET

Bog Standard is a motorcycle and sidecar hidden under a bathroom set comprising a bathtub, sink and laundry bin. Built by motoring enthusiast Edd China (UK), it was presented on the set of *Lo Show dei Record* in Milan, Italy, on 10 Mar 2011, where it reached a top speed of 68 km/h (42.25 mph).

Society Round-Up

If all the displaced citizens in the world in 2016 were brought together to form a single nation, it would be the 21st largest on Earth.

▼ FIRST ASTRONAUT TO VOTE IN SPACE

Russian cosmonauts Yuri Onufriyenko (below left) and Yury Usachov (below right) voted in the Russian presidential election on 16 Jun 1996 using proxies on Earth while travelling on board the *Mir* space station.

The next year, following changes in Texas legislation regarding absentee voting, astronaut David Wolf (USA, above) was able to vote in a US local election using a secure line from *Mir*.

Tallest population

According to the journal *eLife* on 26 Jul 2016, the tallest men are from the Netherlands, with an average height of more than 182.5 cm (5 ft 11.85 in). The tallest women live in Latvia, with an average height topping 168 cm (5 ft 6.14 in).

In terms of the **shortest population**, Guatemalan women had an average height of 149.4 cm (4 ft 10.8 in) according to *eLife*'s survey. East Timor was home to the shortest men, whose height averaged just under 160 cm (5 ft 3 in) as of the same date.

Lowest ratio of men to women

According to the 2016 CIA World Factbook, there are only 84 men for every 100 women in the east African country of Djibouti.

The United Arab Emirates (UAE) has the **highest ratio of men to women**, with 218 males for every 100 females, according to the same source.

Longest-running corporate games

The Juegos Bancarios ("Bank Games") in Mexico have been held annually since 1966. Over the course of 50 years, more than 207,000 employees of financial institutions and banks have taken part.

▲ LEAST HABITABLE CITY ▼

As of Mar 2017, Damascus in Syria has the lowest rating on the Global Liveability Ranking 2016, based on a survey of 140 cities by the Economist Intelligence Unit. It scored 30.2 out of a possible 100, below Tripoli in Libya (35.9). Ratings are based on five factors: Stability, Healthcare, Education, Culture & Environment and Infrastructure.

The **most habitable city** is Melbourne in Australia, which scored 97.5.

Longest career as a lawyer

Palestinian Fuad Shehadeh had served for 66 years 187 days as a professional lawyer in Ramallah, West Bank, Palestinian Territory, as verified on 31 May 2016.

The **longest career as a language teacher** is 55 years, achieved by Ren Zuyong (CHN). He began his career as a Chinese teacher in 1959 and continued to work in Xinghua, Jiangsu, China, until 30 Aug 2014.

Millard M Jordan (USA) is the **longest-serving chief of police**. Between 1962 and his retirement on 6 Jan 2014, Jordan served for 51 years 243 days in Lawtey, Florida, USA, as verified on 25 Feb 2016.

Largest marriage vow renewal ceremony

On 8 Oct 2016, a total of 1,201 couples renewed their marriage vows at an event organized by Western Michigan University in Kalamazoo, Michigan, USA.

Oldest ruling house

The Emperor of Japan, Akihito (b. 23 Dec 1933), is the 125th since Jimmu Tennō, the first Emperor. Jimmu's reign was long held to have begun on 11 Feb 660 BCE, but more likely dates to c. 40 to 10 BCE.

Largest social/global development project competition

Technology festival Campus Party (MEX) attracted 267 completed submissions in Guadalajara in Jalisco, Mexico, on 2 Jul 2016. The award for the winning project – whose goal was to bring internet access to rural villages – was 1,000,000 Mexican pesos ($54,605; £41,046). The aim of such competitions is to promote initiatives that will improve the lives of developing communities by enacting positive and sustainable change.

Highest-altitude award ceremony on land

On 28 Nov 2016, Ram Bahadur Subedi and Puskar Nepal (both NPL) organized the National Box Office Film Fare Awards – which celebrates the Nepalese film industry – to take place at an altitude of 4,627 m (15,180 ft) in Thukla, Solukhumbu, Nepal.

Largest ancient ceremonial Mexican dance

On 17 Jul 2016, a total of 260 participants in Mexicali and Aztec outfits came together to dance at the pre-Columbian pyramid site of Teotihuacán in Estado de México, Mexico.

Most ubiquitous consumer item

Estimates for the global manufacture of plastic bags number in the trillions. In the USA alone, consumers throw away 100 billion plastic bags every year.

First written record of black pudding

The earliest documented reference to food made using blood was in Homer's *Odyssey*, dated to c. 800 BCE. The Greek poem refers to a man who "has filled a sausage with fat and blood and turns it this way and that and is very eager to get it quickly roasted". Black pudding is typically made from pig or cow blood cooked with a filler such as fat, oatmeal and/or meat until it congeals into a sausage.

Most selfie deaths (country)

India accounts for 59.8% of all selfie-related deaths, according to research paper "Me, Myself and My Killfie: Characterizing and Preventing Selfie Deaths". The paper was published by Hemank Lamba (IND/USA) *et al* at Carnegie Mellon University in Pittsburgh, USA, in Nov 2016. The team found that 127 "killfies" had been reported worldwide by the media since Mar 2014; of these, 76 occurred in India. Selfies account for more deaths than shark attacks in the same period.

◄ **MOST CIVILIAN AWARDS**
Tsunejiro Koga (JPN, far left) received 72 civilian awards (*konju housyou*) from 7 Nov 1982 to 30 Sep 2015, as verified on 23 Feb 2016. His collection includes 57 Medals of Honor for generous financial contributions for the well-being of the public, one medal from the Ministry of Justice for Offenders Rehabilitation Activities, and a medal of the Order of the Rising Sun (Gold and Silver Rays).

Highest pilgrimage

A 53-km-long (33-mi) route on Mount Kailash (or Khangrinboqê) in Tibet stands at an altitude of 6,638 m (21,778 ft). Kailash is sacred to followers of Buddhism, Jainism, Hinduism and the pre-Buddhist religion of Bonpo.

The **lowest pilgrimage** is to the ancient city of Jericho in Israel, which is located at 800 ft (244 m) below sea level. Jericho is close to the Dead Sea, the **lowest exposed body of water**, and attracts followers of both the Christian and Jewish faiths.

Most election votes cast in the same year

In 2004, more than 1.1 billion people voted in 58 presidential and parliamentary elections. They ran from the Georgian presidential election on 4 Jan to the third round of the Ukrainian presidential election on 26 Dec.

Saint- Louis- du- Ha! Ha!   6
Rivière- du- Loup   54

▲ **MOST EXCLAMATION MARKS IN A TOWN NAME**
The Canadian municipality of Saint-Louis-du-Ha! Ha! (population: 1,318) in Quebec was named in 1874, and features one more exclamation mark than Westward Ho! in Cornwall, UK. "Ha! Ha!" refers to the French term *ha-ha*, a landscape feature that creates an invisible boundary line – in this case most probably the nearby Lake Témiscouata.

▲ HIGHEST SCORE ON THE DEMOCRACY INDEX

Every year, the Economist Intelligence Unit publishes a list of the countries with the highest levels of democracy. In 2017, Norway (above) achieved a rating of 9.93 out of 10 – the highest score ever given in the history of the index. Norway has topped the democracy list since 2012. Iceland came in second with 9.50.

North Korea (right) received a score of 1.08 out of 10 on the same list – the **lowest score on the Democracy Index**. It has been given the same rating every year since 2010.

▼ MOST DISPLACED PERSONS (CURRENT)

On 20 Jun 2016 – World Refugee Day – the United Nations High Commissioner for Refugees (UNHCR) announced that 65.3 million people had been forced to flee their homes in the previous year as a result of conflict, persecution, human rights violations or starvation. This represents one in every 113 people on Earth, and the equivalent of 24 people displaced every minute. It was the first time that numbers had risen above 60 million since World War II.

More than half of the refugees under the UN's mandate originated from one of three countries: Syria, Afghanistan or Somalia. Here, migrants are shown marching through Slovenia in Oct 2015.

Highest-Earning...

GWR presents the celebrities with the greatest annual income from 1 Jun 2015 to 1 Jun 2016, according to Forbes. The lowest earner listed here has an annual income some 500 times greater than the average personal income in the USA. But for overall wealth, one man still leads the pack...

RICHEST PERSON – $86.9 BN

No one has greater accumulated wealth than Bill Gates (aka William H Gates III, USA). A co-founder of Microsoft, Gates was the wealthiest man alive in 1995–2007, again in 2009, and has been since 2014. As of 3 Apr 2017, his fortune stood at $86.9 bn (£69.1bn). Since 1999, he and his wife have helmed the Bill & Melinda Gates Foundation, which aims to lift millions of people out of poverty, with a focus on eliminating HIV, malaria and other infectious diseases.

> $20 m

TV actor
$22.5 m

Jim Parsons (USA), star of CBS sitcom *The Big Bang Theory* (in which he plays Sheldon Cooper), earned an estimated $22.5 m (£15.4 m), making him the year's top-earning TV actor for the second year in succession.

Model
$30 m

Gisele Bündchen (BRA) made $30.5 m (£20.8 m) in the year to Jun 2016. Alongside deals with the likes of Chanel, Bündchen owns skincare and lingerie ranges. These continue to boost her income, despite the fact that she retired from modelling in 2015.

Track athlete
$32.5 m

With a string of records to his name, including the **fastest 100 m and 200 m**, Usain Bolt (JAM) has also seen his income escalate. Around $30 m (£20.5 m) of his $32.5-m (£22.2-m) earnings came from endorsements. His biggest sponsor is Puma, from whom he earned more than $10 m (£6.8 m).

Bollywood actor
$33 m

India's Shah Rukh Khan – aka SRK – earned $33 m (£22.5 m) in 2015–16. Since debuting in *Deewana* (IND, 1992), he has appeared in more than 80 films and continues to enjoy lead roles in hit movies such as *Dilwale* (IND, 2015).

TV actress
$43 m

For the fifth year in a row, *Modern Family* star Sofia Vergara (COL) is the top-earning TV actress, with an estimated income of $43 m (£29.4 m).

$45–$60 m

Film actress
$46 m

Best known for starring roles in lucrative franchises *The Hunger Games* and *X-Men*, US actress Jennifer Lawrence took home around $46 m (£31.4 m) in 2015–16.

Formula One driver
$46 m

British F1 star Lewis Hamilton earned $46 m (£31.4 m), of which $42 m (£28.7 m) came from race winnings. Hamilton secured his third F1 championship in 2015.

Reality TV star
$51 m

Kim Kardashian West (USA) earned $51 m (£34.9 m). Much of this income came from her mobile game *Kim Kardashian: Hollywood*, which made $71.8 m (£58.3 m) in 2015 alone.

American football player – $53 m

Carolina Panthers quarterback Cam Newton (USA) earned $53 m (£36.2 m) in the 12 months to Jun 2016. Unusually for a sports star, most of Newton's earnings ($41.1 m; £28.1 m) came from his salary and game winnings. "Just" $12 m (£8.2 m) came from endorsements.

Chef
$54 m

Best known for his culinary TV shows such as *Hell's Kitchen*, *MasterChef USA* and *Ramsay's Kitchen Nightmares*, Gordon Ramsay (UK) earned approximately $54 m (£36.9 m).

$60–$75 m

Disc Jockey
$63 m

DJ Calvin Harris (b. Adam Wiles, UK) earned $63 m (£43.1 m). Harris had topped the highest-earning DJ list for the previous two years as well.

Magician
$64 m

David Copperfield (USA) earned an estimated $64 m (£43.8 m) in 2015–16. Most of his income comes from his long-running show in Las Vegas, Nevada, USA.

Actor
$64.5 m

Wrestler-turned-actor Dwayne Johnson (USA, aka "The Rock") earned an estimated $64.5 m (£44.1 m). San Andreas (USA, 2015) and Disney's Moana (USA, 2016) are two of the movies to which he lent his talents in that period.

Musician (male)
$70 m

Country music star Garth Brooks (USA) earned $70 m (£47.9 m) from Jun 2015 to Jun 2016. His income was boosted considerably by profits from his comeback tour, which entered its third year in Sep 2016.

TV personality (female) –
$75 m

Ellen DeGeneres (USA) – TV star, actress and host of her own self-titled chat show since 2003 – earned an estimated $75 m (£51.3 m).

Basketball player
$77 m

Currently with the Cleveland Cavaliers, LeBron James (USA) earned an estimated $77 m (£52.7 m). Around $54 m (£36.9 m) of this came from a range of high-end endorsements with brands such as Nike, Coca-Cola and Samsung.

Radio host
$85 m

"Shock Jock" Howard Stern (USA) enjoyed an income of $85 m (£58.1 m). In Dec 2015, Stern announced that he had signed a new five-year deal with radio station Sirius XM.

Comedian
$87.5 m

Kevin Hart (USA) played more than 100 live shows, each with an average gross of more than $1 m (£684,453), helping him to annual earnings of $87.5 m (£59.8 m).

Athlete
$88 m

Tied with Dr Phil in Forbes' list of the highest earners is Real Madrid superstar Cristiano Ronaldo (PRT). Some $32 m (£21.9 m) of his earnings came from endorsement deals – notably with Nike.

TV personality
$88 m

American television star Dr Phil McGraw – best known for his CBS talk show Dr. Phil – earned an estimated $88 m (£60.2 m) in 2015–16.

> $90 m

Author
$95 m

The top-earning author in 2016 was crime-thriller writer James Patterson (USA), with estimated annual earnings of $95 m (£65 m). This also makes him the **highest-earning living celebrity (male, current).**

Band
$110 m

One Direction (UK/IRL) earned an estimated $110 m (£75.2 m). Most of their income came from the 2015 *On the Road Again Tour*. The boy band are currently on hiatus.

CEO
$131.2 m

In 2015–16, John Hammergren (USA) earned $131.19 m (£89.79 m). He is president, chairman and CEO of McKesson Corporation, which specializes in health care, medical technology and pharmaceuticals.

Celebrity
$170 m

Taylor Swift (USA) hasn't released an album since 2014, but the pop icon's *The 1989 World Tour* grossed $250 m (£164.8 m), boosting her earnings to $170 m (£116.3 m). That's more than double her 2015 income.

Dead celebrity
$825 m

The "King of Pop" lives on – financially, at least. Michael Jackson (USA, 1958–2009) earned $825 m (£636 m) and has topped Forbes' Top-Earning Dead Celebrities list since 2012–13.

Arts & Media

At the 2017 Academy Awards, US sound mixer Kevin O'Connell finally won his first Oscar. His previous 20 nominations had all ended in disappointment.

▲ MOST OSCAR NOMINATIONS FOR A FILM

On 24 Jan 2017, *La La Land* (USA, 2016) received 14 Oscar nominations. This matched the total achieved by *All About Eve* (USA, 1950) and *Titanic* (USA, 1997). The musical comedy-drama, starring Emma Stone and Ryan Gosling, went on to win six Oscars at the 89th Academy Awards ceremony on 26 Feb 2017.

The director of *La La Land*, Damien Chazelle (USA, above, b. 19 Jan 1985), became the **youngest winner of the Academy Award for Best Director**, breaking a record that had stood since 1931. Chazelle was aged 32 years 38 days.

Contents

Confusion reigned at the 89th Academy Awards when a mix-up with the award envelopes led to *La La Land* being incorrectly named as Best Picture. The actual winner was *Moonlight* (USA, 2016).

CONTENTS

Books

Former US president George Bush Sr earned less from his memoirs than his dog Millie did from her "autobiography".

▼ LARGEST LIBRARY
The US Library of Congress in Washington, DC, USA, is home to more than 162 million items spread across approximately 838 mi (1,348 km) of bookshelves. The collections include more than 38 million books and other print materials, 3.6 million recordings, 14 million photographs, 5.5 million maps, 7.1 million pieces of sheet music and 70 million manuscripts.

Washington, DC, is also home to the **largest library of law books**. More than 2.9 million volumes are housed within the Law Library of the US Congress, along with foreign legal gazettes.

Highest annual earnings for an author (current)
According to *Forbes*, thriller writer James Patterson (USA) amassed earnings of $95 m (£65 m) between Jun 2015 and Jun 2016.

First detective novel
According to the British Library, the earliest example of the detective genre is *The Notting Hill Mystery* by Charles Felix (UK), serialized in the magazine *Once a Week* in 1862–63.

The **first female author to specialize in crime fiction** is held to be Mary Fortune (AUS), who penned more than 500 detective stories. Her first story, "The Dead Witness", appeared in the *Australian Journal* on 20 Jan 1866.

The 78 crime novels by Dame Agatha Christie (UK) have sold an estimated 2 billion copies in 44 languages, making her the **best-selling author of fiction**.

Founded in 1800, the US Library of Congress has twice been ravaged by fire. In 1814, it was set alight by British forces, while a blaze on 24 Dec 1851 destroyed two-thirds of its 55,000 volumes.

Q: During World War II, Roald Dahl worked at MI6 with someone who would also become a famous author. Who was it?

A: Ian Fleming

Best-selling work of fiction
Owing to a lack of audited figures, it is impossible to state which work of fiction has sold most. *A Tale of Two Cities* (1859) by Charles Dickens (UK) is reported to have sold more than 200 million copies. Claims have also been made for *Don Quixote* by Miguel de Cervantes Saavedra (ESP), published in two parts (1605 and 1615), but sales of this work can also not be verified.

First audiobook
In Nov 2016, a copy of the first full-length audiobook, dating from 1935, was found in Canada. The album's four shellac LPs featured the text of Joseph Conrad's 1902 novel *Typhoon*. It was recorded by the Royal National Institute of Blind People, and rediscovered by Matthew Rubery of Queen Mary University of London, UK.

Most expensive typewriter
In 1952, Ian Fleming (UK) commissioned a gold-plated typewriter at the completion of *Casino Royale*, his first novel and debut of secret agent James Bond. It sold for £55,750 ($89,473) at Christie's in London, UK, on 5 May 1995.

Most valuable rare book collection gifted
In Feb 2015, Princeton University, New Jersey, USA, revealed that it had been gifted a book collection valued at $300 m (£194 m). Assembled by US philanthropist William H Scheide, it contains Shakespeare folios, the original printing of the American Declaration of Independence, and signed music manuscripts by Bach, Beethoven and Mozart.

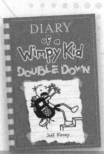

▲ **HIGHEST ANNUAL EARNINGS FOR A CHILDREN'S AUTHOR (CURRENT)**
Having first appeared on educational browser site FunBrain in 2004, *Diary of a Wimpy Kid* has grown into a global franchise with 11 instalments and three feature films. The series helped author and illustrator Jeff Kinney (USA) to estimated earnings of $19.5 m (£13.3 m) between Jun 2015 and Jun 2016, according to *Forbes* magazine. The talented Mr Kinney is also a game designer, actor, movie director, producer and cartoonist.

Most expensive book illustration sold at auction
The Rabbits' Christmas Party, a Beatrix Potter watercolour painted in the 1890s and owned by her brother Bertram, was bought by an anonymous British collector on 17 Jul 2008 for £289,250 ($579,232).

Largest book signing
Vickrant Mahajan (IND) signed 6,904 copies of his book *Yes Thank You Universe* in a single session in Jammu, India, on 30 Jan 2016.

Largest book:
5 x 8.06 m
(width by height when closed)

Most books toppled like dominoes:
10,200
by Sinners Domino Entertainment (DEU), 14 Oct 2015

Largest book pyramid:
70,247
by Perak State Public Library Corporation & Imagika Sdn Bhd (both MYS) on 26 Dec 2015

Longest time to spin a GWR book on a finger:

44 min 20 sec
by Himanshu Gupta (IND) on 17 Apr 2016

Tallest stack of books balanced on head:
62
(weight: 98.4 kg; 217 lb) by John Evans (UK) on 9 Dec 1998

x1 = 5 books

◀ BEST-SELLING PLAYSCRIPT
Published on 31 Jul 2016 to coincide with the official opening of the stage play, the script for *Harry Potter and the Cursed Child* had sold 3,866,156 copies globally as of 6 Aug 2016, according to Nielsen BookScan. Based on an idea by J K Rowling (UK), the series author, it takes place largely in 2020 and centres on the now adult wizard Harry Potter and his son, Albus Severus Potter.

Largest fan fiction archive
Launched in Oct 1998, FanFiction.net hosts stories based on pre-existing books, TV shows, movies and comics. The site has over 2 million users and 8 million published pages, with stories in more than 30 languages. Popular sections include Harry Potter (more than 650,000 stories) and manga series *Naruto* (more than 300,000).

Most published writers per capita
Iceland has a long tradition of storytelling, from the sagas of the Middle Ages to modern smartphone audiobooks, which can be accessed from barcodes attached to public benches. Over the course of their lifetime, one in 10 Icelanders will have a book published. Based on figures from 2012, five books are published for every 1,000 citizens – the **most books published per capita**.

▲ MOST EXPENSIVE PRINTED BOOK
In 1640, the residents of the Massachusetts Bay Colony printed 1,700 copies of the *Bay Psalm Book*, making it the first book printed in British North America. On 26 Nov 2013, US businessman David Rubenstein purchased one of the 11 copies still in existence for $14.16 m (£8.74 m) at an auction at Sotheby's in New York City, USA, with the express intention of lending the book to libraries.

▲ FIRST BOOK PRINTED IN ENGLISH

The Recuyell of the Historyes of Troye is a translation by William Caxton (UK) of a French work composed in 1474 – a rarity at a time when most books were written in Latin rather than English. Formerly the property of the Duke of Northumberland (UK), on 15 Jul 2014 it sold at auction at Sotheby's of London, UK, for £1,082,500 ($1,851,460).

▼ MOST EXPENSIVE BOOK

The *Codex Leicester* is a collection of written observations, musings, theories and illustrations by the Italian Renaissance artist Leonardo da Vinci. He began work on the hand-drawn notebook in around 1508, initially on separate sheets that have subsequently been bound together. In 1994, it was purchased by Microsoft co-founder Bill Gates (USA) for $30,802,500 (£19,246,489) – the highest sum ever paid for any book in any format.

Fan fiction provides a way for buffs of certain books and TV series to publish their own stories using their favourite characters. The roots of the genre can be found in the debut edition of *Star Trek* fanzine *Spockanalia*, produced in the USA in 1967 by Devra Langsam and Sherna Comerford (both USA). The creator of *Star Trek*, Gene Roddenberry (USA), wrote a letter to the fanzine's authors, dated 24 Apr 1968, in which he declared *Spockanalia* to be "required reading [for] every new writer, and anyone who makes decisions on show policy".

Most overdue library book

In 1956, Prof Sir John Plumb (UK) returned a book about the Archbishop of Bremen that had been borrowed from Sidney Sussex College, Cambridge, UK, in 1667–68 (i.e., 288 years earlier). Thankfully for Prof Plumb, there was no fine.

When Emily Canellos-Simms (USA) returned the poetry book *Days and Deeds* to Kewanee Public Library in Illinois, USA, 47 years after her mother had borrowed it in Apr 1955, she paid a fine of $345.14 (£203.29) – the **largest library-book fine paid**. It worked out at a cost of two cents for every day the book had been overdue.

The earliest book to feature engraved maps, as opposed to woodcut prints, was produced in 1477 in Bologna, Italy. It was a medieval translation by Giacomo d'Angelo da Scarperia (ITA) of *Cosmographia* – an atlas and treatise on cartography that had been compiled by the Greco-Egyptian writer Ptolemy around the year CE 150. Da Scarperia's book contains 26 copperplate engravings and can also lay claim to be the first book with maps created by a known artist – Taddeo Crivelli (ITA). It had been thought that the Scarperia translation had been published in 1482, only for documents found in Bologna to prove otherwise.

Wildlife documentary *Planet Earth II* required 117 separate filming expeditions, with 2,089 days spent in the field.

Most Emmy Awards won by an individual
Producer Sheila Nevins (USA), president of HBO Documentary Films, has won 32 Primetime Emmy Awards. In 2016, she took home the Exceptional Merit in Documentary Filmmaking award for *Jim: The James Foley Story*, a biography of the US war correspondent.

Nevins also shares the record for the **most Emmy Award nominations received by an individual** – 74, along with camera operator Hector Ramirez (USA).

Most Primetime Emmy Awards for a TV series
NBC's long-running sketch comedy institution *Saturday Night Live* took home its 50th award at the 2016 ceremony, when co-hosts Tina Fey and Amy Poehler won the Emmy for Outstanding Guest Actress in a Comedy Series.

Saturday Night Live has received a total of 209 nominations – the **most Primetime Emmy nominations for a TV series**.

Highest annual earnings for a reality TV star
According to Forbes, Kim Kardashian West (USA) earned $51 m (£34.9 m) from 1 Jun 2015 to 1 Jun 2016. Some 40% of her income came from her mobile game *Kim Kardashian: Hollywood*, which made $71.8 m (£48.4 m) in 2015 alone.

▼ MOST SUCCESSFUL SCI-FI TV FRANCHISE
Revenue estimates suggested that the *Star Trek* franchise was worth in excess of $6 bn (£4.87 bn) as of 2016. This figure comprises revenue from syndication and DVD sales, plus revenue from books and videogames and a movie gross of $1.73 bn (£1.4 bn). On 7 Oct 2016, William Shatner (above left), who played Captain Kirk on the show, accepted a certificate from *GWR* Editor-in-Chief Craig Glenday.

The **largest TV** was a Sony Jumbotron colour TV screen measuring 24.3 x 45.7 m (80 x 150 ft). It was built for The International Exposition in 1985, held in Tsukuba, Ibaraki Prefecture, Japan.

369

◄ MOST POPULAR SUPERHERO ON TELEVISION

The CW's *The Flash* boasted 3.1 million "demand expressions" per day in 2016, according to Parrot Analytics. This data science company measures worldwide audience demand for TV content across streaming sites, social media and traditional viewing channels.

The **most popular TV show** in 2016 was *Game of Thrones*, with a global average of 7,191,848 daily demand expressions.

▲ HIGHEST ANNUAL EARNINGS FOR A TV ACTRESS IN A CURRENT SERIES

Modern Family star Sofía Vergara (COL) was the top-earning TV actress for the fifth year in a row, with an estimated income of $43 m (£29.4 m) in the 12 months leading up to 1 Jun 2016, according to Forbes. This was a significant increase from the estimated $28.5 m (£18.6 m) Vergara earned in 2014–15.

Most Emmy Awards for a drama series

On 18 Sep 2016, HBO's fantasy drama series *Game of Thrones* (USA) won Emmy awards for Best Writing, Best Directing and Best Drama, bringing its all-time total to 38. This is also the **most Emmy Awards for a fictional series**.

Buoyed by hits such as *Game of Thrones* and *Boardwalk Empire*, in 2015 HBO received the **most Primetime Emmy Award nominations for a network in a single year** – 126.

Most pirated TV programme

Download monitoring website TorrentFreak declared *Game of Thrones* to be the most illegally downloaded TV show for the fifth year running. At its peak, the finale of season 6, which aired on 26 Jun 2016, was being shared across 350,000 torrents simultaneously. In second and third place were AMC's *The Walking Dead* and HBO's *Westworld* (both USA), respectively.

Highest-ever annual earnings for a TV personality

Between Jun 2009 and Jun 2010, Oprah Winfrey (USA) earned an estimated $275 m (£189.5 m) thanks to her magazine, radio contract, production company Harpo and the debut of the Oprah Winfrey Network.

The **highest-ever annual earnings for a TV personality (male)** is $95 m (£62.4 m), a record shared by reality TV judge Simon Cowell (UK) and radio personality Howard Stern (USA) in the 12 months leading up to Jun 2013.

Q: Which hit TV show (debuting in 2016) was set in Hawkins, Indiana, USA?

▲ FIRST SCRIPTED TV SERIES IN VIRTUAL REALITY

Invisible, a sci-fi series that tells the story of the Ashlands, a powerful New York City family with a supernatural gift, is described by its producers as "the first major scripted series designed for 360-degree virtual reality". Each episode was filmed using a static 360° VR camera (pictured above, on the table), submerging the viewer in a full panoramic experience. Co-directed by Doug Liman (inset), *Invisible*'s first season consisted of five six-minute episodes and was made available for the Samsung VR platform in 2016.

▲ HIGHEST ANNUAL EARNINGS FOR A TV PERSONALITY (FEMALE, CURRENT)

In the 12 months leading up to 1 Jun 2016, TV star, actress and host of her own self-titled chat show Ellen DeGeneres (USA) earned an estimated $75 m (£51.3 m), according to Forbes.

The **highest annual earnings for a TV personality (male, current)** is $88 m (£60.2 m), earned by Dr Phil McGraw (USA).

Longest-running sports TV programme with the same presenter
Hosted by Juan Carlos Tapia Rodríguez (PAN), Panamanian boxing show *Lo Mejor del Boxeo* had run for 41 years 334 days as of 8 Dec 2016.

Most prolific science-fiction TV series (by episode)
On 29 Apr 2017, the 819th episode of *Doctor Who* (BBC, UK) was aired. This total encompasses the original run of 694 episodes from 1963 to 1989 and the modern series that returned in 2005, but does not include specials or the 1996 TV movie.

The **youngest Doctor Who** was Matt Smith (UK, b. 28 Oct 1982), who was 26 years old when he filmed his first scenes as the Time Lord.

The **oldest Doctor Who** was William Hartnell (UK, b. 8 Jan 1908), who played the part aged 57 years old and reprised the role for a 10th-anniversary special in 1973, aged 65 years.

In terms of TV shows, the **most prolific Doctor Who** was Tom Baker (UK), who starred in 173 episodes (seasons 12–18) from 1974 to 1981, more than any other actor to play the part. A former monk, Baker was working on a building site when he received the call from the BBC.

TV and radio sets:
10,060
(Göran Ågårdh, SWE)

The Smurfs
memorabilia:
6,320
(Gerda P Scheuers, USA)

Charlie's Angels
memorabilia:
5,569
(Jack Condon, USA)

The Simpsons
memorabilia:
2,580
(Cameron Gibbs, AUS)

Daleks:
1,801
(Rob Hull, UK)

Scooby Doo
memorabilia:
1,116
(Rebecca Findlay, CAN)

Sesame Street
memorabilia:
942
(Sheila Chustek, USA)

▲ MOST EXPENSIVE TELEVISION PROGRAMME

The 10 episodes of the first season of Netflix's lavish drama *The Crown* (2016) cost a widely reported $130 m (£105.6 m). The series follows the life of Queen Elizabeth II (played by Claire Foy) from the 1940s to the present day. Based in part on writer Peter Morgan's 2013 stage play *The Audience*, the series reunited many of the creative team behind the Oscar-winning film *The Queen* (UK/USA/DEU/FRA, 2006), which starred Helen Mirren as the eponymous monarch.

Most spin-off fiction books inspired by a TV show

There have been more than 600 novelizations and original *Doctor Who* stories, with a further 120-plus set in the same universe.

▲ HIGHEST-PAID TELEVISION CAST

As of 22 Sep 2016, the top four male earners on US TV were the male leads of *The Big Bang Theory*: Jim Parsons ($25.5 m; £19.6 m); Johnny Galecki ($24 m; £18.4 m); Simon Helberg ($22.5 m; £17.3 m, all USA); and Kunal Nayyar (IND/USA, b. UK, $22 m; £16.9 m). Co-star Kaley Cuoco (USA) was the second highest-paid female television star, with $24.5 m (£18.8 m), behind Sofía Vergara (see p.370). The combined earnings of these actors alone push *The Big Bang Theory*'s wage bill beyond the $100-m (£79.7-m) mark.

▲ LONGEST CAREER AS A TV PRESENTER

Sir David Attenborough (UK) made his television debut on *Zoo Quest* (BBC UK, inset) in 1954, and presented *Planet Earth II* (BBC UK, above) in 2017, a total of 63 years later. The naturalist has won BAFTA awards for programmes in black and white, colour, HD and 3D.

The **longest-running TV show with the same presenter** is *The Sky at Night* (BBC UK), which was hosted by the astronomer Sir Patrick Moore (UK) for 55 years from its first edition in 1957 to Moore's death on 9 Dec 2012.

Rectify was originally planned to air on AMC, with *The Shield*'s Walton Goggins in the lead role. It was transferred to sister channel SundanceTV, becoming its first original scripted series.

▶ HIGHEST-RATED TV SERIES (CURRENT)

The fourth season of SundanceTV's drama *Rectify* debuted on 26 Oct 2016, garnering a Metacritic rating of 99 out of 100 and a viewer rating of 8.8. The show follows the struggles of Daniel Holden (Aden Young), who returns home after 19 years having been wrongly imprisoned for murder.

The **highest-rated TV series (ever)** is *Breaking Bad: Season 5* (2012), with a Metacritic score of 99 and a viewer rating of 9.6.

Blockbusters

Jaws (see below) is regarded as the first summer blockbuster. It was the first film to exceed $200 million in domestic (US and Canadian) box-office receipts.

▼ MOST PROLIFIC COMPUTER-GENERATED ANIMATION FRANCHISE

The Jul 2016 release of *Ice Age: Collision Course* (USA) makes the franchise the largest computer-generated animation series, and the first to reach five instalments. The movies follow the adventures of a group of animals during prehistoric times. Created by Blue Sky Studios, the series began with *Ice Age* (USA) in 2002. This and its three successors became the highest-grossing animated feature films released in their respective years. To date, the most successful of all the movies in the franchise is *Ice Age: Dawn of the Dinosaurs* (USA, 2009), which had taken $859,701,857 (£683,388,000) at the box office worldwide as of 11 Dec 2016, according to The Numbers.

Fastest editing in a feature film

With 3,007 individual shots crammed into 79 min 59 sec, the action movie *Derailed* (USA, 2002), starring Belgian actor Jean-Claude Van Damme, is the fastest-edited feature film in history, with an Average Shot Length (ASL) of 1.53 sec.

The **slowest editing in a feature film** is that for Aleksandr Sokurov's film *Russian Ark* (RUS, 2002), which consists of a single, continuous tracking shot lasting 91 min 26.3 sec. This gives the film an ASL of 5,486.3 sec – by far the highest recorded for a narrative feature film.

Most expensive Bollywood film

The science-fiction blockbuster *2.0* (IND, 2017), also known as *Robot 2*, is reported to have cost 3 bn Indian rupees ($44.1 m; £36 m) to produce. It stars Akshay Kumar (CAN, b. IND).

HIGHEST BOX-OFFICE GROSS FOR A...

South Korean film

Yeon Sang-ho's zombie disaster movie *Train to Busan* (KOR) broke national box-office records in its home country following its release in Jul 2016. It went on to earn $99,063,777 (£79,566,100) internationally as of 16 Feb 2017, according to The Numbers, making it the most successful South Korean film ever.

Studio

In a press release on 19 Dec 2016, Walt Disney Studios confirmed that it had just become the first studio to gross $7 bn (£5.6 bn) in a year at the global box office. Disney's final worldwide gross for 2016 was $7.605 bn (£6.18 bn), comprising $2.9 bn (£2.36 bn) from the USA and Canada and $4.7 bn (£3.82 bn) from international markets.

A: Captain America: Civil War, at 2 hr 27 min

Film without a villain

The 22nd highest-grossing film of all time as of Jan 2017, Disney/Pixar's *Finding Dory* (USA, 2016) is the most successful film to date to feature a plot line with no clearly defined major antagonist, and the first movie in this category to gross more than $1 bn (£820 m) worldwide. As of 29 Dec 2016, it had grossed $1,022,617,376 (£834,490,000) according to The Numbers.

MOST...

Oscar nominees in a superhero movie

The cast of *Batman v Superman: Dawn of Justice* (USA, 2016) includes no fewer than four Oscar winners (Ben Affleck, Jeremy Irons, Holly Hunter and Kevin Costner) and five more Oscar nominees (Amy Adams, Jesse Eisenberg, Diane Lane, Laurence Fishburne and Michael Shannon), making nine in total – more than any other superhero movie as of Jan 2017.

▲ **MOST EXPENSIVE CLAPPERBOARD**
A clapperboard used during the production of Steven Spielberg's *Jaws* (USA, 1975) was sold at the 2016 Prop Store Live Auction by Prop Store (UK) for £84,000 ($108,875) in London, UK, on 27 Sep 2016. In keeping with the theme of the movie, the clapperboard featured hand-cut "shark's teeth" serrated edges.

▲ **HIGHEST-GROSSING AUGUST DAY AT THE DOMESTIC BOX OFFICE**
Released on 5 Aug 2016 in 4,255 theatres across the USA, *Suicide Squad* (USA) grossed $64,893,248 (£49,004,100) according to box-office intelligence service The Numbers. Within three days, the film had grossed $133,682,248 (£102,227,000) in the USA, the **highest-grossing August weekend at the domestic box office**.

Top 10 highest-grossing films in 2016

Captain America: Civil War (USA): $1,151,684,349

Rogue One: A Star Wars Story (USA/UK): $1,050,441,501

Finding Dory (USA): $1,022,617,376

Zootopia (USA): $1,019,922,983

The Jungle Book (UK/USA): $963,901,123

The Secret Life of Pets (JPN/USA): $875,958,308

Batman v Superman: Dawn of Justice (USA): $868,160,194

Fantastic Beasts and Where to Find Them (UK/USA): $804,702,363

Deadpool (USA): $783,770,709

Suicide Squad (USA): $746,100,054

Source: The Numbers. All figures are gross within the calendar year and correct as of 13 Mar 2017

THE NUMBERS

The Numbers is the web's biggest database of movie financial information, with figures on more than 25,000 movies and 125,000 people involved in the film industry. It was founded in 1997 by Bruce Nash, and is now visited by more than 5 million people every year. As well as movie fans, the major studios, independent production companies and investors use the site and its services to decide which movies to make and when to release them. The site gathers data from the movie studios, retailers, news reports and other sources to compile its database, known as OpusData. The database contains in excess of 7 million facts about the movie business.

Disney movies in annual Top 10 earners

Five of 2016's top 10 highest-grossing films were produced by Disney – if we include their Lucasfilm, Pixar and Marvel Entertainment subsidiaries and their distribution deal with Marvel Entertainment. *Captain America: Civil War*, *Rogue One: A Star Wars Story*, *Finding Dory*, *Zootopia* and *The Jungle Book* were all effectively Disney releases and held all five top positions (see left).

Golden Globe awards won by a film

Musical comedy drama *La La Land* (USA, 2016) was nominated for seven Golden Globe awards and won in every category. It took the gongs for:
- Best Motion Picture: Musical or Comedy
- Best Performance by an Actress in a Motion Picture (Emma Stone)
- Best Performance by an Actor in a Motion Picture (Ryan Gosling)
- Best Director: Motion Picture (Damien Chazelle)
- Best Screenplay: Motion Picture (Chazelle)
- Best Original Score: Motion Picture (Justin Hurwitz)
- Best Original Song: Motion Picture ("City of Stars" by Hurwitz, performed by Stone and Gosling).

◀ HIGHEST-GROSSING FOREIGN-LANGUAGE FILM

Released worldwide in Feb 2016, Stephen Chow's fantasy adventure *The Mermaid* (CHN, 2016) had earned $552,198,479 (£379,654,000) as of 9 Jun 2016, according to The Numbers. The highest-grossing film to be shot and first screened in a language other than English, it is also the **highest-grossing non-Hollywood film**.

◀ MOST PIRATED ANIMATED MOVIE (CURRENT)

Disney-Pixar's *Finding Dory* (USA, 2016) was illegally downloaded more than any other animated film of the year, according to TorrentFreak. Owing to increasing challenges in monitoring online downloads, the company no longer releases download estimates and instead publishes a ranked list.

Deadpool (USA, 2016) is the **most pirated movie (current)**, according to TorrentFreak.

◀ MOST FEATURE-FILM APPEARANCES AS A MARVEL SUPERHERO

Over the course of the 14 feature films released in the "Marvel Cinematic Universe" (MCU) as of Mar 2016, US actors Samuel L Jackson (as Nick Fury) and Robert Downey Jr (as Tony Stark/Iron Man) are tied for the most appearances. Each stars as their signature character in seven MCU movies.

Digital film extras in one scene

The Egyptian procession sequence in *X-Men: Apocalypse* (USA, 2016) features 295,000 people, but only 25 human actors were actually present when the scene was shot. The rest were created using digital visual effects (VFX).

▲ MOST FILM FRANCHISE ENTRIES IN A CALENDAR YEAR

Of the top 100 highest-grossing movies of 2016, a total of 37 were sequels, spin-offs or franchise entries – the third year in a row that this record has been broken. Of the top 20 highest-grossing films, 13 were sequels or franchise entries, including *Kung Fu Panda 3* (CHN/USA, main picture) and *Harry Potter* spin-off *Fantastic Beasts and Where to Find Them* (UK/USA, inset). Six of the top 10 entries were sequels or in a franchise.

▶ BIGGEST INTERNATIONAL OPENING FOR A BOLLYWOOD FILM

Dangal, a vehicle for Bollywood megastar Aamir Khan (IND), tells the true-life story of a family of female wrestlers. It took $31.2 m (£25.28 m) across seven countries at the international box office in the three days after its release on 21 Dec 2016. This beat Khan's own record of $28.8 m (£23.46 m), as grossed by his comedy hit *PK* (IND) in Dec 2014.

▶ MOST FEMALE LEAD ROLES IN THE ANNUAL TOP 100 FILMS

Of the 100 worldwide highest-grossing films released in 2016, a total of 31 feature women in top-billed acting roles. This is the highest number of any year to date, an increase from 20 in 2015. Pictured here, clockwise from above, are: Amy Adams; Janelle Monáe, Taraji P Henson and Octavia Spencer; and Felicity Jones.

Movie Stars

The top 10 highest-earning movie stars took home a collective $471.5 m (£322.72 m) in 2016, according to Forbes.

Highest-grossing actor from cameo appearances only

With movies based on his creations often breaking box-office records, it's perhaps unsurprising that Marvel Comics mastermind Stan Lee (USA) would want to play his part in front of the camera too. The 36 films in which he has made cameo appearances since his cinematic debut in *Mallrats* (USA, 1995), through to his role in *Doctor Strange* (USA, 2016), had grossed $18,777,702,132 (£15,024,000,000) worldwide as of 24 Mar 2017, according to The-Numbers.com.

Most profitable Hollywood actress

No other female actor in Hollywood has returned more profit relative to what they were paid than *Avengers* star Scarlett Johansson (USA), according to Forbes. In her last three major films up to 1 Jun 2016, including *Captain America: Civil War* (2016) and *Lucy* (2014), she grossed $88.60 (£60.64) for every $1 (£0.68) that she received. For the **most profitable Hollywood actor**, see p.382.

Highest-paid James Bond

British actor Daniel Craig's salary for portraying James Bond in *Spectre* (UK/USA, 2015) is estimated to have totalled $39 m (£25.4 m). This makes Craig by far the highest-paid actor ever to have appeared as Bond, even allowing for inflation.

In *Spectre*, Craig is seen wearing clothes and accessories that have a combined retail value of at least £39,060 ($56,220). That also makes Bond the **most expensively dressed movie character**.

Sean Connery and Roger Moore (both UK) both starred as British secret agent 007 seven times, the **most appearances as James Bond**. Connery appeared in the first Bond movie, *Dr No* (UK, 1962), and Moore made his debut in *Live and Let Die* (UK, 1973).

Jesper Christensen (DNK) is the first actor to play the same villain in three separate James Bond films: the **most appearances as a Bond villain**. Christensen appeared as the character Mr White in *Casino Royale* (UK/USA/CZE/DEU/ITA, 2006), *Quantum of Solace* (UK/USA, 2008) and *Spectre*.

▲ **MOST OSCAR NOMINATIONS WITHOUT WINNING**

Long-suffering sound mixer Kevin O'Connell (USA) received a total of 20 Oscar nominations – starting with *Terms of Endearment* (USA, 1983) at the 1984 Academy Awards – without a single win. His luck finally changed at the 2017 ceremony, where he shared a Best Sound Mixing award with Andy Wright, Robert Mackenzie and Peter Grace (all AUS) for *Hacksaw Ridge* (USA/AUS, 2016).

Oldest top-billed star in a billion-grossing film

Actor Harrison Ford (USA, b. 13 Jul 1942) was 73 years 156 days old when *Star Wars Episode VII: The Force Awakens* (USA) was released to cinemas on 16 Dec 2015. The space opera spectacular ultimately grossed $2,058,662,225 (£1,424,280,000) at the worldwide box office, as of 2 Jun 2016.

Oldest Batman

Ben Affleck (USA, b. 15 Aug 1972) was 43 years 223 days old when *Batman v Superman: Dawn of Justice* (USA) was released on 25 Mar 2016, making him the oldest actor to play Batman in a feature film. His nearest rival is Michael Keaton (USA, b. 5 Sep 1951), who was aged 40 years 288 days when he donned the Batsuit for *Batman Returns* (USA/UK), released on 19 Jun 1992.

MOST...

Disney film roles in a calendar year

Actor Idris Elba (UK) provided the voices for Fluke in *Finding Dory*, Chief Bogo in *Zootopia* and the Bengal tiger Shere Khan in *The Jungle Book* (all USA, 2016).

Film appearances as a werewolf

Spanish actor Paul Naschy (aka Jacinto Molina Alvarez) first got a taste for playing the "wolfman" in the film *La Marca del Hombre Lobo*, also known as *Frankenstein's Bloody Terror* (ESP, 1968). He went on to appear as a werewolf in 14 films over the next four decades, taking his lycanthropic character Waldemar Daninsky to the Himalayas in *The Werewolf and The Yeti*, aka *Night of the Howling Beast* (ESP, 1975), to Japan in *The Beast and the Magic Sword* (ESP/JPN, 1982) and to South America for his final werewolf outing in *A Werewolf in the Amazon* (BRA, 2005).

US actor Tom Cruise had been linked with the first *Iron Man* movie, before Robert Downey Jr took the part. Cruise was also one of the actors mooted for *I Am Legend*, before Will Smith claimed the lead role.

◀ ▲ HIGHEST ANNUAL EARNINGS FOR A FILM ACTOR (EVER)

According to Forbes, the greatest amount of money that any movie actor has earned in a single year is $80 m (£50.8 m). This was first achieved by Will Smith (USA, above) in 2007–08, following success with releases such as *I Am Legend* (USA, 2007) and *Hancock* (USA, 2008). It was matched by *Iron Man* star Robert Downey Jr (USA, left) in 2014–15, following the release of *Avengers: Age of Ultron* (USA, 2015).

A: Iron Man (USA, 2008)

◄ YOUNGEST LEADING ACTOR IN A MARVEL CINEMATIC UNIVERSE MOVIE

Tom Holland (UK, b. 1 Jun 1996) was just 20 years 123 days old when principal photography finished on *Spider-Man: Homecoming* (USA, 2017). Turn back to p.xvi to read GWR's interview with Tom.

▲ MOST OSCAR WINNERS TO PLAY A SUPERHERO

In his 10 feature films to date, Batman has been played by three Oscar winners. **1.** George Clooney (USA; *Batman & Robin* [USA/UK, 1997]) won Best Supporting Actor for *Syriana* (USA/UAE, 2005). **2.** Ben Affleck (USA; *Batman v Superman: Dawn of Justice* [USA, 2016]) won best Original Screenplay for *Good Will Hunting* (USA, 1997) and Best Picture for *Argo* (USA, 2012). **3.** Christian Bale (UK; *Batman Begins* [USA/UK, 2005], *The Dark Knight* [USA/UK, 2008], *The Dark Knight Rises* [USA/UK, 2012]) won Best Supporting Actor for *The Fighter* (USA, 2010).

Based on bankability data from The-Numbers.com, we present all the ingredients you need to produce the ultimate blockbuster...

Leading actor:
Tom Hanks (USA)
$9,283,733,292

Leading actress:
Emma Watson (UK)
$7,787,852,895

Supporting actor:
Warwick Davis (UK)
$13,254,450,305

Supporting actress:
Sherry Lynn (USA)
$7,918,738,027

Director:
Steven
Spielberg (USA)
$9,755,487,265

Producer: Kevin
Feige (USA)
$10,896,167,397

Cinematographer:
Andrew Lesnie
(AUS)
$7,960,202,614

Screenwriter:
Steve Kloves
(USA)
$7,575,525,594

Composer:
Hans Zimmer
(DEU)
$26,339,539,415

Source: The-Numbers.com; correct as of 1 Mar 2017

▲ **MOST PROFITABLE HOLLYWOOD ACTOR**
For the second year running, no other Hollywood actor has returned more profit relative to what they were paid than *Captain America* star Chris Evans (USA), according to Forbes. In his last three major films up to 1 Jun 2016, which includes *Captain America: Civil War* (USA, 2016), he grossed $135.80 (£92.94) for every $1 (£0.68) that he received.

▲ **MOST GOLDEN GLOBE AWARDS WON**
Meryl Streep (USA) has received eight Golden Globe awards, winning in 1980, 1982–83, 2003–04, 2007, 2010 and 2012. Her first win was for Best Actress in a Supporting Role in *Kramer vs. Kramer* (USA, 1979). Her latest was for Best Performance by an Actress in a Motion Picture – Drama in *The Iron Lady* (UK/FRA, 2011). In 2017, she was also given the Cecil B DeMille honorary Golden Globe for "outstanding contributions to the world of entertainment".

Streep also has the **most Golden Globe nominations for an actress**, with 30.

Oscar nominees in one movie

Robert Altman's *The Player* (USA, 1992) features 23 Oscar nominees. The cast includes 13 Oscar winners (Tim Robbins, Whoopi Goldberg, Sydney Pollack, Cher, James Coburn, Joel Grey, Jack Lemmon, Marlee Matlin, Julia Roberts, Susan Sarandon, Rod Steiger, Louise Fletcher and Anjelica Huston). It also stars 10 further Oscar nominees (Dean Stockwell, Karen Black, Gary Busey, Peter Falk, Sally Kellerman, Sally Kirkland, Burt Reynolds, Lily Tomlin, Teri Garr and Nick Nolte).

Maui carries a giant fish hook that enables him to shape-shift. At one point in the movie, he momentarily changes into Sven the reindeer from *Frozen* (USA, 2013), which was also produced by Disney.

Star Wars

Four of the top 10 all-time highest grossers at the US box office are Star Wars films. In all, they have earned $2.4 bn (£1.95 bn).

◄ MOST VALUABLE MOVIE FRANCHISE

According to *Fortune* magazine, the value of the Star Wars franchise stood at $41.98 bn (£28.26 bn) as of 24 Dec 2016. Box-office revenue from the eight theatrically released films accounted for only a fifth of this, with the rest generated by home video and digital sales, toys and merchandise, books, games and intellectual property.

Highest box-office gross for a science-fiction film series
As of 16 Jan 2017, the films in the Star Wars series had collectively grossed $7,456,076,338 (£6,117,050,000) worldwide at the box office, according to figures from The-Numbers.

The **highest-grossing Star Wars movie** is *The Force Awakens*, with worldwide box-office takings of $2,058,662,225 (£1.54 bn). The film achieved the **fastest time for a movie to gross $1 bn**, reaching the mark in just 12 days (from its international release date of 16 Dec to 27 Dec 2015). This beat the previous record of 13 days, set by 2015's *Jurassic World* (USA).

Most appearances in Star Wars films
Anthony Daniels (UK) has appeared in all eight theatrically released Star Wars films to date, playing the protocol droid C-3PO. He featured in a brief cameo in *Rogue One: A Star Wars Story*, and is set to return in 2017's eagerly anticipated *Episode VIII – The Last Jedi*.

Most miniatures in a film scene

For the Mos Espa podracing sequences in *The Phantom Menace*, the audience in the Grand Arena consisted of 450,000 hand-painted Q-tips cotton buds.

Most visual effects shots in a Star Wars film

There are 2,200 visual effects (VFX) shots in both *Attack of the Clones* and *Revenge of the Sith*. Ironically, the latter is the only Star Wars film not to be nominated for an Oscar in the Best Visual Effects category to date.

▲ **BEST-SELLING STAR WARS VIDEOGAME**

LEGO Star Wars: The Complete Saga (2007) had achieved sales of 15.29 million as of 23 Feb 2017. The super-selling videogame is a compendium of two previous Star Wars titles: *LEGO Star Wars: The Video Game* (2005) and *LEGO Star Wars II: The Original Trilogy* (2006).

Most actors to play one Star Wars character

Ten actors have played the role of Darth Vader/ Anakin Skywalker. One actor provides the voice, while another plays the role on screen. The first two were David Prowse (UK, Episodes *IV–VI*) and James Earl Jones (USA, Vader's voice in Episodes *IV–VI*, *Rogue One* and possibly uncredited in *Episode III*). Stunt coordinator Bob Anderson (UK) stepped into Vader's costume in *Episode IV*, returning for the next two films. The others were: Sebastian Shaw (UK, *Episode VI*), C Andrew Nelson (USA, 1997 Special Edition of *Episode V*), Jake Lloyd (USA, *Episode I*), Hayden Christensen (CAN, Episodes *II–III*), stuntman Gene Bryant (USA, *Episode III*), Spencer Wilding and stuntman Daniel Naprous (both UK, *Rogue One*).

Most expensive Star Wars action figure

On 19 Jul 2016, a French-edition Boba Fett figure, manufactured by Meccano in support of the release of *The Empire Strikes Back* in 1980, was sold for £26,040 ($34,491) by the UK-based auction house Vectis.

▲ **LARGEST LEGO® STAR WARS SCULPTURE WITH INTERNAL SUPPORT (NUMBER OF BRICKS)**

In May 2013, LEGO unveiled a 1:1 scale model of a Star Wars X-wing starfighter containing 5,335,200 LEGO bricks in Times Square, New York City, USA. It included steel supports and took a year to build.

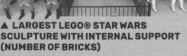

Star Wars: Episode IV – A New Hope
Release date: 25 May 1977 (USA)
Box-office takings: $786,598,007

Star Wars: Episode V – The Empire Strikes Back
Release date: 21 May 1980 (USA)
Box-office takings: $534,171,960

Star Wars: Episode VI – Return of the Jedi
Release date: 25 May 1983 (USA)
Box-office takings: $572,705,079

Star Wars: Episode I – The Phantom Menace
Release date: 19 May 1999 (USA)
Box-office takings: $1,027,044,677

▲ **HIGHEST-GROSSING LIVE-ACTION FILM WITH A FEMALE STAR**
Rogue One: A Star Wars Story – in which Felicity Jones (UK) takes top billing as Jyn Erso – had grossed $1,050,789,328 (£844,652,000) worldwide as of 12 Apr 2017. This eclipsed the $864 m (£523.9 m) earned by *The Hunger Games: Catching Fire* (USA, 2013), which starred Jennifer Lawrence as Katniss Everdeen.

Most Oscar nominations for a Star Wars film

A New Hope was nominated for 10 Academy Awards and won six: Art Direction, Costume Design, Original Score, Sound, Film Editing and Visual Effects.

The **fewest Oscar nominations for a Star Wars film** is one, achieved by *Attack of the Clones* (for Visual Effects) and *Revenge of the Sith* (for Makeup). Neither movie won.

Most expensive Star Wars memorabilia (off-screen item)

A Panavision PSR 35-mm camera used by George Lucas during principal photography for *A New Hope* in 1976 was sold at auction house Profiles in History in Dec 2011 for $625,000 (£398,933), including buyer's premium. The camera had been acquired by actress Debbie Reynolds, whose daughter Carrie Fisher played Princess Leia in the film.

Most expensive Star Wars memorabilia (on-screen item)

On 1 Oct 2015, a model of a Rebel Blockade Runner ship pursued by an Imperial Star Destroyer in the opening moments of *A New Hope* fetched $450,000 (£296,920), including buyer's premium, at auction house Profiles in History in Calabasas, California, USA. The 16-in (40.6-cm) miniature came from the collection of Grant McCune, Chief Model Maker on the film's Miniature and Optical Effects Unit.

Star Wars: Episode II – Attack of the Clones
Release date: 16 May 2002 (USA)
Box-office takings: $656,695,615

Star Wars: Episode III – Revenge of the Sith
Release date: 19 May 2005 (USA)
Box-office takings: $848,998,877

Star Wars: Episode VII – The Force Awakens
Release date: 18 Dec 2015 (USA)
Box-office takings: $2,058,662,225

Rogue One: A Star Wars Story
Release date: 16 Dec 2016 (USA/UK)
Box-office takings: $1,050,789,328

Star Wars: Episode VIII – The Last Jedi
Scheduled release date: 15 Dec 2017 (USA)

▶ LARGEST STAR WARS COSTUMING GROUP

Founded as a "stormtrooper fan club" in 1997 by Albin Johnson (USA), the 501st Legion had a membership of 11,019 as of 26 Apr 2017. Now all allies of the Galactic Empire plus bounty hunters and "denizens of the Empire" are free to join. According to the handbook, members "celebrate the Star Wars movies through the wearing of costumes, to promote the quality and improvement of costumes and props, and to contribute to the local community".

Most themed LEGO sets for one franchise

There were 46 LEGO Star Wars sets available to buy in 2016, which equates to more than 20,000 LEGO pieces at a combined cost of $2,400 (£1,950). Including sets, exclusives and Minifigures packed with magazines, books, giveaways or promotional items, the total rises to 67 sets.

◀ BEST-SELLING SINGLE OF INSTRUMENTAL MUSIC

"Star Wars Theme/Cantina Band" by Meco, aka Domenico Monardo (USA), was a 1977 disco arrangement of John Williams' (USA) *Star Wars* music. It was awarded platinum status by the Recording Industry Association of America (RIAA) for sales of more than 2 million. The song featured on *Star Wars and Other Galactic Funk* (left).

▲ LARGEST COLLECTION OF STAR WARS MEMORABILIA

Steve Sansweet (USA) has amassed an estimated 500,000 unique Star Wars items at Rancho Obi-Wan in northern California, USA. As of 14 Jan 2017, "only" 131,000 items had been accurately audited and catalogued. This is still enough to beat the previous record by a factor of six – and Sansweet's collection is growing all the time...

Shortest gap between Star Wars film releases

Rogue One: A Star Wars Story was released worldwide on 16 Dec 2016, only 364 days after *The Force Awakens* had first appeared in cinemas on 18 Dec 2015.

▼ LONGEST GAP BETWEEN AN ACTOR'S DEATH AND LAST FILM "APPEARANCE"

CGI technology enabled Peter Cushing (UK, 1913–94) to return to the screen more than 22 years after his death. Cushing's image was recreated so that his role as Grand Moff Tarkin from *A New Hope* could be reprised for *Rogue One: A Star Wars Story*.

Music

It would take 5,447 years to listen to Drake's "One Dance" back-to-back as many times as it has been streamed on Spotify.

▼ **MOST FOLLOWERS ON INSTAGRAM**
As of 21 Feb 2017, singer and actor Selena Gomez (USA) had 110,607,553 followers on the photo-focused social network. This placed her ahead of fellow US singers Taylor Swift (97,854,110) and Ariana Grande (97,365,150). Gomez released three albums with Selena Gomez & the Scene; her first two solo albums, *Stars Dance* (2013) and *Revival* (2015), both debuted at No.1 on the *Billboard* 200 albums chart.

Most valuable vinyl record (single)

Recorded at a home studio in Liverpool, UK, by a pre-Beatles Paul McCartney, John Lennon and George Harrison (alongside drummer Colin Hanton and pianist John "Duff" Lowe), the only known copy of The Quarrymen's (UK) "That'll Be the Day"/"In Spite of All the Danger" (1958) is worth an estimated £100,000 ($124,400).

Youngest professional music producer

Brandon Bailey Johnson (USA) was 12 years 363 days old on the release of his self-produced debut album *My Journey*, on 21 Feb 2015.

MOST...

Simultaneous entries on the UK albums chart

On the Official Albums Chart dated 21 Jan 2016, David Bowie (UK, b. David Jones) placed 19 albums in the Top 100. The iconic musician, who succumbed to cancer on 10 Jan 2016, owned a quarter of the Top 40, including his 25th studio album, *Blackstar*, which debuted at No.1 with sales of 146,168 – enough to give "The Thin White Duke" a 10th chart-topper in the UK.

Selena Gomez is named after Selena Quintanilla-Pérez, the "Queen of Tejano music". Tejano is a form of folk and pop music originating in Mexican-American communities in Texas, USA.

Siblings to have solo hits on the *Billboard* charts

All nine children of Joe and Katherine Jackson – Rebbie, Jackie, Tito, Jermaine, La Toya, Marlon, Michael, Randy and Janet (all USA) – have charted with solo recordings in the USA. Michael Jackson kicked off his family's love affair with *Billboard*'s charts when "Got to Be There" entered at No.89 on the Hot 100 on 30 Oct 1971. Almost 45 years later, Tito Jackson's "Get It Baby" completed the family set when it debuted at No.29 on Adult R&B Songs on 4 Jun 2016.

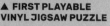

▲ FIRST PLAYABLE VINYL JIGSAW PUZZLE

In Sep 2016, Sugar Coat (UK) released a 7-inch version of "Me Instead" as a playable vinyl jigsaw. Showing a crowded supermarket scene, it was one of a set of 35 designs by the London-based trio to mark the release of their debut single. Other pressings included mirror and faux-fur designs, and one was sprinkled with coal dust.

Simultaneous tracks on the UK Top 20 singles chart

On the Official Singles Chart dated 16 Mar 2017, British singer-songwriter Ed Sheeran had 16 tracks in the Top 20. They included the entire Top 5: "Shape of You" (No.1 for a ninth consecutive week), "Galway Girl" (No.2 – new entry), "Castle on the Hill" (No.3 – non-mover), "Perfect" (No.4 – new entry) and "New Man" (No.5 – new entry).

All 16 tracks appear on the deluxe edition of Sheeran's third studio album, ÷ ("Divide"). It debuted at No.1 on the Official Albums Chart on 16 Mar 2017 after selling 672,000 copies – making it the **fastest-selling UK album by a male artist**.

▲ MOST *DAESANG* AWARDS WON AT THE MNET ASIA MUSIC AWARDS

At the 2016 Mnet Asian Music Awards, boy band EXO (KOR/CHN) won Album of the Year for *EX'ACT*. It was their fifth daesang ("grand prize") at the annual awards ceremony, following previous Albums of the Year in 2013–15 and Artist of the Year in 2014. They matched the feat of BIGBANG (KOR, inset), who won Song of the Year in 2007 and 2015 and Artist of the Year in 2008, 2012 and 2015.

Q: Michael Jackson's nephews Taj, Taryll and TJ are better known as who?

A: R&B pop group 3T

Simultaneous tracks on the US singles chart by a solo artist
Drake (CAN, b. Aubrey Drake Graham) placed 24 tracks simultaneously on the *Billboard* Hot 100 on the chart dated 8 Apr 2017. In the process, he also claimed the all-time record for the **most Hot 100 entries by a solo artist**: 154.

Decades with a Top 20 hit on the US Hot Country Songs chart
Dolly Parton (USA) has had Top 20 hits for six consecutive decades (1960s–2010s). Her first Top 20 entry was "Something Fishy" in 1967, since when she's been a credited artist on a further 73 Top 20 hits. A new version of her 1974 hit "Jolene" with *a cappella* quintet Pentatonix (USA) debuted at No.18 on *Billboard*'s Hot Country Songs chart dated 8 Oct 2016. It was Dolly's 107th chart entry – the **most hits on the US Hot Country Songs chart by a female artist**.

No.1s on the *Billboard* Tropical Albums chart
The "Gentleman of Salsa", Gilberto Santa Rosa (PRI), achieved his 12th chart-topping album with *Necesito un Bolero* on 28 Feb 2015.

World Music Awards for Best-Selling Middle Eastern Artist
Egyptian singer-songwriter and "Father of Mediterranean Music" Amr Diab has been crowned four times: 1996, 2001, 2007 and 2013.

CDs consecutively signed by the artist
Mexican boy band CD9 signed 6,194 CDs non-stop in Mexico City, Mexico, on 25 Apr 2016. The five-piece group autographed special-edition copies of their album *Evolution* during a session that lasted 4 hr 54 min.

Songs on a digital album
On 2 Dec 2016, The Pocket Gods (UK) reclaimed the record for the most songs on a digital album with the release of the 111-track *100xmas30*. The follow-up to *100x30* (2015) and *Shakespeare Verses Streaming* (2016) – both with 100 tracks

– *100xmas30* saw the indie outfit continue their crusade against the digital music industry over royalty payments while taking back the record they lost to Kapten Hurricane (SWE) and their misleadingly titled 101-track digital album *100 Rock Songs* (2016).

◄ HIGHEST-EARNING DEAD CELEBRITY
Michael Jackson (USA, 1958–2009) earned a staggering $825 m (£636 m) in the 12 months to 1 Oct 2016, according to Forbes. Jackson's pre-tax payday was boosted by the $750-m (£578.2-m) sale of his half of the Sony/ATV Music Publishing catalogue, which includes the rights to The Beatles' back catalogue. Jackson's 2015–16 earnings make him the **highest-earning celebrity ever** – dead or alive – over a 12-month period.

EXTREME PERFORMANCES – check out these crazy concerts

Coldest
Charlie Simpson (UK) – Oymyakon, Russia, 24 Nov 2012 – minus 30°C (minus 22°F)

Deepest
Agonizer (FIN) – Pyhäsalmi Mine Oy, Finland, 4 Aug 2007 – 1,271 m (4,169 ft)

Deepest underwater (contained)
Katie Melua (UK, b. GEO) – Troll A gas rig, Bergen, Norway, 1 Oct 2006 – 303 m (994 ft) below sea level

Fastest
Jamiroquai (UK) – Flight ZT6902 from Munich, Germany, 27 Feb 2007 – 1,017 km/h (631.9 mph)

First live to space
Paul McCartney (UK) – Anaheim, California, to the *International Space Station*, 12 Nov 2005

First act to perform on all seven continents
Metallica (USA) – Carlini Base, Antarctica, 8 Dec 2013

Highest on land
Oz Bayldon (UK) – Mera Peak, Nepal, 16 May 2012 – 6,476 m (21,246 ft)

▶ FIRST SONGWRITER TO WIN THE NOBEL PRIZE IN LITERATURE

In 2016, Bob Dylan (USA, b. Robert Zimmerman) was awarded the Nobel Prize in Literature for creating "new poetic expressions within the great American song tradition". The singer-songwriter built his long and illustrious career on songs such as "Blowin' in the Wind", "The Times They Are a-Changin'" and "Like a Rolling Stone". He is the first songwriter to receive the Literature prize, initially awarded in 1901.

◀ MOST UK NO.1 ALBUMS BY A SOLO ARTIST

On 3 Nov 2016, Elvis Presley (USA, 1935–77) scored his 13th No.1 on the UK's Official Albums Chart with *The Wonder of You*, featuring the Royal Philharmonic Orchestra. "The King", who was previously tied with Madonna on 12 solo album chart-toppers, achieved his first UK No.1 with *Rock 'n Roll* on 10 Nov 1956 – one week shy of 60 years before *The Wonder of You*.

◀ SHORTEST SONG TO ENTER THE *BILLBOARD* HOT 100

Created and performed by Pikotaro (aka Daimaou Kosaka, JPN), "PPAP (Pen-Pineapple-Apple-Pen)" lasts for 45 sec. It appeared on the *Billboard* Hot 100 on 29 Oct 2016.

▲ HIGHEST ANNUAL EARNINGS EVER FOR A FEMALE POP STAR

Taylor Swift (USA) is estimated to have earned $170 m (£116.3 m) in the 12 months to 1 Jun 2016, according to Forbes. The singer-songwriter behind multi-million-selling hits such as "Shake It Off", Swift holds numerous records including **most weeks at No.1 on** *Billboard*'s **Artist 100 chart** – 31, as of 25 Mar 2017.

Drake's "One Dance" stayed at No.1 on the Official Singles Chart for 15 weeks. This is the joint-third longest UK chart-topper, three weeks shy of Frankie Laine's "I Believe" (1953).

▶ MOST STREAMED TRACK ON SPOTIFY

As of 13 Apr 2017, "One Dance" by Drake (CAN) had been listened to 1,182,920,493 times on the music-streaming service. The dancehall track, featuring Wizkid and Kyla, appeared on the 2016 album *Views*.

On *Billboard*'s Streaming Songs chart dated 8 Apr 2017, 21 of the 22 tracks from Drake's No.1 album *More Life* (2017) registered a record 384.8 million streams.

Chart-Toppers

On 11 Jan 2016, the day after his death, David Bowie (UK) attracted 51 million views of his recordings on video-sharing platform VEVO.

SPOTIFY

Most streamed in 2016	Holder	Streams	
Male	Drake (CAN)	5,800,000,000	
Female	Rihanna (BRB)	2,900,000,000	
Group	Twenty One Pilots (USA)	2,600,000,000	
Track (male)	"One Dance", Drake feat. Wizkid & Kyla (CAN/NGA/UK)	1,000,000,000	
Track (female)	"Cheap Thrills", Sia (AUS)	623,000,000	
Track (group)	"Don't Let Me Down", The Chainsmokers feat. Daya (both USA)	710,000,000	
Album (male)	*Views*, Drake (CAN)	2,600,000,000	
Album (female)	*ANTI*, Rihanna (BRB)	1,600,000,000	
Album (group)	*Blurryface*, Twenty One Pilots (USA)	1,400,000,000	
"Breakout" artist	ZAYN (UK, right)	894,000,000	

All-time	Holder	Streams	Date
Artist	Drake (CAN)	11,000,000,000	26 Apr 2017
Female	Rihanna (BRB)	6,600,000,000	26 Apr 2017
Track	"One Dance", Drake feat. Wizkid & Kyla (CAN/NGA/UK)	1,100,000,000	26 Apr 2017
Track in 24 hours	"Shape of You", Ed Sheeran (UK)	10,000,000	26 Apr 2017
Track in one week	"Shape of You", Ed Sheeran (UK)	64,000,000	26 Apr 2017
Album	*Purpose*, Justin Bieber (CAN)	4,600,000,000	26 Apr 2017
Album in one week	*÷ ("Divide")*, Ed Sheeran (UK)	374,000,000	26 Apr 2017

◀ RIHANNA
Born Robyn Rihanna Fenty in Barbados, Rihanna has gone on to conquer the pop world. As of 26 Apr 2017, she was the **most streamed female act on Spotify**, with 6.6 billion streams of her songs. "Work", featuring Drake, from the 2016 album *ANTI*, is Rihanna's most popular track with more than 600 million streams.

(AS OF 11 MAY 2017)

Most viewed channels	Holder	Views
Entertainment	T-Series (IND)	17,933,029,645
Male	JustinBieberVEVO (CAN)	15,116,431,053
Female	KatyPerryVEVO (USA)	11,816,049,727
Media	GMM Grammy Official (THA)	9,699,943,749
Group	OneDirectionVEVO (UK/IRE)	7,269,976,966
Community	Trap Nation (USA)	4,609,314,422
Brand	Beats by Dre (USA)	260,037,674

Most viewed videos	Holder	Views
Male	"Gangnam Style", PSY (KOR)	2,834,806,435
Duet	"See You Again", Wiz Khalifa feat. Charlie Puth (both USA)	2,707,093,131
Female	"Shake it Off", Taylor Swift (USA)	2,110,214,601
Group (male)	"Sugar", Maroon 5 (USA)	1,989,872,721
Children's	"Wheels on the Bus" Plus Lots More Nursery Rhymes, LittleBabyBum (UK)	1,869,854,000
Group (female)	"Work from Home", Fifth Harmony feat. Ty Dolla $ign (both USA)	1,543,630,467
Pre-YouTube video (i.e., made before Apr 2005)	"November Rain", Guns N' Roses (USA), 1992	788,028,638
Most viewed in 24 hours	"Gentleman", PSY (KOR)	38,409,306

◀ JUSTIN BIEBER
On 22 Oct 2012, Canadian singer Justin Bieber became the **first musician with a music channel viewed 3 billion times**. He has maintained a global fanbase of "Beliebers" and dominates social media. His VEVO channel is the **most viewed music channel on YouTube**, with 15.11 billion as of 11 May 2017, and the third most viewed channel overall.

MOST WEEKS AT NO.1 (SINGLE)

Territory	Chart company	Song	Artist	Year(s)	Weeks
Brazil	Billboard	"I Want to Know What Love Is"	Mariah Carey (USA)	2009–10	27
France	SNEP	"Happy"	Pharrell Williams (USA)	2013–14	22
UK	Official Charts Company	"I Believe"	Frankie Laine (USA)	1953	=18
Belgium	Ultratop	"Hello"	Adele (UK)	2015–16	=18
Germany	GfK Entertainment	"Rivers of Babylon"	Boney M (JAM/MSR/ABW)	1978	17
USA	Billboard	"One Sweet Day"	Mariah Carey & Boyz II Men (USA)	1995–96	=16
Belgium	Ultratop	"Kvraagetaen"	Fixkes (BEL)	2007	=16
Canada	Billboard	"I Gotta Feeling"	The Black Eyes Peas (USA)	2009	=16
		"Shape of You"	Ed Sheeran (UK)	2017	=16
Australia	ARIA	"Shape of You"	Ed Sheeran (UK)	2017	=15
Netherlands	Stichting Nederlandse	"Shape of You"	Ed Sheeran (UK)	2017	=15

FACEBOOK • INSTAGRAM • TWITTER • MUSICAL.LY (AS OF 11 MAY 2017)

Most Facebook fans	Holder	Fans
Female musician	Shakira (COL)	104,547,254
Male musician	Eminem (USA)	90,634,055
Deceased musician	Michael Jackson (USA)	75,179,320
Music group	Linkin Park (USA)	61,774,733
Media	MTV (USA)	49,177,020
Community	Music	41,721,716
Brand	iTunes (USA)	30,910,151
Entertainment	*The Voice* (NLD)	16,759,244

Most Instagram followers	Holder	Followers
Female musician	Selena Gomez (USA)	120,135,089
Male musician	Justin Bieber (CAN)	86,485,071
Music group	One Direction (UK/IRL)	17,484,094

Most Twitter followers	Holder	Followers
Female musician	Katy Perry (USA)	97,740,227
Male musician	Justin Bieber (CAN)	93,739,524
Music group	One Direction (UK/IRL)	31,747,631
Media	MTV (USA)	15,091,798
Community	Apple Music (USA)	9,046,269
Entertainment	*The X Factor* (UK)	7,017,137
Brand	SoundCloud (DEU)	2,218,096

Most Twitter engagements	Holder	Retweets
Male musician	Harry Styles (UK)	180,607
Group (male)	BTS (KOR)	152,112
Female musician	Beyoncé (USA)	33,038
Group (female)	Fifth Harmony (USA)	11,103

Most Musical.ly followers	Holder	Followers*
Female duo	Lisa and Lena (DEU)	19,100,000
Female	Ariel Martin ("Baby Ariel", USA)	19,000,000
Male	Jacob Sartorius (USA)	16,700,000
Female chart topper	Selena Gomez (USA)	11,100,000
Male chart topper	Bruno Mars (USA)	1,200,000

▶ THRILLER

Michael Jackson's 1982 classic – the **best-selling album** – has been certified 29 times platinum by the Recording Industry Association of America (RIAA). *Thriller* won Jackson eight Grammy awards at the 1984 ceremony, including Album of the Year and Record of the Year for "Beat It" – the **most Grammy awards won by an individual in one year**.

BEST-SELLING ALBUMS BY TERRITORY

Territory	Album	Performer	Year	Units sold*
World	*Thriller*	Michael Jackson (USA)	1982	66 million
USA	*Thriller*	Michael Jackson (USA)	1982	32 million
Japan	*First Love*	Hikaru Utada (JPN)	1999	7.6 million
UK	*Greatest Hits*	Queen (UK)	1981	6.1 million
France	*D'eux*	Celine Dion (CAN)	1995	4.4 million
Brazil	*Thriller*	Michael Jackson (USA)	1982	3.8 million
Italy	*La vita è adesso*	Claudio Baglioni (ITA)	1985	3.8 million
South Korea	*Mis-Encounter*	Kim Gun-mo (KOR)	1995	3.3 million
Germany	*Mensch*	Herbert Grönemeyer (DEU)	2002	3.1 million
Canada	*Thriller*	Michael Jackson (USA)	1982	2.4 million
Spain	*Más*	Alejandro Sanz (ESP)	1997	2.2 million
Australia	*Bat Out of Hell*	Meat Loaf (USA)	1977	1.7 million

◄ **BING CROSBY**
Festive favourite "White Christmas" was sung by Bing Crosby (USA) in the film *Holiday Inn* (USA, 1942) and won an Academy Award for Best Original Song. It was one of four Crosby-crooned songs to win an Oscar between 1937 and 1951 – the **most Oscar award-winning songs sung by the same person**.

BEST-SELLING SINGLES BY TERRITORY

Territory	Song	Performer	Year	Units sold*
World	"White Christmas"	Bing Crosby (USA)	1942	50 million
USA	"White Christmas"	Bing Crosby (USA)	1942	25 million
Japan	"Soba ni Iru ne"	Thelma Aoyama feat. SoulJa (both JPN)	2008	9.2 million
South Korea	"Cherry Blossom Ending"	Busker Busker (KOR)	2012	6.5 million
France	"Petit Papa Noël"	Tino Rossi (FRA)	1946	5.7 million
UK	"Something About the Way You Look Tonight"/ "Candle in the Wind 1997"	Elton John (UK)	1997	4.9 million
Germany	"Something About the Way You Look Tonight"/ "Candle in the Wind 1997"	Elton John (UK)	1997	4.5 million
Canada	"Pour que tu m'aimes encore"	Celine Dion (CAN)	1995	2.1 million
Australia	"Party Rock Anthem"	LMFAO feat. Lauren Bennett & GoonRock (USA/UK/USA)	2011	1 million
Spain	"Amor Gitano"	Alejandro Fernández (MEX) & Beyoncé (USA)	2007	480,000

*all sales figures estimated

MOST AWARDS WON (AS OF 11 MAY 2017)

Award	Artist	Wins
Billboard Music Awards (USA)	Michael Jackson (USA)	40
Grammy Awards (USA)	Sir Georg Solti (UK, b. HUN)	=31
Teen Choice Awards – Music (USA)	One Direction (UK)	=31
American Music Awards (USA)	Michael Jackson (USA)	26
Juno Awards (CAN)	Anne Murray (CAN)	=24
MTV Video Music Awards (USA)	Beyoncé (USA)	=24
Country Music Association Awards (USA)	George Strait (USA)	23
Latin Grammy Awards (USA)	Calle 13 (PRI)	22
ARIA Music Awards (AUS)	Silverchair (AUS)	21
MTV Europe Music Awards	Justin Bieber (CAN)	20
BRIT Awards (UK)	Robbie Williams (UK)	18
Echo Music Prize (DEU)	Helene Fischer (DEU, b. RUS, right)	16
Melon Music Awards (KOR)	Girls' Generation (KOR)	=13
Mnet Asian Music Awards (KOR)	EXO (KOR)	=13
NRJ Music Awards (FRA)	M Pokora (FRA)	11
MTV Video Music Awards Japan	Exile (JPN)	=10
Nickelodeon Kids' Choice Awards – Music (USA)	Selena Gomez (USA)	=10
The Headies (NGA)	Mode 9 (NGA)	9
Sanremo Music Festival (ITA)	Domenico Modugno & Claudio Villa (both ITA)	4

◀ MARIAH CAREY

Mariah Carey (USA) has sung marathon chart-toppers in both the USA and Brazil, duetting with R&B band Boyz II Men on the former and covering a 1984 Foreigner hit for the latter. After "Vision of Love" hit the *Billboard* No.1 spot on 4 Aug 1990, Carey went on to record the **most US No.1 singles by a female artist**. She is tied with Elvis Presley on 18 – only The Beatles, with 20, have scored more.

Arts & Media Round-Up

The Louvre has some 650,000 sq ft (60,386 m²) of gallery space — nearly 10 times the size of the White House.

Fastest time to watch every Shakespeare play

Dan Wilson (UK) wanted to do something challenging to mark his 37th birthday, so settled on seeing all of the 37 plays attributed to William Shakespeare. It took him 328 days, beginning with a secondary-school production of *Julius Caesar* at Lewes Town Hall in East Sussex, UK, on 27 Nov 2014. Last on the list was *Pericles* at the Oregon Shakespeare Festival in Ashland, USA, on 21 Oct 2015 – Dan's 38th birthday.

Highest-grossing year for Broadway theatres

According to The Broadway League, 2016 saw $1.416 bn (£1.146 bn) in ticket sales for Broadway in New York City, USA, from the week ending Sunday, 3 Jan 2016 to the week ending Sunday, 1 Jan 2017. Attendance figures reached 13.61 million.

First live-streamed Broadway show

Roundabout Theatre Company's production of *She Loves Me!* was broadcast from Studio 54 on West 54th Street, New York City, USA, at 8 p.m. (Eastern Time) on 30 Jun 2016.

The next highest-grossing circus show of 2016 was *Varekai*, also by Cirque du Soleil, with estimated takings of $53 m (£43 m).

▲ MOST WATCHED YOUTUBE CHANNEL FOR A MILLENNIAL

As of 4 May 2017, "Ryan ToysReview" had been viewed 12,076,126,791 times since its launch on 16 Mar 2015, more than any other YouTube channel for a "millennial" (i.e., someone born post-2000). It is dedicated to six-year-old Ryan (USA, b. 6 Oct 2010), who uploads videos of himself (or his family) playing with toys or games and assessing them.

▲ LARGEST FINE-ART EXHIBITION DEDICATED TO ONE VIDEOGAME CHARACTER

The *Sonic the Hedgehog 25th Anniversary Collection* at Castle Fine Art in London, UK, on 1–5 Dec 2016 was the largest fine-art exhibition based on a single gaming character. Licensed by SEGA and curated by Washington Green, it featured 25 original, commissioned artworks of Sonic, created by eight artists, with individual valuations of up to £40,000 ($49,912).

Most Laurence Olivier Award wins

Harry Potter and the Cursed Child (2016) was produced for the stage by Sonia Friedman Productions, Sir Colin Callender and Harry Potter Theatrical Productions, and written by Jack Thorne based on an original story by Thorne, J K Rowling and John Tiffany (all UK). It won a record nine awards at the Oliviers on 9 Apr 2017: Best Director (Tiffany), Best New Play, Best Actor (Jamie Parker), Best Actress in a Supporting Role (Noma Dumezweni), Best Actor in a Supporting Role (Anthony Boyle), Best Set Design (Christine Jones), Best Costume Design (Katrina Lindsay), Best Sound Design (Gareth Fry) and Best Lighting Design (Neil Austin).

The Cursed Child was nominated 11 times, sharing the record for **most Olivier nominations received by a production** with the musical *Hairspray* (2008), which took home four of its 11 awards.

Most short films produced

Epiphany Morgan and Carl Mason (both AUS) produced 365 films in 70 cities, as verified on 7 Jun 2016. As part of a project entitled "365 docobites", the pair travelled to five continents during a year. Their goal was to introduce the world to a "stranger a day" through bite-sized documentaries. The series was initially distributed via their website, then picked up for TV distribution by SBS 2 in Australia.

▲ OLDEST CONTINUOUSLY OPERATING MOVIE THEATER (CINEMA)

The State Theatre in Washington, Iowa, USA, opened in 1893 and began screening movies on 14 May 1897; tickets on the day were 15, 25 or 35 cents each. As of 27 Mar 2017, the venue had been in business for 119 years 317 days. It doubled as an opera house until 1931, after which it became a cinema exclusively. The picture below was taken in Nov 1894, around a year after the theatre opened.

Most visited art gallery

According to the annual report by the Themed Entertainment Association (TEA) and AECOM, the Louvre in Paris, France, attracted 8,700,000 visitors in 2015, the latest year for which figures are available.

Most expensive painting sold privately

In Feb 2015, *Nafea Faa Ipoipo* ("When Will You Marry?", 1892) by Paul Gauguin (FRA) reportedly sold privately for around $300 m (£197 m). In doing so, it out-sold *The Card Players* (1890s) by Paul Cézanne (FRA), which had sold in 2011 to Qatar's royal family for $250 m (£158.3 m). In Sep 2015, US business tycoon Ken Griffin reportedly paid $300 m (£197.8 m) for a painting: *Interchange* (1955) by Willem de Kooning (NLD/USA).

The **most expensive painting sold at auction** is *Les femmes d'Alger (Version O)* by Pablo Picasso (ESP), dated 14 Feb 1955. It sold for $179.3 m (£116 m), including a commission of just over 12%, at an auction held by Christie's in New York City, USA, on 11 May 2015. The buyer bid by telephone and chose to remain anonymous.

At the same venue on the same day, Swiss sculptor Alberto Giacometti's 1947 bronze work *L'homme au doigt* ("Pointing Man") sold for $141,285,000 (£91.4 m) – the **most expensive sculpture sold at auction**. The 180-cm (70.8-in) statue shows a man – tall and spindly (Giacometti's trademark style) – with one arm outstretched.

Highest-grossing music festival

During the weekends of 7–9 Oct and 14–16 Oct 2016, the inaugural Desert Trip festival, staged at the Empire Polo Club Grounds in Indio, California, USA, grossed $160,112,532 (£131.3 m) from 150,000 ticket sales, according to Pollstar's annual report. Headline acts at the star-studded festival included veteran rockers Neil Young, Paul McCartney, Bob Dylan, The Who and The Rolling Stones.

▲ MUSICIANS ON SNAPCHAT

Pictured above, pop/rock quartet 5 Seconds of Summer (AUS; @wearefivesos) were the **most popular group on Snapchat** as of 10 Mar 2017. Meanwhile, UK pop quartet Little Mix (@littlemix_offic) – seen below – were the **most popular female group on Snapchat** as of the same date.

The DJ/producer/radio personality/record label executive DJ Khaled (USA; @djkhaled305) was the **most popular musician on Snapchat**, as of 10 Mar 2017. As of the same date, Taylor Swift (USA; @taylorswift) was the **most popular female musician on Snapchat**.

Largest audience for a live videogame music concert

On 13 Aug 2015, at the Beijing Exhibition Theatre in China, Video Games Live (VGL) performed to 752,109 people, 750,023 of whom were watching a live stream via Youku. There were 2,086 people at the concert itself. This beat VGL's own record of 320,000, who had watched their Amazon/Twitch-sponsored event at the San Diego Comic-Con in 2013.

Oldest videogame music composer

Koichi Sugiyama (JPN, b. 11 Apr 1931) was aged 85 years 46 days as of 27 May 2016, when *Dragon Quest Heroes II* was released.

First movie based on an app

As of 21 Feb 2017, *The Angry Birds Movie* (USA/FIN, 2016) had earned a worldwide box-office take of $349,334,510 (£280.7 m) according to The Numbers.

▲ FASTEST THEATRICAL PRODUCTION

Sharpe Academy of Theatre Arts (UK) staged a production of the musical *Annie* in just 15 hr at the Watersmeet theatre in Rickmansworth, Hertfordshire, UK, on 29 Aug 2016. The company only learned what they would be performing at 6 a.m., when a sealed box was opened on stage to reveal the script. The house lights went down at 9 p.m., with the paying audience counting down in time to a digital clock on stage. The show received a standing ovation.

▼ HIGHEST SINGLE-WEEK BOX-OFFICE GROSS ON BROADWAY

Eight performances of *Hamilton* (USA, 2015) grossed $3,335,430 (£2,701,610) for the week ending 1 Jan 2017, at the Richard Rodgers Theatre in New York City, USA. On 3 May 2016, the show secured the **most Tony Award nominations for a musical** (16). It wound up with 11, one less than the record for **most Tony Awards won by a musical**, by *The Producers* in 2001. *Hamilton*'s Lin-Manuel Miranda (inset) won for Best Score and Best Book.

Hamilton is based on the life of Alexander Hamilton, one of the USA's Founding Fathers.

Oldest...

From long-lived pets to the oldest fragments of our planet, we explore Earth's 4.55-billion-year history to celebrate record-breaking longevity in its many forms.

0-100 years

Dog
29 years 5 months

The greatest reliable age recorded for a dog is 29 years for an Australian cattle dog named Bluey, owned by Les Hall of Rochester, Victoria, Australia. Bluey was obtained as a puppy in 1910 and worked among cattle and sheep for nearly 20 years before being put to sleep on 14 Nov 1939.

Cat
38 years 3 days

Creme Puff was born on 3 Aug 1967 and lived until 6 Aug 2005 – an amazing 38 years! Creme Puff lived with her owner, Jake Perry, in Austin, Texas, USA.

Goldfish
43 years

A goldfish named Tish, owned by Hilda and Gordon Hand of Carlton Miniott, North Yorkshire, UK, lived for 43 years. Hilda's son Peter won Tish at a fairground stall in 1956.

Olympic medallist
72 years 280 days

On 26 Jul 1920, at the Antwerp Olympics, Oscar Swahn (SWE, b. 20 Oct 1847) became the **oldest Olympic medallist**, aged 72 years 280 days. On 4 Jul 1912, Swahn had been in the victorious men's 100 m running deer (double shots) shooting team at the Olympic Games in Stockholm, Sweden, aged 64 years 258 days. That win made him the **oldest Olympic gold medallist**. The 100 m running deer was a target shooting competition at the Olympics from 1908 to 1948.

Reigning monarch
91 years 11 days

Her Majesty Queen Elizabeth II (UK) was born on 21 Apr 1926 and became the world's oldest monarch on 23 Jan 2015, aged 88 years 277 days. As of 2 May 2017, she was 91 years 11 days old.

Message in a bottle
108 years 138 days

The oldest bottled message spent 108 years 138 days at sea after being released by the Marine Biological Association (UK) in the North Sea (52°4.8'N; 003°37'E) on 30 Nov 1906. The message was found at Germany's Amrum island on 17 Apr 2015.

Person
122 years 164 days

Jeanne Louise Calment (FRA) was born on 21 Feb 1875 to Nicolas (1837–1931) and Marguerite (née Gilles, 1838–1924). She died 122 years later at a nursing home in Arles, southern France, on 4 Aug 1997.

Zoo
265 years

The oldest continuously operating zoo is the Tiergarten Schönbrunn in Vienna, Austria. It was first opened to the public in 1779, although initially it had been created in 1752 as a crown menagerie.

Amusement park
434 years

Bakken, located in Klampenborg, north of Copenhagen in Denmark, opened in 1583 and is the world's oldest operating amusement park. It claims to have more than 150 attractions, including a wooden roller-coaster built in 1932.

Topiary garden
c. 327 years

Levens Hall in Cumbria, UK, has topiary designs that were initially planted and trained in the 1690s. The shapes include "Chess Pieces", the "Judge's Wig" and the "Great Umbrellas".

500–8,000 years

Wrestling competition
557 years

The Kırkpınar wrestling festival has been held annually since 1460 near Edirne in Turkey. Participants coated in oil vie for the Golden Belt.

Existing parliament
1,087 years

The Icelandic Althing was founded in 930 CE. This body, which originally comprised 39 local chieftains at Thingvellir, was abolished in 1800 but restored by Denmark to a consultative status in 1843 and a legislative status in 1874.

Hotel
1,312 years

The Nishiyama Onsen Keiunkan in Yamanashi, Japan, is a hot-spring hotel that has been operating since 705 CE.

Tree
c. 5,200 years

A Great Basin bristlecone pine (*Pinus longaeva*) known as Prometheus was cut down from Wheeler Peak in Nevada, USA, in 1963. Although 4,867 rings were counted in it, the tree was in a harsh environment that had slowed its growth. Its true age has been estimated at c. 5,200 years old.

Egyptian hieroglyphs
c. 5,300 years

The oldest known examples of Egyptian hieroglyphs were unearthed in 1999 in Abydos, 300 mi (483 km) south of Cairo. Imprinted on clay seal impressions and ivory tags, they have been dated to between 3400 BCE and 3200 BCE.

Plant cultivated for drink
8,000 years

Grapes (*Vitis vinifera*) are among the oldest cultivated plants that are used primarily for drink. The earliest documented evidence proving that grapes were cultivated to make wine dates to 6000 BCE in Mesopotamia (modern-day Iraq).

Plants cultivated for food
11,500 years

The first domesticated plants are the eight species of Neolithic founder crop. Domesticated by early Holocene farming communities in south-west Asia's Fertile Crescent region, they date back to 9500 BCE and consist of the flax plant, four species of pulse and three species of cereal.

Cave art
40,800 years

In 1903, prehistoric rock art was discovered in the El Castillo cave in Puente Viesgo in Cantabria, Spain. Alongside paintings of animals and handprints is one red disc that is at least 40,800 years old. Nearby is a hand stencil that dates back at least 37,300 years.

Ice core
740,000 years

The oldest continuous ice core covers 740,000 years of climate history. It is 3,139 m (10,298 ft) long, with a 10-cm (4-in) diameter. The core was drilled at Dome C in Antarctica by the 10-nation EPICA (European Project for Ice Coring in Antarctica) and announced on 9 Jun 2004.

Stone tools
3.3 million years

Published in the journal *Nature* in 2015, compelling evidence has been presented of stone tools that date back as far as 3.3 million years. The stone flakes, cores and anvils were unearthed in 2011, near Lake Turkana in Kenya, by Sonia Harmand of Stony Brook University (USA) and her team.

Vomit
160 million years

On 12 Feb 2002, a team of palaeontologists led by Prof Peter Doyle (UK) announced their discovery of the fossilized vomit of an ichthyosaur, a large, fish-like marine reptile.

Dated dinosaur
240 million years

The existence of *Nyasasaurus parringtoni* was established from a partial skeleton in a deposit of fossils present within the Manda Beds near Tanzania's Lake Nyasa. The skeleton is some 240 million years old and was around the size of a Labrador dog. *N. parringtoni* was formally described in Dec 2012.

Vertebrate
530 million years

The oldest documented vertebrate is *Haikouichthys*. Regarded as an early fish, it had a distinct head and tail, as well as gills and a dorsal fin.

Mountain range
3.6 billion years

The Barberton Greenstone Belt, or Makhonjwa Mountains, in South Africa is formed from rocks up to 3.6 billion years old. The mountains have a maximum altitude of around 1,800 m (5,905 ft) above sea level.

Fragment of Earth
4.374 billion years

Tiny, diamond-like crystals of zircon ($ZrSiO_4$) from the Jack Hills in Western Australia are the oldest minerals so far dated on Earth. A 2014 study estimated their age to be 4.374 billion years (±6 million years). This means that these zircons were created "only" around 160 million years after Earth itself was formed.

Sci-Tech & Engineering

By 1900, human knowledge was doubling every century, according to US polymath Richard Buckminster Fuller. Today, on average, it doubles every 13 months.

▲ LARGEST DISH RADIO TELESCOPE

The Five-hundred-metre Aperture Spherical radio Telescope (FAST) in Pingtang County, Guizhou Province, China, became operational on 25 Sep 2016. Boasting a diameter of 500 m (1,640 ft), it dwarfs the previous record holder, the Arecibo Observatory in Puerto Rico, which has a diameter of 305 m (1,000 ft). The dish incorporates 4,450 triangular panels, each with a side length of 11 m (36 ft). It took five years to complete FAST, at a cost of 1.2 bn yuan ($180 m; £138 m). Astronomers will use the highly sensitive dish to search for signals from stars and galaxies and what China's official press agency Xinhua News refers to as "interstellar communication signals" – in other words, signs of intelligent life.

Contents

In 2016, a scientist who worked on FAST noted that if the dish were filled with wine, it would hold enough to give each person on Earth four bottles.

Edge of Space

According to NASA, the average mass of Earth's atmosphere is around 5.1 quadrillion (5.1×10^{15}) tonnes — some 1 million times lighter than our planet's own mass.

First image of a sprite

Sprites are atmospheric electrical phenomena associated with lightning. These unusual flashes shoot upwards from the tops of thunderstorms to altitudes of 100 km (62 mi) above the surface of Earth. Historical reports of these atmospheric features were not regarded as genuine until the first image was taken, accidentally, on 6 Jul 1989, when Professor John R Winckler of the University of Minnesota was testing a low-level-light TV camera for an upcoming rocket launch and recorded bright columns of light towering above distant thunderheads.

Largest meteor-burst communications network

Meteor-burst communications exploit the effects of meteors (aka "shooting stars") upon the Earth's upper atmosphere, at 76–100 km (47.2–62 mi) in altitude. When a meteor burns up as it enters the atmosphere, it leaves a trail of ionized particles in its wake. These brief trails can reflect radio waves and so can be used to create temporary long-range communications links between radio stations up to around 2,250 km (1,400 mi) apart. SNOTEL (SNOwpack and TELemetry) is a series of sensors designed to monitor snowpack and other climate data in the western USA, and began operation in the 1970s. It consists of more than 730 stations, which use meteor-burst communications to send their data for analysis.

▲ HIGHEST ALTITUDE BY A COMMERCIAL ASTRONAUT

On 4 Oct 2004, Brian Binnie (USA) piloted *SpaceShipOne* to an altitude of 367,486 ft (112,010 m) above the Mojave Desert in California, USA. Binnie's flight also broke the record for the **highest altitude by a winged aircraft**, which had been held since 1963, when NASA research pilot Joe Walker achieved a height of 107.96 km (67.08 mi) in an X-15.

The Kármán Line divides aeronautics missions from space missions and is adhered to by both NASA and the Fédération Aéronautique Internationale (FAI).

◀ FIRST MAN-MADE OBJECT TO ENTER SPACE

The boundary of space is known as the Kármán Line, after Theodore von Kármán (USA, b. HUN). Kármán realized that the altitude of 100 km (62 mi) above sea level is the height at which a vehicle would need to travel at faster than orbital velocity in order to gain enough aerodynamic lift to sustain flight. On 20 Jun 1944, a test flight of a German V-2 missile, designed to strike London, UK, reached an altitude of 174.6 km (108.49 mi).

Q: How long does it take a Global Positioning System (GPS) satellite to orbit Earth?

A: About 12 hr

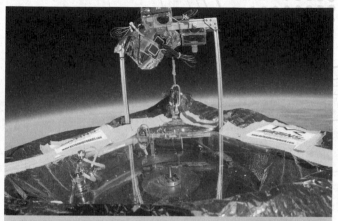

▲ FIRST VINYL RECORD PLAYED IN THE STRATOSPHERE

Third Man Records (USA) used the *Icarus Craft*, a turntable designed by Kevin Carrico, to play a vinyl copy of *A Glorious Dawn* at an altitude of 2,878 m (9,442 ft) on 2 Jul 2016. The record was the 3-millionth pressing by the label, which was co-founded by musician Jack White (USA). It features the voices of Carl Sagan and Stephen Hawking, arranged to music by John Boswell as part of the Symphony of Science project.

On 23 Apr 2015, Matt Kingsnorth and Phil St Pier (both UK) achieved the **highest model X-Wing launched by balloon**. It rose to a height of around 36,190 m (118,733 ft).

The **highest altitude for a Raspberry Pi-powered teddy bear** (on a Raspberry Pi-powered weather balloon) is just over 41 km (25.48 mi), by Babbage the Bear on 24 Aug 2013. The Raspberry Pi Foundation and Dave Akerman (both UK) organized the event.

HIGHEST ALTITUDE...

Survivable by a human in an unpressurized environment

The Armstrong limit was first conceived of by Harry Armstrong (USA), a pioneer in aviation medicine. It represents the altitude at which water boils at normal human body temperature (37°C; 98.6°F) and corresponds to an atmospheric pressure of just 0.0618 atm (atmosphere: 1 atm represents typical atmospheric pressure at sea level). It occurs at an altitude between 18,900 m and 19,350 m (62,000–63,480 ft), making this the absolute highest altitude at which a person could theoretically survive without a pressure suit or a pressurized capsule. At or above the Armstrong limit, your lung fluids, saliva and tears would boil away.

Exosphere	c. 700–190,000 km
Exobase	c. 700–1,000 km
Thermosphere	80–c. 700 km
Satellite	
Hubble Space Telescope	
International Space Station	
Aurora Borealis	
Kármán Line	100 km
Mesosphere	50–80 km
Meteors	
Stratosphere	12–50 km
High-altitude balloon	
Fighter jet	Alan Eustace
Ozone Layer	20–30 km
Troposphere	0–12 km
Passenger aeroplane	
Hot-air balloon	

(Not to scale)

▲ FIRST STRATOSPHERIC SKYDIVE

On 16 Nov 1959, as part of Project Excelsior, US pilot Joe Kittinger skydived from a purpose-built helium balloon that had risen to a height of 76,400 ft (23,287 m). This was the first of a series of three jumps performed by Kittinger from an open gondola attached to the balloon. The image above shows his third jump, on 16 Aug 1960, when he set the then record for the **highest freefall parachute jump**.

Paper plane launch

Students from Kesgrave High School, along with their science teacher David Green (all UK), let fly a paper plane at 35,043 m (114,970 ft) above Elsworth in Cambridgeshire, UK, on 24 Jun 2015. The plane rose attached to a helium balloon; an electrical current, triggered from the ground, then severed the string affixing the plane, thereby "launching" it.

▶ FASTEST METEOR SHOWER

The Leonids occur from 15 to 20 Nov each year. They enter Earth's atmosphere at around 71 km/sec (44 mi/sec) and begin to glow at an altitude of around 155 km (96 mi). Their high speed results from the fact that the motion of the parent meteoroid stream, from comet 55P/Tempel-Tuttle, is almost directly opposite to the orbital motion of Earth around the Sun. This results in an almost head-on impact between the tiny particles and Earth.

◀ FASTEST SPEED IN FREEFALL

Felix Baumgartner (AUT) fell to Earth at 1,357.6 km/h (843.6 mph) during the death-defying Red Bull Stratos mission above New Mexico, USA, on 14 Oct 2012.

The skydive, from a balloon floating at the edge of space, made Baumgartner the **first human to break the sound barrier in freefall**. His feat broke eight world records that had endured for 52 years, including Joe Kittinger's **highest freefall parachute jump**, set on 16 Aug 1960 (see opposite). That record, and the record for **highest manned balloon flight**, is now held by Alan Eustace (see p.416).

Baumgartner's leap from the stratosphere attracted more than 8 million concurrent views on YouTube.

To be exposed to (equivalent)

On 14 Dec 1966, Jim LeBlanc (USA) was a NASA volunteer test subject testing space suits inside a depressurization chamber in Houston, Texas, USA. When an equipment failure disconnected the hose that kept his space suit pressurized, LeBlanc was instantly exposed to a partial vacuum equivalent to an altitude of 120,000 ft (36,576 m), with a pressure of just 0.0068 atm. He blacked out. It took 87 sec for the chamber to be repressurized to 14,000 ft (4,267.2 m) equivalent altitude, at which point LeBlanc woke. Later, he recalled feeling his own saliva boiling off his tongue just before he passed out.

In sustained horizontal flight

USAF Captain Robert C Helt (pilot) and USAF Major Larry A Elliott (RSO) reached 85,068 ft (25,929 m) in sustained horizontal flight aboard a Lockheed SR-71A "Blackbird" at Beale Air Force Base, California, USA, on 28 Jul 1976. This is more than twice the average Boeing 747 cruising altitude of 35,000 ft (10,668 m).

Reached by a projectile fired from a gun

On 19 Nov 1966, an 84-kg (185-lb) projectile was fired to an altitude of 180 km (112 mi) from the HARP (High Altitude Research Project) gun at Yuma in Arizona, USA. The weapon consisted of two barrels with a calibre of 42 cm (16.5 in) fused into a single elongated barrel 36.4 m (119 ft 5 in) long and weighing 150 tonnes (165.3 tons).

◄ HIGHEST MANNED BALLOON FLIGHT

On 24 Oct 2014, Alan Eustace (USA) performed a stratospheric skydive from 41,419 m (135,889 ft) above New Mexico, USA. It took Eustace 2 hr to ascend, in a pressure suit that was tethered directly beneath a balloon – rather than inside a capsule (as employed in 2012 by Felix Baumgartner) or a gondola. By contrast, it took just 15 min for him to fall to Earth again. Eustace was a senior executive at Google at the time of his jump, which was carried out in secret without any publicity.

Untethered (in non-orbital flight)

Several astronauts have performed tasks in orbit while unconnected to a spacecraft. In terms of non-orbital activities, however, the record is held by Austria's Felix Baumgartner. After ascending to a height of 39,068.5 m (128,177 ft) above New Mexico, USA, in a helium-filled balloon on 14 Oct 2012, he perched on the ledge of a capsule in the final moments before making his death-defying leap to Earth (see p.415).

▲ HIGHEST ATMOSPHERIC PHENOMENA

Of all the phenomena visible in our skies, the very highest are the aurorae, also known as the Northern and Southern Lights (Aurora Borealis and Aurora Australis, respectively). Often visible at night from low and high latitudes, these beautiful coloured, shimmering lights are the result of charged particles from the Sun interacting with the upper atmosphere. The lowest aurorae occur at altitudes of around 100 km (62 mi), while the highest extend up to around 400 km (248 mi).

Comets

A comet consists primarily of ice, gas, dust and rock. This composition has earned it the nickname "dirty snowball".

Largest comet
Discovered in Nov 1977, the comet known as 95P/Chiron has a diameter of 182 km (113 mi).

Largest observed coma
The Great Comet of 1811 – discovered on 25 Mar that year by Honoré Flaugergues (FRA) – had a coma (see p.418) with an estimated diameter of around 2 million km (1.2 million mi).

Longest measured comet tail
The tail of Comet Hyakutake measured 570 million km (350 million mi) long – more than three times the distance from Earth to the Sun. A team lead by Geraint Jones of Imperial College London discovered the prodigiously long tail on 13 Sep 1999. To do so, the scientists used data gathered by the ESA/NASA spacecraft *Ulysses* after its chance encounter with the comet on 1 May 1996.

Closest approach to Earth by a comet
On 1 Jul 1770, Lexell's Comet, travelling at 138,600 km/h (86,100 mph) relative to the Sun, was within 2,200,000 km (1,360,000 mi) of Earth.

Largest recorded impact in the Solar System
From 16 to 22 Jul 1994, more than 20 fragments of Comet Shoemaker–Levy 9 struck the planet Jupiter. The "G" fragment exploded with the energy of around 600 times the world's nuclear arsenal, equivalent to six million megatons of TNT.

▼ LEAST DENSE SOLID
As reported in *Nature* on 27 Feb 2013, a team from Zhejiang University in China, led by Professor Gao Chao (CHN), has made a graphene aerogel with a density of just 0.16 mg/cm³ (0.04 grains/cu in). More than seven times lighter than air (which weighs 1.2 mg/cm³, or 0.3 grains/cu in), it can balance on a blade of grass (see above). Below is a block of aerogel without graphene. Among many applications, aerogel is used to gather dust from comets' tails.

As it nears the Sun, a comet's nucleus heats up and its ice begins to sublime, turning into a huge cloud of gas (or "coma") larger than many planets. The solar wind and radiation act on the coma, creating a tail that points away from the Sun and may be millions of kilometres long (see p.417).

The average comet is the size of a small town

When it passed through the Solar System in 1997, Hale-Bopp expelled 250 tons (226.7 tonnes) of gas and dust – almost one-and-a-half times the weight of a blue whale – every second

▲ MOST COMETS VISITED BY A SPACECRAFT

As of Oct 2016, three spacecraft have each visited two comets. The European Space Agency's (ESA) *Giotto* (**1**) encountered 1P/Halley in 1986 and then 26P/Grigg–Skjellerup in 1992. NASA's *Deep Impact* (**2**) visited 9P/Tempel in 2005 and then (under the name *EPOXI*) encountered 103P/Hartley in 2010. NASA's *Stardust* spacecraft (**3**) visited 81P/Wild in 2004 and 9P/Tempel in 2011.

Largest source of comets

Beyond the orbit of Neptune lie the Kuiper Belt, the Scattered Disc and the Oort Cloud, which are collectively known as Trans-Neptunian Objects. The Oort Cloud is a spherical cloud of thousands of billions of cometary nuclei. It surrounds the Sun at a distance of around 50,000 AU (Astronomical Units: 1 AU = the distance from Earth to the Sun), or around 1,000 times the distance from the Sun to Pluto. It is believed to be the source of most of the comets that visit the inner Solar System.

Most distant observations of a comet

On 3 Sep 2003, astronomers at the European Southern Observatory in Paranal, Chile, released an image of Halley's Comet at 4.2 billion km (2.6 billion mi) from the Sun. It shows Halley as a fuzzy dot with a brightness magnitude of 28.2, nearly a billion times fainter than the faintest objects visible with the naked eye.

Most comets discovered by a spacecraft

The ESA/NASA spacecraft *SOHO* (*Solar and Heliospheric Observatory*) was launched on 2 Dec 1995 to study the Sun from L1 – the place between the Sun and Earth where the gravities of the two bodies cancel each other out. Its detection of comets has been purely serendipitous but, as of 13 Sep 2015, *SOHO* had discovered 3,000 of them.

First comet observed being destroyed by the Sun

On 6 Jul 2011, NASA's Solar Dynamics Observatory took a series of images showing Comet C/2011 N3's last moments as it disintegrated in the atmosphere of the Sun. The comet, which had only been discovered two days earlier, had an estimated nucleus size of approximately 9–45 m (29–147 ft) across. In its final seconds, Comet C/2011 N3 was a mere 100,000 km (62,137 mi) from the Sun's surface and travelling at a velocity of around 2.1 million km/h (1.3 million mph) before it broke up and was vaporized.

Most spacecraft to visit a comet

In 1986, Comet 1P/Halley entered the inner Solar System as part of its 75–76-year elliptical orbit around the Sun. Five spacecraft (collectively nicknamed the "Halley Armada") were sent to encounter the comet as it approached perihelion – the point at which it was closest to the Sun. *Giotto* (see opposite and p.420) took the first close-up images of the comet's nucleus, sustaining major damage from dust particles in the coma during its flyby. The Soviet Union sent *Vega 1* and *Vega 2*, both of which had deployed a lander and a balloon on Venus before proceeding to Halley. Japan sent *Suisei* and *Sakigake*, which came within 151,000 km (93,827 mi) and 6,990,000 km (4,343,384 mi) of the nucleus, respectively.

◀ FIRST SAMPLE RETURNED FROM A COMET

The earliest sample returned from a comet came from Comet Wild 2. The *Stardust* spacecraft, which launched on 7 Feb 1999, encountered the comet on 2 Jan 2004. Flying through its coma (a cloud of dust and gas around the comet's centre), *Stardust* swept up precious tiny samples of cometary dust in an aerogel collector. The valuable material was returned to Earth on 15 Jan 2006. Its ongoing analysis is providing insights into the chemical make-up of this icy primordial body.

▲ SMALLEST COMET VISITED BY A SPACECRAFT

Launched on 12 Jan 2005, NASA's *Deep Impact* spacecraft was re-tasked as the EPOXI mission on 3 Jul 2007 with the goal of studying extrasolar planets and performing a flyby of comet 103P/Hartley. The flyby occurred on 4 Nov 2010. "Small" in cosmic terms, the comet is around 2.25 km (1.39 mi) long with a mass of some 300 million tonnes (330.6 million tons).

▲ FIRST COMET VISITED BY A SPACECRAFT

NASA's *International Cometary Explorer* passed through the plasma tail of comet Giacobini-Zinner, around 7,800 km (4,846 mi) from its nucleus on 11 Sep 1985. The first comet encountered at close range was 1P/Halley, which was visited by an armada of five probes in 1986. ESA's *Giotto* was the only craft to pass the comet at close range – 596 km (370 mi) from the nucleus, on 14 Mar 1986.

▲ DARKEST OBJECT IN THE SOLAR SYSTEM

The least reflective body discovered in the Solar System to date is Comet Borrelly. This 8-km-long (5-mi) comet nucleus was imaged by the *Deep Space 1* unmanned spacecraft on 22 Sep 2001. Dust coating the surface of Borrelly makes it so dark that it reflects less than 3% of the sunlight it receives. By way of comparison, Earth reflects around 30% of the sunlight it receives.

Longest orbital survey of a comet

On 6 Aug 2014, ESA's *Rosetta* spacecraft entered orbit around comet 67P/Churyumov–Gerasimenko. On 12 Nov 2014, it released the lander *Philae* (see **first image from the surface of a comet**, opposite). As the comet was heading away from the Sun, the power available to *Rosetta*'s solar panels decreased. It was theoretically possible to put *Rosetta* into hibernation and revive it once the comet approached the Sun again. However, it was not certain that the spacecraft would survive. Instead, ESA opted to end the mission by impacting on the comet's surface, taking images and data until the last possible moment. At 10:39 UTC (Coordinated Universal Time) on 30 Sep 2016, *Rosetta* landed in the Ma'at region of the surface, ending the mission after 2 years 55 days of operations at 67P/Churyumov–Gerasimenko.

▼ FIRST IMAGE FROM THE SURFACE OF A COMET

ESA's *Philae* lander touched down on the comet 67P/Churyumov–Gerasimenko on 12 Nov 2014. Among its instruments was a set of cameras known as the Comet Nucleus Infrared and Visible Analyser (CIVA), designed to capture 360° panoramas of the landing site. Shown below is the first image released, on 13 Nov 2014: a mosaic from two of the CIVA cameras, showing the cliff face *Philae* landed next to and part of the lander itself.

The last contact with the *Philae* lander was on 9 Jul 2015, a total of 239 days after its landing. That interval represents the **longest time survived on a comet by a spacecraft**.

Seen far left is an artist's impression of ESA's *Rosetta* spacecraft. It carried the *Philae* lander, also shown above, which separated off to visit the comet 67P/Churyumov–Gerasimenko (see opposite).

▲ FASTEST ATMOSPHERIC ENTRY INTO EARTH'S ATMOSPHERE

On 15 Jan 2006, NASA's *Stardust* sample return capsule returned to Earth after a seven-year mission to collect material from the comet Wild 2. It entered the atmosphere travelling at a velocity of 29,000 mph (46,660 km/h) and was visible in some parts of the USA as a streak of light (above) before touching down, by parachute, in Utah, USA.

3D Printing

In a 2016 survey of 102 aviation experts, 70% said they expected that aircraft spare parts would be printed directly at airports by 2030.

Set to launch in 2020, European Space Agency (ESA) rocket Ariane 6 will feature many 3D-printed pieces, according to Airbus. This process may reduce costs by as much as 50%.

First 3D printing patent

On 12 Jul 1967, Wyn Kelly Swainson (USA) filed a patent titled "Method of Producing a 3D Figure by Holography" in Denmark. It envisaged a system whereby a three-dimensional object could be scanned using a pair of laser interferometers and its dimensions transferred to a computer. The computer would then feed the data on the object's shape to a second pair of lasers, which would reproduce it by selectively hardening a 3D shape in a tank of light-sensitive plastic.

First dress made from 3D-printed fabric

In Jun 2000, designer Jiri Evenhuis (NLD) created a "Drape Dress" out of 3D-printed fabric made from nylon particles, in a process known as Selective Laser Sintering (SLS). The dress is in the Museum of Modern Art in New York City, USA.

▼ FIRST 3D-PRINTED AIRCRAFT

On 1 Jun 2016, at the Berlin Air Show in Berlin, Germany, Airbus unveiled *THOR*, which was completely 3D-printed save for its electrical systems. Weighing just 21 kg (46 lb), *THOR* (which stands for *Testing High-tech Objectives in Reality*) is an unmanned demonstrator that had its first flight in Nov 2015. The aircraft is powered by two 2-hp (1.5-kW) electric motors and is mostly printed from plastic polyamide. Chief engineer Gunnar Haase, who conducted *THOR*'s inaugural flight, said that it "flies beautifully [and] is very stable".

Heaviest object 3D-printed using simulated lunar soil

On 31 Jan 2013, the European Space Agency (ESA) revealed plans for a base on the Moon that will be mostly 3D-printed using lunar soil. To prove its viability, the ESA consortium 3D-printed a 1.5-tonne (1.65-ton) building block in a vacuum chamber. The block, which has a honeycomb structure, was created from simulated lunar soil mixed with magnesium oxide and binding salt.

First 3D-printed car

In Sep 2014, designer Michele Anoé (ITA) got to watch as the chassis and body of his "Strati" car were printed in five days at the International Manufacturing Technology Show (IMTS) in Chicago, Illinois, USA. Anoé had seen off more than 200 entrants to win the "3D Printed Car Design Challenge", the brainchild of crowdfunded Local Motors of Phoenix in Arizona, USA. Local Motors completed the car's design with help from Oak Ridge National Laboratory (USA) and Saudi manufacturing company SABIC.

▲ LARGEST 3D-PRINTED PROSTHETIC BEAK

Grecia the toucan was brought to the Zoo Ave animal sanctuary in Alajuela, Costa Rica, on 7 Jan 2015 with half of his beak missing. Thanks to fundraising efforts, Grecia was fitted with an 18-g (0.63-oz) full-length prosthetic beak around 19 cm (7.48 in) long. Since his operation in Jan 2016, Grecia can now feed himself and preen his feathers. He began singing again just days after receiving his beak.

▼ LARGEST SOLID 3D-PRINTED ITEM

A trim tool measuring 2.33 m³ (82.28 cu ft), designed for use during the manufacture of the Boeing 777 aeroplane wing, was printed by Oak Ridge National Laboratory and the Boeing Company (both USA) in Oak Ridge, Tennessee, USA, on 29 Aug 2016. It took 30 hr to print out the tool on the Big Area Additive Manufacturing (BAAM) machine.

3D printing has its roots in the 1980s, with the invention of stereolithography: the creation of objects from layers of photopolymers hardened by UV light

3D printers don't just print in plastic: metal, glass, ceramics, chocolate and even cheese, hummus and pizza dough can all be printed

The first pop-up restaurant to serve exclusively 3D-printed food (eaten with 3D-printed utensils) opened in Apr 2016 in the Netherlands

The Aston Martin DB5 in *Skyfall* (UK/USA, 2012) was made using a VX4000 3D printer

The first Global 3D Printing Day was celebrated in 2013; for the 2015 celebration, The Culinary Institute of America 3D-printed an edible Yoda

In 2014, Yoshitomo Imura (JPN) was jailed for 3D-printing a revolver

Smallest 3D-printed medical device

Researchers around the world are trying to find pain-free alternatives to needles to make injections easier for the recipient. One example is the 3D-printed micro-needle produced by teams at the University of Akron and University of Texas (both USA). Measuring 1 mm across, it is in fact an array of 25 needles made from propylene fumarate. Each tip is 20 μm wide – a fifth of the width of a human hair.

First 3D-printed motorcycle

At 2015's RAPID show, TE Connectivity (CHE/USA) unveiled an orange and blue replica Harley-Davidson motorcycle; 76 of its 100 components had been 3D-printed. The process used 4.32 mi (6.95 km) of ABS plastic filament. Multiple printers worked together for 1,700 hr to create the parts.

Longest object 3D-printed in metal

In Oct 2016, researchers at Cranfield University (UK) announced that they had created a double-sided aluminium spar measuring 6 m (20 ft) and weighing 300 kg (661 lb). It was printed on the team's 10-m-long (32-ft 9-in) Wire + Arc Additive Manufacturing (WAAM) 3D printer.

▲ LARGEST 3D-PRINTED BOAT

The annual Seafair Milk Carton Derby in Seattle, Washington, USA, challenges entrants to build the best boat out of recycled milk jugs. In Jun 2012, a team from the Washington Open Object Fabricators group (WOOF) entered the 42nd Derby with a 3D-printed creation made from melted milk jugs fashioned into a single piece of floating plastic. The boat, which measured 7 ft (2.13 m) long and weighed 40 lb (18.14 kg), came second in its category.

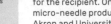

▲ FIRST 3D-PRINTED BRIDGE

On 14 Dec 2016, a 3D-printed bridge was inaugurated in Castilla-La-Mancha park in Madrid, Spain. Spanning 12 m (39 ft 4 in) long by 1.75 m (5 ft 8 in) wide, it was built by a team from the Institute for Advanced Architecture of Catalonia (ESP). The pedestrian bridge is constructed from eight segments consisting of layers of fused concrete powder micro-reinforced with thermoplastic polypropylene.

▲ FIRST 3D-PRINTED CORAL REEF

In 2012, experts from international consortium Reef Arabia sank two 3D-printed coral reefs off the coast of Bahrain. Weighing some 1,100 lb (500 kg) each, the artificial reefs are made from a non-toxic patented sandstone-like material designed to be more attractive to coral larvae and other marine creatures. And, unlike traditional concrete artificial reefs, their 3D counterparts are pH neutral.

▲ EARLIEST MONARCH RECONSTRUCTED USING 3D PRINTING

In 2010, *National Geographic* commissioned model-maker Gary Staab (USA) to create an accurate 3D-printed replica of the Egyptian pharaoh Tutankhamun (c. 1341–23 BCE). He used CT scans of Tutankhamun's mummy, which were converted into a 3D computer model and printed using a stereolithography machine. The printed model was then shipped to Staab's studio in Missouri, USA, where he applied colour and texture details.

Fastest 3D-printed robot

In May 2015, engineers at the University of California, Berkeley, USA, used specially 3D-printed components to build the X2-VelociRoACH – a robotic cockroach. Thanks to its flexible parts, the artificial insect can scuttle around at 11 mph (17.7 km/h). This is faster than an average human jogging.

Most 3D-printed 3D printer

With 3D printers now printing everything from car parts to food, it will come as no surprise to hear that you can actually 3D-print your own 3D printer. The open-source RepRap Snappy 1.1c printer, designed by Garth Minette (USA), was made using 2.4 kg (5 lb 4 oz) of plastic filament to print 86 of its 110 pieces.

First 3D-printed pills

Produced by Aprecia (USA), Spritam is a pharmaceutical drug designed to relieve symptoms associated with seizures. In Jul 2015, it was 3D-printed for the first time. The pills' porous 3D structure allows them to dissolve in just 4 sec, much faster than standard over-the-counter medicines.

On 15 Jan 2016, the American Museum of Natural History in New York City, USA, unveiled its latest exhibition: a 3D-printed full skeleton of a titanosaur dinosaur. The creature was discovered in the Patagonian Desert in Argentina and is believed to have lived during the Late Cretaceous period. At 122 ft (37 m) long, the replica skeleton is slightly too large for its exhibition room. Its neck and head extend out towards the lift, where it can surprise visitors.

The titanosaur was 3D-printed from a lightweight fibreglass material. Mounting the original fossils would have been impossible owing to their sheer weight.

▼ MOST POPULAR 3D PRINTER

According to 3D Hubs, a Dutch company that facilitates transactions between 3D-printer owners and potential users, the Prusa i3 was the most used globally in Jul, Aug and Sep 2016. A total of 2,795 Prusa i3s were used, accounting for 8.3% of all 3D-printing jobs. The Prusa i3 is open source and part of the RepRap project. The first model was designed in 2012 by Josef Průša (CZE).

Photography & Imaging

On average, more photographs are taken every two minutes today than were taken in the whole of the 19th century.

FIRST...

Hoax photograph

In *Self-Portrait as a Drowned Man* (1840), Hippolyte Bayard (FRA) shows himself slumped to one side, as if he had committed suicide. He created the image as a protest for never receiving what he believed was his rightful credit for inventing photography. Instead, the process was attributed to Louis-Jacques-Mandé Daguerre (FRA) and William Henry Fox Talbot (UK).

Durable colour photograph

James Clerk Maxwell (UK) first suggested a three-colour method of producing a chromatic image in 1855. On 5 May 1861, an image of three colour separations of a tartan ribbon was created from a photograph taken by Thomas Sutton (UK).

Underwater colour photograph

In 1926, *National Geographic* photographer Charles Martin and Dr William Longley took a colour shot of a hogfish (*Lachnolaimus maximus*) in the Florida Keys, USA. Martin used a specially designed waterproof camera housing, and the scene was lit with magnesium flash powder ignited on a raft on the water's surface.

▼ LARGEST PANORAMIC IMAGE

As measured on 6 Aug 2015, the panoramic image with the highest resolution comprises 846.07 gigapixels and shows the Malaysian city of Kuala Lumpur in all its glory. It was created by Tan Sri Dato' Sri Paduka Dr Lim Kok Wing and Limkokwing University of Creative Technology (both MYS) in Kuala Lumpur. The image was taken from the Kuala Lumpur Tower. A gigapixel is 1 billion pixels – more than 80 times greater than the resolution of an iPhone 7 camera (see p.430).

It is a measure of the exceptionally high resolution of the panorama below that the picture (left) of a building remains so sharp, despite being magnified to such a great degree.

▲ FIRST SELFIE
Robert Cornelius (USA) took this self-portrait in Oct 1839. It is a daguerreotype – an early photographic process employing an iodine-sensitized silvered plate and mercury vapour. He would have had to sit for up to 15 min to allow the necessary exposure time as he posed in the back yard of his family's lamp and chandelier store in Philadelphia, USA. On the back, Cornelius wrote: "The first light Picture ever taken. 1839."

Orbital images of Earth
On 14 Aug 1959, orbiting at 17,000 mi (27,358.8 km), NASA's *Explorer 6* satellite took the first image of Earth. Its "camera" was a scanning device with a small analogue electronic processor called "Telebit". It took 40 min to transmit back to Earth the 7,000 pixels each frame of an image comprised. The first image was of the crescent Earth.

Image of bonds forming in a chemical reaction
In May 2013, researchers at the US Department of Energy's Lawrence Berkeley National Laboratory in California, USA, took the first high-resolution images of carbon atoms breaking and reforming bonds in a chemical reaction. The team were making graphene nanostructures, and used an Atomic Force Microscope (AFM) for close study.

LARGEST...

Digital image of the Moon
For four years, starting on 11 Dec 2011, NASA's Lunar Reconnaissance Orbiter (LRO) captured the north pole of the Moon in stunning detail, using two Narrow Angle Cameras (NACs) and a Wide Angle Camera (WAC). The LRO team created a 680-gigapixel composite picture of the Moon's north pole region from a total of 10,581 images.

▲ FIRST HOLOGRAM
Hungarian-British physicist Dennis Gabor developed the theory of holography in 1947. However, it was the invention in 1960 of the laser – whose coherent light could capture a holographic image – that enabled Emmett Leith (USA) and Juris Upatnieks (USA, b. LVA) of the University of Michigan to produce the first hologram. Created in 1962, its main subject was a toy train.

▲ OLDEST SURVIVING AERIAL PHOTOGRAPH

On 13 Oct 1860, James Wallace Black (USA) took this shot of Boston in Massachusetts, USA, from the tethered *Queen of the Air* hot-air balloon at an altitude of c. 2,000 ft (609 m).

The **first-ever aerial photograph** was taken by Nadar, aka Gaspard-Félix Tournachon (FRA), in 1858. He photographed the French village of Petit-Bicêtre (now Petit-Clamart) from 80 m (262 ft) in a tethered air balloon. None of his aerial shots survive.

▲ FIRST JPEG

JPEG (Joint Photographic Experts Group) is one of the best-known digital-image formats. It was developed to standardize techniques for digital-image compression and is utilized in imagery on the internet and digital cameras. The earliest images that use the JPEG compression method are a set of four test images used by the JPEG Group called *Boats*, *Barbara*, *Toys* (above) and *Zelda*, created on 18 Jun 1987 in Copenhagen, Denmark.

◄ FIRST UNDERWATER PHOTOGRAPHIC PORTRAIT

French zoologist Louis Marie-Auguste Boutan first used his self-invented submarine camera in 1893. But it was not until 1899 that he created a special flash, enabling him to make an underwater image of a recognizable subject. Produced that year, his portrait of Romanian oceanographer and biologist Emil Racovitza was taken on a dive in Banyuls-sur-Mer in the south of France.

Print from a pre-digital film photograph

For the Diamond Jubilee of the UK's Queen Elizabeth II, a 100 x 70-m (330 x 230-ft) print of a photograph taken of the Royal Family during the Silver Jubilee was erected in front of Sea Containers House in London, UK. Eight specialists took more than 45 hr to position the separate sections, finishing on 25 May 2012.

Total number of photos taken each year

- 1930: **1 bn**
- 1960: **3 bn**
- 1970: **10 bn**
- 1980: **25 bn**
- 1990: **57 bn**
- 2000: **86 bn**
- 2012: **380 bn**
- 2015: **1 tr**
- 2017: **1.3 tr** (est.)

350 million
new photos are added to Facebook every day

60 million
new photos are added to Instagram every day

€2.16 m (£1.73 m; $2,8 m):
price paid for the most expensive camera, a prototype Leica 35-mm film camera, on 12 May 2012

12
iPhone 7 = 12 megapixels

168
Fuji Velvia 35-mm film pixel resolution equivalent = 168 megapixels

12
Number of Hasselblad cameras left on the Moon by Apollo astronauts

Les Horribles Cernettes

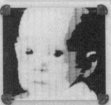

▲ FIRST IMAGE POSTED TO THE WORLD WIDE WEB

On 18 Jul 1992, computer scientist Silvano de Gennaro (ITA) photographed his girlfriend Michele Muller with her comedy doo-wop band Les Horribles Cernettes. A few weeks later, his colleague Tim Berners-Lee (UK) asked for an image to test some new features of his pet project, the World Wide Web, so Silvano sent over the picture as a 120 x 50-pixel GIF.

▲ FIRST DIGITAL IMAGE

Russell Kirsch (USA) created this image of his son, Walden, in 1957 at the National Bureau of Standards in Washington, DC, USA. At the time, Kirsch was working on the first internally programmable computer in the USA, the Standards Eastern Automatic Computer (SEAC). He developed equipment that translated his picture into binary code. The image measured 176 by 176 pixels.

▲ FIRST IMAGE ON INSTAGRAM

On 16 Jul 2010, Instagram's co-founder and CEO Kevin Systrom (USA) uploaded a picture of a golden retriever to the app, which was then known as "Codename". The names of the dog and its owner are not known, but the foot in the picture belongs to Systrom's girlfriend. The image was taken at a taco stand named Tacos Chilakos in Todos Santos, Mexico.

▲ OLDEST KNOWN SURVIVING PHOTOGRAPH

The earliest documented photograph still in existence was taken by Nicéphore (born Joseph) Niépce (FRA) in 1827, using a camera obscura. It shows the view from the window of his home, the estate Le Gras in France's Burgundy region. Rediscovered in 1952, the image is now in The Gernsheim Collection at the University of Texas in Austin, USA.

Photographic negative

A print called *The Great Picture* was created over the nine months leading up to 12 Jul 2006 by six photographic artists known as The Legacy Project. It shows the control tower, buildings and runways at the US Marine Corps Air Station El Toro in Southern California, USA. Aided by 400 volunteers, artists and experts, the team turned an old aircraft hangar into a giant pin-hole camera. They applied 80 litres (21.1 US gal) of gelatin-based silver halide emulsion to a seamless canvas 111 ft (34 m) wide and 32 ft (9.8 m) high. The image was developed using 2,300 litres (607 US gal) of developing fluid and 4,500 litres (1,188 US gal) of fixing solution.

Photograph

On 18 Dec 2000, Shinichi Yamamoto (JPN) printed an image 145 m (475 ft 8 in) long and 35.6 cm (14 in) wide. It was taken from a negative 30.5 m (100 ft) long and 7 cm (2.75 in) wide, created with a hand-made panoramic camera.

▼ FIRST PHOTOGRAPH TO FEATURE A HUMAN

This image was taken by Louis Daguerre (FRA), *c.* 1838. The long exposure necessary for early photographs meant that the Paris street scene on the Boulevard du Temple appears almost empty, apart from a man standing still because his boots are being cleaned. He and the shoe-shiner are the first humans to be captured for posterity.

Fireworks

Firework colours result from the burning of metal salts — e.g., copper chloride produces blue; calcium chloride creates orange.

First documented firecracker

The origin of gunpowder dates back some 2,000 years to China, where a cook reportedly mixed the required chemicals in a fire by chance. However, the first known firework, the Chinese firecracker, is credited to a monk named Li Tian. He lived in the 9th century during the Tang dynasty (618–907 CE), near the city of Liuyang in Hunan Province, China. Li Tian discovered that he could create a noisy explosion by packing gunpowder into a hollow bamboo stem. In the tradition of using loud noises at auspicious times to ward off evil spirits, he bound together several crackers to create the now-traditional New Year firecrackers. Chinese people celebrate this invention every 18 Apr with sacrifices to Li Tian.

First use of rockets

Propelled by gunpowder, "flying fireworks" (containing charcoal, saltpetre and sulphur) were described by Zeng Gongliang of China in 1042. The first use of true rockets reportedly dates from 1232, when the Chinese and Mongols were at war. In the battle of Kai-Keng, the Chinese repelled the Mongol invaders with a barrage of "arrows of flying fire".

Tallest building from which fireworks have been launched

On New Year's Eve, the **tallest building** – the 828-m-tall (2,716-ft 6-in) Burj Khalifa in Dubai, United Arab Emirates (see p.436) – hosts a display in which fireworks shoot from its sides and top. In less than 10 min, more than 1.6 tonnes (3,527 lb) of fireworks are released.

Shortest unintentional firework display

The fireworks display held on 21 Aug 2009 off the Dorset coast, UK, was set up as a world record attempt but ended quickly and unexpectedly. It was planned as a carefully choreographed bonanza, with 110,000 fireworks mounted on a barge between two piers in the English Channel. Unfortunately, the initial rocket launches set fire to the entire barge full of fireworks, which exploded and burned brightly for just 6 sec – although it *did* result in a world record...

▲ TALLEST PYROTECHNICS STRUCTURE

On 7 Dec 2014, the Municipality of Jilotepec in the Estado de México, Mexico, erected a 66.5-m-tall (218-ft 3-in) pyrotechnic frame. Dwarfing both Nelson's Column in London, UK, and the Arc de Triomphe in Paris, France, it featured rotating images, a flying coronet, fireworks set to music and images of key figures from Jilotepec's history.

▲ LARGEST INDOOR FIREWORKS DISPLAY

The Singapore National Day Parade is celebrated on 9 Aug. In 2016, both the preview and main celebration shows in the National Stadium employed 98 pyrotechnic boxes, each housing 14 fireworks on average. Each box was connected to ignition wires at 36 points by the stage and 26 along the sides of four ramps leading to the main stage. In all, 1,372 fireworks were mounted.

Most fireworks launched from a pyrotechnics suit

On 13 Jun 2014, a barrage of 642 fireworks was fired from a pyrotechnics suit worn by Laurent Nat (FRA) in Grenoble, France.

LARGEST...

Aerial firework shell

The "shell" of an airborne firework includes its container, stars (pellets containing metal salts that explode into colours on ignition), a bursting charge and a time-delay fuse. The Yonshakudama firework is fired during Japan's Katakai-Matsuri Festival, held every 9 and 10 Sep in Katakai, Niigata Prefecture, Honshu. First launched on 9 Sep 2014, its shell measures 120 cm (3 ft 11.2 in) in diameter and weighs 464.8 kg (1,024 lb 12 oz) – about as heavy as a grand piano. It was created by Masanori Honda's Katakai Fireworks Co. (JPN).

Chocolate firework

Nestlé (CHE) created a firework 3 m (9 ft 10 in) high and 1.5 m (4 ft 11 in) in diameter, housing 60 kg (132 lb) of Swiss Cailler chocolates. It was released in Zürich, Switzerland, on 31 Dec 2002.

Catherine wheel

Lily Fireworks Factory (MLT) created a Catherine wheel with a diameter of 32.044 m (105 ft 1.5 in) – some four times longer than a London double-decker bus. Its spread was verified in Mqabba, Malta, on 18 Jun 2011.

Brocade	Chrysanthemum	Bees	Peony
A star burst within which clusters of other stars weave	Stars with tails in a larger globe-shaped explosion	Many different points of light that spread to follow diverse paths	A spherical burst giving rise to an explosion of changing colours

▶ LARGEST SPARKLER CANDLE

On New Year's Eve 2015, Yuriy Yaniv from Kiev, Ukraine, set alight an unusual composite firework of his own creation. It comprised 10,000 sparklers (inset) bound tightly together in a ceramic pot with cardboard, dirt and kitchen tin foil. On ignition, the 50-kg (110-lb) candle created a gigantic tower of sparks some 2 m (6 ft 6 in) in diameter.

Pyrotechnic image

Fireworks by Grucci (USA) constructed a 65,526-m² (705,316-sq-ft) image from fireworks in honour of the 20th anniversary of the Dubai World Cup horse race at the Meydan Racecourse in Dubai, UAE, on 28 Mar 2015. The image depicted the country's national flag.

Firework map of the world

On 31 Dec 2013, a firework display was staged in Dubai, UAE, to celebrate the New Year. It incorporated the man-made "World Islands" archipelago, located offshore in the Persian Gulf. Comprising 300 islands, this artificial feature was designed in the shape of the seven continents of the world. During the display, air-burst shells outlined each continent in a pyrotechnic depiction of Earth's landmasses. The development covers an area of 6 x 9 km (3.7 x 5.6 mi) and is surrounded by an oval-shaped breakwater island. All the available shoreline (some 232 km; 144 mi) was used in the display.

◀ LARGEST FIREWORK DISPLAY

On 1 Jan 2016, Iglesia ni Cristo (PHL) staged a display of 810,904 fireworks at the "Countdown 2016" New Year celebrations. The event was held at the Philippine Arena in Ciudad de Victoria in Bocaue, Bulacan, Philippines. The display began at the stroke of midnight 2016 and lasted for 1 hr 1 min 32.35 sec in pouring rain.

Fish
A burst of stars that swiftly become independent lights

Stars
One glowing globe of light, possibly featuring different colours

Strobe
A sequence of rapid, bright flashes

Willow
An extended burst of stars that slowly descend

▲ LONGEST STRAIGHT-LINE FIREWORKS DISPLAY

Each year, near the end of August, the beautiful Cavallino-Treporti beach near Venice, Italy, is the venue for Beach on Fire, a fireworks display spanning a huge area. The event held on 27 Aug 2016 was produced for Parco Turistico – a local tourist consortium – by Parente Fireworks (both ITA) and stretched along 11.38 km (7.07 mi) of the 13-km (8-mi) beach, from Punta Sabbioni to the Cavallino Lighthouse.

▼ FIRST MULTI-SENSORY FIREWORK DISPLAY

The firework display for New Year's Eve 2013–14 in London, UK, incorporated a taste-and-smell experience. Around 50,000 people standing between Westminster Bridge and Hungerford Bridge enjoyed coloured fireworks paired with fruity flavours. Red pyrotechnics were paired with a strawberry-flavoured cloud. Other colours were complemented by clouds of coloured apple-, cherry- and strawberry-flavoured mist, with peach snow, "floating oranges" (thousands of bubbles filled with Seville-orange-flavoured smoke) and edible banana confetti. Food scientists Bompas & Parr (UK) were behind the creation.

▲ LARGEST FIREWORK ROCKET

On 27 Sep 2014, a 97.01-kg (213-lb 14-oz) firework rocket was launched at the Western Pyrotechnic Association convention in Hawthorne, Nevada, USA. It was built by Dave Ferguson and the BFR Boys (all USA). The diameter of the rocket's burst size was put at more than 360 m (1,181 ft).

The mass volley of fireworks (see below) was launched from 400 different sites along Dubai's shoreline and synchronized by 100 computers across the city. The event cost around $6 m (£3.6 m).

▶ MOST FIREWORK SHELLS LAUNCHED PER MINUTE

The New Year's Eve fireworks in Dubai, United Arab Emirates, on 31 Dec 2013 featured 479,651 shells fired in 6 min – a rate of 79,941 fireworks per min. The firework spectacular took 10 months to plan and involved the contributions of 200 technicians from US company Fireworks by Grucci.

Sci-Tech & Engineering Round-Up

According to NASA, the energy released by the Sun is equivalent to 100 billion tons (90.7 billion tonnes) of dynamite exploding every second.

Roundest natural object

On 16 Nov 2016, an international team of astronomers announced their discovery of the most spherical natural object yet measured in the universe. Kepler 11145123 is an A-type star around 5,000 light years away. Over a period of 51 months, the team observed the star's natural oscillations and used asteroseismology to measure its size. They discovered that the star, which has a mean radius of 1.5 million km (900,000 mi), has polar and equatorial radii that differ by only 3 km (1.8 mi).

◀ **MOST VERTICALLY AGILE ROBOT**

Salto ("saltatorial locomotion on terrain obstacles") has a vertical jumping agility – the height of one jump, multiplied by the frequency with which that jump can be made – of 1.75 m (5 ft 8 in) per sec. ("Saltatorial" refers to anatomy adapted for leaping.) Salto is 26 cm (10.23 in) tall when extended and can jump 1 m (3 ft 3 in) high. It was created by a team from the University of California in Berkeley, USA.

100%

▲ FIRST PERSON TO BE CRYONICALLY SUSPENDED

Following his death from kidney and lung cancer, psychology professor Dr James Hiram Bedford (USA, 1893–1967) was cryopreserved by the Cryonics Society of California, USA. He was placed in a dewar (a vacuum-insulated vessel) containing liquid nitrogen at -196°C (-320°F) and taken to the Cryo-Care Equipment Corporation in Phoenix, Arizona, USA. The picture above shows the capsule being prepared. On 25 May 1991, after several relocations, his body was moved from its original dewar to a higher-tech chamber (inset).

▲ SOFTEST ROBOT

"Octobot" was made by researchers from Harvard University in Cambridge, Massachusetts, and Weill Cornell Medicine in New York City (both USA) and unveiled in Aug 2016. It is the first robot made only with soft components – i.e., no hard parts such as batteries. Octobot does not need to connect to a power source as it runs on hydrogen peroxide, which breaks down in the presence of a platinum catalyst and generates the gas that powers it. The robot's parts were 3D-printed.

First use of facial-recognition glasses at a sports event

In 2011, police in Brazil began testing facial-recognition glasses as part of their preparations for the 2014 FIFA World Cup. Almost undetectable to the casual observer, the glasses were fitted with a small camera that captured 400 facial images per sec and compared them with a database of 13 million faces. In the event that the data matched up to a criminal, a red signal would appear on a small screen connected to the glasses, prompting the officer to take action.

Least dense 3D-printed structure

In Feb 2016, researchers from Kansas State University, State University of New York (both USA) and Harbin Institute of Technology (CHN) 3D-printed an aerogel made of graphene with a density of just 0.5 mg/cm³. Aerogels are light and porous structures in which solid materials are mixed with a liquid to form a gel. The liquid is then removed and replaced with a gas. The aerogel was 3D-printed at -25°C (-13°F), enabling the production of a more complex 3D structure.

First evidence of an antibiotic produced by a bacterium in the human body

Discovered by researchers from the University of Tübingen, Germany, in Jul 2016, lugdunin is an antibiotic that can be produced by *Staphylococcus lugdunensis* – a bacterium present in the human nose. Antibiotics are compounds that can inhibit the growth of bacteria or even kill them. They are now seen as essential for human well-being, since some infections caused by bacteria are lethal. Some bacteria (commonly referred to as "superbugs") are able to develop resistance to standard antibiotics. Because of this, scientists have been looking for new and alternative antibiotics. Lugdunin is active against several bacteria, including MRSA (Methicillin-Resistant *Staphylococcus aureus*) – one of the antibiotic-resistant superbugs.

◀ **LONGEST ELECTRICAL DISCHARGE TO STRIKE A SWALLOWED SWORD**
A 1.16-m (3-ft 9.6-in) discharge made contact with a sword swallowed by "The Space Cowboy", aka Chayne Hultgren (AUS), in Perth, Western Australia, on 20 Apr 2013. The electric generator that was used in this attempt was a large Tesla coil capable of producing 500,000 volts. Dr Peter Terren operated the apparatus during the attempt.

◀ **LONGEST ELECTRICAL DISCHARGE TO STRIKE A SWALLOWED SWORD**

A 1.16-m (3-ft 9.6-in) discharge made contact with a sword swallowed by "The Space Cowboy", aka Chayne Hultgren (AUS), in Perth, Western Australia, on 20 Apr 2013. The electric generator that was used in this attempt was a large Tesla coil capable of producing 500,000 volts. Dr Peter Terren operated the apparatus during the attempt.

In MIT's plasma experiment (right), the heat inside the reactor exceeded 35,000,000°C (63,000,032°F).

▲ **HIGHEST PLASMA PRESSURE IN A FUSION REACTOR**

Nuclear fusion reactions can produce very high quantities of energy. Inside a nuclear fusion reactor, scientists try to reproduce the reactions taking place within stars. To do so, gaseous molecules have to be in "plasma" state, i.e., superheated, stable under high pressure and confined in a fixed volume. In Sep 2016, scientists from the Massachusetts Institute of Technology (MIT) created a pressure of 2.05 atmospheres inside the Alcator C-Mod tokamak nuclear fusion reactor of the Plasma Science and Fusion Center at MIT in Cambridge, Massachusetts, USA.

Oldest feathers in amber

On 8 Dec 2016, an international team of scientists led by the China University of Geosciences published their analysis of a sample of amber containing preserved feathers. Some 99 million years old, it housed part of a tail covered in small brown feathers with a white-ish underside. It had probably belonged to a juvenile coelurosaur.

Largest stellarator

The Wendelstein 7-X is a type of experimental nuclear fusion reactor. Its purpose is to maintain a controlled nuclear-fusion reaction, although by means of a different technique to tokamak fusion reactors (see above). It measures 15 m (49 ft 2 in) across, weighs 725 tonnes (799 tons) and has an internal plasma volume of 30 m³ (1,059.4 cu ft). Known as a stellarator, it uses superconducting magnetic coils to contain plasma with temperatures of up to 130,000,000 K (129,999,727°C; 233,999,540°F). Its main construction was completed in Apr 2014, and the reactor produced its first plasma on 10 Dec 2015, when 1 mg of helium was heated to 1,000,000°C (1,800,032°F) for 0.1 sec. The Wendelstein 7-X is located at the Max Planck Institute of Plasma Physics in Greifswald, Germany.

▲ HIGHEST BRIDGE

The cable-stayed Beipanjiang Bridge Duge in Dugexiang, Guizhou, China, has a clearance at mean high water of 565 m (1,854 ft) above the Beipan River. That's taller than the CN Tower in Toronto, Canada. It opened to traffic on 29 Dec 2016, becoming not only the highest bridge but also the first bridge ever to surpass a height of 500 m (1,640 ft). It is also the first cable-stayed bridge to become the world's highest bridge.

The concrete, four-lane road bridge has an overall length of 1,341 m (4,400 ft) and a total height of 269 m (883 ft). Its longest span stretches for 720 m (2,362 ft).

◄ LONGEST SOLAR-POWERED ROAD

On 22 Dec 2016, French authorities opened 1 km (0.62 mi) of road in the village of Tourouvre-au-Perche, Normandy, that was paved with 2,880 photovoltaic panels. At a cost of about €5 m ($5.2 m; £4.2 m), it is expected to carry some 2,000 vehicles each day. Tests will be carried out over two years to see if the solar-powered road can generate enough electricity to power street lamps in the village.

Smallest extracellular needle-electrodes

On 25 Oct 2016, scientists at the Toyohashi University of Technology in Japan announced that they had created extracellular needle-electrodes measuring just 5 micrometres in diameter. A micrometre is one-millionth of a metre. Mounted on 1- x 1-mm (0.03- x 0.03-in) blocks, these silicon needles, which are small enough to be used in the narrow spaces between brain tissue, are expected to advance brain research and may help in the development of a fully working brain-machine interface.

Designed and built by Jeroen Domburg (NLD), this diminutive Game Boy is 54 mm (2.12 in) long, as confirmed in Shanghai, China, on 15 Dec 2016. It fits on a key chain, and boasts a selection of the original Game Boy games.

Jeroen's creation is nearly 19 times shorter than the **largest Game Boy**, which is 1.01 m (3 ft 3.7 in) tall, 0.62 m (2 ft 0.4 in) wide and 0.2 m (7.8 in) deep. Made by Ilhan Ünal (BEL), it was measured in Antwerp, Belgium, on 13 Nov 2016.

100%

▲ **LARGEST LED SCULPTURE**
Taking the form of a giant Christmas tree ball decoration consisting of 23,120 LED lights, the biggest LED sculpture was created by LLC ZodiacElectro (RUS) in Moscow, Russia, on 12 Dec 2015. It was created as part of the run-up to the Russian New Year celebrations.

Thinnest photodetector
A photodetector converts light into electrical energy. On 9 Nov 2016, scientists at the Center for Integrated Nanostructure Physics – part of the Institute for Basic Science in South Korea – announced that they had created a photodetector 1.3 nanometres (nm) thick. A nanometre is 0.000000001 m, or some 50,000 times smaller than the width of a hair. Featuring molybdenum sandwiched between graphene, it can be used in smart devices and wearable electronics.

▼ **LIGHTEST COMMERCIALLY AVAILABLE 14-INCH LAPTOP**
Made by LG Electronics (KOR), the LG Gram 14 weighed 826 g (1 lb 13 oz) when compared with competitors by SGS Testing Services on 14 Dec 2016.

LG Electronics also makes the **lightest commercially available 15-in laptop**. It weighs 980 g (2 lb 2.5 oz), according to research by Frost & Sullivan published on 29 Jun 2016.

Most Expensive...

Money may not be able to buy you love, but it can certainly buy a lot of other things. From polished diamonds to priceless works of art, towering feats of architecture to an extremely expensive cheese sandwich, here are some of the costliest objects on Earth... and beyond.

$0–$1,000

Cinema ticket
$17.91

In London, UK, the average price of cinema admission in 2016 was £12.19 ($17.91), according to Mercer's annual Cost of Living survey.

Taxi ride
$32.10

According to the 2015 UBS Prices & Earnings report, a 5-km (3-mi) taxi ride in the Norwegian capital of Oslo would cost passengers an average fare of $32.10 (£21.65). The same ride in New Delhi, India, would cost just $1.54 (£1.03).

Sandwich
$214

The "Quintessential Grilled Cheese" was selling for $214 (£132.64) at Serendipity 3 in New York City, USA, as of 29 Oct 2014. It is served on French Pullman champagne bread with white truffle butter and ultra-rare Caciocavallo Podolico cheese, and accompanied by a dipping sauce of lobster tomato bisque.

Chocolate bar (auction)
$687

A 100-year-old Cadbury's chocolate bar was bought for £470 ($687) at auction on 25 Sep 2001. It had been taken on Captain Robert Scott's first expedition to the Antarctic in 1901–04 and remained wrapped inside a cigarette tin.

Post-it note (auction)
$940

A Post-it note featuring the pastel-and-charcoal work *After Rembrandt* by R B Kitaj (USA) sold for £640 ($940) at auctions on 13–20 Dec 2000. It was one of a series made by artists to celebrate the Post-it note's 20th anniversary.

Hamburger
$5,000

A 777-lb (352.44-kg) hamburger available on the menu at Juicys Outlaw Grill in Corvallis, Oregon, USA, was selling for $5,000 (£3,115.87) as of 2 Jul 2011.

LEGO® brick
$12,500

On 3 Dec 2012, a 14-carat-gold LEGO brick was sold by collector website Brick Envy, Inc (USA) to an anonymous buyer for $12,500 (£7,752). The 25.6-g (0.9-oz) brick was a gift given to long-serving LEGO staff between 1979 and 1981.

Sheepdog (auction)
$21,392

Owned by Padraig Doherty (IRL), Cap the border collie was bought aged 16 months for £14,805 ($21,392) at auction in Skipton, North Yorkshire, UK, on 13 May 2016. Farm dogs that have been trained for herding usually sell for around $2,000 ($2,890).

Pop-star outfit (auction) –
$300,000

A white peacock jumpsuit commissioned for Elvis Presley (USA) in 1973 and designed by Bill Belew was bought for $300,000 (£153,560) by an American investor. The 2008 sale was held by online auctioneer gottahaveit.com.

Pigeon (auction)
$398,493

On 18 May 2013, pigeon breeder Leo Heremans (BEL) sold his racing pigeon Bolt for €310,000 ($398,493; £261,696) at auction. The bird, named after multiple record-breaking sprinter Usain Bolt, was thought to have been used for breeding.

Jewel (auction)
$71.2 m

The Pink Star, an oval-shaped 59.6-carat diamond, was sold for $71.2 m (£56.8 m) at a Sotheby's auction in Hong Kong on 4 Apr 2017. Found in an African mine in 1999, it is the largest polished diamond in its class to be auctioned.

Work by a living artist (auction)
$58.4 m

On 12 Nov 2013, *Balloon Dog (Orange)* by Jeff Koons (USA, b. 21 Jan 1955) was sold in New York City, USA, for $58.4 m (£36.4 m). The 12-ft-high (3.6-m) stainless-steel sculpture was bought anonymously.

Wedding
$55 m

In 2004, Vanisha Mittal and Amit Bhatia were married at a six-day event in Versailles, France, at a cost of $55 m (£28.5 m) – paid by Vanisha's billionaire father Lakshmi. Performers at the reception included Shah Rukh Khan and Kylie Minogue.

Car (auction)
$38.1 m

A 1962 Ferrari 250 GTO Berlinetta sold for $38,115,000 (£22.7 m), including buyer's premium, on 14 Aug 2014 at the Bonhams Quail Lodge Auction in Carmel, California, USA. Eight of the 10 most expensive auctioned cars are Ferraris.

Guitar (auction)
$2.7 m

A Fender Stratocaster signed by a host of music legends fetched $2.7 m (£1.6 m) at a charity auction on 17 Nov 2005. Stars who signed the guitar included Eric Clapton, Keith Richards and Brian May (all UK).

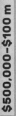

Soccer player
$116.4 m

On 9 Aug 2016, Manchester United (UK) signed French midfielder Paul Pogba from Juventus (ITA) for €105 m (£89.1 m; $116.4 m). Pogba had previously been a youth player at United, before leaving for the Turin giants in 2012.

Sculpture (auction)
$141.28 m

Sculpted by Alberto Giacometti (CHE), *L'homme au doigt* ("Pointing Man", 1947) was sold on 11 May 2015 for $141,285,000 (£91.4 m). The 1.8-m (5-ft 10-in) bronze statue is a tall and spindly figure – in trademark Giacometti style – with one arm extended.

Substance
$163 m

In Dec 2015, Designer Carbon Materials (UK) sold 200 micrograms of nitrogen-atom-based endohedral fullerenes for £22,000 ($32,611) in Oxford, UK. At this price, a gram would have cost £110 m ($163 m). The substance can be used in tiny atomic clocks.

Painting (private sale)
$300 m

In Feb 2015, *Nafea Faa Ipoipo* ("When Will You Marry?", 1892) by Paul Gauguin (FRA) reportedly fetched $300 m (£197 m) in a private sale.

Film
$425 m

Avatar (USA, 2009) had an estimated production budget of $425 m (£261.3 m), according to The Numbers. During the making of his sci-fi epic, director James Cameron (CAN) pioneered the groundbreaking "Reality Camera System". The money proved to be a sound investment – as of 5 Apr 2017, *Avatar* had earned the **highest box-office gross**, raking in a colossal $2.78 bn (£2.23 bn) worldwide.

> $500 m

Aircraft
$1.3 bn

The US-made B-2 Spirit cost in excess of $1.3 bn (£780 m) per unit. A long-range multi-role bomber, the B-2 has special coatings and a flying-wing design that make the craft almost invisible to radar.

House built
$2 bn

Completed in 2010 at an estimated cost of $2 bn (£1.29 bn), Antilia is a 27-storey personal skyscraper and the home of Indian businessman Mukesh Ambani in Mumbai, India. It has a total living floor area of 37,000 m² (400,000 sq ft) plus three helipads, a health spa and a theatre.

Warship
$13 bn

Scheduled for commission in 2017, the USS Gerald R Ford cost around $13 bn (£10.1 bn). The supercarrier can launch up to 220 airstrikes a day from its two runways. It will have 500 fewer crew than a Nimitz-class carrier, saving $4 bn (£3.12 bn) during its lifetime.

Man-made object on Earth
$27 bn

The Itaipu hydroelectric dam on the Paraná River between Brazil and Paraguay cost $27 bn (£20.2 bn) in 1984. Four dams joined together, its total length is 7,235 m (23,737 ft). In 2016, it generated 103.1 terrawatt-hours of energy.

Man-made object
$150 bn

Initial construction on the International Space Station ran from 1998 to 2011, with an estimated final cost of $150 bn (£93.8 bn; €104.7 bn).

Transport

By 1900, around a third of all vehicles on the
road were electric-powered. New York City
alone had a fleet of more than 60 electric taxis.

▲ LARGEST COZY COUPE

Brothers John and Geof Bitmead (both UK) have created a 2.7-m-long (8-ft 10.3-in)
Cozy Coupe, as verified at Attitude Autos in Ambrosden, Oxfordshire, UK, on 14 Aug
2016. The vehicle, a scaled-up version of the iconic children's toy car made by Little
Tikes, is based on a heavily modified Daewoo Matiz and includes an engine. Here, Geof
is seen behind the wheel of the record-breaking car, while his granddaughter, Lili,
looks on in a toy Cozy Coupe.

Contents

X496 H

Designed by Jim Mariol, a former engineer at Chrysler, the first Cozy Coupe appeared in 1979. In 1991, it was the USA's best-selling car, shifting 500,000 units and outselling "real" automobiles.

Trains & Railways

Stray dogs have learned to navigate Moscow's subway system and now use the trains to get around the Russian capital.

Highest sustained train speed (1,000 km)

On 26 May 2001, a French SNCF TGV train recorded an average speed of 306.37 km/h (190.37 mph) across a distance of 1,000 km (621 mi) between Calais and Marseille. The train covered the 1,067 km (663 mi) in 3 hr 29 min, with a top speed of 366 km/h (227 mph).

Highest railway line

Most of the 1,956-km-long (1,215-mi) Qinghai–Tibet railway in China lies 4,000 m (13,123 ft) above sea level. Its highest point, at 5,072 m (16,640 ft), is more than half the height of Mount Everest. Passenger carriages are pressurized and oxygen masks are available. It was completed in Oct 2005. The line also boasts the **highest-altitude railway tunnel**. Built in 2001–03, the Fenghuo Mount tunnel lies at an altitude of 4,905 m (16,092 ft), where the line passes over the Qinghai–Tibet Highland.

The **highest railway station** is Tibet's unstaffed Tanggula station on the Qingzang line, at 5,068 m (16,627 ft) above sea level. It has a 1.25-km-long (0.77-mi) platform.

▼ **LONGEST CHILDREN'S RAILWAY LINE**

The 11.7-km-long (7.27-mi) narrow-gauge Children's Railway runs through the woods on the Buda side of Budapest in Hungary, between Hűvösvölgy and Széchenyihegy stations. Operated by children aged 10–14 under adult supervision, it stops at the seven stations in between for a one-way trip of around 50 min. The railway has run continuously since the first 3.2 km (2 mi) of track was inaugurated on 31 Jul 1948.

Q: When did the production of steam locomotives end in China?

A: 1988

▲ STEEPEST RAILWAY GRADIENT

The Katoomba Scenic Railway in the Blue Mountains of New South Wales, Australia, has a 52° slope. The 310-m-long (1,017-ft) funicular was originally built for mining purposes in 1878 but was converted into a recreational ride for tourists in 1945. It runs at a speed of 4 m/sec (9 mph) and can carry 84 passengers.

Largest railway station (platforms)

Built between 1903 and 1913, Grand Central Terminal at Park Avenue and 42nd Street in New York City, USA, has 44 platforms. They are set on two underground levels, with 41 tracks on the upper level and 26 on the lower.

Highest railway bridge

The deck of the Najiehe bridge in Liuchangxiang, Guizhou, China, is some 310 m (1,017 ft) above the original level of the Wujiang River below. The truss arch has a main span of 352 m (1,154 ft).

Oldest model railway club

Based near King's Cross in London, UK, The Model Railway Club held its inaugural meeting on 3 Dec 1910. The members still meet weekly.

FIRST...

Underground railway system

The first section of the UK's London Underground opened on 9 Jan 1863. The initial stretch of the Metropolitan line ran 6 km (3.73 mi) between Paddington and Farringdon Street. To build the line, the "cut and cover" system was used, with streets along the route dug up, tracks laid in a trench, and then re-covered with a brick tunnel and new upper road surface.

◄ LONGEST DRIVERLESS METRO NETWORK

The Dubai Metro has two lines, with a total length of 74.694 km (46.41 mi). It was built by the Roads and Transport Authority in Dubai, UAE, and officially inaugurated on 9 Sep 2011.

The single **longest driverless metro line** is the Dubai Metro Red Line, which is 52.1 km (32.37 mi) long.

Steam locomotive
On 3 Jul 1938, the "Class A4" No.4468 *Mallard* reached 125 mph (201 km/h) at Stoke Bank, near Essendine in Rutland, UK. Indeed, it briefly achieved 126 mph (202.7 km/h), but did not maintain this speed for the required distance.

Propeller-driven train
The *Schienenzeppelin* ("Rail Zeppelin") reached 230 km/h (143 mph) during a test run between Hamburg and Berlin in Germany on 21 Jun 1931

Diesel train
A British Rail "Class 43" high-speed train (HST) hit 238 km/h (148 mph) on 1 Nov 1987, travelling between Darlington and York in the UK

▲ BUSIEST STATION

Shinjuku Station in Tokyo, Japan, is the world's busiest station. An average of 3.64 million passengers per day pass through the stop, which serves the city's western suburbs via a range of intercity, commuter rail and metro services. The station first opened in 1885 and underwent a major overhaul in 1933.

Internal combustion electric railcar

In 1903, the North Eastern Railway built an electric railcar powered by an internal combustion engine in York, UK. Numbered 3170, it was the first of two similar "Autocar" vehicles. The railcar was intended to use electric motors rather than less efficient steam engines. In order for the motor to run, the necessary electricity supply was generated on board the vehicle by a petrol-powered internal combustion engine. Both cars operated until 1931, when they were withdrawn from traffic – one was scrapped, and the coach body of 3170 was used as a holiday home. It was rescued in 2006 and has been the subject of a comprehensive restoration programme, including the construction of a new running underframe.

Steam locomotive to run on rails

The earliest steam locomotive to operate on rails was built by engineer Richard Trevithick (UK) at Penydarren Iron Works in Merthyr Tydfil, UK. It made its maiden trip on 21 Feb 1804.

▼ LARGEST HIGH-SPEED RAIL NETWORK

As of Jan 2017, China had more than 20,000 km (12,430 mi) of high-speed rail track – that's more than all the high-speed networks in the rest of the world combined. Plans are already underway to add another 15,000 km (9,320 mi) to the network by 2025. Trains on these routes run at an average speed of 200 km/h (124.27 mph).

"Indoor" speed by a train	Train on any national rail system	Speed by a maglev train	Railed vehicle
On 9 Feb 2009, a speed of 362 km/h (225 mph) was reached by an ETR 500 Y1 train in the Monte Bibele tunnel in Italy	The Société Nationale des Chemins de fer Français (SNCF) TGV POS Set No.4402 reached a speed of 574.8 km/h (357.2 mph) on 3 Apr 2007 (see p.450)	A Series L0 (A07) train owned by the Central Japan Railway Company reached 603 km/h (374.69 mph) on a test line in Yamanashi, Japan, on 21 Apr 2015	A four-stage rocket sled system accelerated an 87-kg (192-lb) payload to 10,385 km/h (6,453 mph) in 6.031 sec at Holloman High Speed Test Track in New Mexico, USA, on 30 Apr 2003

▼ MOST NORTHERLY RAILWAY STATION

Karskaya station is situated deep in the Arctic Circle on Russia's Yamal Peninsula, an area rich in natural gas and oil resources. It is the terminus of the 572-km-long (355.4-mi) Russian broad-gauge 1,520-mm (4-ft 11.8-in) line from the junction at Obskaya via Bovanenkovo. The line, which was privately built, is owned and operated by Gazprom and was opened to Karskaya in Feb 2011.

◄ FIRST PUBLIC ELECTRIC RAILWAY STILL IN OPERATION

The Volk's Electric Railway, which runs for around 1 mi (1.62 km) along the seafront at Brighton in the UK, first opened for business on 4 Aug 1883. It was designed by Magnus Volk (UK). The **first public electric railway** entered service on 16 May 1881 at Lichterfelde near Berlin in Germany. It was 2.5 km (1.5 mi) long, ran on 180-V current and carried 26 passengers at 48 km/h (30 mph).

All-female rush-hour carriages

Women-only train carriages have been a part of Japanese rail travel for a number of years, but in Jul 2002 the West Japan Railway Company (JR West), headquartered in Osaka, Japan, introduced the first such carriages for rush hour.

Underwater rail link joining two continents

On 29 Oct 2013, the Marmaray tunnel opened between Europe and Asia across the Bosphorus Strait in Turkey. The 8-mi-long (12.8-km) rail tunnel was designed to carry commuters between the Asian and European sides of Istanbul, as part of the "Marmaray" project to rebuild and improve transport connections in this major cultural city. The underwater section of the tunnel was built from 11 cast concrete sections, each around 135 m (443 ft) long. These were lowered some 58 m (190 ft) to the seabed, where they were joined, sealed, covered with earth and pumped dry – making a total undersea tunnel length of 0.86 mi (1.4 km).

◄ MOST SOUTHERLY OPERATING RAILWAY

The Southern Fuegian Railway or El Tren del Fin del Mundo ("The Train at the End of the World") in Tierra del Fuego, Argentina, was originally built c. 1902 to serve a prison. Today, tourist trains run 7 km (4.3 mi) along it, from Fin del Mundo station to El Parque Nacional station in the Tierra del Fuego National Park.

◄ FIRST MOUNTAIN RACK RAILWAY

The Mount Washington Cog Railway in Bretton Woods, Coös County, New Hampshire, USA, was built by Sylvester Marsh (USA) and opened on 3 Jul 1869. Known as the "Cog", the line still operates today, transporting passengers from Marshfield station a distance of 3 mi (4.8 km) up to the summit of Mount Washington.

▼ FASTEST TRAIN ON A NATIONAL RAIL SYSTEM

A French SNCF modified version of the TGV called V150 (with larger wheels than usual and two engines driving three double-decker cars) reached 574.8 km/h (357.2 mph) on 3 Apr 2007. The peak speed was achieved near the village of Le Chemin, between the Meuse and Champagne-Ardenne TGV stations. This is the highest speed recorded by a train on any national rail system (as opposed to a dedicated test track).

Urban Transport

More than half — approximately 55% — of the London Underground system is actually located overground.

▲ **FASTEST LIFT**
Designed by the Mitsubishi Electric Corporation (JPN), the high-speed lift NexWay travels at a speed of 73.8 km/h (45.85 mph). That makes it approximately as fast as a gazelle. NexWay was installed in unit OB-3 of the 632-m-tall (2,073-ft) Shanghai Tower in China on 7 Jul 2016.

First escalator

US inventor Jesse W Reno created an escalator as a temporary amusement ride for the Old Iron Pier on Coney Island in New York, USA, in Sep 1895. Reno's "inclined elevator" had a vertical rise of 6 ft 10 in (2.1 m) and an inclination of 25°, with riders sitting astride cast-iron slats atop a belt moving at 74 ft 9 in (22.8 m) per min. Approximately 75,000 visitors rode it during its fortnight-long installation.

The **first fully operational spiral escalator** was installed by the Mitsubishi Electric Corporation at a trade fair site in Osaka, Japan, in 1985. It was far more complex and expensive than a straight escalator, owing to multiple centre points and additional guide rollers.

Highest "modal split" for bicycles (by city)

The term "modal split" refers to the percentage of travellers using specific modes of transport, such as cars or bicycles. Some 50% of all trips in Groningen, Netherlands, are by bike, rising to 60% in the city centre. The town is known as the "World's Cycling City". In the 1970s, city planners encouraged non-automotive trips in the city centre by limiting vehicle movement there, leading residents to opt for cycling or walking instead.

In terms of promoting bike use via targetted development of infrastructure, however, the **most bicycle-friendly city** is Copenhagen in Denmark. The Danish capital has seen heavy investment in cycling facilities (such as new bicycle bridges and ramps), resulting in a 70% increase in cyclists since 1990, while car trips in the city centre have decreased by 25%. The Copenhagenize Index 2015 analysed cycling data from 122 cities to reach this conclusion.

Highest use of public transport in a city

Hong Kong is one of the world's most densely populated cities, with up to 57,120 persons per km² (more than twice as dense as Manhattan's 26,000 persons per km²). An efficient and advanced transit system keeps everyone moving. Some 80% of all transport trips are made by public transit in the city, where there are 11.3 million public transit passenger boardings daily.

According to the latest available figures published by *The Economist*, as of 2014 car-crazy Japan had 628.4 vehicles for every kilometre (0.62 mi) of road. The United Arab Emirates trailed in a distant second, with 479 vehicles per km. Asian and Middle Eastern countries dominated the upper reaches of the list, making up nine of the top 10 most crowded road networks.

Longest moving walkway (ever)

The **first moving walkway** was also the longest ever. It appeared at the 1893 World's Columbian Exposition in Chicago, Illinois, USA. Operated by the Columbian Movable Sidewalk Company, the walkway ferried visitors arriving by steamboats, and ran 1 km (0.6 mi) along a pier and onwards to the Exposition entrance. It transported up to 31,680 people per hr. Passengers could either stand while moving at 2 mph (3.2 km/h) or sit on benches and travel at 4 mph (6.4 km/h). It was destroyed by fire in 1894.

Between 2001 and 2010, the Metropolitan Transportation Authority of New York dropped 2,500 old subway trains into the Atlantic Ocean. These man-made reefs now teem with marine life.

The **longest moving walkway (current)** in a city is 207 m (679 ft) long, and is located below the parks and gardens of The Domain in Sydney, Australia. Officially opened on 9 Jun 1961, and constructed by the Sydney Botanic Gardens Trust as a futuristic novelty, it was rebuilt in 1994. The walkway is gently inclined and moves at 2.4 km/h (1.5 mph), taking slightly more than 5 min to complete one length.

TOP 10 LONGEST ROAD NETWORKS

	Absolute	Distance (km)	Per capita (1,000 people)	Distance (km)
1	USA	6,586,610	Pitcairn Islands	139.13
2	India	4,699,024	Western Sahara	22.71
3	China	4,106,387	Cyprus	17.8
4	Brazil	1,580,964	Saint Pierre and Miquelon	16.26
5	Russia	1,283,387	European Union	10.14
6	Japan	1,218,772	Wallis and Futuna	7.49
7	Canada	1,042,300	Liechtenstein	7.19
8	France	1,028,446	Saint Kitts and Nevis	6.67
9	Australia	823,217	Jersey	6.35
10	South Africa	747,014	American Samoa	6.0

Source: CIA World Factbook

Q: Seven of the world's 10 busiest railway stations are located in which city?

A: Tokyo, Japan

◄ LARGEST CONTINUOUS PEDESTRIAN SKYWAY NETWORK

Harsh winters combined with the need to improve access to downtown Minneapolis in Minnesota, USA, has led to the design of a series of elevated pedestrian walkways across the city. Officially known as the Minneapolis Skyway System, this 13-km-long (8-mi) climate-controlled network of aerial passages links 69 city blocks. An estimated 260,000 users walk through the Skyway each day.

Largest elevator in an office building (by capacity)

Each elevator car in the Umeda Hankyu Building in Osaka, Japan, can carry 80 passengers, or a total weight of 5.25 tonnes (11,574 lb). Built by Mitsubishi in 2009, each cabin is 3.4 m (11 ft 1 in) wide, 2.8 m (9 ft 2 in) long and 2.59 m (8 ft 6 in) tall.

Tallest elevator shaft in a building

At 578.5 m (1,898 ft) high, the high-speed elevator NexWay at the Shanghai Tower Unit FR/FLH 1 and 2 (see p.455) is even taller than the elevator at the Burj Khalifa skyscraper – the world's **tallest building**, in Dubai, UAE.

The elevator at AngloGold Ashanti's Mponeng Gold Mine in South Africa's Gauteng province drops 7,490 ft (2,283 m) in a single 3-min descent, making it the **tallest elevator shaft**. A second lift then takes miners even lower, to 11,800 ft (3,597 m). Each day, 4,000 workers are ferried down to the mine in three-level steel cages, at speeds of up to 40 mph (64.3 km/h).

Most escalators in a metro system

The metro subway system of Washington, DC, USA, has 618 escalators. They are maintained by the costliest in-house escalator service contract in North America, with 90 technicians.

▲ LONGEST COMMUTE FOR A CITY

After evaluating 50 million users and 167 metropolitan areas, a 2015 study by Google-owned traffic app Waze discovered that commuters in Manila, Philippines, faced average one-way journeys of 45.5 min. Even car-clogged urban sprawls such as Los Angeles and New York were less congested than the Filipino capital: average journey times in those two US cities came to only 35.9 min and 38.7 min respectively.

Rome's Colosseum had lifts to bring wild animals into the arena. They were raised and lowered manually by more than 200 slaves.

Elevator music was introduced in the 1920s to calm nervous passengers using lifts for the first time

Mirrors were added to lifts to distract riders from the slow speeds of early elevators, and also to make the space seem larger

Pressing the "close" button rarely makes the lift doors shut sooner – the button was added to give riders the feeling that they're in control

The Otis Elevator Company transports the equivalent of the world's population every five days

Statistically, elevators are one of the safest forms of transport; it's safer to take the lift than it is to use the stairs

Largest car-sharing market

Innovations in mobile technology have led to a huge growth in car-sharing networks around the world. As of Oct 2014, Europe was the world's largest car-sharing market, accounting for 46% of global membership (or 2,206,884 users) and 56% of the world's car fleet.

Most expensive taxi ride

According to the 2015 UBS Prices & Earnings report, the Norwegian capital of Oslo has the priciest cab journeys. A 5-km (3-mi) trip costs an average of $32.10 (£21.65). The same distance taxi ride in New Delhi, India, would cost just $1.54 (£1.03) – a 20th of the price.

▲ LARGEST PUBLIC TRANSIT CABLE-CAR NETWORK

The Mi Teleférico system in La Paz, Bolivia, features 10 km (6.2 mi) of aerial ropeways on three separate lines. Owing to the city's rugged and mountainous topography, traditional transit systems such as subways and light rail systems are not feasible here. The cable cars carry more than 60,000 riders daily, saving commuters 652 million min in 2015 alone and preventing the release of 8,000 tons (7,257 tonnes) of emissions annually.

◀ BUSIEST PEDESTRIAN CROSSING

With an estimated 1 million pedestrians each day, the Shibuya Crossing – located outside Shibuya subway station in Tokyo, Japan – is the world's busiest. Five streets converge at the intersection, and an estimated 100,000 people pass through here each hour at peak periods. In approximately 30 min, enough people would have walked across it to fill the Yankee Stadium in New York City, USA.

▲ LARGEST BICYCLE-SHARE PROGRAMME

The Hangzhou Public Bicycle programme in Hangzhou, China, is the world's largest bicycle-sharing system. Inaugurated in 2008 with just 2,800 bicycles and 60 stations, it has expanded prodigiously since then. In Sep 2016, it boasted a total of 84,100 bikes and 3,572 stations. China is home to nine of the world's 10 largest cycle-share networks.

▼ FIRST SELF-DRIVING TAXI SERVICE

On 25 Aug 2016, self-driving taxis began serving the public. Starting with a fleet of six vehicles, riders in Singapore are able to hire "robo-cars" and travel within a 6.5-km² (2.5-sq-mi) district called "one-north". The software firm behind this service, nuTonomy (SGP), believes that self-driving taxis could reduce the number of cars in Singapore from 900,000 to 300,000. The taxis are fitted with cameras (right) that read traffic lights.

Customized Cars

Invisible cars aren't just for Bond films. In 2009, British art student Sara Watson spray-painted an old Skoda so that it seemed to merge with the car park around it.

Lowest camper van

On 18–22 Aug 2008, at the Bug Jam 22 festival in Podington, Bedfordshire, UK, designer Andy Saunders and engineer Jim Chalmers (both UK) took a 1980 T25 Volkswagen (VW) Camper Van measuring 7 ft 8 in (2.34 m) high and converted it into a 3-ft 3-in (0.99-m) version. The finished vehicle, known as *Van Cake*, is fully roadworthy and capable of speeds up to 80 mph (128.75 km/h).

Hairiest car

Maria Lucia Mugno and Valentino Stassano (both ITA) have spent more than 150 hr sewing strands of human hair to the interior and exterior of Maria's Fiat 500. Weighed at a public weighbridge in Padula Scalo, Salerno, Italy, on 15 Mar 2014, the Fiat was covered with 120 kg (264 lb 8 oz) of human hair.

President Donald Trump's *Cadillac One* was due for delivery on 30 Mar 2017. Exact details of the car were classified, but the doors were reported to be so heavy they had to be opened from the outside.

▼ THICKEST DOORS ON A CUSTOM CAR

The United States presidential limousine *Cadillac One*, or "The Beast", boasts 8-in (20.32-cm) doors that weigh as much as the outer cabin door of a Boeing 757. First used on 20 Jan 2009, they have no key holes and are opened by a secret mechanism known only to the US Secret Service. Other customizations to the car include a set of rocket-propelled grenades, on-board oxygen tanks, night-vision optics, pump-action shotguns and bottles of the president's blood type. The interior is 100% sealed in order to protect its occupants from chemical attack.

Lowest roadworthy car

Mirai measures 45.2 cm (17.79 in) from the ground to the highest part of the car. It was unveiled on 15 Nov 2010 by students and teachers of the Automobile Engineering Course at Okayama Sanyo High School in Asakuchi, Japan. They beat the record of 48.26 cm (19 in) held by the appropriately named "Flatmobile", created by Perry Watkins (UK) in 2008.

Smallest roadworthy car

Created by Austin Coulson (USA) and measured in Carrollton, Texas, USA, on 7 Sep 2012, the smallest roadworthy car measures 2 ft 1 in (63.5 cm) high, 2 ft 1.75 in (65.4 cm) wide and 4 ft 1.75 in (126.3 cm) long. The vehicle is licensed for public roads with a speed limit of 40 km/h (25 mph), and is often driven during local veterans' military parades.

FASTEST...

Motorized log

On 20 Jan 2016, Bryan Reid Sr (CAN) steered *Cedar Rocket* to 47.64 mph (76.66 km/h) on the set of HGTV Canada's *Timber Kings*, at the Wild Horse Pass Motorsports Park in Chandler, Arizona, USA. Bryan mashed up a Mazda RX-8 with a single log of western red cedar from British Columbia, Canada.

Motorized shopping trolley

Matt McKeown (UK) achieved a speed of 70.4 mph (113.29 km/h) in a motorized shopping trolley on 18 Aug 2013 at Elvington airfield in North Yorkshire, UK. He souped up his shopping trolley with a modified Chinook helicopter starter engine and a 250-cc Honda engine.

▲ MOST EXPENSIVE SET OF CAR TYRES

On 10 May 2016, a set of four tyres were sold by the Dubai office of ZTyre.com to a private buyer for AED 2,202,000 ($599,350; £415,647). Designed by Zenises CEO Harjeev Kandhari, the Z1 high-performance tyres were fitted with sets of diamonds using 3D-printed white gold casing by jewellers Joaillier Privé. The tyres were then decorated with gold leaf.

◄ FASTEST BUMPER CAR

Colin Furze (UK) restored and modified a vintage bumper car – aka dodgem – that went on to clock a top speed of 161.476 km/h (100.336 mph). The 1960s-style bumper car was souped up with a 600-cc Honda motorbike engine and driven by BBC Top Gear's The Stig at Bentwaters airfield near Ipswich, Suffolk, UK, on 23 Mar 2017. The average speed of a bumper car is usually 8 km/h (5 mph).

MOST PEOPLE CRAMMED INTO A...

Fiat 500

14

††††††††††††††

Smart car

20

††††††††††††††††
†††††

Citroën 2CV

20

††††††††††††††††
†††††

VW Beetle – classic

20

††††††††††††††††
†††††

VW Beetle – new

25

††††††††††††††††
††††††††††

Mini – classic

27

††††††††††††††††
†††††††††††

Mini – new

29

††††††††††††††††
†††††††††††††

VW Camper Van

50

††††††††††††††††
††††††††††††††††
††††††††††††††††
†††††

▲ OLDEST SAUSAGE CUSTOM CAR

"Wienermobiles" are synonymous with the Oscar Mayer (USA) meat-production company. The first custom model was built in 1952 by the Gerstenslager Company (USA), who fixed a 22-ft-long (6.7-m) likeness of a hot dog on a bread bun to a Dodge truck chassis. An original 1952 Wienermobile can be found at the Henry Ford Motor Museum in Dearborn, Michigan, USA.

Bed

Created by Hotels.com and steered by professional racing driver Tom Onslow-Cole (UK), a Ford Mustang GT adapted into a motorized double bed reached a maximum speed of 83.8 mph (135 km/h) at Emirates Motor Sports Complex in Umm al-Quwain, UAE, on 13 Dec 2016. It smashed the previous record of 69 mph (111 km/h), achieved by serial customizer Edd China (UK, see p.464) on 7 Nov 2008.

Milk float

On 25 Jun 2014, a milk float created by Weetabix On the Go Breakfast Drinks and driven by Rob Gill (both UK) achieved 84.556 mph (136.081 km/h) at Bruntingthorpe in Leicestershire, UK.

◄ FASTEST BATH TUB

Between Sep 2014 and Apr 2015, Hannes Roth (CHE) devoted more than 300 hr to the creation of a mobile bath tub. He attached a tub to a go-kart chassis and fitted a 120-hp Yamaha R6 engine into the basin. At the Dynamic Test Center in Vauffelin, Switzerland, Roth achieved an average speed of 186.82 km/h (116.08 mph) over his two fastest runs, and a top speed of 189.9 km/h (117.99 mph).

Postman Pat van

Racing enthusiasts Tom Armitage and David Taylor (both UK) bought a coin-operated ride based on the popular children's TV series and added modifications including a racing wheelbase, slick tyres and a 500-cc four-stroke engine. On 30 Aug 2012, the converted van completed a quarter-mile drag racing run at York Raceway in East Yorkshire, UK, in 17.419 sec, with a terminal speed of 84.28 mph (135.6 km/h).

▲ MOST VALUABLE GOLD-PLATED CAR

The Sultan of Brunei's car collection includes more than 500 Rolls-Royces and Bentleys alone. For his wedding chariot, the Sultan had a Rolls-Royce Silver Spur limousine customized with a 24-carat gold-plate finish. It came with a rear coach seat cloth canopy, gold coats of arms and faux-oak bumper bars. It was valued at $14,000,000 (£9,746,110). The car is shown here at the wedding of one of his daughters.

▼ LONGEST STRETCHED SUPERCAR

Conceived and commissioned by Dan Cawley and designed and built by Chris Wright (both UK), this 7-m-long (23-ft) supercar was made by cutting a Ferrari 360 Modena in half and adding a 2.89-m (9-ft 6-in) midsection, raising the seating capacity to eight people. It had a reported top speed of 166 mph (267 km/h), achieving 0–60 mph in less than 6 sec. The inset shows the car's gull-wing doors.

The *Big Banana Car* was constructed by UK-born Steve Braithwaite in 2009–11. The "banana" measures 22 ft 10.5 in (6.97 m) in length and 10 ft 2 in (3.09 m) in height. It is built on to a truck chassis using rebar (reinforced steel bars), chicken wire and polyurethane foam, which was sculpted, covered in fibreglass and painted. The banana car has a top speed of 85 mph (136.79 km/h).

The *Big Banana Car* has been driven across the USA, from Providence, Rhode Island, to Miami, Florida.

Office

Former presenter and mechanic on the Discovery Channel's *Wheeler Dealers*, Edd China (UK) is the king of crazy customizations. On 9 Nov 2006, China created a roadworthy desk and drove it at a maximum speed of 87 mph (140 km/h) across Westminster Bridge in London, UK. The record attempt took place as part of GWR Day.

China is also responsible for the **fastest garden shed**. His creation *Gone to Speed* can reach 58.41 mph (94 km/h), and was presented on the set of *Lo Show dei Record* in Milan, Italy, on 1 Apr 2011.

▲ FASTEST MOTORIZED HOT TUB

On 10 Aug 2014, Phillip Weicker and Duncan Forster (both CAN) drove their creation *Carpool DeVille* to an average speed of 52.28 mph (84.14 km/h) over their two best runs, reaching a maximum speed of 54.8 mph (88.19 km/h) in Wendover, Utah, USA. They had taken a 1969 Cadillac DeVille and replaced the car's interior with a fibreglass tank. A liquid-to-liquid heat exchanger with engine coolant heated the Jacuzzi water to 102°F (38.88°C) in around 35 min.

Monster Trucks

These outsized mechanical monsters
typically weigh around 10,000 lb
(4,535 kg) and are around 12 ft wide,
12 ft tall and 20 ft long (3.6 x 3.6 x 6 m).

First monster truck
Bigfoot #1, a modified Ford F-250 pick-up truck
standing on 48-in-tall (1.21-m) tyres, was built by
Bob Chandler in St Louis, Missouri, USA, in the mid-
1970s. *Bigfoot* made its initial public appearance
in 1979, introducing the concept of the "monster
truck" for the first time.

First monster truck backflip
in a scored competition
Cam McQueen (CAN) successfully performed
a reverse flip at the Jacksonville Monster Jam
in Jacksonville, Florida, USA, on 27 Feb 2010.
Monster Jam is a live motorsport event tour
series whose season runs from January to
March. It is sanctioned by the United States Hot
Rod Association, with the Monster Jam World
Finals held each year in Las Vegas, Nevada, USA.
Champions have been crowned in the "Racing" and
"Freestyle" disciplines each year since 2000.

Fastest speed for a monster truck
Driving the Ram Truck-sponsored *Raminator*, the
USA's Mark Hall reached a speed of 159.49 km/h
(99.1 mph) – about 1.5 times the maximum speed of
a cheetah, the **fastest land mammal** – on 15 Dec
2014. The feat took place at the Circuit of the
Americas in Austin, Texas, USA.

Miceli took
the nickname
"Madusa" when she was
a professional wrestler
(she once held the World
Wrestling Federation title,
fighting under the name
Alundra Blayze). It's
short for "Made in
the USA".

◀ FIRST FEMALE MONSTER JAM DRIVER
Debrah Miceli, from Florida, USA, became
the first ever female driver in a Monster Jam
competition in 1999. The name of her truck
is *Madusa*, a moniker that doubles as one of
Debrah's nicknames. She's also known as
the "Queen of Carnage".
Five years later, Debrah became the
**first female Monster Jam World Finals
champion**. She shared in a three-way
tie for the Freestyle contest held
in Las Vegas, Nevada, USA, in
Mar 2004.

Fastest quarter-mile in a monster truck

On 17 Mar 2012, Randy Moore of Tennessee, USA, covered a quarter mile (402 m) from a standing start in 13.175 sec in *War Wizard*. His top speed was 96.8 mph (155.8 km/h). The venue was the zMAX Dragway in Charlotte, North Carolina, USA.

Longest time between winning the Monster Jam World Finals Freestyle Championship

In 2003, Jim Koehler (USA) won the Monster Jam World Finals freestyle title in *Avenger*. Eight years later, in 2011, he repeated the feat. Koehler's achievement was then equalled by Adam Anderson (USA, b. 5 Dec 1985), driving *Taz* in 2008 and *Grave Digger* in 2016.

Anderson's 2008 victory also saw him become the **youngest driver to win a Monster Jam World Finals Championship**, aged just 22.

Longest ramp jump in a monster truck

Joe Sylvester (USA) jumped a distance of 72.42 m (237 ft 7 in) in the 10,000-lb (4,535-kg) *Bad Habit* in Columbus, Pennsylvania, USA, on 1 Sep 2013. When Sylvester hit the ramp, he was travelling at around 85 mph (136.7 km/h). "The level of risk is about as high as you can go in a monster truck," he admitted candidly afterwards. "If you crash at that speed and from that height it's pretty devastating."

▲ **FIRST MONSTER TRUCK TO JUMP OVER A BOEING 727**

In 1999, the USA's Dan Runte jumped over a Boeing 727 aeroplane in *Bigfoot 14*, covering a distance of 62 m (203 ft) – around three times the length of a bowling lane. The record-breaking leap took place in Smyrna, Tennessee, USA.

▲ **TALLEST LIMOUSINE**

From the ground to the roof, the world's highest limo measures 3.33 m (10 ft 11 in). Built by Gary and Shirley Duval (AUS), it incorporates an eight-wheel independent suspension system and sits astride eight monster truck tyres. The car has two separate 8-litre Cadillac engines and took slightly more than 4,000 hr (166 days) to build.

Q: On average, how many cars are crushed at Monster Jam each year?

A: 3,000

▲ FIRST ELECTRIC MONSTER TRUCK

Unveiled in Nov 2012, *Bigfoot 20* (aka *Electro-Foot*) is the first monster truck to be fully powered by an electric motor. The 5,000-kg (11,000-lb) behemoth features a custom-made 350-hp (260.9-kW) electric motor powered by 30 Odyssey batteries; six more power the steering system and brakes. Built by *Bigfoot 17* driver Nigel Morris (UK), *Bigfoot 20* debuted at the SEMA show in Las Vegas, Nevada, USA, on 30 Oct 2012.

▲ MOST CONSECUTIVE BACKFLIPS BY A MONSTER TRUCK IN A SCORED COMPETITION

Driving *Mohawk Warrior*, George Balhan of Illinois, USA, completed two consecutive monster truck backflips without stopping in a Monster Jam freestyle competition in Las Vegas, Nevada, USA, on 23 Mar 2012. The truck is named after George's own distinctive hairstyle.

▲ LONGEST MONSTER TRUCK

Brad and Jen Campbell (both USA, above) of Big Toyz Racing built a monster truck that measured 32 ft (9.75 m) long when inspected at Last Stop in White Hills, Arizona, USA, on 10 Jul 2014. The *Sin City Hustler* was originally constructed to ferry tourists around Las Vegas. It is currently operated by Russ Mann (USA).

Forklift truck:
FLT 90-2400

Kalmar LMV (SWE) made three super-sized forklifts, each weighing 116,500 kg (256,838 lb) and measuring 54 ft 5 in (16.6 m) long – including forks – and 15 ft 10 in (4.85 m) wide

Production pick-up truck:
7300 CXT

Made by the International Truck & Engine Corporation (USA), this truck weighs 14,500 lb (6,577 kg). It is 21 ft 6 in (6.55 m) long and 9 ft (2.74 m) high

Monster truck:
Bigfoot 5

(See opposite) Created by Bob Chandler (USA), this behemoth stands 15 ft 6 in (4.7 m) tall and weighs 17,236 kg (38,000 lb)

Semi truck:
Tractomas TR 10 x 10 D100

Manufactured by Nicolas Industrie SAS (FRA), this truck has a total weight of 71 tonnes (156,528 lb) and was launched in France on 28 Oct 2005

Dump truck (two-axle):
BelAZ 75710

Made by BelAZ (BLR), this truck has a rated payload capacity of 450 tonnes (992,080 lb)

Longest monster truck jump in reverse

Black Stallion, driven by Michael Vaters of Hagerstown, Maryland, USA, jumped a distance of 70 ft (21.3 m) – the length of two London buses – in reverse gear in Indianapolis, Indiana, USA, in 2002.

Most monster trucks jumped in a monster truck

Tom Meents (USA) leaped over six Monster Jam monster trucks in *Maximum Destruction* at the MetLife Stadium in East Rutherford, New Jersey, USA, on 23 Apr 2016.

Most cans crushed with a vehicle in three minutes

Ian Batey (UK) flattened 61,106 cans in a 20,000-lb (9,071-kg) monster truck for Burn Energy Drink (UAE) in 3 min at the Jumeirah Beach Residence in Dubai, UAE, on 6 Mar 2010.

MOST WINS OF THE...

Monster Jam World Finals

Tom Meents (USA), who currently drives *Maximum Destruction*, has won a total of 11 Monster Jam World Finals (in Racing and Freestyle) since records began in 1999.

Monster truck national championships

As of the end of 2016, Mark Hall (USA) had won 25 national monster truck competitions – more than any other driver. His wins comprise 12 monster truck thunder drags, six nationals racing, five nationals freestyle and two monster truck nationals.

Monster Jam freestyle stadium event consecutively in one season

Behind the wheel of *Team Hot Wheels Firestorm*, Scott Buetow (USA) completed six straight freestyle stadium wins after his victory in the event Melbourne, Australia, on 8 Oct 2016.

▲ LARGEST MONSTER TRUCK

Bigfoot 5 is 15 ft 6 in (4.7 m) tall with 3-m-tall (9-ft 10-in) tyres, and weighs 38,000 lb (17,236 kg). It is one of a fleet of 17 Bigfoot trucks created by Bob Chandler of St Louis, Missouri, USA, and was built in the summer of 1986. Now permanently parked in St Louis, *Bigfoot 5* still makes occasional appearances at exhibitions in local shows.

▼ FIRST MONSTER TRUCK DOUBLE BACKFLIP OUTSIDE A SCORED COMPETITION

Not content with performing just one reverse flip, Tom Meents (USA) completed a double backflip in his 10,000-lb (4,535-kg) *Maximum Destruction* truck during a Monster Jam event in Foxborough, Massachusetts, USA, on 20 Jun 2015. It took him four attempts to finally pull off this incredibly demanding stunt. Pictured right, you can see a frame-by-frame breakdown of Tom's record-breaking reverse flips.

Classified as a "futuristic SUV", the spiky-topped, 1,500-hp (1,118.5-kW) *Max D* is one of the most distinctive trucks on the circuit.

Military Vehicles

Truk Lagoon in the Pacific is home to the wrecks of more than 30 Japanese warships sunk during the US offensive Operation Hailstone during WWII.

First tank
Built by William Foster & Co. Ltd of Lincolnshire, UK, the No.1 Lincoln first ran in early Sep 1915 and became known as Little Willie. Tanks first saw action a little over a year later, at the Battle of Flers-Courcelette in France on 15 Sep 1916. The Mark I "Male" tank was developed from Little Willie and was part of the Heavy Section, Machine Gun Corps (now the Royal Tank Regiment). It was armed with a pair of 6-pounder guns and four machine guns and weighed 28.4 tonnes (62,611 lb), while its 105-hp (78-kW) motor gave it a top road speed of 3–4 mph (4.8–6.4 km/h).

The **oldest tank design** was created by Leonardo da Vinci (1452–1519). The Italian artist and inventor drafted an early concept for a wheeled, wood-covered machine with provision for outward-facing guns (see panel, p.472).

Highest rate of tank production
The M-4 Sherman battle tank was first rolled out by the USA in 1942, at the height of World War II. Designed with ease of production, reliability and maintenance in mind, more than 48,000 units were turned out over a three-year period.

▼ LARGEST ROCKET ARTILLERY BY TUBE COUNT
First unveiled in 2013, the Jobaria ("Monster") Defense Systems Multiple Cradle Launcher is a 122-mm (4.8-in) rocket artillery system developed by the UAE and Turkish contractor Roketsan. The Jobaria's 10-wheel semitrailer supports four rocket launchers with a total of 240 rockets with a maximum range of around 37 km (23 mi). One full salvo from the Jobaria can devastate an area of 4 km² (1.5 sq mi).

The Maus tank (see opposite) was too heavy to cross bridges. It was designed to ford rivers in pairs, with one tank providing the other with electric power via a cable, and air supplied through a large snorkel.

Q: How many tanks fought in the **first tank vs tank battle** on 24 Apr 1918?

A: Six

Heaviest tank

First built in 1923, the 75-tonne (165,346-lb), 12-man Char de Rupture 2C bis was a French tank that carried a 15.5-cm (6.1-in) howitzer. Powered by two 250-hp (186-kW) engines, it had a maximum speed of 12 km/h (7.5 mph).

An even heavier tank was developed by the Germans during World War II, although it never saw active service. Tipping the scales at 188 tonnes (414,469 lb), the Panzerkampfwagen VIII Maus ("Mouse") was two-and-a-half times heavier than a Space Shuttle. By 1945, only two prototypes of the Maus existed. They were obtained by Soviet forces, who paired the hull of one machine with the turret of the other. The combined vehicle is now on display at Kubinka Tank Museum in Russia.

Longest-range infantry fighting vehicle

Combat Vehicle 90 (CV90) is a series of tracked armoured infantry fighting vehicles designed for the Swedish armed forces and produced by BAE Systems. Each carries a crew of three, plus eight troops, and has a 40-mm (1.57-in) Bofors Autocannon as its main armament. Since development began in 1984, improvements have led to the CV90 Armadillo variant boasting a maximum on-road range of up to 900 km (559 mi) and a top speed of 68 km/h (42 mph).

▲ HEAVIEST FIFTH-GENERATION FIGHTER BY TAKE-OFF WEIGHT

Fifth-gen fighters possess advanced avionics and all-aspect stealth capabilities. As of 2016, there were only three types (although Russian and Chinese prototypes also exist), all produced by Lockheed Martin: the F-22 Raptor, F-35B Lightning II and F-35A Lightning II. The F-22 Raptor is the heaviest, with a fully loaded take-off weight of 38,000 kg (83,775 lb). The USA has banned its export to protect its design.

◀ LARGEST VARIABLE-SWEEP-WING AIRCRAFT

Code-named "Blackjack" by NATO, the Russian Tupolev Tu-160 first came into service in 2005. The strategic supersonic bomber has variable-sweep wings, also called "swing wings". They sweep back in flight, changing the shape of the aircraft and making it more efficient at higher speeds. The Tupolev Tu-160's wings have a span of 36.5 m (119 ft 9 in) when swept and 55.7 m (182 ft 8.9 in) when spread.

Leonardo da Vinci designed a fighting vehicle in 1487 inspired by the shell of a turtle

During World War II, the British briefly considered building a battleship using pykrete – a material made by combining sawdust (or wood pulp) with ice

Highest military budgets for 2015:

USA: $596 bn

China: $215 bn

Saudi Arabia: $87.2 bn

Russia: $66.4 bn

UK: $55.5 bn

= $50 bn

2015 US military budgets, by investments:

$40 bn
Aircraft-related systems

$22 bn
Shipbuilding/maritime systems

$17.2 bn
Missiles/munition/missile defence

$6.6 bn
C4I systems (Command, Control, Communications, Computers and Intelligence)

$6.2 bn
Space systems

▲ LARGEST SURFACE COMBAT SHIP WITH A WAVE-PIERCING HULL

Wave-piercing hulls are long and thin, and designed to cut through the waves on the ocean surface rather than ride on top of them. This makes for a smoother and more stable ride. Commissioned on 15 Oct 2016, the USS *Zumwalt* is the first of its class of destroyer. Measuring 185 m (606 ft 11 in) in length, the *Zumwalt* is a fully stealth-capable combat ship.

Largest gun

In the siege of Sevastopol in the USSR (now Ukraine) in Jul 1942, German forces used a gun with a calibre of 80 cm (31.5 in), incorporating a barrel 32.5 m (106 ft 7 in) long. Internally it was named Schwerer Gustav. The complete assembly of the gun was 42.9 m (141 ft) long and weighed 1,344 tonnes (2,963,000 lb). The range for a 4.8-tonne (10,582-lb) projectile was 46.7km (29 mi).

Largest cruiser fleet

With the battleship's demise in the latter half of the 20th century, cruisers are the largest class of surface combat ship in use today. Three nations have cruisers in active service: the USA, with 22; Russia, with three; and Peru, which has one. The cruisers operated by the US Navy are all of the Ticonderoga guided-missile class. Their armament includes a vertical launch system for surface-to-air, cruise, anti-submarine and anti-ship missiles.

Most expensive military aircraft (programme)

By 2012, costs of the Lockheed Martin F-35 Lightning Joint Strike Fighter had escalated to $336.1 bn (£207 bn). The 50-year, multinational programme has an estimated cost for the USA of $0.85-1.5 tr (£530-927 bn) over the course of its lifetime.

The **most expensive military aircraft (per unit)** is the US-made Northrop Grumman B-2 Spirit. The stealth bomber, which can deploy both conventional and thermonuclear weapons, costs in excess of $1.3 bn (£780 m) per unit.

▲ LARGEST SUBMARINE

On 23 Sep 1980, NATO announced the launch of the 941 Akula-class submarine at the Russian shipyard at Severodvinsk, on the White Sea. The deep-sea behemoths were believed to measure 171.5 m (562 ft 8 in) – two-and-a-half times the length of a 747 jumbo jet. They were armed with 20 multiple-warhead SS-N-20 missiles with a range of 8,300 km (4,500 nautical mi). Akula is Russian for "shark".

◀ FASTEST MILITARY HELICOPTER

The first Chinook helicopter took to the skies on 21 Sep 1961. More than 1,200 variants have since been built, with at least 20 countries currently operating them. The CH-47F Chinook has a top speed of 315 km/h (195.7 mph). Tandem rotors at the front and back of the airframe negate the need for a tail rotor. Used mainly to transport equipment and troops, the CH-47F is armed with three mounted machine guns.

◀ LARGEST WARSHIP CONSTRUCTED FROM GLASS-REINFORCED PLASTIC

The Hunt-class ships of the UK's Royal Navy are active minehunters with a secondary role as offshore patrol vehicles. Their hulls are made from glass-reinforced plastic (GRP) rather than metal, which creates a low magnetic signature. This serves to protect them against mines able to detect and target conventional metallic hulls. Hunt-class ships measure 60 m (196 ft 10 in) long and displace 750 tonnes (826 tons).

Most expensive supercarrier

Scheduled for commission in 2017, the USS *Gerald R Ford* cost $13 bn (£8.1 bn) to build. The 1,092–ft (332.8-m) carrier, which can support 75 fighter planes, is equipped with a new type of catapult, the Electromagnetic Aircraft Launch System (EMALS). It can launch up to 220 airstrikes a day from its two runways.

▲ FIRST MAIN BATTLE TANK WITH AN UNMANNED TURRET

The Russian T-14 Armata was first unveiled to the public during the 2015 Moscow Victory Day Parade, after a four-year period of trial and development. The tank's crew of three sits inside an internal armoured capsule, while the main gun is fully unmanned and controlled from within the crew compartment (inset). The T-14 weighs around 48 tonnes (105,822 lb) and is 8.7 m (28 ft 6 in) long, excluding the main gun.

▲ HEAVIEST MILITARY TILTROTOR AIRCRAFT (CURRENT)

The American Bell Boeing V-22 Osprey has a maximum, fully loaded vertical take-off weight of 52,600 lb (23,859 kg). With its rotors tilted upwards, the Osprey is capable of vertical take-off and landing. In flight, its rotors tilt forward (inset), enabling speeds of up to 565 km/h (351 mph) – much faster than a conventional helicopter.

Transport Round-Up

At any given time, there are 60,000 people flying in the skies above the USA.

Lombard Street has featured in several iconic films, including Alfred Hitchcock's chilling Vertigo (USA, 1958), The Love Bug (USA, 1968) and even the animated Inside Out (USA, 2015).

▲ MOST CROOKED ROAD

Originally constructed in 1922, Lombard Street in San Francisco, California, USA, would give an ancient Roman a heart attack! Over the course of a famous 400-m (1,312-ft) stretch between Hyde Street and Leavenworth Street in Russian Hill, the red-bricked road follows eight hairpin turns that twist a total of 1,440°. Traffic can only move one way along Lombard Street – down the hill's steep 1:3.7 gradient – and there is a 5-mph (8-km/h) speed limit.

Longest continuous road

Australia's Highway 1 circumnavigates the whole country via a network of fully interconnected roads. Its total length is 14,523 km (9,024 mi), making it 3,500 km (2,175 mi) longer than its nearest rival, the Trans-Siberian Highway. More than a million people travel along at least part of Highway 1 every day. It passes through every state in the country.

The **longest one-way road** is also located in Australia. The M2 Southern Expressway in Adelaide, South Australia, has a total length of 21 km (13 mi). Built to ease congestion on the Main South Road, it runs northbound into Adelaide city in the morning before switching to southbound in the afternoon.

Longest straight road

Built originally as a private road for King Fahd (SAU), the stretch of Highway 10 connecting Highway 75 in the Haradh area to Highway 95 in the west of Saudi Arabia is 240 km (149 mi) long. It cuts through the desert with no bends left or right, or any appreciable gradient up or down. The super-straight stretch has an estimated driving time of around 2 hr.

Longest network of roads

According to the latest available figures in the CIA World Factbook, the USA had 6,586,610 km (4,092,729 mi) of graded roads in 2012. India had the next longest road network, with 4,699,024 km (2,919,838 mi).

Oldest functional traffic light

Designed by Teddy Boor (USA), a four-faced signal with a rotating red-and-green lamp was installed on the corner of Main and Long Streets in Ashville, Ohio, USA, in 1932. It continued to operate until 1982, when it was transferred to the town's museum. The traffic light still works today.

▲ FIRST OPEN-TOP DOUBLE-DECKER ROPEWAY CABIN

Peaking at 1,898 m (6,227 ft) above sea level, the Stanserhorn mountain in Switzerland offers a dramatic view of the Alps that includes 10 lakes and even, on a clear day, neighbouring Germany. And there can be few better ways to enjoy it than on the 6-min 24-sec journey in the open-top "CabriO" cable car. The upper deck can accommodate up to 30 people – provided they have a head for heights!

Steepest street

Located in Dunedin, New Zealand, Baldwin Street rises a total of 69.2 m (227 ft) over its length of 350 m (1,148 ft). The street has an average gradient of 1:5, with a true gradient near the top of 1:2.86. It is laid with specially grooved concrete to enable cars to grip the surface.

Shortest street

Ebenezer Place in Wick, Caithness, UK, measured 2.05 m (6 ft 9 in) long when measured on 28 Oct 2006. That's about half as long as a Volkswagen Beetle car, or approximately a quarter the length of a London Routemaster bus.

Longest bus route

Operated by Peruvian company Ormeño, the world's longest bus route measures 6,200 km (3,852 mi) – around 14 times the length of the Grand Canyon – and connects Lima in Peru to Rio de Janeiro in Brazil. Known as the Transoceánica, the route takes passengers through the Amazon and the Andes on a 102-hr (four-plus days) trip. The bus climbs to the dizzying height of 3,500 m (11,482 ft).

Largest roundabout

Circled by the Persiaran Sultan Salahuddin Abdul Aziz Shah road, a roundabout in Putrajaya, Malaysia, measures 3.4 km (2.1 mi) in circumference and has 15 entry/exit points. The royal retreat of Istana Melawati, the Putra Perdana office of the Prime Minister and the Putrajaya Shangri-La five-star hotel can all be found within the roundabout's centre.

▲ LARGEST ROTATING BOAT LIFT

Officially opened by Queen Elizabeth II on 24 May 2002, the Falkirk Wheel in Falkirk, UK, is 35 m (114 ft) tall, 35 m wide and 30 m (98 ft) long. It links the Forth & Clyde and Union canals, and can transfer more than eight boats at a time. Previously, boats travelling between the two canals had to pass through 11 locks, which took almost a day; the Wheel reduces that time to 15 min. Forged from 1,200 tonnes (1,322 tons) of steel, it required 1,000 construction staff to assemble. It only uses 1.5 kW of energy to turn – the same amount needed to boil eight household kettles.

Longest ring road

Highway One, or A01, is a 1,300-mi (2,092-km) two-lane road encircling a huge area at the centre of Afghanistan, linking 16 of its 34 provinces.

Longest ice-skating trail

As of 14 Feb 2014, the naturally frozen Lake Windermere Whiteway in Invermere, British Columbia, Canada, measured 29.98 km (18.63 mi).

▼ LARGEST AIRLINE BRAND (RETAIL RSP, CURRENT)

Headquartered in Atlanta, Georgia, USA, Delta Air Lines' 800-strong fleet of planes fly to 323 destinations in 57 countries. In 2015, Delta made estimated sales of $26,752,484,100 (£18,044,400,000), based on retail selling price (RSP) figures retrieved from the Euromonitor International Passport database on 19 Aug 2016. The second-largest brand was United Airlines (USA), with estimated sales of $24,226,918,500 (£16,340,900,000) over the same period.

US carrier Delta Air Lines flies more than 180 million passengers annually. This is more than the populations of the UK, Spain and France combined.

First car ferry
Built by the Canadian Pacific Railway Company's BC Coast Service, the *Motor Princess* was launched in 1923. It was in service for nearly 60 years before being retired in 1980.

Tallest boat lift
The 124-m-high (407-ft) Krasnoyarsk Dam is located on the Yenisei River in Russia. Its ship lift comprises a flooded chamber in which the ship sits while it traverses the 124-m height on a 9-m-wide (29-ft 6-in) tracked slope 1,510 m (4,954 ft) in length. The chamber is 113 m (370 ft 8 in) long and 26 m (85 ft 3 in) wide, and can carry ships weighing 1.5 tonnes (1.6 tons). The lift moves its cargo at 1 m/s (2.2 mph).

Highest airport
Daocheng Yading Airport is situated at an elevation of 4,411 m (14,472 ft) in the Tibetan Autonomous Prefecture of Sichuan Province, China. The airport opened on 16 Sep 2013.

◄ **BUSIEST AIRPORT FOR DOMESTIC AND INTERNATIONAL PASSENGERS**

According to the Airports Council International (ACI), in 2015 101,489,887 people flew in or out of Hartsfield-Jackson Atlanta International Airport in Atlanta, Georgia, USA. This placed it well ahead of Beijing Capital International Airport in Beijing, China, which was second-busiest with 89,938,628.

In 2015, Hartsfield-Jackson Atlanta International also saw 882,497 "traffic movements" – flights taking off or landing – making it the **busiest airport by number of aircraft**.

Largest airport (area)

King Fahd International Airport near Dammam, Saudi Arabia, measures 780 km² (301 sq mi). This is larger than the nearby country of Bahrain.

Busiest beach airport

Despite being submerged daily by the incoming tide, the beach airport at Barra in the Western Isles, UK, handles more than 1,000 flights per year.

▲ LARGEST BUS RETROFIT PROGRAMME

The double-decker bus is an iconic symbol of the city of London in the UK. Now its distinctive bright-red fleet has turned green. In Jul 2014, the city's transit department, Transport for London (TfL), embarked upon an extensive retrofit programme for its older buses. The exhaust systems on 1,015 buses, travelling on 50 different routes, are now equipped with a Selective Catalytic Reduction (SLR) system that reduces nitrogen oxide emissions. TfL aims to increase the programme to include 1,800 of its buses.

Busiest airport for cargo

According to figures compiled by the ACI, Hong Kong International Airport handled cargo totalling 4,460,065 tonnes (4,916,380 tons) in the 12 months leading up to 31 Dec 2015.

Closest airports

The airports on the neighbouring islands of Papa Westray and Westray in the Orkneys, UK, are just 1.76 mi (2.83 km) apart. Both have been given airport codes by the International Air Transport Association: PPW and WRY respectively. The flight between the two airports takes an average of just 96 sec.

▲ TALLEST SIT-DOWN HYDROFOIL

Hydrofoil technology helps to raise boats and other vessels above the water as they move through it. On 22 Aug 2015, water-skiing legend Mike Murphy (USA) rode a sit-down hydrofoil measuring 11 ft 2.6 in (3.42 m) tall at Long Beach in California, USA. He demonstrated the usable height of the hydrofoil by breaking the surface of the water with the "wing", then maintained control for a farther 100 ft (30.48 m).

Smallest...

You could fit the smallest country into the smallest continent nearly 17.5 million times. But can the smallest cat that ever existed really have been four times smaller than the smallest police dog? And what is the smallest unit of length in the universe? GWR presents a whistlestop tour of relative size, from stellar to sub-atomic.

Our Sun is 11.6 times larger than the **smallest known star** (see below left).

< 150,000 km

Star
119,660 km

The smallest known star is 2MASS J05233822-1403022, observed 40 light years from Earth. It has a diameter of around 119,660 km (74,353 mi), around 0.086 times that of the Sun (top right).

Continent
4,000 km

Some sources argue that Oceania, or Oceania/Australasia, is the smallest continent, but the definitions of what territories this includes vary widely. For most sources, including GWR, the record holder is Australia, with a west-to-east width of some 4,000 km (2,485 mi) and an area of 7.69 million km² (2.96 million sq mi). It is also the sixth largest country.

Extrasolar planet
1,930 km

An extrasolar planet (or exoplanet) is one that orbits a sun other than our own. Kepler 37b orbits the star Kepler 37, around 210 light years from Earth. Its discovery by NASA's *Kepler* spacecraft was announced on 20 Feb 2013. Kepler 37b is only around 1,200 mi (1,930 km) across, smaller than the planet Mercury.

Spherical world
396.6 km

Mimas, one of Saturn's moons, is just 396.6 km (246.4 mi) across. It is the smallest known body whose shape has been rounded owing to its own gravity. Mimas is also the 20th largest moon in the Solar System.

Country
0.44 km²

The smallest independent country is the State of Vatican City or Holy See (Stato della Città del Vaticano), an enclave within the city of Rome in Italy. It has an area of 0.44 km² (0.17 sq mi) and is smaller than the Pentagon – itself the world's **largest office building.**

< 5 m

Pressurised manned spacecraft
3.34 x 1.89 m

The Mercury spacecraft was used for six NASA manned missions between 1961 and 1963. It carried a single astronaut inside a conical capsule that was 3.34 m [10 ft 11.5 in] high and 1.89 m [6 ft 2 in] in diameter.

Aircraft
2.69 m

Designed and built by Robert H Starr (USA), the biplane *Bumble Bee II* was 8 ft 10 in (2.69 m) long, with a wing-span of 5 ft 6 in (1.68 m), and weighed 179.6 kg (396 lb) empty. It could accommodate one person.

Roadworthy car
63.5 x 65.4 x 126.3 cm

Created by Austin Coulson (USA), the most diminutive roadworthy car measures 63.5 cm high, 65.4 cm wide and 126.3 cm long (25 x 25.75 x 49.75 in). It was measured in Carrollton, Texas, USA, on 7 Sep 2012.

Woman (ever)
61 cm

Pauline Musters, known as Princess Pauline, was born in Ossendrecht, Netherlands, on 26 Feb 1876 and measured 1 ft (30 cm) at birth. She died of pneumonia with meningitis on 1 Mar 1895 in New York City, USA, at the age of 19. A post-mortem examination revealed her height to be 2 ft (61 cm).

Man (ever)
54.6 cm

Chandra Bahadur Dangi (NPL) was 54.6 cm (21.5 in) tall when measured at CIWEC Clinic Travel Medicine Center in Lainchaur, Kathmandu, Nepal, on 26 Feb 2012.

< 50 cm

Dinosaur
39 cm

The feathered *Microraptor zhaoianus* measured 39 cm (15.3 in) long, of which 24 cm (9.4 in) was its tail. A fossil specimen found in China in 1999 has been dated to 110–120 million years ago.

Police dog
28 cm

Chihuahua/rat terrier cross Midge is 28 cm (11 in) tall and 58 cm (22.8 in) long. She worked as an official Law Enforcement Work Dog (or "Police K9") with her owner, Sheriff Dan McClelland (USA), at Geauga County Sheriff's Office in Chardon, Ohio, USA. Midge passed her Ohio Certification as a Narcotics Dog on 7 Nov 2006 and retired, along with Sheriff McClelland, on 1 Jan 2017.

Arcade machine
12.4 x 5.2 x 6 cm

In 2009, computer engineer Mark Slevinsky (CAN) built a fully playable arcade machine measuring 12.4 x 5.2 x 6 cm (4.88 x 2.05 x 2.36 in). He wrote his own operating system, FunkOS, to program its *Tetris*, *Space Invaders* and *Breakout* clones.

Cat
7 cm

Tinker Toy, a male blue point Himalayan-Persian, measured 7 cm (2.75 in) tall and 19 cm (7.5 in) long when fully grown (aged 2.5 years). His owners were Katrina and Scott Forbes of Taylorville, Illinois, USA.

Bird
5.7 cm

Male bee hummingbirds (*Mellisuga helenae*) of Cuba and the Isle of Youth measure 5.7 cm (2.24 in) long, half of which is taken up by the bill and tail. Males weigh 1.6 g (0.056 oz), but females are slightly larger.

< 5.5 cm

**Human bones
2.6–3.4 mm**

The stapes or stirrup bone, one of the three auditory ossicles in the middle ear, measures 2.6–3.4 mm (0.1–0.13 in) long and weighs 2–4.3 mg (0.03–0.066 grains).

Commercially available stitched teddy bear 9 mm

Cheryl Moss (ZAF) hand-crafted a teddy bear that measures just 9 mm (0.35 in) tall. She has been making "Microbears" for several years and selling them in specialist teddy-bear stores.

**Working drill
17 x 7 x 13.5 mm**

The smallest cordless drill measures 17 x 7 x 13.5 mm (0.66 x 0.27 x 0.53 in) and holds a twist drill that is 11.75 mm (0.46 in) long. The 3D-printed tool was designed and produced by Lance Abernethy (NZ) on 21 Mar 2015.

**Comic book
2.58 x 3.7 cm**

Written by Martin Lodewijk (NLD) and published in Jun 1999, a special issue of *Agent 327* entitled "Dossier Minimum Bug" measured just 2.58 x 3.7 cm (1 x 1.4 in). A total of 2,000 copies of the 16-page, full-colour comic were produced and sold with a free magnifying glass.

**Revolver
5.5 cm**

The C1ST is a working revolver 5.5 cm long, 3.5 cm high, 1 cm wide (2.1 x 1.3 x 0.4 in) and weighing 19.8 g (0.7 oz). It is made by SwissMiniGun (CHE).

Unit of length
1.6 x 10⁻³⁵ m

The smallest measurable length in the universe is the Planck length, which is 1.6×10^{-35} m across. It is equivalent to around a millionth of a billionth of a billionth of a billionth of a centimetre across (a decimal point followed by 34 zeroes and a one). This is the scale at which quantum foam is believed to exist. Quantum theory holds that space-time is composed of infinitesimally tiny regions in which new dimensions come into being and vanish at incredible speed, rather like foam bubbles. These quantum foam bubbles are tiny compared even to atomic nuclei.

Man-made object
1 atom

By using field ion microscopy, the tips of probes of scanning tunnelling microscopes have been shaped to end in a single atom. The last three layers constitute the world's smallest man-made pyramid, consisting of seven atoms, three atoms and one atom.

Nanocar
3-4 nanometres

In 2005, scientists at Rice University, USA, led by James Tour, revealed a "car" made from a molecule of mostly carbon atoms that contains a chassis, axles and four wheels made from buckyball molecules. The entire assemblage measures just 3-4 nanometres across – slightly wider than a strand of DNA.

Replica guitar
10 micrometres

A guitar based on a Fender Stratocaster and carved from a block of silicon measured 10 micrometres long – one-twentieth of the thickness of human hair. It was made in 1997 in just 20 min by scientists at Cornell University, New York, USA. Each of its strings was 0.05 micrometres thick, equivalent to a line of 100 atoms.

Sculpture of a human
80 x 100 x 30 micrometres

The smallest sculpture modelled on a real person is *Trust* by Jonty Hurwitz (UK), a 3D-printed piece depicting a woman and measuring 80 x 100 x 30 micrometres. The statue, inspired by the artist's first love 27 years after they met, was verified on 13 Feb 2015 at the Karlsruhe Nano Micro Facility in Germany.

< 1 mm

Sports

Michael Phelps (USA) has won the same number of Olympic gold medals – 23 – as India, Nigeria, Egypt and Portugal combined.

▲ FASTEST 400 M

At the 2016 Rio Olympics, Wayde van Niekerk (ZAF) won the men's 400 m final in 43.03 sec on 14 Aug, smashing the 17-year-old record of 43.18 sec by Michael Johnson (USA). Van Niekerk's time was even more amazing for the fact he set it in the outermost lane 8, making it harder to see his competitors and so judge the pace of his race properly.

On 12 Mar 2016, van Niekerk became the **first athlete to achieve the "sub-10, -20, -44"**. He recorded a time of 9.98 sec for the 100 m at the Free State Championships in Bloemfontein, South Africa, meaning that he had broken three notable sprint barriers: running under 10 sec in the 100 m, under 20 sec in the 200 m and under 44 sec in the 400 m. No other athlete has ever done this in competition.

Contents

Usain Bolt (JAM) has challenged van Niekerk to a 300 m race. They hold the second- and third-fastest times for the rarely run distance, behind Michael Johnson's 30.85 sec.

FIFA World Cup Preview

In anticipation of the 2018 FIFA World Cup in Russia, we present the pick of GWR's World Cup records.

Most appearances at the World Cup before hosting

Russia (or its predecessor state, the Soviet Union) has appeared at 10 World Cup tournaments since 1958. After several unsuccessful bids, the country was finally chosen to host a tournament in 2018.

Fisht Olympic Stadium in Sochi, one of the venues selected for Russia 2018, is the **first stadium chosen to host both the Winter Olympics and the World Cup**. It was constructed for the Winter Olympics and Paralympics in 2014 and is set to host six World Cup games in 2018.

The qualification stages for Russia 2018 brought together the **most national federations** of any qualification process so far, with 210 countries represented. Of these 210 federations, only 32 will be involved in the finals in Russia.

The Dutch national soccer team has reached the final of the World Cup on three occasions, and the semi-finals another two times, but has never actually won the trophy.

▼ MOST WORLD CUP WINS

South American footballing superpower Brazil has won the World Cup five times. The country's first win came in 1958 and was followed by wins in 1962, 1970, 1994 and 2002 (pictured below). Brazil is also the only country to have appeared at every single tournament since the inaugural event in 1930.

The other World Cup-winning countries are Germany and Italy (four wins each), Argentina and Uruguay (two wins) and England, France and Spain, who have each won once.

A: 1966. The trophy was on display in London, UK, and disappeared in March of that year. It was recovered within a week, however.

▶ MOST WORLD CUP MATCHES PLAYED

German midfielder Lothar Matthäus was called up to his national team for every World Cup tournament between 1982 and 1998. He was only an occasional substitute in 1982 and 1998, but played a key role in the German team's performances in 1986 (finalists), 1990 (winners) and 1994 (quarter-finalists), putting in a total of 25 appearances.

First World Cup goal

Part-time car mechanic Lucien Laurent (FRA) scored the first-ever World Cup goal, in a game between France and Mexico at Estadio Pocitos in Montevideo, Uruguay, on 13 Jul 1930. His 19th-minute volley was the opener in France's 4–1 victory over Mexico. This match was one of the opening games of the 1930 World Cup.

An impressive 70 goals were scored at the 1930 tournament, despite only 18 matches being played – an average of 3.89 goals per game. The **highest goals-per-game in a World Cup** is 5.38, however, set at the 1954 tournament in Switzerland. In 1962, the average dropped to 2.89 per game, and it hasn't risen above three per game since.

Most expulsions in a single World Cup match

Portugal's second-round victory over the Netherlands on 25 Jun 2006 was one of the most famously ill-tempered matches in World Cup history. The "Battle of Nuremberg" (named after the city in which it was held) saw four players sent off (two from each team) and 16 yellow cards handed out altogether. It was another famously violent World Cup match – 1962's "Battle of Santiago" – that inspired the introduction of the red-card and yellow-card system in the first place, by the English referee Ken Aston.

▲ MOST MINUTES PLAYED IN THE WORLD CUP

Famously reliable Italian defender Paolo Maldini was in the starting 11 for every game Italy played at World Cup tournaments between 1990 and 2002. He was never substituted, even when games went into extra-time or penalties (which happened often for his defence-heavy team). In total, Maldini played 2,217 min of World Cup football (that's 36 hr, or a day and a half).

Fastest goal in a World Cup match

Hakan Şükür (TUR) scored within 11 sec of kick-off during Turkey's match against South Korea at the 2002 World Cup on 29 Jun.

An unfortunate Sead Kolašinac (BIH) achieved the flipside of this record on 15 Jun 2014, scoring the **fastest own goal in a World Cup match**. He found his own team's net after only 2 min 8 sec of play. Bosnia and Herzegovina went on to lose 2–1 to their opponents, Argentina.

FIFA WORLD CUP
RUSSIA 2018

The 21st World Cup will be hosted by Russia from 14 Jun to 15 Jul 2018; matches will be played in 12 stadiums across 11 cities. Will any of these World Cup records be broken?

Most red cards by a team: 11 for Brazil (10 straight red cards and one double yellow card) since 1938

4

Most red cards in a single game: four were issued during Portugal vs Netherlands (two for each team) on 25 Jun 2006

2.91

Average goals per match in a World Cup finals game; for the **highest-scoring World Cup** tournament, see p.489

2.21

Lowest average goals per match, set during the famously defensive 1990 finals in Italy

16

Most shots saved in a single World Cup finals match, set by Tim Howard (USA) playing against Belgium on 1 Jul 2014

Youngest referee: Francisco Mateucci (URY), aged 27 years 62 days when officiating Yugoslavia vs Bolivia on 17 Jul 1930

◄ **OLDEST PLAYER IN THE WORLD CUP**
Colombian goalkeeper Faryd Mondragón (b. 21 Jun 1971) was aged 43 years 3 days when he came on as a late substitute during Colombia's comfortable 4–1 group-stage victory over Japan in Cuiabá, Brazil, on 24 Jun 2014. Mondragón's appearance broke the record set by striker Roger Milla (CAM) at the 1994 World Cup (see below).

Longest World Cup clean sheet
During the 1990 tournament, keeper Walter Zenga (ITA) played 518 min without letting in a goal.

Oldest goal scorer in a World Cup
Legendary Cameroonian striker Roger Milla was aged 42 years 39 days when he scored a late goal against Russia in Stanford, California, USA, on 28 Jun 1994. Milla's appearance in this game, which was Cameroon's last match in the 1994 tournament, made him the oldest player at a World Cup until the record was broken by Faryd Mondragón (see opposite).

The **youngest goal scorer** is Pelé (see above), who was aged just 17 years 239 days when he scored the only goal in Brazil's 19 Jun game against Wales in the 1958 World Cup.

◄ **MOST WORLD CUP FINALS GOALS (INDIVIDUAL)**
Expert finisher Miroslav Klose (DEU) scored 16 goals in the course of his 24 World Cup appearances for Germany between 2002 and 2014. At the 2006 World Cup, he scored five goals to win the coveted "Golden Boot" trophy (awarded to the highest-scoring player of the tournament). He is also one of only 46 players to have scored a hat-trick in a World Cup game since the first tournament in 1930.

▲ **YOUNGEST PLAYER IN A WORLD CUP-WINNING TEAM**
Pelé (BRA, b. 23 Oct 1940; above right) started the 1958 World Cup in Sweden having played only once for his country. His first appearance set a record for **youngest World Cup player** (which stood until 1982, see p.492). He followed this up with **youngest goalscorer** (see opposite page) before becoming the youngest player in a World Cup-winning team on 29 Jun, aged 17 years 249 days. Pelé's career earned him seven GWR titles, which we presented to him in 2013 (above left).

Largest attendance at a football match
An amazing 173,850 people crammed into the Maracanã Stadium in Rio de Janeiro, Brazil, for the final of the 1950 World Cup on 16 Jul.

The match saw hosts Brazil lose to rivals Uruguay in a shock 2–1 result. The defeat was seen as a national catastrophe in Brazil, where it is still remembered as the "Maracanaço" (which roughly translates as the "Maracanã disaster").

▲ **FIRST TO WIN THE WORLD CUP AS BOTH CAPTAIN AND COACH**
In 1974, Franz Beckenbauer (above left, then 28 years old) captained West Germany to victory in the World Cup final against the Netherlands. Almost exactly 16 years later, Beckenbauer, now 44 (above right) and manager of the national team, presided over West Germany's victorious run in the 1990 World Cup.

The **first person to win as both player and coach** was Brazil's Mário Zagallo, who was part of the Brazilian team that won in 1958 and 1962 as well as the manager of the team that won in 1970.

▶ YOUNGEST PLAYER IN A WORLD CUP

Norman Whiteside (b. 7 May 1965) was picked to start in Northern Ireland's first group-stage game of the 1982 World Cup, against Yugoslavia, aged just 17 years 41 days. The match, which was held in Zaragoza, Spain, on 17 Jun, ended goalless. Whiteside went on to play in all of Northern Ireland's games during the 1982 tournament (including the team's shock win over the host nation, Spain).

The Argentine superstar Lionel Messi considers Maradona to be "the greatest there's ever been".

◀ MOST GOALS SCORED IN THE WORLD CUP AS CAPTAIN

Attacking midfielder Diego Maradona scored six goals at World Cup tournaments during his eight-year stint (1986–1994) as the captain of the Argentinians. The team reached the World Cup final twice during his time as captain – in 1986 (when they won) and in 1990 (when they lost to West Germany). These two runs mean that Maradona also holds the record for **most World Cup appearances as captain** (16).

Club Soccer

Paul Pogba (FRA), the most expensive footballer, cost Manchester United €105 m (£89.1 m; $116.4 m) in 2016.

Longest unbeaten streak by a newly promoted Bundesliga team
RB Leipzig (DEU) went 13 matches unbeaten from 28 Aug to 3 Dec 2016. They almost lost their first game, salvaging a last-minute draw, but went on to win eight games in a row from 30 Sep to 3 Dec. Leipzig's run finally came to an end when they lost 1–0 to Ingolstadt.

Youngest coach in the Bundesliga
Julian Nagelsmann (DEU, b. 23 Jul 1987) was aged 28 years 203 days when he took over at TSG 1899 Hoffenheim on 11 Feb 2016.

Longest unbeaten streak by a Ligue 1 team
Paris Saint-Germain went 36 games without defeat in the French top division from 15 Mar 2015 to 20 Feb 2016. They won 32 games and drew four, scoring 98 goals at an average of 2.72 per game. The longest previous unbeaten streak had been 32 games by Nantes in 1994–95.

First all-foreign Serie A match
When Internazionale met Udinese (both ITA) on 23 Apr 2016, all 22 starting players were non-Italian. Inter came out on top, winning the game 3–1.

Most consecutive Champions League home match victories
Bayern Munich (DEU) won 16 Champions League home matches in a row between 17 Sep 2014 and 15 Feb 2017, scoring 58 goals in the process.

Most consecutive wins in La Liga
Real Madrid (ESP) won 16 consecutive games in the top division of Spanish football between 2 Mar and 18 Sep 2016. This equalled the mark set by their great rivals FC Barcelona from 16 Oct 2010 to 5 Feb 2011.

Most goals scored by an individual in the UEFA Champions League
On 18 Apr 2017, Cristiano Ronaldo (PRT) netted a hat-trick during the second leg of Real Madrid's quarter-final tie against Bayern Munich, bringing his total of Champions League goals to 100. His first 15 were scored for Manchester United (UK).

▲ **MOST ENGLISH PREMIER LEAGUE (EPL) GAMES UNDEFEATED WHEN SCORING**

James Milner (UK) scored in 47 EPL games without suffering defeat between 26 Dec 2002 and 19 Mar 2017. His record stood at 37 wins and 10 draws while playing for Leeds United, Newcastle United, Aston Villa, Manchester City and Liverpool (all UK).

▲ MOST APPEARANCES IN UEFA CLUB COMPETITIONS

On 14 Mar 2017, keeper Iker Casillas (ESP) made his 175th UEFA club competition appearance for Porto (PRT) against Juventus (ITA) in Turin, Italy. Casillas, who played for Real Madrid from 1999 to 2015 before joining Porto, has also made the **most UEFA Champions League appearances**: 168.

▶ LARGEST SECOND-LEG COMEBACK IN A CHAMPIONS LEAGUE KNOCKOUT TIE

On 8 Mar 2017, FC Barcelona (ESP) fought back from a 4-0 first-leg deficit to win 6-1 against Paris Saint-Germain (FRA) at the Camp Nou in Barcelona, Spain, for a 6-5 aggregate victory. The Catalan side scored three goals in the final seven minutes, with Neymar netting twice before Sergi Roberto (pictured) scored the decisive goal in the 95th minute.

The previous largest Champions League comeback had been achieved by Deportivo de La Coruña (ESP) in 2004. They beat AC Milan 4-0 in the second leg of their tie, having lost 4-1 in the first.

▲ **MOST CONSECUTIVE WINS OF THE UEFA EUROPA LEAGUE**
Sevilla (ESP) won their third consecutive UEFA Europa League title on 18 May 2016, beating Liverpool (UK) 3–1 in the final at St Jakob-Park in Basel, Switzerland. Manager Unai Emery (ESP) was involved in all three triumphs – the **most wins of the UEFA Cup/Europa League by a manager**, tying with Giovanni Trapattoni (ITA).

Most different clubs coached in the UEFA Champions League

Carlo Ancelotti (ITA) coached seven sides in Europe's premier soccer competition from 1997 to 2016: Parma, Juventus, AC Milan (all ITA), Chelsea (UK), Paris Saint-Germain (FRA), Real Madrid (ESP) and Bayern Munich (DEU).

Most yellow cards for a team in an English Premier League match

On 2 May 2016, nine players from Tottenham Hotspur (UK) were booked during a 2–2 draw against Chelsea at Stamford Bridge in London, UK.

Highest margin of victory in Major League Soccer (MLS)

On 21 May 2016, the New York Red Bulls beat local rivals New York City FC 7–0. This matched LA Galaxy's 8–1 win over FC Dallas on 4 Jun 1998, and Chicago Fire's 7–0 rout of the Kansas City Wizards (all USA) on 4 Jul 2001.

◄ MOST SERIE A GOALS SCORED IN A SINGLE SEASON BY AN INDIVIDUAL

Argentinian hitman Gonzalo Higuaín broke a long-standing Serie A record when he scored 36 times for Napoli (ITA) during the 2015–16 season. The previous best of 35 goals had been set by Gunnar Nordahl (SWE) for AC Milan (ITA) in 1949–50. Higuaín scored a hat-trick against Frosinone on the final day of the season to beat it, finishing with a spectacular overhead kick.

International Soccer

The "Viking clap" popularized by Iceland fans at Euro 2016 originated with fans of Scottish club side Motherwell.

Oldest player at an Africa Cup of Nations finals tournament

Egyptian goalkeeper Essam El-Hadary (b. 15 Jan 1973) played in the 2017 Africa Cup of Nations final against Cameroon aged 44 years 21 days. His hopes of a record fifth tournament victory were dashed as Cameroon ran out 2–1 winners at the Stade de l'Amitié in Libreville, Gabon, on 6 Feb.

Oldest player at a UEFA European Championships

Gábor Király (b. 1 Apr 1976) was aged 40 years 74 days when he played for Hungary in their first-round match against Austria at the Stade Matmut Atlantique in Bordeaux, France, on 14 Jun 2016. He made his debut against the same side in 1998.

After missing a penalty in the 2016 Copa América final shoot-out, Lionel Messi announced his international retirement. A huge campaign by fans persuaded him to reverse his decision.

◄ MOST GOALS SCORED BY A SUBSTITUTE IN A COPA AMÉRICA MATCH

On 10 Jun 2016, Lionel Messi came off the bench for Argentina to score three times against Panama at Soldier Field in Chicago, Illinois, USA. He equalled the feat of Paulo Valentim, who scored a hat-trick for Brazil against Uruguay at the Estadio Monumental in Buenos Aires, Argentina, on 26 Mar 1959.

◄ FASTEST GOAL SCORED IN A FIFA WORLD CUP QUALIFIER

On 10 Oct 2016, Christian Benteke found the net for Belgium against Gibraltar just 8.1 sec after kick-off at the Estádio Algarve in Algarve, Portugal. Gibraltar started with the ball, but after just two touches Benteke was through on goal. He scored twice more as Belgium went on to win the match 6–0.

► MOST UEFA EUROPEAN CHAMPIONSHIP GOALS (INDIVIDUAL)

At Euro 2016, Cristiano Ronaldo notched his ninth Championship goal during Portugal's 2–0 semi-final victory over Wales on 6 Jul. He equalled the mark set by Michel Platini (FRA), who scored nine goals at the 1984 European Championships.

Ronaldo has also achieved the **most UEFA Euro Finals tournaments scored in by a player** – four, from 2004 to 2016.

Longest winless streak by an international soccer team

Andorra failed to win a game in 86 attempts from 17 Nov 2004 to 13 Nov 2016. On 22 Feb 2017, they beat San Marino 2–0 in a friendly.

Most games won by a coach with the same international soccer team

Germany won 97 games under Joachim Löw (DEU) between 16 Aug 2006 and 26 Mar 2017 – most notably the final of the 2014 World Cup.

Highest annual earnings for a footballer (current year)

Cristiano Ronaldo (PRT, see above) earned an estimated $88 m (£60.2 m) in the 12 months to 1 Jun 2016, according to Forbes.

▲ FIRST BROTHERS TO PLAY AGAINST EACH OTHER IN THE UEFA EUROPEAN CHAMPIONSHIPS

Granit and Taulant Xhaka found themselves on opposing sides when Switzerland played Albania in a European Championship group game in Lens, France, on 11 Jun 2016. Younger brother Granit came out on top, with Switzerland winning 1–0 and Taulant being substituted. The brothers were born in Switzerland to Albanian parents.

▶ MOST GOALS AT THE FIFA FUTSAL WORLD CUP BY AN INDIVIDUAL

Alessandro Rosa Vieira (BRA, far right), better known as Falcão, scored 48 goals from 18 Nov 2000 to 21 Sep 2016. Widely regarded as the greatest indoor footballer ever, he won the Futsal World Cup twice and was runner-up once. In his final game ever, Falcão scored a hat-trick in defeat to Iran to reach 10 goals at the 2016 World Cup.

Most games as coach of the same international soccer team

Óscar Tabárez (URY) has managed Uruguay 171 times in two separate spells: 1988–90 and 2006–17. The previous best was 167, by German coach Josef "Sepp" Herberger.

Most frequently played international soccer fixture

As of 2 Sep 2016, Argentina and Uruguay had played each other 187 times. Argentina had won 87 times and Uruguay 57, with 43 draws.

Most penalty shoot-out defeats in the Copa América by a team

Argentina have been knocked out of the Copa América on penalty kicks five times: in 1995, 2004, 2011, 2015 and 2016.

▲ SMALLEST COUNTRY BY POPULATION TO QUALIFY FOR THE UEFA EUROPEAN CHAMPIONSHIPS

Iceland qualified for the 2016 European Championships with a population of just 331,918. At the finals in France, they reached the knockout stages, beating England 2–1 before losing 5–2 to France in the quarter-finals on 3 Jul.

American Football

Betting on the annual Super Bowl coin toss is a popular tradition in the USA. After 51 games, tails led heads 27–24.

▼ LARGEST POINTS COMEBACK IN A SUPER BOWL MATCH

On 5 Feb 2017, the New England Patriots recovered from a deficit of 25 points to win Super Bowl LI at the NRG Stadium in Houston, Texas, USA. They had trailed opponents the Atlanta Falcons 28–3 in the third quarter before coming back to win 34–28 in overtime.

Quarterback Tom Brady (pictured below and inset) achieved the **most passes completed in a Super Bowl game** – 43 – and the **most yards gained passing in a Super Bowl game** – 466. It was Brady's fifth Super Bowl victory, equalling Charles Haley's record for the **most Super Bowl wins by an individual player**. Brady was also voted Most Valuable Player (MVP) for the fourth time – the **most Super Bowl MVP awards**.

All teams and players USA, unless otherwise indicated.

Highest completion percentage in an NFL season

Quarterback Sam Bradford of the Minnesota Vikings achieved a completion percentage of 71.6% in 2016, eclipsing the mark of 71.2% set by Drew Brees in 2011.

Highest field goal percentage in an NFL career

As of 31 Dec 2016, Justin Tucker had converted 168 of 187 field goals for the Baltimore Ravens, giving him a success rate of 89.8%.

Most pass completions by a rookie in an NFL season

Carson Wentz completed 379 passes for the Philadelphia Eagles in 2016. Wentz beat the previous best of 354, set by Sam Bradford for the St Louis Rams in 2010.

Most seasons passing for 5,000 yards in an NFL career

New Orleans Saints quarterback Drew Brees has passed for more than 5,000 yards in a season five times: in 2008, 2011–13 and 2016.

▲ **FIRST NFL PLAYER TO SCORE POSTSEASON TOUCHDOWNS BY RUSHING, RECEIVING AND KICK-RETURNING IN ONE GAME**

On 14 Jan 2017, Dion Lewis scored three different kinds of touchdown during the New England Patriots' 31-16 win over the Houston Texans. Gale Sayers (1965) and Tyreek Hill (2016) have also done this, but only in the regular season.

First NFL quarterback to pass for 4,000 yards in his first two seasons
Jameis Winston passed for more than 4,000 yards for the Tampa Bay Buccaneers during the 2015 and 2016 seasons.

Most fourth-quarter comebacks by a quarterback in an NFL season
Matthew Stafford registered eight fourth-quarter come-from-behind victories for the Detroit Lions during the 2016 season.

Youngest NFL coach
On 12 Jan 2017, Sean McVay (b. 24 Jan 1986) became the youngest NFL head coach of the modern era when he was appointed by the Los Angeles Rams aged 30 years 354 days.

Most times passing and running for touchdowns in one NFL game
On 8 Sep 2016, Cam Newton threw a touchdown pass and ran for one touchdown for the Carolina Panthers against the Denver Broncos. It was the 32nd time in Newton's career that he had done so – one more than Steve Young (1985–99).

Heaviest NFL player to throw a touchdown pass
On 26 Dec 2016, Dontari Poe threw a touchdown pass for the Kansas City Chiefs during their 33-10 victory against the Denver Broncos. He weighs 346 lb (156.94 kg; 24 st 10 lb).

Poe's 1-yard scoring run in the Chiefs' 33-3 win against the San Diego Chargers on 22 Nov 2015 also makes him the **heaviest NFL player to score a rushing touchdown**.

▲ MOST CONSECUTIVE FIELD GOALS BY AN NFL KICKER

Adam Vinatieri converted 44 consecutive field goals while playing for the Indianapolis Colts during the 2015 and 2016 seasons. Vinatieri surpassed the previous mark of 42, set by Mike Vanderjagt (CAN) in the 2002–04 seasons.

The **most consecutive extra points by an NFL kicker** is 523, achieved by the New England Patriots' Stephen Gostkowski in 2006–16.

▲ MOST PENALTIES BY A TEAM IN AN NFL GAME

The Oakland Raiders gave away 23 penalties for a total of 200 yards against the Tampa Bay Buccaneers on 30 Oct 2016. Three sides had previously given away 22 penalties: the Brooklyn Tigers and the Chicago Bears in 1944, and the San Francisco 49ers in 1998. Despite the penalty count, the Raiders won in overtime, 30–24.

Baseball

In 2016, the New York Mets and the Miami Marlins sold the most expensive hot dogs in Major League Baseball: $6.25 (£5.10).

All teams and players USA, unless otherwise indicated.

The Cleveland Indians not only lost the 2016 World Series, they also gained an unwanted record – the **longest World Series drought (current)**: 68 years. They last won the title in 1948.

Youngest person to hit 500 home runs in an MLB career

On 7 Aug 2016, the New York Yankees' Alex Rodriguez announced his retirement from baseball. "A-Rod" hit 696 home runs in his career, passing 500 on 4 Aug 2007, aged 32 years 8 days. He also hit the **most grand slam home runs in an MLB career**: 25.

Longest postseason baseball match (nine innings)

On 13 Oct 2016, Game 5 of the National League Division Series between the Los Angeles Dodgers and the Washington Nationals lasted for 4 hr 32 min. The Dodgers came out 4–3 winners at Nationals Park in Washington, DC, USA.

▼ LONGEST WORLD SERIES DROUGHT

On 2 Nov 2016, the Chicago Cubs clinched the World Series with a dramatic 8–7 victory in Game 7 against the Cleveland Indians at Progressive Field in Cleveland, Ohio, USA. This ended one of the most celebrated title droughts in US sports. The Cubs' last World Series victory came on 14 Oct 1908 – a gap of 108 years 19 days.

Most pinch-hit home runs in an MLB match by a team

On 8 Apr 2016, the St Louis Cardinals hit three pinch-hit home runs (i.e., by substitute batters) against the Atlanta Braves at Turner Field in Atlanta, Georgia, USA. Jeremy Hazelbaker, Aledmys Díaz (CUB) and Greg Garcia helped the Cardinals to a 7–4 victory.

The Cardinals went on to score the **most pinch-hit home runs in an MLB season by a team**. They hit 15, one more than the San Francisco Giants and the Arizona Diamondbacks managed in 2001.

Most valuable baseball franchise

The New York Yankees were valued at $3.4 bn (£2.36 bn) by Forbes as of 31 Mar 2016 – the 19th consecutive year that the club had topped the baseball business standings. In second place were the Los Angeles Dodgers, valued at $2.5 bn (£1.73 bn).

Most runs batted in during a World Series game

The Chicago Cubs' Addison Russell batted in six runs during Game 6 of the 2016 World Series against the Cleveland Indians on 1 Nov. This equalled the mark set by Bobby Richardson in 1960, Hideki Matsui (JPN) in 2009 and Albert Pujols (DOM) in 2011.

Oldest baseball player to reach 30 home runs in one season

David Ortiz (DOM, b. 18 Nov 1975) hit his 30th home run of the season aged 40 years 280 days, for the Boston Red Sox during their 4–3 loss to the Tampa Bay Rays in St Petersburg, Florida, USA, on 24 Aug 2016.

Oldest MLB player to hit his first career home run

On 7 May 2016, pitcher Bartolo Colón (DOM, b. 24 May 1973) hit his first major league home run playing for the New York Mets against the San Diego Padres. He was aged 42 years 349 days.

▲ MOST STRIKEOUTS IN AN MLB MATCH

Max Scherzer threw 20 strikeouts in a single game for the Washington Nationals against the Detroit Tigers on 11 May 2016. The Nationals won the game 3–2. Only two other pitchers have matched Scherzer's achievement: Roger Clemens (twice for the Boston Red Sox, in 1986 and 1996) and Kerry Wood (for the Chicago Cubs in 1998).

◀ YOUNGEST PITCHER TO START A MAJOR LEAGUE BASEBALL (MLB) POSTSEASON GAME

Aged 20 years 68 days, Julio Urías (MEX, b. 12 Aug 1996) took the ball for the Los Angeles Dodgers against the Chicago Cubs in Game 4 of the National League Championship Series on 19 Oct 2016.

The **youngest MLB player** was also a pitcher: Joe Nuxhall (b. 30 Jul 1928) played for the Cincinnati Reds aged 15 years 316 days on 10 Jun 1944.

▲ MOST MLB HOME RUNS HIT IN SEQUENTIAL FIRST GAMES

Rookie shortstop Trevor Story hit at least one home run in his first four games for the Colorado Rockies in 2016. Story hit two on his MLB debut against the Arizona Diamondbacks on 4 Apr at Chase Field in Phoenix, Arizona, USA. He followed up with homers on 5 Apr and 6 Apr, also against Arizona, before hitting two more against the San Diego Padres on 8 Apr.

▲ LOWEST EARNED RUN AVERAGE (ERA) IN AN MLB SEASON

In 2016, Zach Britton of the Baltimore Orioles pitched 67 innings while allowing only four earned runs, giving him an ERA of 0.54. This is the lowest ERA recorded by any MLB pitcher with at least 50 innings pitched in a season.

Basketball

The first basketball game, in Springfield, Massachusetts, USA, on 21 Dec 1891, used peach baskets for hoops. The score was 1–0.

All records are National Basketball Association (NBA) or Women's National Basketball Association (WNBA). All teams and players are USA, unless otherwise indicated.

First player to lead all five statistical categories in a Finals series

LeBron James scored 208 points, 62 assists, 79 rebounds, 18 steals and 16 blocks in the Cleveland Cavaliers' 4-3 Finals win over the Golden State Warriors from 2 to 19 Jun 2016. The Cavaliers came from 1-3 games down to clinch the decisive Game 7 at the Oracle Arena in Oakland, California, USA, on 19 Jun. This is the **largest comeback in a Finals series**.

▼ MOST CONSECUTIVE FIELD GOALS (WNBA)

Forward Nneka Ogwumike scored 23 field goals in a row for the Los Angeles Sparks during a three-game period on 7-14 Jun 2016.

Most three-point field goals converted by an NBA team in a game

The Cleveland Cavaliers converted 25 three-point field goals during a 123–98 playoff win against the Atlanta Hawks on 4 May 2016.

The Golden State Warriors made the **most three-point field goals in a season (team)** in 2015-16: 1,077.

Most defensive rebounds in a career

Kevin Garnett grabbed 11,453 defensive rebounds over the course of a 22-year career with the Minnesota Timberwolves, Boston Celtics and Brooklyn Nets from the 1995–96 season to 2015–16.

Most consecutive free throws in a game

Two players have hit 24 straight free throws in a single NBA game: DeMar DeRozan on 4 Mar 2016 and Dirk Nowitzki (DEU) on 17 May 2011.

Most turnovers in a season

James Harden committed 374 turnovers while playing for the Houston Rockets during the 2015–16 season.

▲ MOST THREE-POINT FIELD GOALS MADE IN AN NBA PLAYOFF GAME

Klay Thompson netted 11 three-point field goals playing for the Golden State Warriors on 28 May 2016. The record-breaking tally took place during a 108–101 victory over the Oklahoma City Thunder in Oklahoma, USA, during Game 6 of the Warriors' playoff series.

Most three-point field goals made in an NBA game by both teams

Between them, the Dallas Mavericks and Golden State Warriors converted 39 three-point field goals on 25 Mar 2016.

Most free throws in a WNBA career

Tamika Catchings converted 2,004 free throws for the Indiana Fever in 2002–16. The prolific Catchings also recorded the **most rebounds in a WNBA career** – 3,316 – and the **most steals in a WNBA career** – 1,074. In addition, she won four consecutive gold medals at the Summer Olympic Games (see p.555).

▲ MOST POINTS SCORED IN THE FIRST QUARTER OF AN NBA MATCH

The Cleveland Cavaliers' Kevin Love scored 34 points in the first quarter of a game against the Portland Trail Blazers on 23 Nov 2016.

The NBA record for **most points scored in any quarter** (37) was set by Klay Thompson of the Golden State Warriors against the Sacramento Kings on 23 Jan 2015.

Most points scored in a WNBA Finals career
Minnesota Lynx forward Maya Moore has scored 268 points in WNBA Finals matches. She beat Diana Taurasi's tally of 262 with 18 points against the Los Angeles Sparks on 9 Oct 2016.

▶ MOST CONSECUTIVE NBA GAMES TO SCORE A THREE-POINT FIELD GOAL

Stephen Curry made a three-point field goal in 157 straight games for the Golden State Warriors from 13 Nov 2014 to 3 Nov 2016.

Curry also scored the **most three-point field goals by an individual in an NBA Finals** (32), while playing for the Warriors against the Cleveland Cavaliers in 2016.

The prolific point guard recorded the **most three-point field goals in an NBA regular season** (402) in 2015–16. He has also had the **most consecutive seasons leading the NBA three-point field-goal chart** (four), in 2012–13, 2013–14, 2014–15 and 2015–16 – all for the Golden State Warriors.

Even with Stephen Curry, there's always room for improvement. As an incentive to tighten up his game, Curry's mother fines him $100 (£80) every time he commits a turnover on the court.

Ice Hockey

In 1932, Maple Leaf Gardens in Toronto, Canada, became the first ice hockey arena to use a four-sided game clock.

▶ PATRICK KANE

The Chicago Blackhawks' Patrick Kane (b. 19 Nov 1988) had a 2015–16 season to remember. He scored in 26 consecutive matches and became the first US-born player to win the Hart Memorial Trophy since its inception in 1923–24. Kane is also the **youngest player to score a Stanley Cup-winning goal in overtime**. He found the net against the Philadelphia Flyers in Game 6 of the Stanley Cup aged 21 years 202 days on 9 Jun 2010.

All records relate to the National Hockey League (NHL) contested in the USA and Canada. All teams and players are USA, unless otherwise indicated.

Fastest four goals

On 3 Apr 2015, the St Louis Blues and the Dallas Stars combined to score four goals in 49 sec during a game in Dallas, Texas, USA. The goal glut broke the 1983 record of 53 sec, which had been set by the Toronto Maple Leafs (CAN) and the Chicago Blackhawks.

In the same game, the teams scored three goals in 38 sec from the start of the second period – the **fastest three goals by both teams from the start of a period**. Final score: 7–5 to St Louis.

▲ **MOST CONSECUTIVE GAME WINS FOR A GOALTENDER TO START A SEASON**
With a 5–0 win against the Detroit Red Wings on 12 Nov 2016, Carey Price of the Montreal Canadiens (both CAN) became the first NHL goalie to win his first 10 games of a season.

Shortest time between goals
Columbus Blue Jackets forward Nick Foligno and Minnesota Wild forward Mikael Granlund (FIN) scored just 2 sec apart in a game played in Columbus, Ohio, USA, on 5 Jan 2016. The 2-sec gap between goals tied a record set by Boston's Ken Linseman and St Louis' Doug Gilmore on 19 Dec 1987.

Most matches won in a season by a goaltender
The Washington Capitals' Braden Holtby won 48 games in 2015–16, matching Martin Brodeur (both CAN) for the New Jersey Devils in 2006–07.

Longest point streak by a rookie defenseman
Shayne Gostisbehere recorded one or more points for 15 consecutive games in his first professional NHL season for the Philadelphia Flyers from 19 Jan to 20 Feb 2016. In ice hockey, players are awarded points for goals and assists.

Most consecutive shootout goals by both teams in a game
The Florida Panthers and the New York Islanders scored nine straight goals to open a shootout in Sunrise, Florida, USA, on 27 Nov 2015. The 10th shooter missed for the Islanders, and the Panthers emerged with the win.

Eight games on 27 Nov 2015 ended in overtime or a shootout, tying the **most overtime games in one day**, previously set on 22 Feb 2007.

Most hits by a player in one season

Hits are an aggressive defensive manoeuvre in which players use their bodies to separate an opposing player from the puck. Matt Martin (CAN) made 382 hits for the New York Islanders during the 2014–15 season. He broke his own record of 374, set during 2011–12.

Derek Stepan, Fabian Brunnström (SWE), Alex Smart and Real Cloutier (both CAN) all scored three goals on NHL debut.

Most penalty minutes in a playoff game

Deryk Engelland accrued 42 penalty min for the Calgary Flames against the Vancouver Canucks (all CAN) in a Stanley Cup playoff match on 17 Apr 2015. He matched the mark set by Dave "The Hammer" Schultz (CAN) for the Philadelphia Flyers against the Toronto Maple Leafs (CAN) on 22 Apr 1976.

The **most penalty minutes in an NHL game** is 67, achieved by Randy Holt (CAN) for the Los Angeles Kings against the Philadelphia Flyers on 11 Mar 1979.

Most overtime goals in a regular-season career

Alex Ovechkin (RUS) scored his 19th regular-season game-winning goal during overtime, playing for the Washington Capitals in a 6–5 win over the Toronto Maple Leafs (CAN) on 3 Jan 2017. This tied him with Jaromír Jágr (CZE). Ovechkin has scored more than 1,000 points for the Capitals since 2005.

Longest postseason drought by a team

The Edmonton Oilers (CAN) missed the playoffs for a 10th consecutive year following the 2015–16 season. The only other team to miss the playoffs for 10 years in a row was the Florida Panthers in 2002–11.

▲ **YOUNGEST CAPTAIN OF A TEAM**
Connor McDavid (b. 13 Jan 1997) was named captain of the Edmonton Oilers (both CAN) aged 19 years 266 days on 5 Oct 2016. McDavid was 20 days younger than Gabriel Landeskog (SWE, b. 23 Nov 1992) had been when he was named as captain of the Colorado Avalanche in 2012.

Rugby

Fiji's gold at the men's rugby sevens tournament at Rio 2016 was the country's first ever Olympic medal.

Most rugby union Five/Six Nations grand slam wins

England's victory in the 2016 Six Nations was the 13th time they had completed a grand slam by winning every game they played in the tournament. Their previous grand slams were achieved in 1913–14, 1921, 1923–24, 1928, 1957, 1980, 1991–92, 1995 and 2003.

Most penalty goals kicked in a rugby union Five/Six Nations match

On 19 Mar 2016, Maxime Machenaud (FRA) kicked seven successful penalties against England at the Stade de France in Paris, France. He became only the eighth player ever to achieve this feat in the competition.

Most rugby union Rugby Championship matches won

Formed in 2012 to replace the Tri-Nations, the Rugby Championship features New Zealand, Australia, South Africa and Argentina. On 8 Oct 2016, New Zealand won their 24th game in the competition. The All Blacks have only ever lost twice in the history of the tournament, with one draw.

▼ MOST TRIES IN A SUPER LEAGUE SEASON

New Zealand-born winger Denny Solomona scored 40 tries for the Castleford Tigers (UK) from 7 Feb to 25 Sep 2016, finishing with his seventh hat-trick of the year in the final regular-season game against Widnes Vikings. Solomona beat the previous record of 36, set in 2004 by Lesley Vainikolo. In Dec 2016, Solomona switched codes to join rugby union side Sale Sharks.

On 8 Oct 2016, Denny Solomona made his international debut for Samoa when they played Fiji in Apia, Samoa. It was the first ever home fixture for the Samoan rugby league team. Fiji won the game 20–18.

Most rugby league State of Origin matches played

Known as the greatest rivalry in Australian sport, the State of Origin is an annual three-game series played between two state representative sides: Queensland and New South Wales. Hooker Cameron Smith (AUS) made 39 appearances for Queensland in 2003–16. In that time, he missed just one game, in 2010, owing to injury.

Most NRL appearances by a forward

One-club man Corey Parker (AUS) made 347 appearances for the Brisbane Broncos from 24 Mar 2001 to 16 Sep 2016.

Most consecutive wins in international rugby union

New Zealand and England may share the Tier 1 record for consecutive wins (see opposite), but the overall record is held by a lesser-known rugby nation: Cyprus. Nicknamed "The Mouflons", after a native wild sheep, they won 24 games on the spin between 29 Nov 2008 and 1 Nov 2014 before suffering a 39–20 defeat to Latvia.

Most points scored in a single Olympic rugby union tournament (individual)

At Rio 2016, rugby returned to the Olympics for the first time since 1924. With her 10 tries in the women's tournament, winger Portia Woodman (NZ) racked up 50 points. She won a silver medal, with the All Blacks losing 24–17 to Australia in the final on 8 Aug 2016.

▲ **MOST POINTS SCORED IN AN ENGLISH PREMIERSHIP RUGBY UNION CAREER**

Fly-half Charlie Hodgson (UK) retired in 2016 having racked up 2,623 points in the English Premiership. Over the course of a 16-year career at Sale Sharks (2000–11) and then Saracens (2011–16), Hodgson scored 39 tries, 332 conversions, 550 penalties and 38 drop goals. He also won 38 international caps for England.

◄ **MOST POINTS SCORED IN THE RUGBY LEAGUE FOUR NATIONS BY AN INDIVIDUAL**

Australian halfback legend Johnathan Thurston amassed 126 points over three Four Nations tournaments: 2009, 2011 and 2016, with injury ruling him out in 2010 and 2014. Thurston also set the record for **most consecutive rugby league State of Origin matches played** – 36, for Queensland from 25 May 2005 to 13 Jul 2016.

▲ **MOST INTERNATIONAL RUGBY UNION APPEARANCES (FEMALE)**
England prop Rochelle "Rocky" Clark had won 122 international caps as of 17 Mar 2017. She broke the record of 115 caps (held by Scotland's Donna Kennedy) on 19 Nov 2016, coming on as a replacement against New Zealand. Clark made her debut against Canada on 28 Jun 2003.

▲ **MOST CONSECUTIVE INTERNATIONAL RUGBY UNION WINS BY A TIER 1 NATION**
New Zealand won 18 consecutive internationals between 15 Aug 2015 and 22 Oct 2016. The All Blacks' run finally came to an end on 5 Nov 2016, when they suffered a 40–29 defeat to Ireland at Soldier Field in Chicago, USA. This feat was subsequently matched by England, who won 18 consecutive games from 10 Oct 2015 to 11 Mar 2017 before losing 13–9 on 18 Mar – also to Ireland.

Tennis

Tennis originated as the French game *jeu de paume* ("game of the palm"), which was played with bare hands not rackets.

Most consecutive main-draw Grand Slam tournaments played

An injured Roger Federer (CHE) withdrew from the 2016 French Open, bringing to an end a sequence of 65 successive main-draw appearances at tennis's four Grand Slam tournaments. On his comeback at the 2017 Australian Open, a resurgent Federer beat Rafael Nadal in the final to secure his 18th title and extend his record for the most Grand Slam singles titles won by a male.

As of 29 Jan 2017, Federer had also achieved the **most Grand Slam singles matches won by a male** – 314. Furthermore, according to Forbes, he earned $68 m (£50.7 m) in the 12 months leading up to 30 Jun 2016, giving him the **highest annual earnings for a male tennis player (current year)**.

▲ **MOST DAVIS CUP DOUBLES MATCHES WON**
On 16 Jul 2016, India's Leander Paes (above front) won his 42nd doubles match in the Davis Cup, with Rohan Bopanna (IND, above rear) in the third rubber of an Asia/Oceania Group I tie against South Korea in Chandigarh, India. Paes equalled the mark set by Nicola Pietrangeli (ITA), who won 42 Davis Cup doubles matches from 1954 to 1972.

Most consecutive weeks as world No.1 (female)
In a record-breaking year for Serena Williams (USA), she drew level with Steffi Graf's (DEU) record of 186 weeks at the top of the WTA rankings. Serena's reign lasted from 18 Feb 2013 to 5 Sep 2016, when she was replaced by Angelique Kerber.

Fewest matches completed to reach a Grand Slam semi-final
At the 2016 US Open, three of Novak Djokovic's opponents retired hurt. Withdrawals by Jiří Veselý (CZE, arm injury), Mikhail Youzhny (RUS, leg) and Jo-Wilfried Tsonga (FRA, knee) meant that Djokovic reached the semi-finals having played just two matches – with a total time of 6 hr 24 min.

Most aces served in a WTA match
Kristýna Plíšková (CZE) hit 31 aces in the second round of the Australian Open in Melbourne on 20 Jan 2016. She went on to lose against Monica Puig (PRI), having squandered five match points.

▶ **MOST GRAND SLAM SINGLES TITLES WON (FEMALE, OPEN ERA)**
On 28 Jan 2017, Serena Williams (USA) beat sister Venus 6–4, 6–4 to win the Australian Open at Melbourne Park. It was Serena's 23rd Grand Slam title, putting her one ahead of Steffi Graf. Since her main-draw Grand Slam debut at the 1998 Australian Open, Serena has racked up the **most tennis Grand Slam singles matches won** – an incredible 316.

When they played each other in the 2017 Australian Open final, the Williams sisters' combined age was 71 years 349 days – the **oldest aggregate age for Grand Slam singles finalists (open era)**.

◀ MOST CONSECUTIVE GRAND SLAM SINGLES MATCHES WON (MALE, OPEN ERA)

◀ MOST CONSECUTIVE GRAND SLAM SINGLES MATCHES WON (MALE, OPEN ERA)

Novak Djokovic (SRB) won 30 consecutive Grand Slam matches from 29 Jun 2015 to 29 Jun 2016. His streak included victories at Wimbledon and the US, Australian and French Opens – a "Career Grand Slam", previously achieved by Australia's Rod Laver in 1969. "Nole" won 90 sets and lost just 11 during his remarkable run.

Most Olympic tennis medals won

Venus Williams (USA) won her fifth Olympic medal at Rio 2016, claiming a silver in the mixed doubles with Rajeev Ram (USA) on 14 Aug 2016. Her other four medals had been gold, winning three doubles titles with her sister Serena and the singles at Sydney 2000. Venus shares the record with Kathleen "Kitty" McKane Godfree (UK), who won five medals in 1920–24.

The 2017 Australian Open was Venus's 73rd Grand Slam – the **most Grand Slam women's singles tournaments played in the open era**. She went on to reach the final.

Longest wheelchair tennis match

On 13 Sep 2016, Jamie Burdekin and Andy Lapthorne (UK) won the bronze-medal match in the men's Paralympic quad doubles after a 4-hr 25-min epic. They beat the Israeli pair of Itai Erenlib and Shraga Weinberg 3–6, 6–4, 7–6 (7–2).

> A triumphant 2016 ended with Andy Murray receiving a knighthood in the Queen's New Year Honours list.

▲ MOST OLYMPIC SINGLES GOLD MEDALS WON

At Rio 2016, Andy Murray (UK) successfully defended the title he had won on home soil at London 2012, becoming the first player to claim a pair of gold medals in the tennis singles. Murray defeated Juan Martín del Potro 7–5, 4–6, 6–2, 7–5 in an epic encounter lasting more than 4 hr. Del Potro's silver was his second Olympic singles medal, having won the bronze in London.

Boxing

Only one man has ever fought for the world heavyweight title in their first professional bout: Pete Rademacher (USA), in 1957.

▲ LONGEST-REIGNING BOXING WORLD CHAMPION (FEMALE)
Momo Koseki's win over Chie Higano (both JPN) on 11 Nov 2016 at Korakuen Hall in Tokyo, Japan, was her 17th successful defence of the World Boxing Council (WBC) atomweight title. She had won the belt with a second-round technical knock-out against Winyu Paradorn Gym (THA) on 11 Aug 2008 in Tokyo. As of her 2016 win, Koseki's reign had lasted 8 years 92 days.

Most Olympic boxing gold medals won (female)
Claressa Shields (USA) and Nicola Adams (UK) have each won two Olympic gold medals, at London 2012 and Rio 2016. Flyweight Adams successfully defended her title on 20 Aug aged 33 years 299 days, becoming the **oldest Olympic boxing gold medallist (female)**.

Middleweight Shields matched Adams' achievement, beating Nouchka Fontijn (NLD) on 21 Aug 2016. Shields won her first gold medal aged just 17 years 145 days – the **youngest Olympic boxing gold medallist (female)**.

The **most Olympic gold medals won in boxing** is three: achieved by László Papp (HUN) in 1948–56, Teófilo Stevenson (CUB) in 1972–80, and Félix Savón (CUB) in 1992–2000.

Most consecutive Olympic boxing gold medals at the same weight category (county)
On 17 Aug 2016, Daniyar Yeleussinov won Kazakhstan's fourth consecutive Olympic welterweight gold medal. This matched Cuba's four consecutive victories at heavyweight, achieved between 1992 and 2004.

Longest time between lineal champions
On 16 Sep 2016, Shinsuke Yamanaka (JPN) became the first lineal bantamweight champion since 1987 – a gap of 29 years 171 days, as measured by *The Ring* magazine. Yamanaka beat Panama's Anselmo Moreno at the Edion Arena in Osaka, Japan, sealing victory in the seventh round after a thrilling fight that featured five knockdowns.

Oldest boxing world champion
On 17 Dec 2016, nearing his 52nd birthday, Bernard "The Executioner" Hopkins (USA, b. 15 Jan 1965) fought his final professional fight against Joe Smith Jr (USA), losing in the eighth round. Hopkins won three titles aged 49 years 94 days when he outpointed Kazakhstan's Beibut Shumenov at the DC Armory in Washington, DC, USA, on 19 Apr 2014.

◀ HIGHEST KNOCKOUT (K/O) PERCENTAGE BY A MIDDLEWEIGHT BOXING CHAMPION

On 10 Sep 2016, Gennady "Triple G" Golovkin (KAZ) stopped the previously undefeated Kell Brook (UK) in the fifth round at the O2 Arena in London, UK. It was his 23rd consecutive victory achieved inside 12 rounds. The hard-hitting Kazakh boasted a career k/o rate of 33 from 36 bouts, or 91.67%.

▼ MOST POWER PUNCHES THROWN IN A SUPER FEATHERWEIGHT BOXING BOUT

A "power punch" is any punch not considered a jab. During the bout between Francisco Vargas and Orlando Salido (both MEX) at the StubHub Center in Carson, California, USA, on 4 Jun 2016, CompuBox counted a combined total of 1,593 power punches thrown – 776 by Vargas, 817 by Salido. Despite 615 of these punches landing, the contest was declared a draw after 12 rounds, with two of the three judges unable to separate the fighters on their scorecards.

The Vargas vs Salido fight was preceded by a traditional "ten count" of the bell in tribute to the boxing legend Muhammad Ali, who had died the previous day at the age of 74.

MOST CONSECUTIVE TITLE DEFENCES

WEIGHT	NAME (NATIONALITY)	DEFENCES	DATES
Heavy	Joe Louis (USA)	25	1937–48
Minimum	Ricardo López (MEX)	21	1991–98
Middle	Bernard Hopkins (USA)	20	1996–2005
Super fly	Khaosai Galaxy (THA)	19	1985–91
Welter	Henry Armstrong (USA)	18	1938–40
Light fly	Yuh Myung-woo (KOR)	17	1986–91
Fly	Pongsaklek Wonjongkam (THA)	17	2001–07
Bantam	Orlando Canizales (USA)	16	1988–94
Cruiser	Johnny Nelson (UK)	=13	1999–2005
	Marco Huck (DEU)	=13	2009–14
Super light	Julio César Chávez (MEX)	12	1989–93
Super feather	Brian Mitchell (ZAF)	12	1987–91
Light middle	Gianfranco Rosi (ITA)	11	1989–94

All figures correct as of 8 Nov 2016

Highest annual earnings for a boxer (current year)

According to *Forbes*, five-division world champion Floyd Mayweather Jr (USA) earned $44 m (£30.1 m) between 1 Jun 2015 and 1 Jun 2016. Of that total, $32 m (£21.9 m) came directly from Mayweather's fight earnings, while $12 m (£8.2 m) was generated by sponsorship deals.

▲ MOST LINEAL WORLD HEAVYWEIGHT CHAMPIONSHIP WINS

In 2016, boxing lost a true legend: Muhammad Ali (USA), who won three "lineal" world titles against undisputed champions at their weight class. A "lineal" boxing title is one that is first held by an undisputed champion but then passes to a fighter who defeats him or her. Ali's first win came in 1964 against Sonny Liston (USA) and his second with the "Rumble in the Jungle" bout against George Foreman (USA) in 1974. Ali's final lineal title came when he beat Leon Spinks (USA, above left with Ali) in New Orleans, Louisiana, USA, on 15 Sep 1978. It is a fitting world record for the fighter known simply as "The Greatest".

Martial Arts

At Rio 2016, Cheick Sallah Cissé (CIV) won taekwondo gold with the match's very last kick – to the head...

First Ultimate Fighting Championship fighter to hold two titles simultaneously

On 12 Nov 2016, reigning UFC featherweight champion Conor McGregor (IRL) faced Eddie Alvarez (USA) at Madison Square Garden in New York City, USA, for the lightweight title. McGregor won in two rounds, making him world champion at two different weights.

The McGregor–Alvarez bout was the headline event of UFC 205, which generated a reported $17,700,000 (£14,061,200). That makes it the **highest revenue earned from ticket sales for a UFC event**.

Most consecutive defences of the UFC flyweight title (male)

Demetrious "Mighty Mouse" Johnson (USA) defended his title eight times between 22 Sep 2012 and 23 Apr 2016. He was the UFC's first flyweight champion, winning the division's inaugural title bout against Joseph Benavidez (USA) on a split decision.

Most medal-winning countries at the Summer Olympic Games in judo

Rio 2016 saw 26 different countries win judo medals between 6 and 12 Aug, including Cuba, United Arab Emirates and Slovenia. Majlinda Kelmendi's victory in the women's -52 kg division was a first Olympic medal for Kosovo.

Most sumo top division wins

Professional sumo has a top division of 42 wrestlers known as the *makuuchi*. Between 8 Jul 2007 and 24 Jul 2016, Hakuhō Shō (MNG, see opposite) racked up 903 wins in this division, the most by any *rikishi* (wrestler). He surpassed the previous record of 879 wins at the 2016 Summer Grand Sumo Tournament in Tokyo, Japan.

▲ **FIRST ATHLETE TO WIN BOXING AND MMA WORLD TITLES**

On 14 Nov 2015, Holly Holm beat champion Ronda Rousey (both USA) to become Ultimate Fighting Championship (UFC) bantamweight champion. In so doing, she became the first athlete – male or female – to hold a world title in Mixed Martial Arts (MMA) and boxing. Holly had previously won the WBA welterweight title back in 2006.

Most Olympic taekwondo gold medals won (overall)
Four athletes have won two Olympic taekwondo gold medals. Ha Tae-kyung (KOR) and Chen Yi-an (TPE) both won golds at the 1988 Games in Seoul, South Korea, and in Barcelona, Spain, in 1992, when taekwondo was still classed as a demonstration sport. Hwang Kyung-seon (KOR) won gold in the women's middleweight division at Beijing 2008 and London 2012, while Jade Jones (UK) won the women's 57 kg title in 2012 and at Rio 2016.

The **most Olympic taekwondo medals won (female)** is three, achieved by Hwang Kyung-seon between 2004 and 2012 and Maria Espinosa (MEX) between 2008 and 2016.

▼ MOST UNDEFEATED TOP-DIVISION SUMO CHAMPIONSHIP WINS

A *zenshō-yūshō* is a sumo tournament victory attained without a single loss. Between 2007 and 2016, Hakuhō Shō (MNG, born Mönkhbatyn Davaajargal, below right) did this 12 times, four more than Futabayama Sadaji (JPN, achieved 1936–43) and Taihō Kōki (JPN, 1963–69). Hakuhō's 12th *zenshō-yūshō* came on 22 May 2016. He beat Kakuryū Rikisaburō by *utchari*, throwing him outside the ring.

In 1968, Hakuhō's father Jigjidiin won Mongolia's first Olympic medal – for wrestling.

◄ HIGHEST-SELLING PAY-PER-VIEW UFC EVENT

Featuring the eagerly anticipated rematch between Conor McGregor (IRL) and Nate Diaz (USA) as its main event, UFC 202 achieved 1,650,000 pay-per-view buys. The event was held in Las Vegas, Nevada, USA, on 20 Aug 2016. The headline bout was eventually won on a majority decision by McGregor, revenge for his second-round loss to Diaz on 5 Mar 2016.

▲ MOST CONSECUTIVE OLYMPIC GAMES TO WIN GOLD IN INDIVIDUAL EVENTS (FEMALE)

Kaori Icho (JPN) won four consecutive gold medals between Athens 2004 and Rio 2016. Her first three golds came in the 63 kg freestyle, with her fourth won in the 58 kg freestyle. An utterly dominant force in women's wrestling, Kaori was undefeated in all competitions for 13 years before finally losing a match in Jan 2016. But she still came out on top in Rio, despite trailing with 5 sec remaining of her final against Valeria Koblova (RUS).

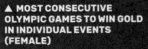

Cricket

On 12 Dec 2016, Shania-Lee Swart (ZAF) scored 160 of her team's total of 169. None of her team-mates scored a single run!

There was one consolation for Pakistan during their record-breaking ODI defeat against England. Mohammad Amir scored 58 off 28 balls to record the highest ODI score by a No.11 batsman.

Highest team score in a Twenty20 International

On 6 Sep 2016, Australia scored 263 for 3 from their 20 overs against Sri Lanka at the Pallekele International Cricket Stadium in Kandy, Sri Lanka. Their innings was built around a destructive 65-ball 145 not out from opener Glenn Maxwell.

Most consecutive balls faced without scoring a run in a Test match

As they battled to save a draw against Sri Lanka on 30 Jul 2016, Australia faced 154 balls – or 25.4 overs – without troubling the scorers. Their efforts were in vain, however, as they lost the match.

Most consecutive days of Test match cricket

Between 21 Jul and 20 Aug 2016, there were 31 consecutive days of Test cricket. The run came to a soggy end when the last three days of South Africa's Test against New Zealand were abandoned because of rain.

◀ HIGHEST TEAM SCORE IN A ONE-DAY INTERNATIONAL (MALE)

On 30 Aug 2016, England scored 444 for 3 against Pakistan at Trent Bridge in Nottingham, UK. Alex Hales (left) top-scored with 171, supported by Jos Buttler (90 not out from 51 balls) and captain Eoin Morgan (57 not out). The mammoth total took England past the previous ODI best of 443, achieved by Sri Lanka for the loss of nine wickets against the Netherlands in Amstelveen on 4 Jul 2006.

▲ FASTEST TIME FOR A BOWLER TO TAKE 100 WICKETS IN ONE-DAY INTERNATIONALS

In dismissing Dhananjaya de Silva (LKA) during a match at Colombo in Sri Lanka on 21 Aug 2016, Mitchell Starc (AUS) claimed his 100th One-Day International (ODI) victim in only his 52nd match. The **fastest time for a bowler to take 100 wickets in ODIs (female)** is Cathryn Fitzpatrick (AUS), achieved in 64 matches between Jul 1993 and Feb 2003.

Most wickets taken in home Test matches (male)

As of Dec 2016, English fast bowler James Anderson had taken 296 wickets in 69 Test matches played on home soil.

Youngest batsman to score hundreds against all Test-playing nations

Born on 8 Aug 1990, Kane Williamson (NZ) was aged 25 years 364 days when he plundered 113 runs against Zimbabwe in Bulawayo, Zimbabwe, on 6–7 Aug 2016. With centuries against all nine Test-playing rivals to his name, Williamson beat the record of 30 years 38 days set by Kumar Sangakkara (LKA) in 2007.

Most matches between Test appearances

On 20 Oct 2016, English spinner Gareth Batty returned to the national side to face Bangladesh. The 39-year-old's previous Test appearance had been on 3–5 Jun 2005 – 142 Tests earlier. Upon his return, Batty took four wickets, helping England to a 22-run victory.

Most runs conceded by opening bowlers in a One-Day International

On 5 Oct 2016, South Africa and Australia contested an ODI at Kingsmead in Durban, South Africa, in which the four opening bowlers conceded a total of 325 runs in 39 overs. Dale Steyn and Kagiso Rabada (both ZAF) and Chris Tremain and Daniel Worrall (both AUS) took just four wickets between them.

Most runs scored in the Indian Premier League (IPL)

Named player of the tournament in 2016, Virat Kohli (IND) has scored 4,110 runs for Royal Challengers Bangalore since the IPL's inception in 2008.

Lasith Malinga (LKA) has taken the **most IPL wickets** – 143 in 98 innings. Malinga's feat is even more remarkable for the fact that he missed two IPL tournaments owing to injury.

◄ **YOUNGEST PLAYER TO SCORE 10,000 TEST MATCH RUNS**

Ex-England captain Alistair Cook (b. 25 Dec 1984) was aged 31 years 157 days when he scored his 10,000th run during his innings of 47 not out against Sri Lanka at Chester-le-Street in County Durham, UK, on 30 May 2016. Cook beat the mark set by Sachin Tendulkar (IND), who was 31 years 326 days when he hit 10,000 on 16 Mar 2005.

▲ **MOST MATCHES AS CAPTAIN IN ONE-DAY INTERNATIONALS (FEMALE)**

Charlotte Edwards (UK) retired in 2016, having captained England in 117 One-Day Internationals since 1997. Over the course of a glittering career in the Test, ODI and Twenty20 arenas, Edwards was responsible for a number of records including the **most runs scored in ODI cricket (female)** – 5,992. Her nine ODI hundreds are also the **most hundreds in an ODI career (female)**.

Golf

Team USA's 17–11 victory in the 2016 Ryder Cup was their first since 2008, and their most decisive victory since 1981.

Lowest score to par at a men's major

On 14–17 Jul 2016, Henrik Stenson (SWE) won the 145th Open Championship at the Royal Troon Golf Club in Ayrshire, UK, with a score of 20 under par. Over four rounds, his total of 264 broke down as 68-65-68-63.

In doing so, Stenson matched the feat of Jason Day (AUS), who won the 97th PGA Championship – held on the Straits Course of Whistling Straits near Kohler in Wisconsin, USA – on 13–16 Aug 2015.

With victory at Rio 2016, Justin Rose became only the fifth golfer to win official tournaments on six different continents. The others are Gary Player, David Graham, Hale Irwin and Bernhard Langer.

▶ FIRST OLYMPIC TOURNAMENT HOLE-IN-ONE

At Rio 2016, golf became an Olympic sport for the first time in 112 years. It was a very happy return for Justin Rose (UK), who hit a hole-in-one on 11 Aug. Selecting a seven-iron at the par-3 fourth hole, he hit a tee shot that pitched 10 ft (3 m) short of the flag before rolling in the hole. Rose shot a round of 67 on his way to victory, becoming golf's first gold medallist since 1904. Jaco van Zyl (ZAF) achieved the second Olympic hole-in-one just two days later.

Q: What bird gives its name to a score of four under par at one hole?

A: Condor

Lowest score after 36 holes at a PGA Tour event

On 12 Jan 2017, Justin Thomas (USA) shot an opening round of 59 at the Sony Open in Hawaii, USA. He followed up with a 64 to register a score of 123 – 17 under par – at the halfway point of the tournament.

The **lowest score after 36 holes at The Players Championship** is 129, by Jason Day (AUS) at TPC Sawgrass in Ponte Vedra Beach in Florida, USA, on 12–13 May 2016. The Players Championship offers the **highest prize fund in golf**: $1.89 m (£1.31 m) in 2016.

Lowest score in a single round at a men's major championship

Golf has four major championships: the Open Championship, the US Open, the PGA Championship and the Masters Tournament. The lowest score in a single round at any of them is 63 – a mark that has been achieved 30 times by 28 golfers. Phil Mickelson (USA) and Henrik Stenson (SWE) joined the club with rounds of 63 at the 145th Open Championship in Ayrshire, UK, on 14–17 Jul 2016. Later that month, Robert Streb (USA) also carded a 63 during the 98th PGA Championship at Baltusrol Golf Club in Springfield, New Jersey, USA, on 29 Jul 2016.

The overall **lowest score in a single round at a major championship** is 61, by Kim Hyo-joo (KOR) at the 2014 Evian Championship on 11 Sep. She was aged 19 at the time and went on to win the tournament.

Most times to host the US Open by a course

Established in 1903, Oakmont Country Club in Pennsylvania, USA, hosted its first US Open in 1927 and went on to stage the major another eight times. The three most recent winners – Dustin Johnson (USA, 2016), Ángel Cabrera (ARG, 2007) and Ernie Els (ZAF, 1994) – were all first-time winners of the event.

Youngest golfer to earn $5 m on the LPGA tour

Born on 24 Apr 1997, Lydia Ko (NZ) was aged just 18 years 303 days when her second-place finish at the Women's Australian Open on 21 Feb 2016 took her career earnings beyond $5 m (£3.47 m).

Korean-born Ko is also the **youngest golfer to win a women's major championship** (aged 18 years 142 days, at the 2015 Evian Championship) and the **youngest golfer ranked world number one** – 17 years 283 days, achieved on 1 Feb 2015.

◄ MOST RYDER CUP TOURNAMENT APPEARANCES BY AN INDIVIDUAL

Phil Mickelson made his 11th appearance for Team USA at the 2016 Ryder Cup, held from 30 Sep to 2 Oct at the Hazeltine National Golf Club in Chaska, Minnesota, USA. Helping his side to a 17–11 victory, Mickelson matched Nick Faldo's 11 consecutive appearances for Europe, which the English golfer made between 1977 and 1997.

◀ LOWEST SINGLE-ROUND SCORE (18 HOLES) AT A PGA TOUR EVENT

Jim Furyk (USA) hit a single-round score of 58 – or 12 under par – during the Travelers Championship in Connecticut, USA, on 7 Aug 2016. Furyk reached the turn in just 27 shots, making seven consecutive birdies on holes 6–12. At the 18th green, he held his nerve to two-putt and clinch the lowest round on the PGA Tour.

▶ LOWEST SCORE TO PAR IN A WOMEN'S MAJOR

At the Evian Championship in Évian-les-Bains in France on 15–18 Sep 2016, Chun In-gee (KOR) recorded a score of 21 under par. She shot rounds of 63–66–65–69 for a total of 263, four shots ahead of compatriots Park Sung-hyun and Ryu So-yeon. In-gee beat the previous best of 19 under, held by five different golfers.

▲ YOUNGEST RYDER CUP CAPTAIN

One of the greatest golfers of all time, Arnold Palmer (USA) died on 25 Sep 2016. He won seven major titles and 62 PGA Tour titles, his flamboyant game bringing the sport to a wider audience and earning him legions of fans known as "Arnie's Army". In 1963, Palmer captained the US Ryder Cup team at East Lake Golf Club in Atlanta, Georgia, USA, aged 34 years 31 days.

Auto Sports

On 27 Nov 2016, Nico Rosberg (DEU) won his first Formula 1 world title – only to retire just five days afterwards!

Stéphane Peterhansel and Jean-Paul Cottret could have won eight Dakar Rallies. In 2014, they received team orders not to challenge leader Nani Roma amid fears the two cars might crash.

▼ MOST DAKAR RALLY WINS

An off-road endurance race open to both amateur and pro drivers, the Dakar Rally originally ran from Paris, France, to Dakar in Senegal, although the race has also been staged in South Africa and South America. The driver-navigator team of Stéphane Peterhansel and Jean-Paul Cottret (both FRA) has won the rally seven times: in 2004–05, 2007, 2012–13 and 2016–17. Not content with victory on four wheels, Peterhansel has also won six times on a motorcycle.

Fastest speed in an NHRA drag racing funny car

In the world of drag racing, "funny cars" are notable for their forward-mounted engine and tilt-up fibreglass or carbon-fibre automative body. At a National Hot Rod Association (NHRA) event in Topeka, Kansas, USA, on 20 May 2016, Matt Hagan (USA) took advantage of a fast track and cool weather to reach a terminal velocity of 335.57 mph (540.04 km/h) from a standing start over 0.25 mi (402.3 m). "When you get conditions like this on a track that's this fast, these cars will really fly," two-time champion Hagan said afterwards.

Most miles led in a NASCAR race

Martin Truex Jr (USA) led the 2016 Coca-Cola 600 for 588 mi (946 km), or 392 of the 400 laps. Truex Jr took the chequered flag for the win, his first of 2016 and his fourth in NASCAR (National Association for Stock Car Auto Racing). The race was held at Charlotte Motor Speedway in Concord, North Carolina, USA, on 29 May.

Most MotoGP race winners in a single season

The 2016 MotoGP season featured an unprecedented nine different winners. They were: Marc Márquez, Jorge Lorenzo, Maverick Viñales, Dani Pedrosa (all ESP), Andrea Iannone, Andrea Dovisioso, Valentino Rossi (all ITA), Jack Miller (AUS) and Cal Crutchlow (UK). Remarkably, rounds 6–13 of the championship featured eight consecutive different winners.

Most points by a driver in a Formula 1 career

By the close of the 2016 season, Mercedes driver Lewis Hamilton had amassed 2,247 world championship points over the course of his career. His nearest rival was four-time world champion Sebastian Vettel (DEU), with 2,108.

Most consecutive World Rally Championship points finishes by a constructor

At the 2002 Monte Carlo Rally on 20 Jan, Ford drivers came third and fourth. It was the start of an incredible 212 consecutive points finishes for the constructor, stretching to the 2017 Monte Carlo Rally on 22 Jan.

Most World Rally Championship race wins by a country

Between 26 Jan 1973 and 22 Jan 2017, France secured 184 race wins at the World Rally Championships. The victories were achieved by 18 different drivers, including two speedy Sébastiens: Loeb (78 wins) and Ogier (39 wins).

▲ YOUNGEST DRIVER TO WIN A FORMULA 1 RACE

On 15 May 2016, Max Verstappen (NLD) won the Spanish Grand Prix at Montmeló in Spain aged 18 years 228 days. The Red Bull tyro – son of former F1 driver Jos Verstappen – became the first Dutch driver to register a victory. He had switched from Toro Rosso to Red Bull Racing just days before the event.

▲ YOUNGEST DRIVER TO 100 FORMULA 1 PODIUM FINISHES

Three-time world Formula 1 (F1) champion Lewis Hamilton (UK) was 31 years 276 days old when he finished third at the Japanese Grand Prix in Suzuka, Mie Prefecture, Japan, on 9 Oct 2016. He became only the third F1 driver to reach the mark, behind legends Alain Prost (FRA, in 1983) and Michael Schumacher (DEU, in 2002). Only Schumacher made 100 podium finishes from fewer starts.

▲ MOST DAKAR RALLY QUAD BIKE CATEGORY WINS BY AN INDIVIDUAL

Marcos Patronelli (ARG) won his third Dakar Rally quad bike race in 2016; he had previously won the event in 2010 and 2013. The 2016 race took place in Argentina and Bolivia over 13 gruelling stages. Quad biking is a family affair for the Patronellis – Marcos's brother Alejandro has won the Dakar Rally twice and came second in 2016.

▲ MOST POLE POSITIONS IN A GRAND PRIX MOTORCYCLE CAREER

From 17 May 2009 to 23 Oct 2016, Marc Márquez (ESP) racked up 65 pole positions. This total comprised 37 MotoGP poles, 14 Moto2 poles and 14 in the 125 cc class. The record changed hands throughout the 2016 season, with Jorge Lorenzo (ESP) eventually matching Márquez's feat by taking pole for the final race in Valencia on 13 Nov.

Cycling

Bicycles designed for racing in velodromes have no brakes. Cyclists slow down by pushing back against the pedals.

Most riders to finish a Tour de France
A total of 174 riders finished the 2016 Tour de France, held on 2–24 Jul. The previous record was 170, set in 2010. Four mass-finish stages of the 2016 race were won by sprinter Mark Cavendish (UK), taking his total to 30 – the **most mass-finish stage wins of the Tour de France**.

Fastest 500 m from an unpaced standing start (female)
Jessica Salazar Valles (MEX) covered 500 m in just 32.268 sec from a standing start at the Pan American Championships in Aguascalientes, Mexico, on 7 Oct 2016. Valles broke the record of 32.794 sec that had been set in Grenchen, Switzerland, almost a year earlier by Anastasia Voynova (RUS) – who had become only the second woman to break the 33-sec barrier.

Meares's silver medal at the Beijing Olympics in 2008 came just seven months after she broke her neck while racing in Los Angeles, USA. Hers was the Australian cycling team's only medal at Beijing.

▶ MOST OLYMPIC TRACK CYCLING MEDALS (FEMALE)
Between 2004 and 2016, Anna Meares (AUS) won six Olympic medals across four different events. Her collection comprises two golds, one silver and three bronze. Behind Meares, there are three women riders with four Olympic medals: Shuang Guo (CHN), Laura Trott (UK) and Sarah Hammer (USA). Trott is the only cyclist whose medal tally comprises only gold.

◀ FASTEST 4 KM TEAM PURSUIT IN TRACK CYCLING (MEN)

Bradley Wiggins, Ed Clancy, Owain Doull and Steven Burke (all UK) completed the 4 km team pursuit in a time of 3 min 50.265 sec on 12 Aug 2016 at the Olympic Games in Rio de Janeiro, Brazil. It was actually the second time that Great Britain broke the record at the Rio Olympics: the first came in the heats, with a time of 3 min 50.570 sec.

Fastest team sprint in track cycling (women)
On 12 Aug 2016, Tianshi Zhong and Jinjie Gong (both CHN) completed the qualification round of the team sprint in 31.928 sec at the Olympic Games in Rio de Janeiro, Brazil. They went on to beat Russia in the final to claim the gold medal.

Most wins of the UCI Cross-Country Mountain Bike World Championships (male)
Nino Schurter (CHE) won the 2016 Union Cycliste Internationale (UCI) Cross-Country Mountain Bike World Championships, held in Nové Město na Moravě in the Czech Republic. It was Schurter's fifth victory in the event, equalling the feat of Julien Absalon (FRA).

Fastest individual B pursuit in track cycling (male)
Stephen Bate (UK) completed the men's individual B pursuit in 4 min 8.146 sec at the 2016 Paralympic Games in Rio de Janeiro, Brazil, on 8 Sep. Paralympic disciplines are categorized according to the level of an athlete's physical restriction. The B classification is for athletes with a visual impairment who compete on a tandem with a sighted pilot at the front. Adam Duggleby (UK) was Bate's partner.

▲ FASTEST 4 KM TEAM PURSUIT IN TRACK CYCLING (WOMEN)

On 13 Aug 2016, at the Rio Olympics in Brazil, Joanna Rowsell-Shand, Elinor Barker, Laura Trott and Katie Archibald (all UK) won the 4 km team pursuit in a time of 4 min 10.236 sec. The team achieved a new world-record time in all three of their races, the last of which saw them beat the USA by more than 2 sec.

▲ MOST UCI MOUNTAIN-BIKE CROSS-COUNTRY WORLD CUP WINS (MALE)

Julien Absalon (FRA) has won seven World Cup titles: in 2003, 2006–09, 2014 and 2016. Absalon won his 33rd World Cup race in securing the seventh title. He had also been hotly tipped to win Olympic gold at London 2012, but suffered a puncture soon after the start of the race and was unable to recover the lost time.

Fastest women's individual C5 pursuit in track cycling

On 8 Sep 2016, Sarah Storey (UK) won the women's individual C5 pursuit in 3 min 31.394 sec at the Paralympic Games in Rio de Janeiro, Brazil. In cycling, C1 denotes significantly reduced functionality, while C5 indicates less marked impairment.

> To prepare for his time trial race in Qatar, Martin trained in his bathroom with the heater on.

▲ MOST WINS OF THE UCI TIME TRIAL WORLD CHAMPIONSHIPS (MALE)

Tony Martin (DEU) has won the UCI Time Trial World Championships four times, in 2011–13 and 2016. In doing so, he matched the mark of Fabian Cancellara (CHE), who won in 2006–07 and 2009–10. Martin won his fourth and most recent title in Doha, Qatar, finishing the 40-km (24.8-mi) course in just 44 min 42.99 sec. In all, he has won seven medals at the event.

Snooker player Mark King (UK) won his first ranking title at the Northern Ireland Open in Nov 2016 – after 25 years of trying.

Most wins of the British Darts Organisation (BDO) Women's World Championships

With her 3–2 victory over Deta Hedman (UK, b. JAM) at the Lakeside Country Club in Frimley Green, Surrey, UK, on 9 Jan 2016, Trina "Golden Girl" Gulliver (UK) claimed her 10th BDO women's world title. Her wins included the first seven championships held, in 2001–07.

Most continents in which an individual has won an Olympic medal

Double trap and skeet shooter Kim Rhode (USA) won her sixth Olympic medal at Rio 2016. She has won medals on five continents: Australia, North and South America, Asia and Europe.

Most Horseshoe Pitching World Championships (male)

Alan Francis (USA) won his 21st title in the men's division at the Horseshoe Pitching World Championships in 2016. His closest rival, Ted Allen (USA), won his 10th and final title in 1959.

Most professional snooker matches played by an individual

Over the course of a glittering career that saw him win six World Championships, Steve Davis (UK) played 1,453 professional matches between his 1978 debut and his retirement in 2016.

▼ YOUNGEST TEN-PIN BOWLER TO WIN A MAJOR PROFESSIONAL BOWLERS ASSOCIATION TITLE

Anthony Simonsen (USA, b. 6 Jan 1997) was aged just 19 years 39 days when he won the 2016 United States Bowling Congress (USBC) Masters at Woodland Bowl in Indianapolis, USA. Simonsen, noted for his two-handed bowling delivery (see below), defeated amateur Dan MacLelland (CAN) 245–207 in the final, hitting strikes with eight of his first nine shots.

In 2008, a project was set up to teach Bolivian bowlers the two-handed style. The scheme was a notable success, with teams winning competitions in Argentina and Brazil.

▲ FIRST INDEPENDENT OLYMPIAN TO WIN A GOLD MEDAL

Following his country's suspension by the International Olympic Committee, Kuwaiti soldier Fehaid Al-Deehani competed at Rio 2016 as part of the Independent Olympic Athletes team. He won gold in the men's double trap shooting on 10 Aug 2016, beating Marco Innocenti (ITA) 26–24 in the final. His compatriot Abdullah Al-Rashidi won bronze in the men's skeet, also competing as an independent.

Most wins of the Masters snooker

On 22 Jan 2017, Ronnie O'Sullivan (UK) defeated Joe Perry (UK) 10–7 in the final of the Masters invitational snooker tournament at Alexandra Palace in London, UK. It was the seventh time that "The Rocket" had won the event – following wins in 1995, 2005, 2007, 2009, 2014 and 2016 – one more than Stephen Hendry (UK).

Most World Croquet Championships appearances by an individual

Three players have each made 14 appearances at croquet's blue-riband event: Robert Fulford (UK, in 1989–2013), Stephen Mulliner (UK, in 1989–2016) and David Openshaw (UK, in 1989–2016).

Highest earnings in a Professional Bowlers Association ten-pin bowling career

Walter Ray Williams Jr (USA) made career earnings of $4,638,519 (£3,576,290) between 1980 and 2016.

▲ MOST POINTS SCORED IN 70 M 72-ARROW OUTDOOR RECURVE (MALE)

On 5 Aug 2016, Kim Woo-jin (KOR) scored 700 out of a possible 720 points at the Sambódromo in Rio de Janeiro, Brazil. Using a recurve bow with curved limbs, he beat the previous record set by Im Dong-hyun (KOR) at London 2012 by a single point. Kim set his mark in the ranking round of the men's individual event, only to suffer a shock second-round defeat to Riau Ega Agatha (IDN).

▲ MOST CENTURY BREAKS IN A SNOOKER WORLD CHAMPIONSHIP MATCH

During his World Championship semi-final match against Alan McManus (UK) at the Crucible Theatre in Sheffield, UK, on 28–30 Apr 2016, Ding Junhui (CHN) rattled in seven centuries in a virtuoso display of break-building. He won the match 17–11, but went on to lose in the final against Mark Selby (UK).

▼ HIGHEST MATCH AVERAGE IN A PREMIER LEAGUE DARTS MATCH

In beating Michael Smith (UK) in Aberdeen, UK, on 25 Feb 2016, Michael van Gerwen (NLD) achieved a three-dart average of 123.4.

On 1 Jan 2017, he also recorded the **highest match average at the PDC World Championships**: 114.05, during his semi-final in London, UK. Van Gerwen's opponent, Raymond van Barneveld (NLD), lost with a match average of 109.34 – the fourth-highest ever at the event!

Van Gerwen started playing darts regularly aged 13. Within two years, he was European Youth Champion.

Weightlifting

After winning gold at Rio 2016, Óscar Figueroa (COL) left his shoes upon the mat as a way of announcing his retirement.

Olympic weightlifting events comprise two disciplines. The "snatch" is a barbell lift with one continuous motion; in the "clean & jerk", the lifter pauses in a squat position before standing.

Heaviest weight squat-lifted (female, assisted)

On 8 Jul 2016, Samantha Coleman (USA) squat-lifted 661 lb (299.82 kg) at a United Powerlifting Association-sanctioned event in Rosemount, Minnesota, USA. She also bench-pressed 391 lb (177.35 kg) on the same day. Coleman is one of only a handful of women to have deadlifted more than 600 lb (272.15 kg). She wears a tiara while lifting to symbolize the "beauty in strength".

Heaviest weightlifting 77 kg snatch (male)

Lü Xiaojun (CHN) lifted 177 kg (390 lb 3.49 oz) at the Rio Olympics on 10 Aug 2016. Unfortunately, even this wasn't enough for Lü to win overall gold. He finished with a silver medal behind Nijat Rahimov (KAZ), who achieved the **heaviest weightlifting 77 kg clean & jerk** with his lift of 214 kg (471 lb 12.62 oz). Rahimov eclipsed the previous record of 210 kg (462 lb 15.52 oz), set in 2001 by Russian Oleg Perepetchenov.

Heaviest weightlifting +105 kg snatch (male)

Behdad "Salimi" Salimikordasiabi (IRN) lifted 216 kg (476 lb 3.17 oz) at the Rio Olympics on 16 Aug 2016. However, triumph turned to heartbreak for Salimi in the final of the +105 kg clean & jerk. All three of his attempts were ruled invalid by the judges, leaving the Iranian weightlifter without a score and therefore removing any hope of a medal in the overall category.

◀ HEAVIEST WEIGHTLIFTING 63 KG TOTAL (FEMALE)

Deng Wei (CHN) enjoyed a dream Olympic debut at Rio 2016. On 9 Aug, she achieved the **heaviest weightlifting 63 kg clean & jerk** with 147 kg (324 lb 1.27 oz). With a snatch of 115 kg, Deng posted a total of 262 kg (577 lb 9.77 oz) – earning her both a gold medal and two world records.

▲ HEAVIEST WEIGHT SQUAT-LIFTED (MALE, UNASSISTED)

On 16 Oct 2016, Ray Williams (USA) squat-lifted 456 kg (1,005 lb 4.92 oz) at the USA Powerlifting Raw Nationals in Atlanta, Georgia. This was the first 1,000-lb "raw" squat – Williams didn't wear a "squat suit" or knee wraps, merely a weightlifting belt and knee sleeves. He attributes his strength to a diet of "cornbread and buttermilk".

Heaviest weightlifting +105 kg total (male)

In an event filled with drama and record-breaking lifts (see opposite), Lasha Talakhadze (GEO) posted a combined total of 473 kg (1,042 lb 12.64 oz). He lifted 215 kg (473 lb 15.9 oz) in the snatch and 258 kg (568 lb 12.68 oz) in the clean & jerk. Talakhadze took the gold medal ahead of Gor Minasyan (ARM) and compatriot Irakli Turmanidze (GEO).

The previous best at +105 kg was 472.5 kg (1,041 lb 10.94 oz), achieved by Hossein Rezazadeh (IRN). The Iranian still holds the record for the **heaviest weightlifting +105 kg clean & jerk**, with 263.5 kg (580 lb 14.69 oz) set at the Athens Olympics on 25 Aug 2004.

▲ HEAVIEST WEIGHTLIFTING 56 KG TOTAL (MALE)

Long Qingquan (CHN) lifted 307 kg (676 lb 13.10 oz) at Rio 2016 on 7 Aug. Aided by a 170-kg (374-lb 12.57-oz) lift with his last attempt in the clean & jerk, he won gold with a total score higher than Halil Mutlu's (TUR) existing record of 305 kg (672 lb 6.55 oz), set at Sydney 2000.

Heaviest Paralympic powerlift (+107 kg, male)
In the heaviest weightlifting category at the 2016 Rio Paralympics, Iran's Siamand Rahman bench-pressed 310 kg (683 lb 6.92 oz) on 14 Sep.

The lightest weight category was won by Nazmiye Muratlı (TUR) on 8 Sep 2016. Her lift of 104 kg (229 lb 4.49 oz) was the **heaviest Paralympic powerlift (-41 kg, female)**.

Most wins of the Arnold Strongman Classic
On 4–5 Mar 2016, Žydrūnas Savickas (LTU) won the Arnold Strongman Classic. It was his eighth title, following previous victories in 2003–08 and 2014. The Arnold Strongman Classic is an offshoot of the Arnold Sports Festival, originally a bodybuilding competition named after its co-creator Arnold Schwarzenegger.

▶ **HEAVIEST WEIGHTLIFTING 85 KG TOTAL (MALE)**
On 12 Aug 2016, Kianoush Rostami (IRN) lifted 396 kg (873 lb 0.49 oz) to win the gold medal in the 85 kg category at Rio 2016. He lifted 217 kg (478 lb 6.44 oz) in the clean & jerk, and achieved a 179-kg (394-lb 10-oz) snatch, breaking his own combined world record by 1 kg (2 lb 3.27 oz).

Track & Field

Rio 2016 was the first Summer Olympic Games held wholly during winter in the host country, and the first in South America.

Fastest one mile (female, indoors)

On 17 Feb 2016, Genzebe Dibaba (ETH) won the women's indoor mile at the Globen Galan IAAF World Indoor Tour event in Stockholm, Sweden, in a time of 4 min 13.31 sec. The previous best of 4 min 17.14 sec by Doina Melinte (ROM) had stood for 26 years, and had been set 12 months before Dibaba was born.

On a record-breaking night at the Globen Galan, Djibouti's Ayanleh Souleiman ran the **fastest 1,000 m (male, indoors)**: 2 min 14.20 sec. He beat the time of 2 min 14.96 sec, set by Wilson Kipketer (DEN) on 20 Feb 2000.

Fastest 10,000 m (female)

Almaz Ayana (ETH) won the women's 10,000 m – and her first Olympic gold medal – in 29 min 17.45 sec on 12 Aug 2016. The previous best of 29 min 31.78 sec, set by Wang Junxia (CHN) on 8 Sep 1993, had stood for 23 years.

Jamaica's victory in the 4 × 100 m relay at Beijing 2008 was rescinded in 2017 after Nesta Carter failed a drug test. Had it stood, Bolt would also have recorded the first Olympic track sprint triple treble, with 100 m, 200 m and 4 × 100 m wins at three Games.

◀ **USAIN BOLT**

At Rio 2016, this legendary Jamaican sprinter won the Olympic 100 m and 200 m events for the third successive time, following his victories at Beijing 2008 and London 2012. His three wins in each event gives him the records for the **most** (and **most consecutive**) **Olympic 100 m and 200 m gold medals**.

Bolt has also run the **fastest 100 m** and **200 m**, with times of 9.58 sec and 19.19 sec respectively.

The International Association of Athletics Federations (IAAF) Diamond League, which began in 2010, involves 14 meetings each year featuring 32 disciplines (16 for men and 16 for women). No athlete, male or female, has had more victories in Diamond League meetings than Sandra Perković (HRV). She enjoyed 34 wins in the discus between 12 Jun 2010 and 1 Sep 2016.

Fastest 3,000 m steeplechase (female)

On 27 Aug 2016, Ruth Jebet (BHR) smashed an eight-year-old record for this distance, winning in 8 min 52.78 sec at the IAAF Diamond League meeting in Paris, France. The Kenyan-born distance runner had won Olympic gold in the event just 12 days earlier in Rio.

▲ MOST CONSECUTIVE OLYMPIC LONG-DISTANCE DOUBLES

At the London 2012 and Rio 2016 Games, Mo Farah (UK, b. SOM) won two consecutive Olympic long-distance doubles (5,000 m and 10,000 m). This matched the feat of Lasse Virén (FIN) at Munich 1972 and Montreal 1976. By winning the 5,000 m at two Olympics in a row, Farah and Virén share the record for the **most consecutive Olympic 5,000 m gold medals (male)**.

Farah's medal collection also includes the **most European Athletics Championships gold medals (male)**: five. He won the 5,000 m at Barcelona 2010, Helsinki 2012 and Zurich 2014, and added the 10,000 m in 2010 and 2014. In recognition of his achievements, Farah was knighted in the UK's 2017 New Year Honours list.

A: They were filled with steel balls, so that they rattled and made the "sound of victory" for visually impaired athletes

▲ FASTEST 100 M (T44, FEMALE)
On 17 Sep 2016, Sophie Kamlish (UK) completed the 100 m T44 sprint in 12.93 sec at the Rio 2016 Paralympic Games in Brazil. Unfortunately for Kamlish, she just missed out on a gold medal on the day. In the last track athletics final staged at Rio 2016, she was beaten to the bronze medal by Trinidad and Tobago's Nyoshia Cain, who ran the race six-hundredths of a second faster than her.

Fastest 100, 200 and 400 m (aggregate)
Wade van Niekerk (ZAF) made history in 2016 by recording the first "sub-10, 20, 44" races (see pp.485–87). However, the sprinter with the fastest combined times for the 100 m, 200 m and 400 m is Michael Johnson (USA), with an aggregate of 72.59 sec, achieved between 1994 and 1999. Van Niekerk has a total of 72.95 sec, while 100 m and 200 m world record holder Usain Bolt has a time of 74.05 sec.

Most Olympic 3,000 m steeplechase medals
Mahiedine Mekhissi-Benabbad (FRA) gained his third medal in the Olympic 3,000 m steeplechase at Rio 2016. He picked up a bronze, having previously won silver in 2008 and 2012.

Most IAAF Diamond Race athletics titles
At the end of every Diamond League season, the athlete with the most points in each discipline is awarded the Diamond Race. From 2010 to 2016, Renaud Lavillenie (FRA) won seven Diamond Race titles in the pole vault.

The **most IAAF Diamond Race athletics titles (female)** is five, by Valerie Adams (NZ) in the shot put in 2011–14 and 2016. Adams's record was equalled by Sandra Perković (HRV) in the discus in 2012–16.

Fastest wheelchair 100 m (T53, female)
Huang Lisha (CHN) completed the T53 wheelchair 100 m in 16.19 sec at the 2016 Paralympic Games in Rio de Janeiro, Brazil, on 8 Sep. The T53 class covers athletes with full use of their arms but no trunk functionality.

The **fastest wheelchair 400 m (T53, female)** is 54.43 sec, by Hongzhuan Zhou (CHN), recorded at the Rio Paralympics on 11 Sep 2016.

Farthest club throw (F32, female)
Maroua Brahmi (TUN) threw a club 26.93 m (88 ft 4 in) at the Rio Paralympic Games on 9 Sep 2016. Two days later, at the same event, Joanna Butterfield (UK) achieved the **farthest club throw (F51, female)**: 22.81 m (74 ft 10 in). F32 denotes coordination impairment; F51 denotes limb deficiency, limited muscle power or restricted movement.

Farthest javelin throw (F40, male)
Paralympian Ahmed Naas (IRQ) threw a javelin 35.29 m (115 ft 9 in) on 11 Sep 2016. F40 denotes short stature.

Farthest hammer throw (female)
Poland's Anita Włodarczyk threw 82.98 m (272 ft 2 in) at the Skolimowska Memorial in Warsaw, Poland, on 28 Aug 2016. It was the second time she had broken the record in a month, having thrown 82.29 m (269 ft 11 in) en route to Olympic gold on 15 Aug.

Most IAAF Hammer Throw Challenge wins (male)
Paweł Fajdek (POL) won three IAAF Hammer Throw Challenges, in 2013 and 2015–16. In doing so, he matched the achievement of Hungary's Krisztián Pars in 2011–12 and 2014.

Highest pole vault (female, indoors)
Jennifer Suhr (USA) successfully cleared a height of 5.03 m (16 ft 6.03 in) in Brockport, New York, USA, on 30 Jan 2016. She broke her own mark of 5.02 m (16 ft 5.63 in), set on 2 Mar 2013.

▲ FASTEST WHEELCHAIR 800 M (T52, MALE)
Raymond Martin (USA) finished the T52-classification 800 m in a wheelchair in a time of 1 min 51.64 sec at the US trials in Charlotte, North Carolina, USA, on 2 Jul 2016. He is shown above competing in the 1,500 m trial, which took place on the same day.

Four years earlier, on 1 Jul 2012, Martin had achieved the **fastest men's wheelchair 200 m (T52, male)**, in 30.18 sec in Indianapolis, USA.

▲ MOST OLYMPIC ATHLETICS GOLD MEDALS WON (FEMALE)
On 19 Aug 2016, Allyson Felix (USA) won her sixth Olympic gold medal in the 4 x 100 m relay. The US team recovered from a dropped baton in the Rio heats to win the final from lane 1. Felix had previously won the 4 x 100 m relay at London 2012, and was part of triumphant 4 x 400 m relay teams at Beijing 2008, London and Rio. She also has an individual gold from the 200 m in 2012.

▶ FASTEST 100 M HURDLES (FEMALE)

The USA's Kendra Harrison completed the women's 100 m hurdles in a time of 12.20 sec during the Diamond League meeting at the Olympic Stadium in London, UK, on 22 Jul 2016. In doing so, Harrison beat a record that had stood since 20 Aug 1988, when Yordanka Donkova (BGR) set a time of 12.21 sec in Stara Zagora, Bulgaria.

Most IAAF Race Walking Challenge wins (male)

Wang Zhen (CHN) won the Race Walking Challenge twice, in 2012 and 2016. The feat had previously been achieved by Robert Korzeniowski (POL) in 2003–04, Paquillo Fernández (ESP) in 2005–06 and Jared Tallent (AUS) in 2008 and 2013.

▼ MOST APPEARANCES IN IAAF DIAMOND LEAGUE MEETINGS

Nigeria's Blessing Okagbare has appeared at Diamond League meetings 50 times, competing in the 100 m, 200 m and long jump disciplines between 3 Jul 2010 and 9 Sep 2016. Hot on her heels are Kenyans Viola Kibiwot (competing in the 1,500 m and 5,000 m events) and Asbel Kiprop (in the 800 m and 1,500 m), both of whom have made 48 appearances.

Okagbare won a bronze medal in the long jump at Beijing 2008. She has since won gold at the Commonwealth Games, the African Championships, the IAAF World Relays and the All-Africa Games.

Marathons

In 2016, Patrick Downes and Adrianne Haslet completed the Boston Marathon just three years after losing limbs in the terrorist bombing of the 2013 race.

Fastest time to run the Tokyo Marathon (female)

On 26 Feb 2017, Sarah Chepchirchir (KEN) completed the Tokyo Marathon in Japan in 2 hr 19 min 47 sec. In just her third competitive marathon, she eclipsed her personal best by more than four minutes. Chepchirchir beat the previous Tokyo best of 2 hr 21 min 27 sec, set by Helah Kiprop (KEN) on 28 Feb 2016.

On the same day as Chepchirchir's record run, Wilson Kipsang (KEN) achieved the **fastest time to run the Tokyo Marathon (male)**: 2 hr 3 min 58 sec. On a redesigned course, he smashed the previous best by 1 min 44 sec.

On 23 Apr 2017, more than 50,000 runners lined up for the UK's London Marathon – the **largest annual single-day fundraising event (single location)**. Check out these fleet-footed fancy-dress runners, in order of finishing times:

1. Swimmer
Joe Spraggins (UK) – 2:42:24

2. Elf
Ashley Payne (UK) – 2:58:16

3. Fast-food item
Gary McNamara (UK) – 2:59:35

4. Viking
Paul Richards (UK) – 3:03:11

5. Monk
Malcolm Treby (UK) – 3:03:32

6. Three-person costume
Graham O'Loughlin (IRL), Evan Williams and Ian Williams (both UK) – 3:13:09

7. Crustacean (male)
Simon Couchman (UK) – 3:13:18

8. Wonder Woman (female)
Rebecca César de Sá (UK) – 3:16:19

9. In a full-body animal costume (male)
Laurence Morgan (UK) – 3:16:36

10. Nun
Daniel Jordan (UK) – 3:17:12

11. Wearing wellington boots
Damian Thacker (UK) – 3:21:27

▶ YOUNGEST WINNER OF THE NEW YORK CITY MARATHON (MALE)

On 6 Nov 2016, Eritrea's Ghirmay Ghebreslassie (b. 14 Nov 1995) won the men's New York Marathon aged 20 years 358 days.

Ghebreslassie is also the **youngest winner of the World Championship marathon (male)**, having taken gold in Beijing, China, aged 19 years 281 days on 22 Aug 2015.

Fastest aggregate time to complete every annual World Marathon Majors marathon

Between 2006 and 2015, Hermann Achmüller (ITA) completed the Tokyo, Boston, London, Chicago, New York and Berlin marathons in a total aggregate time of 14 hr 16 min 32 sec.

Fastest race walk 50 km (female)

On 15 Jan 2017, Inês Henriques (PRT) won the Portuguese Race Walking Championships in Porto de Mos in 4 hr 8 min 26 sec. This was the first official IAAF women's world record in this discipline.

First triplets to compete in the Olympic marathon

Identical sisters Lily, Leila and Liina Luik – the "Trio to Rio" – competed in the 2016 Olympic marathon for Estonia. It was Lily who finished first, coming home in 97th place.

12. Bishop
Max Livingstone-Learmonth (UK) – 3:21:32

13. Monk (female)
Sarah Dudgeon (UK) – 3:21:33

14. Chef (male)
Terry Midgley (UK) – 3:22:27

15. Mr Potato Head
Philip Powell (UK) – 3:24:19

16. Cartoon character (female)
Rebecca Vincent (UK) – 3:24:28

17. Witch (female)
Nicola Nuttall (UK) – 3:26:13

18. French maid (male)
Kevin Day (UK) – 3:26:43

19. Nun (female)
Victoria Carter (UK) – 3:26:53

20. Two-person costume
Alex Smith and Chris Stone (both UK) – 3:33:22

21. Fruit (female)
Lorna Pursglove (UK) – 3:41:25

22. In a sleeping bag (male)
David Smith (UK) – 3:44:01

547

◄ MOST WINS OF THE
BERLIN MARATHON BY AN
INDIVIDUAL (FEMALE)
Aberu Kebede of Ethiopia
won her third Berlin Marathon
in 2016, having previously
triumphed in 2010 and 2012.
She matched the tally set by
Jutta von Haase (GDR/now
DEU – 1974, 1976, 1979), Renate
Kokowska (POL – 1988, 1991,
1993) and Uta Pippig (DEU –
1990, 1992, 1995).

Most barefoot half marathons run on consecutive days
Salacnib "Sonny" Molina (USA) completed 11 barefoot half marathons on
8–18 Sep 2016. The orthopaedic nurse travelled across the USA in search of
races, eventually running 18 official half marathons in 30 days – all barefoot.

Most wheelchair New York City Marathon wins (female)
Tatyana McFadden (USA, b. RUS) has won the New York City Marathon five
times, in 2010 and 2013–16. This equals the mark set by Edith Wolf-Hunkeler
(CHE), who came home first in 2004–05 and 2007–09. McFadden, who was born
with spina bifida, competes in the T54 class and is a seven-time Paralympic
gold medallist.

She also shares the record for **most consecutive wheelchair London
Marathon wins (female)**, having won the race four times in 2013–16. This is
the same as Italy's Francesca Porcellato, who triumphed in 2003–06.

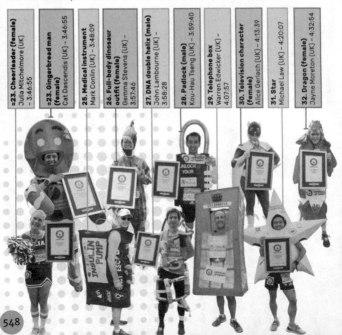

=23. Cheerleader (female)
Julia Mitchelmore (UK)
– 3:46:55

=23. Gingerbread man
(female)
Cat Dascendis (UK) – 3:46:55

25. Medical instrument
Mark Conlin (UK) – 3:48:09

26. Full-body dinosaur
outfit (female)
Gemma Stevens (UK) –
3:57:46

27. DNA double helix (male)
John Lambourne (UK) –
3:58:28

28. Padlock (male)
Kou-Hau Tseng (UK) – 3:59:40

29. Telephone box
Warren Edwicker (UK) –
4:07:57

30. Television character
(female)
Alice Gerlach (UK) – 4:13:39

31. Star
Michael Law (UK) – 4:20:07

32. Dragon (female)
Jayne Moreton (UK) – 4:32:54

▶ FASTEST HALF MARATHON (FEMALE)

On 1 Apr 2017, Kenya's Joyciline Jepkosgei won the Prague Half Marathon in the Czech Republic in a time of 1 hr 4 min 52 sec. En route to victory, she set records for the **fastest road-run 10 km (female)** at 30 min 4 sec; **15 km** at 45 min 37 sec; and **20 km** at 1 hr 1 min 25 sec. It was only Jepkosgei's fifth race over the distance.

Most Olympic marathon medals won by a country

Between 1904 and 2016, the USA won 13 Olympic medals in the marathon. They dominated early editions of the men's event, winning seven medals by 1924 – including a clean sweep at St Louis 1904. But in recent years Kenya and Ethiopia have been dominant in the road race, and at Rio 2016 Kenya briefly equalled the USA's tally of 12 medals when Eliud Kipchoge took gold – only for Galen Rupp (USA) to cross the line in bronze-medal position just 1 min 21 sec later. In doing so, Rupp became only the third US man to win a medal in the marathon since 1924.

▲ FASTEST MARATHON (FEMALE, WOMEN-ONLY RACE)

On 23 Apr 2017, Mary Keitany (KEN) won her third London Marathon title, in 2 hr 17 min 1 sec. This was the fastest time in a women-only marathon by 41 sec, and second only to Paula Radcliffe (UK), whose **fastest marathon (female)** of 2 hr 15 min 25 sec in 2003 used male pacemakers.

33. Wearing chainmail (upper body)
Thomas Langdown (UK) – 4:50:16

34. Toilet roll (female)
Susan Ridgeon (UK) – 4:54:00

35. Car (male)
Thomas Bolton (UK) – 4:55:09

36. Star Wars character (male)
Jeremy Allinson (UK) – 4:59:12

37. Three-dimensional aircraft (male)
Paul Cousins (UK) – 5:03:15

38. Carrying a household appliance (white goods)
Ben Blowes (UK) – 5:58:37

39. Five-person costume
David Hepburn, Megan Walker, Ceyhun Uzun, Andrew Sharpe, Holly Bishop (all UK) – 6:17:26

40. Carrying a 100-lb pack
Marc Jenner (ROM, b. UK) – 6:47:03

549

FASTEST WORLD MARATHON MAJORS

Marathon	Fastest male			Fastest female		
Berlin	Dennis Kimetto (KEN)	*2:02:57	28 Sep 2014	Mizuki Noguchi (JPN)	2:19:12	25 Sep 2005
Boston	Geoffrey Mutai (KEN)	2:03:02	18 Apr 2011	Bizunesh Deba (ETH)	2:19:59	21 Apr 2014
Chicago	Dennis Kimetto (KEN)	2:03:45	13 Oct 2013	Paula Radcliffe (UK)	2:17:18	13 Oct 2002
London	Eliud Kipchoge (KEN)	2:03:05	24 Apr 2016	Paula Radcliffe (UK)	*2:15:25	13 Apr 2003
New York	Geoffrey Mutai (KEN)	2:05:06	6 Nov 2011	Margaret Okayo (KEN)	2:22:31	2 Nov 2003
Tokyo	Wilson Kipsang (KEN)	2:03:58	26 Feb 2017	Sarah Chepchirchir (KEN)	2:19:47	26 Feb 2017

denotes fastest male and female marathon times

◀ ELIUD KIPCHOGE

On 6 May 2017, Eliud Kipchoge (KEN) completed Nike's "Breaking2" marathon challenge in 2 hr 25 sec at the Monza Grand Prix circuit in Italy. Although Kipchoge's time was faster than Dennis Kimetto's (KEN) **fastest marathon (male)** – 2 hr 2 min 57 sec – it did not count as an official IAAF record owing to the use of in-out pacemakers.

Most Ultra-Trail Mt Fuji podiums by an individual

Fernanda Maciel (BRA) has finished in the top three of the Japanese ultramarathon three times: runner-up in both 2014 and 2015, she finally won in 2016. The Ultra-Trail Mt Fuji is run over a 165-km (102.5-mi) course with a 46-hr time limit.

Most wins of the Berlin Inline Skating Marathon (male)

Skater Bart Swings (BEL) won the Berlin Inline Skating Marathon in four consecutive years from 2013 to 2016.

Swings was also responsible for the **fastest time to complete the Berlin Inline Skating Marathon** – 56 min 49 sec, on 26 Sep 2015.

> David Weir has also triumphed in the New York City Marathon, winning the 2010 event in 1 hr 37 min 29 sec.

▲ MOST WHEELCHAIR LONDON MARATHON WINS (MALE)

David Weir (UK) won his seventh men's wheelchair London Marathon title on 23 Apr 2017, winning in 1 hr 31 min 6 sec. He had previously triumphed in 2002, 2006–08 and 2011–12. Weir's seventh victory took him one clear of Dame Tanni Grey-Thompson (UK), earning him the **most overall wheelchair London Marathon wins**.

Swimming

At the 1900 Paris Olympics, a men's 200 m obstacle event required swimmers to climb over poles and swim under boats.

Fastest long-course 100 m breaststroke (male)

On 7 Aug 2016, Adam Peaty brought home the UK's first gold medal of the Rio Olympics in a time of 57.13 sec. The breaststroke swimmer had broken his own world record in the heats on the previous day, before setting an even quicker mark in the final.

Peaty also holds the title for the **fastest long-course 50 m breaststroke (male)** – 26.42 sec, achieved at the FINA World Swimming Championships in Kazan, Russia, on 4 Aug 2015.

Fastest 100 m butterfly – S13 (female)

On 8 Sep, Rebecca Meyers (USA) won gold at the 2016 Paralympics in 1 min 3.25 sec. Four days later, Meyers, who has the rare genetic disorder Usher syndrome, set two more records: the **fastest 200 m freestyle – S13 (female)** – 2 min 7.64 sec – and the **fastest 400 m freestyle – S13 (female)** – 4 min 19.59 sec.

Most swimming medals won at a Summer Paralympics by an individual (male)

Daniel Dias (BRA) won 24 medals in swimming events at the 2008, 2012 and 2016 Paralympic Games – a total of 14 golds, seven silvers and three bronzes. Born with malformed upper and lower limbs, Dias only took up swimming at the age of 16, learning four styles in just two months.

Fastest long-course 100 m backstroke (male)

On 13 Aug 2016, Ryan Murphy (USA) swam the backstroke leg of the Olympic 4 x 100 m medley relay final in 51.85 sec. His US team won gold.

▼ MOST GOLD MEDALS WON IN THE FINA SWIMMING WORLD CUP (MALE)

Between 2009 and 2016, Chad le Clos (ZAF) amassed an astonishing 116 gold medals at the Fédération Internationale de Natation (FINA) World Cup. This is almost double his closest rival, Roland Schoeman (ZAF), who has 64 golds. Le Clos won two silvers at Rio 2016, and followed this up on 8 Dec in Windsor, Canada, by setting the **fastest short-course 100 m butterfly**: 48.08 sec.

▲ FASTEST LONG-COURSE 800 M FREESTYLE (FEMALE)

At Rio 2016 on 12 Aug, Katie Ledecky (USA) won the 800 m in 8 min 4.79 sec. It was her fourth gold medal and second world record at the Games. On 7 Aug, Ledecky had won the 400 m freestyle event in a time of 3 min 56.46 sec – the **fastest long-course 400 m freestyle (female)**.

Fastest long-course 100 m butterfly (female)

At Rio 2016, Sarah Sjöström claimed Sweden's first ever gold medal in a women's swimming event. Sjöström won the final of the 100 m butterfly in 55.48 sec on 7 Aug.

Fastest short-course 200 m breaststroke (male)

At the German Short Course Championships in Berlin on 20 Nov 2016, Marco Koch (DEU) swam the 200 m breaststroke in 2 min 0.44 sec. Koch overcame the disappointment of Rio 2016, where he could only finish seventh in the 200 m breaststroke final on 10 Aug.

Fastest long-course 100 m freestyle (female)

On 2 Jul 2016, Cate Campbell (AUS) swam the 100 m in 52.06 sec at the Australia Grand Prix in Brisbane, Australia. Campbell went on to compete at Rio 2016, where she was part of the Australian quartet who recorded the **fastest long-course 4 x 100 m freestyle relay (female)** – 3 min 30.65 sec. Her team-mates were Emma McKeon, Brittany Elmslie and Cate's sister, Bronte Campbell (all AUS).

▲ MOST GOLD MEDALS WON BY A FEMALE AT THE FINA WORLD CUP

Nicknamed the "Iron Lady", Katinka Hosszú (HUN) won 225 gold medals at the FINA World Cup between 2012 and 2016. On 3 Aug 2015, Hosszú swam the **fastest long-course 200 m individual** medley (female) – 2 min 6.12 sec – at the FINA World Championships in Kazan, Russia.

A: 10 – making her the **youngest competitor** ever in this event

▶ MOST OLYMPIC MEDALS WON

Michael Phelps (USA) retired after Rio 2016, having become the most decorated athlete in Olympic history. Over the course of four Games, Phelps won 28 medals, 10 more than nearest rival, gymnast Larisa Latynina (USSR/now UKR). His record haul included 23 gold medals – the **most gold medals won at the Olympics**.

Most silver medals awarded in a single Olympic swimming race

Held on 12 Aug 2016, the men's 100 m butterfly final at the Rio Olympics was one of the closest swimming events in the history of the Games. Behind the winner, Singapore's Joseph Schooling, three swimmers tied for second place in 51.14 sec: Michael Phelps (USA), Chad le Clos (ZAF) and László Cseh (HUN).

▲ OLDEST OLYMPIC SWIMMING INDIVIDUAL GOLD MEDALLIST

Anthony Ervin (USA, b. 26 May 1981) won Olympic gold in the men's 50 m freestyle aged 35 years 78 days at Rio 2016, on 12 Aug. Ervin won his first gold at Sydney 2000, meaning that he also holds the record for the **longest time between Olympic swimming individual gold medals** – 15 years 325 days.

Water Sports

Freediving is also known as "apnea". The term derives from the Greek word *apnoia*, which means "without breathing".

Most consecutive international rowing races won by a men's coxless pair

The New Zealand duo of Hamish Bond and Eric Murray are one of the most dominant teams in the history of rowing. Between 19 Jun 2009 and 11 Aug 2016, they went eight seasons unbeaten, winning 69 consecutive races, six World Championships and two Olympic gold medals. At London 2012, Bond and Murray won their event in 6 min 8.50 sec, obliterating the decade-old record for **fastest coxless pairs rowing (men's class)** by more than 6 sec.

Fastest row double sculls lightweight class (female)

At the World Rowing Cup regatta in Poznań, Poland, on 19 Jun 2016, the Dutch duo of Maaike Head and Ilse Paulis set a time of 6 min 47.69 sec. This surpassed the previous mark of 6 min 48.38 sec, set by the British pair of Charlotte Taylor and Katherine Copeland on 20 Jun 2015.

First tie for an Olympic medal in canoeing/kayaking

On 20 Aug 2016, the final of the men's Olympic 200 m K-1 sprint was too close to call. The bronze medal was shared between Saúl Craviotto (ESP) and Ronald Rauhe (DEU), who both finished in 35.662 sec.

▼ FIRST BACKFLIP LANDED IN A SURFING WORLD CHAMPIONSHIPS EVENT

On 14 May 2016, Gabriel Medina (BRA) made competitive surfing history when he landed a backflip during Round 2 of the Oi Rio Pro in Barra da Tijuca, Rio de Janeiro, Brazil. Medina, who became Brazil's first ever surfing world champion in 2014, received perfect scores of 10 from all five judges for his ground-breaking flip. He went on to take third place in the event.

In 2009, Medina became the **youngest surfer to win a World Qualifying Series event**. He won the Maresia Surf International aged 15 years 202 days – just 10 days after turning pro!

Longest freedive (dynamic apnea, with fins)

On 3 Jul 2016, Mateusz Malina (POL) and Giorgos Panagiotakis (GRE) both swam a horizontal distance of 300 m (984 ft 3 in) underwater in Turku, Finland. This is equivalent to six lengths of an Olympic 50-m (164-ft) pool in a single breath!

Deepest freedive (free immersion/free apnea, women)

On 6 Sep 2016, Jeanine Grasmeijer (NLD) reached a depth of 92 m (301 ft 10 in) at Kralendijk in Bonaire, Leeward Antilles. Free-immersion divers cannot use any form of propulsion equipment.

Most KPWT Freestyle World Championships by a woman

Gisela Pulido (ESP) won 10 kiteboarding World Kite Tour (previously PKRA) Freestyle Championships: in 2004–11, 2013 and 2015. In 2012 and 2014, Pulido was runner-up to Karolina Winkowska (POL), who came second in 2015.

▲ **MOST CONSECUTIVE GOLD MEDALS IN A TEAM OLYMPIC EVENT (FEMALE)**

Synchronized diver Wu Minxia (CHN, above front) won her fourth consecutive gold medal at Rio 2016, equalling the record shared by basketballers Lisa Leslie, Sue Bird, Tamika Catchings and Diana Taurasi (all USA). It was Wu's fifth Olympic gold overall – the **most gold medals won at the Olympics for diving (female)**.

▲ **MOST INTERNATIONAL WATER POLO TITLES HELD SIMULTANEOUSLY (MALE)**

When it comes to water polo, Serbia's men are in a league of their own. On 20 Aug 2016, they beat rivals Croatia 11–7 to win Olympic gold, completing a set of five international titles comprising the 2014 World Cup, 2015 World League, 2015 World Championships and 2016 European Championships.

D. KOZAK GER HUN

▲ MOST OLYMPIC GOLD MEDALS IN CANOE SPRINT AT A SINGLE GAMES (FEMALE)

On 16–20 Aug 2016, Hungary's Danuta Kozák went on a golden winning streak at the Rio Olympics. She won three 500 m canoe titles, in the K-1, K-2 and K-4. Kozák became only the third canoeist ever to claim three golds at a single Games, joining Vladimir Parfenovich (USSR/now BLR, 1980) and Ian Ferguson (NZ, 1984).

Most points scored in a WSL Surfing World Championship season (female)

Tyler Wright (AUS) dominated the 2016 World Surfing League (WSL) Women's Championship Tour, winning five of the 10 events on her way to the title. Her tally of 72,500 ranking points eclipsed the previous best of 66,200, by Hawaii's Carissa Moore in 2015.

▲ MOST OLYMPIC SYNCHRONIZED SWIMMING GOLD MEDALS (INDIVIDUAL)

At Rio 2016, Natalia Ishchenko (above left) and Svetlana Romashina (above right; both RUS) won gold in the team and the women's duet event, bringing their Olympic total to five golds each. This equalled the record set by former team-mate Anastasia Davydova (RUS) between Athens 2004 and London 2012. All three swimmers competed together in the team event in London.

Winter Sports

On 30 Sep 2016, Japan's Yuzuru Hanyu pulled off the first quadruple loop jump in a men's figure skating competition.

Most participants at a Bandy World Championship

A close relative of ice hockey, bandy is played with a ball instead of a puck. Teams of 11 players compete on a field of ice roughly the size of a soccer pitch. The 2017 World Championship in Sweden featured 18 nations – including Mongolia, Holland and a team of Swedish-based Somalis – matching the mark set in 2016.

Since its inauguration in 1957, the **most wins of the Bandy World Championship (men)** is 24, a combined total achieved by the Soviet Union (1957–79, 1985 and 1989–91) and Russia (1999–2001, 2006–08, 2011 and 2013–16).

The **most wins of the Bandy World Championship (women)** is seven, achieved by Sweden. Bar 2014, they have won every tournament since its inception in 2004.

Most consecutive Biathlon World Cup overall titles won (male)

Martin Fourcade (FRA) secured his sixth consecutive biathlon title in 2017 – three more than Raphaël Poirée (FRA) and Frank Ullrich of the former East Germany.

The **most Biathlon World Championship medals won (male)** is 45, achieved by Norway's Ole Einar Bjørndalen from 1997 to 2017.

Highest score in figure skating – free dance (ice dance)

On 31 Mar 2016, the French duo of Gabriella Papadakis and Guillaume Cizeron scored 118.17 points at the ISU World Championships in Boston, Massachusetts, USA.

On 9 Dec 2016, Tessa Virtue and Scott Moir (both CAN) recorded the **highest score in figure skating – short dance (ice dance)**: 80.50, at the ISU Grand Prix of Figure Skating Final held in Marseille, France.

Most wins of the Canadian Curling Championship by a province

Commonly known as the Brier, the Canadian Curling Championship was first held in 1927. Alberta's victory in 2016 was their 27th, equalling the mark set by Manitoba in 2011.

▲ **HIGHEST SCORE IN FIGURE SKATING – SHORT PROGRAMME (FEMALE)**

Evgenia Medvedeva (RUS) scored 79.21 at the International Skating Union (ISU) Grand Prix of Figure Skating Final in Marseille, France, on 9 Dec 2016.

On 27 Jan 2017, Medvedeva followed up with the **highest score in figure skating – long programme (female)**: 150.79, recorded at the ISU European Championships in Ostrava, Czech Republic.

▲ MOST SKI JUMPING WORLD CUP INDIVIDUAL VICTORIES (FEMALE)

On 16 Feb 2017, Sara Takanashi (JPN) won her 53rd FIS World Cup event in Pyeongchang, South Korea. She made her World Cup debut on 3 Dec 2011, aged 15 years 56 days, and won her first event on 3 Mar the following year. Takanashi has won the overall title four times: in 2013, 2014, 2016 and 2017.

▼ MOST CONSECUTIVE FIS ALPINE SKI WORLD CUP TITLES (MALE)

Austria's Marcel Hirscher won six consecutive Fédération Internationale de Ski (FIS) Alpine Ski World Cup overall titles, in 2012–17. In doing so, he claimed the outright record for **most FIS Alpine Ski World Cup overall titles won (male)**, surpassing the achievement of Marc Girardelli (LUX, b. AUT). Girardelli won his five overall titles in 1985–86, 1989, 1991 and 1993.

On 22 Dec 2015, Hirscher had a narrow escape when a drone carrying a camera crashed into the piste inches from him during a World Cup slalom race in Madonna di Campiglio, Italy.

First person to win the 500 m and 1,000 m at a World Single Distances Speed Skating Championships (male)

Pavel Kulizhnikov (RUS) completed a sprint double at the 2016 championships in Kolomna, Russia, on 13–14 Feb. He had won gold and silver in 2015, missing out in the 1,000 m by 0.04 sec.

Also in Kolomna, Denis Yuskov (RUS) achieved the **most consecutive 1,500 m World Single Distances Speed Skating Championships titles (male)** with three, following his victories in 2013 and 2015.

Most wins of the snowmobiling International 500 by a manufacturer

The "I-500" snowmobile race is staged over an arduous 500-mi (804-km) course at Sault Ste Marie in Michigan, USA. Bunke Racing took the chequered flag on 4 Feb 2017 – marking a 26th victory for manufacturer Polaris (USA).

Most skiing World Cup victories (women)

On 21 Jan 2017, Lindsey Vonn (USA) achieved her 77th FIS World Cup victory in a downhill competition, on the Kandahar course at Garmisch-Partenkirchen in Germany.

It was Vonn's 39th win in the downhill category – the **most downhill skiing World Cup race wins by an individual (female)**. Her victory came only weeks after she severely fractured her right arm in a training crash.

▲ **FASTEST SHORT-TRACK SPEED SKATING 1,500 M (WOMEN)**
Choi Min-jeong (KOR, above front) set a time of 2 min 14.354 sec at the ISU World Cup Short Track Speed Skating Series event in Salt Lake City, Utah, USA, on 12 Nov 2016. Alongside Shim Suk-hee, Kim Ji-yoo and Kim Geon-hee (all KOR), she also recorded the **fastest short-track speed skating 3,000 m relay** – 4 min 4.222 sec.

Winter Olympics Preview

The 2018 Winter Olympics will be held in Pyeongchang, South Korea. Who will join these incredible record-breakers?

Most Winter Olympic appearances by an athlete

Ski-jumper Noriaki Kasai (JPN) and luger Albert Demchenko (RUS) both competed at the seven Games from Albertville 1992 to Sochi 2014.

Demchenko (b. 27 Nov 1971) is the **oldest individual medallist at a Winter Olympic Games**. He won a silver medal on 9 Feb 2014 aged 42 years 74 days.

Most gold medals won at a single Winter Olympic Games

Eric Heiden (USA) won five speed-skating events at the 1980 Winter Olympics at Lake Placid in New York, USA. His victories came in the 500 m, 1,000 m, 1,500 m, 5,000 m and 10,000 m.

The **most gold medals won at a single Winter Olympic Games (female)** is four, achieved by speed-skater Lidiya Skoblikova (USSR/now RUS) in the 500 m, 1,000 m, 1,500 m and 3,000 m events at Innsbruck 1964.

▼ MOST MEDALS WON AT THE WINTER OLYMPICS (FEMALE)

Three female cross-country skiers have won 10 medals at the Winter Olympics: Raisa Smetanina (USSR/now RUS, 1976–92), Stefania Belmondo (ITA, 1992–2002) and Marit Bjørgen (NOR, below right, 2002–14). Six of Bjørgen's medals are gold – the **most gold medals won at the Winter Olympics (female)**. She shares the record with speed-skater Lidiya Skoblikova (USSR/now RUS, 1960–64) and cross-country skier Lyubov Yegorova (RUS, 1992–94).

In 2015, Marit Bjørgen made history by winning all three World Cup crystal globes – awarded for overall, distance and sprint – for a second time. She had previously achieved the feat in 2004–05.

Q: Who designed the opening ceremony of the 1960 Winter Olympics?

A: Walt Disney

PyeongChang 2018

Most consecutive individual Olympic medals

Luge rider Armin Zöggeler (ITA) – known as Il Cannibale ("The Cannibal") for the way he devoured his opposition – won a medal at six consecutive Winter Olympics from 1994 to 2014.

First Winter Olympic medallist from the southern hemisphere

At Albertville 1992, New Zealand skier Annelise Coberger won silver in the women's slalom. She became the first medallist from the southern hemisphere, 68 years after the first Winter Olympics had taken place.

Most Winter Olympic ice hockey medals won by an individual

Canada has won every women's ice hockey final except the first at Nagano 1998. Forward Jayna Hefford and centre Hayley Wickenheiser were in all teams, earning themselves four golds and a silver.

Most Winter Paralympic Games gold medals won

Ragnhild Myklebust (NOR) won 22 golds between 1988 and 2002 in cross-country skiing, ice-sledge speed-racing and biathlon. She also took home three silvers and two bronze.

The **most Winter Paralympic Games gold medals won (male)** is 16, achieved by Gerd Schönfelder (DEU) in alpine skiing in 1992–2010. He also won four silvers and two bronze.

Most siblings to compete in a single Winter Olympic event

At Calgary 1988, Mexico's two teams in the two-man bobsled were crewed by four brothers: Jorge, Eduardo, Roberto and Adrián Tamés.

▲ **YOUNGEST INDIVIDUAL GOLD MEDALLIST AT A WINTER OLYMPICS**

Tara Lipinski (USA, b. 10 Jun 1982) won the ladies' singles figure-skating event in Nagano, Japan, on 20 Feb 1998, aged 15 years 255 days.

The **youngest Olympic gold medallist** is South Korea's Kim Yun-mi (b. 1 Dec 1980). At Lillehammer 1994, she won gold in the women's 3,000 m short-track speed-skating relay aged 13 years 85 days.

▲ FIRST WINTER OLYMPICS

The Winter Olympics were first held in Chamonix, France, between 25 Jan and 5 Feb 1924. The Games were established to support snow- and ice-based sports not suited to the summer. In front of 10,004 paying spectators, a total of 247 men and 11 women from 16 nations competed in events including speed skating, curling and ice hockey (above). On 26 Jan 1924, Charles Jewtraw (USA) became the **first Winter Olympic gold medallist**, winning the 500 m speed-skating competition at the Stade Olympique de Chamonix.

▲ MOST MEDALS WON AT THE WINTER OLYMPICS

Between 1998 and 2014, Norway's Ole Einar Bjørndalen won 13 Winter Olympic medals in the biathlon – an event combining cross-country skiing and rifle shooting. This tally includes eight golds: the **most gold medals won at the Winter Olympics**. Bjørndalen shares this record with cross-country skier Bjørn Dæhlie (NOR), whose golds were won in 1992–98.

At Sochi 2014, Bjørndalen triumphed in the biathlon 10-km sprint event aged 40 years 12 days – making him the **oldest individual gold medallist at a Winter Olympic Games**.

Extreme Sports

According to a 2015 report, 100 hours of GoPro action-camera video footage is uploaded to YouTube every minute.

▼ FASTEST DOWNHILL STANDING SKATEBOARDING

On 31 May 2016, Swedish skateboarding legend Erik Lundberg set out to beat the existing downhill skateboarding record speed of 129.94 km/h (80.74 mph). The downhill course, in Quebec, Canada, was 1 km (0.62 mi) long, with a gradient reaching a steep 18%. After a few practice runs to learn its intricacies, Lundberg achieved a speed of 130.63 km/h (81.16 mph). The key? Staying as still as possible...

Fastest speed in speed skydiving (male)
Developed in the mid-2000s, speed skydiving requires competitors to leap from a plane in an attempt to achieve the fastest possible rate of free fall. On 13 Sep 2016, Henrik Raimer (SWE) achieved a speed of 601.26 km/h (373.6 mph) during round 5 of the Fédération Aéronautique Internationale (FAI) World Championships in Chicago, Illinois, USA. He went on to become Speed Skydiving World Champion.

Farthest hang-gliding declared goal distance (female)
On 7 Jan 2016, Yoko Isomoto (JPN) guided a Class 1 Wills Wing T2C hang-glider from Forbes to Walgett in New South Wales, Australia – a distance of 367.6 km (228.41 mi).

Greatest height gain in a hang-glider (male)
Anton Raumauf (AUT) gained 4,359 m (14,301 ft 2 in) over Burgsdorf and Helmeringhausen in Namibia on 3 Jan 2016, as ratified by the FAI.

Stopping a skateboard at 130 km/h demands incredible balance and skill. Skateboarders stand up slowly, spread their arms and unzip their suits so that the loose material acts as a kind of parachute.

◄ **HIGHEST JUMP ON A POGO STICK**

On 15 Oct 2016, Biff Hutchison (USA) jumped 11 ft 0.5 in (3.36 m) into the air – twice the height of the average human – on a pogo stick in Burley, Idaho, USA. His previous record height of 10 ft 6 in (3.2 m), shared with Dalton Smith (USA), had been matched by Nic Patiño (USA) at Pogopalooza 2016 in Swissvale, Pennsylvania, USA, on 8 Jul 2016.

Longest pickup-truck ramp jump

On 25 Aug 2016, Bryce Menzies (USA) soared above a US ghost town in a ramp-to-ramp jump of 115.64 m (379 ft 4 in). He set the record in a Pro 2 truck during rehearsals for a TV show at Bonanza Creek Ranch in New Mexico, USA. For more ramp-jumping trucks, see pp.465–69.

▲ LONGEST POWER-ASSISTED BICYCLE BACKFLIP

On 13 Aug 2016, X Games star Kevin "KRob" Robinson took on the bicycle backflip record in a live ESPN special at Providence in Rhode Island, USA. To go beyond his target of 64 ft (19.5 m), Robinson had to reach a speed of 43 mph (69.2 km/h) before take-off, which he did with a tow from an all-terrain vehicle. He was thrown from his bike trying to land his first attempt, but came back minutes later to nail a monster jump of 84 ft (25.6 m).

Fastest speed on a gravity-powered street luge

Mike McIntyre (USA) reached a speed of 164 km/h (101.9 mph) at the L'Ultime Descent world record speed event in Les Éboulements, Quebec, Canada, on 10 Sep 2016. McIntyre beat the 2008 mark of 157.41 km/h (97.81 mph) set by Canadian Cédric Touchette.

Most whitewater rafting world championships (male)

Victory for the Brazilian men's team at the 2016 International Rafting Federation (IRF) World Championships was their sixth in total. They had also taken gold in 2007, 2009 and 2013–15. Win number six took Brazil past the legendary Team Bober of Slovenia, winners of the first five rafting World Championships in 1995–99.

Fastest 1 km ice swim (male)

Petar Stoychev (BUL) swam 1 km (0.62 mi) in 12 min 15.87 sec at the 2nd Ice Swimming Aqua Sphere World Championships in Burghausen, Bavaria, Germany. Judit Wittig (DEU) achieved the **fastest 1 km ice swim (female)** in 13 min 13.58 sec at the same event, held on 6 Jan 2017.

▲ MOST WINS OF THE MOUNTAINBOARDING WORLD BOARDERCROSS CHAMPIONSHIP

In boardercross, mountainboarders race down specifically designed narrow tracks with plenty of twists and turns. Matt Brind (UK, above, front) has won the World Boardercross Championship three times, in 2014–16. The only other man to have won the title is Kody Stewart (USA), in 2013. Stewart finished runner-up to Brind at the 2016 championship held in Bukovac, Serbia.

X Games

At Austin 2016, Jackson Strong left hospital to win the Moto X Best Trick only hours after crashing in the QuarterPipe.

First married couple to compete against each other at the Summer X Games

Held over a half-mile (0.8-km) dirt course at the Circuit of the Americas race track near Austin in Texas, USA, the Harley-Davidson Flat-Track event is a fast and furious motorcycle race held at the Summer X Games. The startlist for its inaugural event on 4 Jun 2015 included Jared and Nichole Mees (both USA) – husband and wife professional racers. A mechanical fault on the final lap ended Jared's chance of gold, but he returned the next year to win the race.

Held on 2 Jun, the 2016 event included Cory and Shayna Texter (both USA) – the **first brother and sister to compete against each other at the Summer X Games**. The siblings competed in the heats but neither was able to progress to the final. It was Shayna who earned the family bragging rights, finishing in 21st place – one spot higher than her brother.

▼ YOUNGEST FEMALE X GAMES GOLD MEDALLIST IN SKATEBOARD STREET

Born on 19 Jul 1999, Brazilian high-school student Pâmela Rosa was aged just 16 years 221 days when she took gold at X Games Oslo in Norway on 25 Feb 2016. In a display of consistent technical skating, Rosa scored 80.33 in the first of her three runs, which proved enough to see off the competition. It was her third consecutive medal in the event: she won silver in 2014 and 2015.

Pâmela Rosa's favourite skateboarding trick is the frontside feeble, in which skaters grind rails on the back trucks of their board. Correct weight distribution is crucial to pulling off the trick.

▲ **MOST CONSECUTIVE X GAMES MEDALS WON IN SKATEBOARD PARK (MALE)**
Pedro Barros (BRA) has racked up nine consecutive podium finishes since his X Games debut in 2010, culminating in gold in Austin 2016. His tally stands at six golds and three silvers. Together with his father and fellow skating pro Léo Kakinho (BRA), Barros built a giant bowl in his backyard that has become a magnet for local skaters in his home town of Florianópolis, Brazil.

Highest single-day attendance at the Winter X Games

On 30 Jan 2016, a total of 49,300 spectators flocked to Aspen in Colorado, USA, for the third day of Winter X Games Twenty. The weather was as extreme as the action, but a heavy snowstorm could not deter fans. They were rewarded with events including Skier and Mono Skier X and men's Snowboard SuperPipe, plus music from DJ Snake and deadmau5.

Most Summer X Games medals won without winning gold

Between 1998 and 2016, Simon Tabron (UK) reached the podium 14 times without once getting the gold. His medal tally stands at six silver and eight bronze medals, all achieved in the BMX Vert discipline. At the 2016 X Games, Tabron's best-run score of 86.00 over his two runs was good enough for silver, but he couldn't overhaul compatriot Jamie Bestwick's 90.66. Incredibly, this was the fifth time that Tabron had finished second behind Bestwick.

Most Snowboard Slopestyle medals won at the Winter X Games (female)

With her silver at the 2016 Winter X Games, Jamie Anderson (USA) had accrued a total of 11 medals in 2006–16. She took bronze in her Slopestyle debut in 2006 and has reached the podium with every subsequent appearance. In total, Anderson can claim four gold medals, five silvers and two bronzes. At Aspen 2016, she registered a best-run score of 89.00, which put her in second place behind Canadian Spencer O'Brien on 91.00.

Most gold medals won at the Winter X Games (female)

When it comes to women's Snowboard Cross, there is only one name to beat: Lindsey Jacobellis (USA). From 2003 to 2016, she won 10 gold medals in the event at the Winter X Games held in Aspen, Colorado, USA. This tally could well have been higher had she not lost two years of competition owing to injury.

While dominating the X Games for more than a decade, Jacobellis has twice suffered heartbreak at the Winter Olympics. At the 2006 games in Turin, Italy, she was holding a three-second lead approaching the end of the course when she fell attempting a method grab, losing the gold medal to Tanja Frieden (CHE). Jacobellis also took a tumble while in the lead of her heat at Sochi 2014, failing to even qualify for the final.

▲ MOST X GAMES GOLD MEDALS WON IN BMX STREET (MALE)

Garrett Reynolds (USA) has dominated the BMX Street event since it first appeared at the X Games in 2008, winning eight out of a possible nine gold medals. The only time Reynolds missed out on top spot was at Los Angeles 2013, when he had to settle for silver behind Chad Kerley (USA). His runs have included some of the most complicated tricks seen in BMX riding.

▲ HIGHEST SCORE IN WINTER X GAMES SNOWBOARD SUPERPIPE (FEMALE)

Back-to-back 1080s and a McTwist helped Chloe Kim (USA) to a score of 98.00 in the Snowboard SuperPipe at X Games Oslo on 26 Feb 2016 in Oslo, Norway. Born on 23 Apr 2000, Kim was 15 years 309 days when she won her third gold medal – making her the **youngest X Games triple gold medallist**.

Sports Round-Up

At the peak of her signature backward somersault, US gymnast Simone Biles leaps almost twice her own height.

Most racquetball World Championships (men)

Since 1984, the International Racquetball Federation (IRF) World Championships have been held every two years. On 23 Jul 2016, Rocky Carson (USA) won his fifth consecutive men's singles title. He defeated Daniel de la Rosa 15–11, 5–15, 11–5 in the final.

The **most racquetball World Championships (women)** is three, achieved by a trio of players: Michelle Gould (USA) in 1992, 1994 and 1996; Cheryl Gudinas (USA) in 2000, 2002 and 2004; and Paola Longoria (MEX) in 2012, 2014 and 2016.

Brent Harvey announced his retirement from AFL football on 7 Oct 2016, after North Melbourne refused to renew his contract. Harvey planned to stay on at the club in a mentoring role.

Most consecutive Olympic beach volleyball matches won by an individual

From Athens 2004 to Rio 2016, Kerri Walsh Jennings (USA) won 22 successive matches in the Olympic beach volleyball contest. She won three consecutive golds with Misty May-Treanor before suffering her first Olympic loss to Brazil's Ágatha Bednarczuk and Bárbara Seixas in the semi-finals at Rio 2016. Walsh Jennings and new partner April Ross went on to take bronze.

Most wins of the Women's Softball World Championship

Since its first appearance in 1965, the Women's Softball World Championship has been held 15 times. On 24 Jul 2016, the USA won their 10th title, defeating Japan 7–3 in Surrey, Canada. It was the sixth consecutive USA–Japan final. The combined total of 10 runs made the game the **highest-scoring Women's Softball World Championship final**.

Most EHF Handball Champions League goals scored by an individual

Between 1998 and 11 Mar 2017, Kiril Lazarov (MKD) scored 1,164 goals in the EHF Champions League.

▲ **MOST AUSTRALIAN RULES FOOTBALL GAMES PLAYED**

On 30 Jul 2016, North Melbourne's Brent Harvey surpassed the legendary Michael Tuck (both AUS) when he made his 427th appearance in the AFL. By the season's close on 10 Sep, Harvey had increased his total to 432 games. He made his debut in Round 22 of the 1996 season, aged 18 years 112 days. Over the course of his career, "Boomer" scored 518 goals and 334 behinds, achieved 1,689 marks and ran an estimated 7,300 km (4,536 mi) on the pitch.

▲ **MOST ACES SERVED IN A WOMEN'S OLYMPIC VOLLEYBALL MATCH**
Ekaterina Kosianenko served eight aces during Russia's 25–13, 25–10, 25–16 victory against Argentina at Rio 2016 on 6 Aug. Setter Kosianenko, who plays for Dinamo Moscow, went one better than Zoila Barros and Yanelis Santos (both CUB), who hit seven aces in matches lasting five sets.

Most wins of badminton's World Team Championships for Women

Instituted in 1956, badminton's Uber Cup has been won by China 14 times. They triumphed at every event between 1984 and 2016 save three: 1994, 1996 and 2010. In 2016, China beat South Korea 3–1 in the final to record their latest victory.

Most Olympic badminton medals won (male)

Having already won gold at London 2012, Zhang Nan (CHN) added a men's doubles gold and a mixed doubles bronze to his collection at Rio 2016. Only three other men have won three Olympic badminton medals: Kim Dong-moon (KOR, 1996–2004), Lee Chong Wei (MYS, 2008–16) and Fu Haifeng (CHN, 2008–16).

Ahead of them all is women's player Gao Ling (CHN), who collected two golds, a silver and a bronze in 2000–04 – the **most Olympic badminton medals won by an individual.**

Most participants in the FIVB Volleyball World League (men)

The men's 2016 competition had 36 teams, four more than in 2015. Serbia won the title for the first time.

▲ **YOUNGEST OLYMPIC TABLE TENNIS MEDALLIST**

On 16 Aug 2016, Mima Ito (JPN, b. 21 Oct 2000) sealed victory for Japan in the Olympic table tennis bronze medal play-off by defeating Singapore's Feng Tianwei. Ito joined team-mates Ai Fukuhara and Kasumi Ishikawa on the podium aged 15 years 300 days. Ito had won the women's singles title at the 2015 International Table Tennis Federation (ITTF) World Tour German Open aged 14 years 152 days, making her the **youngest winner of an ITTF World Tour singles title.**

▲ YOUNGEST WINNER OF THE WOMEN'S WORLD OPEN SQUASH CHAMPIONSHIP

Egypt's Nour El Sherbini (b. 1 Nov 1995, above right) was aged 20 years 181 days when she won the Women's World Championship in Kuala Lumpur, Malaysia, on 30 Apr 2016. El Sherbini – who in 2009 became the youngest ever World Junior Champion when she won the title at the age of 13 – came from two sets down to defeat world No.1 Laura Massaro (UK) 6–11, 4–11, 11–3, 11–5, 11–8.

Most wins of the FIVB Volleyball Women's Club World Championship

On 23 Oct 2016, Turkish side Eczacıbaşı VitrA successfully defended their Fédération Internationale de Volleyball (FIVB) title. They are the first side to win the title more than once since its inception in 1991.

Most IHF Super Globe wins (men)

Three club sides have won the International Handball Federation (IHF) Super Globe twice: BM Ciudad Real (ESP, 2007 and 2010), Barcelona (ESP, 2013–14) and Füchse Berlin (DEU, 2015–16). Berlin beat PSG by a point to retain the title.

Most consecutive appearances in the men's IHF Beach Handball World Championships final

Brazil have reached every Beach Handball World Championship final save the first, in 2004. In 2016, they made their sixth consecutive appearance, but were beaten by Croatia. Brazil have won four finals.

▲ MOST KABADDI WORLD CUP WINS (MEN)

India (above, grappling an opposing player) have hosted and won the Kabaddi World Cup every year the competition has been held: in 2010–14 and 2016. Their sixth victory came courtesy of a 62–20 defeat of England in the final of the 2016 tournament, held on 17 Nov. The event adheres to the "Punjab Circle Style" as opposed to the "Standard Style".

India also holds the record for **most Kabaddi World Cup wins (women)** with four, achieved in 2012–14 and 2016.

Most women's Hockey Champions Trophy wins

Argentina won the 2016 women's title, taking their tally to seven. Las Leonas ("The Lionesses") had also triumphed in 2001, 2008–10, 2012 and 2014.

Midfielder Luciana Aymar featured in the first six wins – the **most wins of the women's Hockey Champions Trophy by an individual**.

Most men's Hockey Champions Trophy wins

Australia have won the Champions Trophy 14 times: in 1983–85, 1989–90, 1993, 1999, 2005, 2008–12 and 2016. They won their most recent title after a penalty shoot-out victory against India at the Lee Valley Hockey and Tennis Centre in London, UK.

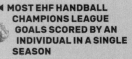

◄ MOST EHF HANDBALL CHAMPIONS LEAGUE GOALS SCORED BY AN INDIVIDUAL IN A SINGLE SEASON

Mikkel Hansen (DNK, near left) scored 141 goals for Paris Saint-Germain Handball (FRA) during the 2015–16 European Handball Federation (EHF) Champions League season. The prolific left-back scored nine goals in his opening game against Flensburg (DEU) and hit double figures six times – twice in the Final4 against Kielce (POL) and THW Kiel (DEU).

Most consecutive Olympic appearances by a gymnast

Uzbekistan's Oksana Chusovitina made her seventh consecutive Olympic appearance, at Rio 2016, aged 41 years 56 days. She made her debut at Barcelona 1992 representing the Olympic Unified Team, winning gold in the team event.

Most Olympic equestrian medals won by an individual

At Rio 2016, Isabell Werth (DEU) rode Weihegold Old to gold and silver in the team and individual dressage events respectively. This brought her tally of Olympic medals to 10: six gold and four silver. Werth's first Games was Barcelona 1992, when she won two medals on Gigolo.

▲ **FASTEST TIME TO COMPLETE AN IRONMAN TRIATHLON (MALE)**

An Ironman triathlon is a gruelling one-day sporting event comprising a 2.4-mi (3.86-km) swim, a 112-mi (180.25-km) bicycle ride and a 26.22-mi (42.20-km) marathon run. On 17 Jul 2016, Jan Frodeno (DEU) completed the Challenge Roth Ironman in Roth, Germany, in 7 hr 35 min 39 sec. Frodeno beat the previous record by almost 6 min, despite crashing into a ditch on the second lap of the bike circuit.

▶ **MOST ITU WORLD TRIATHLON SERIES EVENT WINS (MEN)**

On 2 Jul 2016, Alistair Brownlee (UK) won his 21st International Triathlon Union (ITU) World Series event in Stockholm, Sweden. In the finale to the 2016 World Series in Cozumel, Mexico, on 18 Sep, Alistair slowed down in order to help his exhausted brother Jonny over the line (right).

At Rio 2016, Alistair successfully defended the Olympic triathlon title he had won at London 2012 – earning him the **most Olympic triathlon gold medals** (2).

Acknowledgements

Editor-in-Chief
Craig Glenday

Senior Managing Editor
Stephen Fall

Layout Editors
Tom Beckerlegge, Rob Dimery

Senior Project Editor
Adam Millward

Project Editor
Ben Hollingum

Gaming Editor
Stephen Daultrey

Information & Research Manager
Carim Valerio

VP Publishing
Jenny Heller

Head of Pictures & Design
Michael Whitty

Picture Editor
Fran Morales

Picture Researcher
Saffron Fradley

Talent Researchers
Jenny Langridge, Victoria Tweedy

Artworker
Billy Waqar

Proofreading/fact-checking
Ben Way, Matthew White

Design
Paul Wylie-Deacon,
Matt Bell at 55design.co.uk

Original illustrations
Maltings Partnership,
Sam Golin

Production Director
Patricia Magill

Publishing Manager
Jane Boatfield

Production Assistant
Thomas McCurdy

Production Consultants
Roger Hawkins

Original Photography
Richard Bradbury, Jonathan
Browning, James Cannon,
Mark Dadswell, Al Diaz,
James Ellerker, Paul Michael Hughes,
Ranald Mackechnie, Olivier Ramonteu,
Kevin Scott Ramos, Ryan Schude

Cover Development
Paul Wylie-Deacon at 55 Design

Indexer
Ben Way

Printing & Binding
Worzalla Printing Co, USA

Consultants
Dr Mark Aston, James Burns, Rob
Cave, Martyn Chapman, Nicholas Chu,
Steven Dale, Warren Dockter,
Dick Fiddy, David Fischer, Mike Flynn,
Ben Hagger, Dave Hawksett,
T Q Jefferson, Eberhard Jurgalski,
Bruce Nash (The Numbers),
Ocean Rowing Society International,
Dr Paul Parsons, Clara Piccirillo,
James Proud, Dr Karl P N Shuker,
Ian Sumner, Matthew White,
Robert D Young

Head of Records Management, APAC: Ben Backhouse
Head of Records Management, Europe: Shantha Chinniah
Records Managers: Mark McKinley, Christopher Lynch, Matilda Hagne, Daniel Kidane, Sheila Mella
Records Executive: Megan Double
Senior Production Manager: Fiona Gruchy-Craven
Project Manager: Cameron Kellow
Country Manager, MENA: Talal Omar
Head of RMT, MENA: Samer Khallouf
Records Manager, MENA: Hoda Khachab
B2B Marketing Manager, MENA: Leila Issa
Commercial Account Managers, MENA: Khalid Yassine, Kamel Yassin
Official Adjudicators: Ahmed Gamal Gabr, Anna Orford, Brian Sobel, Glenn Pollard, Jack Brockbank, Lena Kuhlmann, Lorenzo Veltri, Lucia Sinigagliesi, Paulina Sapinska, Pete Fairbairn, Pravin Patel, Richard Stenning, Kevin Southam, Rishi Nath, Seyda Subasi-Gemici, Sofia Greenacre, Solvej Malouf, Swapnil Dangarikar

AMERICAS
SVP Americas: Peter Harper
VP Marketing & Commercial Sales: Keith Green
VP Publishing Sales, Americas: Walter Weintz
Director of Latin America: Carlos Martinez
Head of Brand Development, West Coast: Kimberly Partrick
Head of Commercial Sales: Nicole Pando
Senior Account Manager: Ralph Hannah
Account Managers: Alex Angert, Giovanni Bruna, Mackenzie Berry

Project Manager: Casey DeSantis
PR Manager: Kristen Ott
Assistant PR Manager: Elizabeth Montoya
PR Coordinator: Sofia Rocher
Digital Coordinator: Kristen Stephenson
Publishing Sales Manager: Lisa Corrado
Marketing Manager: Morgan Kubelka
Consumer Marketing Executive: Tavia Levy
Senior Records Manager, North America: Hannah Ortman
Senior Records Manager, Latin America: Raquel Assis
Records Managers, North America: Michael Furnari, Kaitlin Holl, Kaitlin Vesper
Records Manager, Latin America: Sarah Casson
HR & Office Manager: Kellie Ferrick
Official Adjudicators, North America: Michael Empric, Philip Robertson, Christina Flounders Conlon, Jimmy Coggins, Andrew Glass, Mike Janela
Official Adjudicators, Latin America: Natalia Ramirez Talero, Carlos Tapia Rojas

JAPAN
VP Japan: Erika Ogawa
Office Manager: Fumiko Kitagawa
Director of RMT: Kaoru Ishikawa
Records Managers: Mariko Koike, Yoko Furuya
Records Executive: Koma Satoh
Marketing Director: Hideki Naruse
Designer: Momoko Cunneen
Senior PR & Sales Promotion Manager: Kazami Kamioka
B2B Marketing Manager PR & Advertising: Asumi Funatsu
Project Manager Live Events: Aya McMillan

Digital & Publishing Content Manager: Takafumi Suzuki
Commercial Director: Vihag Kulshrestha
Account Managers: Takuro Maruyama, Masamichi Yazaki
Senior Account Executive: Daisuke Katayama
Account Executive: Minami Itoa
Official Adjudicators: Justin Patterson, Mai McMillan, Gulnaz Ukassova, Rei Iwashita

GREATER CHINA
President: Rowan Simons
General Manager, Greater China: Marco Frigatti
VP Commercial, Global & Greater China: Blythe Fitzwiliam
Senior Account Manager: Catherine Gao
Senior Project Manager: Reggy Lu
Account Manager: Chloe Liu
External Relations Manager: Dong Cheng
Digital Business Manager: Jacky Yuan
Head of RMT: Charles Wharton
Records Manager: Alicia Zhao
Records Manager / Project Co-ordinator: Fay Jiang
HR & Office Manager: Tina Shi
Office Assistant: Kate Wang
Head of Marketing: Wendy Wang
B2B Marketing Manager: Iris Hou
Digital Manager: Lily Zeng
Marketing Executive: Tracy Cui
PR Manager: Ada Liu
Content Director: Angela Wu
Official Adjudicators: Brittany Dunn, Joanne Brent, John Garland, Maggie Luo, Peter Yang

British Library Cataloguing-in-publication data: a catalogue record for this book is available from the British Library

US: 978-1-912286-42-3

US: 978-1-68412-146-5

Records are made to be broken – indeed, it is one of the key criteria for a record category – so if you find a record that you think you can beat, tell us about it by making a record claim. Always contact us before making a record attempt.

Check **www.guinnessworldrecords.com** regularly for record-breaking news, plus video footage of record attempts. You can also join and interact with the Guinness World Records online community.

Guinness World Records Limited has a very thorough accreditation system for records verification. However, while every effort is made to ensure accuracy, Guinness World Records Limited cannot be held responsible for any errors contained in this work. Feedback from our readers on any point of accuracy is always welcomed.

Guinness World Records Limited uses both metric and imperial measurements. The sole exceptions are for some scientific data where metric measurements only are universally accepted, and for some sports data. Where a specific date is given, the exchange rate is calculated according to the currency values that were in operation at the time. Where only a year date is given, the exchange rate is calculated from 31 Dec of that year. "One billion" is taken to mean one thousand million.

Appropriate advice should always be taken when attempting to break or set records. Participants undertake records entirely at their own risk. Guinness World Records Limited has complete discretion over whether or not to include any particular record attempts in any of its publications. Being a Guinness World Records record holder does not guarantee you a place in any Guinness World Records publication.

OFFICIALLY AMAZING

THE JIM PATTISON GROUP

▼ PICTURE CREDITS

Rosen, Getty, Alamy; **132–36** John Wright/GWR, Getty, Alamy, Jonathan Browning/GWR, Ryan Schude/GWR, Richard Bradbury/GWR, Reuters; **137–41** DPA/PA, Cristian Barnett/GWR, Alamy, Jaroslaw Nogal, Al Diaz/GWR, John Wright/GWR, Shutterstock; **142–46** James Ellerker/GWR, Paul Michael Hughes/GWR, Getty, Oliver Ramonteu/GWR, Alamy; **147–51** Photolure, Sam Christmas/GWR; **152–56** John Wright/GWR, Paul Michael Hughes/GWR; **157–61** John Wright/GWR, Shutterstock, Richard Bradbury/GWR, Paul Michael Hughes/GWR, Ken Butti, Ranald Mackechnie/GWR; **162–66** Cliff Roles, Shutterstock, Ranald Mackechnie/GWR, Kevin Scott Ramos/GWR; **167–71** SWNS, Gil Montano/GWR, Philip Robertson, Paul Michael Hughes/GWR, Sarah Mirk, SWNS, Alan Place, Alamy; **172–76** Maltings Partnership; **177–79** Kevin Scott Ramos/GWR; **180–84** Maltings Partnership; **185–89** Alamy; **190–94** Shutterstock, Alamy; **200–04** Getty, Shutterstock, Reuters; **205–09** Alamy; **210–15** Ryan Schude/GWR, Getty, Kevin Scott Ramos/GWR, Alamy, Ranald Mackechnie/GWR, Kevin Scott Ramos/GWR; **216–20** Maltings Partnership; **221–23** Kevin Scott Ramos/GWR; **224–28** Michael Roach, Ranald Mackechnie/GWR, iStock, Shutterstock, Kevin Scott Ramos/GWR, James Ellerker/GWR; **229–33** Shutterstock, Paul Michael Hughes/GWR, Jonathan Browning/GWR; **234–38** Anders Martinsen, Shutterstock, Getty; **239–43** Rod Kirkpatrick, Jeff Holmes, Ranald Mackechnie/GWR, Richard Bradbury/GWR, Paul Michael Hughes/GWR, Shutterstock; **244–48** Carla Danieli, Tim Anderson, Shutterstock, Alamy, Definate Films, Matthew Horwood, Ken Bohn; **249–53** Shutterstock, Paul Michael Hughes/GWR, Kevin Scott Ramos/GWR, Ranald Mackechnie/GWR; **254–58** Alamy, C Y Photography, NewsFlare, Mark Dadswell/GWR; **259–63** Shutterstock, Getty, Kevin Scott Ramos/GWR; **264–69** Giuseppa Laratro; **270–74** Maltings Partnership; **275–77** Barcroft Media; **278–82** Kevin Light, Shutterstock, Alamy, Getty; **283–87** Shutterstock, NASA, Alamy, PA; **288–92** Alamy, Shutterstock; **293–97** Rod Mayer; **298–302** NASA, Shutterstock, Willems Johan, Antje Ackermann & C Michel, Alamy, Red Bull; **303–07** Stuart Bailey, Getty; **308–12** Maltings Partnerships;

313–15 Getty; **316–20** Shutterstock, Alamy, Getty; **321–25** Shutterstock, iStock, Alamy; **326–30** Shutterstock, Alamy, Getty; **331–35** Shutterstock, NTT Docomo, Alamy; **336–40** Sotheby's, Getty, Shutterstock, Alamy; **341–45** Getty, Grey Flannel Auctions, Shutterstock, Andrew Lipovsky, Reuters, Alamy; **346–50** Paul Michael Hughes/GWR, Shutterstock, Reuters, Toilography, Reuters; **351–55** Reuters, NASA, Shutterstock, Alamy, Getty; **356–60** Maltings Partnership; **361–63** Alamy, Shutterstock; **364–68** Alamy, Getty, Shutterstock, Kathy Bushman, Sotheby's; **369–73** Alamy, Paul Michael Hughes/GWR, Shutterstock, BBC, Getty; **374–78** Shutterstock, Alamy; **379–83** Getty, Shutterstock, Alamy; **384–88** Shutterstock, Alamy, Ryan Schude/GWR; **389–93** Shutterstock, Getty, Alamy; **394–98** Getty, Alamy; **399–403** Kevin Scott Ramos/GWR, Errisson Lawrence, Washington Green Fine Art Group, Joan Marcus, Shutterstock; **404–08** Maltings Partnership; **409–11** Alamy; **412–16** SPL, YouTube, Shutterstock, SPL, Getty, Alamy; **417–21** Alamy, Getty, NASA, ESA, Shutterstock; **422–26** Alamy, Lindner Fotografie, Hermann Jansen, Shutterstock, IAAC, AMNH/D Finnin, Carlos Jones, University of Washington; **427–31** Panaxity, Shutterstock, Gilman Collection, SEAC Photographic Collection; **432–36** Seah Kwang Peng, YouTube, Shutterstock, Alamy, Getty; **437–41** Bob Mumgaard, Getty, Alamy; **442–46** Maltings Partnership; **447–49** Richard Bradbury/GWR; **450–54** Shutterstock, Hattons Model Railways, Boris Lux, Alamy, Getty; **455–59** Shutterstock, Getty, Alamy; **460–64** Getty, Shutterstock, Roderick Fountain, Barcroft Media; **465–69** Getty, James Ellerker/GWR, Richard Bradbury/GWR, Robert Chandler, Drew Gardner/GWR, YouTube; **470–74** YouTube, Getty, Shutterstock, Crown Copyright, TopFoto, Alamy; **475–79** iStock, Michael Garnett, Mike Boettger, Shutterstock, Getty, Alamy; **480–84** Maltings Partnership; **485–87** Alamy; **488–92** Shutterstock, Alamy, Getty; **493–95** Getty, Shutterstock, Alamy; **496–98** Alamy, Getty; **499–501** Getty, Shutterstock; **502–04** Shutterstock, Getty; **505–07** Getty; **508–10** Alamy, Getty; **511–13** Alamy, Getty, Shutterstock; **514–16** Alamy, Getty, Shutterstock;

Guinness World Records would like to thank the following for their help in compiling this edition:

ABC Australia (Emma Mungavin); Hans Åkerstedt (1st Vice-President, FAI Ballooning Commission Bureau); Alex Burrow Events (Alex Burrow, Garret Wybrow); Carmen María Alfonzo; Andrew Kay and Associates (Andrew Kay, Margot Teele); Mark Archibald; Sophie Barling; BBC (Kez Margrie, Cheryl Taylor); Billy Oscar Bell; Kerry Bell; Leon Stanley Bell; Ronnie Albert Bell, Bender Media Services (Susan Bender, Sally Treibel); Claudia Bienek (Berlin Zoo); Brandon Boatfield; Joseph Boatfield; Luke Boatfield; Ryan Boatfield; Iain Borden; Andrea Braff; Corrinne Burns; Raymond Butler; CCTV China (Pia Ling, Serena Mei, Guo Tong, Wang Wei); Ted Chapin; Quay Chu; John Corcoran; Lydia Dale; Discovery Communications (Bente Engebretsen, Alena Kararic, Kerrie McEvoy, Nesta Owens and Jonathan Rudd); Emirates (Andy Grant); Endemol Shine Italia (Stefano Torisi, Orsetta Balsamo); Enriched Performers (Sarah Riches); E-Vision (Fatiha Bensalem); Benjamin Fall; Rebecca Fall; John Farnworth; Caroline Feer; Marco Fernandez de Araoz; Jono Field; FJT Logistics Ltd (Ray Harper, Gavin Hennessy); David Fletcher; Justin Garvanovic; Karen Gilchrist; Oliver Granger; Chelsea Greenwood; Pete and Victoria Grimsell; Grizzly Media (Adam Moore); Philine Hachmeister (Berlin Zoo); Markus Haggeney (Sports and Events Director, FAI – Fédération Aéronautique Internationale); Hampshire Sports and Prestige Cars; Amy Cecilia Hannah Alfonzo; Sophie Alexia Hannah Alfonzo; Haven Holidays; Danny Hickson; High Noon Entertainment (Jon Khoshafian); Isabel Hofmeyr; Jonathan Holt (Archive and Library Officer, The Tank Museum, Bovington, UK); Marsha Hoover; Colin Hughes; Chayne Hultgren; Tom Ibison; ICM (Colin Burke, Michael Kagan); Integrated Colour Editions Europe (Roger Hawkins, Susan Hawkins); ITV America (David Eilenberg, Eric Hoberman, Adam Sher);

Al Jackson; Gavin Jordan; Richard Kakayor; Dani Kane; Stephen Kish; Jane Klain (The Paley Center for Media); Haruka Kuroda; Kurz; Orla Langton; Thea Langton; Frederick Horace Lazell; Liam Le Guilliou; Asha Leo; LEONHARD KURZ Stiftung & Co. KG; Lion Television (Simon Welton, Susan Cooke, Sarah Clarke); Bruno MacDonald; Mart Maes (WeMakeVR); Missy Matilda; Dave McAleer; Claire McClanahan; Brad Miller; Amara, Florence, Joshua and Sophie Molloy; Dr Laura O'Brien (Lecturer in Modern European History at Northumbria University); One Stop Party Shop (Mike Jones, Rob Malone); Nick Patterson; Alice Peebles; Terry Phillip (Reptile Gardens); Prof Alistair Pike (Dept of Archaeology, University of Southampton); Trieste Pinzini (ID); POD Worldwide (Yip Cheong, Christy Chin, Alex Iskandar Liew); Prestige (Jackie Ginger); PrintForce.Com (Mark McIvor); R and G Productions (Eric Bron, David Charlet, Stéphane Gateau, Patrice Parmentier, Jérôme Revon); Rightsmith (Jack Boram, Laura Dorsey, Mica Imamura, Masato Kato, Jackie Mountain, Omar Taher, Sachie Takahashi); Lindsay Roth; Eric Sakowski; Milena Schoetzer (Team Assistant, FAI – Fédération Aéronautique Internationale); Dr Jennifer Sessions (Associate Professor of History at the University of Iowa); Natasha Sheldon; Ben Shires; Bridget Siegel; Dr Andrew W M Smith (Senior Lecturer in Contemporary History and Politics at the University of Chichester); Gabriel Smith; Scarlett Smith; Glenn Speer; Claire Stephens; Andy Taylor; TC Soho (JP Dash, Steve Langston); TG4 Ireland (Siobhan Ní Bhradaigh, Lís Ní Dhálaigh Karina Feirtéar); Julian Townsend; Turner (Zia Bales, Susanna Mazzoleni, Marco Rosi); United Group (Vladimir Gordić); UPM Paper; Martin Vacher (Spotify); Marawa Wamp; Whale and Dolphin Conservation (Marta Hevia); Lara White; Sevgi White; Brian Wiggins; Linda Wiggins; Paul Wiggins; Beverley Williams; Hayley Wylie-Deacon; Rueben George Wylie-Deacon; Tobias Hugh Wylie-Deacon; Cherry Yoshitake; Evan Younger; XG-Group

517–19 Alamy, Getty; **520–22** Alamy, Getty; **523–25** Getty, Alamy; **526–28** Getty, Shutterstock, Alamy; **529–31** Red Bull, Alamy, Paul Michael Hughes/GWR, Getty; **532–34** Red Bull, Alamy, Getty; **535–37** Shutterstock, Getty, Alamy; **538–40** YouTube, Alamy; **541–45** Alamy, Getty, Shutterstock, Alamy; **546–50** Alamy, Reuters, Shutterstock; **551–53** Alamy, Shutterstock; **554–56** Shutterstock, Alamy, WSL; **557–59** Alamy, Getty; **560–62** Alamy, Shutterstock, Getty; **563–65** ESPN; **566–68** Alamy, Red Bull, ESPN; **569–73** Silvio Avila, Getty, Alamy, Getty.

▼ COUNTRY CODES

Code	Country
ABW	Aruba
AFG	Afghanistan
AGO	Angola
AIA	Anguilla
ALB	Albania
AND	Andorra
ANT	Netherlands Antilles
ARG	Argentina
ARM	Armenia
ASM	American Samoa
ATA	Antarctica
ATF	French Southern Territories
ATG	Antigua and Barbuda
AUS	Australia
AUT	Austria
AZE	Azerbaijan
BDI	Burundi
BEL	Belgium
BEN	Benin
BFA	Burkina Faso
BGD	Bangladesh
BGR	Bulgaria
BHR	Bahrain
BHS	The Bahamas
BIH	Bosnia and Herzegovina
BLR	Belarus
BLZ	Belize
BMU	Bermuda
BOL	Bolivia
BRA	Brazil
BRB	Barbados
BRN	Brunei Darussalam
BTN	Bhutan
BVT	Bouvet Island
BWA	Botswana
CAF	Central African Republic
CAN	Canada
CCK	Cocos (Keeling) Islands
CHE	Switzerland
CHL	Chile
CHN	China
CIV	Côte d'Ivoire
CMR	Cameroon
COD	Congo, DR of the
COG	Congo
COK	Cook Islands
COL	Colombia
COM	Comoros
CPV	Cape Verde
CRI	Costa Rica
CUB	Cuba
CXR	Christmas Island
CYM	Cayman Islands
CYP	Cyprus
CZE	Czech Republic
DEU	Germany
DJI	Djibouti
DMA	Dominica
DNK	Denmark
DOM	Dominican Republic
DZA	Algeria
ECU	Ecuador
EGY	Egypt
ERI	Eritrea
ESH	Western Sahara
ESP	Spain
EST	Estonia
ETH	Ethiopia
FIN	Finland
FJI	Fiji
FLK	Falkland Islands (Malvinas)
FRA	France
FRG	West Germany
FRO	Faroe Islands
FSM	Micronesia, Federated States of
FXX	France, Metropolitan
GAB	Gabon
GEO	Georgia
GHA	Ghana
GIB	Gibraltar
GIN	Guinea
GLP	Guadeloupe
GMB	Gambia
GNB	Guinea-Bissau
GNQ	Equatorial Guinea
GRC	Greece
GRD	Grenada
GRL	Greenland
GTM	Guatemala
GUF	French Guiana
GUM	Guam
GUY	Guyana
HKG	Hong Kong
HMD	Heard and McDonald Islands
HND	Honduras
HRV	Croatia (Hrvatska)
HTI	Haiti
HUN	Hungary
IDN	Indonesia
IND	India
IOT	British Indian Ocean Territory
IRL	Ireland
IRN	Iran
IRQ	Iraq
ISL	Iceland
ISR	Israel
ITA	Italy
JAM	Jamaica
JOR	Jordan
JPN	Japan
KAZ	Kazakhstan
KEN	Kenya
KGZ	Kyrgyzstan
KHM	Cambodia
KIR	Kiribati
KNA	Saint Kitts and Nevis
KOR	Korea, Republic of
KWT	Kuwait
LAO	Laos
LBN	Lebanon

LBR	Liberia	SAU	Saudi Arabia
LBY	Libyan Arab Jamahiriya	SDN	Sudan
LCA	Saint Lucia	SEN	Senegal
LIE	Liechtenstein	SGP	Singapore
LKA	Sri Lanka	SGS	South Georgia and South SS
LSO	Lesotho		
LTU	Lithuania	SHN	Saint Helena
LUX	Luxembourg	SJM	Svalbard and Jan Mayen Islands
LVA	Latvia		
MAC	Macau	SLB	Solomon Islands
MAR	Morocco	SLE	Sierra Leone
MCO	Monaco	SLV	El Salvador
MDA	Moldova	SMR	San Marino
MDG	Madagascar	SOM	Somalia
MDV	Maldives	SPM	Saint Pierre and Miquelon
MEX	Mexico	SRB	Serbia
MHL	Marshall Islands	SSD	South Sudan
MKD	Macedonia	STP	São Tomé and Príncipe
MLI	Mali	SUR	Suriname
MLT	Malta	SVK	Slovakia
MMR	Myanmar (Burma)	SVN	Slovenia
MNE	Montenegro	SWE	Sweden
MNG	Mongolia	SWZ	Swaziland
MNP	Northern Mariana Islands	SYC	Seychelles
MOZ	Mozambique	SYR	Syrian Arab Republic
MRT	Mauritania	TCA	Turks and Caicos Islands
MSR	Montserrat	TCD	Chad
MTQ	Martinique	TGO	Togo
MUS	Mauritius	THA	Thailand
MWI	Malawi	TJK	Tajikistan
MYS	Malaysia	TKL	Tokelau
MYT	Mayotte	TKM	Turkmenistan
NAM	Namibia	TMP	East Timor
NCL	New Caledonia	TON	Tonga
NER	Niger	TPE	Chinese Taipei
NFK	Norfolk Island	TTO	Trinidad and Tobago
NGA	Nigeria	TUN	Tunisia
NIC	Nicaragua	TUR	Turkey
NIU	Niue	TUV	Tuvalu
NLD	Netherlands	TZA	Tanzania
NOR	Norway	UAE	United Arab Emirates
NPL	Nepal	UGA	Uganda
NRU	Nauru	UK	United Kingdom
NZ	New Zealand	UKR	Ukraine
OMN	Oman	UMI	US Minor Islands
PAK	Pakistan	URY	Uruguay
PAN	Panama	USA	United States of America
PCN	Pitcairn Islands	UZB	Uzbekistan
PER	Peru	VAT	Holy See (Vatican City)
PHL	Philippines	VCT	Saint Vincent and the Grenadines
PLW	Palau		
PNG	Papua New Guinea	VEN	Venezuela
POL	Poland	VGB	Virgin Islands (British)
PRI	Puerto Rico	VIR	Virgin Islands (US)
PRK	Korea, DPRO	VNM	Vietnam
PRT	Portugal	VUT	Vanuatu
PRY	Paraguay	WLF	Wallis and Futuna Islands
PYF	French Polynesia	WSM	Samoa
QAT	Qatar	YEM	Yemen
REU	Réunion	ZAF	South Africa
ROM	Romania	ZMB	Zambia
RUS	Russian Federation	ZWE	Zimbabwe
RWA	Rwanda		

Round-Up

The following entries were approved and added to our database after the official closing date for this year's submissions.

Largest bank card mosaic

A mosaic of an ICBC (ARG) gold bank card comprising 32,400 individual bank cards was created by ICBC on 14 Mar 2016. The finished display stretched for more than 151 m² (1,625 sq ft).

Largest disposable cup mosaic

To showcase the launch of their new internet campaign, on 9 Apr 2016 Vodafone Mobile Services Ltd (IND) created a 627-m² (6,749-sq-ft) mosaic of their logo using disposable cups in Lucknow, India. It took 250 employees four-and-a-half hours to place the c. 140,000 paper cups.

Largest notebook

On 26 Apr 2016, a notebook measuring 0.99 m² (10.65 sq ft) was presented at the Business Design Centre in Islington, London, UK. It was created by stationery firm Nuco and was an exact-to-scale replica of one of their existing products. The finished notebook weighed almost 40 kg (88 lb 2.9 oz).

Largest shirt mosaic

On 1 Jun 2016, detergent giant Ariel unveiled a mosaic of 4,224 shirts with a total area of 1,482.03 m² (15,952 sq ft) at a plant in Louveira, São Paulo, Brazil. The mosaic was in support of the home nation's Olympic hopefuls at the Games in Rio de Janeiro.

Largest gathering of people dressed as ghosts

On 12 Jun 2016, the Marina Bay Sands convention centre in Singapore was haunted by 263 people dressed as ghosts. The ghostly goings-on were part of a red-carpet event to promote Sony Pictures' new film *Ghostbusters* (USA/AUS, 2016).

Most spoons balanced on the body

On 26 Jun 2016, Dalibor Jablanović (SRB) balanced 79 spoons on his body in Stubica, Serbia. Although he achieved this before Marcos Ruiz Ceballos set his mark of 64 spoons (see p.269), Dalibor's record was not ratified until after the closing date for submissions.

Largest light bulb image

On 17 Jun 2016, LG Electronics and Invisible, Inc (both KOR) displayed an artwork comprising 18,072 light bulbs in Gimpo City, South Korea. The design of a refrigerator surrounded by fruits and vegetables was created by artist Serge Belo (CAN).

Most valuable teapot

A teapot owned by the N Sethia Foundation (UK) was appraised at

Mosaics are always popular here at GWR – there are largest variants made from batteries, éclairs, socks, soap, umbrellas, popcorn, shoelaces and dumbbells, among many others!

Q: Who was the most searched-for person on the internet in 2016, according to Google?

A: Donald Trump

$3 m (£2.3 m) in London, UK, on 9 Aug 2016. The "Egoist" teapot was hand-made by jeweller Fulvio Scavia (ITA), with cut diamonds covering the body and a 6.67-carat ruby in the centre.

Highest margin of victory in an Olympic gymnastics all-around final (female)

Simone Biles (USA) took gold at the Rio Olympics with an overall score of 62.198 on 11 Aug 2016 – a margin of victory of 2.100 over second-placed Alexandra Raisman (USA), who scored 60.098.

According to Google's annual report of the year's online trends, Biles was the **most searched-for sportswoman on the internet (current)**. She came fifth in the overall list of most searched-for people in 2016. The **most searched-for sportsman on the internet (current)** was swimmer Michael Phelps (USA), who ranked third overall.

Most LED lights lit simultaneously

Students at the University of Nevada in Las Vegas, USA, simultaneously lit 1,590 LED lights on 31 Aug 2016. They stood in formation to spell out the letters 'UNLV' in red.

Most points scored in 30 m 36-arrow outdoor recurve (male)

Kim Woo-jin (KOR, see p.536) scored 360 points with 26 Xs at the 48th National All-Star Archery Tournament in Yecheon, South Korea, on 5 Sep 2016. Many archers have scored 360 out of a possible 360 in this event, so the record is decided on the number of Xs achieved. An X is recorded when the arrow lands within the inner ring of the gold.

Fastest time to build a six-level LEGO® pyramid (team of two)

On 17 Sep 2016, Shana and Richard Wilkins (both USA) built a six-level LEGO pyramid in 14.72 sec in Richmond, Virginia, USA. It was the first record set at Brick Fest Live!, during the launch of *Guinness World Records LIVE!* in the USA.

At the same event, Thomas "Tommy" Ladd (USA) achieved the **most LEGO bricks removed from a baseplate and held in the hand for 30 seconds** – 16, on 18 Sep.

On the same day, Brick Fest Live! host Evans Elias Richards (USA) set the **fastest time to assemble three LEGO Minifigures** – 18.44 sec.

Largest cereal bowl

On 17 Sep 2016, a bowl of organic granola weighing 1,589.4 kg (3,504 lb) was offered as a "ZONK!" prize on a food-themed episode of the CBS game show *Let's Make a Deal* in Los Angeles, California, USA.

Heaviest bell pepper

Verified by Le Potager Extraordinaire on 22 Sep 2016 in Arnage, France, a *Capsicum annuum* grown by Mehdi Daho (FRA) weighed 621.07 g (1 lb 5.90 oz). The record-breaking pepper was verified ahead of the 2016 edition of the National Giant

Fruit and Vegetable Competition, held annually in Oct in the Vendée department of France.

Largest projected image

To celebrate the opening of the annual "Circle of Light" international festival in Moscow, Russia, LBL Communication Group (RUS) created a giant projected image with a total surface area of 50,458 m² (543,125 sq ft) on 23 Sep 2016.

Largest display of cheese varieties

On 23 Sep 2016, Philippe Marchand (FRA) displayed 2,140 cheeses of 730 varieties in Nancy, France, beating the previous best of 590 varieties (see p.237). The event took place during National Gastronomy Week, and the cheese was subsequently donated to Nancy's food bank.

Largest drumming lesson

On 3 Oct 2016, the Bang the Drum project organized by Inspire-works, Street Child United and London schools (all UK) attracted 1,827 participants at the Copper Box Arena in Queen Elizabeth Olympic Park in London, UK.

Most Unmanned Aerial Vehicles (UAVs) airborne simultaneously

Intel Corporation (USA) managed to get 500 UAVs airborne at the same time over Krailling, Germany, on 7 Oct 2016.

Most consecutive crossings of a pool of non-Newtonian fluid

On 26 Nov 2016, a total of 107 people crossed a pool filled with a mixture of cornflour and water at the Pure & Crafted Festival in Muldersdrift, South Africa. The event was organized by Gaviscon (ZAF). A non-Newtonian fluid possesses a variable viscosity based on applied stress or force – meaning that it is possible to cross it without sinking.

Most mechanical energy produced by pedalling on static bicycles in one hour

On 26 Nov 2016, a total of 300 participants cycled for 1 hr on 100 stationary bikes to produce 8,999 watt hours of energy at Burj Park in Dubai, UAE.

Highest catch of a cricket ball

Kristan Baumgartner (UK) caught a cricket ball dropped from 62 m (203 ft 4.9 in) in Windsor, Berkshire, UK, on 30 Nov 2016. This beat the mark of 46 m (150 ft 11 in) set by former England cricket captain Nasser Hussain (see p.261).

Largest cricket lesson (single venue)

Cricket Australia hosted a lesson for 488 people in Sydney, Australia, on 2 Dec 2016. The lesson signalled the launch of the national junior summer participation programme.

Largest Rube Goldberg

Rube Goldberg machines take their name from an American cartoonist who became famous for drawing fiendishly complex machines performing simple tasks. On 2 Dec 2016, Latvian firm Scandiweb turned on the Christmas lights in Riga, Latvia, with the aid of a contraption featuring 412 individual mechanical steps. The finale was initiated by a sound meter, which was triggered by the shouts and screams of the crowd.

Largest flower arrangement/ structure

A flower arrangement in the shape of an Airbus A380 airplane measured 72.95 x 78.34 x 21.98 m (239 ft 4 in x 257 ft x 72 ft 1 in), achieved by Dubai Miracle Garden (UAE) in Dubai, UAE, on 2 Dec 2016.

Largest human image of an organ

On 6 Dec 2016, a group of 3,196 students from GEMS Cambridge International School (UAE) came together to form the shape of a pair of human lungs in Abu Dhabi, UAE. The event, sponsored by Novartis Middle East FZE (UAE), was held to raise awareness of chronic obstructive pulmonary disease (COPD).

Most people wrapping presents simultaneously

On 13 Dec 2016, a total of 876 employees of UK firm Jewson wrapped presents in Birmingham, UK.

Most expensive seal sold at auction

A seal belonging to Emperor Qianlong (1735–96) of the Qing dynasty was sold to an anonymous buyer for $22 m (£17.34 m) on 14 Dec 2016. Qianlong had reportedly owned 1,800 similar seals.

Most people playing Monopoly (single venue)

On 12 Jan 2017, a total of 733 people played the classic acquisitional board game at an event organized by Rustic Cuff and Addicted 2 Cuffs (both USA) at the Renaissance Hotel in Tulsa, Oklahoma, USA. Participants played the officially licensed Rustic Cuff edition of Monopoly, with properties designated as jewellery pieces.

First trio to row the Atlantic Ocean

From 14 Dec 2016 to 2 Feb 2017, team American Oarsmen – comprising Mike Matson, David Alviar and Brian Krauskopf (all USA) – rowed the Atlantic east to west from La Gomera to Antigua in 49 days 14 hr 4 min. They covered a distance of 4,722 km (2,550 nautical mi) on board *Anne*.

Most horror-movie sequels

With the simultaneous release of *Witchcraft XIV: Angel of Death*, *Witchcraft XV: Blood Rose* and *Witchcraft XVI: Hollywood Coven* in Jan 2017, the *Witchcraft* horror series (USA) boasts 15 direct sequels to the original. It began in 1988.

Longest ODI career (female)

The 90-match One-Day International (ODI) career of Clare Shillington (IRL) spanned 19 years 195 days, from 8 Aug 1997 to 19 Feb 2017. She had scored 1,276 ODI runs in 79 innings at an average of 17.72, registering six 50s and a top score of 95 not out.

Most burpees in one hour – female

Fitness trainer Kathryn Beeley (AUS) completed 1,321 burpees in 60 min on 27 Feb 2017 at the MissFit gym in Brisbane, Queensland, Australia. Beeley beat the previous best of 1,272, set by fellow Australian Eva Clarke in 2015 (see p.147).

Fastest 100 m on a space hopper – female

On 9 Mar 2017, Ali Spagnola (USA) bounced her way to 100 m glory in 38.22 sec at UCLA's Drake Stadium in Los Angeles, California, USA. Spagnola beat the existing time of 39.88 sec set by Dee McDougall (see p.158).

Largest bust (sculpture)

The "Adiyogi" Shiva, created by the Isha Foundation (IND), is a statue of the Hindu deity Shiva measuring 34.24 m high, 24.99 m wide and 44.9 m long (112 ft 4 in x 81 ft 11 in x 147 ft 3 in), as verified on 11 Mar 2017 in Tamil Nadu, India. The statue was unveiled by Prime Minister Narendra Modi on 24 Feb.

Longest professional ice hockey match

During the playoffs of the GET-ligaen in Norway, a match between Storhamar Hockey and Sparta Warriors on 12–13 Mar 2017 lasted 217 min 14 sec. The marathon tie, played at Hamar OL-Amfi in Hamar, Norway, went to an eighth period of overtime before Storhamar's Joakim Jensen finally netted the winner. This beat the previous professional record of 176 min 30 sec, achieved by the NHL's Detroit Red Wings and Montreal Maroons, who played six overtime periods on 24–25 Mar 1936.

Largest Easter egg tree

On 16 Mar 2017, an Easter egg tree consisting of 82,404 painted hen eggs was presented by Associação Visite Pomerode (BRA) at the 90 Osterfest in Pomerode, Santa Catarina, Brazil.

Youngest club DJ

On 20 Mar 2017, Itsuki Morita (JPN, b. 26 Nov 2010) played a set at the restaurant and bar L&L in Osaka, Japan, aged 6 years 114 days. Itsuki used the Pioneer XDJ-AERO DJ system for his hour-long performance, played to a 30-strong audience.

Largest human image of an airplane

To celebrate the 11th anniversary of the ESTACA Graduate School of Aeronautical and Automotive Engineering in Laval, France, 474 students dressed in blue came together to depict an airplane on 21 Mar 2017. They beat the 350 mark set by Ethiopian Airlines on 29 Jun 2016.

Tallest stack of tortillas

Ben Leventhal (USA) created a stack of tortillas measuring 58.03 cm (22.85 in) high at Mashable House at SXSW in Austin, Texas, USA, on 10 Mar 2017.

Largest tree hug

On 21 Mar 2017, a total of 4,620 people hugged trees in Thiruvananthapuram, Kerala, India. The attempt, organized by the news broadcaster Asianet News Network and the Jawaharlal Nehru Tropical Botanic Garden and Research Institute, was held on the United Nations' "International Day of Forests". Each participant had to hug one tree for at least 60 sec to qualify.

Most haikus about one town

The Luton Haiku team, led by Tim Kingston and also including Andrew Kingston, Stephen Whiting and Andrew Whiting (all UK), have been posting weekly online haikus about Luton in Bedfordshire, UK, since 23 Jan 2007. The collected poems of *Clod Magazine* numbered 2,700, as of 24 Mar 2017, and have been bound up in a series of printed volumes.

Highest score in figure skating – total score (women)

On 31 Mar 2017, Evgenia Medvedeva (RUS, see p.557) won the women's title at the International Skating Union (ISU) World Championships in Helsinki, Finland, with a combined score of 233.41.

The next day, Yuzuru Hanyu (JPN) achieved the **highest score in figure skating – long**

programme: 223.20. On his way to the title, he skated to "Hope and Legacy" by Joe Hisaishi.

Fastest University Boat Race (women's)
On 2 Apr 2017, Cambridge secured the Women's Boat Race Trophy by beating Oxford in a time of 18 min 33 sec in London, UK.

Longest duration holding weight (outstretched arms)
On 11 Apr 2017, Anatoly Ezhov (BLR) held a 20-kg (44-lb) kettlebell with outstretched arms for 2 min 35 sec in Arkhangelsk, Russia. Strongman Ezhov beat his existing record by 2 sec.

Longest frame in a professional snooker match
On 12 Apr 2017, Fergal O'Brien (IRL) and David Gilbert (UK) played a deciding frame lasting 2 hr 3 min 41 sec during the final qualifying round of the Betfred World Snooker Championship at the Ponds Forge International Sports Centre in Sheffield, South Yorkshire, UK. It was O'Brien who emerged from the marathon frame victorious, winning it 73–46 and the match 10–9.

Largest origami rhinoceros
On 19 Apr 2017, Liu Tong and The MixC (both CHN) created an origami rhinoceros measuring 7.83 m (25 ft 8 in) long and 4.06 m (13 ft 3 in) high in Zhengzhou, Henan Province, China. The paper used measured 14 x 14 m (45 ft 11 in x 45 ft 11 in) and weighed more than 100 kg (220 lb).

Highest pinfall in tenpin bowling in 24 hours by a pair
On 22 Apr 2017, Trace and Steve Wiseman (both USA) knocked down 35,976 pins in Louisville, Kentucky, USA. Trace passed the previous best at 7.12 p.m., using his great-grandfather's ball.

Largest permanent hedge maze
The Butterfly Maze at the Sunhu tourist resort in Ningbo, Zhejiang Province, China, has a total area of 33,564.67 m² (8.29 acres) and a total path length of 8.38 km (5.2 mi). Inspired by the Chinese story "The Butterfly Lovers", the maze features towers, bridges and underpasses. It was opened on 22 Apr 2017.

Most popular raccoon on Instagram
Pumpkin the raccoon had 1.1 million followers on the photo-sharing social media site, as of 3 May 2017. She lives with two dogs, Oreo and Toffee, and their owners Laura and William Young in The Bahamas.

Most retweeted message on Twitter
In his attempts to secure a lifetime supply of Wendy's Chicken Nuggets, Carter Wilkerson (USA) had a message retweeted 3,430,655 times, as verified on 9 May 2017. This was more than the famous "Oscar selfie" taken by Ellen DeGeneres.

Most Pulitzer Prizes and citations
On 10 Apr 2017, *The New York Times* received Pulitzer Prizes for International Reporting, Breaking News Photography (Daniel Berehulak, AUS) and Feature Writing (C J Chivers, USA). This took the newspaper's total prizes and citations to 122.